Engraved by James Fittler A.R.A.

WHITE   KENNETT, S.T

Christus   *Prebendarius*

ISBN 978-1-332-32910-6
PIBN 10314818

1 MONTH OF
FREE
READING

at

www.ForgottenBooks.com

By purchasing this book you are eligible for one month membership to ForgottenBooks.com, giving you unlimited access to our entire collection of over 700,000 titles via our web site and mobile apps.

To claim your free month visit:

www.forgottenbooks.com/free314818

PAROCHIAL ANTIQUITIES

ATTEMPTED IN

THE HISTORY

OF

AMBROSDEN, BURCESTER,

AND OTHER ADJACENT PARTS

IN THE

COUNTIES OF OXFORD AND BUCKS.

———◆———

BY WHITE KENNETT, D.D.

VICAR OF AMBROSDEN,

AFTERWARDS BISHOP OF PETERBOROUGH.

Vetera Majestas quædam, et (ut sic dixerim) Religio commendat. Quinct. de Inst. Orat. i. 6.

A NEW EDITION, IN TWO VOLUMES,

GREATLY ENLARGED FROM THE AUTHOR'S MANUSCRIPT NOTES.

———◆———

VOL. I.

———◆———

OXFORD,

AT THE CLARENDON PRESS.

MDCCCXVIII.

ADVERTISEMENT.

THE present edition of Bishop Kennett's Parochial Antiquities contains much additional matter, and that too from the pen of the Author himself.

The Bishop's own Copy, enriched in almost every page with Manuscript Notes, was given by the late Mr. Gough to Mr. Archdeacon Churton, with a wish, that it should become the property of the Bodleian Library, when there was no longer any one of his family who was distinguished by the father's taste for antiquarian research. But the Archdeacon with great liberality has anticipated that event; and by presenting the Book to the Bodleian Library, through the Delegates of the Clarendon Press, has enabled them to give to the Public an enlarged and improved edition, at a time when the original one was become so scarce, as almost to have disappeared.

That the difference between the first and the present edition may be more clearly seen, the original text is preserved entire; and the Author's Manuscript Additions are printed in columns at the foot of the page, which contains that portion of the History to which they refer. The authorities cited have been examined; all the charters and documents which could be traced have been collated; such quotations from them as were found imperfect, or in any respect inaccurate, have been corrected; and a very copious Index of Persons and of Places will be found at the end of the second volume.

To the Author's Appendix relating to the History of Allchester has been added another, containing a History of Chilton, in the county of Buckingham, by the late Rev. Thomas Delafield, from a MS. in the Bodleian Library. The public have derived so little benefit from the labours of the Historian and Topographer, in either of the Counties of Oxford or Buckingham, that the publication of all such inedited works cannot fail to be acceptable; and the more so in this case, as the Parish of Chilton and the Manor of Borstall are contiguous to the places treated of in the Parochial Antiquities.

It would be unjust not to acknowledge the kind permission of the Dean and Chapter of Christ Church to examine the chartularies deposited in their Chapter House, as well as the ready access to all their documents connected with the Work, which was afforded by the Right. Rev. the Warden and Fellows of All Souls College, by Sir John Aubrey, Bart. and by John Coker, Esq. of Bicester.

It remains only to add, that the Print prefixed to the work is engraved from an original Portrait in the possession of the family of Sir John Bayley, one of the Judges of the Court of King's Bench, who is a descendant of Bishop Kennett's, and on whose application it was allowed in the most obliging manner to be put into the hands of Mr. Fittler.

B. BANDINEL.

Bodleian Library, March 16, 1818.

TO

THE HONOURED

SIR WILLIAM GLYNNE, BART.

PATRON OF THE CHURCHES OF AMBROSDEN AND BURCESTER.

———————◆———————

SIR,

THIS Discourse has a title to your patronage, as you are the patron of those two churches, which are the particular subject of it.
But I have more express reason to offer up these Collections into
your hands, because you are the heir of that patron, to whose favour
I owed this benefice, and have yourself not only protected my func-
tion, and defended my rights; but out of your own property have
augmented my small revenues; and by your generous contribution
have supported me in the great labour and expence of gathering together these materials, and digesting them in this method.

As to the performance, I am under no concern to vindicate it
from the slights and ridicules that may be cast upon it by idle witty
people, who think all history to be scraps, and all antiquity to be
rust and rubbish. I say this only, next to the immediate discharge
of my holy office, I know not how in any course of studies I could
have better served my patron, my people, and my successors, than
by preserving the memoirs of this parish and the adjacent parts,

which before lay remote from common notice, and in few years had been buried in unsearchable oblivion. If the present age be too much immersed in cares or pleasures, to take any relish, or to make any use of these discoveries; I then appeal to posterity: for I believe the times will come, when persons of better inclination will arise, who will be glad to find any collection of this nature; and will be ready to supply the defects, and carry on the continuation of it.

I doubt, there is but one argument against such historical attempts; that is, men have degenerated from the piety, and integrity, and industry of their forefathers, and therefore do not love to be upbraided with the memory of them; and lead such a vicious, at least such a useless life, that they desire no other mercy from after ages, but silence and oblivion; and therefore must fear and hate that sort of learning, which may hereafter call them fools, and other proper names. So that antiquity has indeed the like enemies with religion; those despise it, who are sensible they live contrary to the rules and the examples of it.

Whereas, men would have some appetite to the notice of ancient things and persons, if they had a spirit to improve the arts, and imitate the virtues of their good old ancestors. And they would delight to read any account of former ages, if they could themselves hope to make any good figure in future story.

This, Sir, makes me confident, that whoever are fond to be ignorant of past times; yet your family, and all the long descendants from it, will ever prize antiquities, and love a faithful relation of any matters of fact. For will not your posterity rejoice, to find upon record the good and laudable deeds of their predecessors? Will it not divert them to read, how the first Baronet of their name raised a beautiful and regular seat at Amersden? How he kept there a hospitable and well-governed house, and by his prudence and charity reformed a rude and licentious people? How he rescued the patronage of this church from the hands of one, whose principles betrayed him into no affection for it? How he twice conferred the same church with no regard to interest or importunity? How, out of his own proper soil, he enlarged the bounds of the churchyard; and made a like addition to the adjoining garden of the vicar? How, by his countenance and kind endeavours, he recovered an estate (before embezzled) to the proper pious use of supporting and adorning the parish church? How he was pleased to accept a share in that new trust, and what a conscience he made in the discharge of it? How just he was to the interest and the honour of his other church at Burcester? How he filled it with an incumbent of exemplary goodness, and serviceable learning? And how he made it a greater beauty of holiness, by giving a very noble service of communion-plate, and all other decent ornaments for the Lord's table and the pulpit?

When they come to the history of his son and heir, what fuller satisfaction will they have, in reading his character of virtue and honour, of generosity and public spirit! How will it please them to observe, that he had an early education to good principles and good letters! That he always shewed a respect to scholars, a reverence to divines, and a veneration to the Church of England; and that even his good nature could not betray him into a kind opinion of any other sect or party! That he managed his private affairs with discretion and ease; and administered public justice in calmness and with courage! That he was often projecting and promoting the strength and beauty of his parish church, and set an example of constant access to and good behaviour in it! That he was encouraging and as-

b 2

sisting the improvement of the vicar's manse, and making some augmentation to his slender portion of glebe! That in a neighbouring church of his patronage, for the two first turns of presentation, he referred the choice of fit persons to the sole judgment of the Bishop, and by such deference did his lordship and himself most particular honour! And how will it please them to be put in remembrance of a great many other good and glorious actions, which I might now foretel, and they will hereafter find completed!

And I have the vanity to hope, that some of those who shall succeed in the benefice I now enjoy, will be glad to recollect, that they had a certain predecessor, who seemed to have some zeal for the good estate of his church and parish, who was at some charge and pains to search into histories and records, upon no other motive, but the love of his parochial charge, and the benefit of posterity.

My thanks for all your favours, and my prayers for the happiness of yourself, your hopeful son, and all your dear relations, is the duty of

Your obliged Clerk

and faithful Servant,

WHITE KENNETT.

THE

AUTHOR'S PREFACE.

I AM only concerned to let the reader prepare himself, with some short account of the occasion and the method of these historical collections.

The occasion was this. Upon the death of Mr. Owen Jones, 21. May 1685. I was presented to this church of Ambrosden, by the worthy patron the late Sir William Glynne, baronet, and found some disturbance in the parish, about the manner of expending and accounting for the annual profits of certain lands and tenements allotted to *pious uses.* I was soon sensible, my duty obliged me to reconcile all differences; and was more especially inclined to consult the interest of my church, and to secure the firm title, and the just disposal of a *public charity.*

With these thoughts, I applied myself to the two proper advocates of such a cause; my diocesan, and my patron. They *both* agreed in the opinion, that the church and people were abused; and *both* promised their assistance to promote a regulation of that abuse. In order to which, they enjoined me to make a more diligent search into the matters of right and fact; and to draw up a short *state of the case,* that they might more fully discover the corruption, and more easily proceed to some redress. Upon this, with difficulty I obtained a sight of some papers and records reposited in the church chest, and made this abstract of them, Sept. 26, 1685.

There be lands and tenements within the manor of Blackthorn, in the parish of Ambrosden, commonly called by the name of *the church houses,* and *the church land*,* now in the occupation of Robert George and other tenants,

----

* Any lands given to the pious use of rebuilding, repairing, and maintaining any cathedral, or parochial church, were called *fabric-lands,* mentioned in the Act of Oblivion, 12. Car. II. cap. 8. and they were more anciently called *tymber-lands.* In the good old ages of devotion, most persons, by their last will, gave somewhat to the use of the church where they lived. Mr. Blount cites this copy of a will for example—" *In Dei nomine*

at the vearlv rent of 14*l.* 12*s.* received and expended by the churchwardens, with consent of some feoffees. The time of this donation, and the name of the benefactor, are unknown. There is a dark tradition, that the said estate was bequeathed by the last will of a certain inhabitant of this parish. But upon search in the registry of Lincoln, made by a predecessor in this church, no such instrument could be found. And, possibly, the donation might be as ancient as the allotment of manse and glebe to the parish priest; when, at the dedication of the church, the lord of the soil might offer such a portion of ground to the maintenance of a residing priest, and such another portion to the repair and support of his new founded church. That by such distinct assignment he might comply with the old custom of dividing the tithes and oblations, and the appropriating at first a *fourth*, as afterward a *third* part to the reparation of churches.

However, the settlement of this estate to such uses was proved to be immemorial and ancient, by reference made to a deed bearing date MCCCXXXVI. wherein was a mention of those lands as belonging to the peculiar uses of the said church, and excepted from the endowment of the vicar. A copy of which deed was produced in a trial before the *commissioners for charitable uses*, in 12. Jac. I. I confess, I have seen no such original or transcript: but if they mean the form of ordination of the vicarage of Ambrosden, which bears the like date 1336, then the cottage there excepted from the endowment of the vicar, yielding the annual rent of VI*s.* III*d.* and reserved to the rector and bonhommes of Ashcrugge, cannot be understood of this estate, but was a part of the church glebe detained from the vicar, and reserved (as it now belongs) to the appropriator.

But leaving the original donation undetermined, it is certain the said lands were quietly enjoyed, and the profits honestly employed to the public uses of the church, till the year 1568, 10. Queen Eliz. when Hugh Councell and Robert Pister procured a precept from the queen to hold an inquisition at Thame, com. Oxon. on December 12. in claim of the said estate at Blackthorn, as escheated to the crown, (under the title of *concealed lands,*) because given and

" amen—*Die Veneris anno Dom.* 1423. *Ego Richardus Smyth de Bromyard condo testa-*
" *mentum meum in hunc modum—Imprimis lego animam meam Deo et Beatæ Mariæ et*
" *omnibus sanctis, corpusque meum sepeliendum in cœmiterio beatæ Edburgæ de Bradway.*
" *Item lego fabricæ ecclesiæ cathedralis Hereford* XII*d. Item lego fabricæ capellæ Beatæ*
" *Mariæ de Bromyard* XL*d. Item lego fratribus de Woodhouse* XX*d. Residuum vero bono-*
" *rum"* &c.

employed to superstitious uses, and so forfeited to the crown by an act 1. Edw. I. cap. 14. This inquisition was so hastily and corruptly returned, that the verdict was, that the said lands were in seisin of the queen, from whom a grant by letters patent was made to the said informers Hugh Councell and Robert Pister, in consideration of sixteen pounds, the annual rent being at that time twenty marks.

Yet these fraudulent purchasers could never gain possession; for immediately upon complaint made in a petition of the inhabitants to the queen's majesty, the inquisition was declared to be false, and the conveyance void. When the purchasers were thus condemned, they still kept up a pretended title; and by several mediate conveyances, in the 10th year of king James I. the said lands were claimed by Thomas Bowler, Richard Stanton, Judith Hern, Thomas Cross, and William Haws; some of which being in possession as tenants of the estate, pretended to the sole right and property of it, and for two years forcibly detained and denied all rent, and acknowledgment for it. Therefore in 12. Jac. I. 1614. the parishioners, and others, obtained a *commission for charitable uses*, in pursuance of an act 43. Eliz. cap. 4. to be held in the city of Oxford by John, lord bishop of Oxon. Sir Michael Dormer, Sir George Tipping, knights, Anthony Blinkoe, doctor of laws, chancellor of the diocese, &c. This cause was brought before the said commissioners, who, after a full hearing, decreed an ejectment of the intruders, and adjudged them to pay for the mediate rents thirty pounds, and ten pounds for waste made by the cutting down some elms on the premises, and so resettled the lands to the former uses of the church, appointing a certain number of feoffees, with authority to nominate successive persons to the same continued trust.

But the false claimers appealed from this decree of the commissioners to the Court of Chancery, where, after dilatory and expensive proceedings, a decree was at last obtained, 14th June, 10. Car. I. confirming the precedent order of commissioners, and disannulling all other claims and pretensions. This long depending suit was so chargeable to the parishioners, that for their satisfaction the new feoffees leased out the lands at a moderate corn rent, taking a fine of forty pounds, which was equally distributed to reimburse the defendants' charges. And when that lease expired, the lands were farmed out for near the full rent in money, received by the churchwardens, and accounted for every year at Easter. But by the iniquity of the late times, and the combination of some church and parish officers, these two abuses have shamefully crept in.

1. The profits of this estate, which were at first designed, and have been

since declared for the sole benefit of the church, have been converted to several other uses: as, to finding the communion bread and wine; defraying the
charges of ecclesiastical visitations; helping in the repair of bridges, and
amendment of highways; contributing to sufferers recommended by letters patent; rewarding the ringers upon public festivals; and other accidental occasions, which should have been rather served by imposed rates, or by voluntary
contributions. So as what is properly a *church stock*, is now perverted into a
parish stock; and when appropriated to sacred, is now prostituted to profane
and common uses.

2. Whereas the fund arising from the said lands and tenements ought to be
reposited in a church chest, formerly provided for that purpose, and thence to
be taken out, and disbursed with the order or full consent of the feoffees; this
reasonable practice is now laid aside; the churchwardens alone receive the
rents, and divide the money in proportion to the townships or hamlets of the
said parish, taking two parts of the dividend for Blackthorn, one for Arncott,
and one for Amersden: which sums the respective churchwardens keep in
their several hands, and account at Easter for those separate shares, with collu-
sion and great disorder.

It is therefore thought necessary, for the honour of God and the interest of
the church, that the profits should be applied to the alone proper use of supporting and adorning the parish church. And that the issuing rents should be
safely reposited in a common chest, to be expended by the care of the churchwardens, at the direction of the feoffees.

This abstract I delivered to the right reverend John Fell, lord bishop of
Oxford, who for piety, justice, and charity, and especially for patronising his
clergy, and defending the rights of the church, was (at least) equàl to the primitive examples of Christian prelates. His lordship consulting the peace of
the parish, drew up with his own hand *a form of regulation*, to be subscribed
by the feoffees, and practised without further trouble. But they refused to
comply with any sort of proposals, and called their own perverseness an *old
custom*, which was not to be broken. Upon which contempt, his lordship,
after a second ineffectual admonition, commanded me to have recourse to the
commissioners for charitable uses: to whom I made complaint at their first
session in the Guild Hall, within the city of Oxford; and after several hearings
the court were so well convinced of the abuses and injuries done to the church,
that on Wednesday, March 1, 168⅔, they declared their opinion agreeable to
the verdict of a jury, to dissolve the present feoffment, to constitute a new trust

in more faithful hands, and to oblige the churchwardens for seven years last past, to refund the several sums of money, which they had not employed to the use and service of the church. This judgment of the court had been fully executed, but that before the next sessions, Sir William Glynne, baronet, in pure tenderness and charity, interceded with the chief commissioners to remit all penalty for past miscarriages, and only to prevent the like abuses for the future. Accordingly, in compliance to his generous request, at the next sessions, Wednesday April 20, 1685, Mr. Justice Holloway declared the judgment of the court, to dissolve the late feoffment, and to constitute new trustees, for disposal of the profits to the sole uses of the church; and in conclusion did observe, they should have inquired more narrowly into the past miscarriage, which would have fallen heavy upon some of the late churchwardens, but that an honourable person had interceded for them.

This was the occasion which first engaged me in inquiries and searches after papers and records, which might any way relate to my church and parish. When I had once began to be thus inquisitive, the slow discoveries which I gradually made did not so much satisfy my mind, as they did incite it to more impatient desires. So that diverting from my ordinary course of studies, I fell to search for private papers and public evidences, to examine chartularies and other manuscripts, and by degrees to run over all printed volumes, which I thought might afford any manner of knowledge of this parish, and the adjacent parts of the country. Had I proposed the antiquities of this whole county, I should perhaps have sooner gathered up sufficient materials for it. But confining myself to such a narrow circuit, I often read much to very little purpose. And when I applied myself to those courts of record, where I thought such remains were most likely to be found, I felt the exaction for searching and transcribing to be so great, and perceived the notes to be so imperfect, that I began to want ability and courage to go on. At least I became sensible, that undertakings of this nature should be encouraged and supported by several hands, as the cause of a community should be managed by a public fund. And I well know, those gentlemen whose seats or estates lay within the compass of my design, would have readily contributed to any just proposals made to them. But I thought it somewhat more suitable to my profession and my temper, if I could thus serve the country without wages; and therefore (except the voluntary kindness of my patron) I never asked or received any other gratuity, than the pleasure of doing good for its own sake. This was my design.

As to the method, I proposed to make it as obvious and regular, as such disjointed matter would allow. Where I wanted authorities, I resolved my conjectures should be short and modest. Therefore I passed hastily over the unknown state of these parts under the primitive Britains; but looked more narrowly for some footsteps of the Romans; and perhaps have made some discoveries of their marches, their garrisons, coins, ways, and customs; which may give diversion to the English reader; and may afford some light to the sense of Greek and Latin writers. I went on to the invasion of the Saxons, and to their times of disorder and confusion; where I think I have done justice to the memory of some forgotten places; have better settled the bounds of the Mercian and West-Saxon kingdoms; have fixed the session of certain councils and synods of that age; and have reconciled some accounts of time, which our authors had confounded and mistaken. I went through all the revolutions of Danes and Saxons with the same regard to curiosity and truth; and seem to have hit upon several things, which had escaped the observation of common writers.

When I came to the Norman Conquest, I found the subject matter more copious, and the authorities more express; and therefore thought it convenient to proceed by way of annals, that I might keep to the exact periods of life and action, which are the soul of history, and the criterion of all truth. In this part of the performance, I have endeavoured to be very accurate in the descent of families, and the conveyance of estates. I have corrected a great many traditional errors, and have gathered up considerable materials, when any diligent and judicious person shall undertake to improve the history of the Baronage of England. I have traced many temporary usages and local customs, many feudal services and particular tenures, many other ancient rites and manners, not unserviceable to those gentlemen, who would know the reason and original of what they are to call the *common law*.

I have been more especially curious in transmitting all those charters and authentic deeds, which were pertinent to my subject, and lay dispersed in obscure and distant places; and have thereby preserved some thousands of charts and muniments, which are ready for the hands of those, who shall collect and publish some other volumes of a Monasticon Anglicanum, a work that above any other will illustrate and adorn the antiquities of this church and nation. And further, as occasion offered, I have made some digressions into the search of a few particular subjects, as consecration to religious uses, appropriation of tithes, institution of churches, dependance of chapels, office of rural deans, and such like: arguments, wherein I was most desirous to satisfy myself, and to inform the world.

When I had brought down the series of affairs to the end of the reign of Hen. VI. I found the volume growing incapable to hold the remaining matter, unless I had contracted it into a compass too narrow for the projected design. So that I broke off at the year 1460, but have carefully preserved all the other memoirs, and shall endeavour to adjust them in such a method, as that I may hereafter give them to the public in a *second part*; or rather may leave them to my successor in the church of Ambrosden, to whom I shall desire my executors to deliver all such papers and materials as I leave collected for that purpose.

There was one manuscript communicated to me by my very worthy friend Mr. Blackwell, B. D. which (though of modern age and no great authority) immediately relating to these parts, I thought good, with consent of the owner, to join as an Appendix to this work, under the title of " The History of All-chester, near Bircester, in Oxfordshire," &c. wrote in the year 1622.

While I was running over the sheets from the press, I met with a great many terms and phrases, which would create trouble to a curious reader, and, if unexplained, would leave several writs and deeds obscure and useless. To obviate this danger, I made an alphabet of those obsolete words and forms of speech, to shew in short the sense and application of them; wherein, by pointing at the original of our English tongue, with the several innovations and corruptions in it, and giving new light to some ancient customs, laws, and manners, I have left matter to be applied by some more able pen to the noble uses of improving the excellent Glossary of Sir Henry Spelman, which would be a work of infinite service, and of equal honour to this nation. A new edition might be made more copious and exact from some of the author's own manuscripts, from some volumes since published, and from many records since recovered from dust and darkness. It is a labour that requires an expert, industrious, patient hand. I wish I might recommend it to the leisure of my singular friend Mr. Edmund Gibson, a master of those studies, and of much other useful knowledge. Some persons may imagine, that the large Latin Glossary of Du Fresne is so comprehensive of all antiquated words and phrases, as to supersede any additions and improvements to the archæology of Spelman: but with all deference to the indefatigable pains and great fidelity of that noble lord, I dare affirm, that in all the old terms which were of more peculiar use in

this island, he has barely transcribed, or, what is worse, abridged the explica-
tions of Spelman.   It is excuse enough, that he was a foreigner; for indeed,
none but a native can perfectly understand the idioms of any tongue, or the
customs of any country.   Therefore the elder Vossius wisely declared, *Satius
esse edi glossaria ab unoquoque gentis suæ scriptore, quia is facilius certius-
que, quid e suæ nationis genio proficiscatur, perspiciet.* (Præfat. ad lib. de vitiis
Sermon.)   And the learned Du Fresne, after his immense labour, confessed,
*Optandum esse ut in singulis nationibus prodeant viri docti, qui linguæ suæ
idiomata, vim eorum, notionem, origines, sed et desuetas, et pridem obsoletas
voces ad amussim investigent explicentque.* (Præfat. ad Gloss. Lat. p. xx.)

And indeed there is no greater argument, why the Antiquities of England
should be more and more illustrated than this; to correct the mistakes, and
reconcile the contradictions of foreign writers.   Why should Pabebrochius conjecture, we had no charters, or other written instruments of conveyance in the
time of Bede?   When Bede himself does mention the hereditary right of monasteries to some territories by royal edicts, and privileges of the religious,
confirmed by the subscription of bishops, abbots, and secular powers.   Why
should Du Fresne assert, that after the Norman Conquest there were no deeds
of donation by kings or private subjects in the Saxon idiom; but all in the
French, or in the Latin tongue and letter?   When for three or four reigns after
the Conquest, there be found several charters and other public acts in the
Saxon character and language.   Why should the French editors of Eadmer
stumble upon *Balæum ejusque exscriptorem Lelandum?*   When nothing is more
ridiculous than to make Leland the transcriber of Bale: they might as well
have made Bale the transcriber of Pits.   Why should Picard, in his late anno-
tations upon Anselm, betray his own ignorance, and leave his author under the
censure of mistake?   Anselm in one of his Epistles, (l. 3. Ep. 90.) being then
at Lyons, in his return from Rome, anno 1105, excused himself for not coming into England, because he could not attend at court, and *crown the king*
before his submission to the pope.   The annotator wonders at this expression,
and takes pains to prove, that the king had been solemnly crowned five years
before.   Whereas if he had known any thing of the English court, he must
needs have known the custom of that age, open court and common councils
held at the three principal festivals, Christmas, Easter, and Whitsuntide: when
it was one ceremony to have the crown put upon the king's head by the archbishop of Canterbury.   It were endless to recount the absurd and gross errors
committed in the relation of English affairs by those authors, who meddle with

a province not their own. I only point at these few, to shew the necessity of having all our antiquity and history explained and improved by scholars of our own nation, and not betray our land to the evil and false report of strangers.

And truly I cannot but congratulate the present age, that a genius to our national antiquities seems now to invigorate a great many lovers of their country, from whose attempts and advances in this kind of knowledge the world may expect much public service. Particularly from my industrious and judicious friend Mr. Thomas Tanner, who may do great honour to his native county of Wilts. when he has perfected the great and good design of publishing and improving that too long concealed treasure, *Opus Johannis Lelandi de Scriptoribus Britannicis.*

Any writer without the countenance of friends, is like a poet without a patron, cold and heavy. But antiquities expose the lovers of them to so much labour and expence, that they, above all other studies, do want a support and reward from men of wealth and honour. And indeed they have met of late with some favour and encouragement, to help to bear their fatigue, and to excite their progress. In Oxford, they have been especially promoted by the Rev. Dr. Charlett, Master of University College, to whom this work and the author of it are very much obliged.

I am sensible there be some who slight and despise this sort of learning, and represent it to be a dry, barren, monkish study. I leave such to their dear enjoyments of ignorance and ease. But I dare assure any wise and sober man, that *historical antiquities*, especially a search into the notices of our own nation, do deserve and will reward the pains of any English student; will make him understand the state of former ages, the constitution of governments, the fundamental reasons of equity and law, the rise and succession of doctrines and opinions, the original of ancient, and the composition of modern tongues, the tenures of property, the maxims of policy, the rites of religion, the characters of virtue and vice, and indeed the *nature of mankind.* I wish the excellent parts of many other writers were not spent upon more frivolous arguments, where by subtleties, and cavils, and controverting quibbles, they serve only to weaken Christianity, and (what otherwise were pardonable) to expose one another.

PAROCHIAL ANTIQUITIES

ATTEMPTED IN THE

HISTORY OF AMBROSDEN, BURCESTER,

AND

OTHER ADJACENT VILLAGES

IN THE

COUNTIES OF OXFORD AND BUCKS.

THE subject and the times, which I am first to deal with, are obscure; but my endeavours shall be, not to represent them fabulous.
National antiquities are deeply buried; but parochial are sunk farther into the most remote oblivion. The most diligent enquirer
might break off with the same complaint, which the wise Gildas
made, in prefacing his zealous epistle, that *if any written memoirs
were ever left, they have been burnt at home, or carried away into
foreign lands*[a]. Yet I consider, that in all searches for the rise and
original of things, there is room for conjecture, before there is
allowance for matter of fact. Therefore I shall step back, and
guess at some things, which I do not pretend to assert. From the
date of the Conquest I know my authorities to be very good, and
shall from that time digest the whole story into exact annals. But

[a] Historia Gildæ, sect. 2. edit. Gale.

till then, I shall loosely discourse in general of these parts, through the great epochs of this nation, the time of the Britains, the Romans, the Saxons, the Danes, and the Saxons restored.

CHAP. I.

BRITAINS.

I PROFESS not to determine, whether, among these our true an-cestors, the site of these parishes had any inhabitants, much less the names of places, which it now retains. Possibly these parts had not the honour of ruined Troy, of being converted into corn fields; but lay in primitive nature, an uncultivated desert. Whether any *Indigenæ* kept always here in the navel of the land, as Cesar reports their pretences[b], or whether no mansion till foreigners arrived; and those, whether Scythæ, or Celtæ, Germans, Gauls, or Spaniards, the three nations from which Tacitus[c] thought us derived, according to the nigher position of our coasts to those countries, are beyond all knowledge to resolve. This only is agreed, that those people, which Dio called Bodunni, and the Romans Dobuni, dwelt within the tract, that now makes up most part of this county, and that of Glocester: and the circuit of these north-east parts was called Do-buni Dofu[d], from the fat and fertile soil. In the declining part at least of this dark age, there were at no great distance some British towns, that must occasion this adjacent country to be the better inhabited. From the account which Cesar[e] and Strabo[f] give, some look upon all British cities preceding the Roman invasion, to have been rather necessitous and moving stations, than any fixed archi-tecture of walls and houses. But however rude their military en-

---

[b] De Bell. Gall. l. 5.   [c] Tacitus Vit. Agric. sect. 11.   [d] Hist. Alcester MS.
[e] Cæsar de Bell. Gall. l. 5.   [f] Strabo Geog.

campments were, it is probable their more public resort and abode was in places of artificial, though less regular strength and beauty. For even Cesar allows them the same way of building with the Gauls[g]. Why should not the twenty-eight British cities mentioned by Gildas, and enumerated by Nennius, and their number increased by Huntingdon, &c. have their foundation in the pure British age, though their improvement might be owing to the Roman arts? If such immense ruins are now visible, which the most learned do believe the remains of heathen British Temples; how can we think them ignorant in their own accommodations, when they were so pompous in providing for their gods? Among such original British Cairs, there was Cair-Draithon, which Huntingdon makes Cair-Draiton, which I durst not ascribe to either of those two parishes in this county, which still retain that name, though no antiquaries can find better where to place it. But the Cair-Dauri of Huntingdon, which Alfred of Beverley calls Cair-Dorim, and Beda, Civitas Dorcinia, is by all interpreted Dorchester, the city of waters, in Leland's word Hydropolis. Cair-Gretholin, Grethlin, or Wetheling, which Hum. Lhuyd assigns to Warwick, might perhaps be more aptly fixed at Watlington in this county, which, without considering the affinity of name, did seem to a late diligent surveyor to have been an old British city[h]. Henley is likewise taken for a most ancient British town, from Hen *old* and Lhey *a place*, which Camden[i] and Dr. Plot[k] suppose to be the head town of the people called Ancalites, who submitted to Cesar. The fortifications on Long-Witenham hill are by Leland[l] thought to be the marks of the British Sinnodunum. Not to recount the disputes of the antiquity of Oxford, whether Cair-Mempric and Cair-Vortegern be monkish fancies, whether the Iren of Gildas his studies be mistaken for Ichen or Ruyd-Ychen, the pretended ancient name of this place; whether this and more be truth or pretence, let men of leisure satisfy them-

[g] De Bell. Gal. l. 5.   [h] Dr. Plot. Nat. Hist. Oxford, ch. 10.   [i] Britan. Dobuni.
[k] Nat. Hist. Oxf. ch. 10.   [l] Lel. Cygnea cantio.

selves from copious authors[m]. It is enough at present to infer, that long before the visit of the Romans, these parts were known and peopled, which may pass into the more easy conjecture, if we reflect on the pieces of money dug up at Wood-Eaton, 1676; one of which had CUNO on the one side, and on the reverse CAMU, denoting it to be coined by Cunobelin, a king in Britain, under the reign of Augustus at Camulodunum, now Maldon in Essex[n]. There was another dug up at Little-Milton, presumed to be the coin of Prasutagus, king of the Iceni[o]. Nor is it so probable, these coins were dropt in after ages, as nearer to the time of their stamp, when current among the British inhabitants, populous in these parts. But I hasten to be relieved from the dangers of ignorance and error.

———————

C H A P. II.

R O M A N S.

CESAR, in his first expedition upon this island, was no doubt confined to the eastern parts of Kent. And in his second descent, he is generally supposed to have made no great progress, because his own Itinerary describes no far advancing marches, and because Dio, Tacitus, Lucan, Horace, &c. reflect upon this as an imperfect attempt. Hence Camden was the first of our writers who dared to bring Cesar as far as Coway-stakes, nigh Oatlands in Surry, where the Roman army passed the Thames[p]. But without the vanity of assuming honour to these parts, I think it next to certain that Cesar came in to the limits of this county, and brought his forces cross the Thames at Walingford. The author who confirms me in this opinion is the judicious Mr. Somner[q], who suggests to me several of

———

[m] Selden on the 11th Song of Drayton's Polyolb. Stillingfleet Orig. Britan. Hist. et Antiq. Oxon. Nat. Hist. of Oxfordshire, &c.   [n] Plot. ib.   [o] Ib.   [p] Camden Britann. in Atrebat.   [q] Saxon Diction. in voce Walingford.

those arguments, which I would briefly deliver. First, Comius the Atrebatian was sent over by Cesar to dispose the Britains to subjection, as a man of great authority among them, whose interest must lie chiefly among those Britains, who were in effect his own countrymen, who inhabited that part of the island, which is now called Barkshire: which Comius at his first arrival was imprisoned by the Britains, but on Cesar's first victory was released, and, upon retreat of the Romans, was left behind as an agent of Cesar, when he spent his time no doubt among his old friends the Atrebatii, and might inform Cesar that he had prepared him an easy reception in those parts. In the next summer's expedition, this encouraged Cesar to march higher into the country, where the interest of Comius might facilitate his conquests: this might bring him to the Atrebatii in Berks, and to one of their chief stations in Walingford, which is much the more probable, because after this passage over the Thames, king Cassibelan sent this Comius as a mediator to Cesar, which was the more proper, if the conqueror was in those parts, for which the ambassador was most concerned. Secondly, after Cesar had crossed the Thames, the people who submitted themselves do seem to prove, that his presence and his conquests extended hither. For upon the yielding of the Trinobantes or men of Middlesex, they were the inhabitants about this middle of the land, who followed their example: among them the Bibroci in the hundred of Bray, com. Berks: the Segontiaci, who had their Cair-Segont, now Silcester, in Hampshire: and the Ancalites, who were the next neighbours to Walingford on the other side of the river, and had their head town at Henly in this county. Thirdly, this tradition of Cesar's coming over at Walingford was current in the time of king Alfred, who, giving a Saxon interpretation of the history of Orosius, makes this express comment on Cesar's wars in Britain, that *his third battle was by the river Thames, nigh a shallow called Wallingford*[r] Which authority of so ancient a native writer ought to weigh much

---

[r] Alfredi interpret. Oros. l. 6. c. 9.

with English antiquaries. Fourthly, though Cesar did intend and did possibly attempt a passage at that place, where the Coway Stakes were by the Britains pitched down on the bank, and at the bottom of the river: yet the Romans could not ford it over at this place, because of the stratagem which galled their foot, and made them retreat to find out a more passable part of the river, as is plain from Orosius, who is herein followed by the venerable Bede, who, speaking of those stakes, observes, that the Romans, when they found them, were forced to avoid them, &c. So as, declining this difficulty, they might well march higher up the river, and cross it at or near Walingford, and on the other side encountered the forces of Cassibelan, and put them to flight. Fifthly, Gulielmus Pictaviensis was informed of this tradition, who, writing the acts of his patron William the Conqueror, draws the parallel between him and Cesar, and endeavouring to shew how much greater success attended the Duke, than ever waited on the Roman general, he gives this instance, *When Cesar came to the river Thames to force a passage into the dominion of Cassibelan, his enemies opposed him on the other side, so as the Roman soldiers passed over with loss and danger. But when the Norman Duke came into the same country, the princes and the people came there to meet him, and his forces had a free and open passage cross the river* [s]. Which must allude to the town of Walingford; for there it was that Stigand archbishop and other grandees made their application to him, and there he passed the Thames, came to Oxford, took his road to Berkamsted, and thence to London [t]. Farther, the very name of this town is no light argument of this matter; for Antonine calls it Calleva, and from Ptolomy it is rendered Callena; Camden restores it Gallena, and from Hum. Lhuyd would have it a British name, Gual-Hen, Vallum Antiquum. Yet I see no reason why it may not be supposed a Roman appellation, or at least by the Britains imposed in memory of the Gauls here passing the Thames, and defeating the forces of Cassibelan:

[s] Gesta Ducis Norman. p. 210.   [t] Ib. 235.

especially when the Saxons changed the name into ⲅuallenȝaꝼoꝼb and ꝼallenȝaꝼoꝼb; their addition of *ford* implying it to have been a fordable passage cross the stream. Why may not Walingford be *Gallorum transitus*, as well as the ancient Nant-Gallum, the Saxon Walbroke, be so called from the passage and defeat of Levius Gallus, colleague of Alectus, an. 294 [u]. Lastly, the eminence of this place during the government of the Romans in this isle may add weight to the former reasons. It is not unlikely that Comius of Arras or Artois, before his mission by Cesar, had been king of the Atrebatii in Britain, and had his principal city upon this bank of the Thames, called Gallena Atrebatium, the metropolis of those people. For the Britains seizing and imprisoning him at first arrival seems too great a rudeness even for barbarous people to have been guilty of, if they had not looked upon him as a deserter, rather than a legate. Or, however, if he did not bear that precedent relation to our British Atrebatii, yet having been made king of the Atrebates in Gaul, during his service in those wars, it is likely he applied himself to the same people in this island; and by their information and assistance might conduct Cesar, through their country, to the most passable part of the Thames. And if he were not their original prince, yet, upon this conquest, he was appointed their king by Cesar: which is evident by two several coins found in these parts, and represented by Camden [x], one of gold, that exhibits on the one side a horseman armed, and inscribed REX; on the reverse, COM. which that author interprets COMIUS king of the Atrebatii: the other of silver with a crescent and this inscription, REX CALLE; and on the reverse a vulture or other bird. He conjectures that CALLE might allude to the city Callena or Gallena, Walingford; and the accurate Mr. Burton refers REX to Comius king of the Atrebatii [y]. It was certainly a place of great figure and resort, while the Roman arms prevailed, and is mentioned at least four

[u] Mat. West. p. 123.   [x] Camden Britan. inter numismata.   [y] Burton Comment. on Anton. Itinerary, p. 225.

times in the Itinerary of Antoninus as a public station : and Camden, upon frequent view of the place, does impute the remains of
fortification to the labour of the Romans [z]. These several conjectures may arise to as much proof, as any matter of fact not expressly
recorded is capable of, at so great a distance of time. Let all abound
in their own sense : I am myself satisfied by these reasons, that
Walingford was the place where Cesar crossed the Thames, and came
into the borders at least of this county; on which I would not have
insisted, if any of our antiquaries had before applied themselves to
the resolution of it.

Having thus advanced the opinion of Cesar's access to this county, I shall now keep to these north-east parts, the confines of my intended subject. And here, since the plainest tokens of the abode
and dominion of the Romans were either forts and garrisons established by them, or coins reposited, or highways made, or customs
remaining; it is easy to discover all these marks of Roman antiquity, and thence to infer, that these adjacent parts were full of
men and action, under those masters of the world.

C H A P. III.

ROMAN GARRISONS.

THE next Roman expedition into Britain was under the command of Aulus Plautius, sent hither by the emperor Claudius, about
the forty-fourth year from our Saviour's birth. His first victory
over Cataratacus and Togodumnus, sons of Cunobelin, was in these
parts, as appears from the consequence of it : for, upon the flight
of these British princes, that part of the Bodunni or Dobuni, who
were subject to the Catuellani, submitted to the conquerors, and re-

[z] Britan. Atrebatii.

ceived garrisons to secure their fidelity[a]. These Bodunni were the people of Glocester and Oxfordshires, thought to be so called from the British Bodu or Bodun, *deep*, (from whence possibly Bodicott, of a deep situation in this county,) as by other authors called Dobuni, from the like British word. *Dwfn* now signifies *deep* in the Welch tongue. The Catuellani were the inhabitants of Buckingham, Bedford, and Hertfordshires. So as the Bodunni, which, because nearest to the Catuellani, were in subjection to them, must be the people of the north-east parts of this county, adjoining to that of Bucks. This is the more apparent from the progress of the Romans: for, after their leaving a garrison to awe the Bodunni, they marched toward a river, on the other side of which the Britains were encamped, supposing the enemy could not pass the waters to them: but Plautius sending over the Germans, who were used to rapid streams, surprised the Britains, wounded their chariot-horses, and put them to a disordered flight. This action seems to have been on these banks of the river Ous, at or near Buckingham, it being plain that Plautius had pursued the Britains hither eastward, and after this defeat, and a second unsuccessful rally, they still retired to the more eastern parts, till they came toward the mouth of the river Thames. After another victory over the Britains, and the death of Togodumnus, Plautius thought fit to pursue a flying enemy no farther, but invited the emperor to come himself, and reap the glories of a triumph, having first placed sufficient garrisons in those places, which he had already subdued; some of which garrisons must be fixed here in the north-east borders of the Bodunni, and the adjacent parts of the Catuellani.

By long ages and the silence of historians, places are as much subject to death, as the men who resided in them. I ought not to guess where these garrisons were fixed without some authority, or fair presumption for it. The injustice is as great to set up new, as to remove the ancient landmarks. Cirencester, on the edge of Glo-

[a] Dio. b. 60. f. 677.

cestershire, seems to have been as well the first as the greatest of the Roman stations, which the Britains had before made a place of strength and confluence. This Corinium is by Ptolomy recorded as the metropolis or chief city of the Dobuni [b], and was after called Corinium Dobunorum [c]. But the presumption is very fair, that another of these garrisons of Plautius was at Alcester, adjoining to Ambrosden, lying as the frontier of the Boduni and Catuellani, and from whence the army of Plautius might agreeably pursue the Britains to Buckingham, or the adjacent banks of the Ouse. Of this station that still retains the name of Alchester, Camden was content to observe this only, that the name did denote the antiquity of it, the Saxons having called it Ealƀceaᵼᵼeþ, because, before their arrival, it had been an ancient military station. But others have since thought, there is some reason and some authority to attribute this garrison to the Roman Allectus, supposing it Allecti Castrum. An opinion ingeniously delivered, and with much shew of truth, by a modern author, in a short discourse, an. 1622, which begins with this account of the antiquity of that place [d]. *Alchester, All-cair, or Cair-allect, was a walled town, that stood in the north-east part of Oxfordshire, part of that country, which, before the division of shires, was called Dobuni Dofu, because of the deepness and fatness thereof: built, as may be collected from many probabilities, (besides the first syllable of his name) by Caius Allectus, one of the thirty tyrants, who, by slaying his dear friend and emperor Carausius, obtained the sole government of Britain. Allectus usurping the title of Emperor, as may appear by his brass money still extant, for his better defence as well against Carausius whilst he lived, as also against Constantine then coming in, had built and fortified the walled town of All-chester in the heart of the land, that if he were put to the worst at the sea-side, yet he might have where to reinforce himself in the main land,*

[b] Ptol. Geog. l. 8. c. 2. [c] Raven Geog. Par. 1688. [d] The History of All-chester, near Bircester in Oxfordshire, with such other occurrents as are contiguous and appendant to the same. Ad Franciscum Crane Equitem Auratum Aulicum. MS. 4to.

and having advertisement of Constantius his coming near at hand by sea, hastened to the south-seas, near the Isle of Wight, to intercept his landing, leaving the first syllable of his name in Allsford, Allington, Allingham, for his way and passage as well as in All-chester for his residence. But Constantius having gained the benefit of a misty foggy time, landed his men, put them in good order, and, like a valiant resolute captain, burnt up his ships, that neither the enemy might be strengthened by his vessels, nor his vassals have any hopes to save themselves by flight; and so, before Allectus had any certain intelligence where he was, gave Allectus, that ambitious bloody tyrant, a set battle by the sea-side, and put him to a shameful flight, whom Asclepiodotus slew shortly after; but where, except it were at a plain called Allesfield, now Ellsfield, between All-chester and the city of Oxford, which cometh near to his name, and importeth a battle fought, I cannot nor will not determine. In the forefront of All-chester, Allectus, for his better defence, built a sconce or watch-tower, the ruins or rudders whereof still appear in a plat of meadow ground, now the soil of Thomas Moyle, Esq. but formerly of a knight of the name of Maund; where in our days has been digged up much Roman money, brick and tile, and pavement of curious and wrought tile, of the bigness of sixpence, being delicately laid there. Before it, was some inward hollow place which the Romans called Tyslanicum; the country people call it still very properly Rully or Rulla, yet without any knowledge of what it meaneth. For Rulla is a diminutive of Runa, which cometh of Ruo to rush; that as Aries was a kind of engine to batter down walls withal: so also the engine Rulla was broad-headed like a plough-staff, which thereupon is called Rullum, and seemed to beat off the enemies from the walls thereof. The engine, therein kept, giving name to the tower. The ground where Allchester stood was neither too fat to make it foul, nor too lean to make it barren, but reasonably fertile, well-meadowed about it, and washed with a sweet little current of water, that floweth out of two little heads arising some three or four miles off. For Allchester there is not one stone left upon another; what happened to Troy, happened to it. As it stood in Plough-hundred, so is it all ploughed over, and corn doth grow where it stood, as in this rhyme:

> In Oxfordshire, by Graven-hill wood
> Stood Allchester, so fair and good;
> Allectus walls are brought full low,
> Where once they stood now corn doth grow.

Allectus slew his emperor and friend Carausius, not by secret practices, but by open battle at a place some two miles distant from the walls of Allchester, called after his name; and the field fought there Carausfield, now Cavers-field. The entrenched sconce of Carausius his camp where it lay, still appears in the plain upon Bayards-green. What this writer can mean by the word Tyslanicum I apprehend not, nor can I be informed. All I can say is this, in transcribing quotations we must keep to the very words, though we do not understand them.

This relation is credible, though by the defect of histories there is no authority, but inference and conjecture. The story of Carausius and Allectus in short is this. The guard of our sea-coasts from the infestation of northern pirates was by the Romans committed to a standing admiral, under the title of *Comes Littoris Saxonici per Britanniam*. He was guardian or warden of the ports; and the disposition of garrisons under this officer has given great assistance to the ancient topography of this isle[e]. Which command, about the third year of Dioclesian, was, on petition of Carausius a native of Britain or Ireland, given to him. Who took this opportunity of insinuating to his countrymen, that if they would receive him for their king, he would expel their foreign masters, and restore their native liberty. Upon this prospect he was admitted to the government of this isle, and renounced all tribute and subjection to the Roman state: who, resenting this defection, sent over Basianus; but Carausius, by assistance of the Scots and Picts, killed him, and defeated his forces[f]:

---

[e] Notitia dignitatum Imperii, &c. drawn up in the reign of Theodosius, jun. or in that of Arcadius and Honorius.   [f] Joh. Fordun Scot. Hist. l. 2. c. 39.

maintaining his supreme power for seven years, when, about the year 292, he was slain by Allectus; and though many historians hint at this as a private and treacherous murder, yet is it more likely, as the author of the MS. conjectures, that it was by a decisive battle. For even one of our best historians does represent Allectus delegated by the Roman senate, and coming over hither with an army, and succeeding Carausius, slain in open fight[g]: this British histories attest[h]. From which action, Caversfield, sometime Carausfield, now corruptly Casefield, might be as well denominated, as the river Carun from the same person[i]; on the banks whereof Carausius, in repairing the wall of Severus, built a round house, of which the relics are now said to be known by the name of Arthur's oven, and Julius Hoff. Allectus, after three years reign, was conquered and slain by Asclepiodotus, an. 294, or 295. Nor do Allchester and Ellsfield only bear allusion to his name, but his coins or medals, which in other parts are very rare, have been so often found in this part of the country, that it is an argument he had here his frequent marches, if not his fixed stations.

Before I pass from the presumed original which this unknown author gives to Allcester, I ought to inform posterity, that this MS.* is now in the custody of my worthy friend Mr. Samuel Blackwell, B. D. late Vicar of Burcester, and now Rector of Brampton in the county of Northampton. It had been in the hands of Dr. Plot, before he published his Natural History of this county. *I have met* (says he) *with some notes in a MS. now by me, that says, it was the seat of Allectus the Emperor. Allectus was slain (as this author will have it) at Ellsfield near Oxon. For the credit of this relation, it having no foundation in the Roman story, I shall leave it to the reader's judgment. Yet I shall add thus much for its reputation, that the Roman military ways are very agreeable to it*[k]

* This MS. was by Mr. Blackwell given to me, and is now in my custody. Apr. 25, 1720.

[g] Mat. West. sub. an. 292.   [h] Holinshead, l. 4. c. 23.   [i] Nennii Hist. Brit. cap. 19.   [k] Nat. Hist. Oxf. ch. 10.

CHAP. IV.

ROMAN COINS.

ANOTHER obvious proof of places frequented by the Romans, is the digging up, or casually finding, medals and other relics of that age and nation. For wherever those victorious lords did spread themselves, they must either by design or accident leave those marks behind them, so as it has been justly made an argument for the negative, to disprove any part inhabited by the Romans, if none of their antiquities could be there found. Thus the vast woody tract called by the Britains Cord-Andred, beginning in Kent and running through Sussex into Hampshire, secured all that large extent from being visited by the Romans: and therefore Mr. Lambert observes, that no monuments of antiquity are to be met with in the weald of Kent or Sussex[1]. The same reflection may be made upon our Chiltern-hills, upon our Bernwood forest, and upon all those parts of England, which were of old uncultivated woods and deserts. But all along their own high ways and open stations, they left much greater quantities of this hidden treasure than has been ever yet discovered: for it was not only accidentally dropped, but industriously secured before they fought, and when at last they deserted the island, they buried their money in hopes of an opportunity to return and raise it up. Of these remains, Leland mentions very many Roman coins found at Dorchester[m]. Dr. Plot reports, that about fourteen years before his writing the Natural History of this county, there were several Roman urns and coins took up in Drunshill, formerly a part of the forest of Stow-wood[n]. And among other places, where the like curiosities are found, he mentions these neighbouring parishes,

---

[1] Peramb. of Kent, p. 211.   [m] J. Lel. Itin. Burton Copy, MS. p. 57.   [n] Plot's Nat. Hist. of Oxf. cap. 13. p. 313.

Stratton-Audley, Fringford, and Tusmore. But there is no one part of this county, wherein such abundance of this treasure has been found, as in the adjoining site of Allcester, of which many instances are given in the Manuscript History of that place. *In the year of grace 1616, an earthen pot full of brass money, bearing the stamp, name, and picture, some of Carausius, some of Allectus, was found under the root of a tree in Steeple-Claydon parish, by the great pond there, in the woods of the worthy knight, Sir Thomas Chaloner, Chamberlain to the hopeful beam of Great Britain, Prince Henry, while he lived: which may seem instead of many authors to give credit to my history. For it seemeth to be hid there, what time they went to the field there hard by; and the hiders being either put to the flight or killed, it so continued till it was found by Sir Thomas his woodward William Richardson. Sir Thomas Chaloner taking me the coin to be informed of the inscription what it meant, I found that the one coin had this inscription on the right side,* IMP. CARAUS. P. F. AUG. *which I interpret thus,* Imperator Carausius Pius Felix Augustus. *And the other coin had* IMP. C. ALLECT. P. F. AUG. *which I likewise thus interpret,* Imperator Caius Allectus Pius Felix Augustus: *both Emperors' pictures being on the right side coronated laureate, and on the other side both coins had the picture of Pallas, with an olive leaf in her right hand, reaching it out in token of peace offered: and a spear in her left hand, that if peace were refused, then wars should ensue: and has in hieroglyphical manner on the same side of the coin, importing each Emperor's name in his own coin. In the midst of that ploughed field, Allchester, which still retaineth that name, though the city be gone, one Fynmore, a husbandman of Wendlebury, ploughing very deep, lighted upon a rough round stone, which being digged out was found to be hollowed within, and seamed and cemented together, and being opened, there was nothing found there but a green glass of some three quarters full of ashes, close stopped up with lead over the mouth, which warranted it to be the urna or burnt ashes of some great man, most like Carausius slain hard by. One George Maund, of Chesterton aforesaid, took me a piece of money there found,*

(i. e. *in the field where Allchester stood,*) *bearing the picture and name of Constantine, who was second from Allectus, on the right side thereof was this inscription,* CONSTANTIUS AUGUSTUS, *and on the other side the portraiture of a castle, the sun and stars in chief about, and some word by the side of the castle; in my judgment it was* GALLITAS; *it is the arms at this day of the castle of Walingford.* Most likely the inscription was GALL......ITAS, for GALLENA CIVITAS, the city of Walingford. For nummary authors observe, that a castle or walled city was the portraiture of a Roman colony or garrison: and what comes nearest to this stamp, there is a coin of Constantius bearing a castle with a star and crescent, which is made to be the insignia of Byzantium[o]. *Another piece of brass money bearing the name and stamp of* DOMICIAN AUG. GERMAN. *was found in Allchester by the same gentleman at the same time, which, together with a piece of the mouth of the glass, wherein the urna or burnt ashes were kept, he sent me this year,* 1622. *In the plain plat of meadow ground adjoining to Allchester in our days have been digged up much Roman money, brick and tile, and pavement of curious wrought tile of the bigness of sixpence, being delicately laid there.* Thus far the writer of that MS. The pavement last mentioned does argue this place to have been the tent or station of Allectus, or some other supreme general. Dr. Plot[p] speaks of this *pavement* (under the character of the *most eminent of Roman antiquities*) *made of small bricks or tiles not much bigger than dice, with which they paved the place, where they set the prætorium or general's tent, as Suetonius[q] mentions of Julius Cesar. If of small square marbles, they were called* lithostrata; *if of bricks or tiles,* pavimenta tessellata, *or opus musivum.* Of both sorts he found several ploughed up about Great Tew, Steeple-Aston, &c. in this county; and concludes, they must argue *some Roman generals did here encamp, either in time of Agricola, Lieutenant of Vespasian, or at least of Paulinus that defeated*

[o] Numismata Ducis Croy Tab. 66. xix. edit. Ant. 1654.   [p] Nat. Hist. of Oxford, ch. 10.   [q] Jul. Cæs. c. 46.

Boadicea. Some of these pretty curiosities are by that worthy collector of them reposited in the Musæ. Ashmol. Leland reports that King Edward the First, in the eighth year of his reign, brought out of France some porphyry marble, with which he adorned the sepulchre of his father at Westminster : and from the broken pieces of it were made a tesselated pavement in the same place ʳ.

Dr. Plot speaks of several *earthen pots found in these parts, some for the use of urns, some of lamps, some of lacrymatories, and others for vessels of oil and aromatic liquors.* And what is of more immediate concern, he relates, that *in the parish of Wendlebury a great square stone hollowed round in the middle, dug up in or near the old city of Allchester, in which there was set a glass bottle fitted to it, containing nothing but somewhat like ashes, and covered over above with another flat pot.* This urn he saw at a house in the town, where it was used for a hog-trough, but the glass had been broken long before, nor could he get any certain description of it.

This area or site of Allchester has been for many ages an arable part of the common field of Wendlebury : so as the teeth of time and of the plough may be thought to have consumed all the Roman relics : yet by walking over the ground, I find it easy to collect many fragments of brick, tile, urns, vessels, and other materials, all of Roman make, and enough to distinguish this from any adjacent soil. Great variety and plenty of Roman money, of such especially as is dated from the decline of that empire, has been within few years gathered and dispersed. The largest collection is said to have been in the hands of Mr. Lee, the proprietor of Bignel farm in the parish of Burcester ; who, in his voyage from the West-Indies, was carried prisoner into France, and died in that kingdom. The late Rector of Wendlebury, Mr. Bond, was by his parishioners furnished with a considerable number of them. And within a few years wherein I have applied myself to some inquiry, I have bought up more than one hundred several pieces, most of which have been

ʳ J. Lel. MS. Collect. tom. 1. p. 365.

found by the children of Wendlebury in following the plough, or by turning the clods of earth. They call them Allcester-coin, and are proud of receiving more passable money for them. The most remarkable of those in my custody shall be represented in a table.

There be footsteps still remaining of this garrison at Allcester, in the names of the two neighbouring villages Chesterton and Wendlebury: of which the former lies contiguous to the site of the old city, and seems to have sprung up from the ashes of it, preserving the memorial and the name of *castrum* or *cestre*. The other, though a small village, has swallowed up the city, and keeps the site of it within its own bounds, on the east part of the common field. This Wendlebury seems to derive its name from the Vandals, who might have their station in this place. For these northern people being of Gothic original, came out of Scythia, and settled on the coasts of the Baltic sea toward Germany. They were employed as auxiliaries to the Romans in the decay of that empire, and being called Vandals, from the word [s] *wandalen* to wander, this station of theirs might be called Vandalburg, or (according to the promiscuous use of V and W) Wandalburg, and the termination of Burg passing into Bury: this place, in Doomsday-book Wandesberie, might with ease and softness corrupt into Wendelbury. This conjecture appears the better grounded, when we consider that Zosimus [t] reports the Vandals were sent as stipendiary soldiers into Britain by Probus the Emperor, whose coins have been here found. Gervase of Tilbury mentions an old intrenchment in Cambridgeshire called Vandelsburg, because a work or fortification of the Vandals. The same place is by Ingulphus called Wendlingburough, and Wendlyngburgh [u], which answers exactly to the present parish.

---

[s] Sheringham de Angl. origine, p. 210.   [t] Zoz. Histor. l. 1.   [u] Histor.
Ingulphi, edit. Gale, p. 3?

C H A P. V.

ROMAN HIGHWAYS.

A THIRD reason to infer the acquaintance of the Romans with any place is, when any of their highways did lead through it. And though this indeed be no immediate proof, since a long tract of any road may extend through desert and unpeopled places; yet when this is strengthened by the two former arguments, it imports the greater likelihood, that the Romans should settle most upon their own roads, to be in places of better defence and greater resort. For it is the tracing out these port ways, that has enabled our later antiquaries to establish the site of Roman forts and stations in this isle, which, for want of this advertence, had been miserably displaced and confounded.

From hence we may presume the Romans had a familiar notice of this country, because one of their more eminent and chief ways led through the parish of Ambrosden; and some other of their lesser streets were nigh adjoining. Most of our modern writers have rejected, as a legendary tale, the account of four main roads, drawn out as it were to measure and divide the land by the British king Molmutius Dunwallo, or by his son Belinus. In the seven Molmutian laws recited by Mr. Selden[x], the second relates to highways; but these laws seem invented rather than preserved. So that most are now persuaded these four principal ways were each a Roman labour, done for the conveniencies of march and conveyance: and some assert the beginner of them to have been the famed Agricola[y], and that their continuation and improvement were an exercise, both to the captived Britains and to the Roman soldiers. But no more of this, because other writers have made it a common place, to which I would not prostitute a reader's patience.

[x] Janus Angl. cap. 4.   [y] Tacit. Agric. vit. 30.

An accurate observer thought it once a new discovery, that one of these prime stratæ called Ikenild* or Ickenild street, passed through this county, entering at Chinnor and passing over the Thames at Goring, and still retained its old name at many places, as Ikenild, Icknil, Acknil, Hackney, &c. [z] But the same ingenious author seems to retract this opinion. *Whether that in Staffordshire be the true Ickenild street, or that in Oxfordshire, deserves consideration. That in Oxfordshire seems to have been so called, because it tends toward the Iceni of Norfolk, &c. This of Staffordshire, because made through the county of the other Iceni. I look upon this of Staffordshire the more remarkable of the two, and so to be that Ickenild street, which is usually reckoned one of the four basilical or great ways in England, and not that in Oxford* [a].* Ours however was one of the Roman ways, though none of the four by eminence so called. But I inquire the less into it, because its course did not directly touch upon these parts. One of these chief ancient ways was called Erming-street, which though Hen. Hunt. would have to lead from north to south, yet others have most justly assigned its course from west to east [b]: beginning at St. David's in Wales, and so directing not to Southampton as some pretend, but to London, and so to the eastern shores of Kent. This Erming-street is thought the same, which was since, and is now called Akeman-street-way, a road pointing east and west, upon which on the south side was close adjoining the ancient city of Allchester. The MS. history of that place asserts it thus. *Allchester standeth in the very heart of Akeman-street-way, one of the four great ways that parteth the land of Britain. Our chronicles generally call it Ermyn-street of the British word Army-*

---

* *Centum acræ terræ in manerio de Newnham com. Oxon. jacent in quatuor particulis, una particula jacet in uno ley et extendit versus orientem in Tethingwey, et altera pars jacet versus Mongewell, et tertia pars extendit versus occidentem. In campo de Niwenham quinque acras quæ se extendunt in viam quæ dicitur Ykenhilda. b. f. lxx. a.*

[z] Nat. Hist. of Oxf. ch. 10. §. 22.   [a] Nat. Hist. of Staff. ch. 9. §. 14.   [b] Burt, Com. Ant. Itin. p. 94.

inth, because it crosseth mountains and wayless places for the better direction for travellers. Those that call it Akeman-street-way say, that it took its name from them, that, being full of ache and aching, made it their way to the hot baths in Somersetshire for ease of their pains. The present name of Akeman-street is justly here derived from its passage to Bath, which city by several of the old writers is called Acamannum[c]. And the other derivation here given of Erming-street seems more natural than what Mr. Selden[d], and from him Mr. Burton[e], would affix to it. *Ermingstreet (say they) being of English idiom, seems to have had its name from* Iᵽmunᵽull, *in that signification whereby it interprets an universal pillar worshipped for Mercury,* President *of ways.* Mr. Camden was misinformed in the tract of this way, and made to believe that Akeman-street was the military way which led from Walingford to Banbury, of which some remains appeared in Otmoore[f]. This he resolved into the oral tradition of the common people, which indeed does still continue among the borderers on Otmoore, who now call the paved way, which crosses their deep marsh by the name of Akeman-street, though its course be indeed as directly opposite, as north and south to east and west, and did either terminate at Allchester, or there cut the Akeman-street, and continued on to Banbury. And the country people could have no other reason for this false appellation, but only that the greater adjoining road to Acmancestre having been always so called, they came thence to attribute the like name to any other way, that was of the like make and use, and seemed a branch of the former. Dr. Plot was the first writer who restored the true directions of Akemanstreet, in which he was instructed by the current tradition, and by many visible marks[g]. *The true Akeman-street, or as some call it Akeham-street, and others Akerman-street, enters this county at a village called Blackthorn, whence it passes on without any raised bank, close by Allchester as far as Chesterton, as described by the*

---

[c] Sim. Dun. p. 161, &c.   [d] Notes on Polyolb. Song 16. p. 256.   [e] Comment. Ant. Itin. p. 95.   [f] Camden, Dobuni.   [g] Nat. Hist. Oxf. ch. 10. §. 33.

shaded or pointed lines in the map: whence it goes to Kirtlington
town's end, and so over the river Cherwell near Tackley, and thence
in a straight line to Woodstock-Park, which it enters near Wotton-
gate, and passes out again at Mapleton-well near Stunsfield-stile,
whence it holds on again as far as Stunsfield, and all this way on a
raised bank, as described in the map by two parallel lines; where break-
ing off (but still keeping its name) it goes on over the Evenlode to
Wilcot, and so to Ramsden; a little beyond which village, at a place
called Witty-green, it may be seen again for a little way; but from
thence to Astally, over Astall-bridge, and so through the fields till it
comes to Brodwell-grove, it is scarce visible, but there it is as plain
again as any where else, holding a straight course into Glocestershire,
and so towards the Bath, the old Akemancester. I need add no more
to this accurate description, but I would define its more particular
course through the parish of Ambrosden, and the parts contiguous
to it. This way comes down from the hill in Tuchwic grounds, in
the common road from Ailesbury to Burcester, and passing over that
mershy vale, which gave name to the neighbouring town of Mersh
it leaves there some tracks of a stony ridge now visible and useful,
and crosses the rivulet at a place called Worden-pool or Stean-ford,
from that passage pitched or paved with stones, where it enters upon
the county of Oxford, and the parish of Ambrosden, and continuing
on near the north-east corner of Blackthorn-green by the pond, it
there leaves some other tokens of bank and stone, and so ascends to
Blackthorn-hill, formerly Windmill-hill, whence it ran in the present
Bicester road, till in Wrechwic-green, which was the common field
of the manor of Wrechroych, it turns to the left hand, and in the
second ground (as now divided) it extends by the north-side of
Gravenhull-wood, in and near the way that now leads to Wendlebury, and passing the brook at the fordable place called Langford,
it bears close to the north-side of Allchester field, and so to Ches
terton, &c.

The city of Allchester having had for long time a fixed garrison
of Roman forces did occasion many other public ways, leading to

other of their stations, of which the most apparent is that before mentioned over Ottmore, which the country people persuaded Mr. Camden to take for the true Akemanstreet. It is thus corrected and described by Dr. Plot[h]. *There seems also to have been cast up another Roman way between the old city of Allchester in the parish of Wendlebury, and the city of Calleva, whereof there is part to be seen at this day running quite cross Otmoor, and coming out of the moor under Beckley-park-wall, which it is plain has been paved (as indeed it had need) by the stones yet found upon and about the ridge, and no where else on the moor. From Beckley it passes on to, and may be plainly seen in the wood near Stockers, where, cutting the London road to Worcester, it goes plainly through the fields to Stafford-grove, and thence over Bayards watering place, toward Heddington quarry-pits, leaving Shot-over-hill on the left hand, and the pits on the right. At the foot of Shot-over-hill it enters Magdalene college coppices, over the eastern part of Bullington-green, as I gather by its pointing, for it is not to be seen there, it having been ploughed down as well in the green as fields thereabouts, as may be seen by the marks of the ridge, and furrow yet remaining upon it: whence I guess it passes on towards the two Baldens, and so for Walingford, going over the river at Benson, alias Bensington, where it may be seen again running west of the church; and is there called by the name of Medlers-bank.* The same diligent and well informed observer speaks of several other branches of Roman way, *one going out of the main road about the parish of Beckley, and passing more westward through Stow-wood, and more particularly through the grounds called Principal, where the way is to be seen entire and perfect, having formerly been paved, as appears by a ditch cut through the bank, where the stones lie archwise, &c. so leading to Oxford. Another such Roman way seems designedly made for a passage immediately from Allchester to Oxford, whereof there is a part still remaining about Noke, &c. And out of Akemanstreet there are several branches; two near Kirklington, one at the town's end,*

---

[h] Nat. Hist. Oxf. ch. 10. §. 27, 28.

which, though presently discontinued, yet points just upon the port-way running east of North-brook, the two Heyfords, Sommerton, and Souldern, for six miles together; and another that by its pointing seems to have come out of Akemanstreet, nearer the place where it passes the river Cherwell, crossing the port-way, and running at the broadest place, scarce a mile distant from it, as far as Fritwell, where on the north-side of the town it inclines toward the port-way as if it joined with it again somewhere about Souldern, &c.

Beside these and other branches mentioned by this author, there appears to have been two other roads leading directly from Allches-ter, one declining from the old Akemanstreet at Chesterton, and passing through Middleton-stony, where there is a barrow or large hillock cast up, that seems one of the Roman tumuli or sepulcers, thence falling into Wattle-bank or Avesditch, it might lead to Ban-bury, as is the tradition of the inhabitants near Allchester, and so on to Warwick, the Roman præsidium. Another of these streets turned from Akemanstreet on the east side of the brook, through the grounds called Langford, cutting the lane which leads to Bicester on the south side of Candle-meadow, and thence passing through the lower end of Dunkins-ground, where, upon the late digging of a pond, has appeared the plainest evidence of a paved way, so passing through Lanton went on to Stratton, so called because placed on a Roman street, and where Roman coin has been discovered, thence proceed-ing to Buckingham, and to the old Lactodorum, Stony-Stratford.

CHAP. VI.

ROMAN CUSTOMS.

I MAY offer one more argument for the conversation of the Ro-mans in these parts, that they have left here one of their customary exercises called Quintan, though generally corrupted into Quintal;

by the French termed Quintaine, by the old English, Quintane and Whintane; which sportive custom is still retained in our village of Blackthorn, through which lay the Roman way, where there is seldom any public wedding without this diversion on the common green, with much solemnity and mirth. The ingenious Dr. Plot, among the ancient customs still retained here, when abolished and quite lost in most other counties, reckons this *running at the Quinten, Quintain, or Quintel, so called from the Latin [Quintus], because, says Minshew, it was one of the ancient sports used every fifth year amongst the Olympian games, rather perhaps because it was the last of the πένταθλοι, or the Quinque certamina gymnastica, used on the fifth or last day of the Olympics. How the manner of it was then I do not find, but now it is thus. * They first set a post perpendicularly into the ground, and then place a slender piece of timber on the top of it on a spindle, with a board nailed to it on one end, and a bag of sand on the other; against this board they anciently rode with spears; now, as I saw it at Deddington in this county, only with strong staves, which violently bringing about the bag of sand, if they make not good speed away, it strikes them on the neck and shoulders, and sometimes perhaps knocks them from their horses; the great design of this sport being to try the agility both of horse and man, and to break the board, which whoever does, is for that time accounted* princeps juventutis. *For whom heretofore there was some reward always appointed.*
Eo tempore (says Matthew Paris[d]) juvenes Londinenses, statuto

---

* Escuage might well have taken that name from the manner of summons used in the empire, which was by erecting a post or pillar, and hanging a shield at the top thereof, an herald proclaiming, that all who held in this manner should at such a day attend the emperour in his voyage to Rome for taking the crown of Italy or king of Romans, which the Ligurine poet thus expresseth:

——— ——— Ligno suspenditur alto
Erecto clypeus, hinc præco regius omnes
Convocat a Dominis feudalia jure tenentes.
Gunter de Gest. Tred. 1. l. 2. p. 301.
Spelman of Feuds. MS. cap. 22.

Those sports which were first military grew into peaceable and ludicrous diversions. So the old mommyng was formerly an hastiludia, now a mere Christmas masquerade. Vide Hist. Croyland contin. p. 495.

d Mat. Par. sub initium an. 1253. edit. Watsiana, p. 863.

Pavone pro bravio, ad stadium quod Quintena vulgariter dicitur, vires proprias et equorum cursus sunt experti. *Wherein it seems the king's servants opposing them were sorely beaten, for which, upon complaint, the king fined the city. Whence one may gather that it was once a trial of manhood between two parties; since that, a contest amongst friends who should wear the gay garland; but now only in request at marriages, and set up in the way for young men to ride at, as they carry home the bride, he that breaks the board being counted the best man*[e]. *I must beg leave to acquaint the reader, that since the printing the 21st-sect. of it, I have found the Quintan amongst the Roman exercises, (which yet perhaps they might borrow from the Greeks) by the name of Quintana, so called by reason the Romans in their tents made first four ways in manner of a cross, to which adding a fifth on one side, it was called Quintana*[f]. *In this way they set up a great post about six foot high, suitable to the stature of a man, and this the Roman soldiers were wont to assail with all instruments of war, as if it were indeed a real enemy; learning upon this, by the assistance of the Campidoctores, how to place their blows aright. And this they otherwise called* exercitium ad palum, *and sometimes* palaria, *the form whereof may be seen in Vulturius*[g]. *Which practice being in use during their government here, in all likelihood has been retained among us ever since, being only translated in times of peace from a military to a sportive marriage exercise*[h].

To this agreeable description of the Quintan, because no other authors have made it their particular inquiry, I shall farther add. Matthew Westminster transcribed this account of the Quintan from Matthew Paris; but in the common edition of his Flores Histor. it is *ad Quindenam* instead of *ad Quintenam*[i], by which error readers have mistaken it for a *term of days* instead of a *solemn sport*. Dr. Watts in his glossary gave an apt explication of it, *a ludicrous and*

---

[e] Dr. Plot. Nat. Hist. Oxf. ch. 8. §. 21, 22, 23.   [f] Vid. Guid. Pancirollum rer. memorabilium, lib. 2. tit. 21.   [g] In Augustanis monumentis, p. 237.   [h] Plot. Oxf. ch. 8. §. 53.   [i] Mat. West. sub an. 1253.

sportive way of tilting, or running on horseback at some mark hung up on high, moveable, and turning round, which, while the riders strike at with lances, unless they ride quickly off, the versatile beam strikes upon their shoulders[k]. Sir Henry Spelman, from being himself a spectator of it, reports, *a piece of board fixed at one end of a turning beam, and a bag of sand at the other, by which means, striking at the board whirls round the bag, and endangers the striker*[l]. As far as I am yet informed, I find this sport is now continued in no part of the country, but where the Roman ways did run, or where some Roman garrisons had been placed, which last honour does seem to belong to Deddington, where Dr. Plot observed the celebration of it. For though this learned author does acknowledge, that *after long search he could find nothing of Deddington, till about the reign of King Edward the Second*[m]. *When he takes the old castle to be the very place, no question, to which Aymer de Valence Earl of Pembroke, brought Piers de Gaveston*[n], *&c.* Yet in one of those elaborate volumes of the Baronage of England, to which he does acknowledge himself beholding for the account of these things[o], I find that in the tenth of Richard the First, *Warine, son of Warine Fitzgerold, gave one hundred marks for the seisin of the manor of Deddington in com. Oxon. as his mother had at the time of her death*[p]. This Warine held the manor of Heyford in this county, which from this family was called Heyford-Warine. His mother's name (not mentioned by Dugdale) was Maud de Chesny, who in her widowhood granted to the canons of St. Edburg in Burcester five seams or quarters of bread-corn out of the said manor of Heyford, to make hosts or consecrated bread: which gift was assented to by the said Warine her son[q]. This manor of Deddington had then a castle fortified in it, which soon after belonged to Wido de Diva, whose possessions king John seized into his hand, and in the sixth of his reign sent a precept to the Sheriff

---

[k] Watts in Glossar. verbo Quintena. [l] Spelman Glossar. in verbo. [m] Nat. Hist. Oxf. ch. 10. §. 122. [n] Ib. §. 135. [o] Ib. §. 134. [p] Dugd. Bar. tom 1. p. 411. [q] R. Dodsworth MS. vol. 132. f. 9.

of Oxfordshire, to restore without delay all his lands and chattels, except the castle of Deddington, which the king would keep in his own hands[r]. But I designed no such digression here; the antiquity and conveyance of Deddington will hereafter fall to a more proper place.

I return to the sport of Quintan; which in the Christian expeditions to the Holy Land was an exercise of the soldiers when they lay in their camp, *their tents being beautified with several sorts of orna-ments, some posts were fixed in the ground*, on the top of which were shields fastened to a turning beam, on which they practised on horse-back the sport of Quintan*[s]. When Giraldus Cambrensis returned from Paris in the year 1180, passing through Artois in Flanders, he came in Whitsunweek to Arras, where a great tumult happened on this occasion; *Philip Earl of Flanders, in this his chief city, in the market-place, had a Quintan erected, to wit, a strong beam hung upon a post, where the stoutest young men on horses tried their strength by breaking their lances, or striking through the shield on the end of the beam*[t]. Du Fresne recites it as a custom in the town of Meziers in Champaine, that the millers of that place were bound once in a year to strike three blows at the Quintan, as a feat of activity[u]. Here in England it was sometime a sport upon the water, as well as on the land; being thus represented by William Fitz-Stephen monk of Canterbury, who wrote a short Latin description of the city of Lon-don, in the reign of Henry the Second. *In Easter holidays they have a sort of naval battles, a shield is hung upon a mast fixed in the*

---

* 1550, June 4. Sir Rob. Dudley, third son to the earl of Warwick, married Sir John Robsart's daughter; after which mar-riage there were certain gentlemen that did strive who should first take away a goose's head, which was hanged alive on two cross posts. Diary or Journal of King Edw. VI.

See Sir Hen. Spelman of Feuds and Te-nures, ch. 23. p. 27.

[r] R. Dods. MS. vol. 103. f. 8.   [s] Robert. Mon. Hist. Hieros. l. 3. p. 51.   [t] Gi-rald. Cambrens. de rebus a se gestis. pars 2. c. 4. Whartoni Ang. Sacra pars 2da. p. 479. [u] Du Fresne Glossar. in voce.

middle of the river, for which a boat without oars is to be carried down to it by the force of the stream, and at the head of the boat stands a young man ready to strike at the shield with his lance: if he break his lance and keep his standing, he is then a victor ; but if he be repulsed without breaking his lance by a full blow, he then falls into the water, and the boat is drove down by the tide ; but to prevent his drowning, there be two other boats on each side the beam to take up the person: upon the bridge, wharfs, and penthouses, stand great numbers to see and laugh at this diversion[x]. This seems to be the same sport which was afterward called *arietum levatio,* I suppose so called, because such manner of violent striking did seem to resemble the Roman ways of playing their battering rams: or else because the shield or board upon the striking end might be made in fashion of a ram's head, or because they fastened the horns of a ram on the returning end to make the blow more comical. None of our glossographers have explained this term, though it is evident it was a customary English sport, and often forbid by ecclesiastical authority. In the year 1233, among the articles of inquisition directed to the archdeacons in this diocese of Lincoln, one inquiry was to be, *an alicubi eleventur arietes, vel fiant scotalla, &c.* And in the constitutions of that great preserver of church discipline Bishop Grosthead, it was commanded that in every church should be published a prohibition, *ne quisquam levet*[*] *arietes super rotas, vel alios ludos statuat, in quibus decertatur pro bravio, nec hujusmodi ludis quisquam intersit*[y]. The same words are repeated in the provincial statutes of Walter Bishop of Durham, an. 1255. Wherein the description and allusion seem to determine it the same, or a very like sport with the Quintan. It is certain this diverting exercise was used in different manner, at different times and places: and the present use of this manly recreation in the village of Blackthorn does a little vary from

---

* Quære of the Saxon word for a Ram, Þænþol.

[x] Stow, Survey of London, 4to. p. 69.   [y] Append. ad Fasciculum inter opuscula Rob. Grossetest. p. 413.

the customary method of other places : for here they set up a roll, or that instrument of agriculture which is drawn to smooth and break the clods of the earth, whether cut round or octangular, which latter form Dr. Plot observes as peculiar to these parts about Burcester [z], and at the erect end they hang a strong rafter board, which turns upon the spindle of the roll, to one end of this moving beam or balance they nail a slab or broader piece of thick board, and at the other end they hang a leathern bag or satchel of gravel or rubbish of equal poise, which flies round, and smites the inexpert rider.

As we may plainly trace the Romans, so is it possible that Christianity was here planted among the remaining Britains, who at last were most populous, where Roman garrisons lay nearest to protect them. One of our historians founds a long story on a Christian church and patron of it, within the county of Oxford, above one hundred and fifty years before the coming of Austine the monk [a]. And by better authority we after find, that one of the most fatal mischiefs, occasioned by the incursion of the Angles, was the persecution of the British converts in these parts. For when the Angli took possession of Mercia, wherever they prevailed, the British Christians were martyred or expelled [b]. That our religion flourished early in these parts does appear from the saints who were here buried, and whose shrines did long invite the ignorant and superstitious : of whom there was St. Brenwold at Bampton, St. Hycrith a virgin at Cheselhampton, and St. Donanverdh at Beckley [c].

Before I pass from the Romans in these parts, I would farther inform the world, that in the beginning of March 169⅔, in Kingstonfield within the parish of Aston-Rowant, at the bottom of a small stream called Colebrook, about a furlong from the lower branch of the Ikenild-street way, was taken up a large earthen pot in which were contained, 1. A Roman urn that would hold the quantity of

[z] Nat. Hist. of Oxf. ch. 9. §. 79.   [a] Jo. Brompton inter X. script. p. 735.
[b] Hen. Hunt. Hist. l. 2.   [c] E Libello de Locis in quibus sancti requieverunt, apud Jo. Leland Collect. vol. 2. p. 369. MS.

TAB 1.

Fig. A.

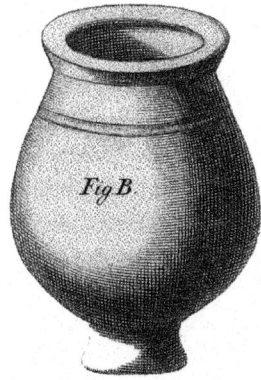

Fig. B.

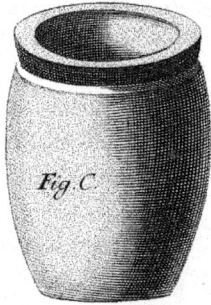

Fig. C.

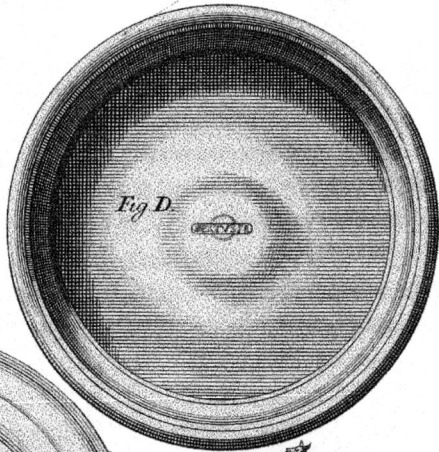

Fig. D.

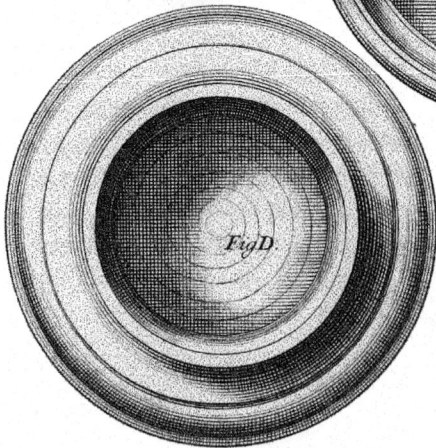

Fig. D.

Summa spei Juveni
et ad optima quæque nato
HENRICO WORSLEIO suo
Tabellam hanc dicat,
W. Kennett.

two quarts, narrow at the mouth, which was stopped with lead, and
filled with pieces of bones, entire at the taking up, and broke in vain
hopes of treasure in it : represented by the figure *A*. 2. A smaller
urn or lacrymatory unstopped and empty, as figured *B*. 3. A little
pot or vessel of finer earth, containing about one quarter of a pint,
which seems to have been filled with aromatic liquor, of which a
strong scent does still remain, as in the figure *C*. 4. A patine of curious red earth about six inches diameter, with this inscription cross
the centre, SEXTUS FE. the potters name, represented D. the
three last of which are now in my custody.

C H A P. VII.

S A X O N S.

As to the time of the Saxons coming in, the edition of Bede by
Chifletius, and most other printed copies, place it in the year 409.
Mr. Camden is confident it was before an. 449. But Mr. Whee-
lock's Saxon Bede assigns the very year 449, which seems abundantly proved the right date by a very learned writer[d]. Though
these usurpers of our country were swallowed up in the same common name of Saxons, yet they were three different sorts of people,
Saxons, Jutes, and Angles, of which the latter took possession of
this midland country, and were the most noble of all the intruding
party, not only as under king Egbert they gave name to the whole
united kingdom, but as our ancestors were always proud of the appellation of Angles, when their enemies in contempt called them Sassons.

The poor remaining Britains struggled for their liberty, and the
best defender of it was the person, who most likely gave name to the
parish of Ambrosden, Aurelius Ambrosius, whom Gildas makes of

[d] Stillingf. Orig. Brit. ch. 5. p. 316.

Roman *extract, and to have survived his royal murdered parents*[e]
Some of our other historians report him the son of Constantine king
of Britain, by a Roman lady, born about 435, and educated by Gui-
theline archbishop of London : who being forced to retire to Aremo-
rica was thence recalled by the oppressed Britains, and, defeating
the Saxons under the conduct of Hengist at Wipped-fleet in Kent,
he marched to York, thence to Winchester, Salisbury, &c. to en-
courage and recruit the Britains.   Now in this circuit of travels, it is
probable he encamped nigh those places which the Romans had garrisoned and made populous : so as Allchester being lately deserted by
the Romans, and possessed as a tenable fort by the Britains ; Ambrosius may be well supposed to have visited this place, and to have
encamped his marching army on the rising plain, where Ambrosden
now stands : and by this encampment, or some other action, might
leave his name to it : the termination being British and Roman, Am
brosdun and Ambrosdunum.   Dun being the British final syllable
to those places which were situate on a hill or an ascent : and the
Romans letting their proper names be adapted to the British, made
these names end in Dunum, which Dun the English converted into
Don, as Meldon, Ambrosdon, &c.   This is but surmise, yet the
more credible, because the same Ambrosius gave a like name to Am-
brosburg or Ambrosberie, or Amesbury in Wiltshire : which in the
primitive age of English writers was called Urbs Ambrosii[f], (whatever tales some monks have told, and made it long before Pagus Am-
bri[g]) and might be denominated from some victory here obtained, or
his coronation, or burial, or monument after his death, or memorial
by himself erected in honour to the slaughtered Britains, making the
parish to be called Ambrosius Vicus[h], and Stonehenge, Ambrosii
monumentum[i], and Ambrosius Mons.   And though many labour to
give a different account of that stupendous structure, yet none have
denied but that Ambrosius had a relation to that place.

[e] Histor. Gildæ. edit. Gale, p. 17.   [f] Spelman Concil. tom. 1. p. 494.   [g] Gal-
fred. Mon. Rich. Broughton, &c.   [h] Baudrandi Lex.   [i] Pol. Virg. l. 3.

There be other places of like sound, and possibly of like allusion to the camps or seats of action of this victorious prince. A parish in Worcestershire, though corruptly called Ombresly, is truly Ambresley or Ambresloy, as in a donation of lands by Egwyn bishop of Worcester, to the monastery of Evesham in that county[k]. In a royal charter to the church of Ely, there be lands given in Amerdene or Amersden[l], which is likewise called Amberdene in a donation to the abbey of Tilly in Essex[m]. I am not fond of remote and uncertain derivations, and give the reader leave, upon any better grounds, to reject what I guess the primitive name of Ambrosden, Ambrosii Dunum.

In this part of the country, the Britains did long resist the encroaching Saxons. After the kingdom of the West Saxons was established in the persons of Cerdic and Cynric, an. 519[n], they made several attempts to enlarge their conquests in these parts, and after the death of Cerdic, an. 534, Cynric had a greater progress to his arms, and from 551, for five following years, gave several defeats to our midland Britains, who, in the year 556, united all their strength, and at Beranbyrig now Banbury in this county, they fought with king Cynric and Ceawlin his son, to regain the honour they had lost in five preceding years; where they were so numerous as to divide their army into nine battalions, placing three in the front, a like number in the flank, and as many in the rear, with their archers and horse men disposed according to the Roman discipline: by which conduct they so well received the fury of the Saxons, that when the night parted them, the victory was still depending[o]: and though historians conceal it, yet the event seems to prove a success to the Britains, who kept their fortified places in this county to the year 571[p], or as some writers to 580, when king Ceawlyn and Cuthwulph his brother fought with the Britains at Bedford, and after a defeat took from them their strongest garrisons, of which three were in these

[k] Spelman. Concil. tom 1. p. 209.   [l] Mon. Ang. tom. 1. p. 91.   [m] Ib. p. 889.
[n] Chron. Saxon.   [o] Hen. Hunt. edit. Sav. p. 311.   [p] Chron. Saxon.

parts, Egelesburh, Eilesberi, now Ailsbury: Bennington, Benesing-tun, now Benson: and Egonesham, Henesham, now Ensham. From which time, though this whole county was reputed within the district of Mercia, yet most of it was subjected to the kings of the West Saxons.

The next action of remark in these parts was at Beamdune or Bampton on the edge of this county, where king Cynegil and Cwichelm fought with the Britains, and slew above two thousand of them, in the year 614[q]. It is true, Mr. Camden lays the scene of this action at Beandun, now Byndon in Dorsetshire[r]: and another ingenious writer at Bampton in Devonshire[s]. But if we consider the many conflicts in this age between the Britains and Saxons in these parts, and that the Britains were yet powerful, and at their own dis-posal here, before Mercia was brought into the subjection of Penda, about 626; and that the West Saxon kings had their frontier garri-sons at Cirencestre and Ensham frequently infested by the bordering Britains; it is much more probable the forementioned battle was at Bampton in this county, a place of great antiquity, and once of mi-litary strength, and called by the like name Bembune, in a charter of Leofric chaplain to Edward the Confessor[t]. To these reasons of conjecture there is at last a full authority to determine all dispute; *Kinigilsus et Quichelinus multa strenue fecerunt contra Britones, po-tissime apud Bampton juxta Oxoniam*[u].

After Mercia was reduced into a kingdom by Penda, he had the same difficulty to defend these borders from the West Saxons, as the Britains before had: and after three years settlement fought with Cynegils and his son Cwichelm at Cirencester[x], and there being no decisive victory, a league was here made between them. During this peace in these parts came Birinus, a missionary from pope Ho-norius in the year 634, and having converted most of the West

---

[q] Chron. Saxon. sub. an.   [r] Camden in Durotriv.   [s] Gibson, explicat. loc.
in Chron. Sax.   [t] Plot. Nat. Hist. Oxfordsh. ch. 10. §. 121.   [u] Polycron.
Ran. Higden. sub. an. 611   [x] Chron. Saxon. sub. an.

Saxon people, he baptized their king Cynegils at Ðoɲc-ceaɲʈɲe, Dorchester in this county: which city the new Christian prince gave to Birinus for an episcopal see: in which he settled, and exercised his jurisdiction through the whole West Saxon kingdom : in the next year he baptized at the same place Cwichelm, who reigned with his father Cynegils, and died within the year.

It is not unlikely this part of the country was before concerned in the mission of Augustine the monk, about 597, who passed through this county to his place of conference with the Britains, in the remoter parts of Mercia, called from him Augustine-Ac, or Austin's Oak : placed by Brompton in the confines of the West Saxons and the Britains, and from thence to Whalley in Blakeburnshire, Com. Lanc. if we can believe those monks[y]. We are told, that when this apostle of the English came into the county of Oxford, to a village called Cumpton, i. e. Long-Cumpton in Warwickshire, at the edge of this county, the parish priest waited on him, and complained of the lord of the manor refusing to pay his just tithes, upon which Augustine reproved him, and convinced him by a miracle of a dead body raised from the grave; who confessed himself to have been patron of the church in the time of the Britains, and to have been excommunicated for the like default above 150 years before[z], &c. Though Mr. Selden[a], in prejudice to the right of tithes, does reject this whole story as an absurd legend; yet certainly we may lay aside the miraculous part, and believe the person was in this place, though he did no mighty work there. Indeed, if all the circumstances of this relation were true, it would prove Christianity and the discipline of the Church to have flourished here among the Britains very early, and to have continued in good order till the said visit of Austin. But if we renounce all the monkery of this tale, and keep only to the matter of fact, his passing through these parts, it is enough to infer,

[y] Mon. Ang. tom. 1. p. 899.   [z] Jo. Brompton, p. 136.   [a] Selden of Tithes, cap. 10. §. 2.

that those adjoining places, through which his road must lie, did embrace the opportunity to repent and be baptized.

It is however certain, that Birinus resided at his see of Dorchester, and planted Christianity in all adjacent parts : where, as Bede relates, *many churches were built and dedicated by him* [b]. He extended his pious care to the Mercians, among whom Cuthred king of Kent, whose captivity made him no more then a titular prince [c], was baptized at Dorchester by this bishop, an 639 [d].. He is said to have instituted secular canons in his cathedral church, who continued till, in the reign of king Stephen, Alexander bishop of Lincoln converted them into canons regular [e]

Tradition and some slender authority report, that Birinus bore a particular relation to the town of Bisister, which from him, they say, was called Birini-castrum, Birincestre, Burincastre, or Berncestre [f]. It is true, authors differ much in the etymology of this town. W. Harrison seems to refer it to the little rivulet of that name, which rises near it, and runs through it, formerly called Bure, now commonly Rea. *The Isis taketh in a rivulet called the Bure, which falleth into it about Otmoore side ; but forasmuch as it riseth about Bircester, the whole course thereof is not above four miles.* And again, *The last river of all is the Reie alias Bure, (Lat. Burus) whose head is not far above Bircester alias Burcester and Burncestre, and from whence it goeth by Bircestre to Merton, Cherleton, Fencote, Addington, Noke, Islip, and so into Cherwell* [g]. But it is not likely so insignificant a stream should give name to a place which, in its most ancient appellation, Berncestre, bears no affinity to it. Skinner writes it Buрenceaрᴄeр and Beрneceaрᴄeр, *which perhaps* (says he) *is derived from the Anglo-Saxon* Beрn *horreum, and* ceaᴦᴄрe *urbs, as if a grange or repository of corn* [h]. But this too seems a trifling fancy. The

---

[b] Eccles. Hist. l. 3. cap. 7.   [c] Will. Malms. p. 11.   [d] Chron. Saxon. sub an.
[e] Ex Legenda Sanct. apud Rog. Dods. MS. vol. 155. f. 161.   [f] Hist. Allchester MS.
[g] W. Harrison, Description of Brit. p. 48.   [h] Skinner, Etymol. Angl. in voce.

name Berton did indeed signify a granary or store-place of corn :[l] as Berton by St. Martins in Canterbury, the granary of the monks of St. Austins; and West-gate-court nigh the same city, before called Berton de West-gate[i]. For which reason I do not find this name affixed to any principal towns, but to those farms and mansion houses that were in possession of the monks, and by them assigned to that use. Dr. Plot is pleased to ascribe another derivation. *About 'this time,* 614, (it should be at least 634,) *the town of Berencester, alias Berncester, in Saxon* Buɲenceaɼceɲ *and* Beɲnaceɼceɲ, *which I take to have been its primitive names, seems also to have been raised, and to have taken its name, as some have thought, from the same bishop Birinus,* quasi Birini castrum. *But I much rather believe it so called from Bern-wood or forest mentioned by Bede, Florilegus, and Wigorniensis', upon the edge whereof it was then seated, nor is now far off it: after which perhaps from St. Eadburg, to which the priory there was, and parish church is now dedicated, it changed its name to Burg-cestre, and since that to Burcester, now Bissester.* But still this is a conjecture not grounded on any tradition; nor indeed is the suppo-sition true: for it was never seated upon the edge of the forest Bern-wood, the nearest part of which was three miles distant from it, the borders of it coming no farther than the edge of this county to Pid-ington, Arncot, &c. the utmost village on the north-side was Bor-stal, held under the Saxon kings by the tenure of a horn, which made the possessor of it the forester of Bern-wood[k]. Possibly this town of Berncester might owe its name to the same reason as Bern-wood did. For this. Buɲne-puɒa or Beoɲne-puɒa, being a woody tract and forest of the widest extent, and greatest eminence seems to have been called from the Saxon Beoɲn, an epithet of dignity and remark: so perhaps this adjoining town being a place of greatest strength to the West Saxons against the Britains or Mercians, and at last against the Danes, it might be honoured with the title of their Beoɲn-ceɼceɼ, *castrum primarium,* their principal fort and garrison.

---

[l] Somner, Gloss. ad X. script.   [k] Ex evidentiis de Borstall MS.

But after all surmises, the first appears most fair, that Birinus did
denominate this town.   The MS. of Allchester gives this opinion :
Birinus, bishop of Cair-Dor, which Beda calleth Dorcinia, and Le-
land Hydropolis, now called Dorchester in Oxfordshire, sometime
walled about and castled, but all now ruined and gone, a round hill
there still appearing, where the superstitious ensuing ages built Bi-
rinus a shrine, teaching them that had any cattle amiss, to creep to
that shrine for help, &c.   From him too Bircester, Birini castrum,
sometime a walled town, though no step thereof appears now, built to
withstand the incursions of the Danes and Pagans.   This author is
indeed too early in attributing the cause of Birinus his building this
town for a defence against the Danes, when their first arrival was not
till about 789.   It seems however in the age of Birinus to have been
a frontier garrison of the West Saxons against the Mercians, and
might from him assume a name, because built by his advice and assistance out of the ruins of Allchester and Chesterton, or because of
a church here built and endowed by him in the extreme parts of his
jurisdiction. · The variation in the name of this town might be some
little argument to derive it from this bishop; for, as he has run the
changes of St. Birine, St. Beryn, St. Burine, &c.[1], so has the place
followed the like turn of initial syllables, Birinecester, Beryncester,
and Burincester.

· An. 643, Kenwalch succeeded in this kingdom of the West Saxons,
who, despising Christianity, and turning off his wife the sister of
Penda king of the Mercians[m], was nigh these parts invaded by him,
an. 645, and in open battle conquered and forced to flee to the king
of the East Angles, in whose court residing three years, he was baptized an. 646[n], and returned to his kingdom an. 648.   During his
abdication, these parts were in subjection to the Mercian kings,
Penda and Wulpher his son, of which this latter was converted and
baptized by the pastoral care of Birinus, and inviting Ethelwold
king of the West Saxons to Dorchester, was godfather to him at his

---

[1] Rob. Gloc. &c.   [m] Beda Histor. Eccles. l. 3. cap. 7.   [n] Chron. Saxon.

baptism by the same Birinus. Kenwalch at his restoration gave away all that part of his kingdom which lay on this side of the Thames to Cuthred his brother's son, to hold as a principality or province under him, computed at three thousand hides by the Saxon chronicle, at so many villages by Hen. Hunt. [o], and at near the third part of hi kingdom by Malmsbury [p]. This donation is said to be at Æsces dune, which I take to be Ashendon in the forest of Bern-wood, included in this grant: within which forest were several places denominated from the wood and the nature of it, as Aclea or Oakley, Æscesdon or Ashendon, Wodsham, Wotton, Woddesdon, &c.

Birinus, after he had enjoyed his pontificate fourteen years, died at Dorchester, and was there buried, an. 648 [q], or 650, in which year Agilbert a native of Gaul came out of Ireland, his place of theological studies, whose learning and industry were so well esteemed by king Kenwalch, that he desired him to accept that see, and be the bishop of this kingdom [r]. But the king understanding no more than his own Saxon language, and being weary of a barbarous or foreign tongue, he instituted another see at Winchester, an. 662, and gave it to Wine, a Saxon born, ordained in France. This erection of a new see seems owing in great part to the necessity of affairs: for in the preceding year 661, Kenwalch was defeated by Wulfer * king of Mercia at Poꝛꝛenꞇeꝑ-bȳpꞇꝟ, which I take to be Pottersbury in Northamptonshire, upon which victory Wulfer destroyed all this country as far as Æscesdune or Ashendon [s]: which must make Dorchester an unsafe place for a see of the West Saxon kingdom. However, this indignity and diminution of authority Agilbert so much resented,

* See the charter confirmed by Wulfer king of Mercia *in villa que vocatur Thama,* which by the names of other places mentioned in the said chart must be the town of Thame in Oxfordshire, which 'it seems was sometime the residence of the said king Wlfere. Mon. Ang. tom. 1. p. 76.

[o] Hen. Hunt, l. 2. p. 317.   [p] De gestis Regum, lib. 1. p. 13.   [q] Tho. Rudburn Hist. Maj Winton, cap. 3. 5.   [r] Bcd. Hist. Eccles. l. 3. cap. 7.   [s] Sax. Chron. sub. an.

that he left his see, and retired first to Northumberland[t], and thence
to Gaul, where he died bishop of Paris[u]. By which means Dorchester was deprived of the episcopal chair till the year 670, when
Eleutherius was ordained by Theodore archbishop of Canterbury to
the see of Winchester, vacant four years upon the expulsion of Wine,
an. 666, who removed to the old seat at Dorchester, and was there
buried an. 676[x].

In the year 672. died Kenwalch king of the West Saxons, and left
his kingdom among several petty princes[y], of whom Cuthred governed on this north side the Thames. During their reign Hedda a
monk of Streneshall, now Whitby, succeeded to the see of Dorchester an. 676, being consecrated at London by Theodore archbishop
of Canterbury[z], who again removed the see to Winchester, an. 677,
and by the authority of pope Agatho translated the body of Birinus
from the the old church at Dorchester to the new one at Winchester,
then dedicated to the honour of the Holy Trinity. This second removal of the ancient see was again owing to the distress of the times:
for Etheldred king of Mercia, succeeding his brother Wulfer an.
675, was victorious against the kings of Kent and Northumberland,
and had reduced all on this side the Thames to his own subjection,
so as the whole country was now first united to the Mercian kingdom. Hereupon in the year 680, (a record in the Monasticon mistakes 678[a], others postpone it to 683[b],) Theodore archbishop of
Canterbury, who had lately divided the bishopric of York, and instituted other sees to oblige king Etheldred, whose favour he did
servilely court, came now to new model the ecclesiastic state of the
kingdom of Mercia: and holding a council at Hatfield, he divided
the see of Litchfield into five distinct bishoprics, removing Sexwulph, who was before the single bishop, to Chester, and ordaining
Cudwin to Litchfield, Bosel to Worcester, Ethelwin to Lindsey, and

---

[t] Wharton, Ang. Sac. tom. 1. p. 191.   [u] Beda.   [x] Tho. Rudburn Histor. Maj.
[y] Bede, Hist. Eccles. 1. 4. cap. 12.   [z] Ib.   [a] Mon. Ang. tom. 1. p. 136.
[b] Rad. de Diceto. sub. an.

Eata a monk of the monastery of Hilda at Whitby to Dorchester. So as the disposition of the ecclesiastic state depending always on the revolutions of the civil government; from hence it happened, that *the see of Dorchester, which from the time of Birinus belonged to the West Saxons, pertained from the time of this council to the Mercians*[c].

This southern part of Mercia was by king Etheldred committed to Berthwald a son of his brother Wulfer[d], who under the title of king had the command of this county, who, with the joint authority of Etheldred, convened a synod at Berghford or Bregforde, now Burford in this county, at which were present the two kings Etheldred and Berthwald, Theodore archbishop of Canterbury, Sexwulph bishop of Litchfield, Bosel bishop of Worcester, &c. Where king Berthwald gave by charter to Aldhelm abbot of Malmsbury, forty cassates of land at Sumerford in Wiltshire. Which Aldhelm, afterwards bishop of Sherborn, now only priest and abbot, was here present, and at command of this synod wrote a book against the error of the British Christians in the observation of Easter, and other different rites wherein they disturbed the peace of the church: the reading of which book reclaimed many of those Britains who were under the West Saxons. After which he wrote that excellent treatise De Virginitate, and some other tracts, being a man of great learning and a neat stile[e]. This was the same synod which Sir H. Spelman indefinitely calls *Synodus Merciana*, an. 705[f], not knowing how to fix the place or time, because he had met with no other notice of it but what he found in Bede. The charter of Berthwald, recited from the Malmsbury register in the Monasticon[g], reports it, *Actum publice in synodo juxta vadum Berghford mense Julio tricesimo die mensis ejusdem indictione* XIII, *anno ab incarnatione Domini,* DCXXXV. Where the year 635 is a gross mistake, and can be reconciled neither to the persons, nor to the other note of time, the

---

[c] Ran. Higden. Polycron. p. 206.   [d] Will. Malms. de Pontif. l. 5.   [e] Beda Hist. Eccles. l. 5. cap. 19.   [f] Concil. Brit. tom. 1. p. 199.   [g] Mon. Ang. tom. 1. p. 51.

thirteenth indiction. Therefore the same charter, with little difference of words, preserved by William Malmsbury, restores the right
date and recites the witnesses. *Actum publice in synodo juxta vadum Bregforde mense Julio* xxx, *die mensis ejusdem, indictione* xiii,
anno ab incarnatione Domini dclxxxv. *Subscripserunt Theodorus
archiepiscopus, Ethelredus rex Merciorum; Berthwaldus subregu
lus, Kenfrithus patricius, Sexuulfus Lichfeldiæ, et Bosel Wigor
niæ episcopi*[h]. So as the error in the Monasticon was only by
omission of the numeral letter l. dcxxxv for dclxxxv, which in
another edition of Malmsbury runs into the additional mistake of
one year, dclxxxvi[i], but in the MS. leger-book of Malmsbury it is
right dclxxxv[k].

After this time our county was an unmolested part of the Mercian
kingdom, during the reign of Ethelred, who turned monk in the year
703, and of his successor Kenred, who resigned to Coelred an. 708,
who fought with Ina, king of the West Saxons, at Wodnesburch in
Wiltshire: where the event being with equal loss[l], the peace was renewed, and Coelred was buried at Litchfield an. 716, to whom succeeded Ethelbald, who in the year 723 invaded Æthelheard king
of the West Saxons, besieged his chief town of Sumurtun or
Somerton in the county of Somersetshire, took and demolished
it, and committed many other outrages, putting several parts of
that country under tribute and contribution; which so provoked
the princes and the people, that Cuthred successor to Æthelheard,
*being no longer able to endure the proud exactions and insolences
of the Mercian king*, raised an army and marched into these borders
of Mercia in the year 752[m]. King Æthelbald met him at Beorg-
ford[n], Beorhtford[o], Borford[p], or Burford in this county : where they
began a most desperate battle, Æthelbald had a standard whereon
was the figure of a golden dragon, carried before him by Æthelhun,

---

[h] Gul. Malms. l. 5. de Pontif. edit. Wharton, p. 11.   [i] Edit. Gale, p. 346.   [k] In
Musæo Bib. Bod.   [l] Mat. West. sub. an.   [m] Chron. Saxon.   [n] Ib.   [o] Flor. Wig.
[p] Mat. West.

who was killed with a lance by the standard-bearer of king Cuthred, which taking of the colours was a great encouragement to the West Saxons[q]; but the victory was long depending, till at last king Æthelbald was forced to fly, and leave a joyful victory to Cuthred, who by this defeat recovered the greatest part of this county. Dr. Plot conjectures, *this battle was fought on the place still called Battle-edge, west of the town, betwixt it and Upton. In memory of which victory perhaps the custom (yet within memory) of making a dragon yearly, and carrying it up and down the town in great jollity on Mid-summer eve, to which (I know not for what reason) they added a giant, might likely enough be first instituted* [r].

Cuthred king of the West Saxons died an. 754 [s], to whom Sigebright succeeded, but for his injustice was allowed only the province of Hampshire, and deprived of the rest of his kingdom, which was given to Cynwulph, who, after the death of Æthelbald king of Mercia, slain at Seccandune or Secckington in Com. Warwic. by Bearnred [t], enjoyed his West Saxon kingdom in great security and strength [u]. In the year 756, the usurper of Mercia Bearnred was expelled by the defection of the people, who restored Offa a young prince of the royal family, whose piety and valour made him so considerable, as to translate the metropolitan see from Canterbury to Litchfield, and after several successful attempts upon the kingdoms of Kent and Northumberland, he did at last resolve to recover this county of Oxford from the West Saxon kings, and enlarge his Mercian kingdom to its ancient limits the banks of the Thames. Upon which, in the year 775 [x], or 778 [y], or 779 [z], he brought an army cross the frontiers about Souldern or Fretwell in this county, where ran a branch of a Roman way, called now the Port way, and in some part Wattle-bank ; *but* (says Dr. Plot) *in an old terrier of Sir Thomas Chamberlain's, it is called Avesdich, perhaps a corruption of*

q Mat. West.　　　r Nat. Hist. Oxf. ch. 10. §. 116.　　　s Chron. Saxon. sub. an.
t Higden. Polycron. sub. an.　　u Mat. West. sub. an.　　x Chron. Saxon.　　y Flor.
Wig. et Higden. Polycron.　　z Mat. West.

Offa's-ditch, the great king of the Mercians, whose kingdom might at first be terminated here, though I find at length he extended it as far as Benson, as thinking it for his honour and profit both, that the West Saxons should have nothing north or west of the Thames[a] : and marched to * Benningtun or Bynsingtun, (most corruptly printed Resington[b]) now Bensington or Benson nigh Dorchester, which (says Camden) Marian calls *Villam Regiam, and which, from the time it was taken from the Britains by Ceaulin, had been possessed by the West Saxons for two hundred years*[c]. But this report of Mr. Camden, though transcribed and assented to by another worthy author[d], is not true; for this town, after its taking by Ceaulin, had often changed its masters, and was last regained from the Mercians upon their defeat at Burford, an. 752, and was maintained by them as one of their oldest and strongest garrisons. This place king Offa now besieged, and Kenwulph king of the West Saxons, coming up to the relief of it, was in open battle defeated, and obliged to fly beyond the Thames[e] : king Offa took the town, and in a passion for its long defence, dismantled the place[f]; and for the reward of his victory was again possessed of this whole county. Soon after this reduction, he took away from the monks of Malmsbury the manor of Piretune[g], perhaps Pyrton nigh Watlington, which his son Egferth restored[h] : (which the British Cedwalla king of the West Saxons had given to them) and gave Hethrop and Kidington in this county to the abbey of Worcester[i]. About this time he resettled the see of Dorchester, which, on the continued contests between the two kingdoms, seems to have had a long interruption in the succession of bishops, and had one Berthun ordained to reside here, who dying

---

* Anno DCCLXXVII. Kinewlfus Rex gem Merciorum circa Benetune, sed ab eo West-Saxonum pugnavit contra Offam re- fugatus est. Cron. Mailros.

[a] Nat. Hist. Oxf. ch. 10. §. 35.   [b] Higden. Polycron. edit. Gale, p. 250.   [c] Camden's Brit. in Dobun.   [d] Plot. Nat. Hist. Oxf. ch. 10. §. 114.   [e] Mat. West.   [f] Jo. Brompton, p. 770.   [g] W. Malms. de Pont. p. 243.   [h] Chartular. MS. Mon. Meldun.   [i] Mon. Ang. tom. 1. p. 134.

in the year 785 [k] Higebright was by the same king Offa elected to succeed him, whose diocese in the year 794 did extend through the counties of Oxford, Buckingham, Huntingdon, Cambridge, Northampton, and half of Hertfordshire [l]. In which year king Offa returning from Rome held a council at Verulam, founded the monastery of St. Alban's, and among other endowments gave to it Wneslowe, (now Winslow in Com. Buck.) which the historian calls the king's village in Demesn, and says it was twenty miles distant from Verulam [m]. King Offa died in August 794 [n], leaving Egferth or Egbert his son and heir: who died within the year, after whom Cenwulph king of Mercia was a strong and victorious prince: he dying an. 819 left his kingdom to Kenelm, who being slain the same year gave place to Ceolwulph, deprived an. 821, and succeeded by Beornwulf; who in the year 823 was defeated by Egbert king of the West Saxons at Ellendune, (which place cannot be fixed at Wilton [o], since one of our historians says expressly it was in Hampshire [p], perhaps Ellingham in that county,) upon the success of this battle king Egbert gained the kingdom of Mercia, by which means this county of Oxford was again united to the West Saxon kingdom. Shortly after, Ludecan usurped a regal power in Mercia, but was slain by the East Angles, an. 825, when the Mercians set up Wiglaf to redeem them from their subjection to the West Saxons; but in the year 827 king Egbert conquered Wiglaf and recovered Mercia, which in the next year he gave back to Wiglaf, to hold it as a deputed and tributary king [q]: who, after thirteen years enjoyment, left it to Berthwulph, a like vassal to the West Saxon kings, an. 838, in whose reign these parts were infested by the Danes.

[k] Flor. Wigorn. sub. an.   [l] Mat. West. sub. an. 794.   [m] Ib.   [n] Chron. Sax.
[o] Gibson. locorum explicatio.   [p] Ran. Higden. Polycron. p. 252.   [q] Will. Malms.
de gestis Reg. Ang. p. 33.

C H A P. VIII.

D A N E S.

 THE first ships that landed the Danish pirates in this island are
said to have arrived here an. 787 [r]. Their depredations, at first confined to the sea coasts, were soon carried on to the inland parts.
But they made no advance to this county till the year 851, when,
landing at the mouth of the Thames with three hundred transport
ships, they destroyed Canterbury and London [s], and marched on to
the eastern part * of this county of Oxford, where king Berthwulph
met them with an army, but was defeated by them, and forced to
fly beyond sea [t], where he died an. 852 [u]. Upon this victory, the
Danes after their usual spoil and devastation marched southward,
and, crossing the Thames, came to Oakley in Surry, where they were
encountered by Ethelwulph king of the West Saxons, and Ethelbald
his son, and received an absolute defeat [x]. After which Burrhed succeeded to the kingdom of Mercia, who strengthened himself by an
alliance with king Ethelwolph, and secured these parts from the incursion of the Danes, whose cruelty was most exercised in the
eastern and the northern parts, from which they came and took up
their winter quarters at Notingham, in the year 867 [y]. Upon which
invasion of this kingdom of Mercia, king Burrhed called in the assistance of his brother-in-law Ethelred king of the West Saxons, and

* In carta Bertulphi regis Merciorum
fact. abbat. de Croyland anno 851. Propo-
sita ergo tali querela vestra per fratrem As-
killum commonachum vestrum palam coram
prælatis et proceribus totius regni mei Mer-
ciæ apud Beningdon ultimo congregatis, &c.

where by Beningdon or Benigndon we may
justly presume is meant Bensingtun, com.
Oxon. the court of the Mercian kings.
Vid. Ingulph. Histor. p. 12. Archbishop
Ceolnoth and others cured there by mi-
racle; ib.

[r] Chron. Saxon.   [s] Ib.   [t] Will. Malms. p 33.   [u] Ran. Higden. Polycron.
[x] Chron. Saxon.   [y] Ib.

led up his army to Notingham, and there besieged the Danes, and after some slight repulse was content to make a league with them. So as these parts were again quiet till the year 871, when the Danes, designing an irruption upon the West Saxon kingdom, came to Reading and took possession of it; upon which Ethelwulph earl of Berkshire raised some forces, and while the Danish generals Hingar and Hubba, within three days after the seizure of the town, led out a party to plunder the country at Inglefield in Berks, Ethelwulph fell upon them, routed the whole party, and slew the two leaders of them [z]. Within four days king Ethelred and his brother Alfred brought up a numerous army, and in a battle with the Danes forced them to retire within their garrison of Reading; from whence they made a successful sally, killing Ethelwulph earl of Berkshire, and obliging the Saxons to raise their siege: who upon this repulse made their retreat to Easceasdune, which might possibly be Aston nigh Walingford in Berks; but I rather take it to be Ashendon in the fo- rest of Bernwood, which might seem a safer retreat to the discouraged Saxons: the Danes pursued them hither under the conduct of Bagsey and Halden, and within four days in a set battle by the cou- rage of Alfred, and the piety of Ethelred, after a whole day's fight, the Saxons were masters of the field, and absolute victors, leaving many thousands of the Danes there slain, and pursuing the re- mainder of them to their garrison of Reading. All historians inter- pret this place to be a *hill of ashes;* they represent it fit for an open and wide campaign, set with thorns and bushes, the Danes drawn out upon the rising ground, the Saxons with disadvantage encamped in the vale: the flight of the Danes all that night and part of the next day before they could reach to their fortifications at Reading [a]: which description and circumstances do all exactly answer to that part of the forest of Bernwood, which still retains that name, and was so considerable as to give a title to the hundred of Ashendon.

The Danes after this defeat and flight to Reading, within fourteen

---

[z] Ran. Higden. Polycron.   [a] Rog. Hoved. Annal. p. 416.

days got into a new body at Basing in Hampshire, whither king
Ethelred pursued them, and after a long engagement was defeated
by them[b]. Upon which it seems natural for the Saxons to retreat
toward the forest of Bernwood, in which they had so lately been victorious: and being followed by the Danes, they might encamp nigh
the borders of that forest, at Meretune in this county, close by the
Roman fort of Allchester, hoping for some assistance or security from
that place. Hither came the Danes and divided their army into two
bodies, and fell upon the Saxons, who were encamped on the west
side of Graven-hill, where the signs of entrenchment do still remain.
The Danes at first onset were broke and scattered; but they rallied
again, beat the Saxons, and kept masters of the field. There have
been different opinions of this place of battle; many have affixed it
to Merdon in Wilts; and Cressy with his wonted judgment calls it
Merton in Surry: one, who is well instructed in antiquities, does *believe, we should look for this place in some part of the West Saxon
kingdom: and in Wiltshire* (says he) *there be two villages which bear
a resemblance to this name,* 1. *Merdon in Swanborrow hundred, about
thirty miles directly west from Basing, about three miles from Wode-
nesdike; and here those that place this town in Wiltshire fix it. But
I rather think it to be,* 2. *Merton in Kinwerdeston hundred upon
the borders of Hampshire, because it is not so far out of the Danes
road between Basing and Wilton; but equally distant from those two
places, and not far from Bedwin, in the Saxons' time the metropolis
of Berkshire and Wiltshire*[c]. This my industrious friend seems concerned for the honour of his native county; and when he comes to
adorn the history and antiquities of it, he may perhaps discover more
certain tokens of this place of battle. But at present I readily in-
cline to the opinion of Dr. Plot, as thus delivered. · *As for the en-
trenchments in Merton-woods, I guess them cast up by king Æthelred
and his brother Alfred, who* cum paganis pugnantes apud Mertune [d],
fighting with the Danes at Merton, (as I find this town was anciently

---

[b] Rog. Hoved. Annal. p. 416.   [c] T. Tanner e Coll. Reg. Oxon.   [d] Flor. Wigorn.

written in the leiger-book of Ensham[e]*) overcame them and put their whole army to flight.* That the Danes had somewhat to do hereabout, is further evinced from one of the spurs in the hands (if I misremember not) of George Sherman of the town of Bisseter, not far from this place, which I took no care to get engraven, because already done by Olaus Wormius[f], where the reader may see the exact figure of it. All which put together, and that this place is near the meeting of two military ways, I am pretty well satisfied that this battle between Æthelred, his brother Alfred, and the Danes, was much rather here than at Merdon in Wiltshire as some have thought it[g]. Some fair reasons may be added to confirm this opinion. 1. There was another of these Danish spurs found upon digging the foundation of a garden wall belonging to the seat of Sir William Glynne, Baronet, an. 1674, which might well be dropped on the same occasion: for the Danes dividing their army into two bodies, one of them might rally and engage on that rising ground, where the church of Ambrosden and the said seat are now built, at a small distance from, and within view of the other supposed place of battle. 2. The noble Ethelwerd calls it Merantune[h], and mentions Heahmund bishop there slain (bishop of Sherborn[i]) and buried at Cegineshamme, which no doubt should be Aegineshamme (now Ensham) then a *famous place*[k], and fit for the sepulture of bishops, soon after honoured with a cell of religion; so as the interment of this prelate at Ensham may well argue that his death and the battle were in these parts. 3. This part of the county of Oxford had been long within the circuit of the West Saxon kingdom; and if king Egbert did restore it to the Mercians an. 828, yet the Mercian kings were from that time tributary to the West Saxon, as Burrhed now was to Æthelred: so that it was enough proper for Æthelred, after a grievous defeat in

---

[e] E registro de Ensham, MS.　　[f] Mon. Dan. l. 1. cap. 7. p. 50. fig. E.　　[g] Nat. Oxf. ch. 10. §. 77.　　[h] Ethelwerdus, lib 3. p. 43. edit. Savil.　　[i] Mat. West. sub an. 871.　　[k] Mon. Ang. tom. 1. p. 259.

Hampshire, to cross the Thames and repair to these borders of Mercia
for the assistance of his vassal and ally king Burrhed; the more likely,
because after this battle Burrhed and the Mercian people were necessitated to a league and tribute to the Danes [i], for which there seems no
occasion, if this scene of action and terror had been more remote from
their own country. 4. That hill, on the west side of which we presume
to have been this seat of action, has long been called Graven-hull (now
Graven-hill) which name from the Saxon ʒɲeꝼen-hul implies a sepulchre of the dead, and a number of graves in this place, most likely
of the bodies slain in this battle, whom the Danes, that were masters
of the field, took care to bury in this adjoining ground, it being their
custom to inter their dead in woods and groves [k]. And this seems
to be pretty evident from the composition of the name. For the
two words whereof it is made have each of them something in their
original to attest it. As for the first, the Gothic ᚱᚴᛆᛒᛆᚾ, fodere,
with the Saxon ʒɲæꝼ, which in general signifies *lucus, cavea, dume-*
tum; and in a more restrained sense, *sepulchrum;* with the *I*slandic
or old Danish grafa *fodere,* (which brings it nearer home,) puts it
out of all doubt. And the second part of the' word, which is the
product of the Gothic ʰᚾᛆᚷᛆᚾ. *tegere, operire,* seconded by the
*I*slandic eʒ þil, *tego,* and the Saxon helan, *tegere,* does strongly confirm it. For though there be diggings or *gravings* made for several
uses, yet a *digging* joined with *covering* cannot well agree to any
thing but the burial of the dead. And this no doubt was the original of our *hill,* by which we commonly mean *any rising ground;*
whereas, if we look back to the originals, there is nothing more evident than that it ought to be restrained to such *risings* as are caused
by burial of the dead; which in the northern parts are called *raises.*
For the Saxons had other ways to express a *mountain,* and other
things, wherein a *rising* without any limitation is simply implied.
Besides, that this termination points out to us something concerning

---

[i] Ethelwerd. cap. 3. p. 644.   [k] Olai Wormii Mon. Dan. l. 1. cap. 6.

the *dead*, is further evinced from the use the Saxons made of it to signify *hell*, *inferi*, *tartarus*, by which we know formerly was signified no more than the *grave*.

After this battle, one of the Danish officers called Somerled marched back with a party to Reading, destroying the town and all he could find in it[l]. From which station now demolished the Danes removed to London, and there took up their winter quarters, an. 873[m], where our Mercians made their peace with them, upon the terms of so much tribute or Dane-geld to be paid to them. In the following spring, Alfred king of the West Saxons, who succeeded his brother Etheldred, buried at Winburn in com. Dors. fought several battles wih the Danes, of which the most sharp was at Abendon in com. Berks[n], by which the Saxons were so much weakened, that they were glad to purchase a peace with the Danes, and hire them to withdraw from these parts. Upon which compact the Danes retired beyond the Humber, to the island Torkesey in com. Linc. where, within this year, 873, our Mercians made a second bargain with them[o]; but the Danes, not able to forbear their trade of plunder, broke the articles[p], and for satisfaction king Burrhed raised an army, and stood battle nigh Repton in Derbyshire; but being there defeated, he was forced to fly beyond the seas, and take sanctuary at Rome[q]. Upon his desertion the victorious Danes committed this kingdom of Mercia to Ceolwulph a thane and a subject of Burrhed, an. 874, upon servile conditions, to assist them in their robberies, to provide provision for their flying armies, and to resign the kingdom whenever they should please to demand it[r]. Accordingly in the year 877 they took away the greater part of this kingdom, all beyond the Humber, and gave it to Healfdene one of their own commanders[s]: leaving Ceolwulph in possession of these parts: who, being a very weak and unactive prince, was content to deliver up his

---

[l] Chron. Joh. Brompton, p. 809.   [m] Chron. Saxon.   [n] Joh. Brompton, p. 810. [o] Chron. Saxon.   [p] Jo. Brompt. p. 810.   [q] Ethelwerd. l. 4. c. 3.   [r] Chron. Saxon.   [s] Ethelwerd. l. 4. c. 3.

government to king Alfred before the end of the same year 877 [t], by
which means this county was again united to the West Saxon kingdom.

In the year 879 the Danes removed their quarters from Chippen-
ham in Wiltshire to Cirencester in Glocestershire, and kept a station there for twelve months, by which neighbourhood the western
parts of this county must suffer greatly [u].   An. 886 Mercia, that had
lately been a kingdom, was now reduced into a province, and committed to the government of Æthelred, who had married Æthelfled
a daughter of king Alfred [x].   An. 897, in a raging pestilence that
now swept away many of the nobility and prime clergy, Ealheard
bishop of this diocese died of the infection at his see of Dorchester [y]
To omit the founding or restoring of an University at Oxford by king
Alfred, I meet with nothing more in his reign of immediate concern
to these parts, unless, that before his death, an. 901, he did in his
last will bequeath to Osferth his kinsman the villages of Beccaule,
Ritherumfield, Diccanlingum, Suttune [z], &c. which I take for Beck
ley, Rotherfield, Ducklington, Sutton, &c. in this county.

To king Alfred succeeded his son Edward, much opposed by his
uncle's son Æthelwald, who in the first year of competition for the
crown was forced to cross the seas; but returning in the next year,
902 [a] or 904 [b], he brought a numerous army into these parts, and,
destroying all before him with fire and sword, he frighted the city of
Oxford into a surrendry to him; but king Edward marching hither
with greater force made him retire, and pursued him into the east;
where nigh St. Edmundsbury he gained a complete victory over
him, and soon after reduced those cities which had rebelled against
him; among which the chief were London and Oxford [c].   An.
905, in a council held in the province of the West Saxons, Kenulf
was elected bishop of this see of Dorchester, and was consecrated,

[t] Will. Malms. de gest. Reg. l. 1. p. 33.   [u] Chron. Saxon.   [x] Ælfredi M. vita,
p. 42.   [y] Chron. Saxon.   [z] Ælfredi M. vita, p. 194.   [a] Mat. West, sub an.
[b] Chron. Saxon.   [c] Mat. West.

with six other bishops elect, by archbishop Plegmund at Canterbury[d]. An. 907 the Danes, who had of late kept within their bounds in the east parts of England, and on the north of Humber, by the appointment of king Edward met him at Yttingaford, Ittingeford, or Ichyngford, which I take to be *I*ckford in com. Buck. on the edge of this county; where a league was made between them[e]. By which means these parts were unmolested till the year 911, when the Danes fell into this country with their wonted violence; but by an army of the West Saxons and Mercians they were drove back, pursued, and beat in the north. An. 912 died Æthelred earl of Mercia, whose province was committed to the government of his widow Ethelfleda[f] by her brother king Edward, excepting the cities of London and Oxford, and all the lands belonging to them[g], which the king retained in his own hands, as a pledge of his sister's fidelity, and to keep in subjection the whole province.

An. 914 the Danes from Northampton and Leicester fell into the north-east parts of this county, and marched on with plunder and destruction to Hocneratune[h], Hokenertune[i], Hocheneretune[k], Hochemeretune[l], now Hokenorton, and made great slaughter of the English Saxons in this place, and other adjoining parts. At which time were cast up those military works still known by the name of Tadmerton-castle and Hooknorton-barrow, the former being large and round, and is therefore judged a fortification of the Danes; the latter, being smaller and rather a quinquangle than a square, is thought done by the Saxons[m]. Historians differ much in the time of this action; Brompton and Huntingdon would have it in the tenth of Edward sen. 911, which others compute 910[n]; the Saxon Chronicle relates it 917; but the account of Flor. Wigor. 914, (where he calls it Hokeneretune, *villam regiam*) must be right, if Ethelfleda, after this defeat, took care to repair and defend[o] the city

[d] Mat. West.   [e] Chron. Saxon.   [f] Mat. West. sub an.   [g] Chron. Saxon.
[h] Ib.   [i] Flor. Wigor.   [k] Hen. Hunt.   [l] Jo. Brompt.   [m] Nat. Hist. Oxf. ch. 10.
§. 75.   [n] Hist. et. Antiq. Un. Oxf. p. 42.   [o] Hist. et Antiq. Un. Oxon. ib.

of Oxford, supposing she died on the 19th of the kalends of July, an. 915, and was buried at Glocester[p]. When the Danes after this pillage returned to their quarters at Leicester and Northampton, within the same year came out another strong party and ravaged on to Ligetun, now Leyton in Com. Bedf. where they were encountered by the Saxons of those parts, and drove back with great loss of men and taken prey[q].

While they kept their head quarters at Northampton and made frequent incursions into this country, the Saxons had a partition wall and trench to keep out the enemy from these parts, which work was perhaps before raised for the boundary between the Mercian and West-Saxon kingdom, and therefore the whole or a branch of it called Avesdich, a corruption of Offa's-ditch[r]; which seems to have run on to Wansdike in Wiltshire, running from the north-east to south-west through a great part of that county, which Mr. Camden alway believed to have been the limits of the Mercian and West-Saxon kingdom in those parts[s]. The extreme parts of it in this county were at Mixbury, where near the church does still appear a large fortification square, and encompassed with a ditch 170 paces one way, and 128 the other[t], which by the Normans was called Beaumont, from the fair ascent and prospect of it; within this parish was afterward a castle, of which the tradition and its name in the site of it do still remain. From whence it ran to Fritwell, where Dr. Plot has observed a Saxon barrow, *called Ploughly-hill, standing just within Oxfordshire on the port way, and (which is somewhat more than ordinary) giving name to the hundred where it stands*[u]: from whence it continued to Ardulvesle, now Ardley, where was another rampire, by the Normans converted into a castle, *the foundations whereof are yet to be seen in a little wood west of the town, which, if any heed may be given to the tradition of the place, flourished about*

p Rog. Hoved. Annal. p. 422.   q Chron. Saxon. Jo. Brompt. Hen. Hunt.   r Nat. Hist. Oxf. ch. 10. §. 35.   s Camden. in Belgis.   t Nat. Hist. Oxf. ch. 10. §. 35. u Ib. §. 48.

the time of king Stephen[x]. It passed from thence to Midlington-stony, where (most likely upon the ruins of a Saxon work) was erected another castle formerly belonging to the family of Camvil, and long remaining, after most other castles in this county were demolished: so to Northbrook and to Kirklington. The ruins of the bank and trench are visible in several parts, and the road from Midlington to Heyford bridge is cut through it, the bank rising on each side to a considerable height.

Many towns and villages in these parts, of which the names and ruins now remain, are thought to have been destroyed by the Danes in these times of calamity. As, 1. the old town of Berincester, which was first built on the west part, or in kings-end, where the site of it may be now tracked through the close or grove of Mr. John Coker, gent. a kind encourager of this attempt. 2. Fulwell in the parish of Mixbury, and Woolaston near adjoining. 3. Shelswell nigh to Newton-Purcell. 4. Bainton within the precincts of Stoke-line. 5. Saxenton in the parish of Bucknell, where the foundations of building do more especially appear in a ground called the Ball-yards.

Camden thinks it was in this year 914, *that the Danes broke with fury into the forest of Bernwood, and that then perhaps was ruined the city of Burgh, an ancient place, as Roman money there found does witness, which was afterward a royal village of Edward the Con fessor, though it be now a small country town, and instead of Buri-hill is by contraction called Brill*[y]. This etymology of the place is indeed more natural than what another writer would force upon it, as if Brill was a corruption of Burr-hill, from the burrs there growing[z]. But I rather think the true denomination of this place, formerly called Bruheham, Bruhel, Brehull, was from Bruel a thorny place, from Bruer a thorn, whence a thicket or bushy place was called Bruere, as the abbey of Bruer, *abbatia de Brueria* in the forest of Whichwood: and a wood in our old Latin was called Bruil-

---

[x] Nat. Hist. Oxf. ch. 10. §. 136   [y] Camden. Britan. in Cattieuch.   [z] Skinner in Etymol. Lex.

lus, as in a charter of Henry the Third to the church of Chichester, the king grants *bruillos nostros Cicestre, viz. bruillum qui vocatur bruillus regis, et bruillum qui vocatur denemarsh*[a]. From which reason this town, so situate in the forest of Bernwood, might be properly called Bruill, and at last Brill. Mr. Camden seems not only mistaken in the derivation of this place, but in his historical remark upon it, there being no authority or tradition that this place was ever called Burgus, or ever sacked by the Danes. And therefore Speed conjectures that this demolition by the Danes is to be meant of Tame in this county[b]. But this opinion stands on no better grounds: and *I* should sooner think the Burgus or Burg they report now to be destroyed was far remote from the forest of Bernwood, and could be no other than the old Medeshamsted, called Burgh and Burgus, now Peterborough, once at least destroyed by these Pagans[c].

In the next year after the desolation of this county by the Danes, an. 915[d], * or 918[e], king Edward raised a great army in these parts, and before the feast of St. Martin marched to Buckingham, where he lay one month, and caused two forts to be built and garrisoned on each side the Ouse : and then advancing toward the Danes he struck such a terror into them, that Turketil their general, with the garrisons of Bedford and Northampton, were glad to make their submission and their peace[f]. In the year following, the Danes, falling back to their violation of all truces, and their constant trade of plunder, king Edward, with a new army from these parts, marched to Bedford, besieged and took it[g]. After which he built the town of Tocester for a barrier to hinder the Danes incursion into this country: who were so sensible of this restraint to be put upon them, that they came out in a great body from Northampton, and besieged

* *Anno 916. Elfieda construxit Chirebiri, et Warebiri, et Runconen.   Cron. Mailros.*

[a] Mon. Ang. tom. 3. p. 125.   [b] Theat. Hist. Brit. in Bucks.   [c] Chron. Sax. sub an. 963.   [d] Jo. Brompt. et Mat. West.   [e] Chron. Sax.   [f] Ib. et Jo. Brompt.   [g] Chron. Sax.

the new town of Tocester; but the garrison, recruited by the neighbouring inhabitants, made a stout defence, and by frequent sallies
drove away the Pagan army; who upon this repulse broke into the
adjoining parts of the county of Bucks, plundered the villages, drove
away the cattle, and killed many of the inhabitants between the
town of Eilesberie, now Ailsbury, and the forest of Bernwood [h]. But
they were soon pursued and drove to their winter quarters by king
Edward, who lay with his army at Passenham or Passham in Northamptonshire, while the new town of Tocester was better secured
by a stone wall: and within the compass of the same year, the Danes
were so weakened and dispersed, that they chose to promise allegiance, and live in subjection to king Edward [i]: who thereby settled
the peace of these parts till his own death at Faringdon on the edge
of this county, and the death of Ælfweard his son at Oxford immediately after, an. 924[k], or 925[l].

Upon the death of Edward, Æthelstan his eldest son succeeded,
and during his whole reign guarded these parts from all disturbance
by the Danes; who in January 938 held a council at Dorchester in
this county, *in civitate celeberrima quæ Dornacestre appellatur,* and
there gave a charter subscribed by four tributary kings, two archbishops, and fourteen bishops, to the convent of Malmsbury, granting to them ten cassates of land in Wdetun, five in Ewulm, &c. (perhaps Wood-eaton and Ewelm in this county [m].) He died an. 940[n],
or 941[o], buried at Malmsbury, to whom succeeded his brother Edmund; in the first year of his reign the Danes, presuming on the
weakness of a new prince, made an excursion into those parts of
Buckinghamshire, which border on the north-east parts of this
county, and, finding all places surprised and unprovided, they committed great outrages upon men and cattle between Ailsbury (which
Leland conjectured might be the Eadsbirig built by Elfleda princess

[h] Mat. West. sub an. 918. [i] Mat. West. sub an. 981. et Higden. Polycron. sub
an. eod. [k] Mat. West. Higden. Polycron. &c. [l] Chron. Saxon. [m] Will.
Malms. de Pontif. l. 5. apud Gale, p. 364. apud Wharton, p. 31. [n] Hen. Hunt.
Rog. Hoved. &c. [o] Sax. Chron. Ran. Higd. &c.

of the Mercians [p]) and the forest of Bernwood. But king Edward
soon frighted them to their places of retreat, and, pursuing them
northward, took from them their garrisons of Stanford, Lincoln,
Nottingham, &c.[q] and so resettled the peace and security of these
parts; being further employed in reduction of the Danes in the
north till his death, an. 946[r]. To him succeeded his brother Edred,
who kept the whole scene of action on the other side the Humber,
and having accepted the submission of Wulstan archbishop of York,
translated thither from the see of Dorchester, and finding him afterwards false to him, he brought him away a prisoner into these parts
an. 952, and in the year 953[s], or 954[t], restored his episcopal dignity
to him at the town of Dorchester in this county: and died 955[u], in
which year his uncle Edwy was crowned in Kingston; but in the
next year, 956, Edgar was made king of Mercia, and, upon the death
of Edwy 957, had the dominion of all England[x]. His peaceful reign
left nothing of remark in these parts, but only that Escuin bishop of
Dorchester subscribed a charter to the church of Malmsbury an.
962[y], or 964[z], and an. 970, Osketyl archbishop of York, who like
his predecessor Wulstan had been translated from this see of Dorchester, resided now at Tame in this county, and dying there on All-
Saints day was buried at Bedford by his cousin Turketil abbot of
that place[a]. King Edgar made his kinsman Elfere governor of this
province of Mercia, who by his sacrileges and irreligious humour
brought a great calamity on these parts[b].

King Edgar died an. 975, leaving Edward his son to succeed him;
in the third year of his reign an. 977, a great synod or council was
held at Kirtlington in this county, which had been a place of great
eminence and antiquity, a frontier town between the kingdoms of
Mercia and the West Saxons, and of great resort from the port way
that led through it, and had a very ancient church dedicated to St.

[p] J. Leland. Collect. MS. vol. 2. p. 240, 244.   [q] Chron. Saxon.   [r] Sim. Dun.
[s] Rog. de Hoved. p. 2423.   [t] Sim. Dun. p. 156.   [u] Chron. Saxon.   [x] Sim. Dun.
[y] W. Malms. de Pont. l. 5. Wharton.   [z] Ib. edit. Gale.   [a] Chron. Saxon.   [b] Sim.
Dun. et Chron. Saxon.

Mary[c]. There has been much doubt and controversy about the name and situation of this place of council. In the Saxon Chronicle it is called Kýntlingtune, which the expert editor grants to be a mistake for Kýptlingtune [d], as Spelman does record it [e]. Florence of Worcester calls it Kirtlinege, and says by mistaken conjecture that it was in the east part of England [f]. From him Hoveden places it in East-England, but further corrupts the word into Kirding [g], which Brompton with as little care and truth writes Kerling [h]. Sir Henry Spelman, submitting to the authority of Flor. Wig. and Hoved. grants the place to have been among the East Angles, yet can find no village in those parts of that name, till at last he remembers in an old catalogue of the villages of Cambridgeshire, there did occur one by the name of Kirtling, which he takes to be the same that is now called Katlage, then the seat of baron North. All which is a forced and improbable guess. And therefore one that has done service in these matters does restore the just honour to Kirtlington in this county [i], which opinion, besides the propriety of name, he confirms by the burial of Sidemanne bishop of Criditon in Devonshire, at Abendon in com. Berks: which could not have been otherwise agreeable, if his death had happened in any of the eastern counties. It is true that bishop Sidemanne was buried in the monastery of Abendon, and therefore it is an unhappy mistake in Sir Henry Spelman, in his Latin translation of the Saxon, to insert Criditon as his burial place, without authority of the original. He desired indeed to be buried at his episcopal see, but because that was too remote, he was, by order of king Edward and archbishop Dunstan, carried to the next religious place, which was Abingdon on the edge of this county, and there interred on the north side of the porch or cloister of St. Paul [k]. But besides this identity of name and sepulture at Abendon, there be other reasons, that do abundantly evince this

---

[c] Mon. Ang. tom. 2. p. 1007.   [d] Gibson. locorum explicatio.   [e] Concil. Brit. tom. 1. p. 493.   [f] Flor. Wigor. sub an. 977.   [g] Ran. de Hoved. p. 427.   [h] Chron. Jo. Brompt. p. 870.   [i] Gibson. locorum explicatio.   [k] Hist. Cenob. Abend. apud Wharton, p. 166. et Chron. Saxon.

synod to have been held in this place. 1. The occasion of this assembly was to redress grievances that arose in these parts, from the
expulsion of monks and the settlement of secular clergy in all the religious cells of Mercia, by Elfere governor of this province[1]; so as
the business of the synod arising in these parts, their convening must
be here, and not among the East Angles. 2. The person who most
concerned himself in procuring this synod, and soliciting the cause
of the monks (next to the zealous archbishop Dunstan) was Æthelwald bishop of Winchester, who had first been abbot of Abendon,
and after his preferment to that see had consecrated them a new
church of St. Mary's in Abendon, and had persuaded king Edgar to
expel the secular priests, and introduce monks to that abbey[m];
which monks Elfere had again disturbed, so that one of the prime
agents in this synod, bearing so near a relation to Abingdon, and the
interest of that abbey being one of the chief affairs then depending,.
it must needs follow, that the synod should be convened in some
place convenient for such a scene of affairs, which could never be in
any of the eastern parts of England, but might well be appointed
within twelve miles of Abendon. 3. In those little remains we have
of the result of this synod, we find but one act, which is, that king
Edgar and the bishops did there ordain, that the country people
might go in pilgrimage to the church of St. Mary's in Abendon[n],
which had been absurd if not done among the inhabitants of these
parts. The two following synods, held near the same time upon the
like occasion at Calne and Ambresbury in Wiltshire, prove the former to have been toward the same part of the kingdom[o]. In short,
from the continual preserved name, from the commodious situation,
from all circumstances thereto agreeing, I think it most certain that
this micle ᵹemoᴛ, this great synod, was held at Kirtlington within three
miles of Burcester.

In the year 878 king Edward was murdered at Corf in Dorset-

---

[1] Sim. Dun. sub an. 975. Ran. Higden. sub an. 976, &c.   [m] Hist. Cenob. Abend.
p. 166,   [n] Spelman. de Concil. tom 1. p. 493.   [o] Jo. Brompt. p. 870.

shire, and buried at Warham, from whence his body was taken by our Elfere earl of Mercia, and buried at Shaftsbury[p]; which earl died in the year 983, when his son Elfric succeeded to the government of these parts : who, within two years, 985[q], was banished the kingdom by king Ethelred, but was soon recalled, and in the year 991 was one of the chief instruments to promote a dishonourable peace with the Danes, and to begin that yearly pension which was afterward so great a burden and scandal to this nation[r]. And the next year being made one of the admirals at sea, he declined to fight, and betrayed our navy to the Danes[s]: for which baseness in the year following, 993, the king put out the eyes of his son Elfgar[t]. An. 993 *, or 995, Escwin bishop of Dorchester gave to the church of Canterbury and Elfric archbishop the manor of Risbergh[u], (not Kisberge as falsely printed in another author[x]) now Monks-Risborough in com. Buck. then of Bokeland tenure[y]. And in the year 997 Elfgive the queen gave the two manors of Niwentune and Brutewelle, now Newington and Brightwell in this county of Oxford, to the said church of Canterbury, free from all secular service except the threefold necessity[z]. An. 1002 the king commanded all the Danes to be murdered on the feast of St. Brice, which orders were executed with greatest violence in this county, and especially at Oxford, where the churches were no protection from a general massacre[a]. An. 1003 the king raised a great army in Wiltshire and Hampshire against the Danes, and made Elfric earl of Mercia general of them, who at the the time of battle feigned himself sick, and betrayed all to the Danes[b]: for which king Ethelred deprived him

* An. 993, K. Ethelred gave to the abby of Abingdon some lands in Erncote (now Arncot in Amersden,) to which char-ter see the witnesses, under the year MCCCXX in this work.

[p] Chron. Saxon. [q] Ib. et Mat. West. [r] Hen. Hunt. sub an. [s] Chron. Saxon. [t] Ib. [u] Mon. Ang. tom. 1. p. 21. [x] Thorn. Evident. inter X. Script. p. 222. [y] Ib. et Wharton. Ang. Sac. tom. 1. p. 101. [z] Ib. [a] Hist. et Antiq. Oxon. p. 43. [b] Chron. Sax.

of his honour, and gave this province to a more perfidious governor, Edric surnamed Streone [c]

An. 1005 Ailmer earl of Cornwall, who had before founded the abbey of Cerne in Dorsetshire, gave thirty-six mansions in others places in exchange with Ethelward his son in law, for thirty mansions at Eynsham in this county, *in loco celebri juxta fluvium qui vocatur Temis, quod apud incolas regionis illius Egnesham vocatur.* Upon which he founded an abbey of the Benedictine order, and among other endowments gave to it ten mansions of common field in Erdintune, which he exchanged with his kinsman Godwyn for five mansions at Stodelege, and ten mansions at Cestertune, now Stodley and Chesterton in this county [d], and was buried in this monastery [e].

An. 1006 about Christmas, the Danes from Hampshire fell into Berkshire, plundered Reading [f], and utterly destroyed Wallingford [g]. An. 1008 died Alfelm bishop of Dorchester, who had succeeded Escwin; and Ednoth abbot of Ramsey was now elected to that see [h].

An. 1009 the incensed Danes marched through the Chiltern country and broke into the east parts of this county [i], passing on to Oxford, and firing that city [k]. About this time king Ethelred by the advice of Alphege archbishop of Canterbury, and Wulstan archbishop of York, held a general council at Ænham, wherein many decrees were established for the policy of church and state [l]. This place of council I take to be Ænsham in this county, for these reason. 1. This Ægnesham had been a British city [m], and was just before called *locus celebris* [n], and was now made more eminent by the accession of a new religious house. 2. King Ethelred kept the greatest part of his residence in this county, chiefly at Hedington near Oxford [o], and at Islip, and therefore may be justly supposed to have some time removed his court at Egnesham, and there at one

[c] Mat. West. sub an. [d] Mon. Ang. tom. 1. p. 259. [e] Ib. p. 254. [f] Flor. Wigorn. sub an. [g] Chron. Saxon. [h] Histor. Rames. cap. 69. et Mon. Ang. tom. 1. p. 240. [i] Chron. Jo. Brompt. p. 287. [k] Hen. Hunt. p. 361. [l] Spelman. Concil. tom. 1. p. 510. [m] Chron. Saxon. sub an. 571. [n] Mon. Ang. tom. 1. p. 259. [o] Mon. Ang. tom. 1. p. 984.

of the three solemn times to have entered into council with his nobility and clergy. 3. Another council was nigh the same time held
by king Ethelred at Wudestoc[p], now Woodstock in this county,
which may argue the other to have been in some place adjoining.
4. This council began with so many orders and constitutions for
the discipline of monasteries, that from thence it seems to have been
held in a place of religion, and the more likely Egnesham, because
this abbey being lately founded, and committed by the founder
to the patronage of king Etheldred[q]; these laws of monastic government seem to bear a peculiar relation to this place. 5. The
feast of St. Mary was now enjoined to be solemnly observed above
all other festivals, which perhaps might be on the occasion of
their assembling in or near this abbey dedicated to the Virgin
Mary.

Upon the mention of Heddington, I ought to recite what a worthy person has lately observed of it. *From King Edward the Confessor's being born at Islip, it is easy to collect, that his father king
Ethelred must necessarily have had a royal seat there, as in all proba-
bility at Heddington near Oxford; for though tradition now goes, that
it was but the nursery of the king's children, whereof there remains yet
upon the place some signs of foundations in a field near the town, called Court Close: yet it is plain, that king Etheldred did sometimes at
least reside there himself, for he concludes a charter, or some such like
instrument, wherein he grants privileges to the monastery of St.
Frideswide here in Oxon. of his own restoration in English thus,*
[Ⱦⱨⰵⱄ privilege was with in Heddington] *and after in Latin, scripta
fuit hæc cedula jussu præfati regis in villa regia quæ . . . . . appellatur,* &c.[r] To which I need only add, that this grant was made to
the convent of St. Frideswide (which the King calls *myn owne myn-
ster in Oxenford*) before the year 1005, while Elfric was archbishop
of Canterbury, and Alfric Earl of Mercia, who are witnesses to this

---

p Lambard, Ἀρχαιον. 4to. fol. 82.   q Mon. Ang. tom. 1. p. 259.   r Plot, Nat.
Hist. Oxf. ch. 10. §. 12.

donation : and at the same time the king granted to the said monastery, some possessions within that royal village, .   . [of ꝏeꝺꝺington
anꝺ of alle tꜧe lonꝺe tꜧat tꜧeꞧeto be⸗ . . . . . anꝺ in felꝺe anꝺ all otꜧer
tꜧing anꝺ ꞧꝑtꜧe tꜧat . . . . .] within which concession was the free
chapel of Heddington, exempt from all customs due to the bishop
and archdeacon, which Maud the empress afterward confirmed to
that church of St. Frideswide[s].

An. 1010 the Danes came again into this county, and after
great destruction in these north-east parts, marched from hence to
Buckingham, and Bedford, and Temsford[t]. An. 1011, among the
counties that, upon conquest and composition, paid a constant tribute to the tyrannic Danes, this of Oxford is recounted[u]. An. 1012
Alphege archbishop of Canterbury, having been taken away captive
by the Danes, was martyred by them on Sunday the 13th of the
kalends of May, and his body soon after interred in the church of
St. Paul's, London, by the pious care of Eadnoth Bishop of Dorchester[x]. An. 1013 Swane king of Denmark marched with his
army from Gainsborough in Lincolnshire into these parts of Mercia,
and on this side of Watling-street he gave command to his soldiers
to plunder the country, to burn the villages, to deface the churches,
to murder the men, and to ravish the women[y]: in which impious
and sanguinary method he went on to Oxford, and frighted the city
into surrendry, taking pledges of them : and within the same year,
being repulsed from London, he came back to Wallingford, and
marched thence to Bath, with the like military execution, returning
this way into the north, and striking such a terror into king Ethelred, that he first sent away his queen and children into Normandy,
and retired thither himself after Christmas, leaving Swane in full
possession of this kingdom : who died at Candlemas, an. 1014,
and left his son Cnute elected by the Danes; but the Saxons recalled their old master King Ethelred, who, an. 1015, invited the

---

[s] Mon. Ang. tom. 1. p. 384.   [t] Chron. Sax. sub an. et Mat. West.   [u] Chron.
Sax. sub an.   [x] Histor. Rames. cap. 69.   [y] Sim. Dun. sub an.

Danes to a conference at Oxford, where Edric earl of Mercia caused two of their Noblemen, Sigeferd and Morcar, to be treacherously murdered, whose death when the Danes endeavoured to revenge, they were overpowered, and some of them having taken sanctuary in the tower of St. Frideswide church were there burnt: of which barbarous breach of faith, a full relation was once preserved in the register of that monastery [z]. An 1016 Edric earl of Mercia perfidiously went over to Cnute with forty ships, and joining with him at the beginning of January marched along with the Danish forces, crossing the river at Creeklade, destroying many towns in Warwickshire; and passing through these parts advanced to Buckinghamshire with infinite fury and spoil [a]. King Etheldred died at London, on St. George's day, and his son Edmund Ironside succeeded, who in this first year of his reign, after several engagements with the Danes, pursued them into Mercia, and followed them into Essex, where at Assandune was a battle fatal to the English, where Eadnoth bishop of Dorchester, while he was singing mass, had first his right hand cut off for the sake of his pastoral ring, and was then killed in the field [b], whose body the monks of Ramsey fetched off, and would have conveyed to their monastery: but on the road, the monks of Ely robbed them of the corpse [c]. After his death Ethric monk of Ramsey was elected to the see of Dorchester [d]. About the feast of St. Andrew king Edmund died [e], or was murdered at London [f], or, as some historians, at Oxford [g].

An. 1018, Cnute having absolute possession of this kingdom, some disputes arose between the English and Danes upon the observation of king Edgar's laws: to end this controversy, king Cnute assembled a council at Oxford, where an agreement was made [h]. The next great council of king Cnute was at Cirencester on

[z] Will. Malms. de gest. Reg. l. 2. p. 71.   [a] Sim. Dun. sub an.   [b] Hist. Eccles. Eliens. cap. 13.   [c] Histor. Rames. cap. 72, 73.   [d] Mon. Ang. tom. 1. p. 240.   [e] Chron. Sax. Sim. Dun. &c.   [f] Knighton. Brompt. &c.   [g] Hist. et Antiq. Un. Oxon. p. 43.   [h] Sim. Dun. sub an.

the edge of this county, an. 1020 [i]; and another at Oxford an. 1022, when the laws of king Edward the First were translated into Latin, and enjoined to all subjects Danes and English [k]. After which nothing of moment happened in these parts, till the death of Ethric bishop of Dorchester [l], buried in the monastery of Ramsey, an. 1034 [m], who had a great interest in king Cnute, and was often admitted to his private councils, upon the experience of his being a just, prudent, and active prelate [n]. To him succeeded Ædnoth junior, elected from the said abbey of Ramsey, which had now given three bishops to this see of Dorchester [o].

On the death of king Cnute, an. 1036, a great council was convened at Oxford, to settle the disputes of succession, where by the interest of Leofric earl of Mercia, and other of the nobility on this north side of the Thames, Harold Harefoot was advanced to the crown [p], who, an. 1039, died at Oxford [q], and was buried at Westminster; having done great injuries to learning and religion in these parts [r]. To him succeeded Hardi-Cnute, who dying at Lambeth, an. 1041, made way for restoration of the Saxon line, in the person of Edward son of Ethelstan and Emma.

CHAP. IX.

SAXONS RESTORED.

THE birth of Edward the Confessor gave him a relation to these parts, of which the latest history is thus given. *The town of Islip, Saxon Lightᵹlepe or Lihtᵹlepe, must needs be of good repute in these days, for Camden says expressly, and so do several other authors, that king Edward the Confessor was born there, which they prove from his*

[i] Chron. Sax.   [k] Mat. West. sub an.   [l] Chron. Sax.   [m] Flor. Wigorn. sub an.   [n] Histor. Rames. cap. 81.   [o] Ib. cap. 92.   [p] Chron. Saxon. [q] Hen. Hunt. et Chron. Sax.   [r] Hist. et Antiq. Un. Oxon. p. 44.

*original charter of restoration of the abbey of Westminster, wherein he gives to this his new church the town of * Islip, with the additional clause of [the place where he was born] which, though it is true, I*

* Rectores Ecclesiæ de Islip, com. Oxon. Hugo de Glaston clericus ad ecclesiam de Ighleslep ad pres. abb. et Conv. Westm. Rot. Hug. Wells. pont. 12.

Walt. de Tudinton subdec. ad eccl. de Yfleslep ad pres. abb. et conv. West. Rot. Rob. Grosthead, anno 18. (1252.)

Mag. Rob. de Legum clericus pres. per abb. et conv. West. ad eccl. de Islep, vac. per mortem Walt. de Tudington, 11. kal. Jun. pont. 17. i. e. 1296. Reg. Ol. Sutton.

Tho. de Heyford, acol. pres. per abb. et conv. Westm. ad eccl. de Islep. vac. per mortem magri Rob. de Leyham. 8. id. Sept. 1318. Reg. D'Alderby.

Dom. Rob. de Hemmyngburgh, presbiter, pres. per Regem ad eccl. de Islep, (ratione vac. abb. Westmin.) vac. per mortem domini Hen. de Iddebury. 2. id. Dec. 1333. Reg. Burgwersh.

Permutatio inter Adam. Rikeman rectorem ecclesiæ de Islyp et Joh. Sulthorn rectorem de Bromley, Roff. dioc. 8. kal. Nov. 1366. Reg. Bokyngham.

Permutatio inter dom. Johannem de Sulthorn rectorem ecclesiæ de Islip, et magistrum Willelmum Horsleye rectorem ecclesiæ de Aldyngton, Cant. dioc. 19. Jun. 1369. Reg. Bokyngham.

Steph. Payne, capellanus, pres. per abb. et conv. West. ad eccl. de Isleep per mortem domini Will. Horsle. 19. Mart. 1411. Reg. Reppingdon.

Johannes Wouburn clericus pres. per abb. et conv. Westm. ad eccl. de Islepe per resign. domini Steph. Payne. 3. Dec. 1413.

Tho. Clyff clericus pres. per abb. et conv. Westm. ad eccl. de Islep per resign. domini Joh. Wobourne. 17. Nov. 1417. ib.

Magister Tho. Haywood presbiter pres. per abb. et conv. Westm. ad eccl. de Islepe per resign. domini Rog. Assar ex causa permutationis de ipsa cum decanatu ecclesiæ collegiatæ S. Johannis Cestr. Cov. et Lichf. dioc. 8. Feb. 1443. Reg. Alnewyk.

Magister Tho. Haywod presbiter pres. per dominum Walterum Devereux mil. ad ecclesiam de Bosworth per resign. domini Willelmi Kynwolmersch, ex causa permutationis de ipsa cum ecclesia de Islep, Linc. dioc. 18. Sep. 1446. ib.

1450. 5. Jun. Magister Willelmus Danges pres. per abb. et conv. Westm. ad eccl. de Islepe per resign. magistri Willelmi Kynwolmersh. Reg. Lumley.

Dominus Tho. Wylcock presbiter pres. per abb. et conv. Westm. ad eccl. de Islep per mort. domini Willelmi Browne. 25. Feb. 1465. Reg. Chedworth.

Magister Simon Stalworth presbiter pres. per abb. et conv. Westm. ad eccl. de Islep per mortem Magistri Tho. Wyllcok. 4. Jun. 1479. Reg. Rotherham.

Magister Ricardus Norton presbiter pres. per abb. et conv. Westm. ad eccl. de Islep per resign. domini magistri Simonis Stallworth (subdecani Linc.) 24. Jul. 1485.

Magister Simon Stalworth canon. Linc. ad ecclesiam de Algerkirk per resign. magistri Ricardi Norton. 24. Jul. 1495.

Dominus Robertus Weston capellamus pres. per abb. et conv. Westm. ad ecclesiam de Islipe per resign. magistri

could not find in Mr. Dugdale, yet here remaining some footsteps of
the ancient palace, and a chapel now put to profane use, called the
king's chapel, and the town still belonging to the church of Westmin-
ster, there is no great doubt to be made of the thing, tradition itself
being not like to be erroneous in a matter of this nature, though there
were no such charter to prove the thing alledged, which yet we have
reason to believe there is or was, though not produced by Mr. Dug-
dale[s]. To this account may be added, that a great part of the original Saxon charter, though not discovered by Mr. Dugdale, nor
known to any later writer, is yet preserved, and for the curiosity of
it deserves to be here recorded.

Eþpanꝺ Kınᵹ ᵹꝛet Þlꝛẏ Bıshop, ⁊ Lẏꝑꝺ eꝑl ⁊ alle mıne þeıᵹneꞃ on Oxne-
ꝼoꝑꝺeꞃẏne ꝼꞃenꝺlıc, ⁊ ıch cẏþe ou þ ıc hæbbe ᵹıꝼen Cꝛıꞃꞇ ⁊ Saınꞇe Peꞇꝛe ınꞇo
Þeꞃꞇmınꞃꞇꝛe ꝺaꞇ coꞇhıꝼ ꝺe ıc ꝑaꞃ boꝑen ınne bı naman Lıꝺꞃlepe ⁊ ane hẏꝺe aꞇ
Ꝙeꝑꞃce, ꞃcoꞇꝼꝑe anꝺ ᵹaꝼolꝼꝑe, mıꝺ allen þanu þınᵹan þa þeꝑ ꞇo bılımpaꝺ on
poꝺe ⁊ on ꝼelꝺe, on maꝺe ⁊ on paꞇeꝑe mıꝺ chꝩꝑchen ⁊ mıꝺ chꝩꝑch-ꝼocne ꞃꝑa
ꝼul ⁊ ꝛ ꝑa ꝼoꝑꝺ ⁊ ꞃꝑa ꝼꝛee, ꞃꝑa ıꞇ me ꞃılꝼon on hanꝺe ꞃꞇoꝺ, ⁊ ꞃꝑa alꝼ ıue Imme
mın moꝺeꝑ on mınꝑe ꝼꞃımbıꝑꝺe ꝺaꝛe ꞇo ꝼoꝑme ᵹıꝼe ıꞇ me ꞃaeꝼ ⁊ ꞇo ꞃe kınꝺe
bıquaꝺ [t].

Edward King greeteth Wlsy Bishop, and Gyrth Earl, and all my

Ricardi Norton. 8. Sept. 1508. Reg.
Smith.

Dominus Willelmus Dycher pres. per
abb. et conv. Westm. ad eccl. de Islype per
resign. domini Roberti Weston. 10. Mar.
1511. ib.

Magister Willelmus Shraggar pres. per
abb. et conv. Westm. ad eccl. de Islepe
per resign. domini Willelmi Dycher. Maii.
1517. Reg. Atwater.

Magister Petrus Polkyn, LL. D. pres.
per resign. magistri Willelmi Shragger. 1.
Mar. 1518. pensio 16 libr. solvend. resignanti. ib.

Ecclesia de Islip sequestratur per mortem Humph. Parkins. 22. Apr. 1578. Reg.
Grindall. Archiep. Cant.

Willelmus Wilson institutus in ecclesia
de Islip. 25. Apr. 1578. ad pres. Geo. Fur-
mer armig. ratione concess. sibi per Joh.
nuper abbatem Westm. ib.

1598. 7. Jul. Thomas Ravis. S. T. P.
Decanus Ædis Christi Oxon. ad eccl. de
Islip per resign. Hug. Lloide presbiteri
LL. D. ad pres. Gabriel Goodman S. T. P.
Decani Westm. et capituli. Reg. Whitgift.
Archiepi. Cant.

[s] Plot. Nat. Hist. ch. 10. §. 12.   [t] MS. num. 24. James in Musæo Bib. Bod. p. 75.

nobles in Oxfordshire. And I tell you that I have given to Christ and St. Peter into Westminster that small village wherein I was born, by name Githslepe, and one hyde at Mersce, scot-free and rent-free, with all the things which belong thereunto, in wood and field, in meadows and waters, with Church, and with the immunities of the Church, as fully and as largely, and as free as it stood in mine own hand; and also as my mother Imme, upon my right of primogeniture, for my maintenance gave it me entire, and bequeathed it to the family

Besides this charter, there is another standing memorial of the birth of king Edward at Islip, the relics of the font wherein he was baptized, lately removed from the ruins of a royal chapel in that town; of which this account is given by an eye witness of it. *In the chapel above mentioned, not many years since, there stood (as was constantly delivered down to posterity) the very font, wherein that religious prince, king Edward the Confessor, received the sacra ment of baptism: which, together with the chapel in these latter days being put to some indecent at least, if not profane use, was care- fully and piously rescued from it, by some of the right worshipful family of the Browns of Nether-Kiddington, where it now remains in the garden of that worthy gentleman Sir Henry Brown, Baronet, set handsomely on a pedestal, as exactly represented, tab. 16. fig. 6, and adorned with a poem rather pious than learned, which yet I think I had put down, but that it is imperfect* [u]. This font of stone seems a much nobler relic of religion, than that other of solid brass for the use of baptizing the royal family in Scotland, brought away among other spoils of war by Sir Richard Lee, and placed in the church of St. Albans, A. D. 1543 [x]. To this gift of Islip and of lands in Mersh to the church of Westminster, king Edward in the twenty-fifth and last year of his reign, A. D. 1066, recites a prece- dent donation of the manor of Langtun now Lanton adjoining to Ambrosden, which continues to that church, and is at present held in lease by William Oakely Esq. *Ad usus fratrum ibi Deo servien-*

---

[u] Dr. Plot's Nat. Hist. Oxf. ch. 10. §. 121.   [x] Camdeni Brit. in Catticuch.

tium de meo jure quod mihi soli competebat absque ullius reclamatione vel contradictione ista, inprimis Langtun, cum omnibus ad se pertinentibus. Gibtslepe cum omnibus ad se pertinentibus, &c.[y] This place of the donor's nativity is called Hiltesleape[z], in the pipe rolls of the thirteenth of Henry the Second, Ileslepe in a charter of the same king Henry the Second[a], Ighteslep in a presentation of the abbey of Westminster, in the sixth of Henry the Third[b]. The initial Saxon Ᵹ being cast away in this and other names of places, as Gipeswic now Ipswich, and Gifteley[c] now Ifley near Oxford. The same king Edward granted two manses and a half in Wdeton, (Wood-eaton adjoining to Islip) to Thola widow of Orc, to whom king Cnute had given seventeen manses at Abbodesbury[d].

This pious king bore a more especial relation to these parts, by his frequent residence at Brill in com. Buck. where he had a royal palace[e], to which he retired for the pleasures of hunting in his forest of Bernwood. It is to this prince, and to his diversion at this seat, that we must ascribe the traditional story of the family of Nigel, and the manor of Borstall on the edge of the said forest. Most part of the tradition is confirmed by good authority, and runs to this effect. The forest of Bernwood was much infested by a wild boar, which was at last slain by one Nigel a huntsman, who presented the boar's head to the king, and for a reward the king gave to him one hide of arable land called Derehyde, and a wood called Hulewode, with the custody of the forest of Bernwood, to hold to him and his heirs from the king, *per unum cornu quod est charta prædictæ forestæ,* and by the service of paying ten shillings yearly for the said land, and forty shillings yearly for all profits of the forest, excepting the indictments of herbage and hunting, which were reserved to the king[f]. Upon this ground the said Nigel built a lodge or mansion house called Borestalle, in memory of the slain

[y] Mon. Ang. tom. 1. p. 61.   [z] Dugd. Bar. tom. 1. p. 451.   [a] Mon. Ang. tom. 2. p. 954.   [b] R. Dodsw. MS. vol. 117. p. 41.   [c] B. Twine MS. notat. cap. 2. p. 252.   [d] Sir Hen. Spelm. of Feuds MS. in Bibliotheca Bodleiana.   [e] Camden. in Cattieuch.   [f] Ex Chartulario de Borstall MS.

boar. For proof of this, in the *chartulary of Borstall, (which is a transcript of all evidences in the reign of Henry the Sixth, relating to the estate of —— Rede esq. then owner of Borstall, a large folio in vellum)'there is a rude delineation of the site of Borstall house and manor, and under it is the sculpture of a man, presenting on his knees to the king the head of a boar on the top of a sword, and the king returning to him a coat of arms, *bearing argent, a fesse gules, two crescents, a horn verd:* which distinction of arms, though it could not agree with the time of Nigel, yet it is most likely he did receive from the king a horn, as a token and charter of his office of forester, and his successors by the name of Fitz-Nigel did bear those arms. The same figure of a boar's head presented to the king was carved on the head of an old bedstead, lately remaining in that strong and ancient house: and the said arms of Fitz-Nigel are now seen in the windows, and in other parts: and what is of greatest authority, the original horn, tipt at each end with silver gilt, fitted with wreaths of leather to hang about the neck, with an old brass ring that bears the rude impress of a horn, a plate of brass with the sculpture of a horn, and several less plates of brass with flower-de-luces, which were the arms of Lisures, who intruded into this estate and office soon after the reign of William the Conqueror, has been all along preserved under the name of Nigels horn, by the lords of Borstall, and is now in the custody of Sir John Aubrey baronet,

---

* Hæc laudantur a clarissimo linguarum septentrionalium instauratore Georgio Hickesio in Dissertatione Epistolari his verbis: Sic reverendus et doctissimus vir, Whitus Kenettus, de vetusta omne genus literatura præclare meritus, in illo antiquitatis penu, libro suo, qui inscribitur PAROCHIAL ANTIQUITIES, ex veteri Chartulario Borstaliensi, tradit S. Eadwardum confessorem dictum, ob vægrandem occisum aprum, dedisse præfecturam saltus sive Sylvæ, cui Brenwode nomen in pago Buck- inghamensi, cum una hida terræ præclaro Cynegetæ NIGEL vocato et hæredibus ejus ab iis tenenda per unum cornu quod est charta prædictæ forestæ. Nigel ille ex Cynegeta gregario, Cynegatarum sive venatorum regiorum tribunus factus erat, Cornuque venatorium istud quod apud sedis Borstaliensis dominum vidit Kenettus, non tantum ut donationis sed ut Cornici us officii Symbolum Nigello datum esse videtur.

who has been pleased with great courtesy to communicate the notice of these things.

The village of Brill was the king's demesne, and now or soon after it was let out in soccage, for the reserved rent of one hundred capons yearly for the king's table. Among those manors which the kings held in demesne, they had mansions or palaces in the largest and best situate of them, where they often resided, having constant provisions brought in by their feudatory tenants ; by such change of stations they made a sort of constant progress through their whole kingdom, kept up the better acquaintance with their people, and provided for the more easy administration of justice, which then attended the king's court and person. These places which had royal seats had the honour to be called Villæ Regiæ, which title was given to Brill[g]; and while king Edward the Confessor did here divert himself, there happened an accident, which was turned into one of the miracles of that religious prince. The story is distinctly told by Will. Malms. *One Wulwin surnamed Spillicora,* (it should be de Spillicote) *son of Wulmar de Nutegarshale,* (it should be Lutegarshale, now Ludgershall) *cutting down fuel in the wood Bruelle* (now Brill) *after hard labouring fell into a sleep, and by a settlement of blood in his eyes lost his sight for seventeen years, and then upon the strength of a dream he went round to eighty seven churches to beg relief from the respective saints, and at last came blind to the king's court at Windsor, and was cured by a touch of the king's hand ; after which he was keeper of the king's palace at Windsor for several years after the death of his royal healer*[h]. Ailred abbot of Rievaulx recounts this among the other miracles of Edward the Confessor, and varies but little in the circumstances of it: he represents the occasion to have been a royal palace then built at Bruheham, (by which name Brill is sometimes called) and many country labourers being sent out by the chief workmen to fell timber in the adjoining woods, lying down to sleep in the heat of the

g Camdeni Brit. in Atrebat.   h W. Malms. p. 91.

day, one of them called Wulfwin rose up blind, and being long after cured by the hand of king Edward was made keeper of his palace nigh St. Peter's church[i].

An. 1046[k], (not 1040, as mistaken in a late writer[l],) Emma the king's mother had been suspected of adultery with Alwin bishop of Winchester, of which falsely imputed crime the queen purged herself by the trial of *fire ordeal*, walking barefoot over nine hot plough shares without hurt: which miraculous proof of innocence was to be ascribed to the assistance of St. Swithin, patron of the church of Winchester, and therefore in a grateful acknowledgment the queen and bishop gave each nine manors to the said church, when among those given by the bishop was Witeney, now Whitny or Witney in this county[m].

About the same time the see of Criditon was removed to the city of Exeter, and given to Leofric the king's chaplain, to whom the king gave the monastery of St. Mary and St. Peter in that city, to which he recovered many of the lost possessions, and for an augmentation of lands to the maintenance of those monks who should pray for the souls of his lord the king and himself, he gave six lands in six several manors, of which the first was þ lanð aꞇ Bæmꞇune[n], now Bampton* in this county, which still belongs to the church of Exeter

---

* Vicarii ecclesiæ de Bampton.

Dominus Johannes Holrigge institutus in vicar. de Bampton per mortem domini Thomæ de Boulegh ad pres. president. et capituli Exon. 3. Maii 1367. Reg. Bokynham.

Johannes Widelond capellanus pres. per decanum et capit. Exon. ad vicar. eccl. de Bampton per mort. Joh. Holrygg. 9. Jun. 1400. Reg. Beaufort.

Magister Edmundus Willesford S. T. P. presbyter pres. per dec. et capit. Exon. ad vicariam in eccl. de Bampton per resign. domini Willelmi Clerk. 5. Dec. 1498. Reg. Smith.

Magister Ricardus More decr. doctor, presbyter pres. per dec. et capit. Exon. ad vicar. eccl. de Bampton per mort. magistri Joh. Pope. 21· Sept. 1499. ib.

Magister Will. Wood A. M. presbyter

---

[i] X. Script. Alred. Ab. p. 892.   [k] Chron. Jo. Brompt. p. 94.   [l] Nat. Hist. of Oxf. ch. 10. §. 120.   [m] Mon. Ang. tom. 1. p. 980.   [n] Mon. Ang. tom. 1. p. 221.

In the same year, 1046[o], though one historian makes it 1049[p], and another 1050[q], died Eadnoth bishop of Dorchester, who had founded the church of St. Mary's at Stow in Lincolnshire[r], as a cell to the abbey of Eynsham in this county : and was succeeded by Ulf a chaplain to the king, by birth a Norman ; who in the year 1047, going to a council held by the pope at Verceil in the duchy of Millan, for his ignorance in discharge of his office, should have had his epis-copal staff there broken, if he had not purchased his pardon with a very great sum of money[s]. After his return he became odious as a foreigner and an evil counsellor of the king, and under that cha-racter was banished with Robert archbishop of Canterbury, William bishop of London, and other Normans an. 1052[t], but was afterwards recalled, and in the year 1067 died at Winchester, and was buried at Dorchester[u]

In this reign of the Confessor, the manors of Burcester, Ambros-den, Stratton, Weston, and many adjoining villages were a part of the large estate of Wigod de Walengford, a noble thane, who kept his residence at the town from whence he had his title, where at this

---

pres. per dec. et capit. Exon. ad vicar. eccl. de Bampton per resign. mag. Ric. More. 20. Sept. 1500. ib.

Dominus Tho. Hoye, presbyter, pres. per dec. et capit. Exon. ad vicar. eccl. de Bamp-ton per mort. magistri Roberti Holcote. 15. Dec. 1500. ib.

Magister Joh. Southwode S. T. B. pres. per dec. et capit. Exon. ad vicar. ecclesiæ de Bampton per resign. magistri Edmundi Wylleford. 19. Dec. 1506. ib.

1585. 22. Nov. Hen. Walmysley, A. M. ad vicar. de Bampton. Reg. Whitgift, ar-chiepiscopi Cant.

1595. 16. Maii. Humphr. Hargrave ad vicar. de Bampton per resign. Rob. Sib-thorp, A. M. ad pres. decani et capituli Exon. ib.

1595. 14. Jul. Rob. Joye, A. M. ad vi-car. de Bampton, per mort. Henr. Doltin. ib.

1598. 7. Jul. Joh. Howson, presbyter, A. M. ad vicar. ecclesiæ de Bampton, quare Humphr. Hargrave nuper habuit jam de-functus, ad pres. decani et capituli Exon. ib.

---

[o] Chron. Saxon.   [p] Flor. Wigorn.   [q] Mat. West.   [r] Mon. Ang. tom. 1. p. 262.   [s] Chron. Saxon. et Hen. Hunt. p. 365.   [t] Mat. West. sub an.   [u] Sim. Dun. p. 197.

time were 276 houses, of which a mint-master had one, free from all geld while he coined money; but at the general survey in the next reign, thirteen of these houses were diminished, and eight had been demolished to make a castle[x]. This Wigod de Walengford gave to the church conventual of Egnesham in this county, two hides of land in Fulbroc[y], now Fulbrook, nigh to Teynton, which Edward the Confessor gave to Deorherst com. Gloc. a cell to the abbey of St. Dennys in France[z].

An. 1066, on the day before Epiphany king Edward died at Westminster, succeeded by king Harold, who, dying in the field on Oct. 14, surrendered life and crown to the victorious William duke of Normandy, from whose reign I shall adjust the history and antiquities of these parts into short and faithful annals.

An. MLXVI.   1. WILLIAM CONQUEROR.

AMONG the Normans who were engaged in this expedition, those, who were soon after rewarded with lands in these parts[a], were 1. Robert de Oily, to whom the king gave in marriage the estate of Wigod de Walengford and two other honors, including Burcester, Ambrosden, Bucknel, Stratton, Weston, Blechesdon, &c. 2. Roger de Iveri to whom, for his friendship and sworn fraternity, the said Robert de Oily gave one of the said honors, of which the head or capital seat was Beckley, containing Ambrosden, Mixbury, Northbrook, &c. 3. Odo bishop of Baieux and earl of Kent, to whom his royal brother gave Somerton, Fritwell, Fringford, &c. 4. Jef-

---

[x] Lib. Doomsday.   [y] Regist. Egnes. MS. p. 158.   [z] Mon. Ang. tom. 1. p. 548.
[a] Ex tab. Mon. de Bello. et ex Regist. Doomsday, &c.

fery de Magneville who had the manor of Wendlebury. 5. Judith
niece to the Conqueror, who had Merton and Pidington. 6. Milo
Crispin, who had Chesterton, Gadington, &c. 7. William earl of
Warren, who had Kirtlington and Midlington. 8. Walter Giffard, to
whom, with the earldom of Bucks were given Oakley and many adjoining parishes in com. Buck. with Caversham, Craumersh, Stoke,
Bix, &c. in this county. Those other Normans who now entered the
kingdom, and in after reigns came to possessions in this part of the
county were, 1. The family of Chanvill, who enjoyed the manor and
castle of Midleton. 2. Basset, who had the lordship of Hedington,
the manors of Burcester, Wrechwick, Stratton, &c. 3. S. Walery,
who came to the honor granted to Roger de Ivery, which from the
later family was after called the honor of St. Walery. 4. De Lizures, who intruded into the manor of Borstall, and the custody of
the forest of Bernwood, which of right belonged to Nigel de
Borstall.

After the decisive battle near Hastings, the Conqueror carried his
forces into Kent, and, marching back from thence, passed by London possessed by the party of Edgar Atheling, and came to Walingford, where the lord of that town Wigod de Walengeford went out
to meet him [b], delivered the town to him, and entertained him there,
till archbishop Stigand and many of the grandees of Edgar's faction
came and offered their submission [c]. For which service and merit of
the lord of that place, the victorious prince, in policy to ingratiate
with the Saxons, and to reward his Normans, gave Aldith only
daughter of the said Wigod in marriage to Robert de Oily, who,
after her father's death, which happened nigh the same time, in right
of her became possest of that great estate, wherein Burcester was in
the honor of Walingford, and Ambrosden in that honor which was
after called S. Walery. From Walingford the Conqueror led his
army through this part of the country with great spoil and mischief
in his road to Bercamsted, at which place prince Edgar, the earls

---

[b] Gul. Pict. Gest. Ducis Norman. p. 21.　　　[c] Ib. p. 285.

Edwin and Morcar, the bishops of York, Worcester, Hereford, &c.[d] waited on duke William, and resigning up all their interest invited him to London, and on Christmas day he was crowned at Westminster by Aldred archbishop of York[e].

An. MLXVII. 1, 2. *William Conqueror.*

Soon after his coronation, the king designed a journey to the north for the quiet of those parts, and in his way thither came to Oxford, which city refused to yield to him, and a soldier from the wall gave him a most contemptible affront[f]: upon which provocation the king stormed it on the north side, and, gaining an easy entrance, he gave the greatest part of it to Robert de Oily, who at the survey had, within the walls and without, forty two houses inhabited, and eight lying waste[g]. About which time the king fearing that his new subjects might turn Walingford, as they had Oxford, into a garrison against him, he commanded the lord of it, Robert de Oily, to fortify it with a new castle, for prevention of that danger: in which castle Aldred abbot of Abbendon was imprisoned in the year 1071[h].

An. MLXVIII. 2, 3. *William Conqueror.*

In the late expedition, Robert de Oily brought over with him Roger de Ivery, a fellow adventurer and sworn brother, for they had mutually engaged by oath to be sharers of the same fortune. This was a sociable practice of that age, for so Eudo and Pinco, though not allied, were upon that invasion sworn brothers in war, and co-partners in the reward of their service[i]. According to this compact, when the said Robert de Oily had two honors given to him, beside the estate which came by his wife, he freely gave one of those honors (of which Beckley was the capital seat, and within which Am-

[d] Sim. Dun. p. 193.   [e] Chron. Tho. Wikes.   [f] Mat. Par. sub an.   [g] Lib. Doomsday.   [h] Hist. Cœnob. Abend. Wharton. Ang. sac. tom. 1. p. 168.   [i] Dugd. Bar. tom. 1. p. 439.

brosden was included) to this Roger de Ivery. The history of it is
thus imperfectly delivered by Mr. John Leland. Robertus de Oleio,
that cam into England with William Conqueror, had gyven to him
the Baronies of Oxford and Saint Waleries. This Robert had one
John de Eiverio, that was exceeding familiar with him, and had been
in the warres as sworen brother unto him, and had promised to be
partaker of Robert's fortunes, whereupon be enriched him with
possessions, and as sum think gave him S. Waleries[k]. This gift of
the barony, which was after called S. Waleries, I wonder Mr. Leland
should express as a doubtful thing, and seem to resolve it into an
uncertain tradition; when there were the plainest records to prove
it, of which he could not well miss, having so ample a commission to
search in all places for the books and writings of his scattering age.
It is more strange he should call him John de Eiverio, when for this
he could have no authority, but his own conjecture. Yet this error
is continued without notice in the monasticon, and is again asserted
by Mr. Dugdale[l]. Whereas we find in records no one of that family
named John; and it is certain, the sworn companion of Robert de
Oily was Roger de Ivery. He is so registered in Doomsday inquisition, and Mr. Camden has rightly so called him[m]. And what may
put it beyond all dispute, is this transcript from the old register of
Oseney. *Memorandum quod Robertus de Oleio et Rogerus de Iverio
fratres jurati et per fidem et sacramentum confederati venerunt ad
conquestum Angliæ cum rege Willielmo Bastard. Iste rex dedit dicto
Roberto duas Baronias, quæ modo vocantur Baronia Doylivorum et S.
Waleria*[n]. This Roger was the son of Waleran de Ivery, who held
one knight's fee in the bailiwic of Tenechebrai in Normandy, by
the service of cup-bearer to the duke, and three other fees within the
said liberty, as also eight fees and a half of the town and castle of

[k] Jo. Lel. Itin. vol. 2. f. 17. MS. et Mon. Ang. tom. 2. p. 136.   [l] Dugd. Bar. tom. 1.
p. 460.   [m] Britan. in Dobun.   [n] Regist. Mon. Oseney per William Sutton Abb.
MS. penes Decan. et Capit. Æd. Christi Ox. f. 1.

Ivery[o]. He enjoyed the same honour of cup-bearer to William king of England, which his father had done to him while duke of Nor mandy : he married Adeline eldest daughter of Hugh de Grentmaisnil and Adelidis his wife: which Hugh coming in with the Conqueror, and fighting stoutly in that memorable battle, was this year made an administrator of justice through the whole kingdom, jointly with Odo bishop of Baieux and William Fitz-Osbern : and nigh this same time was made governor of Hantshire and sheriff of Leicestershire[p]. This family de Ivery was descended from one Rodulph half brother to Richard, the first duke of Normandy, who killing a monstrous bear, when hunting with his brother duke, was by him for that service rewarded with the castle of Ivery on the river l'Evre, and had from thence the title of Comes de Ibreio. *Cum Richardus primus ducatum Norman. esset adeptus, venatum ibat. Adfuit Rodolphus uterinus frater ducis, qui ursum belluam immanissimam prostravit, vocaturque hodie vallis, in qua occidit ursum, vallis Ursonis. Dedit præterea illi castrum Ivereium, unde vocatus est Comes*[q]. Mr. Dugdale ought to have allowed this family a place in his baronage of England, since this first Roger de Ivery with Roger his son, and Jeffery younger brother of the said Roger, did successively enjoy a full barony of D'Oyly's gift, which from them was called Baronia de Iverio, as it was after Baronia de S. Walerico. This omission is more excusable than that gross mistake committed by the author of the Introduction to the old English History, who in his Appendix offering a catalogue of all the chief tenants in Doomsdaybook, under the county of Oxford, mentions Hugo de Luri vel Luci, when it is plainly, Terra Hugonis de Ivri. AMERESDONE; and again, Roger de Luri vel Lauri, and uxor Rogeri de Luri. And farther in the counties of Gloucester, Warwickshire, Hunt. Northam. he transcribes it Lury, and hits right only in Bucks, where he truly calls him Roger de Iveri[r].

[o] Norman. Script. p. 1018.   [p] Dugd. Bar. tom. 1. p. 425.   [q] Gul. Gemet. p. 288.
[r] Dr. Rob. Brady Introd. &c.

An. MLXIX. 3, 4. *William Conqueror.*

The great Gospatric being deprived of his earldom of Northumberland, it was now by the king bestowed on Waltheof son of the famous earl Siward, by Elfled his wife, daughter of earl Aldred; and that he might be the more firmly won over to the Norman interest, the Conqueror gave him in marriage to his niece Judith [s], and with her the manors of Pidington within the parish of Ambrosden, and of Merton next adjoining, restoring at the same time his father's earldoms of Huntendon and Northampton. This Judith was the daughter of Lambert de Lenes by Maud countess of Albemarle, who was the daughter of Halwyn de Comitis Villa by Arlota his wife, and thereby sister to duke William by the mother [t].

On Easter Monday the king at Winchester gave the church of Deorhurst in com. Gloc. as a cell to the abbey of St. Dennys in France, and confirmed the donation of Teynton in this county, given by his predecessor king Edward, to which charter one of the witnesses was Rogerus de Ivri [u].

An. MLXXI. 5, 6. *William Conqueror.*

The king, being jealous of the fidelity of these parts, commanded Robert de Oily to build a castle on the west side of the city of Oxford, as he had done at Walingford [x]. The date of this action is thus entered in the Oseney Register. *An. ab incarnat. Dom. mil. septuages. primo ædificatum est castellum Oxon. temp. regis Willielmi prædicti a Roberto de Oily. Iste Robertus de Oleio dedit fratri suo Rogero prædicto baron. quæ modo vocatur S. Walerici.* But observe, though this gift of the barony be here mentioned jointly with the building of the castle, yet it was not indeed given to Roger de Ivery till after the year 1074.

---

[s] Orderic. Vital. p. 523.　　[t] Vincent's Heraldry, Brooks, &c.　　[u] Mon. Ang. tom. 1. p. 547.　　[x] Wood. Antiq. Oxon. sub an.

An. MLXXII.   6, 7. *William Conqueror.*

Upon the death of Ulf or Wulfin bishop of Dorchester, Remigius was preferred to this see.   And at a council held this year in London, this episcopal seat was transferred from Dorchester, as too obscure a place, to the city of Lincoln [y].

An. MLXXIII.   8, 9. *William Conqueror.*

Robert de Oily, having now finished his castle in Oxford, built within the walls of it a chapel dedicated to St. George *, and established there a fraternity of secular priests; whom he endowed with several rights and possessions in these parts.   He gave them the churches of Cudelinton, Weston, Cestreton, &c. with two parts of the tithe of his demesne in Berencestre, Wrechwike, Blechesdon, Weston, Bukenhull, Ardulfley, Northbroc juxta Somerton, &c. two parts of all the tithe of Beckele, the whole tithes of Aclee, Horton, and Mercote; half a hide of land in Stodele belonging to Beckele, and two hides of land with wood and other appurtenances in Ernicot now Arncot in the parish of Ambrosden.   In the first charter of R. de Oily, as now preserved in the Oseney Register, there is no mention of the particular places; but when they were all after converted and confirmed to the abbey of Oseney, they are expressed in several successive charters.   It seems not so plain whether Robert de Oily had the whole estate entire, or whether he had divided it with his

---

* Notum sit omnibus fidelibus sanctæ ecclesiæ tam presentibus quam futuris, quod ego Robertus de Olleyo, volentibus et concedentibus Alditha uxore mea et fratribus meis Nigello et Gilberto, dedi et concessi Deo, et ecclesiæ S. Georgii in castello Oxenforde et canonicis in ea Deo servientibus, quam ecclesiam pro salute, &c. omnes res, tenementa, decimas et possessiones subscriptas, videl. ecclesiam S. Mariæ Magdalenæ, quæ sita est in suburbio Oxenforde, cum tribus hidis terræ in Walton, &c.   Ex collectan. R. Glover, e registro de Osney. MS.

y Histor. Ingulphi. p. 93.

sworn brother Roger de Ivery. This latter might be supposed from
their being both reputed equal founders and benefactors in the
Oseney register. *An. Dom. mil. septuages. quarto fundata est eccle-
clesia S. Georgii in castello Oxon. a Roberto de Oleio primo et Rogero de Iveri tempore reg. Willelmi Bastard, qui in dicta ecclesia canonicos seculares instituerunt, et diversos redditus de duabus baroniis
prædictis eisdem assignarunt de ecclesiis, terris, &c.* [z] If this were
true, then the two parts of the tithe of Berncester, Wrechwike, Blechesdon, Weston, Bukenhull, &c. must be the gift of Robert de
Oily: and the tithes of Beckele, Horton, half hide in Stodle, and
two hides in Ernicote, must have been the donation of Roger de
Iveri, because within the limits of the barony given to him. But it
appears more likely, that Roger de Iveri was not yet instated in his
barony, and therefore could not immediately grant, but only confirm
the precedent gift of Robert de Oily, who had first settled the pious
uses, and then gave him the barony so charged. This may be con-
cluded from the first charter of Roger de Iveri. *Sciant præsentes et
futuri quod ego Rogerus de Ivereio pro salute domini regis et totius
regni nec non pro salute domini mei Roberti de Olleyo et Aldithe
uxoris suæ et meorum salute concessi et præsenti carta mea confirmavi
Deo et ecclesiæ S. Georgii quæ sita est in castello Oxon. omnes terras
et tenementa decimas redditus et possessiones quas dictus Robertus de
Olleyo dedit, et concessit, et assignavit* [a]· This evidence does imply,
that all was an antecedent donation of Robert de Oily, while both
the baronies remained in his own hands, one of which when he soon
after bestowed on his devoted friend Roger de Iveri, the uses before
assigned were again fully confirmed. It is no objection, that Roger
de Iveri was called a founder and endower of that chapel, or that
Jeffery de Iveri does after call these grants the gift and concession of
his father Roger de Iveri. For it is evident to any that converse with
old charters, that those barons and knights, who held the fee of estates
belonging to monasteries, were by courtesy called the founders of

Regist. Oseney MS. fol. 1.   [a] Ib. f. 1.

such houses, and the donors of such lands, because heirs and lords of the fee, and confirmers of what their predecessors gave. That the whole endowment of these secular canons was the act of Robert de Oily, without the concurrence of the other, is farther evinced from the titles of those lands, as they stood registered in the Oseney-book: where some of them are said to have been the gift of Robert de Oily, and the confirmation of Roger de Iveri; others are expressed as the sole grant of d'Oily. *Abbas Osen. habet in Ernicote de dono Roberti de Olleyo, et confirmatione Regum Angliæ et episcoporum et capituli Lincoln, duas hidas terræ pertinentes ad ecclesiam S. Georgii ut patet in charta ejusdem Roberti superius. Quæ ecclesia S. Georgii data fuit fratribus Osen. et habet ibidem visum Francipleg. et totum regale servitium* [b]. *Abbas de Osen. habet ecclesiam de Weston de dono Doylivorum cum confirmatione episcoporum et capituli Lincoln, ut patet supra in titulo fundationis Osen* [c]. *In ista balliva de Weston, continentur hæc, Westona, Blechesdon, Berecestre, Cestreton, Wrechwike, Bochenhull, Ardulfsle, Ernicote, Northbroc juxta Somerton.*

An. MLXXV.   9, 10. *William Conqueror.*

Waltheof earl of Northumberland, Northampton, and Huntington, lord of the manors of Pidington and Merton, was drawn into the plot of Ralph de Ware earl of Norfolk [d]; and though archbishop Lanfranc attested his innocence, yet by the instigation of his wife, who affected another marriage [e], he was beheaded without the walls at Winchester, and his body after translated to the abbey of Croyland, where, agreeable to the faith of that age, miracles were soberly reported of him [f]. The execution of this Saxon baron is observed as the first example of beheading in this island. After his death the earldoms of Northampton and Huntendon remained to his countess dowager Judith, with the manors of Pidington and Merton [g].

---

[b] Regist. Oseney MS. f. 32.   [c] Ib. f. 316.   [d] Rog Hoved. p. 457.   [e] Sim. Dun. p. 207.   [f] Hist. Ingulph. p. 72   [g] Doomsday-book.

An. MLXXVI.   10, 11.   *William Conqueror.*

At or before this time Hugh de Grentemaisnil, father of Adeline,
wife of Roger de Iveri, among other large possessions given by him
to his restored monastery of St. Ebrulf in Normandy, granted the
church of Charlton upon Otmoore, with the tithes and five virgates of
land, and one villain ; as also the church of St. Laurence at Merston,
in com. Northampt. with all the tithe and land belonging to the
church, &c. which grants William the Conqueror confirmed to those
monks by a large charter dated at Winchester, an. MLXXXI [h]. This
monastery of St. Ebrulf or St. Evroul of the Benedictine order was
built by one Ebrulf in the reign of king Clothair the First, an. 578
and, being almost destroyed, was restored in the year 1050 by Robert de Grentesmaisnil and Hugh his brother [i] : at which time Robert de Grentesmaisnil became a monk under the government of
Theoderic then abbot, was soon after made prior [k], and an. 1059, on
the death of Theodoric, was elected abbot.   And four years after being banished by William duke of Normandy, he appealed to pope
Nicholas ; but having no redress, he was at last received by Robert
duke of Calabria, who gave him a little church nigh Bresse upon the
shore of the Adriatic sea, where he founded a new monastery, and
was himself abbot for seventeen years [l].   All the donations of Hugh
de Grentesmaisnil to his said abbey of St. Ebrulf were confirmed by
Robert Blanchmaine earl of Leicester, who married Petronil daughter of Hugh de Grentesmaisnil, grandson of the said restorer, in the
reign of king Richard the First [m].

Nigh this time Roger de Ivery had the whole barony, of which
Beckley was the capital seat, given to him by Robert de Oily, who
had sworn to divide his fortunes with him.   About the same time the

[h] Oderic. Vital. p. 603, et Mon. Ang. tom. 2. p. 966.   [i] Neustria Pia, p. 104.
[k] Gul. Gemet. sub an. 1051.   [l] Neustria Pia, p. 105.   [m] Dugd. Bar. tom. 1.
p. 88.

said Roger de Iveri founded a monastery of the Benedictine order dedicated to St. Mary, near the castle of Yuri in Normandy, which castle Asceline Goel had extorted from the hands of William de Bretoil, who, to recover the custody of it, in the following year besieged it, and made a garrison of the new monastery, which the said Asceline Goel in a sally took, and set fire to it. *Abbatia juxta castrum Ibreicense sita (Gallice Yuri et la Chaussee Dioc. Ebroic. Ord. Benedict.) fundat. a Rogero de Ibreio viro illustrissimo, &c.* [n]

The king, having founded another Benedictine monastery at Caen in Normandy, had it now dedicated to St. Stephen, and amply endowed by charter, to which were witnesses Hugh de Grentesmaisnil, William Crispin, &c. [o]

An. MLXXVIII. 12, 13. *William Conqueror.*

About this time Judith countess of Huntendon, who held the manors of Merton and Pidington, founded the nunnery of Helenestow, or Elnestowe, not in com. Berks. as mistaken in the Monast. but in com. Bedf. and had the church dedicated to the Holy Trinity, Virgin Mary, and St. Helen : giving to it the whole village of Helenestow, and the village of Wilsamstede, and five hides and a half in Meldon [p].

An. MLXXIX. 13, 14. *William Conqueror.*

Roger de Iveri, lord of that honor which contained Beckele, Ambrosden, &c. died about this time, and left Adeline his widow, who by inheritance from her father held lands in Charlton, Otendon, and Islip : and three sons, of which Roger the elder succeeded in the barony, and in the office of cup-bearer to the king. Hugh the second had the manor of Ambrosden ; and Jeffery the youngest, after the decease of the two other, came to the whole possessions [q].

---

[n] Neustria Pia sub Abbat. Iveri.   [o] Neustria Pia, p. 227. et Mon. Ang. tom. 2. p. 956.
[p] Mon. Ang. tom. 1. 360. et Joh. Leland. Collect. MS. vol. 1. p. 324.   [q] Doomsdaybook and Oseney Register.

An. MLXXXI.   14, 15. *William Conqueror.*

About this time Judith the countess of Huntendon and Northampt. taking great delight in her village of Saltrey in the county of Hunt. did give and enclose a wood for the monks of that place, and procured for them a royal charter of very large immunities within the precincts of that place[r]. This Judith had been offered by her uncle the king in marriage to Simon St. Liz, son of Randolph le Rich, a noble Norman : but she nicely refused him, because he was lame of one leg[s]; whereat the king in anger gave away the earldoms of Huntendon and Northampton to the said Simon, in marriage with Maud eldest daughter of earl Waltheof and the said Judith ; whose second daughter Alice was married to Ralph de Todneio, lord of Flamsted, and a third to Robert a fifth son of Richard de Tonebridge[t].

An. MLXXXII.   15, 16. *William Conqueror.*

Now began the general survey of all parts of England, except the three most northern counties, which were so desolated by wars and incursions, that no account could be taken of them. This was done in imitation of king Alfred's policy, who, when he divided his kingdom into counties, hundreds, and tithings, had an inquisition taken and digested into a register called Dome-boc, reposited in the church of Winchester, thence called Codex Wintoniensis. This new survey was from the model of the other, and was for some time kept in the same church, and was possibly a corruption of the same name, Dome-boc into Doomsday-book[u]; though some will have it named from *Domus Dei*, the church where it was first preserved : others from giving final judgment in the tenure of estates : hence by Latin writers often termed *liber judicialis*. The itinerant commissioners

[r] Mon. Ang. tom. 1. p. 850.   [s] Ingulph. Hist. edit. Savil. p. 903.   [t] Dugd. Bar. tom. 1. p. 58.   [u] Ælfredi vita, l. 2. cap. 28.

for these parts seem to have been the same persons who were appointed for Worcester and other midland counties: viz. Wulstan bishop of Worcester, Remigius bishop of Lincoln, Walter Giffard earl. of Buckingham, Henry de Feriers, and Adam brother of Eudo, &c. [x] These inquisitors upon the oaths of the sheriffs, the lords of each manor, the presbyters of every church, the reves of every hundred, and six villains of every village, were to inquire into the name of the place, who held in king Edward's time, who the present possessor, how many hides in the manor, how many carucates in demesne, how many freemen, how many tenants in soccage, how many in villenage, how much wood, meadow, and pasture, how many mills and fish-ponds, how much added or taken away, what the value, and how much taxed for in king Edward's time, what now, and what advance could be made of it? This inquisition was not finished till the twentieth of this reign, being registered in two books now kept in the treasury of the Exchequer, in the lesser of which is the description of Essex, Norfolk, and Suffolk, and at the end of it is this short note, an. 1086. *An. regni W. 20, facta est hæc descriptio non solum per hos tres comitatus, sed etiam per alios.* In this search of the land, Oxfordshire was surveyed in order the fourteenth county, which we may suppose to have been dispatched about two years after the circuit began. Their method of entering this return was, first to entitle the estate to its owner, as *terra regis, terra Roberti de Oilgi*, &c. then to specify the hundred, of which there were more in number, and of different names than now remain, nor alway containing one hundred villages according to their first institution [y]. Under the hundred followed the tenant, the place, and the description of it. But in the orthography of names of places, the Norman scribes were oft mistaken, seldom copying out the name from any other writing, but only taking it from the mouth of the Saxon informers, whose pronunciation could

---

[x] Dugd. Bar. tom. 1. p. 257.   [y] Jo. Ross, Warw. MS.

not be fit to dictate to foreigners: nay these new lords did purposely deprave and contract the Saxon words out of pure detestation of that language, which their master had so great ambition to extirpate, that he would not suffer lawyers to plead, nor so much as children to be instructed in it [z]. This is a great unhappiness, that the most ancient record of places cannot be now with certainty appealed to, for the true and proper names of them. Of this mischief Mr. Lambard [a], Mr. Dugdale [b], and others, have justly complained. From hence we have reason to infer a mistake in their way of writing Ambrosden, which is there made Ameresdone, which possibly might be occasioned from the softer pronunciation of the Saxons, and the common use of contracting words by the Norman pens. I scarce doubt but the place was Ambrosdun among the remaining Britains, and very nigh to the same sound among the Saxons. I confess we have no direct authority, but in the most early records after the conquest, we alway find it Ambrosden and Ambresdon, which must needs be from good tradition, or by transcript from Saxon deeds: for it could be no corruption, because these latter names are more harsh than the former: whereas we may take for granted, that every corruption of words, after the Normans prevailed, was into a more soft and easy pronunciation. I shall set down the original tenure of Burcester, and some few adjacent parishes.

Terra ROBERTI DE OILGI, Peritune hund.

Idem Rotbertus ten. Bernecestre *pro* 2 *maner. Ibi st.* 15 *hidæ et dim. Terra* 22 *car. De hac terra* 3 *hidæ st. in dnio. et*

Robert de Oily holds Berncestre for two manors [c]: there are 15 hides and a half; land of 22 carucates, of which land 3 hides are in demesne, wherein are 6 carucates and 5 servants, and 28 villains, with 14

---

[z] Hen. Spelm. Codex Legum MS. sub Gul. 1.   [a] Lambard Perambul. Kent. p. 342.
[b] Antiq. Warwic. Pref.   [c] Now the two manors of Burcestre and Wrechwick.

ibi 6 *car. et* 5 *serui, et* 28 *uilli cum* 14 *bord. hnt.* 16 *car. Ibi* 2 *molini. de* 40 *solid. et* 12 *ac. prati. Silua* 1 *qr. 'lg. et una lat. T. R. E. valuit* 15 *lib. Modo* 16.

Gislebertus ten. de Ro. BVCHEHELLE. *Ibi st.* 7 *hidæ. Terra* 10 *car. Nc. in dnio.* 2 *car. et* 3 *scrui. et* 6 *villi tum* 3 *bord. hnt.* 5 *car. Silua* 1 *qrent. lg. et dim. q'. lat. Valuit* 10 *lib. Modo* 7 *lib.*

Aluuardus ten. de Ro. STRATONE. *Ibi st.* 5 *hidæ. Terra* 6 *car. Nc. in dnio.* 1 *car. cum* 1 *seruo. et* 8 *villi cum* 2 *bord. hnt.* 2 *car. Ibi* 25 *acr. prati. Valuit* 40 *sol. ct post ct modo* 60 *sol.*

Gislebertus ten. de Ro. WESTONE. *Ibi st.* 10 *hidæ. Terra* 12 *car. Nc. in dnio.* 4 *car. et* 5 *servi ct* 17 *villi cum* 11 *bord.*

borderers, and they have 16 carucates. There are two mills[d] of 40 shillings rent, and 12 acres of meadow. A wood of one quarentine[e] in length, and one in breadth. In the time of king Edward it was worth 15 pound, now it is worth 16.

Gilbert holds of the said Robert Buchehelle (or Bucknell.) There are 7 hides, and land of 10 carucates : now in demesne there are two carucates and 3 servants, and 6 villains, with 3 borderers who have 5 carucates. There is a wood of one quarentine in length, and half a quarentine in breadth, it was worth 10 pounds, it is now worth 7.

Alward holds of the said Robert Stratone (now Stratton-Audley.) There are 5 hides; and lands of 6 carucates : now in demesne there is 1 carucate with 1 servant and 8 villains, with two borderers who have two carucates : there are 25 acres of meadow. It was worth 40 shillings, and afterwards and now 60 shillings.

Gilbert holds of the said Robert Weston. There are 10 hides, and land of 12 carucates, now in demesne four carucates, and 5 servants, and 17 villains, with 11 borderers who have 8 carucates. There are

---

[d] One mill where it now remains, and the other seems to have been at the north end of the close or grove adjoining to the seat of John Coker, gent.   [e] A quarentine was forty perches, or a furlong.

hnt. 8 car. Ibi 2 molini. two mills of four shillings rent, and thirty
4 solid. et 30 acr. prati. acres of meadow. It was worth eight
Valuit. 8 lib. modo 12 lib. pounds, now it is worth 12 pounds.

Idem Gislebertus ten. The same Gilbert holds of Robert Bli-
de Ro. BLICESTONE. *Ibi* cestone, (or Blechingdon) there are 8
st. 8 hidæ. terra 6 car. hides, and land of 6 carucates, now in de-
Nc. in dnio. 2 car. et 5 mesne there be two carucates, and 5 ser-
servi. et 9 villi cum 7 vants, and 9 villains, with 7 borderers who
bord. hnt. 4 car. Ibi 11 have 4 carucates. There are 5 acres of
acr. prati. Pastura 6 q'. meadow, and pasture of 6 quarentines in
lg. et 3 q'. lat. T. R. E. length and three in breadth. In the time
et post valuit 4 *lib. Modo* of king Edward and afterwards, it was
100 *sol. hanc redemit* worth four pounds, now one hundred shil-
Robertus de rege. lings. Robert redeemed it from the king.

I recommend a farther abstract of the names of hundreds and
manors, under those tenants who bare the nearest relation to these
parts.

TERRA **ROBERTI DE OILGI**, PERITUNE HUND.

WATELINTONE,	*Watlington.*	CERTELINTONE,	*Kirtlington.*
BERNECESTRE,	*Burcestre.*	TEWA,	*Duns Tewe.*
ETONE,	*Aston.*	CHEDELINTONE,	*Kidlington.*
DRAITONE,	*Draiton.*	GARINGES,	*Goring.*
SCIREBVRNE,	*Sherborn*	HOCHENARTONE,	*Hooknorton.*
LEVECANOLE,	*Leuknor.*	WITEFELLE,	*Whitfield.*
BVCHEHELLE,	*Bucknell.*	FULEWELLE,	*Fulwell.*
ESEFELDE,	*Ellsfield.*	HARDEWICH,	*Hardwick.*
STRATONE,	*Stratton-Audley.*	WESTONE,	*Weston on the Green.*
BLICESTONE,	*Blechingdon.*	DOCHELINTONE,	*Ducklington.*
BENTONE,	*Bampton.*	PEREIVN,	*Water-perry.*
ROWESHAM,	*Rousham.*	LVDEWELLE,	*Ludwell.*
ESTHCOTE,	*Astcot.*	CHENETONE,	*Kencot.*

HALIWELLE,	*Holywell.*	*murum quam extra; et* VIII. *man-*
siones habet vastas, et XXX. *acras*
Idem Robertus habet XLII. *domus*	*prati juxta murum, et molin.* X.
hospitatas in Oxeneford tam intra	*solid.*

TERRA ROGERII DE IVERI, PERITUNE HUND.

MISSEBERIE *,	*Mixbury.*	BECHELIE,	*Beckley.*
ESTHALLE,	*Astall.*	NORTONE,	*Cheping-Norton*
FVLEBROC,	*Fulbrook.*	SCIRBVRNE,	*Sherborn.*
ETONE.		ELTONE,	f. *Holton.*
NORTBROC,	*Northbrook.*	LEGE,	N. *Leigh or S. Leigh.*
HORSPADAN,	*Horspath.*	HANTONE,	*Hampton-Gay.*
HANSITONE,	*Hensington.*	WISTELLE.	
TROP,	*Heathrop.*	CODESLAVE,	*Cutslowe.*
CHENEFELDE,	*Clanfield.*	ROVESHAM,	*Rousham.*
BERTONE,	*Barton.*		

IN PRIMO GADRE HUND.

NORBROC,	*Norbrook.*	STOCHES,	*Stoke Line.*

IN SECUNDO GADRE HUND.

WALTONE,	*Walcot.*	VLFGARCOTE,	*Woolvercot.*

TERRA EPI' BAIOCENSIS IN LEVECANOL HUND.

SVMERTONE,	*Somertone.*	FERTWELLE,	*Fritwell.*
SEXINTONE,	*Sexinton.*	FERINGEFORD,	*Fringford.*
FINEMERE,	*Finmere.*	CESTITONE,	*Chesterton.*
HORTONE,	*Horton.*	COVELIE,	*Cowley.*
BRISTELMESTONE,	*Brighthamton.*	SANFORD,	*Sanford;* &c.

* Rogerus de Ivri ten. de rege Misse-	Nunc in dominio I car. cum I servo et XVIII
berie. Ibi sunt XVII hide terre XV carucat.	villani cum XI bord. habent vicar.

TERRA MILONIS CRISPIN. IN SECUNDO GADRE HD.

GADINTONE,   *Godington.*   HASELIE,   *Haseley.*

IN DIMID. BESENTONE HD.

CELGRAVE,	*Chalgrave.*	GERSEDVNE,	*Gersington.*
MAPELDREHAM,	*Mapledurham.*	CVCHESHAM,	*Cuxham.*
SVMERTONE,	*Somerton.*	HEGFORD,	*Heyford.*
CESTRETONE,	*Chesterton.*	NIWEHAM,	*Newnham.*
BRVTVVELLE,	*Brightwell.*	ALCRINTONE,	*Alkerton; &c.*

TERRA GISLEBERTI DE GAND.

HANEBERGE,   *Hanborough.*   LAVVELME,   *Ewelm.*

TERRA GOISFRIDI DE MANNEVILE.

CANINGEHAM,   *Kingham.*   WANDESBERIE, *Wendlebury.*
REICOTE,   *Ricot.*

TERRA HVGONIS DE IVERI, IN DORCHECESTRE HD.

AMBRESDONE*, *Ambrosden.*

TERRA JVDITHÆ COMITISSÆ. IN DIMID. BESENTONE HD.

MERETONE,   *Merton.*   PETINTONE,   *Pidington.*

---

* Terra Hugonis de Iveri ÞULO ðe IVRI ʒen. ðe reʒe ÆꝒBRESÐONE. Ibi s'ʒ x hiðe ʒ'ʒa xvɪ caʒ.' N'c in dnio ii caʒ' ꝡ iii ʒeʒuɪ ꝡ xxɪii villi cū xɪ boʒd' h'nʒ xɪiii caʒ'. Ibi ʟxv ac' p'ʒɪ. Valuit vɪɪi lib'. Modo x. lib'. Ælueua libe' tenuit T. R. E. Ex libro Domesd.

Hugo de Iveri holds of the king Ambresdone. There are ten hides land of 16 carucates. Now in demesne two carucates and three servants, and twenty four villanes, with eleven borderers. They have fourteen carucates. There be sixty-five acres of meadow. It was worth eight pounds, now ten pounds. Ælveva held it free in the time of king Edward.

Terra vxoris ROGERIJ DE IVERI.

LETELAPE,   *Islip.*   OTENDONE,   *Oddington.*

Terræ de feodo WILLI Comitis. In Levecanole hd.

FERTEWELLE,   *Fritwell.*   MIDELTONE,   *Midlington.*

The possessors of lands in the county of Bucks which lay nearest to these parts, were as follows,

Terra COMITIS MORITONIENS. In Lamve hd.

MERSA,   *Mersh.*

Terra WALTERIJ GIFARD. In Ticheshele hd.

CREDENDONE,   *Crendon.*   EDDINGRAVE,   *Adyngrave.*
CILTONE,   *Chilton.*   DORTONE,   *D'orton.*

In Esseden hd.

ASSEDONE,   *Ashendon.*   WICHENDONE,   *Winchington.*

In Mvselai hd.

ACHELEI,   *Oakley.*

Terra MILONIS CRISPIN. In Votesdone hd.

VOTESDONE,   *Wadsdon.*   MERSTONE,   *Merston.*

Terra HENRICI DE FEIRERES. In Essedene hd.

GRENNEDONE,   *Grendon,* &c.

An. MLXXXII. 16, 17. *William Conqueror.*

Maud, wife of William the Conqueror, founded a monastery for

nuns at Caen in Normandy, dedicated to the holy Trinity; and a
charter of endowment was now given by the said Conqueror and
Maud his queen, to which was witness Rogerius de Iverio, pincerna,
Roger de Iveri cup-bearer to the king, lord of the honor of Iveri in
these parts [f].

An. MLXXXIV. 18, 19. *William Conqueror.*

Between the time of survey taken in these parts and this year,
Robert de Oilly married his only daughter Maud to Milo Crispin,
who had before great possessions in the counties of Oxon and
Bucks, and in right of this wife had now the custody of the castle
and town of Walingford, with that whole honor, within which was
included the manor of Berncestre, &c. And the king, now keeping
his Easter at Abingdon, was there splendidly entertained by Robert
de Oily, while these two only were admitted to sit at the king's
table, Osmund bishop of Sarum, and Milo de Walengfort *cognomento* Crispinus [g]. At the same time Henry the king's youngest son
was left to be educated at Abingdon, where he was accommodated
by the care of Robert de Oily, who by the king's command was to
supply him with all provisions for himself and his retinue [h]. Walter
Giffard earl of Bucks now founded a Benedictine priory at Lon-
guevil in Normandy, dedicated to St. Faith [i]; to which he gave his
manor of Newington in com. Buck. which soon after became a cell
to the said priory, and from this relation was called Newinton-Lon-
gaville [k]. Within this same year Judith countess, either by death, or
by a religious habit, left the manors of Merton and Pidington to
Simon St. Liz earl of Northampton and Huntendon, who had
married Maud her eldest daughter; which S. Simon and Maud his
wife did in this year found at Northampton a priory of Cluniac

---

[f] Neustria Pia, p. 661.　　　　[g] Ex Lib. Mon. Abingd. excerpt. in Twine MS. C. 2.
p. 252. in bib. C. C. C. Oxon.　　　[h] Liber Abend. citat. in Hist. et Antiq. Un. Oxon.
sub an.　　　[i] Neustria Pia, p. 661.　　　[k] Mon. Ang. tom. 3. p. 111.

monks dedicated to St. Andrew[l] : as a cell to the abbey of Charite in France[m] : and gave to it the church of Brackley, with the land and tithe of the said church[n].

An. MLXXXV. 19, 20. *William Conqueror.*

The king having founded the Benedictine abbey of Battaill in Sussex, hy the advice and direction of Remigius bishop of Dorchester[o], did now[p] by charter grant to it, among other large possessions, the manor of Craumareis, now Croamish, in this county[q].

An. MLXXXVI. 20, 21. *William Conqueror.*

It seems probable that Hugh de Iveri, lord of the manor of Ambrosden, died about this time, and left the said manor to his elder brother Roger de Iveri, who being cup-bearer to the king did now wait upon him into Normandy, and being there made keeper of the castle of Roan, he gave a notable proof of his courage and fidelity on this occasion. It happened that in a town of Normandy called l' Aigle, from an eagle's nest there found, a great quarrel arose between the king's sons, which raised so great a clamour, that the king himself was forced to come from his own lodgings and part them : the night following Robert the elder brother with his whole retinue left his father, and marched away to Roan, where he attempted to seize the castle ; but Roger de Iveri, having some notice of the design, diligently fortified the place, and sent away messengers to his master the king to inform him of this rebellious assault[r].

An. MLXXXVII. 21. *William Conqueror.* 1. *William Rufus.*

Milo Crispin, lord of the honor of Walingford and manor of Burcester, &c. nigh this time gave to the abbey of Bec in Normandy the

---

[l] Mon. Ang. tom. 1. p. 679.   [m] R. Dods. MS. vol. 79. f. 10.   [n] Mon. Ang. ib.
[o] Mat. West. sub an.   [p] Jo. Lel. MS. vol. 2. p. 346..   [q] Mon. Ang. tom. 1,
p. 315.   [r] Ordericus Vital. lib. 4. p. 546.

manor of Swinescumb in this county, and the tithes of his demesne of the said honour of Walingford[s]. King William the Conqueror died on Sept. 9th[t]; upon whose death the nation was divided on the point of succession : many of the barons were for Robert the elder brother, among whom was Hugh de Grentmaisnil sheriff of Leicestershire, who raised forces, and committed great spoils in that county[u]: and his kinsman Roger de Iveri, lord of the manor of Ambrosden, who by this means incurred the king's displeasure, and was forced to fly beyond sea, where, after a short time of banishment, and the loss of his whole estate in England, he died in sorrow and disgrace. This affliction is by the monks of Worcester imputed to his robbing them of the manor of Hampton in the county of Glocester, of which Hemmingus one of that convent gives this account. *Simili modo tempore Willielmi regis Rogerius de Iveri invasit terram in Gloeceastrescire quæ Hamtun nominatur, domino Wlstano episcopo existente in legatione regis apud Ceastram. Nec ipse impune super rapina gavisus est. Nam vivens cum esset ditissimus, et pincerna regis carissimus, regalem incurrit iram, vixque fuga vitam ad modicum protexit, omnesque suas possessiones permaximas perdidit, et exul a patria ignominiose post parvum tempus obiit[x].* This manor of Hamtun had been given to the abbey of Worcester by Aldred bishop of that see, in the year 1061[y], and when took away by Roger de Iveri was never again restored[z].

An. MLXXXVIII. 1, 2. Will. Ruf.

Jeffery de Iveri, youngest son of Roger de Iveri sen. and Adeline his wife, seems to have been soon restored to his brother's barony in England, and thereby to the manor of Ambrosden, within which he confirmed two hides of land in Arncot, and all other donations within his said barony, which had been made to the secular priest

---

[s] Mon. Ang. tom. 2. p. 954. b.   [t] Annal. Waverl. sub an. p. 489.   [u] R. de Diceto.
[x] Mon. Ang. tom. 1. p. 134. b.   [y] Ib. p. 140. a.   [z] Ib. p. 134. b.

of St. George's in the castle of Oxford, and had been ratified by his father and brother [a].

An. MLXXXIX. 2, 3. Will. Rufus.

Adeline, widow of Roger de Iveri, sen. who held in dowry the manors of Islip and Oddington, with lands in Charlton upon Otmoore, did nigh this time give unto the abbey of Bec in Normandy a mill in her said village of Islip, which was after confirmed by Henry the Second; *Ex dono Adeline uxoris Rogeri de Ivereyo unum molendinum in villa quæ dicitur Iteslepe* [b]. She likewise gave the manor of Brocthrop to the abbey of St. Peter's in Glocester; but in the recitation of this gift she is miscalled, Adeliza for Adelina, *Adeliza uxor Rogeri de Ybreyo dedit Brocthrop ecclesiæ S. Petri Glouc.* [c], and in a confirmation of king Stephen, in the third year of his reign, her name is again mistaken, *Brocthrop ex dono Atheline de Hibreio* [d]. In which parish of Brocthrop Roger de Iveri her husband, and Hugh his brother, had given several acres of land [e].

An. MXC. 3, 4. Will. Rufus.

Robert de Oily, who was now a witness to the foundation charter of the new cathedral church of Salisbury, died within the month of September in this or the following year, and was buried at Abingdon, on the north side of the high altar in the abbey-church, his wife Aldith lying interred on his left hand. The monks of that place gave this account of him, that being constable of the castle of Oxford in the reign of William the Conqueror and William his son, he had an arbitrary power in this county, and was always supported by the king's favour, upon which he grew rich, and very injurious to many churches; among others, he robbed their church of a meadow without the walls of Oxford, converting it to the use of his soldiers in the castle: but by the prayers of the monks he was cast into a fit

---

[a] Regist. de Oseney MS.　　[b] Mon. Ang. tom. 2. p. 954. a.　　[c] Ex Chartulario Mon. S. Petri Gloc. MS.　　[d] Mon. Ang. tom. 3. par. 1. p. 8. a.　　[e] Mon. Ang. tom. 1. p. 111.

of sickness, and so frighted in a dream, that by his wife's persuasion
he came to Reginald, abbot of Abbendon, and before the high altar
gave to them Tadmertune of ten pounds annual rent; after which,
to expiate for his past sacrilege, he contributed much to the building of St. Mary's church in Abingdon, and at his own charge repaired several other parish churches, as well within the walls as with
out; and built a bridge on the north side of the city [f]. Leaving no
heir male of his own body, his brother Nigel de Oily succeeded to
the castle of Oxford and to the honor of D'Oyly, of which the capital seat was at Hokenorton. But as before noted, his honor of Walingford, with the manor of Burcester, &c. descended to Milo Crispin in right of his wife Maud, only daughter of the said Robert.

An. MXCI.   4, 5: *Will. Rufus.*

Adeliza wife of Hugh de Grentesmaisnil, and mother of Adeline
de Iveri, died at Rhemes in France on the fifth of the ides of July,
and was buried in her husdand's monastery of St. Ebrulf at Utica, on
the right hand of Mainer abbot of that house [g]. About this time
William, son of Nigel lord of Borstall, and forester of Bernwood,
having been unjustly dispossessed of his lands and his office, by the
predecessors of Fulk de Lizures, a Norman family, who came in with
the Conqueror, was forced to become a feudatory tenant to the said
Fulk, and to receive this charter from him. *Fulco de Lisuris omni-*
bus hominibus Francis et Anglicis suis salutem. Sciant tam presentes
quam futuri me Fulconem de Lisuris reddidisse et concessisse Williel-
mo filio Nigelli de Borstalle terram suam scilicet terram que fuit pa-
tris sui et officium forestarii de Bernwode cum omnibus pertin. suis,
tenendum de me et hæredibus meis illi et hæredibus suis libere et
quiete reddendo inde annuatim XL[s]. *de officio forestarii, et* X[s]. *de terra*
sua, ita ut ille et hæredes sui teneant jure hæreditario de me et hæ-
redibus meis, bene et in pace, liberé et quiete sicuti antecessores sui
tenuerunt melius et liberius de me et antecessoribus meis. Test. Willi-

[f] Mon. Ang. tom. 1. p. 106. b.   [g] Neustria Pia, p. 119.

elmo de Lisuris filio suo et uxore ejus Alicia de Alb. et Hugone de Li-
suris, et Fulcone de Lisuris filio suo, et Willielmo de Lisuris filio suo,
et Hugone Camerario ac Roberto filio Nigelli. Radulpho filio Ro-
berti, Waltero filio Nigelli[h]. Some will have this charter referred to
this time, but it does indeed belong to the reign of king John.

A short account of the right and property of Nigel and his heirs,
and violent intrusion of Fulk de Lisures is thus recorded among the
ancient memoirs of Borstall.

Quidam Willmus filius Nigelli fuit seisitus jure hæreditario de una
hida terræ arabilis in Borstall vocat. Derehyde que nunc vocatur la
Vent et de uno bosco vocat. Hulwode, cum custodia forestæ de Bern-
wode in com. Buck. cujus quidem Willi antecessores ante conquestum
Angliæ tenuerunt jure hæreditario terram boscum et ballivam prædic-
tas de domino rege per unum cornu quod est charta prædictæ forestæ
et per servitium reddendi domino regi pro terra prædicta x[s]. *et pro fo-*
resta prædicta XL[s]. *per annum pro omnibus proficuis forestæ præ-*
dictæ exceptis indictamentis de viridi et venatione quæ domino regi
omnino reservabantur, et postea in conquestu Angliæ antecessores Ful-
conis de Lisuris in dominium forestæ bosci et terræ se intruserunt sub-
sequenterque prædictus Fulco et Willus de Lisuris filius ejus per char-
tas suas separatim factas terram et ballivam prædict. prefato Willo
filio ejus et hæred. suis per redditus prædictos tenend. successive con-
cesserunt et confirmaverunt.

An. MXCII.   5, 6. *William Rufus.*

Upon the translation of the see of Dorchester to Lincoln, the new
cathedral church in that city was to be dedicated on the seventh of
the ides of May; but two days before the appointed time, bishop
Remigius died and obstructed that solemnity : his death is by writers
imputed to a judgment of God upon his simony and corruption[i].
The king would have kept this bishopric in his hands, as he did other
revenues of the church ; but being struck into a better sense of re-

[h] Ex Chartular. de Borstalle MS. penes Dom. Joh. Aubrey, Bar.   [i] Sim. Dun. p. 217.

o 2

ligion by a long sickness at Alvestan and Glocester, he gave this see
to his chancellor Robert Bloet on the first Sunday in Lent in the following year, 1093 [k]

An. MXCIII.   6, 7.   *William Rufus.*

The manor or village of Pidington within the parish of Ambrosden (not the church, as mistaken by Mr. Dugdale[l], for it was at
this time a distinct manor, but not a distinct parish, nor was any
church or chapel there erected, till about three hundred years after
this donation) was nigh this time given by Simon earl of Northampton to the monastery of St. Frideswide in Oxford, by this charter.
*Comes Simon omnibus hommibus suis tam Francis quam Anglis tam
Clericis quum Laicis salutem. Sciatis me dedisse deo et S. Marie et
ecclesiæ S. Frideswidæ Oxoniæ, et canonicis ibidem deo servientibus
in liberam et perpetuam elemosynam villam Pidentonam in Oxfen-
fordscire pro salute mea, et patris et matris meæ et omnium antecessorum et successorum meorum ita ut Johanna in vita sua teneat et servitium inde debitum canonicis prædictis reddat ; post decessum vero
prefatæ Joannæ villa prædicta eisdem canonicis remaneat in perpetuam possessionem et elemosynam cum omnibus pertinentiis suis in bosco
et in plano et in pascuis cum omnibus pertinentiis aliis quæ ad eandem
villam pertinent, &c.* [m]

This Joan mentioned in the charter was called Joan de Pidington,
the wife of Guido de Ryhale[n], who held the manor of Pidington
from the said Simon earl of Huntendon during her life.   She and
her husband founded the hermitage of St. Cross at Mussewell, within
the said manor.

An. Dom. MXCIII.   6 Will. Ruf.   *rium de Cherleton cum pertinentiis suis.* Mon.
Robertus Bloet cancellarius regis factus est   Ang. tom. 1. p. 460. i. e. de Charlton com.
episcopus Lincolniæ et dedit eodem anno idem   Kanc.
Robertus monachis de Bermondseye mane-

---

[k] R. de Diceto, p. 491.   [l] Dugd. Bar. tom. 1. p. 58.   [m] Regist. S. Frideswidæ
in C. C. C.   [n] Ex Chartular. de Borstall MS.

An. MXCVIII. 11, 12. *William Rufus.*

Hugh de Grentmaisnil, who had given the church of Charlton and lands within the said parish to his abbey of St. Ebrulf at Utica in Normandy, lay sick at this time [o], (though others report it was in the year 1094 [p],) when Jeffery, prior of St. Ebrulf, sent over for that purpose by Roger the abbot, invested him in the habit of a monk, and prepared him for his death, which followed on the eighth of the calends of March. After which Bernard and David, two monks of that abbey, salted up his body and carried it into Normandy, where, by the care of Roger the abbot and the convent, it was honourably buried in their chapter-house on the south side. His eldest daughter was Adeline, widow of Roger de Iveri, who had a mansion or seat at Fencote in the parish of Cherlton; and at the general survey was possessed by her father's gift of the manors of Islip and Oddington. Robert, elder brother of this Hugh de Grentmaisnil, had a daughter named Agnes, married to Robert de Molins, a Norman, who, disobeying the commands of king Henry the First, was banished out of Normandy, and died in Apulia [q]. From whom descended that John de Molins, who, in the reign of Edward the Third, came to those large possessions in the adjoining parts of the county of Bucks.

An. MC. 13. *William Rufus.* 1. *Henry I.*

The new conventual church of Glocester, rebuilt by Serlo the abbot, was dedicated on Sunday the seventh of July, at which time Robert, son of Nigel de Oily, gave to it the tithe of Chesterton, joining to Burcester [r]; or at least this gift was made before the death of the said abbot, which happened an. 1104 [s]. In the beginning of August William Rufus was killed in his new forest, to whom succeeded his brother Henry the First.

o Neustria Pia, p. 119.   p Dugd. Bar. tom. 1. p. 425.   q Orderic. Vital. p. 578.
r Mon. Ang. tom. 1. p. 113. a.   s Sim. Dun. p. 226 et 228.

An. MCII.   2, 3. *Henry I.*

About this time Guido de Ryhale, and Joan de Pidington his wife, gave Mussewell within the parish of Ambresdon to Ralph, a hermit, who in that proper solitary place built a hermitage, and had the chapel of it dedicated to the honor of St. Cross; which was soon after endowed by the said Guido and Joan his wife, with all the tithe of their demesne in Pidington, and the tithe of pasnage or the profit of feeding hogs within that manor, and of meadow in demesne two acres, one in Westmede, and the other in Langdale[t]. Simon earl of Huntendon was lord of the fee of Pidington, who, with Maud his wife, did about this time confirm to the priory of Daventre several donations made by Robert, son of Vitalis[u].

An. MCIV.   4, 5. *Henry I.*

Nigel de Oily, constable of the castle of Oxford, and lord of the barony of Hooknorton, held at this time in feudatory service from the abbot and monks of Abingdon one meadow at Oxford, one hide at Sandford, and one hide in Ernecote[x], or Arncot, within the parish of Ambrosden, which had been all given to that abbey by Robert de Oily his brother and predecessor. Which hide in Arncot must have been granted before the manor of Ambrosden was given to Roger de Iveri, and possibly at the same time when two other hides in Arncot were given by the said Robert to his chapel of St. George's in the castle of Oxford.

An. MCV.   5, 6. *Henry I.*

Nigh this time, Milo Crispin, lord of the honor of Walingford, and manor of Burcester, &c. gave the tithe of his demesne lands within the said honor, together with the manor of Swinescumb in this county to the abbey of Bec in Normandy[y]

---

[t] Chartular. de Borstall. MS. f. 30.   [u] Mon. Ang. tom. 1. p. 675.   [x] Ex Chartular. Abbendon. apud R. Dods. MS. vol. 105. f. 3.   [y] Mon. Ang. tom. 2. p. 954.

An. MCVI. 6, 7. *Henry I.*

Guy de Ryhale died nigh this time, and left Joan his widow, (who held during life the manor of Pidington, from Simon earl of Hunt.) and Thomas his son and heir, which Joan de Pidington, after her husband's death, confirmed to the church of St. Mary's and canons of Missenden in com. Buck. the hermitage and chapel of St. Cross at Mussewell, annexed to that abbey by Ralph the hermit. *Johanna de Pedintona que fuit sponsa Guidonis de Ryhala omnibus dominis et amicis suis salutem.   Sciant omnes qui sunt et qui futuri sunt quod concessione Guidonis domini mei, et meo assensu Radulphus Heremita locum heremitorium de Mussewella ædificavit, inhabitavit, et possedit, et capellam ibidem in honorem S. Crucis fundavit, quam capellam cum ipso toto loco succedente tempore præfatus Radulphus concessit et dedit ecclesiæ S. Mariæ de Missenden, et canonicis ibidem deo servientibus in perpetuum habendam et possidendam.   Et hanc eandem donationem concessimus, ego et Thomas filius, et hæres prædicti Guidonis jam defuncti, et omnium amicorum, et antecessorum, et successorum meorum ecclesiastica auctoritate confirmari fecimus prefatæ ecclesiæ sanctæ Mariæ, et canonicis ibidem deo servientibus in perpetuam, et liberam elemosinam supernominatam capellam S. Crucis, cum toto adjacente loco, et omnia ad eandem capellam deputata, et pertinentia, totam scilicet decimam de dominio de Pedyngton, in bosco et in plano, scilicet de blado, et de omnibus fructibus terræ qui decimari solent, et de ovibus et porcis, et omnibus aliis animantibus, et decimam de pasnagio, et pasnagium quietum de suis dominicis porcis ejusdem loci ; et communionem pasturæ, tam in bosco quam in plano, et de bosco quod opus fuerit, ad emendationem domorum et sepium suarum ; et de dominico prato duas acras per singulos annos : scilicet quando occidentalis campus seminatur, duas primas acras de prato quod dicitur Westmede ; quando vero orientalis campus seminatur latitudinem duarum acrarum in prato quod dicitur Langdale, juxta fossatum quod dividit inter Pedyngton et Luthegareshalam.   Rogamus autem vos omnes amicos nostros pro Dei amore, et vestra salute, quatenus prædicti ca-*

nonici habeant et teneant, bene et in pace hanc præfatam donationem nostram, sicut liberam elemosinam. Affuerunt hiis actionibus presentes et testes Willus senex sacerdos de Burcestr, cum Willo Capellano suo, et Willo sacerdote de Hambresdun, et Rogero juniore de Pedyngton, et quamplures alii testes [z].

By the ecclesiastical authority, to which reference is made in this charter, is meant the confirmation of Robert Bloet[*] bishop of Lincoln, and Robert archdeacon of Oxford in this form.

Robertus dei gratia Lincoln episcopus, omnibus S. ecclesiæ filiis clericis et laicis salutem. Notum facio universitati vestræ me episcopali auctoritate, confirmasse decimam illam quam Guido de Rihala, et Johanna uxor illius di Pidintona [†] *dederunt, et concesserunt deo et capellæ S. Crucis de Musewella, ad opus canonicorum de Messenden in perpetuam elemosinam, totam scilicet decimam de dominio suo de Pidintona, tam in blado quam in agris, et porcellis, et omnibus aliis rebus domus suæ decimandis* [a].

Robertus archidiaconus Oxon. omnibus clericis et fidelibus Oxen

---

[*] De Chesny.

[†] Malcolmus rex Scotorum dedit ecclesiæ S. Frideswide villam Pydinton in Oxenfordschir pro salute sua, et matris suæ, ita ut Johanna in vita sua teneat, quæ Johanna fuit soror Thomæ Basset. Test. Herberto Epo. Glasg. Reg. S. Frideswide. MS. p. 117.

Ista carta confirmatur per Hen. reg. Ang. ducem Norman. et Aquitan. et com. Andegav. ib.

Ista carta confirmatur per Tho. Ar'ep'um Cant. tempore Malcomi regis Scotiæ. ib.

Confirmatur per Simon. com. Hunt. ita ut Johanna in vita sua teneat. ib.

Alexander ep'us servus servorum, ven.

fratribus Cant. Ar'ep'o, et Cicestr. ep'o salut. Ad aures notras pervenit, quod cum bonæ memoriæ M. quondam Scot. rex villam de Pydenton contulisset eccl'iæ S'ctæ Frideswide ita quidem quod Johanna nobilis mulier in vita sua eandem villam teneret, W. frater ejus, qui sibi in regno successit, eandem villam abstulit, et postmodum David frater ejus qui honorem de Huntendon tenuit prescriptam villam, quæ ad ipsum honorem spectare dinoscitur, injuste detinuit, et nunc comes Simon, qui præscriptæ eccliæ pretaxatam villam scripti sui robore confirmaverat, contra Deum in suæ salutis periculum, detinet occupatam. ib. p. 118.

[z] Ex Chartulario de Borstal. MS. f. 30. et Mon. Ang. tom. 3. pars 1. p. 18.   [a] Chartular. de Borstall. f. 31.

fordshire salutem. Sciatis me quantum ad officium meum pertinet, concessisse et confirmasse decimam illam quam Guido de Rihala, et Johanna uxor illius de Pidentona, dederunt et concesserunt deo, et capellæ S. Crucis de Mussewella ad opus canonicorum Missendenensium in perpetuam elemosinam. Scilicet decimam de dominio suo de Pedyngton, tam in blado quam in agris, et porcellis, et omnibus aliis rebus domus suæ decimandis. Et ut hæc elemosina rata et absque calumpnia sit in posterum, præsentis scripti et sigilli mei attestatione prædictis canonicis illam confirmo. Hiis testibus. Magistro Gilberto de Berecestria. Willo Capellano de Berecestria. Radulpho Heremita, &c. [b]

These charters, with other confirmations of Malcolm and William kings of Scotland, which follow in due order of time, do prove the absolute mistake of the inquisition taken in the 51. of Edward the Third, which reports that abbey founded by William de Mussenden in the year 1293 [c], as also of that other account given of its foundation by the said William de Mussenden knight, in the year 1336 [d], which errors stand in the Monasticon without correction. When it is certain this abbey was of a much more early foundation, and the said Sir William de Mussenden could be only lord of the fee, and a benefactor to it.

An. MCVII. 7, 8. Henry I.

Milo Crispin, lord of the manor of Burcester, lay sick in his castle of Walingford, and having many good offices done to him in his sickness by Faritius, abbot of Abbendon, as a reward he gave to his abbey a public inn, and half a hide of land in Colebrook on the road to London; and sent Gilbert Pipard his steward, and Warine his chaplain to Abbendon, to lay the said donation on the altar of St. Mary, in presence of the abbot and the whole convent [e]. But before the end of the year, this great baron Milo Crispin died with-

---

[b] Chartular. de Borstall, f. 31.   [c] Mon. Ang. tom. 1. p. 542. a.   [d] Ib.
[e] Ib. p. 105. b.

out issue; upon which his own proper estate reverted to the crown,
but the castle and whole honor of Walingford remained in right
of birth to Maud his widow, who from hence was called MATILDIS
Domina de WALENGFORT[f]. Nigh this time seven knights fees of
the said honor of Walingford were held by Gilbert, who seems a
younger son of Ralph Basset, justice of England: which Ralph being raised to this high office from a very mean condition had a large
estate in this country, and gave to Ralph his younger son, a clerk or
chaplain to the archbishop of Canterbury, all his right of advowson to
churches and chapels within his demesne; which right the said
Ralph after gave to the abbey of Oseney, of which he entered him
self a monk: among others was the advowson of the church of Mixbury, now in the deanery of Burcester, as appears by the confirmations of Theobald archbishop of Canterbury, and Robert bishop of
Lincoln[g]. Within the seven knights fees held by Gilbert Basset
were the manors of Burcester, Wrechwike, and Stratton.

An. MCVIII.   8, 9.   Henry I.

Simon St. Liz, earl of Northampton and Huntendon, and Maud
his wife, who had the manors of Merton and Pidington, confirmed
their foundation of the priory of St. Andrews in Northampton, with
additional revenues to it. *Laudante hoc et confirmante Henrico
Anglorum rege, octavo imperii sui anno coram subscriptis testibus, &c.* ✠ *Signum Roberti episcopi Lincoln, &c.* ✠ *Signum Nigelli de Oily, &c.*[h] About the year 1115, this earl Simon went in
devotion to the Holy Land, and in his return died in the abbey of
Charite in France, and was there buried[i], leaving Maud his widow in
possession of the said manors of Merton and Pidington, and Simon
his son and heir in minority; and Waltheof, after abbot of Melros
in Scotland: and one daughter Maud, first the wife of Robert son

---

[f] Mon. Ang. tom. 1. p. 582. a.   [g] Excerpta ex Regist. Oseney per Rog. Dods. MS.
vol. 39.   [h] Mon. Ang. tom. 1. p. 681. b.   ·   [i] Rot. Crendon MS. penes Decan. et
Capit. Æd. Christi Oxon.

of Richard de Lucy, and after the wife of William Albini of Belvoir, and last of all the wife and widow of Robert Fitz-walter. She died at sixty years of age, an. 1140, and had procured the body of her father, earl Simon, to be brought into England, and interred in the abbey of St. Neots in com. Hunt. to which she gave the third part of her manor of Cratesfeld, which she held in frank marriage, to maintain two secular priests to pray for her father's soul [k].

An. MCIX.   9, 10. *Henry I.*

Ralph Basset, justice of England, had lately given to the abbey of Egnesham, the tithe of one hide of land in Estelai (now Astall) in this county, with the tithe of his wool in all other parts. And his son Gilbert Basset, who held the manors of Burcester and Stratton, gave to the same abbey his tithe of Stratton, which was two parts, with the whole tithe of his wool and cheese in all his lands. Which donations, with the tithe of Tame, Banbury, Croppery, Darnford, Minster, &c. were now confirmed by royal charter. *Hoc autem confirmatum est anno ab incarnatione Domini* MCIX. *anno vero Henrici regis decimo apud Westmonasterium in nativitate Domini* [l]

As to this donation of Gilbert Basset, two parts of the tithe in Stratton, it is not thence to be inferred, that he had an arbitrary power of alienating his tithe from the parish church, or that he really intended to impoverish the incumbent : but the case was this. Of old all the tithes of a whole diocese were paid into the bishop for a common fund to maintain the clergy, (who lived in the city with him, and were sent abroad as itinerant priests upon occasional duties,) and to be disposed at his discretion to any other uses of charity and religion. The method of dividing this public stock was prescribed by pope Gregory to his missionary Augustin archbishop of Canterbury, that there should be four distinct portions, one to the bishop and his family : a second to the clergy : a third to the poor :

[k] Dugd. Bar. tom. 1. p. 113.   [l] Mon. Ang. tom. 1. p. 625.

and a fourth to the reparation of churches [m]. But after this upon
the building of rural chapels, the bishops finding their cathedrals to
be soon in lands and other profits sufficiently endowed, they omitted
the trouble of receiving all country tithe, and by degrees let fall their
claim to a fourth part, which was before their own portion. So as
now the priests settled in the new rural churches collected all the
tithe and profit within their own circuit, yet did not at first convert
them to their own proper use, but dispersed them by orders from the
bishop, who generally commanded to observe the old proportion,
one part to the poor, another to the support of the church, and a
third to the priest. This tripartite division was at last settled by a
law of king Alfred, which expressly ratified the custom, *of one part
to the reparation of churches, one for distributing to the poor, a
third to the ministers of God who have care of the church* [n]. So as
still the parochial clergy were but stewards * of the tithe, and had a
claim to no more than the third part. From hence the lords of those
manors, wherein no churches were yet built, did by the bishop's consent receive, as trustees for church and poor, the whole tithes within
their respective manors, who were to answer the same uses, one portion to some stipendiary priest, one to the poor, and one to the repair of the cathedral, or some conventual church. When these lords
for the convenience of themselves or their tenants built distinct
churches on their several manors, they were then by the laws obliged
to allot no more than a third share † to maintain a priest to reside
and officiate : and by the bishop's connivance reserved to themselves
the other two shares for their arbitrary allotment to the support of
the church, and relief of the poor. But in time the lords of each

---

* The priests received and accounted to
the bishop. Def. of Plural, p. 81.
† Laymen could not appropriate the
whole tithes to a parish priest without
the bishop's consent. Def. of Plural, p.
79.

[m] Bed. Hist. Eccles. l. 1. cap. 27.   · [n] Leges Alfredi, num. 24.

manor or parish, being partly weary of this fiduciary right of tithes, and partly by the religious dissuaded from meddling with that which was holy : they did resign to the parish priest two remaining shares, or else did dispose of them to some religious house; yet at first not as an absolute property, but charged with the same uses to the church and poor; and upon this practice depends the custom now obtaining, of the rector or impropriator maintaining the chancel : and upon the same reason were those canons founded which pre- scribed hospitality and charity to monasteries and to parish priests. It seems to have been evidently on those grounds, that Gilbert Basset gave his two parts of tithe in Strattone (for which in law and conscience he stood accountable to the poor, and to the cathedral, or some adjoining church) to another object of piety and charity, the monks of Egnesham.   Hence in very many of the first donations of tithe to monasteries, there is mention only of two parts, which were not alienated from the parochial clergy, but assigned to what they thought the like pious and charitable uses.   Some footsteps of this division of tithes do still remain, and there would have been many more, but that the monks, so endowed with two parts, did either by appropriation get the whole, or else, to spare the trouble and avoid the difference which might arise in dividing, they commuted for a pecuniary pension from the parish priest.

An. MCX.   10, 11. Henry I.

King Henry having married Maud sister of Alexander king of Scotland, and David his brother, gave to the said David to wife Maud the widow of Simon earl of Northampton and Huntendon, and the guardianship of his son and heir Simon the second, in which right he became lord of the manor of Merton, and of the fee of Pi- dington°.   It is to this tenth of Henry the First, or to about the same time, that Mr. Selden refers the donation of Gilbert Basset,

<hr>

° Mon. Ang. tom. 1. p. 679. b.

when he gave for ever to the abbey of Abingdon, with his son Robert entering there into religion, the tithe of his land in Waneting, to be employed ad usum pauperum [p]. But I rather think this gift was much later, in the reign of king Stephen, or Henry the Second. On the third of the nones of July, an. 1110, the king confirmed the foundation of a priory at Coges, com. Oxon. as a cell to the abbey of Fiscamp in Normandy, given by Manasser Arsic lord of the barony of Coges, with several endowments, among which were two garbes or sheaves of tithe at Fretwell [q]

An MCXI. 11, 12. Henry I.

Adeline de Ivery, mother of Jeffery de Ivery, who held in dowry the manors of Islip and Otingdon, lay now desperately sick at her house in Fencot, within the parish of Charlton, and gave to the monks of Abingdon, to pray for her recovery, one hide of land within the said village of Fencot, which gift her daughter Adeliz and king Henry did both confirm; of which the story is thus recorded. *Nobilis quædam matrona Adelina de Hiverio vocata apud locum qui Faincote dicitur, ubi diu irremediabiliter ægrotavit, hidam unam pro suo remedio abbatiæ de Abbandun contulit, an.* XI. *Hen. I. et Adeliz filia ejusdem Adelinæ dictum donum maternum confirmavit. Hiis testibus. Nigello de Oileio, Thoma de S. Johanne, Hugone de Euremon, Galfredo filio Pagani, Galfredo de Magnavilla, Rogerio de Oileio, Roberto de Dunstanvilla. Apud Wudestoc in quadragesima* [r]. Which gift is recited and confirmed in a bull of Pope Eugene the Third, an. 1146. *In Fencota unam hidam* [s]: and is fully expressed, though falsely printed in the charter of Henry the First, *unam hidam in Femcote* (it should be Fencot) *cum pratis et pascuis, et omnibus sibi pertinentibus, sicut Adelina de Suereio* (it ought to have been de Ivereio) *dedit Ecclesiæ in elemosina, et Adeliza filia concessit* [t]. This

---

[p] Seld. Hist. of Tithes, p. 304.   [q] Mon. Ang. tom. 1. p. 574.   [r] Ex Chartul. Abend. apud. Rog. Dods. MS. vol. 105. f. 2.   [s] Mon. Ang. tom. 1. p. 107.   [t] Ibid. p. 106. a.

Adeliz, daughter of Adeline de Ivery*, was married to Alberic de
Ver, junior, lord chamberlain of England, who in his wife's right
came to some possessions in Islip, and Hedingdon, and Draiton,
giving to the monks of Thorney in com. Cant. ten shillings yearly
rent, issuing from his one part of tithe in Islep, *Insuper pro remissione peccatorum meorum, illis de una mea decima scilicet de Islep,
unoquoque anno ad festivitatem S. Michaelis x:. reddam*[u]: with as
much other tithe in Draiton and Hedindon, as amounted to the
tithe of five carucates, which Robert son of the said Alberic confirmed to that abbey: *Decimas de quinque carucis quas pater meus
Deo et S. Mariæ Thorniæ concessit, scilicet Islep, Draitune, et Edin
ton, Deo atque sanctæ Mariæ, atque monachis Thorneiensibus concedo.
Test. Willielmo de Cestreton, &c.*[x]   And therefore it is a palpable
mistake which Mr. Dugdale transcribes from Leland, that Adeliza,
wife of Alberic Ver, was daughter of Gilbert de Clare[y], who had indeed a wife, but no daughter of that name[z].

The same Adeline de Iveri, in or before her time of sickness, gave
to the monks of St. Ebrulf, at Utica in Normandy, her manor of
Cherlton in com. Wilts. (wherein her father Hugh de Grentmaisnil
had before given one villain[a]) thus confirmed, not by king Henry
the Second, (as the editors of the Monasticon have falsely entitled
the charter,) but by king Henry the First.   *H. rex Angliæ archiepiscopis, episcopis, et baronibus, et vicecomitibus, et fidelibus suis*

---

* *Henricus rex Angliæ I. concessit eccl'iæ.
beatæ Mariæ Rading manerium de Rokinton in Warwicsyra quod 'Adelicia de Ivereio eis concessu meo dedit: dat. anno D'ni
1133. Cartular. Rading MS. f. 3.*

*Sciant tam præsentes quam futuri sub
Christiana religione constituti, quod ego Adeliz de Iveri concessi eccl'iæ sanctæ Dei genetricis Mariæ de Rading et fratribus ibidem*

*Deo servientibus pro salute animæ meæ et pa-
tris mei atque matris meæ et omnium antecessorum meorum perpetuo jure possidendam villam nomine Rokinton cum omnibus ad eam
pertinentibus. Et ne hoc aliqua rerum la-
bentium varietate deleri valeat, decrevi istud
presenti scripto assignare et confirmare subscriptis testibus.* Ib. f. 108.

[u] Mon. Ang. tom. 1. p. 248. b.   [x] Ib.
207. b.   [a] Mon. Ang. tom. 2. p. 966. b.   [y] Bar. of Eng. vol. 1. p. 190. a.   [z] Ib.

Francis et Anglis totius Angliæ salutem. Sciatis me concessisse et reddidisse Deo, sancto Ebrulfo, et monachis suis manerium de Ceorlotona, quod Adelina de Ivri eis dedit, et volo et concedo, et firmiter præcipio, ut bene et quiete, et honorificc teneant. Testibus Nigello de Albiniaco, &c.[b] Which witness Nigel de Albini came in with the Conqueror, and died in the beginning of the reign of king Stephen[c]. In this manor of Cherlton was soon after founded a priory, that was a cell to the said abbey of Utica; and after the dissolution of *priories alien* was given by king Edward the Fourth to his collegiate church at Windsor[d]. The said Adeline de Iveri died of this sickness at Fencote, and her body was carried over into Normandy, and buried in that abbey of St. Ebrulf, near the bodies of her father and mother. She had a younger sister Maud, married to Ralph eldest son of Hugh de Mont-Pinchion, who survived her sister Adeline, and lamented over her grave in Utica, when she came with her husband and his father to visit those monks[e]

An. MCXII. 12, 13. Henry I.

Upon the death of the bishop of Hereford*, Robert arch-deacon of Oxford was advanced to that see, being elected on the sixteenth of the calends of June, Ascension day[f]. Nigh this time Jeffery de Iveri, lord of Ambrosden, &c. died without issue, upon which his barony in this county fell to the king, who soon after bestowed it on Guy de S. Walery, who seems the son or younger brother of Ranulph de S. Walery, who came in with the Conqueror. This family derived their name from the town and port of S. Walery or Valery in France, so called from S. Valeric, a disciple of Columban, whom, about an. 589, Clotharius made abbot of a monastery here in the territory of Amiens, nigh the mouth of the river Soam. It was from this port duke William set sail for his English expedi-

---

* This was anno 1173.

[b] Mon. Ang. tom. 2. p. 966. b.   [c] Dugd. Bar. tom. 1. p. 122. b.   [d] Mon. Ang. tom. 3. p. 2. p. 75. a.   [e] Order. Vital. l. 5. p. 585.   [f] R. de Diceto, p. 568.

tion. And some historians, who are fond of a miracle, report the duke was detained here by adverse winds, *et ob hoc vulgus submurmuraret, asserens insanum fore alienum solum velle usurpare ;* till the body of this saint carried in procession brought a fair gale[g]. The first of this family was the duke's advocate in that town, called *Gilbertus Advocatus de S. Gualerico ;* who married Papia the daughter of Richard the second duke of Normandy; whose son was Bernard de St Walery, who had issue Walter de S. Walery, who flourished under duke Robert the Second, and with his son Bernard was present at the siege of Nice, an. 1096[h]. One of this family having been thus by marriage related to the duke came over with him. In the catalogue of those adventurers given by Brompton is Seynt Walery[i]: and in the French annals of Normandy, whereof one very ancient copy in parchment remained in the author's custody[k], in the list of those who were at the conquest of England is Le Sire de S. Valery, and among the names of those who remained alive after the battle is R. de S. Valery, who I suppose was Ranulph de S. Walery, recorded in Doomsday-book for possession of lands in Lincolnshire[l]: and had several houses in Winchester, from whom a street in that city was called *Vicus Sancti Walerici*[m].

As to the family of Iveri, though the direct line was now extinct, yet some collateral branch did long after continue in this county. I would only further observe, that Roger de Iveri, who came in with the Conqueror, gave name to that parish of his possession, now called Iver and Evre in com. Buck. of which the church was dedicated to St. Peter, and two parts of the tithe were given to the chapel of St. George's in the castle of Oxford. *Abbas habet in Evera duas partes de omni re quæ decimari solet de decimis Curiæ de Evera pertinentibus ad capellam S. Georgii sitam in castello Oxon. de dono Roberti de Oileio, et Rogerii de Iverio*[n]. Which manor of Evre, in the ninth of

---

[g] Polycron. R. Higden. p. 285. et Will. Malms. p. 100.   [h] Norman. Scriptor. Append.   [i] Cron. Jo. Brompton, p. 965.   [k] Fox, Act. et Mon. tom. 1. p. 182.   [l] Dugd. Bar. tom. 1. p. 454. a.   [m] Mon. Ang. tom. 1. p. 212.   [n] Regist. Oseu. MS. p. 266.

Richard the First, was granted by the king to Robert Clavering, baron of Werkworth in Northumberland, and of Clavering in Essex, to
hold to himself and his heirs by one knight's fee: and in the first of
king John, he had a confirmation of the manor and advowson of the
church [o].   And Eufemia, daughter of Sir John de Clavering, wife of
Ranulph de Nevil baron of Raby, brought to him this manor in
frank marriage, whose heir Ralph de Nevil in the fourteenth of Edward the Third, obtained a charter of free warren in this his lordship of Evre [p].

An. MCXIII.   13, 14. Henry I.

About this time Maud de Walingford, the relict of Milo Crispin,
was by king Henry given in marriage to Brien Fitz-count, with all
her large inheritance, by which the said Brien became constable of
Walingford, and lord of the fee of Burcester within that honor.   It
seems an unhappy error in Mr. Dugdale, first to confess, *that it does
not directly appear of what parentage this person was, and then adventure to deduce him from Baldwin de Redvers earl of Devon and of
the isle of Wight, who died in the first year of Henry the Second; because the wife of the same Baldwin was named Lucia, notwithstanding there is no mention of any such son that he had [q].*   This conjecture is impossible, for Baldwin de Redvers was not earl of Devon till
the second of king Stephen, nor seems to have been married long
before that time, when his first wife was Adeliza, and his second Lucia, by whom he had three sons, Richard, William, and Henry, and
died in the first of Henry the Second, being then younger than his
presumed son.   Whereas it is most probable, he was a natural son of
Alan Fergant earl of Britanny and Richmond, (who came in with
the Conqueror) by Lucia a daughter of Dru de Baladon, lord of
Overwent in Wales.   For so he is expressly called in the Saxon
Chronicle, *Brian son of the earl Alein Fergan* [r].   And Gervasius calls

[o] Dugd. Bar. tom. 1. p. 107. a.   [p] Ib. p. 294.   [q] Ib. p. 468. b.   [r] Chron.
Sax. sub an. 1127.

him *prudentem Britonem*[s], which might be in allusion to his father the earl of Britain, as well as to his mother and estate, and perhaps his birth in Wales. And Alan earl of Britanny, grandson of Alan Fergaunt, gave, an. 1140, *ten shillings yearly rent issuing from a fair at Merdrcsem, to the church of St. Michael's mount in Cornwall, for the redemption of the soul of Brien his uncle, of whose inheritance he held his lands in Cornwall*[t]. Which must be understood of our Brien Fitz-count[*], (and so Mr. Dugdale does himself determine, *the soul of Brientius filius comitis*[u]) who had an estate in Cornwall, and being at Bristol, an. 1141, gave to the priory of Lanthony two caru-

---

[*] In a learned argument about the descent of the barony of Abergeny I find this passage: ' William conquerour of higher Gwent, gave this title and dignity unto Hamelin de Beaulma, the sonne of Duigo de Buckline, a Norman, that came into England with him; which Hamline builded the castle and priory of Abergenny, and after assured the same unto Brian de Walingford sonne of Eudo E. of Britain, and sonne of Lucy, younger sister to the said Hamlin, from whom it was conveyed to Walter, 2d son of Milo of Glocester.' Ex. MSS. W. Glynne Baronetti.

In a pedigree drawn from the History of Bretaigne in France by Mr. Glover, Somerset Herald, it does appear, that Eudo earl of Ponthieu, brother of Alan duke of Britaigne, by his wife Owen, daughter of Aluin earl of Cornwall, had issue six sons; 1. Geffry, surnamed Graiomen, slain at Dole in the year 1093. 2. Stephen E. of Britaigne, who died A.D. 1138. 3. Derien. 4. Robert. 5. Alanus Niger. 6. Briand, " home fort veillant;" which youngest son I take to be our Brian Fitz-count.

Brienus Eudonis ducis Britanniæ Minoris filius, &c. Vid. Will. Gemet. de ducibus Norman. l. 7. c. 41.

Contigit paulo post obitum Anglorum regis Henrici primi nobilem virum Ricardum Clarensem ab Anglia in Walliam hac (i. e. per Abergevenny) transire; et cum provinciæ illius tunc dominum Brienum videlicet Gualingfordensem cum militibus multis socium habuisset et deductorem. Silv. Girald. Itin. Camb. l. 1. c. 4.

Regnante Will. Conquest. duo filii regis Haroldi regem Hiberniæ Dirmetum pro juvamine conferendo sunt aggressi. Qui cum LXVI. ab Hibernia redeuntes navibus Anglos ocyus repetierunt, rapinis et incendiis populum terræ exterminantes. Quibus Briennus Eudonis ducis Britanniæ Minoris filius cum suis obvius, protinus cum eis sub una die manus conseruit, cæsis Hybernensium bellatoribus septingentis. Tho. Rudborn apud Whartoni Ang. Sac. v. 1. p. 246.

---

[s] Gervas. Chron. sub an. 1153. tom. 1. p. 47. b.   [t] Mon. Ang. tom. 2. p. 902. a.   [u] Dugd. Bar.

cates of land in his village of St. Michael's[x]. Nay farther, Mr. Dugdale, in his family of Fitz-Alan of Bedall, does deduce it from Brian
a younger son to Alan Fergant earl of Britanny and Richmond[y]:
by which he does acknowledge, that Alan Fergant had a son so
called; though indeed as to that descent of Fitz-Alan he is again
mistaken, for they were not derived from Brian Fitz-count, son of
Alan-Fergant, but from Brian a younger son of earl Alan the second, and brother of Conan earl of Britain[z]

In reference to this same person, I ought not to omit another
great mistake of Mr. Selden, who writes thus of him. *Were there
not also earls of Walingford anciently? Malmsbury[a] says, that Robert earl of Glocester went from Arundel to Bristol,* occurrente sibi
medio itineris Briano filio comitis de Walingford. *The same person is
afterward mentioned, and called* Brientius filius comitis marchio de
Walingford[b]. *I conceive this Brian to be the same man which is
called Brientius[c], in that office cited by Mr. Camden[d].* Where Mr.
Selden did not consider, that Malmsbury's expression is not to
be rendered *Brian son of the earl of Walingford,* but *Brian Fitz-
count of Walingford,* lord of that honor and castle; and this only in
right of his wife. His other title of Marchio de Walingford was in
respect of his being warden or constable of Walingford castle, which
he so stoutly defended for the empress Maud against Stephen.

An. MCXIV. 14, 15. Henry I.

At building of the new church in the abbey of Croyland, among
the great number of benefactors, Simon, earl of Northampton the
second, was there on the foundation day, and laid a corner stone
with one hundred marks upon it for the workmen[e]. He enjoyed only
the earldom of Northampton, the other of Huntingdon being given

---

[x] Mon. Ang. vol. 2. p. 4. a.　　[y] Dugd. Bar. tom. 1. p. 53.　　[z] Mon. Ang. tom. 2.
p. 883.　[a] Malm. Hist. Nov. l. 2. p. 104.　　[b] Ib. p. 105.　　[c] Camden. Britan. p. 204.
[d] Selden, Epist. to Mr. Vincent, prefixed to Discovery of Errors in Brook's Catalogue.
[e] Pet. Bles. Contin. Hist. Croyland, p. 119.

to his guardian and father-in-law David, brother to the king of Scotland.

An. MCXV.   15, 16.   *Henry I.*

The king was now at Woodstock, and there by charter confirmed to Faricius and the monks of Abingdon, their cell of Eadwardston in com. Suffolk, given to them by Hubert Munchensi. Testibus, &c. Nigello de Oilei, et Radulfo Basset, &c. *apud Wdestocam, anno ab incarnatione Domini,* MCXV [f]

An. MCXVI.   16, 17.   *Henry I.*

Nigh this time Guy de S. Walery, lord of the manor of Ambrosden, Beckley, and other places which made up the late honor of Iveri, now from this new possessor called the honor of S. Walery; gave to the prior and canons of St. Frideswide in Oxford, his manor of Knyttinton com. Berks, which was then taxed in the hundred of Shryningham, which manor Peter de Ashrugge, after steward of St. Walery, did annex to that honor [g].

An. MCXVII.   17, 18.   *Henry I.*

Brien Fitz-count [*], lord of the manor of Walingford, granted to Osmund Basset one knight's fee, with its appurtenances in Oakly nigh adjoining to Brill, in com. Buck. and the fourth part of one

---

[*] Eccl'ia de Hildendona habet 1 hid. dimid. hid. est de dominio d'ni quam Milo Crispin dedit Waltero abbati ad faciend. hospitium suum ; ipsam eccl'iam dedit eccl'iæ de Evesham Brien. fil. comitis et reddit annuatim 1 marc. et 1 hospitium invenit integrum Abbati per annum, et, si iterum venerit, ignem, salem, et literiam. Cartular. Evesham. Vespasian. B. 24.

R. ep'us Linc. successor A. ep'i Linc. confirmat priori S. Frideswide eccl'iam de Accleya cum capellis de Brehill et Brustall et de Heddingrave. Test. Theobald Cant. ep'o. David Archid'o Buck. Wygod abb'e de Osney. Mag'ro Rob. de Buk. Ric'o precentore. Will'o de Cheyne. W. R. fratre ejus. Mag'ro Rad'o et multis aliis. Ex cartis S. Fridesw. Oxon.

[f] Mon. Ang. tom. 1. p. 469. a.   [g] Ex Regist. S. Frides. in C. C. C. MS. carta 406.

knight's fee in Aspeden, by a special charter confirmed by king
Henry the First, which lands descended to John Basset, son of the
said Osmund, and then to William Basset son of the said John, to
whom and his heirs they were confirmed by king John in the eighth
year of his reign [h].

An. MCXVIII. 18, 19. Henry I.

David, brother of Alexander king of Scotland, and of Maud queen
of England, having married Maud, eldest daughter of earl Waltheof, the relict of Simon earl of Huntendon and Northampton, held
in her right the manors of Pidington and Merton, in the latter of
which he gave the advowson of the church to the abbot and monks
of Egnesham [i] in this county; to whom was soon after reserved an
annual pension of thirty shillings.   Note, this was one of the early
projects which the regulars invented to oppress the secular clergy:
that when the advowson of a church was given to an abbey, they
would not present a priest but on the simoniacal compact of a reserved pension to themselves, whereby the parish priests became tributary to their patrons the abbots and monks.   This grievance had
been considered in the council at London, an. 1102, where by the
twenty-sixth canon it was provided, that the religious should not accept the new advowson of churches without consent of the bishops,
and when legally given to them, should not withhold any of their revenues, and so impoverish the priests [k].   And even the popes inter-
posed to reform this abuse.   Alexander the Third, an. 1170, wrote to
the monks within the diocese of York, that whereas he understood in
churches of their presentation, they used to receive certain pensions to
the lessening of the ancient revenue: he did therefore command them
to restore to the priests their full profits which they had so diminished [l].   And about the same time, writing to the bishop of Worcester, he advised, That whereas monks did so oppress the vicars of

---

[h] Rog. Dodsw. MS. vol. 53. f. 13.   [i] Regist. Egnesham. MS. cartæ 22, et 23.
[k] Spelm. Concil. tom. 2. p. 22.   [l] Rog. Dods. MS. vol. 74. f. 13.

*parochial churches, that they were not left able to keep up hospitality :
he should not institute the clerks presented by them, without an allowance of fit and competent support*[m]. A canon to this effect was
made in the Lateran council, an. 1179. And an. 1189, pope Clement fairly decreed, *That whereas monks endeavoured to convert to
their own use the revenues of churches belonging to their patronage,
either by not presenting fit persons, or by loading them with pensions
when so admitted: if they did not within due time make a free and
unconditionate presentation, it should be lawful for the bishops to fill
up such vacant churches*[n]

An. MCXIX. 19, 20. *Henry I.*

In this year the king was at his palace in Woodstock, and now
made an enclosed park in that place, which by most historians is observed to have been the first in England[o]. In this or the preceding
year died Nigel de Oily, and left his barony and castle of Oxford to
Robert de Oily his son. The said Nigel before his death remitted
to the monks of Egnesham one hide of land which he held of that
abbey, with the consent of Robert Bloet bishop of Lincoln ; giving
them three hides and a half more lying in Mildecumbe for the health
of his soul, and the souls of his wife and children[p]

An. MCXX. 20, 21. *Henry I.*

About this time Robert de Oily jun. married Edith Forne, a beautiful concubine of the king, who gave her in frank marriage the manor of Cleydon in com. Bucks, which match stands thus recorded in
the Oseney register. *Memorandum quod rex Henricus primus filius
Willielmi Bastard dedit Editham filiam Forne Amasiam suam Roberto
de Oileio secundo in uxorem, et cum ea totam Cleydonam in liberum
maritagium*[q].

---

[m] Rog. Dods. MS. vol. 74. f. 13.   [n] Extrav. de Prebendis.   [o] Hen. de Knighton,
p. 2382.   [p] Dugd. Bar. tom. 1. p. 460.   [q] Regist. Osen, MS. p. 228

An. mcxxiii.   23, 24. *Henry I.*

At Christmas the king held a council at Woodstock, where, three days after Epiphany, riding out with Robert bishop of Lincoln at a distance from all other company, the bishop fell from his horse, and, being carried home speechless, died the following day, and his bowels were reposited in the monastery of Eyvesham[r], (I suppose Egnesham,) to which he had been a restorer and benefactor. In Lent following the bishopric of Lincoln was given to Alexander archdeacon of Salisbury[s], who was consecrated at Canterbury on the eleventh of the calends of August[t].

An. mcxxiv.   24, 25. *Henry I.*

Alexander king of Scots died on the sixth[u], or seventh[x], or ninth[y], of the calends of May, and was succeeded by his brother David earl of Huntendon, who in right of his wife had the manors of Merton and Pidington, and with his crown of Scotland continued to enjoy his honors and possessions in England[z]. Of whom there is a rude mistake committed by the composer of the useful index to X. Scriptores. *David regis Scotiæ frater comes Huntingdoniæ dicitur fuisse rex Scotiæ, sed ni fallor falso;* when nothing is more evident than that the same David earl of Huntendon became now king of Scotland.

An. mcxxv.   25, 26. *Henry I.*

The king built a new monastery at Reading com. Berks, and now gave to it a charter of endowment, to which was witness Brien Fitzcount, lord of the honor of Walingford, and of the fee of Burcester. *Signum Brientii filii comitis de Warengeford*[a]. Nigh the same time the king confirming several donations to the priory of St. Andrews

---

[r] Jo. Brompt. p. 987.   [s] Flor. Wigorn. sub an.   [t] R. de Diceto, sub an.   [u] Sim. Dun. p. 251.   [x] Chron. Mailros. sub an.   [y] Chron. Saxon.   [z] Ib.   [a] Mon. Ang. tom. 1. p. 418. b.

in Northampton, mentions one virgate of land in Wendlingbury, the gift of Ilbert de Cogenho [b]

An. MCXXVI. 26, 27. Henry I.

Guy de S. Walery, lord of the honor so called, and of the manor of Ambrosden, impleaded Simon Beauchamp for the whole barony of Bedford; till, by way of composition, the said Simon granted to Guy de S. Walery and his heirs his manor of Aspele within that barony [c], of which the church had been by the said Simon given to the Augustine priory of Newnham [d]. Mr. Dugdale relates, that this Simon de Beauchamp, in the twenty-sixth of Henry the Second, gave a fine of three hundred marks to the king, upon an agreement betwixt him and Guy de S. Walery [e]. A plain mistake of Henry the Second for Henry the First. For not only Guy de S. Walery, but Reginald his son was dead before the twenty-sixth of Henry the Second; it can agree only to the twenty-sixth of Henry the First, before which time Simon Beauchamp succeeded to the barony of Bedford, was after steward to king Stephen, and had then sons of age to hold Bedford against the king. After Michaelmas, David king of Scotland, lord of the manors of Merton and Pidington, came into England, was honorably received by king Henry, and resided here twelve months [f].

An. MCXXVII. 27, 28. Henry I.

The king kept his Lent and Easter at Woodstock, and Whitsuntide at Windsor, where David king of Scotland and all the English barons sware allegiance to Maud the king's daughter, the emperor's widow, who had been brought over in September the year preceding [g]; and was now sent into Normandy with the attendance of Robert earl of Glocester, and Brien Fitz-count lord of Walingford [h]:

<hr/>

[b] Mon. Ang. tom. 1. p. 682. a.   [c] Rog. Dods. MS. vol. 42. f. 106.   [d] Mon. Ang. tom. 2. p. 239. a.   [e] Dugd. Bar. tom. 1. p. 223.   [f] Chron. Saxon. sub an.   [g] Will. Malms. p. 174.   [h] Chron. Saxon. sub an.

where she was married to Jeffery son of Fulk earl of Anjou; a match carried on chiefly by the counsel and interest of the said Brien Fitz-count[i].

An. MCXXVIII. 28, 29. Henry I.

The church of Merton adjoining to Ambrosden had been lately given by David earl of Huntendon, now king of Scotland, to the abbey of Egnesham in this county, and soon appropriated to that religious house; but was on some pretence detained by Guy le Charing, to whom about this time Alexander, bishop of Lincoln, sent a preceptory letter, to restore unto Walter abbot of Egnesham the said church of Meriton, with the tithes and all other profits; or upon default he should be prosecuted in the spiritual court. *Alexander Lincoln. episcopus Guidoni de Charing parochiano suo salutem. Mando tibi et præcipio ut cito reddas ecclesiæ de Egnesham, and Waltero abbati ecclesiam suam de Meritona, cum omnibus rebus quæ ad eam pertinent in terra, et in decima, et in aliis sicut antecessores nostri eam præfatæ ecclesiæ de Egnesham dederunt et concesserunt. Quod ni cito feceris, præcipio ut Walterus archidiaconus nobis justitiam Christianitatis faciat, donec reddas, ne pro recti vel justitiæ penuria amplius audiam clamorem. Vale*[k].*

An. MCXXIX. 29, 30. Henry I.

Robert de Oily, and Edith his wife *, began now to build the

---

* *Notum sit fidelibus sanctæ ecclesiæ tam presentibus quam futuris quod ego Robertus de Olleyo volentibus et concedentibus Editha uxore mea et filiis meis Henrico et Gilberto do et concedo in perpetuam elemosinam ecclesiæ Dei et sanctæ Mariæ genetricis ejus et canonicis in ea Deo servientibus, quam ego consulente et confirmante Alexandro Dei gratia Lincoln. episcopo fundavi in insula quæ dicitur Oseneya, &c. quicquid meum est in prefata insula cum omnibus mensuris quas habui supra waram quæ est de molendinis meis quæ sunt juxta castellum Oxenfordiæ, &c. Testibus Rogero de Amari; Fulcone de Olleio; Hugone Tuvia; Roberto filio Widonis, &c. Collectan. R. Glover. e reg. Osenei.*

---

[i] Will. Malms. p. 175.

[k] Regist. Egnesh. MS. carta 15.

church of St. Mary's in the isle of Oseney, near to the castle of Oxford, for the use of Augustine monks. This pious work was under-
taken at the motion of the wife, who, to expiate the sins of her former unchaste life, solicited her husband to this merit; and, to prevail with him, told him a story of the chattering of birds, and the interpretation of a friar: which legendary dream was afterwards
painted near her tomb in that abbey. ᏲᏢᎬ comming of ᏟᎠᎥᏖᏅ to
ᎧᏚᎬᏁᎬᏢ, anᎠ ᎡaᎠulᏢᏅ waiting on ᏅᎬᏒ, anᎠ tᏅᎬ tᏒᎬᎬ witᏅ tᏅᎬ cᏅatteᏒing
ᏢᏢᎬᏚ, be ᏢaintᎬᎠ in tᏅᎬ waule of tᏅᎬ cᏅircᏅᎬ oᏴᎬᏒ ᏟᎠᎥᏖᏅ tombe in
ᎧᏚᎬᏁᎬᏢ ᏢᏒᎥorie[1]. The foundation stands thus in the register of that
abbey. *An. Dom.* MCXXIX. *Robertus de Oileio secundus, filius Nigelli
de Oileio prædicti, fundavit ecclesiam S. Mariæ in insula Oseneia,
tempore regis Henrici primi filii scilicet Willielmi Bastard conquisi-
toris Angliæ ad petitionem Edithæ filiæ Forne uxoris prædicti Roberti de Oileio fundata est*[m]. How soon this structure was completed, and when Radolph the first prior was admitted, we know not.
But the best part of the endowment was not till twenty years after,
when, an. 1149, the church of St. George's in the castle was translated and annexed to it. In the mean time was given the church of
Steple-Claydon in com. Buck. *Dictus Robertus ecclesiam de Oseneia fundavit, et canonicos regulares in ea constituit, et ecclesiam de
Claidon, et alias quamplurimas eisdem canonicis contulit. Post mortem vero ejusdem Roberti præfata Editha, in libero maritagio suo, plu-
rimas terras præfatis canonicis in Cleidona, et alibi dedit*[n]. Among
these first foundations was the church of Chesterton adjoining to
Burcester. *Abbas habet ecclesiam de Cesterton in Henemarsh, de
dono Roberti de Oilcio fundatoris nostri, et concessione, et confirmatione episcoporum et capituli Lincoln. et Romanorum pontificum.*
But the abbey of Oseney had only the right of patronage to this
church, not the impropriated tithes of it, of which a great part at
least was given by the said Robert de Oily, or rather Nigel his father, to the abbey of St. Peter's in Glocester[o]. And possibly the

[1] Lel. Itin. vol. 2. f. 17   [m] Regist. Osen. f. 6.   [n] Ib.   [o] Mon. Ang. tom. 1. p. 113.

alienation of tithes from this parochial church might occasion one
of the first vicarages in England, if we believe the report of common
lawyers. For Mr. Noy, urging the antiquity of vicarages in this kingdom, that they were before the time of king John, says, *that in Oxfordshire there were four vicarages before his reign* [p]. One of which
might probably be this of Chesterton, another that of Merton,
though indeed we meet with no such early records that makes them
distinct and proper vicarages.   The patronage of the church of Chesterton was in exchange for some greater benefit afterwards restored
to the lord of the manor, and was by Edmund earl of Cornwall
given to his college of Bonhommes at Ashrugge [q]

An. MCXXX.   30, 31. *Henry I.*

The king kept his Easter at Woodstock, where a false accusation
of treason was brought against Jeffery de Clinton, chamberlain and
treasurer to the king, who had given his daughter Lesceline in marriage to Norman de Verdon, and with her the manor of Heth in this
county [r]; the advowson of which church was given by the said Lesceline to the priory of Kenilworth of her father's foundation; and
confirmed by Bertrem de Verdon her son [s]. While the king kept
this solemnity at Woodstock, Ingulf prior of Winchester was here
elected abbot of Abbendon, and consecrated by Roger bishop of
Salisbury, on Sunday the sixth of the ides of June [t].

An. MCXXXI.   31, 32. *Henry I.*

The king now gave at Northampton, and confirmed at Westminster, to William archbishop, and to Christ Church in Canterbury,
the church of St. Mary's in Dover, for canons regular and an abbot
to be elected by the chapter of Canterbury, and consent of the arch
bishop.   To which charter among other witnesses, was Brien Fitz-

---

p Sir G. Palmer's Reports, p. 114.   q Mon. Ang. tom. 3. par. 1. p. 69.   r Chron.
Jo. Brompt. p. 1018.   s Dugd. Antiq. Warwic. p. 157. b.   t Hist. Cœnob. Abend.
apud Wharton. Ang. Sac. Pars 1. p. 199.

count lord of the honor of Walingford, &c.", who was a great favorite of this prince, and a constant attendant on him.

An. MCXXXII.   32, 33. *Henry I.*

Nigh this time the king granted to the prior and canons of St. Frideswide in Oxford the chapels of Hedindon, Merston, and Beneseye, exempt from all taxes and other dues to the bishops, archdeacons, or their officials; which, with the chapel of Elsfield, were confirmed by Alexander and his successors bishops of Lincoln[x].

An. MCXXXIII.   33, 34. *Henry I.*

About this time Fulk, son of William de Lisures, by intrusion of his ancestors lord of the fee of Borstall, went with Roger de Stibinton to Thorney, and there confirmed to those monks the tithe of Stibinton, which the said Roger had given to that abbey[y].   But afterwards Henry de Merch claimed the advowson of the said church of Stibinton, and the right of advowson was disputed, till Eustace son of Henry de Merch quitted and resigned his title to the monks[z] The said Fulk de Lisures soon after gave to the knights templars three acres of lands in Benigfield[a].

An. MCXXXV.   35, 36. *Henry I.*   1. *King Stephen.*

The king having took ship for Normandy on the nones of August,

An. MCXXXIV.   34, 35. *Henry I.*

Simon comes de Northamptun omnibus fidelibus suis et ministris salutem. Sciatis quod ego dedi unam marcam argenti in molendino meo quod habeo apud Huntendon Sc'to Benedicto et ecclesiæ de Ramesie in perpetuam eleemosinam manerium de Waltone quod jure hæreditario meum fuit. Hanc autem donationem feci assentiente domino Waltero de Bolebech de cujus feudo fuit

ipsum manerium, et Hugone filio et hærede ipsius Walteri, et Eustachio filio et hærede meo in presentia christianissimi regis Henrici, anno ab incarnatione Domini MCXXXIV. regni vero ipsius regis Henrici XXXV.   Testibus domino Waltero de Bolebech domino feudi illius et Hugone filio et hærede ipsius; Eustachio filio et hærede meo, &c.   Ex regist. de Ramesie inter collectan. R. Glover, MS.

u Mon. Ang. tom. 2. p. 4. a.   x Regist. S. Frides. in C. C. C. MS. cartæ 416, 417
y Mon. Ang. tom. 1. p. 246. b.   z Ib. p. 247. a.   a Mon. Ang. tom. 2. p. 588. a.

his coronation day, an. 1132, died this year at Lyons en Forest, on the first of December; when Stephen earl of Moreton hasted over to England, got himself crowned by William archbishop of Canterbury on December the twenty-second, and at the end of Christmas went to Oxford, and calling thither a general council, he solemnly confirmed the liberties of the church and laws of the land[b]: to which charter among other witnesses were Brien Fitz-count constable of Walingford, and Robert de Oily[c].

An. MCXXXVI. 1, 2. K. Stephen.

Maud the widow of Simon St. Liz earl of Huntendon, having married David now king of Scotland, had issue by him Henry, who, coming now to age, did his homage at York to king Stephen, and in his mother's right obtained livery of the honor of Huntendon[d], and thereby of the manors of Merton and Pidington, and at Easter was received by the king at London with great honor, and placed at his right hand, till the envy of the archbishop of Canterbury and other barons put such affronts upon him, that in displeasure he returned to Scotland[e]. This Henry married Adeline one of the daughters of William the second earl of Warren, by Elizabeth daughter to Hugh the great earl of Vermandois, and widow of Robert earl of Mellent[f]. And in the next year after Easter, king David and his son came with an army into England, and making a truce till Christmas, then broke it.

An. MCXXXVIII. 3, 4. K. Stephen.

Sir Robert Gait knight, lord of the manor of Hampton, thence called Hampton Gait, now Hampton Gay, possessed a fourth part of the village of Ottendun; and going to Gilbert abbot of Waverlie, he desired and obtained leave to build an abbey of the Cistertian order, in the said village of Ottendun, which accordingly he raised

[b] Jo. Brompt. p. 1021. et Ricard. Hagust. p. 314.   [c] Richard Hagust. p. 315.   [d] Sim. Dun. p. 256.   [e] Ric. Hagust. p. 313.   [f] Dugd. Bar. tom. 1. p. 75.

at his own charge, and endowed it with five virgates of land, which made the fourth part of a knight's fee, and called it from the name of an adjoining wood Ottelei [g]. The foundation charter runs thus. *Notum sit omnibus sanctæ ecclesiæ filiis tam presentibus quam futuris, quod ego Robertus Gait dedi omnem terram de Ottendun, et omnia eidem terræ pertinentia in bosco et plano, prato et pasturis et aquis, liberam et quietam, ab omni servitio seculari, et consuetudine terrena Deo et S. Mariæ ad abbatiam construendam de ordine Cisterciensi, in provincia* Alexandri Lincolniæ episcopi. Testibus, magistro Osberno de Hache, Roberto de Oili constabulario regis, Warkelin Waudardo, Rogero de Aumari, Radulfo de Salchei [h].*

Gilbert and the convent of Waverlie gave to this new abbey of their order one hide of land in Nortun, which Robert de Siffrawast had given to them. *Notum sit universis matris ecclesiæ filiis quod ego Gilbertus abbas, omnisque conventus Waverlie, concessimus conventui Oteleie hidam de Nortuna, nobis a Roberto de Siffrawast in elemosinam datam, quod ut ratum sit nullaque temporis varietate vel posterorum successione violetur, sigilli nostri impressione confirmavimus [i].*

The next additional revenue was made by Edith the wife of Robert de Oily, who with her husband's consent gave, out of part of her own dowry in Weston bordering upon Ottmoore, that demesne which lay on the corner of their wood, and continued on without the intermixture of any other lands: the quantity of which demesne was thirty-six acres, as expressed in a confirmation of Henry the Second. The original charter of donation is this. *Notum sit omnibus sanctæ matris ecclesiæ filiis, quod ego Editha, Roberto de Oili conjugali copula juncta, consilio et voluntate ejusdem Roberti mariti mei de duario meo de Weston, dedi in perpetuam elemosinam Deo et sanctæ Mariæ, et*

---

* Alexander episcopus Linc. precipit ut abbati de Eynesham. MS. Cotton Claud. ecclesia de Meriton isto reddatur Waltero A. 3. f. 129.

[g] R. Dods. MS. vol. 143. f. 41. et Mon. Ang. tom. 1. p. 802. [h] Ib. [i] Rog. Dods. MS. vol. 90. f. 107.

fratribus in Oteleia secundum institutionem Cistertii viventibus domi-
nium illud, quod extremitati nemoris illorum absque alterius terræ
intermixtione continuatur, pro animabus Henrici et Gilberti filiorum
meorum. Testibus, Fulco de Oily, Fulco Luval, Henrico filio Ro-
berti filio Aumari[k].

Mr. Leland says, this abbey was situate upon Otmoore[1]; that corner (I suppose) which lay nearest to the village of Ottendon. The
religious alway affected such low places, out of pretence to the more
solitary living; but I believe rather out of love to fish and fat land.
However this site upon the moor was fitter for an ark than a monastery, and therefore, by Alexander bishop of Lincoln, it was soon
removed to Thame in this county, and the church there dedicated
to St. Mary on the twenty-first of July, an. 1138[m], of which the bishop was now reputed the founder, though it was only a translation
of the other, and the bishop's augmentation to it was only the park
of Thame whereon the abbey was built, and some land which had
belonged to Nigel Kyre[n]. Soon after there was given to this abbey
of Thame some land in Chesterton by Robert de Amory: two hides
in Stok by Peter Talemash, which were of the fee of Reginald de S.
Walery: half a hide in Merton by Hugh Constable: and another
hide in the same place by Jeffery son of Omund[o]. *

Edith, an eminent and devout matron, at her own proper charge
built the monastery of Godestow near Oxford, which at the latter
end of December, 1138, in the fourth of king Stephen was dedicated
by Alexander bishop of Lincoln, to the honor of the Virgin Mary
and St. John Baptist[p]. King Stephen and his queen Maud, with

---

* Robertus filius Almerici dedit Serloni   Jocelino clerico archid'i; Osmundo clerico
abbati de Thame terras in Wulwardhull.   de Cesterton. Ex Cartulario S. Mariæ de
Test. Rob'to archid. Oxon. Rog. Cantor.   Thame. Bib. Cotton. Jul. C. 7. fol. 30.
Linc. Rad. de Noiers; Rob. filio Irbert;

[k] Mon. Ang. tom. 1. p. 802. a.   [l] Leland, Itin. Burton copy MS. p. 191.   [m] Rog.
Dods. MS. vol. 143. p. 41.   [n] Mon. Ang. tom. 1. p. 802.   [o] Ibid.   [p] Ibid.
p. 525. b.

with their son Eustace, were present at laying the first stone[q]; and were each a benefactor to it[r]. John de St. John gave the site of the abbey[s]; and one mill of four pounds in Wulvercot[t]; and two houses and a parcel of land before the gate of the church, in the island between the two rivers; and half a meadow called Lambey, of which the other half was given by Robert de Oily. Roger de Amory gave twenty-five acres of land in Blechingdon to sow yearly, and as many acres to enclose. Alexander bishop of Lincoln gave one hundred shillings yearly rent out of his toll in Banbury. And beside these donations recited in the Monasticon, Robert le Gait knight, with consent of Maud his wife and Philip their son, gave half a hide of land in Hampton[u]; and Guy de S. Walery, lord of the manor of Ambrosden, with the consent of Aubreche his wife and Reginald their son, gave yearly half a mark of silver on the feast of St. Giles, being the anniversary obit of his father[x]. This Edith, the foundress, seems to have been the same with Edith wife of Robert de Oily, she being called *Memorabilis Matrona Deo devota*[y]: and was buried in Oseney abbey in a religious habit, as Mr. Leland an eye witness reports, *Cher lyeth an image of Edith of stone, in th' abbite of a vowess, holding a hart in her right hand, on the north-side of the high altare*[z].

The king, at petition of Walter de Lacy abbot of Glocester, confirmed to that abbey their several possessions; among which the tithe of Cestretone (Chesterton adjoining to Ambrosden) of the gift of

An. MCXXXVIII. 3, 4. *K. Stephen.*
Albertus sanctæ Hostiensis ecclesiæ minister sedis apostolicæ legatus dilecto in Christo fratri W. abbati Eynesham ejusque succ. salutem. Tuis justis postulationibus assensum prebentes privilegium quod ven. frater noster Alexander Linc. episcopus concessit, scil. ut omnes clerici et laici de Oxeneford-scire qui ecclesiam Linc. in diebus Pentecost. adire solebant, ecclesiam de Eynesham requirant et eandem indulgentiam quam ibi perceperunt hic consequantur, nos confirmamus. Actum anno ab incarnat. Domini MCXXXVIII. Cartul. Eynesham. f. 23.

[q] Ex lib. de Godestow, MS.   [r] Mon. Ang. tom. 1. p. 525.   [s] Ib. p. 527. a.   [t] Ib. p. 525. b.   [u] Ex Lib. de Godestow, MS.   [x] Ib.   [y] Mon. Ang. tom. 1. p. 525. a.   [z] Leland's Itin. vol. 2. f. 17. Mon. Ang. tom. 2. p. 136. a.

Nigel de Oily[a]: which indeed corrects the register of donations to that church [b], where Chesterton is said to have been given by Robert son of Nigel, (as before observed *sub an.* 1010.) in the time of Serlo the abbot; when Robert was not come to that estate till after the death of Serlo, and could therefore only confirm his father's precedent gift.

An. MCXXXIX. 4, 5. K. Stephen.

Henry earl of Huntendon, having been deprived of his honor and lands in this kingdom, during the war between his father David king of Scots and king Stephen, was now at Durham upon a peace restored to all his possessions in England; among which were the manors of Pidington and Merton: and had the county of Northumberland given to him, excepting the towns of Newcastle and Bebanburg[c]. Ethelred abbot of Rievaulx, who was bred from the cradle with this earl Henry, gives him the character *of a mild and pious temper, an obliging spirit, and a sincere heart, worthy of so great and good a father* [d].

The king at Midsummer coming to Oxford, had sent to Roger bishop of Salisbury to come to him, whom he suspected for fortifying his castle of Divises: when the bishop, fearing a design to apprehend him, sent for his two nephews the bishops of Lincoln and Ely, and with their and his own retinue came to Oxford in a military manner: where a quarrel arising between them and the king's guards, the bishops of Salisbury and Lincoln were taken prisoners, and forced to resign their castles[e]; of which three had been newly built by the said Alexander bishop of Lincoln, Newark, Stafford*, and Banbury in this county.

Maud the empress, to prosecute her right of succession, landed in July nigh Arundel in Sussex, with her brother Robert earl of Glo-

* Sleford.

[a] Mon. Ang. tom. 3. pars 1. p. 8. a.   [b] Ib. tom. 1. p. 113. a.   [c] Ric. Hagust. p. 330.   [d] Ethelred. Abbas. inter X. Script. p. 368.   [e] Chron. Gervas. p. 1345.

cester, who with small attendance immediately came to Walingford, and firmly engaged the interest of Brien Fitz-count, lord of that honor; who, rejoiced at the news of her arrival, secured the affections of all the adjacent people [f], and fortified his castle of Walingford, resolving upon all possible endeavours to assist the cause of the empress [g]: and in order thereto he fortified his castle of Walingford, which after Michaelmas the king besieged, but being unable to take it, he raised a fort of wood before the castle, which he filled with men and arms for a blockade, and so marched off to Malmsbury [h].

An. MCXL.   5, 6. K. Stephen.

After Christmas the king went to Reading [i]; designing to force the castle of Walingford to a surrendry; but not able to effect it, he marched to Ely [k], and thence to Lincoln, where he was taken prisoner, and afterward exchanged for Robert earl of Glocester: when all these parts returned to his obedience. And Brien Fitz-count, lord of the honor and castle of Walingford, was glad to purchase his peace with him; if we can depend on the authority of Mr. Dugdale, who says, *that he came to a composition with king Stephen for the more secure enjoyment of his wife's inheritance; for in the fifth of Stephen, the record says, that he gave to the king one hundred sixty-six pounds for the office, and part of the lands of Nigel de Oily* [l]. It is however certain, that within the same year he returned to the interest of queen Maud, and was her most vigorous and constant friend.

Gerard de Camvil, lord of the manor and castle of Midleton, (now Midleton-stoney,) near Burcester, in this fifth of king Stephen, gave the monks of Bermundsey two parts of the tithe of Charlton-Camvil, in com. Somerset. which were afterwards leased to the priory of Kyllingworth for two marks yearly, to be paid at Kynwardeston [m].

---

[f] Sim. Dun. p. 266.   [g] Mat. Par. sub an.   [h] Chron. Gervas. p. 1350.   [i] Ib.
[k] Ib.   [l] Dugd. Bar. tom. 1. p. 569. a.   [m] Ex Registro Abbatiæ de Bermundsey abbreviato per Rog. Dods. MS. vol. 55. f. 98. et Mon. Ang. tom. 1. p. 640. b.

Nigh the same time Sir Robert de Gait gave to the abbey of Oseney his church of Hampton-Gay by charter, to which were witnesses Henry de Oily and Robert his brother. He married Maud de Povre, and afterward by consent of the said Maud his wife, and of Philip and Robert his sons, he confirmed the church, and gave the manor of Hampton to the said monks of Oseney ; who, in consideration thereof gave ten marks of silver to the said Robert, one bezan tine to his wife, and a horse to his son Philip, who confirmed his fa ther's donation in the third of Henry the Third [n]

An. MCXLI.   6, 7. K. *Stephen.*

Maud the empress in Rogation week was at Reading[*], 'to which

* *M. imperatrix H. regis filia A. ep'o Linc. et omnibus baronibus de Oxonsyre salutem. Sciatis me dedisse ecclesiæ S. Mariæ de Rading et conventui ecclesiam de Stanton cum omnibus rebus ei pertinentibus in decimis et terris et omnibus aliis rebus in elemosinam sicut eam A. regina uxor patris mei et W. vir ejus dederunt et per cartas suas confirmaverunt. Et volo et precipio ut eam bene et in pace teneant sicut melius alias res suas tenent. Ex Cartular. de Rading. MS. f. 4.*

A. Dei gratia regina presentibus et futuris omnibus ecclesiæ Dei catholicæ filiis salutem. Notum vobis facio me concessisse et dedisse Deo et ecclesiæ S. Mariæ de Rading et fratribus ibidem Deo servientibus centum solidatas terræ in manerio meo Stanton in Oxenefordsir, quod dominus meus rex H. mihi dedit cum omnibus rebus eidem terræ pertinentibus et nominatim Reinaldi Forestarii et hoc ad procurationem conventus et religiosarum personarum illuc convenientium in termino anniversarii domini mei regis H. pro

salute animæ ipsius et animæ meæ omniumque parentum nostrorum tam vivorum quam defunctorum, ita libere et quiete sicut unquam idem Dominus meus rex H. idem manerium tenuit et mihi dedit. Ib' f. 5.

Et præter illas centum 'solidatas terræ dedi ecclesiam ejusdem manerii Stanton cum omnibus rebus eidem ecclesiæ pertinentibus. Notumque sit quod eandem ecclesiam concessi ad continua luminaria ante corpus domini mei nobilissimi regis Henrici. Ib.'

A. Dei gratia regina A. ep'o Linc. amico suo carissimo salutem et amicitias. Sciat dilectio vestra quod manerium meum de Stanton partim divisi et concessi Sctæ Mariæ et conventui de Rading pro anima regis H. domini mei ; et partim concessi fratribus de Templo de Jerusalem et partim concessi Milesendi cognatæ meæ uxori Roberti Marmioni et partim concessi Will'o de Harefluctu pro servicio suo. Et omni tempore ecclesiam de Stanton et omnia quæ ep's Sarum. avunculus in Stanton de me tenebat. Ib. f. 5.

[n] Rog. Dods. MS. vol. 39. f. 96.

place Robert de Oily came to her, and made conditions for deliver-
ing up his castle of Oxford[o]. In pursuance of which agreement the
empress came to Oxford, and took possession of the castle and homage of the city, by which means she had in subjection all the adjacent country[p] : and appointed garrisons to be fixed in several of the
nearest castles, particularly at Cirencester com. Gloc. and Woodstock,
Ratcote, and Bampton in this county[q]. The said Robert de Oily, for
this surrendry of Oxford, had the character *of a soft man, that
abounded in the delights of the world, more than in true virtue*[r].
From whence the empress went to Winchester, and made oath to
the bishop, that in case he would accept her for queen of England,
he should have the disposal of all bishoprics and abbies; for the
observation of which oath, Robert earl of Glocester, and Brien Fitz-
count lord of Walingford, were guarantees[s] : which Brien returned
to the guard of his castle, and there received under his custody William Martel, sewer to king Stephen, taken at Winchester, and put
into his closest prison, called Cloere-Brien, and for his ransom had
the castle of Sherborn delivered to the empress[t]. Gilbert Basset,
who held Burcester and Stratton from the said Brien as a feudatory
tenant, adhered to him, and was faithful to the same cause.

At or before this time Guy de S. Walery possessor of several
lands in this county died, and left son and heir Reginald de S. Walery; who, being a friend and assistant of the empress, was by king
Stephen disseized of the lordship of Haseldone in com. Gloc. which
being given to John St. John of Stanton, was in the time of peace
restored to the said Reginald[u]; who soon after granted and confirmed to the nuns of Godstow Heringesham and Boieham, and one
fishery, with its appendages, and the whole island between the two
bridges, and whatever John St. John had given at dedication of the
church[x].

---

[o] Flor. Wigorn. Contin. sub an.   [p] Sim. Dun. sub an. p. 1354.   [q] Scriptor. Norman. l. 2. p. 958.   [r] Ib. p. 553.   [s] Will. Malms. Hist. Novel. l. 2. p. 188.   [t] Mat.
Par. sub an.   [u] Mon. Ang. tom. 1. p. 811. b.   [x] Ib. p. 525. b.

An. MCXLII. 7, 8. K. *Stephen.*

The empress kept her Easter at Oxford[y], soon after which the bishop of Winchester deserted her, and declared again for king Stephen; at which the empress, being much enraged, marched and besieged his castle of Winchester on the first of August, assisted by
Brien Fitz-count lord of Walingford, who, upon a defeat, attended
the empress to her castle of Devises: from whence they removed to
Oxford, whither in the beginning of October king Stephen came;
and when he had destroyed most parts of the adjacent country[z], he
burnt the city, and besieged the empress in the castle. During the
siege, Brien Fitz-count, to bring relief to the empress, got out and
repaired to his own castle of Walingford, to which many barons of
that party came in, with resolution to give king Stephen battle, or
to raise the siege[a]. But being too dilatory, the empress, near Christmas day, clothed herself in white, and walking by night through the
snow, escaped to Abingdon, and thence to Walingford[b].

Within the time of this siege, the neighbouring inhabitants not
being able to repair to the chapel of St. George's within the castle,
they built the church of St. Thomas without the walls of the said
castle, upon the ground of Jeffery de Ivery, lord of the manor of
Ambrosden; being the half of seventeen acres, which, after the annexion of St. George's chapel to Oseney abbey, was granted or confirmed to those monks by Bernard de S. Walery. *Durante obsidione*
Castelli Oxon a rege Stephano, qui Matildem imperatricem in dicto
castello diu obsedit, ædificata fuit capella S. Thomæ, quia parochiani
S. Georgii in castellum intrare non poterant, et sciendum quod ædifi-
cata est super medietatem decem et septem acrarum, quas nobis dedit
Bernardus de S. Walerico, &c.[c]

While king Stephen formed this siege, to oblige the monks of St.

---

[y] Will. Malms. Hist. Nov. p. 188.   [z] Gervas. Chron. p. 1858.   [a] Hist. Min. Mat.
Par. sub an. ' [b] Annal. Waverl. sub an   [c] Regist. de Oseneia. MS. f. 31.

Frideswyde, he gave to them the chapel of Brehull (now Brill) in com. Bucks, by this charter:

Stephanus rex Angliæ Alexandro episcopo Lincolniæ, et justitiariis, et vicariis, et baronibus, et ministris, et omnibus fidelibus suis Francis et Anglis de Buckinghamshire salutem. Sciatis quia pro anima regis Henrici avunculi mei, et pro salute animæ meæ, et Matildis reginæ uxoris meæ, et Eustachii filii mei, et aliorum puerorum meorum dedi et concessi in perpetuam elemosinam Deo et ecclesiæ S. Frideswydæ, et canonicis regularibus ibidem Deo servientibus capellam de Brehulla, cum omnibus ad illam pertinentibus. Quare volo et firmiter præcipio, quod bene et in pace libere et quiete et honorifice teneant capellam prædictam cum ecclesiis, et capellis, et terris, et decimis, et omnibus aliis rebus ad illam pertinentibus in bosco et in plano in pratis et pasturis, sicut aliquis ante eos melius et liberius tenuit tempore prædecessorum meorum regum Angliæ. Testibus, Willielmo de Ipra, Roberto de Ver, Richardo de Luci, Warino de Luseriis, apud Oxoniam [d].

Nigh which time Maud the empress, to ingratiate herself with the said monks, gave them a like grant of the mother-church of Oakle, with the chapels of Brill, Borstall, and Edingrave. So as in this competition for the crown of England, these religious had the same bribe offered them by both the contending parties; that which side soever they deceived, they might be true to their own interest.

Matildis Imperatrix Henrici regis filia, et Anglorum domina episcopo Lincolniæ, et omnibus fidelibus suis Francis et Anglis salutem. Sciatis me dedisse et concessisse ecclesiæ S. Frideswydæ Oxenford, et canonicis ibidem Deo servientibus ecclesiam de Accleia, cum capellis et omnibus rebus ad easdem pertinentibus, scilicet capellam de Brehulla, et capellam de Borstalle, et de Edigrave, pro anima patris mei et matris meæ, et omnium predecessorum meorum, &c. [e]

The bishop of Lincoln, by another charter at the instance of Maud the empress, gave the said monks leave to appropriate to their own

<hr>

[d] Regist. S. Frideswyde MS. carta 462.   [e] Ib. carta 463.

use the said church of Oaklee, with the chapels of Brehull and Bor-stall [f]. And king Stephen sent other letters to Alexander bishop of Lincoln, to advise, that he had given and confirmed to those monks the chapel of Brehull, with all tithes and customs of his demesne, as freely as his predecessors had ever enjoyed the same [g].

An. MCXLIII. 8, 9. K. Stephen.

Robert de Oily and Edith his wife granted to the knights temp-lars (besides what they had before given to them) land, to the value of six shillings and four-pence per an. toward the dedication of their church of Covele or Cowley nigh Oxford : which was now con-secrated by the bishop of Hereford, with consent of the bishop of Lincoln [h]

Nigh this time Brien Fitz-count, lord of the fee of Burcester, keeping his Christmas at Evre in com. Bucks. with Maud his wife, granted to the abbey of Evesham the church of Hildendon (now Hillingdon) in com. Bucks. &c. by this charter.

Brienus* filius comitis R. Londoniæ episcopo, et Hugoni de Bocheland, et hominibus de Colham de Midlesexa salutem. Sciatis me dedisse et concessisse ecclesiæ S. Mariæ de Evesham, ecclesiam de Hildendon et tertiam partem decimæ de Dominico meo, cum una hida terræ, et unam mansionem cum orto qui ibi pertinet apud Oxebruge, et volo et præci-pio quod pacifice et honorifice habeant ea conventione quam ego et uxor

---

* An. MCXLIII. 8, 9. K. Stephen.

David Rex Scotorum obiit 24 Maii, 1153.

In Londoniis ecclesia S'cti Michaelis de Cornhull pertinet ad ecclesiam de Eve-sham cum tribus domibus et reddit annu-atim ecclesiæ duas marcas, et semel in anno ignem, salem, et literiam. Ecclesia de Hildendona habet 1 hidam; dimidia est

de dominio domini, quam Milo Crispin de-dit Waltero abbati ad faciendum hospitium suum. Ipsam ecclesiam dedit ecclesiæ de Evesham Brienus filius comitis, et reddit annuatim 1 marcam et 1 hospitium invenit integrum abbati per annum et si iterum venerit ignem, salem, et literiam. Ex Car-tulario Abbatiæ de Evesham, fol. 9. Bib. Cotton. Vespasian, B. 24.

[f] Regist. S. Frideswyde MS. carta 417. ford in Musæo Bib. Bod. Ox. MS. p. 17.

[g] Ib. carta 464.   [h] Lieger-book of San-

*mea simus fratres, et participes orationum et beneficiorum illius
ecclesiæ in sempiternum. Hoc fuit in nativitate Domini apud Eure
in redditu de curia London. Teste ipsa Domina Matilda, et Radulfo Basset, et Gilberto Basset, et Gilberto Pipart, et Rogero de
Caisneto, et Warino Capellano, et Hugone filio Milonis, et Rogero filio
Aluredi, et Radulfo Foliot* [i].

This Hugh de Bocheland was seneschal or steward to the said
Brien Fitz-count, and held in Berkshire two knights fees and a half,
and was afterwards sheriff of that county from the sixteenth to the
twenty-second of Henry the Second [k].

An. MCXLIV. 9, 10. K. Stephen.

While Brien Fitz-count, lord of Walingford, maintained that castle
as the strongest garrison for the empress, and frequently sent out
parties for contribution and provisions, Henry bishop of Winchester
had desired of him not to molest any passengers that should be coming to his fair, nor to commit any acts of hostility upon his lands and
tenants. And when this martial baron had allowed his soldiers to
put no distinction in their sallies out to plunder, the bishop wrote
sharply to him, and threatened excommunication.

*Henricus Dei gratia Wintoniæ episcopus et sedis apostolicæ legatus,
Brientio filio comitis, &c.....Memorem esse uxoris Loth quæ respi-
ciens in statuam salis conversa est. Dum semper ad ea quæ retro sunt
respicitis, offendiculum quod præ oculis habetis minus cavetis, eoque
citius corruere potestis. Cum in literis quas novissime vobis direxi,
firmam pacem omnibus ad feriam meam venientibus a vobis et vestris
dari quesierim, nec in literis a vobis mihi directis illa negaretur, &c.
Res autem meæ a vestris interim captæ sint et terræ, et homines mei
inquietati, videtur mihi de vobis et vestris minus confidendum esse.
Et vos (quod tamen mihi confiteri grave est nec cordi meo sedet) nisi
correxeritis, inter infideles Angliæ connumerabo, &c.* [l]

---

[i] R. Dods. MS. vol. 105. f. 16.   [k] Dugd. Bar. tom. 1. p. 680. a.   [l] Inter MSS. R.
Dodsworth.

To which menacing letter the said lord made a stout and generous reply; upbraided the bishop with deserting the cause of the
empress, justified the necessity of his soldiers plunder, and appealed
to any legal method of trial against him.

Henrico nepoti Henrici regis Brientius filius comitis salutem.   Mi-
ror multo et mirandum est, &c.   Vosmet qui estis prælatus S. ec-
clesiæ olim præcepistis mihi, filiæ regis Henrici avunculi vestri ad-
hærere, et eam auxiliari rectum suum acquirere quod vi aufertur, et
hoc quod modo habet retinere, &c.   Non est mirum si capio ex alieno
ad vitam meam et meorum hominum sustentandam, et ad hoc agendum
quod mihi præcepistis ; nec de alieno quicquam cepissem, si mea mihi
relinquerentur, &c.

After which was subscribed this form of challenge in red letters.
Sciant igitur omnes fideles sanctæ ecclesiæ, quod ego Brientius filius
comitis quem bonus rex Henricus nutrivit, et cui arma dedit et hono-
rem, ea quæ in hoc scripto assero contra Henricum, nepotem regis Hen-
rici, episcopum Wintoniæ, et apostolicæ sedis legatum præsto sum
probare vel bello vel judicio, per unum clericum vel per unum laicum [m].

By which it appears that his lands were all seized to the use of
king Stephen, and among the rest no doubt the manor of Burcester,
held in fee from him by Gilbert Basset sen. who paid him his military service, and must suffer with him in the same cause.

An. MCXLV.   10, 11. K. *Stephen.*

Jeffery, abbot of St. Albans, at the motion of Roger the Hermite,
built a monastery for Benedictine nuns in a wood nigh Merk-yate in
com. Bedf. of which the site was granted by the dean and chapter of
St. Paul's in London.   The church was this year consecrated by
Alexander bishop of Lincoln, dedicated to the Holy Trinity, and
called *Cella Monialium S. Trinitatis de Bosco* : where Christiana the
first abbess had the easy reputation of doing miracles [n].   Matthew
Paris complains that this nunnery was by the founder endowed with

[m] R. Dods. MS.   [n] Mon. Ang. tom. 1. p. 350, et tom. 2. p. 872.

several lands taken by violence from his abbey of St. Albans. There was afterward given to it an estate in Burcester, of which the mansion was called Nonnes-Place. In the reign of Edward the Fourth, this land in Burcester, being assessed among the temporals of the abbess of Merk-yate, was computed at the yearly value of LVI^{s}. X^{d}. of which the tenths were rated at V^{s}. VIII^{d}.[o] Mr. Leland reports of Humphrey, an illegitimate son of John Bourchier lord Berners, in the reign of Henry the Eighth, *that he bestowed much cost in translating the house of nuns at Merk-gate to a manor-place;* that is, in pulling down the whole structure of that dissolved cell, and converting it to a mansion house for himself: but he lived not to finish it[p]

An. MCXLVI. 11, 12. *K. Stephen.*

King Stephen after his taking of Faringdon castle[q], and reducing most other parts to his obedience, found the remaining strength and interest of queen Maud to lie chiefly in the garrison of Walingford, which had much annoyed the country by frequent excursions[r], and was vigorously maintained by Brien Fitz-count, lord of that honor. Upon which the king again brought his army to the siege of this castle, where Ranulph earl of Chester came in to him with three hundred horse; but the place was so well defended, that after a long fatigue, the king not able to prevail by stratagem or force, raised or rather repaired an impregnable fort of wood at Craumers, to block up the garrison, and so retreated[s].

An. MCXLVII. 12, 13. *K. Stephen.*

The king at Northampton confirmed the donation of Siwell to the priory of St. Andrews in that town, to which charter was witness

[o] Transcript. Regist. Archid. Oxon. MS. penes Anton. a Wood. [p] Dugd. Bar. tom. 2. p. 133. [q] Annal. Waverl. sub an. 1145. [r] Dugd. Bar. tom. 1. p. 37. b. [s] Chron. Gervas. sub an. 1145, et Rog. de Hunt. et An. Wav. sub an. 1146.

*Richard Camvil[t], lord of the manor and castle of Midleton-stony, who adhered faithfully to king Stephen; and was at the same time and place with Robert de Weston, &c. a witness to another charter of William de Abrincis[u]. This castle of Midleton seems to have been built or repaired by him, for a garrison of the king's. In a very ancient manuscript that gives a catalogue of the monasteries and castles in England, (wrote at least in the reign of Henry the Second, before the building of Burcester priory not there mentioned) among the castles that follow the religious houses, this of Midleton is recorded, Oxenford, Midleton, Bannebyri[x].

An. MCXLVIII. 13, 14. K. *Stephen.*

Richard de Camvil, lord of Midleton, was now witness to a char-

---

* *Symon de Sen Liz comes Norhamtoniæ ep'o Linc. archid. baronibus, justiciariis, vicecom. ministris, clericis, laicis et omnibus sanctæ ecclesiæ filiis per Oxenefordsyram constitutis salutem. Sciant omnes tam præsentes quam futuri me dedisse et concessisse et in perpetuæ possessionis elemosinam confirmasse Deo et ecclesiæ S. Mariæ de Rading pro salute anime mee et parentum meorum ecclesiam de Hanebergha cum terris et decimis et omnibus ecclesiæ pertinentibus sicut rex Henricus dedit et concessit in vita sua. Unde volo et precipio quod ecclesia de Rading et monachi eam in perpetuum possideant, et in pace teneant. Hii sunt testes hujus cartæ. Ricardus de Camvil, &c.*

The chaple of North-Leigh or South-Leigh in com. Oxon. was granted by Richard de Camvil to the abbey of Rading.

Notum sit universis sanctæ ecclesiæ filiis atque fidelibus quod ego Ricardus de Cam-

vill voluntate et petitione Milisent uxoris meæ et Roberti Marmion filii sui donavi et in perpetuam elemosynam concessi Deo et sanctæ Mariæ de Radings et monachis ibidem Deo servientibus capellam de Leya cum duabus virgatis terræ, quarum una fuit de dominio nostro, altera de terra hominum de Leya tam nostrorum quam aliorum hominum villæ, et præter illas terram ad cœmiterium faciendum. Et volumus et concedimus, ut eas liberas omnino et ab omni servitio nobis pertinente et consuetudine seculari quietas teneant et habeant pro salute et incolumitate mea et uxoris meæ Milisent et Roberti filii sui et pro anima Roberti Marmionis et pro animabus omnium nostrorum, ut sint participes omnium beneficiorum domus Rading in eternum in quibus abbas et conventus nos receperunt tanquam speciales fratres domus Rading, &c. Cartular. Abbat. de Radinges. MS. f. 196. b.

---

[t] Mon. Ang. tom. 1. p. 680.   [u] Ibid.   [x] MS. Bib. Bod. num. 648.

ter of king Stephen to his new abbey of Feversham in Kent, dated at Bermondsey [y]. And nigh the same time was witness to another charter of Reginald, son of Roger earl of Hereford, and Emeline his wife, whereby they granted their manor of Eaton to the nuns of Godstow in com. Oxon [z]. Alexander bishop of Lincoln died this year, and was succeeded by Robert Chesny [a]

An. MCXLIX. 14, 15. K. Stephen.

The abbey of Oseney, lately erected and slenderly endowed by Robert de Oily, came now to be established upon the ruins of another convent. The uncle Robert de Oily sen. had, upon his building the castle in Oxford, raised within the precincts of it a chapel of St. George's, after made a parochial church, and in it he settled a society of secular priests, well endowed with tithes and other possessions by him, and confirmed by Roger de Iveri, to whom he soon after gave one of his baronies, as appears sub an. 1074, which charity the seculars had thus long quietly enjoyed. But now two reasons conspired for the dissolution of their fraternity, and the conversion of their lands. One was, the devotion of the age inclining more to regulars, who had a greater form of godliness; and this made it thought a work of piety to eject the seculars from their church of St. George's in the castle, and convey their estate to the Augustine abbot and canons at Oseney: a second reason was the late building of the church of St. Thomas, which made that of St. George's lose the use and service of a parochial church, and so this holy place might be the more easily spared, when the parishioners had no longer any title to it. Upon.these grounds this church of St. George's, with all thereto appertaining, was given to the canons of Oseney, by the grant of Robert de Oily patron, and consent of Theobald metropolitan, and Robert diocesan [b]. A. D. milles. centes. quadrages. nono tempore Eugenii papæ tertii et regis Stephani, et Theobaldi Cantuariensis ar-

[y] Mon. Ang. tom. 1. p. 688.   [z] Ibid. tom. 2. p. 886.   [a] Sim. Dun. sub an.
[b] Regist. de Osen. MS. f. 1.

*chiepiscopi et Roberti de Chesneto Lincolniensis episcopi, et Roberti de
Oileio secundi, qui fuit filius Nigelli de Oileio, data fuit ecclesia sancti
Georgii cum omnibus suis pertinentiis canonicis Oseneye regularibus,
et a Galfrido de Ivereio confirmata, quæ antea data fuit canonicis se-
-cularibus in castello Oxon.*

The charter of Robert de Oily now made to Oseney was not a
new donation, but an assignment of his uncle's gift to new uses, and
what the elder Robert had given to the seculars of St. George's, this
younger Robert transfers to the regulars of Oseney. He recites the
old gift of two parts of the tithe within all the demesnes of both honors, (*utriusque honoris,* which in the margin of the Monasticon is
thus interpreted: *D'oili scil. et de Ibreio, id est, de S. Walerico,*) by
which we are to understand the barony of Hokenorton, and that
other barony given first to Roger de Ivery, thence called *baronia de
Ibreio,* after granted to Reginald S. Walery, thence named *baronia
de S. Walerico.* Within Hokenorton barony[c], *duas partes decimæ
de omni re quæ decimari solet de omnibus dominicis de Hocnorton,
Swerefordia, Berefordia, Wygintona, et de una hida et dimidia in
Edburburia, et de una hida et tertia partæ dimidie hidæ in Cornwelle,
et de Cudlynton, Tropwithulle, Bensintona, et Northleya, et de una
hida dimidia in Bartona Odonis et Rowlesham, de utraque curia et de
Dunstewa, Ludwella, et Heyford.* Within Ivery barony, *duas partes decimæ, &c. de Hampton, cum Northbrook Gaytorum, et Blechesdon, de Weston, Berencestria, cum Wrechwych, Bukenhulle, Ardul-
feya, cum Northbroc juxta Somerton, de Mixebury, &c. de Beckele,
de tota villa Hortone, Morcote et de dimidia hida in Stodleya quæ
pertinet ad Beckeleyam, de Wode-pire, Elsefelda, Ocleya, et Horse
pathe; et duas hidas in Ernicote, cum bosco et aliis pertinentiis.*

What lay within the barony of Hokenorton being still in the tenure of D'oily, was past and confirmed by Robert de Oily jun. but
what lay within the other barony now in possession of Jeffery de
Ivery was by him confirmed in this following charter[d]. By which

---

[c] Regist. de Osen. MS. f. 7. et p. 350.   [d] Ibid.

it plainly appears those other authorities are mistaken, which assert or presume the death of Jeffery de Ivery about the twelfth of Henry the First, and his barony then given to Guy de S. Walery, who had indeed an estate in this county, but the barony of de Ivery was given to his son Reginald in the beginning `of the reign of Henry the Second.

Noverint universi quod ego Galfridus de Ivereio concessi, et hac præsenti carta mea confirmavi Deo et ecclesiæ S. Mariæ de Oseney, et canonicis ibidem Deo servientibus, omnes terras ecclesias reditus decimas et possessiones quas habent in omnibus maneriis meis de dono Roberti de Oileio, et concessione Rogeri de Ivereio patris mei in liberam puram et perpetuam elemosinam, sicut charta prædictorum Roberti et Rogeri quas habent plenius testatur. Et quia volo quod donationes et concessiones prædictorum Roberti et Rogeri ratæ sint et stabiles in perpetuum sigilli mei impressione præsens scriptum signavi. Hiis testibus Roberto Dei gratia Lincolniensi episcopo, Roberto de Oileio juniore, Nigello de Oileio, Gilberto de Amari, Hugone de Tywa, &c.

The two hides of land at Arncot in this parish of Ambrosden were expressly confirmed by Maud the empress[e], *duas hidas de Ernicota;* by king Henry the Second, *duas hidas in Ernicota;* by pope Euge nius the Third, *in Ernicot duas hidas cum nemore et aliis pertinentiis suis;* by king John, *duas hidas de Ernicot;* by Richard bishop of Lincoln, *duas hidas de Ernicote, &c.* There were two other hides of land in Arncot, which had been given to the abbey of Abingdon, possibly by Robert de Oily sen. when he was forced to compound with those angry monks, mentioned with other adjoining gifts in a bull[f] of confirmation by pope Eugenius the Third, A. D. 1146. *In Cestertona unam hidam, in Hernicota duas hidas, in Fencota unam hidam. In Stretona unam hidam et tres virgatas de dono ... de Albeneio.*

It is here proper to observe that Mr. Selden[g], in his History of Tithes, does cite, from the chartulary of the abbey of Oseney, this

---

[e] Regist. de Osen. passim.   [f] Mon. Ang. tom. 1. p. 107.   [g] History of Tithes, edit. 1618. p. 307.

donation by Robert D'oily, of the tithes of his demesnes in Burcen-
cester, Erdinton, &c.   And this he produces for one proof of the
arbitrary disposal of tithes by lay patrons, and their power to alienate
them from the parish church.   It is a pity that learned man should
be so prejudiced against the clergy, as in unkindness to them, not
only to run away with a false opinion, but to defend it with the
falsest matter of fact.   None of his first answerers had the opportunity to confute this gross mistake.   Mountague and Netles durst not
meddle with our national antiquities : and Dr. Tildesly could reach
no farther than the records of Rochester, by which he clearly dis-
proved all the citations of Mr. Selden which related to that diocese.
I think the first who replies to this instance of Robert de Oily's charter, is the reverend and living author of the Historical Discourse of
Tithes [h]; who has in general well refuted that conceit of the arbitrary consecration of tithes by laymen : but as to the particular story
of Burcester, &c. writes thus.   *Mr. Selden reckons these gifts as arbitrary lay consecrations, whereas a charter of Robert d'Oily says
expressly,* Consulente et confirmante Alexandro Dei gratia Lincolniensi episcopo ; *so that it is he advised Robert d'Oily to found it,
and confirmed the endowment at first, though this charter be not now
extant.   And the Monasticon cites another old record saying, Robert
d'Oily founded this church by the approbation of Theobald archbishop of Canterbury, and Alexander bishop of Lincoln.   Also that
other charter of the same Robert d'Oily, cited by Mr. Selden, expressly saith, the bishop of Lincoln advised and confirmed it, and
Theobald archbishop of Canterbury is the first witness to it.   Yet this
he falsely produces for an arbitrary lay consecration, and basely con-
cealing these old testimonies of the bishop's consent to, and confirmation of the founder's grant, (which he must needs see, while he transcribed so much of the charter,) he tells us, this was confirmed long
after by Richard (it* [i] should be Robert Grosthead) bishop of Lin-*

---

[h] Dr. Comber, Hist. Vindication of Tithes, p. 209.   [i] No, it should be Richard, i. e.
Richard Gravesend, and the date should be 1259, in the ninth of his pontificate.

coln, A. D. 1250, *as if this had been the first episcopal confirmation, whereas it is evident he knew it was confirmed by his predecessor from the first foundation, viz.* 120 *years before. What credit can be given to such an historian?* This reverend author has undoubtedly the truth of the argument on his side, but he wanted those records which would have much better guided him in the circumstances of the story, and would have made Mr. Selden's error much the more notorious. The Dr. confesses, that he had no other help than what he received from the Chartularies of Rochester, transcribed by Dr. Tildesly, from the *Monasticon Anglicanum,* and from Mr. Selden his own instruments[k]. Had he seen the register of Oseney, a fair parchment transcript of all their charters and other deeds in large folio, belonging first to the Cotton library, and by Sir Robert Cotton given in exchange for *Annales Burtonenses* MS. to the dean and chapter of Christ Church, Oxon, where now preserved in their treasury;—had he seen this authentic evidence, he would have drawn better conclusions from it, and more effectually exposed the partiality and falseness of Mr. Selden in that tract which least deserves his name. First, he would have found that this charter of Robert de Oili conveyed no new charity of his own, but only confirmed the antecedent donations of his uncle Robert de Oili sen. who, after he had built the castle of Oxford, placed secular canons in the church of St. George's, and endowed them with the several tithes here again recited. So as the application of this story by Mr. Selden stands wholly on a false bottom; he supposes this an original grant of Robert de Oili jun. when it was really made by a predecessor. This fundamental error the Dr. would have more gladly discovered, because he had observed the same disingenuous shuffling in other cases, and had charged Mr. Selden for often citing later confirmations of the lay granter's heirs, as if they were original grants. He gives other instances of it, to which he might justly have added this.

[k] Historical Vindication, p. 200.

Secondly, the Dr. would have been sensible, that the foundation of Oseney should not have been confounded with the grant of these tithes, when there was the distance of twenty years between these two actions, the abbey raised and first endowed in the year 1129, but the appropriations of tithe, before made to the church of St. George's, were not translated and confirmed to Oseney till 1149. So as though Alexander bishop of Lincoln advised and approved the first foundation; yet it was only Robert bishop of Lincoln who consented to this transferring of the tithes.

Thirdly, the Dr. would have perceived, that in this case there was no collation of tithes, or alienation from the parish church to a religious house, but only a transposal from one fraternity to another; and this no way reaches Mr. Selden's design, who would have proved by it, that the parish church might at pleasure of the patron be robbed to enrich abbies. Though indeed, when the bishop of the diocese agreed with the patron of the church to convert any part or the whole of parochial tithes to the use of religious houses, they did not think it an alienation, but only a new assignment of these dues to the same religious use, though to different religious persons.

Fourthly, the Dr. would not have complained, that the charter of Alexander bishop of Lincoln, confirming the foundation of Oseney, is not now extant, when he might there have seen it. *Alexander Dei gratia Lincolniensis episcopus omnibus in Christo, &c. Clarissimi filii nostri Wygodi prioris de Oseneye et fratrum suorum justis petitionibus facile assensum præbentes, &c.*[1]

Fifthly, the Dr. might have produced the old testimonies which he rightly guesses Mr. Selden did basely conceal. He might have cited the charter of Theobald archbishop of Canterbury. *Theobaldus Dei gratia Cantuariensis archiepiscopus fratri Wygodo priori de Oseney salutem. Omnes ecclesias et decimas præsenti carta confirmamus, et authoritate officii quo fungimur corroboramus, &c.* The char

---

[1] Regist. Osen. p. 11.

ter of Robert bishop of Lincoln, diocesan; *Robertus Dei gratia episcopus Lincoln. confirmamus ecclesias de Kudelinton, Cestretone, &c.* The charter of pope Eugenius the Third in the seventh of his pontificate; *Confirmamus duas partes decimarum de dominicis horum maneriorum, Berencestre, Blechesdon, Weston, &c.* Thus was this assignation of tithes to a new monastery no single act of Robert de Oili, but allowed and confirmed by the triple ecclesiastical authority, metropolitical, diocesan, and papal. And often again confirmed by their successors, by Thomas archbishop of Canterbury, by Hugh bishop of Lincoln; and in the vacancy of that see, often by the dean and chapter in express charters.

How strangely would Mr. Selden impose upon his reader, to advance an odd notion prejudicial to the church, and only serviceable to sacrilege and atheism; namely, that parochial tithes were of old purely arbitrary, and left to the absolute pleasure of the lay patron : and, citing but one testimony relating to this county, should represent it palpably false, when he consulted the original records, and must needs have failed in his eyes, or in his conscience.

MCL.   15, 16. K. Stephen.

Simon de Gerardmulin, who held lands in Pidington and Merton in fee from the earl of Huntingdon, died about this time, and left Joan his wife in possession of that estate. Before his death he confirmed to the abbey of Missenden the chapel of St. Cross, which Ralph the Hermite had built at Mussewelle, within the manor of Pidington, by this charter. *Notum sit cunctis fidelibus sanctæ ecclesiæ tam præsentibus quam futuris quod ego Simon de Gerardmulin concilio et consensu uxoris meæ Johannæ do atque concedo in perpetuam elemosinam abbati et canonicis S. Mariæ de Missenden capellam S. Crucis, quam Radulphus Hermita ædificavit apud Mussewellam in fœdo de Pidentona donatione Guidonis filii Pagani antecessoris mei, et totum assartum quod adjacet. Præterea do eis quandam particulam nemoris quæ est inter eandem capellam prædictam et nemus de Bruhella, quæ sicut semita vadit de Harwella usque ad Scottga-*

tam. Hæc supra dicta dedi eis libere et quiete ab omni servitio et consuetudine pro 'salute mea et uxoris meæ et liberorum meorum, et pro anima supradicti Eudonis antecessoris mei. Test. Wigot priore de Osenea [m].

Before this time Roger de Moubray granted the whole lordship of Smite in com. Warw. to Richard de Camvill* of Midleton castle nigh Burcester, and his heirs, to be held by the service of one knight's fee. Which Richard being a devout and pious man, and much affecting the Cistertian monks, whose order had then been but newly trans‑ planted into England; and finding that part thereof which is situate in the valley to be full of woods, and far from any public passage, as also low and solitary, and so consequently more fit for religious per‑ sons; gave unto Gilbert, abbot of the monastery of our blessed lady of Waverly in Surrey, and to the covent of that place, all this his lord‑ ship of Smite, there to found an abby of the Cistertian order: whereupon they presently began to build, and out of their own covent planted some monks here, dedicating the church thereof to the blessed

---

* *Notum sit omnibus—quod ego Ric. de Camvilla donavi et concessi Deo et beato An-dreæ Well. ecclesiæ in perpetuum prebendam ecclesiam de Hengstrig liberam et quietam ab omni servitute et exactione cum omnibus pertinentiis suis. Salvo jure Johannis filii Lucæ qui eo tempore ejusdem ecclesiæ per-sona extabat, et in manu Reginaldi Bathon. epi. quicquid juris in eadem ecclesia habe-bam—resignavi. Reg. Dec. et Cap. Well.*

Hæc donatio confirmatur per Reginal-dum episcopum Bathon. Test. Alexandro decano; Tho. Well. Rob. et Godefrido Bath. archid. ib.

Gerardus de Camvil confirmat donum patris sui Ricardi de ecclesia de Hengstrig in prebenda eccl. Well. 1182. ib.

Cartæ prædictæ Ricardi de Camvil testes sunt, Ricardi Cant. ar'epi; Gislebertus London. Barthol. Exon. Roger. Wigorn. Joh. Cicestr. Ricardus Cestr. Adam. de Sancto Asaph. episcopi; mag. Walt. de Constantiis Oxeneford archid. domini regis sigillarius; Walt. precent. Sarum. Gaufri-dus archid. Berk. mag. Petrus Blesn'. Will. de sancta Fida. Reg. Well. 1. c. inter an-nos 1175 et 1180

Ista donatio confirmatur per Gerardum de Canvil fil. Ricardi de Canvil anno 1182. Testibus Herbert. Cantuar. Ricardo Elien. Petro Bath. Jocelin Cicestr. archidiaconis; Huberto Walteri; Willelmo de Glanvill clerico; Asberto de camera; Bald. cancellar Sar. ib.

---

[m] Regist. de Borstalle, MS. f. xxx.

virgin, and calling it the abby of Cumbe in respect of its low and hollow situation. The word Cwmm in the British signifying vallis or convallis, *as doth also Cumbe and Combe in the Saxon. This was confirmed by Roger de Moubray about the latter end of Stephen's time, and ratified by Robert earl of* Leicester *in Henry the Second's time at the desire of the said Roger, Richard de Camvil, and the monks, who thereupon jointly allowed that the said earl should be reputed the principal founder of this abby.* Thus far the learned Mr. Dugdale [n]: who, from the register of Cumbe assigns only a general time, the reign of king Stephen: but the Waverly annals affix it to this year 1150. *Hoc anno fundata est abbatia de Cumba a viro nobili Richardo Decanvilla,* (it should have been printed *de Canvilla*) vi. id. *Julii* [o].

In allusion to this name of the monastery and the reason of it, *I* remember to have observed, that at Combe in this county of Oxon, though the church and town be now upon the hill, yet was the church first built in the deep adjoining valley, at the east end of the water mill in a ground called Bury Orchard, where the foundations of building and limits of the church-yard are still visible: from which place the materials were removed, and the present church erected on the hill, an. 1395, which church of Cumbe was given by Maud the empress to the monks of Egnesham in this county.

An. MCLI. 16, 17. K. *Stephen.*

Nigh this time Reginald de Gait knight confirmed to the monks of Thame the land in Ottendune, which had been given at the foundation of that abbey by his father Sir Robert Gait. *Sciant universi S. matris ecclesiæ filii quod ego Reginaldus de Gai dedi et concessi abbati de Thama et fratribus suis totam terram de Ottendun, quam Robertus le Gai pater meus in elemosinam dedit, &c.* [p] Which Reginald de Gait seems to have left a daughter married to Fulco de Fontibus, who left issue two daughters co-heirs, Alice married to Hugh Constable, and Petronilla wife of Hugh de Braimuster; and on the

[n] Dugd. War. Ant. p. 115.　[o] Annal. Waverl. p. 157.　[p] Ex Lib. de Thame, MS.

partition of his estate the village of Ottendun was allotted to Hugh de Braimustre, who left issue Odo de Braimustre, who granted to Henry de Colevile one knight's fee in Ottendun and Norton, for thirty-five marks sterling in hand, and the yearly rent of one besantin, or two shillings: which Henry gave the said land to the monks of Thame [q]

An. MCLII.   17, 18. K. Stephen.

Henry, son of David king of Scots, earl of Northumberland and Huntendon, and lord of the manors of Merton and Pidington, died this year and left issue Malcolm, who, in the year following succeeded his grandfather in the crown of Scotland [r]. At or before the death of earl Henry, king Stephen restored the honor of Huntendon to Simon St. Liz [*], the second earl of Northampton [s]: who thereby came possessed of the manors of Merton and Pidington, the former of which he gave to the Knights Templars, excepting the dowry of the wife of Simon de Gerardmulin, which she had in Pidington, and two virgates of land in Merton to hold for her life; by this charter. *Sciant omnes, &c. quod ego Simon comes Northampton. &c. assensu et concessione Simonis filii mei concessi et dedi Deo et Sanctæ Mariæ, et fratribus militiæ templi salvatoris de Jerusalem in perpetuam elemosinam habendam et tenendam Meritonam, cum omnibus appendiciis ejus excepta dote Simonis de Gerarmolin quod habet in*

---

[*] *Simon de Sen Liz, comes Norhamptoniæ episcopo Lincoln. archidiaconis, baronibus, justiciariis, vicecomitibus, ministris, clericis, laicis et omnibus sanctæ ecclesiæ filiis per Oxonefordsyram constitutis salutem. Sciant omnes tam præsentes quam futuri me dedisse et concessisse et in perpetuæ possessionis elemosynam confirmasse Deo et ecclesiæ sanctæ Mariæ de Rading pro salute animæ meæ et parentum meorum ecclesiam de Hanebergha cum terris et decimis et omnibus ecclesiæ pertinentibus sicut rex Henricus dedit et concessit in vita sua. Unde volo et præcipio quod ecclesia de Rading et monachi eam in perpetuum possideant, et in pace teneant. Hii sunt testes hujus cartæ, Ric. de Camvill, &c. Ex Cartular. abbat. Radinge, MS. f. 197. b.*

[q] Ex Lib. de Thame, MS. 967.   [r] Chron. de Mailros sub an.   [s] Chron. Jo. Brompt. p.

Pedinton, et præterea concedo quod prædicta uxor Simonis teneat in vita sua de eisdem fratribus illas duas virgatas terræ quas habet in Meriton, et post mortem ejus redeant illæ duæ virgatæ terræ in liberam possessionem perpetuæ elemosinæ. Hæc autem concessi et dedi pro salute mea et uxoris meæ, et liberorum meorum et pro animabus patris mei et matris meæ et omnium prædecessorum meorum, habenda et tenenda soluta et libera ab omni exactione et secularibus servitiis in bosco et plano et pratis et pasturis et aquis et omnibus aliis apperti-nentibus. Hujus donationis testes sunt Theobaldus Cantuariæ archie-piscopus, Richardus episcopus Londinensis, Robertus episcopus Lin-colniæ, Nigellus Helyensis episcopus, Gilbertus episcopus Hereford. Willielmus episcopus Northwic. Willielmus comes de Warena, Williel-mus comes Cicestriæ, Henricus de Essexia constabularius domini re-gis, Ricardus de Lincolnia, Willielmus de Caisneto[t].

Mr. Dugdale by mistake attributes this donation of the manor of Meriton to Simon St. Liz the elder, who gave the other manor of Pidington to the monastery of St. Frideswide. But it is most certain he died in the reign of Henry the First, whereas the witnesses to this charter prove it made in this latter end of the reign of king Stephen by the second earl Simon, who enjoyed this estate by the favour of king Stephen, in whose cause he died before Walingford, an. 1153, and left Simon the third, his son and heir mentioned in the charter: which third earl Simon gave to the same order of Knights Templars, the church of Southwyke belonging to Sadeles-comb, and the church of Wodmancote[u].

An. MCLIII.   18, 19. K. Stephen.

Brien Fitz-count, lord of Walingford, had maintained that garri-son with obstinate bravery against the fort of Craumers, and all other attempts of king Stephen, who, having lately besieged and took the castle of Newbury, marched from thence to renew the closer siege of Walingford, and reduced the place to that extremity, that Brien

---

[t] Leger-book of Sanford, MS. f. 102.   [u] Mon. Ang. tom. 2. p. 525.

Fitz-count and his friends sent over a messenger to duke Henry
in Normandy, with earnest desires either to come over and relieve
them, or to give them liberty of surrender[x]. Upon which intelligence
Henry duke of Normandy came into England with small forces,
which he soon improved into a formidable army; and having besieged and taken the castle of Malmsbury, marched up to Walingford to relieve his distressed friends, where he first blocked up the
fort of Craumers, so as the garrison of king Stephen could not move,
while that in Walingford had a free passage for victuals and recruits.
Upon the duke's advance, the king had retreated to reinforce his
army, and when he thought his numbers were sufficient, he brought
them up toward Walingford, from whence duke Henry advanced to
meet him; but when both armies were drawn out to battle, William
earl of Arundel proposed a treaty, which the barons of both sides
promoted, on this policy, (as the wise historian observed,) *that the
war might be prolonged, and mutual jealousy might restrain them
both, rather than either of them by conquest should become a more absolute governor*[y]. Such were the very fears that put a stop to the
victories of king Charles the First, because his own friends suspected
the abuse of victorious power. One of the greatest opposers of the
duke's interest was Simon earl of Northampton and Huntendon,
who died at the siege of Walingford in the same week, and of the
same distemper with Eustace the king's son[z]: he was buried in the
priory of St. Andrew's in Northampton, leaving son and heir Simon
the third in minority, and Isabel his widow after married to Gervase
Paganel, baron of Newport, com. Bucks, from which family that
town assumed its name. In the charter of agreement now made between the king and duke, (to which Richard de Camvil of Midleton
was witness,) there is mention that those which held out the castle
of Walingford, (viz. Brien Fitz-count and his retinue,) had done homage to the king, and delivered hostages for their fidelity[a]. But this

[x] Hen. Hunt. sub an. 17. R. Steph.   [y] Hen. Hunt. p. 397.   [z] Chron. Gervas. sub an.
[a] Chron. Jo. Brompt. p. 1039.

valiant and haughty baron, partly out of fear that king Stephen would not be heartily reconciled to him, and partly out of sorrow that both his sons were lepers, and confined to the priory of Bergavenny, *with great devotion took upon him the cross and went to Jerusalem, leaving the inheritance of Overwent, and the castle of Grosmunt, to Walter his kinsman, constable of England, son to Milo de Glocester earl of Hereford, and to the said Milo and his heirs the castle and whole honor of Bergavenny, to be held of him the said Brien and his heirs by the service of three knight's fees*[b]. His wife Maud de Walingford, to avoid the storms of civil war, had before retired into Normandy, and there, taking a religious habit, she granted at Beck to the church of St. Mary's and monks of that place, Great Okeburn and Little Okeburn in com. Wilts. of her own inheritance, with consent of Henry duke of Normandy and Maud the empress. *Testibus Ricardo Cancellario, Roberto de Curceio, Roberto de Novoburgo, &c.* To the original charter was a seal appending with an

An. MCLIII.

The mannor of Staunton com. Oxon. being settled on Adeliza, the relict of K. Hen. I. she granted these several charters to the abbey of Radinges com. Berk.

A. Dei gratia regina præsentibus et futuris omnibus ecclesiæ Dei catholicæ filiis salutem. Notum vobis facio me concessisse et dedisse Deo, et ecclesiæ S. Mariæ de Radinges et fratribus ibidem Deo servientibus C. solidatas terræ in manerio meo Stanton in Oxonefordsire, quod dominus meus rex Henricus mihi dedit cum omnibus rebus eidem terræ pertinentibus et nominatim Reinaldum Forestarium, et hoc ad procurationem conventus et religiosarum personarum illuc convenientium in termino anniversarii domini mei regis Henrici pro salute animæ ipsius et animæ meæ omniumque parentum nostrorum

tam vivorum quam defunctorum ita libere et quiete sicut unquam idem dominus meus rex H. idem manerium tenuit et mihi dedit. **T.**

Notum sit præsentibus et futuris omnibus ecclesiæ catholicæ filiis, quod ego Adel. regina uxor nobilissimi regis Henrici, concessi et dedi Deo et ecclesiæ S. Mariæ de Radinge et fratribus ibidem Deo servientibus C. solidatas terræ in manerio meo de Stanton in Oxenfordsyre ad procurationem conventus et religiosarum personarum illuc convenientium in termino anniversarii domini mei nobilissimi regis Henrici et præter illas C. solidatas terræ concessi eis et dedi ecclesiam ejusdem manerii Stanton cum omnibus rebus eidem ecclesiæ pertinentibus. Et volo atque præcipio ut in pace et libere et quiete teneant cum omnibus liberalibus consuetudinibus cum quibus dominus meus nobilissimus rex Hen-

[b] Dug. Bar. tom. 1. p. 469. a.

impress of her own person in religious habit, with an olive branch in
her right hand, and beads on the left arm, with this inscription in
the oval margin, SIGILLUM MATILDIS DOMINE WARINGFORDIE[c]
This Okeburn was afterwards made a cell to the abbey of Bec in
Normandy, and confirmed to them by king Henry the Second[d], and
by king Edward the Fourth annexed to Windsor college[e]. The date
of this donation by Maud de Walingford was much too early computed in a petition to the king and parliament in the eighth of Edward the Third; *Ubi recitatur quod Matilda de Walengford dedit
maneria et ecclesias de Grand Okeburn et Litle Okeburn abbati de
Becco tempore conquestoris*[f]

*ricus eam in dominio suo tenuit et mihi dedit.
Notumque sit quod eandem ecclesiam concessi ad continua luminaria ante corpus Domini nostri Jesu Christi et ante corpus domini mei nobilissimi regis Henrici. T.*

*A. Dei gratia regina A. episc. Lincoln.
amico suo karissimo salutem et amicitias.
Sciat dilectio vestra quod manerium meum
de Stanton partim divisi et concessi S. Mariæ et conventui de Rading pro anima regis
Henrici domini mei, et partim concessi fratribus de templo de Jherusalem et partim
concessi Milisendi cognatæ meæ uxori Roberti Marmiun et partim concessi Willielmo
de Harefluctu pro servitio suo. At cum
omni tempore ecclesiam de Stanton et omnia
quæ ep. Sarum avunculus in Stanton de me
tenebat, in manu mea detinui; et nunc
sciatis me concessisse beneficia ejusdem ecclesiæ de Stanton conventui de Rading in
elemosynam pro anima Henrici nomini nostri
et pro animabus omnium fidelium defunctorum et represento vobis dominum abbatem de
Rading cum monachis suis ut pro amore*

*Dei et meo benigne eos recipiatis, et quod
vestrum est eis voluntarie faciatis. T.*

*A. Dei gratia regina C. abbati et toti con-
ventui de Rading salutem. Audivi a quibusdam quod vultis ecclesiam de Stanton extra dominium vestrum et manum ponere.
Quare mando vobis quod nolo ut illam vel
aliquid aliud de eleemosyna mea extra manum vestram ponatis. T.*

*Stephanus rex Angliæ A. episc. Lincoln.
et Waltero archidiacono Oxon. salutem.
Mando vobis et præcipio ne ponatis abbatem
de Rading de aliqua tenura unde ecclesia de
Stanton fuit seisita, et tenens tempore regis
Henrici avunculi mei et die quo fuit vivus et
mortuus, et meo tempore postea, et nominatim de mora, et prohibeo ne prædictus abbas
inde placitat unde nominatim præcipere sicut
pacem meam habere voluerit, et abbatia de
Rading et omnes res ei pertinentes sint in
custodia et tutela mea, et præcipio ne capella
de mora fiat donec dirationata fuerit. T.*
Cartular. Abbat. Radinges. MS.

[c] Mon. Ang. tom. 1. p. 582.   [d] Ib. tom. 2. p. 954.   [e] Ib. tom. 3. p. 71.   [f] R. Dodsw.
MS. vol. 40. f. 1.

An. MCLIV. 19. K. *Stephen.* 1. *Henry II.*

King Stephen died October the 25th, succeeded by Henry the Second, who, in the beginning of his reign, in consideration that Brien Fitz-count and Maud his wife had both entered into a religious life, seized on the said honor of Walingford, and directed a precept to the sheriff to charge the constable of Walingford to make a legal inquisition of the tenure and conveyance of the said honor, and a return was made in this form.

Dominis suis dilectissimis domini regis justitiariis et baronibus scaccarii constabularius Walingford salutem. Sciatis me diligenter inquisitionem fecisse de mandato domini regis per vice-comitem ad me transmisso per milites de balliva mea, et hæc est inquisitionis factæ summa. Wigodus de Walengford tenuit honorem de Walengford tempore regis Haroldi, et postea tempore regis Willielmi primi, et habuit ex uxore sua quandam filiam quam dedit Roberto de Oily. Ipse Robertus habuit ex ea quandam filiam Matildem nomine quæ fuit hæres ejus. Milo Crispinus desponsavit eam, et habuit cum ea prædictum honorem de Walingford. Mortuo Milone, dominus rex Henricus primus prædictam Matildem dedit Brientio filio comitis. Idem Brientius et præfata Matilda uxor ejus tempore regis Stephani reddiderunt se religioni, et dominus Henricus filius Matildis imperatricis seisivit prædictum honorem [g].

An. MCLV. 1, 2. *Henry II.*

In this and the following year Richard de Camvil, lord of the manor and castle of Midleton, executed the office of sheriff for the counties of Oxford and Berks, and had a grant from the king of the lordship of Sutton in com. Northampton [h]. In his accounts for this year it appears, that Robert de Oily paid seven pounds six shillings for a writ of pardon [i]. After Easter there was a general council of the bishops and barons convened at Walingford, where solemn oaths

g R. Dodsw. MS. vol. 4.   h Ib. e. Rot. Pip. vol. 24.   i Ib. MS. vol. 73. f. 140.

of fidelity were taken to the king and his heirs[k]. Reginald de S. Walery was now restored to his lordship of Haselden in com. Gloc. of which he had been disseized by king Stephen, and which in the interim had been given to the abbey of Kingswood, who were un- willing to relinquish their claim to it; but after a vexatious suit, considering that the said Reginald was enjoined as a penance by the pope to found some abbey of the Cistertian order, they offered to refund Haselden and several other lands, on condition he should there found such an abbey, which by compact was soon after done; and the abbot, with several brethren, leaving few at Kingswood, translated themselves to Haselden, from whence, for want of water, they again removed to Tettebiri[l]. This Reginald de S. Walery[*] had been a faithful friend, and was now a great favorite of the king, who, on the death of Jeffery de Ivery, bestowed on him that honor, which from him and his successors was called the honor of S. Wa lery; by which means he was now possessed of the manor of Am brosden. Albreda, mother of the said Reginald, surviving her hus band Guy de S. Walery, married Walter de Wahull, and gave forty marks and three palfries for livery of her inheritance, whereof Regi- nald her son had the possession, while she staid in Normandy[m].

An. MCLVI.   2, 3.   Henry II.

About this time, while the honor of Walingford was in the king's hands, he gave a charter of ample privileges to the tenants and traders within this and the other honor of Bercamsted: wherein the inhabitants of Burcester had their ease and interest much concerned.

Henricus Dei gratia rex Angliæ, dux Normanniæ, &c. Episcopis,

---

* Reginaldus de Scto Walerico concedit monachis de Egnesham ecclesiam de Tette- berra pro salute H. regis, et A. reginæ Angl. et pro salute sua et Bernardi filii sui tempore Godefridi abbatis de Egnesham. Ex Cart'ario de Egnesham. Bib. Cotton. Claudius A. 8. fol. 131.

k Chron. Gervas. p. 1378.   l Mon. Ang. tom. 1. p. 811.   m Dugd. Bar. tom. 1. p. 504.

*comitibus, baronibus, justitiariis, et omnibus ministris meis et fideli-
bus totius Angliæ et Normanniæ Francigenis et Angligenis salutem.
Præcipio vobis quod omnes homines et mercatores honoris de Walingford et de Berkhampstede firmam pacem habeant per totam terram
nostram Angliæ et Normanniæ ubicunque sunt. Et sciatis me dedisse
et concessisse eis in perpetuum omnes leges et consuetudines bene et
honorifice sicut melius et honorabilius eas habuere tempore Edwardi
regis et tempore atavi mei regis Willielmi et tempore Henrici avi
mei. Concedo eis etiam quod ubicunque ierint cum mercationibus
emptionibus vel venditionibus suis, per totam terram meam Angliæ et
Normanniæ atque Aquitaniæ et Andegaviæ,* bp water and bp land, bp
wood and bp strand, *quieti sint de thelonio, pontagio, passagio, et
picagio, panagio, et stallagio, et* sheeres *et* hundredes, *et sectis shi-
rarum et hundredarum, de auxilio vicecomitum et servientum, de
geldis et danegeldis de hidagio et* Blodewhite *et* Bredewhite, *et de
murdredis et de variis ad murdredum pertinentibus, et de operationibus castellorum et murorum et fossatorum et parcorum et pontium et
calcearum et omni consuetudine et exactione seculari et opere servili,
ne super hoc ab aliquo inquietentur sub forisfactura decem librarum.
Prohibeo et præcipio super eandem forisfacturam ne quis super hoc
vexet vel disturbet, &c. Test. Theobaldo Cantuariæ episcopo, et aliis.
Datum apud Oxon. primo die Jun.* [a]

This charter was confirmed and enlarged with many additional
privileges by king Henry the Third [o].

An. MCLVII. 3, 4. *Henry II.*

Robert de Oily jun. founder of Oseney abbey, died before this
time, and was by his own appointment buried in the abbey of Eg-

---

An. MCLVI. 2, 3. Henry II. Mixburi concessa abb. de Oseney, 2 Hen °
  Carta Thomæ de Mixburi clerici conju- Ex Cron. Osneiensi. fol. 120. Bib. Cotton.
gati de una virgata terræ et messuagio in Vitellius, C. 15.

[a] R. Dods. MS. vol. 111. f. 40.   [o] Ib.

nesham [p]; leaving Henry his son and heir, who was sheriff of Ox
fordshire and Berks, from the third to the sixth year of this king inclusive : and this year he accounted for v[s]. in lands given to Walter
Bicistre in that town : from Reginald de S. Walery vii[l]. xv[s]. vii[d].
from Henry de Oily xi[l]. xv[s]. from Richard de Chanvil lx[s]. and for
a pardon by the king's writ to Reginald de S. Walery vi[l]. xv[s]. [q]
From whence it may be inferred that Reginald de S. Walery, by this
fine and pardon, came now to the full possession of his barony in
this county ; that Henry de Oily did in this year succeed to the barony of Hokenorton ; and that Richard de Canvill the elder died
and left issue, by Milisent his wife, Richard his son and heir to the
manor and castle of Midleton.   Henry de Essex, sheriff of Bucks
and Bedford, accounted for the rent of the king's firm in Bruhull
(Brill) lx[s]. and in lands given to the brethren of the hospital of
Witsand lx[s] [r]

    Malcolm king of Scotland, having surrendered to king Henry the
city of Carlisle, the town of Newcastle, the castle of Bamburg, and
the whole county of Laudan in Scotland [s], came to the king at
Chester, and, paying his homage, received from him the honor[*] of

---

[*] Malcolmus rex Scotorum dedit ecclesie Scte Frideswide villam Pydynton in
Oxefordscire pro salute sua et matris sue
ita ut Johanna in vita sua teneat. Test.
Herberto Epo. Glasg. Lib. S. Fridesw.
Oxon. [Ista Johanna fuit soror Tho. Basset.]

    Ista carta confirmatur per Thomam Ar'-
e'pum Cant. tempore Malcolmi regis Scotie. p. 117.

    Confirmatur per Simonem com. Hun-
tendon, ita ut Johanna in vita sua teneat.
ib.

    Alexander ep'us, servus servorum Dei ven.

fratribus Cant. Ar'e'po et Cicestr. ep'o, salutem. Ad aures nostras pervenit, quod cum
bone mem. M. quondam Scot. rex villam de
Pydinton contulisset ecclesie S. Frideswide,
ita quidem quod Johanna nobilis mulier in
vita sua eand. villam teneret, W. frater ejus
qui sibi in regno successit eand. villam abstulit, et postmodum David frater qui honorem de Huntendon tenuit, prescriptam villam que ad ipsum honorem spectare dinoscitur injuste detinuit, et nunc comes Simon,
qui prescripte ecclesie pretaxatam villam
scripti sui robore confirmaverat contra—in sue
salutis periculum detinet occupatam. P. 118.

---

[p] Tabella Annalium Osenei Cœnob. apud. J. Lel. collect. vol. 2. p. 285.   [q] R. Dodsw.
MS. ex Rot. Pip. vol. 12. p. 35.   [r] Ib. p. 51.   [s] Mat. West. sub an.

Huntingdon[t], and thereby the fee of the manors of Merton and Pidington. Simon the son of Simon St. Liz the second being then in minority[u].

An. MCLVIII. 4, 5. Henry II.

Hugh de Braimustre, lord of the manor of Ottindon, gave the said manor to his wife's brother Henry de Fontibus, who covenanted to leave him his heir, if he died without issue. *Sciant &c. quod ego Henericus de Fontibus feci hæredem Hugonem de Braimuster et Petronillam uxorem ejus sororem meam et pueros illorum de tota terra mea quam teneo et quam adquisiero, nisi hæredem habuero de muliere desponsata, et pro hac concessione tribuit mihi terram suam de Attendune, &c. Hæc concessio facta fuit anno quarto postquam rex Henricus filius Matildis imperatricis primo coronatus fuit*[x]. In August, the king at Dover confirmed to Alberic Ver the earldom of Oxford by charter, to which was witness Richard de Camvil lord of Midleton castle, who, being possessed of an estate in Stanton in this county, granted to Richard brother of Robert Pipard for his homage and service, all the land which Liger knight, his grandfather, held at the time of his death in the said parish of Stanton, by the gift of Richard de Camvill his father and Milisent his mother, to hold by the service of one third part of a knight's fee, by this charter.

Ricardus de Camvill omnibus hominibus et amicis suis Francis et Anglis salutem. Notum sit vobis me petitione Roberti Pipard reddidisse et concessisse Ricardo Pipard fratri suo et hæredibus suis pro homagio et servitio ipsius Ricardi totam terram quam Ligerus miles avus eorundem tenuit die qua obiit in manerio de Stanton, donatione Ricardi Camvil patris mei et Milisent matris meæ, tenendam sibi et hæredibus suis de me et hæredibus meis per servitium tertiæ partis fœdi militis pro omni servitio quod ad me vel hæredes meos pertinet. Quare volo, &c. Hiis testibus, Willielmo de Stanton, et Milone Ca-

<hr/>

[t] Cron. Mailross, sub. an.　[u] Dugd. Bar. tom. 1. p. 609. b.　[x] Ex Lib. de Thame MS.

pellanis, et Widone de Hamarz, et Radulfo de Beghevill, et Widone de Cahnes, et Roberto de Stanton, et Joanne de Kent clericis, et Godfrido de Leia, et Johanne de Bakepuz, &c. apud Stanton [y]. Simon son of Peter, sheriff of Bucks and Bedford, accounted this year for LII[l]. XI[s]. II[d]. *de veteri firma in Bruhella,* and LX[s]. for lands given to the brethren of Witsand in the said town of Brill [z]. Richard the king's son was now born at Oxford [a].

An. MCLIX. 5, 6. *Henry II.*

Richard de Camvill, lord of Midleton castle, accounted fifteen pounds for the rent of Cornberie forest in this county for five years [b]. Mr. Dugdale not only confounds this Richard de Camvill with Richard his father, but attributes to him the being *lord of the manor of Erdinton in com. Oxon. and giving to the canons of Oseney one messuage there, with free liberty to gather the tithes of his demesnes of that place, and in Berncestre* [c]. When this donation does evidently belong to Richard de Camvill his grandson, who, in right of his wife the daughter of Gilbert Basset, came to the possession of those manors of Erdinton and Berncestre.

About this time Malcolm king of Scotland and earl of Huntendon, confirmed to the Knights Templars their lands in Merton by this charter. *Malcolmus rex Scotiæ omnibus, &c. Sciant tam posteri quam præsentes me dedisse fratribus Templi Salvatoris Meriton in perpetuam elemosinam pro salute animæ meæ et predecessorum meorum et successorum meorum tam bene et honorifice sicut habuerunt die illa qua honorem Huntendoniæ a rege Henrico Angliæ suscepi. Testibus Herberto episcopo, Ernaldo abbate, Waltero Cancellario, Waltero filio Alani, Gilberto de Humframvil, Willielmo de Somervill, apud Scotebi* [d]

This prince in another charter nigh the same time confirmed to

---

[y] Sir Christ. Hatton, Book of Seals, inter R. Dodsw. MS. vol. 68. f. 4.   [z] R. Dodsw. MS. vol. 12. p. 51.   [a] Chron. Jo. Brompt. p. 1047.   [b] Dugd. Bar. tom. 1. p. 627. a.   [c] Ib.   [d] Leger-book of Sanford, MS. p. 102.

the monks of St. Frideswide in Oxford, the village of Pidington within the parish of Ambrosden, given to them by Simon St. Liz the first, earl of Northampton and Huntendon; which confirmation, with other endowments, was ratified to the church of St. Frideswide by pope Alexander the Third, in this bull.

Alexander episcopus servus servorum Dei dilecto filio Roberto priori Oxenfordensi salutem et apostolicam benedictionem. Justis petentium desideriis dignum est nos facilem præbere assensum, et vota quæ a rationis tramite non discordant effectu sunt prosequente complenda. Quapropter dilecte in Domino fili tuis justis postulationibus præbentes assensum, villam de Pidentona cum omnibus pertinentiis suis, quam recolendæ memoriæ Malcolmus rex Scottorum ecclesiæ tuæ devotionis intuitu et scripto proprio confirmavit, ecclesiam quoque de Fretwella, et ecclesiam de Wrmhala, cum pertinentiis suis rationabiliter prædictæ ecclesiæ concessam, tibi et eidem ecclesiæ authoritate apostolica confirmamus et præsentis scripti patrocinio communimus. Statuentes ut nulli omnino hominum liceat hanc paginam nostram confirmationis infringere aut ei aliquatenus contraire. Siquis autem hæc attemptare præsumpserit, indignationem omnipotentis Dei et beatorum Petri et Pauli se noverit incursurum. Datum Tusculani XIII. Kal. Junii[e].

An. MCLX.   6, 7. *Henry II.*

At the beginning of this year the king kept his court at Brill, attended by his chancellor Thomas Becket archdeacon of Canterbury, and Robert bishop of Lincoln, &c. where he granted to the said Robert bishop of Lincoln a charter of free warren in his land of Banbury in this county, as had been enjoyed by his predecessors in the reign of Henry the First.

Henricus rex Anglorum, dux Normanniæ et Aquitaniæ, comes Andigaviæ, justitiariis, vicecomitibus, et omnibus ministris suis Oxenfordscire salutem. Concedo quod Robertus episcopus Lincolniæ habeat

---

[e] Regist. S. Frideswydæ MS. carta 441.

warrenam in terra sua de Banbury *, sicut antecessores sui eam melius et honorabilius habuerunt tempore Henrici regis avi mei. Et prohibeo nequis in ea fuget vel capiat leporem sine licentia ejus super* x[l]
forisfacturam. Teste Thoma cancellario apud Bruhullam [f]. A like
charter in the same form was given for the like privilege in his land
of Thame in this county : both which charters were expressly confirmed in the eighth of Henry the Eighth[g]. At the same time and
place, upon petition of the said Robert bishop of Lincoln, the king
gave to the church of St. Mary's in Lincoln the church of Langeford, and the land which Roger bishop of Salisbury held in the said
village of Langeford. *Testibus, Thoma cancellario, H. de Essexia
constabulario, Warino filio Geroldi camerario, Willielmo filio Hamonis, H. filio Geroldi, apud Bruhellam in foresta* [h].

It seems to have been at the same time that the king released and
quitted to the Knights Templars the payment of assarts, or the yearly
imposition on grounds converted from wood to tillage, of twenty
acres of land in Merton; which remission was confirmed by king
Richard in a charter that mentions *quadraginta acras terræ in Ox-
fordscire apud Merton,* provided the tenants should not trespass in
the king's forests. King John confirmed the same liberty by charter, dated the 14th of July, in the first year of his reign[i].

Richard de Camvill, lord of Midleton castle, was sent beyond sea
with the king's austringers and falconers[k]; and nigh this time was

---

* Banburi. Rob. Bloet episcopus Linc.
olim dederat abbati de Egnesham omnes
decimas majores et minores provenientes de
dominicis episcopatus in parochiis de Banneburi, Cropsedy, Thame, et Middilton.
Hoc confirmatur per Hen. e'pum Linc.

Cartul. Egnesham. f. 76.
Contentio inter magistrum Salonem canonicum Linc. rectorem ecclesiæ de Bannebiri et mon. de Egnesham super decimis
in parochia de Bannebiri, anno 1238. Ib.
f. 57.

[f] Ex Rental. Episcopat. Linc. MS. penes D. D. Halton, Archid. Oxon.   [g] Ibid.
[h] Mon. Ang. tom. 3. p. 267. b.   [i] R. Dods. MS. vol. 25. p. 148.   [k] Dugd. Bar.
tom. 1. p. 627.

witness to a grant of the king to John son of John Mareschal[l].
Fulk de Lisures, from whom Borstall and the forest of Bernwood
were held by William Fitz-Nigel, had now the custody of the forests
of Rokingham, Selveston, and Huntindon [m]

The king made an expedition to Tholous in Gascoin, attended by
many English barons, and by Malcolm king of Scotland and earl of
Huntingdon, lord of the fee of Pidington and Merton [n].

An. MCLXI. 7, 8. Henry II.

The king in Normandy commissioned Rotroc bishop of Evreux,
and Reginald de S. Walery lord of the manor of Ambrosden, to
make inquisition within the several dioceses, what rents, rights, and
customs belonged to the king, and what to the barons [o]. And there
being a scutage this year assest at two marks on every knight's fee
for the army at the siege of Tholous, the collecting in this county
was committed to Manasser Arsic and the said Reginald de S. Walery [p]; who, near this time, confirmed to the monks of St. Frideswide in Oxon his manor of Kniton or Knyttinton in com. Berks.
which had been given by his father Guy de S. Walery, was soon after
ratified by a charter of Henry the Second [q] and again confirmed by
king Henry the Third in the thirteenth of his reign [r].

An. MCLXII. 8, 9. Henry II.

Manasser Arsic, sheriff of Oxford and Berks, accounted for ten
pounds ten shillings for Reginald de S. Walery [s]. This Manasser
Arsic was son of Robert son of Manasser the elder, founder of the
cell of Coges, which barony of Coges continued in this family to the
twenty-ninth of Henry the Third, when the two daughters and heirs
of Robert de Arsic past away the lordship of Coges, and what-

---

[l] R. Dods. MS. vol. 68. f. 4.   [m] Dugd. Bar. tom. 1. p. 597.   [n] Chron. Jo. Brompt.
p. 975. et 1051.   [o] Rad. de Diceto.   [p] R. Dods. MS. vol. 143. f. 1.   [q] Regist. S.
Frideswidæ, MS. carta 426.   [r] R. Dods. MS. vol. 80. p. 175.   [s] Ib. vol. 12. p. 79.

Y 2

ever descended from their father, to * Robert Grey archbishop of York[t].

Within this year Walter Giffard earl of Buckingham and Ermigard his wife founded the abbey of St. Mary's Nutley, within the park of Crendon nigh Thame, for monks of the Augustine order[u] · and gave to it the churches of Kaversham, Risenberg, Chiltune, and chapel of Dortune, Essevendone, Hildesdone, Cheseley, and the tithe of Mersh. *Teste Hugone de Bolebec, Galfrido Willielmi filio, Widone de Rocsfort, &c.*[x] Soon after the king, keeping his court at Brill, did there by charter give to the said abbey the hermitage of Finemere, which was of the fee of Rouland Maleth of Quainton, with license of free ingress and egress, and pasturage of cattle and other privileges in the forest of Brehull. *Hiis testibus; Ranulpho de Glanvill, Hugone de Cressy, Gilberto Pipard, Willielmo de Gerpounvill, apud Bruhull*[y].

An. MCLXIII.   9, 10.   Henry II.

Before this time Gilbert Basset sen. who held in fee of the honor of Walingford the manors of Berncester, Wrechwike, and Stratton, died, leaving Thomas Basset his son and heir, who was this year sheriff of the counties of Oxford and Berks[z]. Which Thomas married Alice the daughter of R. de Dunstanvill, and Cecily daughter of Alan de Dunstanvill was after married to William Basset son of John son of Osmund Basset.

The king held a great council at Woodstock, where he confirmed the foundation of Nun Eaton in com. War. *Testibus Thoma archiepiscopo Cantuariæ, Willielmo episcopo Londiniæ, Roberto episcopo Lincolniæ, Malcolmo rege Scotiæ, Willielmo fratre regis, &c. apud Wodestochiam*[a]. At which place, on the calends of July, Malcolm

* Walter.

[t] Dugd. Bar. tom. 1. p. 539.   [u] MS. Ashmol. vol. 839. f. 68.   [x] Mon. Ang. tom. 2. p. 154.   [y] Ib.   [z] Dugd. Bar. tom. 1. p. 383. a.   [a] Mon. Ang. tom. 1. p. 519. a.

king of Scotland did homage to king Henry, and to Henry his
son[b]: and after his return to Scotland confirmed to the abbey of
Missenden the hermitage of Musewell, within his manor of Pidington
in the parish of Ambrosden, by this charter.

Malcolmus rex Scotiæ cunctis fidelibus suis notum, et catholicæ ma-
tris ecclesiæ' filiis universis salutem. Sciant clerici et laici præ-
sentes et absentes moderni et posteri me concessisse et hac mea carta
confirmasse Deo et ecclesiæ S. Mariæ de Missenden, et abbati et ca-
nonicis ibidem Deo servientibus hermitorium de Mussewelle possiden-
dum libere et quiete, cum omnibus suis pertinentiis in bosco et plano
cum quibus prædicta ecclesia idem heremitorium juste tenebat die ipsa
qua ego regni Scotiæ suscepi gubernacula. Testibus Nicolao cancel-
lario, Waltero filio Alani dapifero, Ricardo constabulario, Willielmo
de Husa, Radulfo de Evrefort, apud Jeddewurth[c].

And at the same time he directed a preceptory letter to the
steward of his honor of Huntendon, to allow quiet possession to the
canons of Missenden, in this form.

Malcolmus rex Scotiæ dapifero suo de honore Huntyndon salutem.
Scias quod volo et præcipio ut abbas et canonici de Missenden teneant
heremitorium de Mussewell, cum suis pertinentiis ita plane et ita libere
et quiete sicut ipsi prædictam elemosinam plenius liberius et quietius
tenuerunt in tempore regis Henrici et regis David. Testibus Ada co-
mitissa matre regis, Nicholao cancellario, Waltero filio Alani dapi-
fero, apud Jeddewurth[d].

An. MCLXIV. 10, 11. Henry II.

About this time Thomas Becket archbishop of Canterbury con-

An. MCLXIII. 9, 10. Henry II.
Conventio facta apud Doveriam inter Henricum regem Angl. et Hen. filium ejus ex una parte, et Theodoricum com. Flandrie et fil. ejus ex altera. 14. kal. Apr. 1163. An. 9. Hen. 2. Hujus conventionis ex parte regis et Henrici filii sui obsides sunt, Reginald. de Scto Valerico pro 100 marcis. Bernardus de Scto Valerico pro 100 marcis. Rogerus de Oilli pro 100 marcis. Rymer. vol. 1. 26.

[b] Rad. de Diceto, p. 536. sub an.   [c] Regist. de Borstall. MS. f. xxxi.   [d] Ibid.

firmed to the Knights Templars their land in Merton by this charter.

Thomas Dei gratia Cantuariæ archiepiscopus Anglorum primas, &c. Universis, &c. salutem. Ad nostram spectat solicitudinem religiosorum virorum quieti providere, et quæ suis sunt usibus a regibus sive a principibus rationabiliter collata nostra auctoritate confirmare. Idcirco fratribus religiosis de Templo Domini militibus terram de Meriton quam comes de Northampton Simon eis in perpetuam dedit elemosinam confirmamus et scripti nostri munimine corroboramus, sicut regis Stephani carta quam habent testatur. Valete[c]

Nigh the same time Wydo de Meriton knight, in consideration of fifteen shillings to himself, two seams of wheat to his wife, and one hundred marks to Simon his son, granted to the Knights Templars two acres of land in Meriton, with other gifts and privileges, by this charter.

Guido de Meriton miles filius Willielmi omnibus, &c. salutem in Christo. Sciatis, &c. me dedisse et concessisse concilio uxoris meæ et Simonis senioris filii mei et omnium hæredum meorum Deo et St. Mariæ et fratribus Templi Salvatoris unam acram terræ secus molendinum de Meriton apud Frankeburg, et unam acram prati ubi incipiunt primo vertere fossam suam per medium pratum suum versus molendinum suum. Dedi itaque et concessi Deo et fratribus illas duas acras liberas et quietas ab omnibus secularibus servitiis sicut in perpetuam elemosinam tanquam ille qui dominus et fundator ; et cum donatione hujus elemosinæ omnes percapturas quas fratres inceperunt versus me in faciendo passagium suum, et in......aquæ et in fossis et in ponte et in omnibus rebus ubicunque præsumpserint quiete clamavi. Pro ipsa elemosina prænominati fratres me et uxorem meam et pueros meos et omnes prædecessores meos in precibus, et in omnibus beneficiis domus percipiant. Ego vero ad hanc domum......ad obitum meum meliorem equum quem concessi. Pro concessione igitur hujus elemosinæ dederunt mihi fratres caritative xv. sol. et uxori meæ ii. summas bladi, et Simoni filio marcas centum ad quasdam chosas emendas. Et præter

[c] Leger-book of Sandford, MS. f. 102.

hoc concesserunt mihi fratres unam libertatem ad suum molendinum scilicet molandi segetem pro multura reddenda pro segete quæ est in tremuta, et meum brasium sine multura. Testes donationis sunt Fulco sacerdos de Meriton, Luvellus de Horspath, et totum falmotum meorum hominum et suorum [f].

Among the barons now convened in the great council of Clarendon, were Richard de Camvil of Midleton castle [g], who was a witness to the recognition of the people's liberties and rights [h]; and Reginald de S. Walery, lord of the manor of Ambrosden, who, being a great enemy to the turbulent and haughty spirit of Thomas archbishop of Canterbury, was sent over with other nobles to Lewis king of France, and to the pope, to represent the king's case to them, that they might give no protection to the bishop who was flying to them [i]: but their message was ineffectual, for the king of France and the pope espoused the bishop's faction, and improved the opportunity to pretend religion, and promote rebellion.

An. MCLXV. 11, 12. *Henry II.*

The king married his eldest daughter Maud to Henry king of the Romans, for which there was an aid or scutage imposed on all that held of the king by military service: on which occasion the sheriff of this county made return, that Thomas Basset held seven knight's fees of the honor of Walingford, within which were included Burcester, Wrechwike, and Stratton; and that Richard de Camvill held one knight's fee *de antiquo feoffamento*, by which was meant his manor of Midleton [k].

Malcolm king of Scotland and lord of the honor of Huntendon died at Gedewurth, on the fifth of the ides of December, in the twenty-fifth year of his age; to whom William his brother succeeded in the kingdom of Scotland and honor of Huntendon, who became thereby lord of the fee of Pidington and Merton [l].

---

[f] Leger-book of Sandford, MS. p. 103.   [g] Quadrilog. l. 5.   [h] Dugd. Bar. tom. 1. p. 627. a.   [i] Chron. Gervas, sub. an.   [k] W. Dugdale, MS. Lit. X. p. 77.   [l] Chron. Mailros, sub an.

About this time John del Osse of Wendlebury gave to the Knights Templars four acres and a half in Long-comsho and Mercot. *Hiis testibus; Rogero decano de Pire, Mattheo capellano de Ambrosden, et Willielmo fratre ejus, Fulcone capellano de Meriton, Willielmo filio Heliæ, Willielmo de Fresne, Willielmo de Bosco, Elia filio Stephani, et Galfrido fratre suo, Radulfo de Herdulvesle, Waltero et Clemente de Mercot. Hoc factum est tempore fratris Johannis existentis præceptoris de Covele, et fratris Alani de S. Laurentio de Meriton* [m]. By another charter he gave to the said knights one acre and a half nigh Sweteman-croft. *Hiis testibus; Waltero capellano de Heyfyrd, Waltero presbytero de Meriton, et Simone fratre ejus, Willielmo de Bosco, Waltero de Merlac, Clemente de Mercot, Rogero clerico de Covele, &c.* [n] The same person gave to the same use Swetemancroft. *Hæc donatio facta fuit tempore fratris Rogeri de Covele. Testes Fulco capellanus de Meriton, et frater capellanus de Covele, et Hugo Sagitarius, et Johannes clericus, &c.* Another donation by John del Osse and Andegave his wife of Leecroft and Hodestaplefurlong nigh Mercot. *Hiis testibus; Waltero capellano de Meriton, Simone milite filio Widonis de Meriton, Waltero milite de Gersindon, Hugone Paupere, Willielmo del Osse, Willielmo de Bosco, &c.*

Walter del Osse sen. who seems to have been the father of John, gave to the said knights one virgate of inland in Chatingathar and Benedashale. *Testibus; Simone presbytero de Oxon, Fulcone presbytero de Meriton, Rogero de Mellet, Radulfo clerico de Leystall, &c.* Hawise del Osse, who seems the widow of the said Walter, gave the knights one acre in Ossemede, nigh Merlake. *Hiis testibus; Nigello de Piry, Fulcone del Osse, Simone de Meriton, Wydone de Cherleton, Petro de Wendleburi, Waltero de Fencot, Hugone de Meriton præceptore, &c.*

Note, the title of *capellanus* given to several of these witnesses had the same sense as the word *curate* now has: he was either a stipendiary vicar or deputy of that religious house to which the church was

---

[m] Leger-book of Sandford, MS.   [n] Ibid.

appropriated; or else the retained assistant of the inducted priest. For in large parishes the incumbent was obliged to keep two or more capellanes or curates, to officiate in part of the duties, though he himself was resident. This was one of the constitutions in the council of Oxford, an 1222; that in all churches where the parochial bounds were large, there should be two or three priests maintained according to the greatness of the parish [o]. And Walter de Kirkham bishop of Durham did ordain in his diocese, an. 1255, that the rector of a church united should maintain as many chaplains, *i. e.* curates, as there used to be of old, while the church was divided [p]. The proper incumbent being styled at first *presbyter*, then *persona*, at last *rector* or *vicarius*: and the retained assistant was called at first *capellanus*, then *vicarius*, and at last *curatus*.

An. MCLXVI. 12, 13. *Henry II.*

In this or the preceding year died Reginald de S. Walery, lord of the honor so called, within which was the manor of Ambrosden. He left issue one daughter Maud, (wife of William de Braose, a potent baron; she was called Matildis de Sancto Walerico; and her younger son bore the name of his grandfather Reginald: for her bold and resolute behaviour to king John, she was miserably famished with her eldest son in Windsor castle, an. 1210[q],) and one son Bernard, who being at his father's death beyond the seas, the king directed this precept to secure his rights and properties till he should return.

Henricus Dei gratia rex Angliæ, dux Normanniæ et Aquitaniæ et Andigaviæ, vicecomitibus et omnibus ballivis suis in quorum ballivis Bernardus de Sancto Walerico terras habet et tenementa. Præcipio vobis quod custodiatis et manu teneatis et protegatis terras et homines et omnes res et possessiones Bernardi de Sancto Walerico in ballivis vestris sicut meas proprias, ita quod nullam molestiam vel injuriam aut gravamen eidem faciatis, nec fieri permittatis, et siquis super hæc in

[o] Concil. Ang. tom. 2. p. 183. [p] Ib. p. 297. [q] Mat. West. sub an.

aliquo forisfecit plenariam eidem inde sine delatione justitiam fieri fa-
-çiatis, et terræ suæ sint quietæ de scyris et hundredis et sectis scyrarum
et hundredorum et omnibus placitis et querelis exceptis murdredo et
latrocinio. Teste Ranulpho de Glanvil[r]. The said Bernard de S.
Walery for livery of his lands paid to the king five marks and a half,
as accounted for by Adam de Catmer sheriff of Oxon and Berks, in
this form. *Oxenfordscire, Adamus de Catmera reddit computum pro*
Bernardo de Sancto Walerico v. marcas et dimid. Bechlea dim. marc.
Hortuna 1 *marc. Haltona* 11 *marc. Horspada dim. marc. Luga dim.*
marc. Esthalla dim. marc. Fulbroc dim. marc[s].

There had been a long controversy depending between the church
of St. Frideswide in Oxford and the cell of Coges, concerning two
parcels of tithe of the demesne of Gilbert Pipard in Fretwell; which
church of Fretwell was dedicated to * St. Olave, and the advowson
of it given by Ralph Foliot to the priory of St. Frideswide: which
controversy, in presence of † Richard archdeacon of Oxford and the
whole chapter (or convention of the clergy) of the rural deanery of
Stoke, was decided on this agreement, that the canons of St. Frideswide should pay yearly to the cell of Coges, in consideration of
that tithe, the sum of one besantine, or two shillings, within the octaves of Michaelmas. Of which issue the archdeacon made this notification.

R. archidiaconus Oxon. Universis sanctæ matris ecclesiæ filiis sa-
lutem. Noverit universitas vestra controversiam quæ diu agitata est
inter ecclesiam sanctæ Frideswydæ et ecclesiam de Coges super duabus
garbis decimæ de dominico Gilberti Pippard de Fretwell in præsentia
nostra et totius capituli in decanatu de Stokes tali transactione in
perpetuum decisam esse, ecclesia siquidem S. Frideswidæ annuatim

* Fulco de Banvill concedit ecclesie suus Fulco dederat eis. Test. Willelmo de
Scti Olavi de Fretewell x acras terre et di- Scto Amande.
mid. in perpetuam elemosinam, quas pater † Robert.

[r] Regist. Osen. MS.   [s] Rog. Dods. MS. vol. 12. et Rot. Pip.

persolvet ecclesiæ de Coges pro eadem decima duos solidos vel bisan-
tium unum infra octavas S. Michaelis[t].

An. MCLXVII. 13, 14. *Henry II.*

In this year was the fourth scutage or tax to the king at a mark
for every knight's fee; when in the return made upon inquisition it
appeared, that Henry de Oily held thirty-two knight's fees and an
half of the old feoffment, and one fee and a half and the twentieth
part of a fee of the new feoffment, and Thomas Basset seven knight's
fees of the honor of Walingford, in which honor the family of Basset
had a great share; Nicholas Basset had ten knight's fees; Turstan
Basset six fees and two parts of a seventh; Osmund Basset one fee
and a fourth part; Fulco Basset one fee.

The church discipline suffered much in these parts by the death
of * Robert bishop of Lincoln, on the seventh of the calends of February[u], when Jeffery, the king's base son, kept the title and tem-
poralties, though a layman, till 1182, at which time being urged by
the pope and archbishop to take orders, he resigned his title, and
the king kept it in his own hands some time after, which long vacancy made a converted monk of Thame pretend to prophecy there
should be no more bishops of Lincoln[x].

About this time William king of Scots, lord of the fee of Pidington, as part of his honor of Huntendon, confirmed to the abbey of
Missenden the hermitage of Mussewell within the manor of Piding-

---

* This Robert de Cheisni bishop of Lincoln gave this charter to the monastery of
Egnesham to testifie the donation of the
church of Newenton made by his brother
Hugh de Cheisny.

*Robertus Lincoln. episcopus universis &c.
Noverit universitas vestra fratrem nostrum
dominum Hugonem de Cheisny filiosque suos*

*nepotes nostros Radulfum et Willielmum con-
cedente et consentiente uxore sua domina
Dionisia ecclesiam de Neuuenton monachis
de Egnesham sub presentia nostra concessisse.
Testibus David. archid. Buck. Rob. Oxon.
archid. Martino thesaur. Magistro Radulfo,
&c.* Ex MS. Bib. Cotton. Claudius A. 8.
Hist. Elien. f. 130.

[t] Regist. S. Frideswidæ, MS. carta 466.
Wikes, sub an.

[u] R. de Diceto, p. 547.　　[x] Chron. Tho.

ton and parish of Ambrosden by this charter.   *Willielmus rex Scotiæ omnibus &c. salutem.   Sciant præsentes et futuri me concessisse et hac carta mea in perpetuam elemosinam confirmasse Deo et ecclesiæ S. Mariæ de Missenden et canonicis ibidem Deo servientibus pro salute mea et antecessorum meorum heremitorium de Musewell perpetuo possidendum libere et quiete cum capella et omnibus pertinentiis suis in bosco et plano in aquis et pratis et cum tota decima de dominio de Peꝗ dyngton in omnibus rebus quæ decimari debent et de decima de padsnagio.   Quare volo et præcipio ut prædicti canonici ecclesiæ de Mussenden habeant et teneant hæc omnia in liberam elemosinam bene et in pace sicut unquam plenius et melius ea habuerunt in tempore D. regis avi mei et regis Malcolmi fratris mei.   Testibus Nicholao cancellario, Willielmo filio Alani dapifero, &c.*[y]*

An. MCXLVIII. 14, 15. *Henry II.*

Simon de Mertoñ knight, son of Wydo, gave to the Knights Tem´ plars one of his vassals, Agnes of Merton, with all that appertained to her.   Foŕ these vassals or servile tenants could be disposed of at the arbitrary pleasure of the lord.

Omnibus &c. Simon de Meriton salutem in domino.   Noverit universitas vestra me pro salute animæ meæ dedisse et quietum clamasse et hac carta mea confirmasse Deo et beatæ Mariæ et fratribus militiæ Templi Salvatoris de Jerusalem Augnetem de Meriton quæ fuit filia Willielmi patris Walteri ejusdem villæ et omnia catalla quæ habet vel habere poterit et omnes proventus qui de ea exierunt vel exibunt, item quod ego et hæredes mei nullam chalengiam poterimus habere de futuro in eam neque in catalla sua neque in proventus suos inde progressos vel progressuros, et præterea volo quod prædicti fratres Templi de premissis præsentibus bonam securitatem et ratam habeant de me et hæredibus meis fideliter tenendis sine omni revocatione et reclamatione dictæ mulieris.   Hanc cartam meam sigilli nostri munimine corroboramus.   Hiis testibus; Domino Waltero Paupere de Meriton, Ha-

y Regist. de Borstall, MS. f. xxxi.

*mundo de Sancta Fide, Fulcone de Meritone, Willielmo de Mort-
lac, &c.* [z]

Nigh which time the said Simon de Meriton, by the consent of
Mabil his wife, granted to Richard, son of John, all his land in the
village of Lydeneston (now Lydston) of the fee of Mabil de Broc
his wife, for the yearly rent of fifteen shillings and one pound of cin-
namon, with one penny and one pair of white gloves at Easter, and
in consideration of two marks of silver in hand ; by this deed.

*Simon de Meriton voluntate Mabiliæ uxoris meæ concessi &c. Ri-
cardo filio Johannis totam terram illam in villa de Lideneston quam
habui ex dono Radulphi filii Galfridi de Lideneston quæ est de fœdo
Mabiliæ de Broc uxoris meæ reddendo inde annuatim quindecem solidos et unam libram cymini cum uno denario et uno pari albarum chi-
rothecarum ad Pascha quem redditum Rogerus filius Radulphi nobis
assignavit. Pro hac concessione dedit dictus Ricardus duas marcas argenti in gersumam, &c. Hiis testibus ; Bardulfo de Cesterton, Thoma
Cossin, Gilberto de Hyda, Johanne le Brun, Waltero de Tywe, Johanne Medico, Lusitano de Cornwall, Roberto de Bradenestun, et
multis aliis* [a]·

An. MCLXIX. 15, 16. Henry II.

Nigh this time Amfride, son of Richard de Oxford, gave to the
monastery of Oseney one hide of land in Chesterton, which con
tained sixty-four acres ; of which the donation and tenure is thus entered in the register of that abbey. *Abbas habet in Cesterton, juxta
Weston unam hidam terræ cum pertinentiis scilicet* LXIV. *acras de*

Theobaldus ar'epus Cant. dedit ecclesiam Sctæ Mariæ de Bix monasterio Sctæ
Trinitatis Lond. Test. Martino abbate de
de Buck. Anselmo abbate de Holm. apud
Cant. Pax Benefactoribus. Ex cart. MSS.
in baga dioc. Cantuar. Quære an sit ec-

clesia de Bix com. Oxon.

Willelmus ar'epus Cant. dedit ecclesiam
S. Mariæ de Bix monasterio Sctæ Trin.
Lond. Test. Johanne epo. Roff. et Helewis
archid. Cant. ib.

[z] Leger-book of Sandford, MS. p. 103.   [a] Regist. Coll. Æn. Nas. Ox. MS. p. 34.

dono Amphridi de Oxon. et confirmatione Roberti filii Amarici, et Ra-dulfi filii ejus in liberam et perpetuam elemosinam.   Ita quod quando dominica terra de Cestreton dat scutagium, dicta terra dabit quintam partem unius scuti, et si dominica terra quieta fuerit ipsa quieta erit [b].*

Reginald de S. Walery having removed the monks of Kings-wood to Haselden, and thence to Tettebiri, where they were incommoded by the want of wood; his son Bernard de S. Walery, lord of the manor of Ambrosden, procured from Roger de Berkley forty acres of land in Mireford, bordering on Kings-wood, and thither again translated that Cistertian abbey: in consideration of which land the said Bernard promised to the said Roger and his heirs his aid and counsel in the king's court, and freedom of toll in his port of St. Walery by this charter. *Bernardus de Sancto Walerico omnibus ho-minibus et amicis suis Franciæ et Angliæ salutem.   Sciant præsentes et futuri quod ego Bernardus concessi Rogero de Bercheley et hæredi-bus suis auxilium et concilium meum in curia domini mei regis Angliæ salva fide mea, et quitantiam in portu Sancti Walerici sibi et hæredi-bus suis et omnibus hominibus mensæ suæ, et ipse dedit et concessit mihi annuente R. filio suo* XL. *acras terræ apud Mireford ad remo-vendam abbathiam meam de Tettebiria, &c.* [c]

An. MCLXX.   16, 17. *Henry II.*

Before this time Sawall de Ossevill, a tenant to Jeffery Mandevil earl of Essex and lord of the manor of Wendlebury, had given to the Knights Templars a grove called East-lyot, lying toward the north part of the old city of Alcester, by this charter.

Sciant &c. quod ego Sawallus de Ossevil dedi et firmiter concessi pro salute animæ meæ et omnium antecessorum meorum lucum quen-dam East-lyot nomine Domino et domui Templi de Jerusalem in perpe-tuam elemosinam solutum et quietum ab omni seculari servitio et secure illum......per mediam terram meam versus septentrionalem partem de

---

[b] Regist. Osen. MS. p. 327.   [c] Mon. Ang. tom. 1. p. 812. b.

ALENCESTRE *usque ad......molendini sui et ego debeo illam warrentizare versus omnes homines, et fratres Templi dederunt mihi de prato suo pro......meorum hominum et illi similiter perceperint de prato meo. Et pro ista donatione et concessione acquietaverunt fratres prædicti de quinque marcis argenti, et hoc feci concessu et testimonio Galfridi domini mei. Testibus; Radulpho de Lesners, Waltero de Mandevill, Willielmo de Iver, Thoma de Hasting, Waltero Camerario, Radulfo Clerico, et aliis.*

Which charter was thus confirmed by Algar earl of Essex. *Algarus comes de Essexa omnibus hominibus et amicis suis salutem. Sciatis me concessisse et hac carta mea confirmasse donationem quam Sawallus de Ossevil fecit domui Templi de Jerusalem scilicet de quodam luco Estlyot nomine sicut carta ipsius Sawalli quam prædicti fratres Templi habent testatur* [d].

Prince Henry, by his father's order crowned king at Westminster on the fourteenth of the calends of July, kept his Christmas at Woodstock, to which place Thomas archbishop of Canterbury was coming to him: but was stopped by express messengers at Southwarc on the fifteenth of the calends of January [e].

An. MCLXXI. 17, 18. *Henry II.*

Bernard de S. Walery, lord of the manor of Ambrosden, seems now to have fallen into the king's displeasure, and to have his lands seized and the rents paid into the Exchequer: for Hugh de S. Germans, sheriff, accounted for fifty pound of the fee of Bernard de S. Walery [f]. But he soon made his peace, and it seems a condition of it, that he gave to the king his manor of Wulvercote, near Oxford and his right of advowson or patronage of the nunnery of Godstow by this charter.

Universis sanctæ matris ecclesiæ filiis Bernardus de Sancto Walerico salutem. Noverit universitas vestra quod ego assensu et volun-

---

[d] Leger-book of Sandford, MS.   [e] R. de Diceto, sub an.   [f] R. Dods. Collect. Rot. Pip. MS.

tate uxoris meæ Avoridis et filiorum meorum Reginaldi Bernardi et Thomæ dedi et concessi in perpetuum domino meo Henrico secundo regi Angliæ sedem abbatiæ de Godestow et totum dominium et jus advocationis ejusdem abbatiæ quod in ea habebam solutum et liberum et quietum de me et de hæredibus meis ab omni servitio et exactione seculari sibi et successoribus suis regibus Angliæ. Ita ut præfata abbatia de cetero habeatur libera et in capite coronæ regis sit, sicut abbatia S. Edmundi et aliæ regales abbatiæ quæ per regnum Angliæ sunt constitutæ. Salvis tantummodo mihi et hæredibus meis ejusdem ecclesiæ orationibus et elemosinæ suffragiis. Manerium etiam totum de Wulgariscote cum omnibus pertinentiis suis dedi et concessi domino meo regi consensu et voluntate præfatæ uxoris meæ et prædictorum hæredum meorum ut quicquid inde fecerit dominus rex de me et hære- dibus meis ratum et inconcussum firmiter observetur. Ita quod neque ego neque hæredes mei regressum habeamus vel calumpniam aliquam versus aliquos de præfato manerio[g].

Which village of Wulvercote and site of the abbey the king gave to those nuns by a charter, wherein he acknowledges to have received them from Bernard de S. Walery.

H. &c. Sciatis me concessisse &c. abbatiæ S. Johannis Bapt. et mo- nialibus ibidem, &c. villam de Wlgaricote et locum in quo ecclesia sua fundata est, &c. ex dono et concessione Bernardi de S. Walerico et hæredum suorum. Qui scilicet Bernardus de S. Walerico prædictam villam et locum illum concessit mihi, &c.[h]

By these and other charters not recited in the Monasticon it does appear, that the second wife of Bernard de S. Walery was Avoris, and not Annora, as she is falsely called by Mr. Dugdale[i], and as it is erroneously printed in the charter of her son Thomas to the said abbey[k]. She seems to have been the daughter of John de St. John lord of Stanton, and to have brought in frank marriage the advow- son of Godstow and the manor of Wulvercote, in which place some

[g] Ex Regist. Godestow, MS.   [h] Ibid.   [i] Dugd. Bar. tom. 1. p. 454. b.   [k] Mon. Ang. tom. 1. p. 526. b.

lands and the site of their house were at the foundation given by her father[1].

An. MCLXXII.   18, 19. *Henry II.*

· Nigh this time Bernard de S. Walery gave to the abbey of Oseney a pool near the Thames with a water course running to the mill belonging to those canons[m] : as also the moiety of seventeen acres and a half of his demesne land in the isle of Oseney[n].   To the hospital of St. Giles's in the suburbs of London he gave several rents and privileges in the hundred of Istlesword[o].   He confirmed and enlarged the gift of his father Reginald to the nuns of Ambresburie, *viz.* Ermundestre and its appertenances in com. Gloc.[p]   He founded an abbey which he called *Locus Dei,* Godestow, between Normandy and Picardy in France[q].   And after the death of his younger son Thomas, he granted this charter to the nuns of Godestow near Oxford.

Bernardus de S. Walerico omnibus S. Ecclesiæ fidelibus tam futuris quam præsentibus et omnibus hominibus suis Francis et Anglis salutem.   Notum sit vobis quod ego Bernardus de S. Walerico dedi et concessi consensu hæredum meorum Reginaldi et Bernardi in perpetuam elemosinam ecclesiæ Dei et S. Mariæ et S. Johannis Baptistæ de Godestow et sanctimonialibus ibidem Deo servientibus pro salute regis Henrici et reginæ A. et filiorum suorum, pro salute quoque mea et uxoris meæ Avoridis et liberorum meorum et pro remedio peccatorum meorum et pro animabus patris et matris meæ uxorisque meæ Matildis et omnium fidelium defunctorum, insulam in qua prædicta ecclesia fundata est quæ vocatur Godestow cum omnibus pertinentiis suis et Lichesiam totam et molendinum de Wulgaricote, et Boicham, et Heringesham, et Labeie et unam piscariam de Werchama, et mansionem Osmundi, et insulam intra duos pontes et Pechesiam, et quinque solidos ad falcandum idem pratum ad festum S. Johannis Baptistæ, et XII. *denarios in Wulgaricote, et* II[s]. *in Eardintune, et* IV[s]. *in*

---

[1] Mon. Ang. tom. 1. p. 525. b.   [m] Ib. tom. 2. p. 140. b.   [n] Ib. p. 141. b.   [o] Ib. p. 381. a.   [p] Ibid. p. 868. b.   [q] Neustria Pia. ·

Leaga, et unam dimidiam hidam de dominio de Wulgaricote, et x.
acras de eadem, et mensuram bladi. Hæc omnia prædictis moniali-
bus concedo bene et in pace et honorifice et sine servitio tenenda libere
et quiete et perpetualiter. Testibus hiis; Alelmo de Frutariis, Wil-
lielmo de Brausa, Hugone Malard, et Baldwino Malard fratre ejus,
Pagano de Westbiri, Waltero Bavil, Ricardo Harenge, et Hugone
dapifero, et Ernulfo clerico, et Waltero Dale, et Elrardo, et Barino,
et Lamberto coco, et Mattheo mareschallo, et Hugone de Caham, et
Bernardo Covele, et Waltero de Wesburi, et Waltero de Burtunc, et
Roberto Chawe, et Mileto capellano, Radulfo clerico de Dumaris,
Rogero de Brausa, Rogero coco, et aliis [r].

An. MCLXXIII. 19, 20. *Henry II.*

King Henry the son, by the instigation of the king of France,
breaking into rebellion against his father, to secure the interest of
Scotland, granted to William king of Scots all Northumberland to
the river Tyne; and to David his brother for the like homage and
service he gave the honor of Huntingdon, and for augmentation
added the county of Cambridge to that earldom[s]; by which means
the said earl David became lord of the fee of Merton and Pidington:
who, joining with his brother king William, raised great commotions
in England, and was chosen governor of the town and castle in Leicester then in rebellion against the old king[t].

Before this time Amory of St. Mary's knight, and preceptor of
the Templars, demised to Hugh de Merton one virgate of land in
Merton, to be held in demesne from the Templars at the yearly rent
of ten shillings. *Universis &c. Americus de S. Maria Chevaler mili-*
tibus Templi in Anglia salutem. Noverit universitas vestra nos de
consilio et assensu capituli nostri in paschate apud...... concessimus et
hac carta nostra confirmavimus Hugoni filio Willielmi de Meriton
unam virgatam terræ cum omnibus pertinentiis suis in Meriton illam
scilicet quam prædictus Willielmus pater suus tenuit, habendam et te-

---

[r] Regist. Abbat. de Godestow, MS.   [s] Chron. Jo. Brompt. sub an.   [t] Ib. sub an. 1174.

nendam filiis et hæredibus suis vel cui assignare voluerint de tenemento dominorum Templariorum libere quiete bene-in pace et integre, reddendo inde annuatim domui nostre x. sol. sterlingorum ad duos anni terminos scilicet ad festum S. Michaelis v. solidos et ad pascha v. solidos pro omni servitio consuetudine et exactione. Salvo domui nostre quod ipse nobis in obitu suo faciat id quod alii liberi homines nostri faciant et in obitu hæredum et assignatorum, &c. Hiis testibus; Fratre Mauritio capellano, fratre Alano Martell, fratre Johanne Lupo, fratre Willielmo de Midleton, fratre Hugone filio Baldwini, fratre Petro de Suavibus, fratre Ricardo de Marisco, fratre Ricardo de Insula, &c.

An. MCLXXIV. 20, 21. *Henry II.*

While the king was detained in Normandy by the rebellion of his sons, Jeffery his base son by Rosamund, bishop elect of Lincoln, raised an immense sum of money through this whole diocese; but either from an honourable sense that the king had no occasion for it, or from a prudent fear of exposing himself to danger by illegal exactions, he had the money refunded to the rural deans, who were to distribute it to those persons of whom it had been levied in their respective districts [u]. This lay prelate had now procured a dispensation for his defect of birth and age from the pope, and the confirmation of it was referred to a great council held at Woodstock in the week before Midsummer, an. 1175, where the case was argued and the dispensation allowed before the two kings, father and son, and Richard archbishop of Canterbury, with eight of his suffragan bishops, &c. [x] Upon which assent granted on the seventh of the ides of July, the said Jeffery bishop elect returned into England on the fifteenth of the calends of August; and on the calends of that month was with solemn procession received at Lincoln [y].

Thomas Basset, lord of the manors of Burcester, Wrechwike, and

[u] Wharton. Ang. Sac. tom. 2. p. 378.　[x] Jo. Brompt. p. 1103.　[y] R. de Diceto, p. 587.

Stratton, in the twenty-first of Henry the Second, was constituted one of the king's justices in his court of judicature[z]. Simon earl of Northampton brought his action in the king's court against David, brother to the king of Scotland, for the honor of Huntendon, which he pleaded to belong to him by right of inheritance[a]; and, after judgment given for him, the king delivered him the castle of Huntingdon and that earldom, by which title he became lord of the manors of Merton and Pidington.

An. MCLXXV. 21, 22. Henry II.

Aubrey Dammartin earl of Bologne, who, in the preceding year was present at the court of Foudringhei, held by Simon earl of Northampton and Huntingdon[b], did now hold in fee from the said earl Simon the manors of Merton and Pidington; in which latter he confirmed the hermitage of Musewell to the abbey of Missenden, by this charter.

Notum sit omnibus tam præsentibus quam futuris quod ego Albricus comes de Damarun dedi et concessi consensu Reginaldi filii et hæredis mei Deo et ecclesiæ S. Mariæ de Missenden et canonicis ibidem Deo servientibus heremitorium de Mussewell cum capella ejusdem loci et cum tota terra sicut eam fossis circumdederunt cum omnibus pertinentiis suis et totam decimam de Pidington et decimam de pasnagio et pasnagium quietum de suis dominicis porcis ejusdem loci et communionem pasturæ tam in bosco quam in plano suis dominicis animalibus ejusdem loci et de bosco quod opus fuerit ad emendationem domorum et sepium suarum. Quare volo et concedo et præsenti carta confirmo ut præfati canonici habeant et teneant in perpetuum prædictam elemosinam liberam et quietam ab omni servitio et consuetudine et exactione pro salute mea et uxoris meæ et omnium antecessorum et successorum meorum. Testibus; Juliano de le Hare, Mattheo Fannel de Lilebone,

---

[z] Dugd. Bar. tom. 1. p. 383.   [a] Jo. Brompt. p. 1094.   [b] Thoroton, Antiq. of Noting. p. 370.

Engelmero de Saintbeierie, Yvone fratre ejus, Simone de Bracle, Radulpho de Wyntena, Waltero de Patre, Roberto de Parys de Sachedon, Willielmo de Wrevilla, Radulpho filio et aliis[c].

. This charter is corruptly printed in the Monasticon, and is set before the other grant of Mussewell by Simon de Gerardmulin, to which it ought to have been postponed. But indeed this inverted position was an error not so much of the editor Mr. Dugdale, nor of the transcriber Mr. Anthony a Wood, as of the ancient writer of the chartulary of Borstall, who, through ignorance or inadvertence, has often confounded the order of those records, and has very frequent literal mistakes, of which there is one apparent in the last recited charter, *decimam de passuagio et passuagium quietum de suis dominicis porcis*, for *decimam de pasnagio et pasnagium quietum*, the running of hogs to feed on acorns. And I believe among the witnesses Waltero de Patre, should be Waltero de Povre.

An. MCLXXVI. 22, 23. Henry II.

The king this year, in a council of his bishops, earls, and barons, granted his daughter in marriage to the king of Sicily, of which many honourable persons were sent to inform that prince; and among others were Richard de Camvill, lord of the manor and castle of Midleton[d]. Bertram de Verdon, lord of the manor of Heth in this county, now founded the abbey of Croxden in com. Staff. and nigh this time confirmed to the canons of Kenilworth that grant of the church of Heth, which Lesceline his mother had made to them.

An. MCLXXVII. 23, 24. Henry II.

A charter of the king to the church of St. Augustin in Canterbury, dated this year, has, among other witnesses, Gilbert Basset eldest son of Thomas Basset lord of Burcester, with Reginald de Courtney his father-in-law, and Thomas Basset his brother, &c.[e] About which time Roger de Sanford, knight, granted to the church of St.

c Cartular. de Borstal, MS. f. xxx.   d Rog. de Hoveden, p. 551.   e Ashmole MS.

Nicholas in Sanford, and to the nuns there serving God, one acre of land in Bruhell (now Brill) which Alred his grandfather had given to his mother in frank marriage, from which they should receive two shillings yearly, or one seam of nuts *in capite jejuni*, on Ash-wednesday[f]. Which Roger de Sanford, by Milisent his wife, had issue Ralph de Sanford knight, whose daughter and heir, Mabile, was married to Thomas Bussell of Sanford, who confirmed his predecessor's charity in the year 1254[g]. This nunnery of Sanford or Litlemoore is in two several volumes of the Monasticon falsely ascribed to the county of Berks[h].

An. MCLXXVIII. 24, 25. *Henry II.*

Simon St. Liz the third, earl of Northampton and Huntendon, lord of the fee of Pidington and Merton, confirmed his father's donation of the latter to the Knights Templars, by this charter.

Simon filius Simonis com. Northampt. &c. Omnibus &c. salutem. Sciatis me concessisse et confirmasse donationem illam quam pater meus dedit fratribus Templi de manerio de Meriton. Et volo et firmiter præcipio quod totam terram illam libere et in pace teneant sicut elemosinam liberam et quietam ab omni sectantia et exactione. Testibus; Roberto Grimbald, et Roberto Foliot, et Simone filio Petri, et Roberto filio Hugonis, et Gaufrido de Normanvill, et Sahero de Quincy[i]

The old king was this summer at Woodstock, where, on the eighth of the ides of August, he knighted Jeffery his younger son duke of Britain[k].

An. MCLXXIX. 25, 26. *Henry II.*

Thomas Basset, lord of the manor of Burcester, one of the king's justices, and in this twenty-fifth of Henry the Second appointed a judge itinerant for Berkshire, Oxfordshire, and several other counties, for his special services to this king in divers wars had the lord-

---

[f] Mon. Ang. tom. 3. p. 13.　　[g] Ibid. p. 14.　　[h] Ibid. tom. 1. p. 481. et tom. 3. p. 13.
[i] Leger-book of Sandford, f. 102.　　[k] R. de Diceto, sub an.

ship of Hedendon, with the hundred of Bolendon, and the hundred without North-gate, Oxford, given him in fee farm for the rent of twenty pound *per annum* to the king's Exchequer[1]. From whence this branch of that great family had the title of Basset of Hedendon, and the third part of the hundred without North-gate was called Basset's fee, and now belongs to Brazen Nose Coll. Oxon[m]. Which Thomas Basset died about this time, and by Alice Dunstanvil his wife, left issue three sons, Gilbert, Thomas, and Alan, as also a daughter wife of Albert de Grelle[n]

An. MCLXXX. 26, 27. Henry II.

Bernard de S. Walery, lord of the manor of Ambrosden, among many other royal favors had the manor of Erdington * (now Ardington in com. Berk.) given to him, which manor had been formerly granted to the abbey of Egnesham, of whom Remigius bishop of

---

* Gilbert Basset granted his demesne meadow in Erdintun, com. Berks, to the abbey of Reading, by this charter.

Sciant præsentes et futuri quod ego Gilebertus Bassette dedi et concessi pro amore Dei et pro salute animæ meæ et animæ patris mei et animæ matris meæ et Thomæ filii mei et omnium antecessorum meorum et successorum abbati et monachis de Rading totum dominicum pratum meum apud Erdetun quod duobus locis continetur et appellatur Lankedal, Tenendum de me et hæredibus meis ad firmam perpetuam reddendo annuatim mihi et hæredibus meis xx solidos ad festum S. Johannis Baptistæ pro omni servitio terreno. Concessi etiam præfato abbati et monachis ut habeant propter prænominatum redditum xxiiii boves cum dominicis bobus meis in omnibus pratis meis et in omnibus pratis ubicunque communem pasturam habeo et habere

debeo in boreali plaga de Erdetun a die quo totum foenum meum dominicum asportatum fuerit, vel secundum oportunitatem temporis asportari poterit usque in diem quo prata ponantur in defensum. Ita ut in quocunque pratorum ex illa parte de Erdetune communi pastura potero warantizare boves meos warantizabo boves abbatis et monachorum de Radinge. Quod si abbas et monachi de Radinge xxiiii boves in prænominata pastura vel habere noluerint vel non potuerint habeant in eadem totidem averia eadem libertate qua boves eis habere concessi. Ut igitur de hac mea donatione et concessa de me et hæredibus meis firmam et perpetuam habeant securitatem et warantum eam sigilli mei impressione confirmavi. Pro hac itaque concessione dederunt mihi præfatus abbas et monachi xv marcas argenti. T. Cartular. abbat. de Radinges. MS. f. LIX. a.

---

[1]Dugd. Bar. tom. 1. p. 383. a.   [m] Regist. Coll. Æn. Nas. MS.   [n] Dugd. Bar. ib.

Lincoln borrowed the use of it for a convenient place of residence :
after whose death it was seized by the king, and was afterward bestowed on this favourite, against whom Godfry and Robert, successive
abbots of Egnesham, brought several actions without effect; and the
disputes of title held for many years, possession being still kept by
this Bernard de S. Walery, by his son Thomas, by Robert earl of
Dreux, and by Richard earl of Cornwall, who successively enjoyed
this barony of S. Walery. The history of it, as inserted in the register of Egnesham, is worthy to be inserted.

*Manerium de Erdinthon in possessione ecclesiæ de Egnesham per
multum temporis mansit. Et quidam Remigius tunc Lincolniæ episcopus petiit illud manerium sibi accommodandum ut ibi possit per aliquod tempus perendinari, et ei concessum est. Et paulo post Remigius
in fata decessit scisitus de dicto manerio tanquam de accommodatione.
Et dominus Henricus rex Angliæ secundus seisivit baroniam dicti episcopi et dictum manerium de Erdinthon, quod manerium dictus dominus rex tradidit cuidam Bernardo de Sancto Walerico quem Gode-
fridus abbas de Egnesham sæpius convenit coram rege de jure suo sed
nihil profecit. Obtulit ei Bernardus homagium, sed recusante abbate
Godefrido Robertus secundus episcopus Lincolniæ suscepit illud salvo
jure abbatis et conventus de Egnesham. Defuncto illo Godefrido successit ei quidam abbas Robertus nomine qui dictum Bernardum implacitavit per breve de recto in curia ejusdem Roberti tunc episcopi Lincolniæ. Sed episcopo ante finem placiti defuncto abbas Robertus in
curia regis Johannis implacitavit, et electi sunt duodecim homines legales de vicineto, quibus ad curiam apud Southwyk conductis, et pro
dicto manerio juramentum præstare paratis suspensæ sunt querelæ
omnes usque ad reditum regis de transmarinis partibus. Abbas Robertus cito postea migravit ad dominum ; successit ei abbas Adam qui
per breve in recto in jus vocavit Thomam de S. Walerico in curia domini Lincolniæ episcopi. Et cum jam comparere oporteret, turbatio
regni exorta est per adventum Lodowysi in Angliam, et siluerunt leges inter arma. Thoma quoque non longe postea defuncto, translata
est per filiam suam hæreditas ad Robertum comitem de Drus quem per*

*literas regias in curia regis in jus tractum cum justitiarii Oxoniam
devenissent et jurati electi essent præsentes et dies quæ instaret ad judicium proferri debuisset, allatæ sunt literæ regis Robertum seisinam
perdidisse omnium quæ habebat in Anglia et custodiam terrarum
suarum traditam fuisse domino Ricardo filio regis*[o].

An. MCLXXXI.   27, 28. *Henry II.*

Henry de Oily *, baron of Hooknorton and lord of the manors of
Weston and Chesterton, gave four hides of land in his village of
Chesterton to the abbey of Egnesham in com. Oxon, by this charter.

*Notum sit omnibus qui sunt et qui venturi sint quod ego Henricus
de Oily concessi et dedi ecclesiæ Dei et S. Mariæ de Egnesham quatuor hidas terræ apud Cestreton villam meam in perpetuum pro anima
patris mei et Edid sororis meæ, duas videlicet in Bruceria et duas in
villa Cestreton liberas et quietas ab omnibus querelis excepto Murdredo et Danegeldo. Testibus; Nicholao capellano meo, Walchelino
presbytero de Weston, Nigello de Oily, Widone de Oily, Leonardo de
Witefeld, Willielmo de Cantelup, Petro de Witefeld, Willielmo filio
Richardi*[p].

An. MCLXXXII.   28, 29. *Henry II.*

Gilbert Basset, baron of Hedingdon and lord of the manors of
Burcester, Wrechwike, and Stratton, who had his mansion seat and
park at Burcester, this year[q] founded there a religious house for a
prior and eleven canons of the Augustine order dedicated to St. Ed-

---

* *Henricus d'Oily omnibus &c. Sciatis me
concessisse et confirmasse donationem quam
pater meus et mater mea abbati et conventui
de Thama fecerunt de terra, videlicet de
Weston quæ juxta nemus de Otteleia jacet
XXXV acras ne quis filiorum meorum aut hæredum post obitum meum abbatem et conven-*
*tum de Thame eo quod abbatia de Otteleia
apud Thamam transposita sit inquietare voluerit. Test. Ricardo Daumari cantor. et
archid. Linc. Radulfo Daumari &c. Ex
Cartulario S. Mariæ de Thama. Bib. Cotton. Julius. C. 7. fol. 14.*

---

[o] Regist. de Egnesham, MS.   [p] Ibid. carta 22.   [q] Dugd. Bar. tom. 1. p. 383. a.

burg, with consent of Egeline his wife, who, surviving her husband
and adding other benefactions, was reputed a co-founder. The foundation is thus entered in a very ancient manuscript that gives a short
account of the houses of religion in the several counties of England.
Com. Oxon. Cœnob. Prioratus S. Edburgæ Burcestriæ pro canonicis
XI. *per Gilbertum Basset et* ...... *Courtney uxorem*[r]. When the first
prior John and his eleven brethren (which institution was to answer
the number of our Saviour and his apostles) were introduced, he
gave them the church of Burcester, with all its appertenances, with
the churches of Ardinton, Comton, and Missenden, with several lands,
messuages, tithes, and privileges in Burcester and Wrechwike, by
this charter.

Omnibus sanctæ matris ecclesiæ fidelibus presentibus et futuris Gil-
bertus Basset salutem. Notum sit universitati vestræ quod ego dedi
et concessi Johanni priori de Bernecestre et canonicis ibidem Deo ser-
vientibus pro salute corporis et animæ domini mei regis Henrici et pro
salute corporis et animæ meæ et uxoris meæ Egelinæ et liberorum
meorum et pro animabus antecessorum et successorum meorum eccle-
siam de Bernecestre cum omnibus pertinentiis suis. Et de incremento
totam terram quæ est inter croftam Gileberti molendinarii et messua-
gium quod fuit Adam et ipsum messuagium usque ad calceiam vivarii
mei cum quinque acris quas prædictus Adam tenuit. Et messuagium
quod fuit Osmundi Favel cum crofta. Et messuagium Willielmi Au-
rigæ et messuagium Alwardi cum crofta in qua ipsa duo prædicta mes-
suagia fuerunt. Et præterea decimam carectam ligni mei, ut sicut
venitur de bosco attrahatur in curiam canonicorum sicut in meam.
Et quoddam pratunculum quod vocatur Hamma quod extenditur de
crofta Serici de Wrechwic per la mulnedam usque illuc ubi novus ri-
vulus descendit in veterem rivulum et ipsam mulnedam ad faciendum
ibi molendinum ubi fuit antiquitus vel si alicubi in confinio per illam
mulnedam melius fieri poterit fiat. Et pasturam in meam dominica
pastura ad tres charucatas boum trahentium una cum bobus meis tra-

---

[r] B. Twine's MS. in C.C.C.

hentibus.   Et ad quatuor centum oves pasturam ad ecclesiam perti-
nentem tam in dominica mea quam in communi pastura.   Et quitan-
ciam de pasnagio, et homines suos de eis tenentes liberos et quietos ab
omni servitio quod ad me pertinet.   Præterea ecclesiam de Ardintona
cum pertinentiis suis, ecclesiam de Comtona cum pertinentiis suis, ec-
clesiam de Missenden cum pertinentiis suis in perpetuam elemosinam
liberam et quietam ab omni seculari servitio et exactione in pratis et
pasturis in mariscis in molendinis in viis et semitis et in omnibus locis
sicut unquam aliqua persona melius tenuit et liberius.   Et ego Gile-
bertus Basset has prædictas ecclesias et possessiones prædictas cano-
nicis prædictis de omni seculari servitio warantizabo, et prædicti ca-
nonici supradictas ecclesias vel possessiones non debent dare vel pro
alia ecclesia vel aliis possessionibus commutare neque ad firmam dare.
Hiis testibus ; Rob. de Witefeld tunc vic. Thoma de Durevall, Ege-
lina uxore mea, Aliz Basset, Henrico de Curtenai, Rob. de Amalri,
Hug. Durevall, Thoma Basset, Fulcone Basset, Jacobo de Gerard-
mulin, Walerano de Chrichlade, Rob. le Waleis, Bartholomeo capel-
lano, Rob. filio Rad. Will. de Covele, Will. filio Rici. Warino pin-
cerna, Hasculfo de Bixa, Thoma Britone, Adam clerico, Ric. clerico
de Calverton, et multis aliis [s].

This first charter of foundation is in a long slip of parchment, with
a seal appending of green wax, with the rude effigies of a man on
horseback and this inscription.   ✠ SIGILLUM GILBERTI BASSET.
There is another ancient copy of this charter entituled *Carta Gileberti Basset de fundatione ecclesiæ de Burcestre,* under the copy is
subscribed, *Cum bulla Celestini papæ de confirmatione ecclesiarum de
Ardyngton, Messenden et Cumpton.*

Soon after the said Gilbert Basset gave to the same prior and canons a second charter in parchment, with seal appending of the
same impress, which recites the chapel of Stratton as an appertenance to Burcestre, with lands in the said parish of Stratton, and
then repeats literally the former donation with the same witnesses.

---

[s] Ex Orig. penes hon. virum D. Gulielmum Glynne Baronettum.

Omnibus sanctæ matris ecclesiæ fidelibus præsentibus et futuris Gilebertus Basset salutem.　Notum sit universitati vestræ quod ego dedi et concessi Johanni priori de Bernecestre et canonicis ibidem Deo servientibus pro salute corporis et animæ domini mei regis Henrici et pro salute corporis et animæ meæ et uxoris meæ Egelinæ et liberorum meorum et pro animabus antecessorum et successorum meorum ecclesiam de Bernecestre cum omnibus pertinentiis suis scilicet capellam de Strattun et in eadem villa de Strattun unam virgatam terræ collectam de terra rusticorum quæ data fuit in dote prædictæ capellæ et de incremento unam virgatam terræ in eadem villa quam Walterus filius Ansgerii et Aeliz uxor Gileberti le Crith tenuerunt et in prædicta Bernecestria totam terram, &c. [t]

There is a third and larger charter made within the same year with the additional gift of forty acres of his demesne, twenty acres in one of the common fields, and twenty in the other, &c.

Omnibus sanctæ matris ecclesiæ filiis præsentibus et futuris Gilebertus Basset salutem in Domino, &c. . . . . Quadraginta acras de dominico meo scilicet viginti in uno campo ex quibus quinque acræ sunt in furlungia quæ descendit in rivulum ultra spinam et quinque acræ in furlungia intra vallem quæ vertitur apud Rugweiam et tres acræ in Copeshlow-furlung, et quatuor acræ et dimid. in Ruxfurlung, et duæ acræ et dimid. quæ vertuntur in Parroc et in altero campo viginti acras scilicet in Heilefurlung et buttes apud Ymbehlowesmer ad complendum numerum viginti acrarum, et præterea unam virgatam terræ in Stratton ad luminare prædictæ ecclesiæ scilicet illam quam Walterus et uxor Gileberti militis tenuerunt cum omnibus pertinentiis suis præter unam croftam ejusdem virgatæ terræ pro qua dedi sæpedictis canonicis alteram croftam quæ vocatur Grescroft in excambium prædictæ croftæ.　Et præterea concessi conventionem factam inter prædictos canonicos sæpedictæ ecclesiæ et homines meos de Wrechwyke videlicet quod sæpe dicti canonici concesserunt prædictis hominibus duas acras prati pro capitalibus suarum croftarum secus rivulum ver

[t] Ex Orig. penes hon. virum D. Gulielmum Glynne Baronettum.

sus molendinum fluentem ad faciendum stagnum et viam ad molendi-
num, et si forte contigerit quod in futuro molendinum non sit prædictis
canonicis necessarium prædictæ acræ prati ad sæpe dictos canonicos
redeant ita quod canonici viam in pristinam planitiem reparent et ho-
minibus meis prædictis terra illorum remaneat, et præterea concessi
sæpedictis canonicis liberam capellam curiæ meæ et de curiis hære-
dum meorum cum oblationibus et omnibus adventionibus ad liberam
capellam pertinentibus, &c.

To this original parchment are the same witnesses, a label appending, the seal broke off[u].

The charter of Gilbert Basset recited in the patent of confirmation
in the ninth of Edward the Second, inserted in the Monasticon, is
made up of those three charters reduced into one, with some small
omissions and alterations[x]. Of the name Edburg, to whom the
church was dedicated, Mr. Cressy[y] reckons up no less than seven
English saints; St. Eadburg of Winchester, St. Eadburg of Kent,
St. Eadburg of Peterburrow, St. Eadburg of Glocester, St. Eadburg of Ailsbury, St. Eadburg of Buggan, and St. Eadburg
daughter of king Edward the elder, though this last seems the
same with her of Winchester. We may suppose the saint of this
priory was the holy virgin of Ailsbury, which town was given to her
and her sister Eaditha by their father Frewald, which sisters here
taking the veil of religion were both reputed saints[z]. Edburg gave
name to a place in the Chiltern Bucks, now called Edburton[a]: as
also to Edburgberie, now Adderbury* com. Oxon. of which place

---

* Personæ et vicarii eccl'iæ de Adderbury, com. Oxon.

Edmundus de Maydenestan rector eccl'iæ de Abberbury. 22. E. 1. Prin. Coll.
vol. 3. p. 596.

Ld. cardinal Nonmacen parson of Adderbury, 1374. Fox, Acts. Mon. vol. 1. p.
430.

Ex libro scripto per Johannem Chalkhill
socium coll. Winton. continent. seriem sociorum ejusdem coll. circa finem est cata-
logus omnium incumbentium ecclesiarum

[u] Ex Orig. penes hon. vir. D. Gul. Glynne Bar.   [x] Mon. Ang. tom. 2. p. 283. b.
[y] Cressy, Church Hist.   [z] Camd. in Catticuch.   [a] Ib.

Mr. Ray had a fanciful mistake, that the town had its name from those stones which are called Orphiomorphits, from the figure of a serpent or adder; and a very worthy author who corrects that sur-

de suo patronatu inter quos hæc de eccl'ia de Adderbury transcripsit vir rev. Matth. Hutton, S. T. P.

Custos et scolares coll. de Winton. receperunt de Will'o Gylle de Witteney 9 marc. de bonis cardinalis quondam rectoris eccl'iæ de Eabberbury pro reparationibus ejusd. eccl'iæ 7 Oct. 22. Ric. 2.

Johannes Wikeham alias Fyvian unus e sociis Novi Coll. nominatus per fundatorem, A. M. et decret. dr. rector de Crondale 1385, et eccl'iæ paroch. de Broughton, Linc. dioc. 1398, erat etiam rector ultimus eccl'iæ de Abberbury quam dimisit 1381. pro Crondale.

Joannes Monke unus ex primis sociis Novi Collegii, A. M. vicarius 1ᵘˢ. de Abberbury, obiit ibidem 1414.

Willelmus Frythe, A. M. et S. T. B. vicarius de Abberbury presentatus 1414, permutat cum rectore capellæ Scti Leonardi 1415, quam rectoriam dimisit 1419, presentatus ad eccl'iam de Colorne, et obiit 1420, sepultus in medio novæ capellæ.

Joh. Love, LL. B. vicar. de Abberbury presentatus 1415, permutavit cum rectore eccl'iæ paroch. de Chesylhurst, in dioc. Roff. 1426.

John Awnsell vicar. Abberbury obiit 1431.

Joh. Clerke, S. T. B. vicarius de Abberbury presentatus 1431, resignavit 1443.

Will. Bedmyster, A. M. vicarius de Abberbury presentatus 1443, obiit ibidem 1462.

Martin Joyner alias Bonolyth, A. M. et ꜱ. T. B. vicarius de Aberbury presentatus

1462, postea S. T. D. et cancellar. eccl. Lincoln. resignavit 1481, electus in custodem Novi Coll. 1475, recusavit.

Will'us Dorset, S. T. B. vicar. de Abberbury 1482, obiit ibid. 1510.

John. Page, A. M. vicar. de Abberbury 1510, ubi obiit 1517.

Rad'us Barnacke, S. T. P. vicar de Abberbury 1517, qui obiit 1526. per resign. mag'ri Read, 1520, factus fuit custos coll. Winton.

Joh. London, LL. D. eccl'iarum Windsor. et Ebor. canonicus, vicar. de Abberbury, Novi Coll. custos, et eccl. cath. de Oseney decanus 1528, resignavit 1542.

Joh. Cottrell, LL. D. vicar. de Abberbury 1542, resignavit 1551.

Will'us Binsley, LL. B. vicar de Abberbury 1551, resign. 1554, fuit is archid. North'ton.

Christoph. Rawlins, S. T. B. vicar de Eabberbury 1554, et fundator scolæ grammaticalis ibidem, obiit ibidem 1589.

Joh. Pryme, S. T. D. vicar. de Eabberbury 1589, obiit ibidem 1596.

Chr. Budd, A. M. vicar 1596, obiit ibidem 1627.

Will. Oldys, S. T. B. vicarius 1627, cæsus a militibus circa ann. 1644.

Will'us Barker, S. T. D. prebendar. Cantuar. vicar. Abberbury, postea rector de Hardwyck.

Will Beaw, A. M. socius coll. Novi presentatus ad vicar. de Eabberbury, postea S. T. B. consecratus in ep'um Landav. Jun. 22. 1679.

mise is (I doubt) as much mistaken; *That the town* (says he) *has not its name from these stones (as Mr. Ray thinks) I dare confidently avouch, Adderbury being only the vulgar name; for, in the court rolls of New College (and other instruments) to which the lordship of the town belongs, it is written Eabberbury, perhaps from St. Ebba the tutelar saint of the church*[b]. But whatever corruptions there may be in the latter records, it is certain that, in the great inquisition of William the Conqueror, this place was called Edburgeberie, which in Edward the Confessor's reign had been the possession of Edwine earl of Mercia, and in the time of survey was the tenure of Robert de Statford[c]: and preserved the like name in many succeeding reigns. Besides this priory of Burcester, the abbies of Evesham in com. Wigorn. of Egnesham com. Oxon. of Berking com. Essex, and several others were dedicated to St. Mary and St. Edburg. The greatest memorial which now remains of this saint at Burcester is a spring or fountain-head called St. Edburg's well, which rises in the west part of the common field belonging to Kings-End; no question but in the superstitious age there was great resort of the lame and blind with their vows and their offerings, the sanctity of waters being such a devout fancy among our ancestors that to restrain the superstition of it, the sixtieth canon in a council under Edgar forbids ρılpeoρɣunʒa, which word though the Latin version has applied to *will-worship,* yet it ought to be rendered *well-worship,* or a fond running to be cured at wells or fountains: as is abundantly proved by Dr. Hammond[d]; who, to the same purpose, quotes a Saxon Penitential, and Homily of bishop Lupus, and the injunctions of Oliver Sutton, bishop of Lincoln, against that practice in this very county. But since the Reformation, our saints lost their honor, and the waters their supposed virtue. So as the current of St. Edburg's well by long neglect was stopt up, till in the year 1666, being a dry summer, by the advice and care of Mr. John Coker gent. the head

---

[b] Dr. Plot's Nat. Hist. of Oxf. ch. 5. §. 94.   [c] Doomsday-book.   [d] Annot. Coloss. ch. 2. v. 23. not. 1. in voce ἐθελοθρησκεία.

of it was opened and cleansed, at which time it gave such a sudden and great supply of water, that had the old adorers now lived, this should have been esteemed another miracle. There was a neat and much frequented walk leading to it from the priory and town, which, in a record about the tenth of Edward the First, is called **Seynt Edburg hes grene way**, and *Via Sanctæ Edburge*[e]. It is now by corruption called Eadburg balk*, *i. e.* the Edburg way balk, it running as a green balk between plough-ridges on each side. It begins at the west part of Kings-End in a narrow passage between two houses of Mr. John Coker, now or late in the occupation of Ralph Edwards on the south, and Edward Bridgman on the north: it extends half a mile in length leading to no other place but directly where it terminates, the head of the spring; the breadth is too much lessened by some encroachments of the plough, and there be some intermissions in the path by a like trespass of the husbandman: it being once a high-way, no propriety is yet claimed of it; but by custom the grass or profit of herbage is allowed to the tithing-man of Kings-End. Nor was this the only well made sacred by St. Edburg; there was another of the like name and reputation in the city of Canterbury, of which we read in the time of Athelred archbishop, Christ-Church recovered six mansions in Canterbury, nigh Edburg-well[f].

An. MCLXXXIII. 29, 30. *Henry II.*

Jeffery the unordained bishop elect of Lincoln did, on the feast of Epiphany at Marleborow before the king and archbishop of Canterbury, renounce his election to that see[g]; which within this same year was given to Walter de Constance the king's clerk, archdeacon of Oxford and canon of Lincoln, who, being consecrated at Anjou by Ri-

* Tadbury-balk.

[e] Ex Autographo penes Joh. Coker, gen. [f] Wharton, Ang. Sac. tom. 1. p. 53. [g] R. de Diceto, p. 614.

chard archbishop of Canterbury, returned and took possession in the following year [h].

An. MCLXXXIV. 30, 31. *Henry II.*

Bernard de S. Walery, lord of Ambrosden, founded a nunnery at Stodley in this neighbourhood, which he endowed with half a hide of land in Horton, by this charter.

Notum sit omnibus tam præsentibus quam futuris quod ego Bernardus de S. Walerico dedi et concessi Deo et ecclesiæ S. Mariæ de Stodley et sanctimonialibus ibidem Deo servientibus dimidiam hidam terræ in Horton eandem scilicet quam Normannus tenuit tenendam in perpetuam elemosinam de me et hæredibus meis liberam et quietam sicut elemosinam ab omnibus servitiis mihi et hæredibus meis pertinentibus pro Henrico et pro uxore sua et pro liberis suis et pro animabus patris et matris meæ et pro anima Matildis uxoris meæ et pro animabus antecessorum meorum et pro me ipso et uxore Avoride et pro liberis meis ut Deus det eis et nobis concedat vitam æternam. Hiis testibus ; Roberto vicecom. Bernardo milite, Johanne de Occeleia, Rogero de Sanford, Herberto de Piry, Ernulfo clerico, Everardo de Abbe, Hugone de S. Germano, et omni curia mea [i].

The church of Horton was before given to the abbey of Egnesham in this county by Walcheline Hareng, and was confirmed by Hugh bishop of Lincoln, with several other churches.

Omnibus Christi fidelibus Hugo Lincolniensis episcopus, &c. Confirmamus ex dono Johannis de S. Johanne ecclesiam de Stanton. Ex dono Davidis regis Scotiæ ecclesiam de Meriton. Ex dono Jordani de Sai ecclesiam de Sulethorn. Ex dono Hugonis de Chaisneto eccle-

---

CORNWELL.

Ego Hawysia de Gray pro anima Joh. de Gray fratris mei quondam Norwic ep'i et voluntate dni. Rob. de Gray filii et hæredis

mei concessi S. Mariæ de Oseney eccl'iam de Cornwell; hiis test. dno. Waltero de Gray Wigorn. ep'o filio meo. Reg. Osen. f. 103.

---

[h] Mat. West. sub an.   [i] Mon. Ang. tom. 1. p. 101.

siam de Niwenton. Ex dono Alexandri de Barton ecclesiam de Barton. Ex dono Petri de Mara medietatem ecclesiæ de Heyford. Ex dono Walchelini Hareng ecclesiam de Horton. Ex dono Stephani de Pinfold et Aliciæ uxoris suæ ecclesiam de Cornwell, &c. [k]

There is another confirmation of the same bishop, that recites the pension * reserved to the monks from this and other churches.

Hugo Lincoln. episcopus, &c. ecclesias et pensiones confirmamus videlicet ecclesiam de Stantona et in ea annuam pensionem unius marcæ argenti. Ecclesiam de Sulethorn et in ea pensionem duarum marcarum argenti. Ecclesiam de Stoches et in ea pensionem unius libræ piperis. Ecclesiam de Horton et in ea pensionem quatuor solidorum........Ecclesiam de Mereton et in ea annuam pensionem xxx. *solidorum* [1]

The Stoches here mentioned is that now called Stoke-Line, where

* *Omnibus Xti fidelibus ad quos presentes literæ pervenerint Hugo Dei gr. Linc. ep'us salutem in Dno. Noverit universitas vestra nos divinæ pietatis intuitu de assensu Rogeri decani et capituli nostri Linc. concessisse dilectis in Xto abbati et conv. Rading viginti marcas annuas de ecclesia de Stanton scil. decem marcas eis de novo per nos concessas et alias decem marcas quas prius habuerunt per manum Th· de Camel personæ ejusdem eccl'iæ et successorum suorum nomine perpetui beneficii percipiendas. Idem autem Thomas et successores sui omnia onera ordinaria ipsius eccl'iæ debita et consueta sustinebunt. Salvis in omnibus ep'alibus consuetudinibus et Lincoln. eccl'iæ dignitate. Quod ut perpetuam optineat firmitatem presenti scripto sigillum nostrum una cum sigillo predicti capituli nostri Linc. duximus apponendum. Hiis T. Ex cartular. Rading. MS. f. 193.*

Omnibus Xti fidelibus ad quos presentes literæ pervenerint Hugo D. gr. Linc. eps. salutem. Noverit universitas vestra nos ad presentationem dilectorum in Xto abbatis et conv. Rading patronorum eccl'iæ de Stanton dilectum in Xto filium Th. de Camel clericum ad eandem eccl'iam admisisse ipsumque in ea canonice personam instituisse, salvis xx. *marcis annuis dictis abb'i et conv. per manum ipsius Thomæ et successorum suorum de eadem eccl'ia nomine perpetui beneficii percipiendas. Idem vero Thomas et successores sui omnia onera ipsius eccl'iæ debita et consueta sustinebunt. Salvis item in omnibus consuetudinibus ep'alibus et Linc. eccl'iæ dignitate. Quod ut ratum sit et firmum presenti scripto sigillum nostrum duximus apponendum. T. Ex cartular. de Rading. MS. f.* 194.

[k] Regist. Egnesham, MS. carta 22.   [1] Ibid. carta 24.

the pension to the abbey was one pound of pepper. This church, with that of Charlbury *, and the chapels of Egnesham, Chersinton †, and Ardinton, were of old exempted from all episcopal dues of pentecostals, synodals, &c. and paid for Peter-pence no more than eight shillings, as appears by certificates of Hugh bishop of Lincoln. *Hugo episcopus Lincoln. salutem. Capellæ de Egnesham et de Chersinton et de Ardinton similiter etiam ecclesiæ de Stoches et de Cherlebiri ab omni onere episcopali ab antiquo liberæ sunt nec solvunt pró denariis beati Petri nisi octo sol. &c.* [m]

The original gift of the church of Horton to the abbey of Egnesham was in this manner.

Notum sit universitati tam futurorum quam præsentium quod ego Walchelinus Hareng dedi et concessi pro salute animæ meæ et uxoris meæ et omnium parentum et antecessorum meorum Deo et S. Mariæ de Egnesham et monachis ibidem Deo servientibus ecclesiam de Horton cum omnibus quæ ad eam pertinent in decimis in terris in pratis et pasturis. Quare volo ut præfati monachi de Egnesham memoratam ecclesiam de Horton cum omnibus pertinentiis suis liberam et quietam ab omni consuetudine et sæculari servitio et exactione sicut elemosinam decet in perpetuum possideant. Hiis testibus; Waltero Mallet, &c. [n]

---

* CHERLEBIRI.

Philippus decan. Linc. et capitulum confirmant mon. de Egnesham appropriationem eccl'iæ de Cherlebyri. 17. cal. Sept. 1293. cartul. Egnesham, f. 114.

Ordinatio vicariæ de Cherlebyri 1296. 13. cal. Jul. Olivero tum ep'o Linc. et S. archid'o Oxon. ib. f. 120.

† CHERSINTON.

Hugo ep'us Linc. confirmat monasterio de Egnesham capellam de Chersinton. Test. mag'ro Rico de Smallclive; mag'ro Ric. Grim; Rob. de Capella, et Theobaldo canonicis Linc. eccl'iæ. Cartul. Egnesham. f. 15.

Dns. ep'us confirmat capellam de Chadelington tanquam membrum eccl'iæ de Cherlebiri. Mag. Phil. de Barton rect. ejusdem eccl'iæ et capellæ. 14. kal. Maii 1292. Reg. Ol. Sutton.

4. kal. Jun. 1295. Mag'r Phil. de Barton rector eccl. de Cherlebiri eandem eccl'iam resignavit, et mandatum est archid'o Oxon. ad inducend. abb. et conv. de Egnesham in eadem. 3. kal. Jun. ib.

[m] Reg. Egnes. MS. carta 24. [n] Ibid. carta 10.

The witness Walter de Malet seems to have been the brother of William de Malet baron, who married Alice sister of Gilbert Basset lord of Burcester, and had with her in frank marriage the lordship of Dadington, alias Dedington, in this county[o].

The same Walcheline Hareng gave to the said abbey of Egnesham two virgates of land in the village of Horton in exchange for two virgates given by his mother Helewise, one in Throp, and the other in Woodeaton.

Notum sit omnibus, &c. quod ego Walchelinus Hareng confirmavi ecclesiæ S. Mariæ de Egnesham duas virgatas terræ in villa de Horton in escambio duarum virgatarum quas mater mea Halewisa concesserat, unam in villa de Tropa. et aliam in Wdeaton. Facta est hæc conventio escambii coram Adelardo Banastre tunc vice-comite, &c.[p]

This church of Horton and land in Woodeaton were after confirmed to the said abbey, together with the church of Tetteburi * in Gloc. by Thomas de St. Walery[q].

In this year died Simon St. Liz, the third earl of Northampton and lord of the manors of Merton and Pidington, who leaving no issue, the king at Windsor, in the following year, delivered the earldom of Huntingdon, with all its appertenances, to William king of Scots, who immediately surrendered it to David his brother, who thereby became lord of the said adjoining manors[r].

An. MCLXXXV. 31, 32. Henry II.

This year an inquisition [s] was made by Jeffery Fitz-Stephen of all the lands and possessions belonging to the Knights Templars: wherein are found these particulars relating to these parts.

---

* Carta Thomæ de S. Walerico monachis de Egnesham super eccl'iam de Tettebur. quam R. de S. Walerico avus suus dederat eis. Teste Clem. priore Osney. Ex cart'ario de Egnesham. Bib. Cotton. Claudius, A. 8. f. 128.

[o] Dugd. Bar. tom. 1. p. 111.   [p] Regist. Egnes. MS. carta 107.   [q] Ibid.   [r] Tho. Walsing. Ypod. Neust. sub an. 1185. et Memoriale Gualteri de Coventre apud J. Lelandi Collect. MS. vol. 1. p. 354.   [s] Mon. Ang. vol. 2. p. 528.

Apud Couele, de dono Matildis reginæ, habentur quatuor hidæ, quarum duæ sunt in dominio, et duæ assisæ ab hominibus. Ailwinus præpositus dim. virgatam pro III[s]. *&c. Hæ sunt pertinentiæ de Couele apud Midletune, ex dono Rogeri de Cundi* 1. *virgata terræ quam archidiaconus de Norwiz tenet pro* v[s]. *Apud Couele duo molendina, quæ Will. molendinarius tenet pro* 1. *marc. Hæc summa summarum, tam de terris assisis, quam de molendinis domui Temp. de Couele pertinentibus* XII. *marc.* XII[s]. x[d].

Apud Meritune, ex dono Simonis comitis sunt VII. *hidæ terræ, quarum duæ sunt in dominio, et* v. *assisæ de hominibus. Walt. filius reg. tenet* 1. *virgatam terræ pro* v[s]. *&c. Hæ sunt pertinentiæ de Meritune apud Hamtune, ex dono Will. Belchii virgata terræ, quam tenet Robertus hæres ejus pro* III[s]. *Apud Blegedun, ex dono Mandegor* II. *virgatas terræ, quas Robertus filius Osberti tenet pro* VIII[s]. *&c. Hæc est summa pertinentiarum de Meritune* III[l]. XVI[s]. VIII[d].

In another account of lands and benefactors taken by John Stillingfleet an. 1434. *Thomas de Saunford miles dedit Templariis manerium de Saunford cum pertinentiis in comitatu Oxonii. Matildis regina Angliæ, dicta bona regina, quondam uxor regis Stephani, dedit eisdem manerium de Couley cum pertinentiis cum duobus molendinis in Oxonio. Simon comes Northamptoniæ dedit eis manerium de Meritone cum pertinentibus eidem. Will. de Bosco dedit eis plures terras in Meritone. Ric. Sifrewaste et Will. Sifrewaste dederunt hospitalariis unum molendinum, et plurima terras et tenementa in Clichware, pertinentes ad Saunforde A. D.* 1136. *et an.* 1. *R. Steph. Matildis regina uxor Stephani dedit manerium de Couley pertinens ad Saunford cum duobus molendinis in Oxonio, ac communem pasturam in foresta de Shottovere et ecclesiam de Stractone in com. Rutlandiæ.*

Before this thirty-second of Henry the Second, Richard de Hay, baron, departed this life, leaving his wife Maud daughter of William de Vernun surviving, and three daughters his heirs, of which Nichola the elder was wife of Gerard de Camvill, soon after lord of Midleton castle[1].

[1] Dugd. Bar. tom. 1. p. 598. a.

An. MCLXXXVI. 32, 33. *Henry II.*

Albert de Greslei, baron of Mancestre in com. Lanc. had taken to
his second wife a daughter of Thomas Basset, sister of Gilbert now
lord of Burcestre, &c. and departing this life in the thirty-second of
Henry the Second or before, left Robert his son and heir; whose
wardship his uncle Gilbert Basset did now obtain from the king, this
his nephew being eleven years of age, and his lands in Swineshed
com. Linc. valued at cii'. beside the stock thereon, at which place
his grandfather Robert de Greslei had founded an abbey of Cistertian monks, an. 1134 [u].

Before this time Aubrey earl of Dampmartin lord of the manors of
Merton and Pidington, which were held in fee from Simon earl of
Huntendon, and recovered by appeal to the king's court as his right
of inheritance, confirmed the manor of Meriton to the Knights
Templars, by this charter.

*Universis &c. Comes Albericus de Dammartun salutem. Sciatis
quod ego caritatis intuitu et pro salute animæ meæ omniumque antecessorum meorum et successorum meorum et pro salute regis Henrici
secundi comitisque Simonis domini mei concessi dedi et charta mea confirmavi fratribus militiæ Templi Salvatoris de Jerusalem Meritonam
cum omnibus pertinentiis suis quas in curia domini regis sicut hære-
ditatem meam recuperavi, habendam et tenendam sicut puram et perpetuam elemosinam solutam et quietam ab omni servitio sæculari consuetudine et exactione salvo fœdo et tenemento Guidonis et hæredum
suorum quod ad opus meum pertinet. Proinde volo et firmiter præcipio quod prædicti fratres militiæ Templi eandem Meritonam habeant
et plenarie teneant in bosco in plano pratis et pascuis aquis et molendinis et in omnibus aliis locis sicut comes Simon dominus meus eandem eis dedit et confirmavit. Et ut hæc mea actio rata in posterum
maneat eam præsentis scripti et sigilli mei impositione communio. Hiis
testibus; domino Ricardo Wintoniensi episcopo, domino Waltero Lin-*

----

[u] Dugd. Bar. tom. 1. p. 608.

cöln. episcopo, domino Ranulpho de Glanvill justitiario domini regis, Ricardo domini regis thesaurario, Huberto Walter, &c. [x]

The first of this family in England was Odo de Damartin, to whom William the Conqueror for his valour and faithful service gave the manor of Effingham with several privileges, in com. Sur. [y]

Walter de Constance bishop of Lincoln having been elected archbishop of Rhemes * in the year 1184 [z]; at a general council convened in May at Egnesham in this county, Richard dean of Lincoln and the chief part of his chapter came thither; and, after a long debate, in the presence of the king and archbishop, they chose Hugh a native of Grenoble, prior of the Carthusian order in England, who was consecrated at Westminster on the feast of St. Matthew [a]. Several other solemn elections of bishops and abbots were made during the said council at Egnesham [b]. In September following the king was at Woodstock, where, in his royal chapel within the park, William king of Scotland with great solemnity married Ermengard daughter of the lord Beaumont, on Friday the nones of September [c].

An. MCLXXXVII. 33, 34. Henry II.

The warden or steward of the honor of Walingford did this year account to the king for several sums, in pardons granted to Gilbert Basset lord of the manor of Burcester, and to Ranulph de Glanvill, Gilbert Pipard, Alan Basset, Robert de Witefelde, and William Paganell [d]

About this time Robert, son of Ralph, son of Robert de Amory, knight, in consideration of one mark and ten shillings in silver, confirmed to the abbey of Oseney the gift of one hide of land in Chesterton [e]; and gave those monks a plat of ground between the king's way and the grange of William Lare, with leave to enclose it with a

* Roan.

---

[x] Leger-book of Sandford, p. 102.   [y] R. Dods. MS. vol. 120. f. 13.   [z] R. de Diceto, sub an.   [a] Ib. 631.   [b] Chron. Gervas, p. 1480.   [c] Chron. Mailros, sub an.   [d] R. Dods. MS. vol. 113. f. 5.   [e] Regist. Osen. MS. p. 329.

wall[f]. Nigh the same time Ralph, son of William, son of Maud de
Weston, gave to the said church of Oseney five acres of land in
Weston, by this charter.

*Sciant præsentes et futuri quod ego Radulphus filius Willielmi filii
Matildæ de Weston dedi ecclesiæ S. Mariæ de Oseneia et canonicis
quinque acras terræ cum pertinentiis de libero tenemento meo quod de
dictis canonicis tenui Weston scilicet in campo versus Cestreton super Cornhulle duas acras et dimidiam &c. et unam dimidiam acram
inter terram Gilberti Maugere, &c. et duas acras et dimidiam
quæ jacent in Berinelande quarum una acra se extendit ad viam quæ
ducit usque ad Cestreton, et una dimidia acræ se extendit usque Wit-
tingden, &c.[g]*

An. MCLXXXVIII. 34, 35. Henry II.

Before the ninth of Henry the First, Gilbert Basset sen.* had
given to the abbey of Egnesham the tithes of his demesne in Stratton; and in the twenty-ninth of Henry the Second, his grandson
Gilbert had given one virgate of land in the same Stratton to the
new priory of Burcester, which latter lying more convenient to collect the tithes made a pretence of quarrel, till the difference being
referred to Philip prior of St. Frideswyds and Richard of Ailsbury,
they made this composition, that the tithes of Stratton should be annexed to the priory of Burcester in exchange for a pension of twelve
shillings *per annum* to the abbey of Egnesham.

*Universis S. matris ecclesiæ filiis Philippus prior S. Frideswydæ et
magister Ric. de Eilesbiria salutem in Domino. Cum causa quæ vertebatur inter abbatiam et monachos de Egnesham et Gilbertum Basset*

* Compositio inter Godefridum abbat.
de Egnesham et priorem de Berencestre
super duabus garbis decimarum de dominico Gilberti Basset de Stratton coram
Philippo priore sanctæ Frideswydæ et magistro Rich'o de Ailesburia, quibus auctoritate Hug. ep. Linc. causa commissa
fuit; anno 1188. Cart'arium de Egnesham.
Bib. Cotton. Claud. A. 8. f. 1.

[f] Regist. Osen. MS. p. 329.   [g] Ibid. p. 319.

et magistrum Gilbertum et Walterum clericos de Bernecestre super duabus garbis decimarum de dominio de Stratton nobis commissa, &c.

Hæc est compositio quæ facta est inter Godefridum abbatem et mo nachos de Egnesham et priorem et canonicos de Berencester super duabus garbis decimarum de dominico Gilberti Basset de Stratton coram Philippo *priore* S. *Frideswidæ et magistro* Ric. *de Ailesbiria quibus autoritate venerabilis patris* Hugonis Lincoln. *episcopi causa quæ inter ipsos super eisdem decimis jacebat commissa fuerat. Partibus siquidem præsentibus hoc modo lis amicabili compositione sopita est, quod videlicet præfatæ duæ garbæ decimarum de dominio de Stratton penes ecclesiam de Bernecester in perpetuum residebunt, easque cononici de Berencester sine molestia vel perturbatione aliqua perpetuo possidebunt, reddendo ecclesiæ de Egnesham* nomine *pensionis* XII. sol. *annuatim infra* XV. *dies post festum* S. Michaelis. *Con venit etiam intra eos quod si præfata ecclesia de Berencester in solutione prænominatæ pensionis* XII. *solidorum infra terminum præscriptum cessaverit, ecclesia de Egnesham ad præscriptas decimas liberum habeat regressum. Hæc compositio facta est anno ab incarnatione Domini* MCLXXXVIII. *apud Stanton in ecclesia ejusdem villæ feria quarta post dominicam in qua cantatur misericordia Domini et postmodo apud* S. *Frideswedam apud Oxeneford plene confirmata. Hiis testibus;* Philippo *priore* S. *Frideswidæ, magistro* Ric. *de Ailesbiria,* Nigello *decano de* Oxeneford, Ernaldo, Radulpho, Hugone *presbyteris,* Waltero *presbytero, magistro* Johanne *de* Tinemuth, *magistro* Rob. *de* Eboraco, Rob. *filio* Petri *de* Mara, Willielmo *fratre suo,* Hugone *de* Draval, Rob. *de* Aumari, Rad. Gibbiun, Gaufr. *de* Bella Aqua, Rob. *filio* Pagani, &c. [h]

Which agreement was confirmed by Gilbert Basset jun. founder of the priory, and lord of Burcester and Stratton, in this form.

Universis sanctæ matris ecclesiæ filiis ad quos præsens carta pervenerit Gilbertus Basset *salutem. Notum sit universitati vestræ me concessisse et præsenti carta mea confirmasse compositionem quæ facta*

[h] Regist. Egnesham, MS. carta 6 ›

*est inter ecclesiam de Egnesham et ecclesiam de Berencester super
duabus garbis decimarum de dominio meo de Stratton, &c.* [k]

This pension of xii'. per annum to the abbey of Egnesham was
charged not on the temporalities of the priory of Burcester, but on
the appropriated tithes of that church.   In a valuation of the spirituals and tenths of the abbey of Egnesham[1] made A. D. 1277, we
find these particulars; *Decanatus de Berencester, de decima in Berencester* xii'. *inde decima* xiv[d].   In the taxation of spirituals made
the nineteenth of Edward the First, A. D. 1291, it is thus registered [m];
Decanatus de Burcestre. Ecclesia de Burcestre deducta portione
xviii [marc.] *Portio abbatis de Egnesham in eadem* xii'.   And in a register of the king's tenths within the archdeaconry of Oxford in the
reign of Edward the Fourth, we find [n] *Spiritualia abbatis de Egnesham, portio in Burcestre* xii'.   In the rental of the abbey of Egnesham we meet with a receipt given for the said pension.

*Noverint universi per præsentes nos Jacobum permissione divina
abbatem monasterii de Egnesham recepisse et habuisse die confectionis
præsentium de priore de Burcestre duodecem solidos legalis monetæ
pro decimis in Stratton, viz. pro termino S. Michaelis archangeli ultimo præterito ante datam præsentium de quibus quidem duodecem solidis fatemur nos inde plenarie fore solutos per præsentes. Sigillo
nostro consignatum* [o].

At the latter end of this same year William del Osse of Cherlton
gave to the Knights Templars the meadow of Chevesle for the health
of the soul of king Henry son of Maud. *Hiis testibus; Waltero fratre
meo, Willielmo de Bosco cognato meo, Simone filio Wydonis de Meriton, et Roberto fratre ejus, Waltero de Merlac, Clemente de Merlac,
Fulcone filio Johannis de Osse, Amarico de Covele, Andrea filio ejus
et capellano qui scripsit hanc cartam, et multis aliis. 'Hæc carta facta
fuit anno* xxxv°. *regni regis Henrici secundi* [p].

[k] Regist. Egnesham, MS. carta 63.   [l] Ibid. p. 4.   [m] Taxatio Spiritual. in Dioc.
Linc. MS. in Bib. Bod.   [n] Transcrip. MS. penes A. à Wood.   [o] Rentale Egnes. MS.
p. 41.   [p] Regist. Sandford, MS.

The same William del Osse gave to the Knights one acre nigh the house of Walter de Merlac toward the great pasture and the meadow called Cowmed. *Hiis testibus; Hugone paupere, Simone de Meriton, Willielmo de Bosco, Johanne del Osse, &c.*

He gave to the same religious use some lands between the house of Walter de Merlac and the great road, *i. e.* the Roman way from Allchester to Walingford, leading over Otmoore, &c. *Hiis testibus; Roberto le Meare tempore illo vice-com. Oxon. Roberto de Amory, Hugone le Povre, Ric. Foliot, Will. de Lewekenore, Ada de Gersindon, Simone de Meriton, Hamone de S. Fide, &c.* He also confirmed a grant made by John his brother; *Testibus; Waltero fratre meo, et Godefrido fratre Heliæ, et Ric. de Camvil, &c.*

An. MCLXXXIX. 35. *Henry II.* 1. *Richard* I.

Henry the second died July the sixth, and his son Richard was crowned at London September the third. There were present at his coronation David earl of Huntindon lord of the fee of Merton and Pidington [q], Gilbert Basset lord of Burcester, and Gerard Camvil heir to Midleton, who (in a pedigree of that family drawn by the most accurate Dodsworth) is called *Gerardus de Campuilla de Midleton castle* [r].

Bernard de S. Walery lord of Beckly, Ambrosden, &c. was with Richard in Normandy at the death of his father; and, having been disseized of his lands, was now restored to them by this precept of the new king.

Ricardus Dei gratia rex Anglorum, &c. Omnibus ballivis suis Angliæ salutem. Præcipimus quod permittatis Bernardo de S. Walerico dilecto familiari nostro habere et tenere totam suam terram quam habet in Anglia cum tali libertate quali eam tenuit tempore domini regis patris nostri. Teste meipso [s].

Before his coronation the king gave to his brother John the honor

---

[q] Chron. Jo. Brompt. inter X. Script. p. 1158.   [r] Dodsw. MS. vol. 6. p. 26.   Regist. Osen. MS.

of Walingford, by which means he became lord of the fee of Burcester, &c.[t] and preferred William de Camvill, a younger son of Richard de Camvill of Midleton castle, to the archdeaconry of Rich-
mund [u]

<h2 style="text-align:center">An. MCXC. 1, 2. Richard I.</h2>

The king at Christmas after his coronation passed over to Normandy, to prepare for his expedition to the Holy Land *; in which
pious adventure, he was attended by Bernard de S. Walery lord of
Ambrosden, and Richard de Camvill lord of Midleton : this latter
was constituted by the king one of the admirals of his navy[x] at
Chinon, (where Henry the Second died;) which navy, setting sail
from divers parts of England, arrived at Lisborn in Portugal, under
command of Robert de Sabloil and the said Richard de Camvill, &c.
and thence to Marseilles, &c.[y]

In the league between king Richard and Tancred king of Sicily,
Richard de Camvill is one of the witnesses to the articles, and one
of the guarantees for observance of them[z]. In this first year's siege of
Acon, a port of Palestine, Bernard de S. Walery was killed, whereby
his son Thomas de S. Walery succeeded to the honor of S. Walery
in this county, viz. Beckley, Ambrosden, Horton, &c....... Nomina
magnatum qui eodem anno in obsidione Accon obierunt. Ranulfus
de Glanvilla justic. Ang. et Bernardus de S. Valerico junior, &c.[a]
While the king was wearied with this siege, through some secret impulse at the intercession and mediation (as he imagined) of St.
George, he was inspired with fresh courage, and thought of this device, to tie about the left leg of a certain number of knights a leathern

---

* Conventio quædam inter Philippum
regem Franciæ et Ricardum regem Ang.
facta Messanæ anno 1190, mense Martii.
Hii autem fidejussores sunt, post comitem,
de predictis conventionibus tenendis——.
Bernardus de Scto Walerico vel ille ex heredibus suis qui Sanctum Walericum tene-
bit, cum toto feodo suo. Rymer. 1. 70.

[t] Chron. Jo. Brompt. p. 1157. [u] Ibid. p. 1161. [x] Rog. de Hoved. p. 666. edit. Savil.
[y] Ibid. p. 670. [z] Chron. Jo. Brompt. inter X. Script. p. 1184. [a] Rog. de Hoved. p. 685.

thong or garter, that, by a sense of glory and assurance of reward, they might be excited to the greater courage. Among which knights (says the late historian) were Sir John St. John, and Sir Richard de Camvill, which some think the first occasion to that order of the garter, instituted by king Edward the Third [b]

Within this year William Mareschal earl of Pembroke gave a fine of two thousand marks to the Exchequer for the moiety of the lands of Walter Giffard late earl of Buckingham, in right of Isabel his wife, daughter and heir to Richard earl of Strigul, whereby he was possessed of the adjoining manors of Mersh and Crendon, &c. and in the second of king John had a grant of the patronage of the abbey of Notley, by delivery of the [c] pastoral staff *.

Within the second of Richard the First died William de Lisures lord of the fee of Borstall, who, in the thirty-third of Henry the Second, had paid xx[s]. to the sheriff of Wiltshire on collection of the scutage of Gallwey; and in the thirty-fifth of Henry the Second had given two hundred marks for the forestership of Northamptonshire: to whom succeeded Jeffery de Lisures his brother, who gave vii[l]. ii[s]. iv[d]. for livery of his lands [d]. The said William granted to William Fitz-Nigel of Borstall his land in that place, held from Fulk de Lisures his father, for the yearly rent of x[s]. by this charter.

Willielmus de Lisuris omnibus hominibus suis Francis et Anglicis salutem. Sciant omnes tam præsentes quam futuri me Willielmum de Lisuris reddidisse et concessisse et hac charta mea confirmasse Willielmo filio Nigelli de Borstalle terram suam illam scilicet quæ fuit patris sui tenendam de me et hæredibus meis illi et hæredibus suis jure hæreditario libere et quiete et honorifice sicut ipse vel antecessores sui tenuerunt liberius et quietius de me vel antecessoribus meis reddendo inde mihi annuatim pro omni servitio et consuetudine x[s]. ad festum S.

---

* Vid. Seldeni not. ad Eadmerum, p. 143.

[b] Barnes, Hist. of Edward the Third, p. 293.   [c] R. Dods. MS. col. è rot. Pip. et Mon. Ang. tom. 2. p. 156.   [d] Dugd. Bar. tom. 1. p. 597. a.

Michaelis. Ut autem hæc concessio et donatio stabilis et firma per-maneat eam præsentis scripti patrocinio et sigilli mei munimine duxi roborandam. Hiis testibus; Hugone de Lisuris, Reginaldo de Basset, Willielmo Basset, Roberto de Grenevile, Roberto de Grendon, Waltero de S. Fide, Willielmo de L'isle, Radulpho filio Burewardi, Fulcone de Lisure, Willielmo Borstard, Widone Malsa, Johanne Fe-rebraz, Thoma de S. Andrea, Willielmo fratre ejus, Reginaldo de Pokebroke, et aliis quamplurimis [e].*

There is another charter of the said William de Lisures to William Fitz-Nigel, granting to him the office of forester of Bernwood for the yearly rent of xl[s]. attested by the same witnesses [f]. It seems to be from this pretended title to Borstall and the custody of Bernwood, that one of this family of De Lisures had it certified, that being forester of fee to the king, he was by his office obliged to attend him in his army, well fitted with horse and arms, *his horn hanging about his neck* [g].

An. MCXCI. 2, 3. *Richard II.*

King Richard, provoked with many indignities offered by Isaac called emperor of Cyprus, made a descent, took the emperor prisoner, and soon conquered his whole island, which he delivered in custody to Richard Camvill lord of Midleton, and Robert de Turnham; *Tradidit insulam de Cypre Richardo de Camuilla et Roberto de Turnham* [h]. From whence Richard de Camvill, without the king's leave, went to the siege of Acon, which held out to this second year, and there died in June. *Eodem mense Junii Richardus de Camuilla, quem rex Angliæ constituerat unum de justitiariis suis in insula de Cypre, infirmabatur, et sine licentia regis venit ad obsidionem Accon et ibi mortuus est* [i]. He left heir Gerard de Camvill his eldest son, who, in the scutage for Wales imposed in the first, but not fully collected till this third year of the king, paid ten shillings for his one knight's

---

.[e] Regist. de Borstall, MS. f. 1.   [f] Ibid. f. 2.   [g] Dugd. Bar. tom. 1. p. 597. a.   [h] Rog. de Hoved. p. 692.   [i] Ibid. p. 694.

fee in Midleton[k]: and left a younger son William, who married Aldred daughter and heir of Jeffery Marmion, and had his principal seat at Arewe in com. Warw. from whom the Camvils of Clifton in Staffordshire descended[l]

The king in his absence had appointed William de Longchamp bishop of Ely chancellor and chief justiciary of England, who had great quarrels with John earl of Moreton the king's brother, which rose first from the earl's defence of Gerard de Camvill lord of Middleton[m], whom the chancellor turned out of his office of sheriff of Lincolnshire, giving it to William de Stutevil, who besieged Camvill in his castle of Lincoln; but the siege was raised by earl John, and an agreement made between him and the chancellor, one article of which was to reinstate our Gerald de Camvill in his shirevalty of Lincoln; to which compact Gilbert Basset lord of Burcester was a witness[n], being one of them who adhered to earl John in all his ambitious quarrels. Before the end of this year the chancellor was deposed and fled beyond sea, where he represented his grievances to the pope, and moved him to write to the archbishops and bishops of England to excommunicate earl John and all his accomplices. And the said William bishop of Ely, as legate and chancellor, wrote to the bishop of Lincoln to put in execution the pope's brief, and sent a list of those whom he would have him declare to be excommunicate, among which were Gerard de Camvill, Gilbert Basset, Thomas Basset, &c. But the bishop was too wise to obey him[o]. *In this

---

* Circa annum 1212. (sic.)

Hugo ep'us Linc. admisit mag'm Simon. de Lond. ad eccl'iam de Langctun ad pres. Radi. abbatis et conv. Westm. salva Hen. de Colewella perpetua vicaria quam habet in eadem qui tenet dictam eccl'iam reddendo annuatim 2 marcas nomine pensionis. Testibus dno. J. Bath. Epo. mag'ro Joh. de Eboraco; mag'ro Regin. de Castre; mag'ro Will. de Tornay; Elya capellano; Hereberto camerario. Dat. per manum Rog. capellani n'ri apud Lond. 3 non. Oct. pont. 4. Ex cartis original. eccl. Westmon.

---

[k] R. Dods. MS. vol. 47. p. 57.   [l] Dugd. Antiq. War. p. 621.   [m] Rog. de Hoved. p. 700.   [n] Ibid. p. 701.   [o] Chron. J. Brompt. p. 1230.

year Hugh bishop of Lincoln visited this part of his diocese, and at
Godestow removed the body of Rosamund from before the high
altar, and had it buried without the church[p]. Her father Walter de
Clifford gave to those nuns of Godestow for the health of the soul of
Margaret his wife, and this Rosamund his daughter, his mill at
Framton in com. Gloc. with a little meadow called Lechton in pure
and perpetual alms[q]. I cannot imagine why Walsingham should attribute to king John this foundation of Godstow for the soul of Rosamund his father's concubine, and impute it to a prophecy of Merlin[r].

Bernard de S. Walery, for the better success of his expedition to
the Holy Land, had in his passage through France laid the foundation of a monastery called Godestow, the name derived from that in
this county, built on the land which he gave for that use to Henry
the Second[s]. *Abbatia loci Dei sita est ad fluvium Brestan qui Pi-
cardos dirimit a Normannis. Fundator Bernardus de S. Walerico
dominus de Gamaches consensu Avor. conjugis et Thomæ filii an.*
M.C.XC.I. The foundation is thus recorded in the French Monasticon. *Abbatia locus Dei (lieu Dieu) dioc. Ambionensis, sed in comitatu Aucensi vulgo Eu ducatus Norman. ordinemque profitetur Cister-
tiensem, cujus fundator primarius producitur vir illustrissimus D.
Bernardus eo nomine quartus dominus S. Walerici cum uxore sua
Alienora pientissima ac nobilissima heroina, an.* 1191[t].

An. MCXCII.   3, 4. Richard I.

Nigh this time Henry de Oily baron of Hokenorton, in considera-

MCXCII.

*Hubertus Dei gratia Sarum episcopus.
Noveritis &c. quod nos dedimus abbati et canonicis regularibus de Parco juxta Thamam
ecclesiam de Bradleia cum capella de Horn-*
*ingham et cum decimis de omnibus aliis perti-
nentiis &c. pro capella leprosarum mulierum
de Maiden Bradley dedicanda, quam villam
Manasserus de Biset dedit dictis leprosis, &c.*
Ex rotulo de Crendon, MS.

p Chron. Jo. Brompt. p. 1235.   q Mon. Ang. vol. 2. p. 884.   r Ypod. Neustria, sub
an. 1216.   s Extraicts de divers Cartularies, &c. tom. 2.   t Neustria Pia.

tion of his body to be buried before the high altar in the church of Oseney, gave to the abbot and monks his chief mansion house in Weston, with a wood and mill, and his meadows near the mill toward Kertlinton, and three crofts, Benecroft, Grascroft, Hegcroft, with offer of exchange in Hokenorton or Kidlington.

Omnibus Christi fidelibus ad quos præsens scriptum pervenerit Henricus de Oily salutem. Noverit universitas vestra me, &c. concessisse ecclesiæ sanctæ Mariæ de Oseneia, ubi corpori meo sepulturam elegi ante majus altare, &c. capitale mansum meum in Westona cum ejus pertinentiis et boscum meum et prata mea juxta idem molendinum versus Kertlington et tres croftas meas scilicet Benecroft, Grascroft, Hegecroft, cum earum pertinentiis et si aptius fuerit excambium iis faciemus in manerio de Hokenorton vel in manerio de Kidlington ubi voluerint et sibi melius expedire viderint, &c. [u]

This part of the country was much concerned in the attempts made by earl John, who, upon his brother's imprisonment, aspired to the crown, and, with many of his accomplices in these parts, besieged the castle of Walingford [x]. Jeffery late elect of Lincoln, now archbishop of York, granted by charter to the abbey of Godestow in this county the priory of St. Clements in York, to be annexed and subordinate to it; but the nuns of St. Clement refused to submit to those of Godestow, which occasioned long and sharp disputes [y].

An. MCXCIII. 4, 5. Richard I.

Thomas de S. Walery, lord of Ambrosden, gave to the abbey of Oseney his whole manor of Mixbury, with his capital court and all appertenances within the village and without, for the health of his own soul, and of Edela his wife, and Bernard his father, and Avoris his mother, and Reginald and Bernard his brothers.

Sciant, &c. quod ego Thomas de S. Walerico dedi et concessi, &c. pro salute animæ meæ et Bernardi patris mei et Avor. matris meæ et

---

[u] Regist. Osen. MS. p. 316. [x] Chron. Tho. Wikes, sub an. [y] Leland, Collectan. vol. 2. p. 275.

Reginaldi et Bernardi fratrum meorum, &c. Deo et ecclesiæ beatæ Mariæ de Oseneia, &c. totum manerium meum Mixebury in liberam et perpetuam elemosinam cum capitali curia et cum omnibus pertinentiis in villa et extra villam, &c. cum homagio et servitiis Roberti Persal et hæredum suorum de fœdo quod de me tenuit in Newenton videlicet xxiv. *solid. per an. de redditu et servitio dimid. milit. scripto et sigilli mei appositione roboravi, &c.*[z] The abbey of Oseney, by the gift of Robert de Oily, had long before enjoyed two parts of the tithe of all the demesne land in Mixbury[a].

In this year's accounts of William Briewerre, sheriff of this county, it appears, that Thomas de S. Walery, for relief of his lands, was indebted to the king one hundred and seventy marks[b].

About this time Gilbert Basset and Egeline his wife gave to their priory of Burcester all their land of Wotesdun and Westcote their demesne, for the health of their own souls and of Thomas their son, for pure and perpetual alms, by this form of donation.

Universis sanctæ matris ecclesiæ filiis ad quos præsens scriptum pervenerit Gilbertus Basset et Egelina uxor sua salutem in vero salutari. Noverit universitas vestra nos divinæ pietatis intuitu concessisse et dedisse et hac præsenti charta nostra confirmasse Deo et ecclesiæ S. Edburgæ de Bernecestria et canonicis ibidem Deo servientibus totam terram nostram de Votesdun et de Westcote cum omnibus pertinentiis suis scilicet dominium nostrum cum vilnagio pro salute animarum nostrarum et pro salute animæ Thomæ filii nostri et antecessorum et successorum nostrorum eis possidendam in puram et perpetuam elemosinam liberam et quietam ab omni exactione et servitio seculari salvo domini regis servitio quantum ad terram illam pertinet. Hanc vero prædictam terram scilicet de Votesdun et de Westcote, ego Gilbertus Basset et Egelina uxor mea et hæredes nostri warantizabimus sæpedictis canonicis contra omnes in perpetuum. Et ut hæc donatio nostra rata et inconcussa permaneat eam sigilli nostri impressione roboravimus. Hiis testibus; Petro abbate de Woburn, Hugone

---

[z] Regist. Osen. MS.   [a] Ibid.   [b] R. Dods. MS. Rot. Pip.

abbate de Osencia, Ada abbate de Mussenden, Thom. Basset, Alano Basset, Henrico filio Geroldi, Rob. de Amari, Reginaldo de Curtenei filio Willielmi, Jurdano de Dantesic, Ric. de Calvertun, Willielmo persona de Scaldeford, Acelino de Peritune, Philippo de Covele, Roberto Boscher, Rogero de Covele, et pluribus aliis [c].

To the original parchment slip is a large seal appending, with impression of a knight on horseback, with drawn sword, and this inscription. ✠ SIGILLUM GILBERTI BASSET. This land at Wodesdon in com. Bucks. seems to have been part of the marriage portion of Egeline de Courtney, the said manor of Wodesdon being in possession of that family, and in the nineteenth of Edward the First, it was assigned as part of the dowry of Alianore, widow of Hugh de Courtney baron [d].

Among the witnesses, Reginald de Courtney son of William must be the son of William son of Reginald de Courtney, born in Normandy, by his first wife; which William married Maud the sole daughter of Robert, natural son of king Henry the First by Maud Avenel, who took him for a second husband, having had by Robert de Abrincis her first husband a sole daughter called Hawise, married to Reginald the father of this William and Egeline wife of Gilbert Basset [e]

An. MCXCIV. 5, 6. Richard I.

The king in his return from the Holy Land was took prisoner, and delivered to the emperor of Germany, from whom he was ransomed at one hundred thousand marks : and this year returned to England, holding a parliament at Nottingham on the thirtieth of March. He did on that day disseize Gerard de Camvill lord of Middleton of his castle and shirevalty of Lincoln, for adhering to the interest of earl John, who, in the king's absence, had used all methods to usurp the

---

[c] Ex Orig. penes hon. Guil. Glynne, Bar.   [d] Dugd. Bar. tom. 1. p. 637.   [e] Ibid. tom. 1. p. 631.

crown, and offered money to prevent or retard his royal brother's return.

Eodem die rex disseisivit Gerardum de Camvilla de castello et vice-comitatu Lincolniensi [f]. Within a week after, at the instigation of William bishop of Ely chancellor, the said Gerard de Camvill was accused for receiving thieves who had robbed the tradesmen in their road to Stanford fair. He was farther charged with treason, &c. but he stoutly answered, he was earl John's man or feudatory te-nant, and would stand to the law of his court. The said Gerard de Camvill was now disseized by the king of the manor of Benham in com. Berks. which king Richard in the first of his reign had given to Richard de Camvill, who left it to a younger son John de Camvill; and he dying without issue, it was enjoyed by this Gerard, till the king upon this seizure gave it to Hugh Wake to hold during his pleasure. On which account there was a trial in the fifty-seventh of Henry the Third, wherein the jury found that manor an escheat to the king, unless the heirs of Richard de Camvill could produce the feoffment of king Richard [g]. Gilbert Basset lord of Burcester, &c. had also adhered to earl John, for which he now purchased the king's pardon for eight pounds; Thomas Basset for his pardon paid four pounds, and Alan Basset four pounds, as appears from the ac-count of escheats within the honor of Walingford [h]. And Gerard de Camvill gave two thousand marks to be repossessed of his estate and castle of Midleton, and to regain the king's favour [i].

This part of the country was now concerned in one of the great tournaments appointed by the king between Brackly and Mixbury, on the plain called Bayards green, (*i. e.* Horse-green) expressed in a letter from king Richard to Hubert archbishop of Canterbury [k] · wherein he acquaints him of his ordering solemn tournaments *in-ter Sarum et Wilton, inter Warwick et Kennelingworth, inter Stan-*

<hr>

[f] Rog. de Hoved. p. 736.   [g] R. Dods. MS. vol. 64. f. 39.   [h] Ibid. vol. 47. f. 70.
[i] Dugd. Bar. tom. 1. p. 627. b.   [k] MS. James, num. 27. in Bib. Bod.

ford et Warniford, inter Brakele et Mixebiri. These tiltings, justs, or feats of arms were[1] instituted, if we may credit Munster, an. 934. It is said the use of them was brought into England by king Stephen, and by this martial people managed with much spirit and much blood. These appear the first that were publicly authorized. The occasion of them was pretended to make English subjects more expert in arms, and that they might not be insulted over by the French, who in these feats did much excel them. One more ingenuous reason was, no doubt, to advance the king's revenue. For in the chart that grants them, the following rates were imposed[m]: an earl for licence of tilting twenty marks of silver, a baron ten marks, every knight that had land four marks, a knight who had no land two marks, &c. The mischief of these bloody sports was found so great, that they were prohibited in three councils by three several popes[n] under the penalty of denying Christian burial: and were restrained by act of parliament in the reign of Henry the Third, under the penalty of the heirs of offenders being deprived of their estates. But the custom could not be broke till the time of Edward the Third. There was another tournament held at this very place in the thirty-third of Henry the Third[o].

Richard d'Amorie held now from the Knights Templars part of the manor of Merton and other appendants in Fencot, Blechesdon, and Hampton-Gay *: the conditions of tenure are expressed in a writing dated this year[p].

---

* *Sciant presentes et futuri quod ego Willelmus de Camphernulphi confirmavi canonicis de Oseney donationem quam Robertus de Gay eis fecit de tota terra illa quam de me tenuit in villa de Hampton Gay, &c.* Reg. Osen.

Sciant presentes et futuri quod ego Johanna de Champernulfi filia et hæres Willi. *de Campo Ernulfi uxor quondam Radulphi de Wylynton in ligia potestate et viduitate mea confirmavi canonicis de Oseney illam concessionem quam Robertus de Gai eis fecit de tota terra illa quam de Willo de Champernon patre meo tenuit in villa de Hampton Gay, &c.* ib.

---

[1] Camden, in Hertford.   [m] Brady, Hist. p. 447.   [n] Guil. Newburg, l. 5. cap. 1. et Rog. Hoved. p. 584.   [o] Mat. Par. p. 769.   [p] R. Dods. MS. vol. 35. p. 61.

Nigh the same time John de Folya gave half a yard land to the Knights Templars in Cherlton, by a charter thus exemplified.

Sciant tam præsentes quam post futuri quod Johannes de Folya dedit Deo et Templo de Jerusalem ubi milites religiose Deo serviunt dimid. virgatam terræ in Cherleton liberam et quietam in perpetuam elemosinam tenendam cum libertatibus eidem terræ pertinentibus. Libertates hujus terræ sunt istæ, scilicet pastura x. *bobus cum vitulis suis et* LXXX. *ovibus et in bosco suo ad omnia negotia sua facienda infra fœdum illud. Hanc chartam tenebat Walterus de Botremer de dominis et militibus Templi finaliter duos solidos dando per annum pro omnibus servitiis Templo pertinentibus. Hujus donationis testes sunt Rad. presbyter de Hungreford, &c.* [q]

The tax for the king's ransom when prisoner to the emperor was twenty shillings on each knight's fee, with all church plate, and all that year's wool of the Cistercian monks, and the order of Semplingham. The collection is entered in this year's account of the sheriffs, though the rate was imposed an. 1193. Gerard de Camvill paid xx'. for one knight's fee in Midleton, and Henry de Oily for no less than twenty-two fees and the third part, and Roger de Chesterton x'. and Philip de Hampton xx'. &c.

Within this year Gilbert Basset lord of Burcester, &c. gave an hundred pounds fine to the king, that his daughter Eustace might be married to Thomas de Verdon, a baron, and lord of the manor of Heth in this county; who, upon his marriage, paid a fine to the king of three hundred marks, to have livery of the lands and castles of his father Bertram de Verdon [r], the son of Bertram who came in with the Conqueror, and held the manor of Fernham-Royal in Bucks. by the service of providing a glove upon the day of the king's coronation for his right hand, and to support his right arm the same day, during the time that the royal sceptre is in his hand [s]. Gilbert Basset gave in marriage with his said daughter one moiety of the manor of Wrechwike [t]

---

[q] Regist. Sandford, MS. p. 77.   [r] Dugd. Bar. tom. 1. p. 472. a.   [s] Ibid.   [t] Ex MS. chartis penes D. W. Glynne, Bar.

An. mcxcv. 6, 7. *Richard* I.

William de Sobinton, sheriff of this county, in stating his accounts to the Exchequer, reckoned eighteen shillings for the rent of Fencote, and eighteen shillings in part of eleven pound for the fee ferm of Pidington, which lately belonged to the earl of Danmartun or Dammartin, and now by escheat was in the king's hands[u].

We meet with other branches of this family : Manassir de Dammartin, one of the itinerant judges in the reign of Henry the Second, an. 1170[x]; Galiena de Dammartin and Bartholomew hér son, patron of the church of Northirn in this reign of Richard the First. There is a charter of this Galiena de Dammartin, made to Robert de Mandevil her son, granting to him some lands in the village of Nortun in com. Essex[y]. Nicholas de Dammartin, witness to the charter of William de Braose to the church of Bergavenny in reign of king John. William de Dammartin, who gave the church of Effingham in Surry to the priory of Merton, and the tithes of Michelham to the abbey of Lewes; and Eudo de Dammartin, son of William, who founded the hospital of St. James in Tanregge in Surry[z]. To the charter of foundation of this hospital a seal is affixed, with impress of a knight on horseback armed and sword drawn, and on the reverse the arms of this family, five bars with a label of three points, inscribed, S. EUDONIS DE DAMMARTIN[a]

Our Aubry de Dammartin left son and heir Reginald, who by marriage came to the earldom of Bologne, of which he was deprived, and of all his goods in France, an. 1211, when he was honourably received by king John, and had his paternal estate delivered to him, with as many other lands as amounted to 300*l.* *per ann.*[b]

Aubry de Ver, earl of Oxford, in the second of Richard the First, had given a fine to the king of five hundred marks for the daughter

[u] R. Dods. Rot. Pip. vol. 13. p. 89.   [x] Chron. Gervas, p. 1110.   [y] R. Dods. MS. vol. 30. f. 32.   [z] Mon. Ang. tom. 2. p. 135. 403. 908.   [a] R. Dods. MS. vol. 30. f. 28. [b] Mat. Par. f. 231.

of Walter de Bolebec, to make a wife for his son, and died the
seventh of Richard the First, leaving heir his son Aubry ; who, by his
father's advice, having married Isabel daughter of Walter Bolebec,
did, by his said wife's consent, confirm to the abbey of Notley in
Crendon the donation which Walter Giffard earl of Buck. made by
the concession of Hugh de Bolebec in the village of Hillesdon, *viz.*
the church with all appertenances, with pasturage for their drawing
cattle, and two hundred acres of pasture.

Notum sit &c. quod ego Albricus de Ver et Isabella de Bolebec filia
Walteri de Bolebec sponsa mea concessimus Deo et ecclesiæ S. Mariæ
de Parco Crendon totam illam donationem quam venerabilis comes
Walter Giffard eis dedit in villa de Hillesdon concessu Hugonis de
Bolebec, scilicet ecclesiam cum omnibus pertinentiis suis et boves de
caruca eorum cum bobus nostris ibique in pastura nostra et ducentas
acras in pastura nostra ibique de nutrimento eorum, &c. [c]

Constance, daughter of Hugh de Bolebec, wife of Elias de Beauchamp, did with her husband's consent give to the said abbey of
Nutley that croft in the village of Hillesdon which Thorold before
held, making a solemn oblation of it on the altar of the church of
Hillesdon [d].

Hugh de Hosdenche confirmed to the church of Hillesdon and

An. MCXCV. 6, 7. Richard I.

Will'us filius Eliæ prepositus Emmæ de
Pery petit versus Will'um Basset feodum
1 mil. in Corfton cum pertin. et feodum 1
militis in Acleia cum pertin. ut jus et hære-
ditatem ipsius Emmæ quæ ei descendit ex
parte Luvet de Brai avi sui qui terram illam
tenuit temp. R. H. avi et post eum Fulco
filius Luvet pater suus qui eam habuit et
tenuit temp. regis H. patris ut jus et hære-
ditatem. Will'us venit et dicit; Rex H.
avus dedit terram illam Osmundo Basset
avo suo pro servitio suo qui eam habuit et
tenuit, et post illum Joh'es Basset pater
suus, et ille post ipsum etiam habet et tenet
ut jus suum. Will'us fil. Eliæ defendit
quod rex H. non dedit Osmundo Basset
terram illam, sed Luvat dedit terram illam
Basiliæ uxori ejus in dotem et post mortem Luvet Osmundus Basset cepit Basi-
liam in uxorem, et sic per eam habuit introitum in terra illa et sic descendit terra
illa. Placita temp. Ric. I. an. 6. rot. 3.

[c] Rotulus de Crendon, MS.   [d] Ibid.

the canons of Notley one virgate of land in Hillesdon, which his father Hugh de Hosdenche gave to the mother church of Hillesdon,
for a chapel to be built on his land at Hillesdon ^e

An. MCXCVI. 7, 8. Richard I.

About this time Thomas de S. Walery, lord of Ambrosden, confirmed to the abbey of Egnesham the church of Tettebury in com.
Gloc. and the manor of Line-Stokes, (now Stoke-Line,) which had
been given by Reginald his grandfather; and the church of Norton,
with half a hide of land in that village; and the wood and village of
Woodeaton of the gift of Walkelin Hareng.

*Thomas de S. Walerico omnibus hominibus suis Francis et Anglis
salutem. Sciant præsentes et futuri quod ego concessi et præsenti
charta confirmavi Deo et ecclesiæ S. Mariæ de Egnesham et monachis
ibidem Deo servientibus in puram et perpetuam elemosinam et pro salute animæ meæ et patris mei et matris meæ et omnium antecessorum
meorum et hæredum meorum ecclesiam de Tettibiri cum omnibus pertinentiis suis et libertatibus sicut eam habent ex dono R. de S. Walerico
avi mei. Concedo et confirmo prædictæ ecclesiæ et monachis de Egnesham terram de Line-Stokes cum omnibus pertinentiis suis habere
de me et hæredibus meis libere et quiete et in pace sicut eam habent
ex dono Rad. Basset et ex concessione R. avi mei. Ecclesiam quoque
de Norton, et dimid. hidam terræ in eadem villa de Norton, nemus et
villam de W'deaton cum omnibus pertinentiis et libertatibus suis sicut
eam possident ex dono Walkelini Hareng eisdem monachis concedo in
perpetuum possidenda libere et quiete et pacifice confirmo. Hujus autem
concessionis et confirmationis meæ præsenti scripto et sigillo meo apposito roboratæ, testes sunt Clemens prior Osen. magister Walterus
sub-prior S. Frideswydæ, magister Alardus de S. Mildrida, Rad. Hareng, Rad. de Norton, Rob. de Estrop, Rog. de Nova Foresta*^f.

From the rolls of escheats to the king this year, it appears that
Thomas de S. Walery paid eighteen pounds for lands in this county:

^e Rotulus de Crendon, MS. ^f Regist. Egnesham, MS. charta 13.

VOL. I.   F f

he married Adela or Edela de Pontieu, heir to the lordship of St. Albine, near Deep in Normandy [g].

An. MCXCVII.   8, 9.   Richard I.

In the year 1194 an aid was imposed for the king's expedition into Normandy twenty shillings on every knight's fee. The collection is recorded in this year's accounts of the sheriff of Oxon. and Berks. when Gerard de Camvill paid for one fee in Midleton, and Thomas de S. Walery for eighteen of his barony in this county.

Jeffery Fitz-Piers earl of Essex, advanced this year to the honor of Justice of England in the room of Hubert archbishop of Canterbury, having marched with a great power into Wales, was, by the bishop of Bangor, so much incensed against Giraldus Cambrensis archdeacon of Brecon, that he disseized him of all his church lands at Brecon; and, passing afterward through Glocester, directed a precept to the archdeacon of Oxon. to take into his hands all the revenues which he had within his said archdeaconry, which must have respect to the church of Chesterton * near adjoining.

G. *filius Petri comes Essexiæ carissimo amico suo archidiacono Oxoniæ salutem. Sciatis quod G. archdiaconus de Brechene inimicus est domini regis; et ideo vobis mandamus quatenus capiatis in manus vestras omnes reditus suos quos habet in archidiaconatu vestro. Teste meipso apud Gloverniam* xx. die Januarii [h].

The said learned archdeacon did afterwards in an epistle to the bishop of Ely, the dean of London, and the archdeacon of Buckingham, complain, that among his other sufferings he had been dis-

---

* Inter opera MSS. Giraldi Cambrensis in bib. Cotton. Cleopatra. D. 5. habetur epistola Giraldi Hugoni Lincolniensi ep'o de quadam causa eccl'iæ suæ de Cestreton, ad quam presentatus fuerat, sed institutionem ab ep'o obtinere non potuit, Willelmo de S. Maria quodam eccl'iam sibi vendicante. Conqueritur Hugonem adversario plus æquo favere et sibi justitiam denegare G. de Barri [i. e. Giraldus Cambrensis archid. Brechon.] obiit 1223. tunc rector de Cestreton. vid. sub an. MCCXXII.

[g] Neustria Pia, p. 893.   [h] Girald. Camb. Ang. Sac. tom. 2. p. 555.

seized of his revenues, *viz.* his prebend of Hereford, and his church of Chestertune[i]

So as the first precept implying he had some ecclesiastical benefice in this county, and his own after confession declaring that he was dispossessed of the church of Chesterton : it is a just inference that he had the benefice of Chesterton in this neighbourhood. Add to this the authority of Mr. Selden, who reports him presented to this church in the reign of Henry the Second by Gerard de Camvill patron, lord of Midleton adjoining to Chesterton. *In an epistle* (says *he) of Giraldus Cambrensis, writ in time of Henry the Second to Hugh bishop of Lincoln, about his parsonage of Chestertune, which he challenged upon presentation of himself made by Gerard of Camvill, a gentleman of great worth in Lincolnshire ; the bishop's institution is spoken of as clearly necessary according to the canons*[k].

The king, in this ninth of his reign, gave the manors of Shalefeld and Aldeford in Surry to Gilbert Basset, as the right and marriage portion of his mother Alice, daughter of Robert Dunstanvil, which occasioned a trial at law in the fourteenth of Henry the Third, between Sibilla de Ferrers widow of Walter son of Walter Dunstanvil, and William Longspe and Idonea his wife, grand-daughter and heir to the estate of Gilbert Basset[l].

Warine Fitz-Gerold, son of Warine chamberlain and treasurer to king Henry the Second, lord of the manor of Heyford in this county, which from this family received the name of Heyford-warine, did now give one hundred marks for the seizin of the manor of Dadinton in this county, as his mother had at the time of her death : his mother's name (not mentioned by Dugdale) was Maud de Chesny, who in her widowhood, having the said manor of Heyford for her dowry, did grant to the canons of St. Edburg in Burcester five seams or quarters of bread corn out of the said manor, to make hosts or consecrated bread ; which gift was assented to by the said Warine her son.

---

[i] Girald. Camb. Ang. Sac. tom. 2· p. 571.   [k] Selden, Hist. of Tithes, p. 382. citat. a Symbolo Electorum, MS. in Bib. Cotton.   [l] Rog. Dods. MS. vol. 12. f. 119.

*Sciant præsentes et futuri quod ego Matildis de Chesneto dedi, &c.
canonicis de Burnecestre, &c. quinque sumas frumenti ad hostias faciendas, &c. et hoc idem concessit Warinus filius hæres meus ex parte
sua, &c.*

See this confirmed by Isabel de Fortibus, daughter of Baldwin son
of Baldwin husband of Margery daughter of the said Warine, *sub an.*
52 H. III.

An. MCXCVIII. 9, 10. Richard I.

Nigh this time Robert, son of Simon de Meriton, knight, with
consent of Christiana his wife and John his heir, gave to the Knights
Templars three acres of land in Meriton, one upon Stonhearst, one
upon Gerdendole, and the other on Fulberwe, in this form of donation[m].

*Sciant, &c. quod ego Robertus filius Simonis de Meriton assensu et
voluntate Christiane uxoris mee et Johannis heredis mei concessi et di-
misi liberavi et hac mea presenti charta confirmavi pro me et pro antecessoribus meis domui de Templo de Meriton et fratribus ejusdem loci
et successoribus suis in puram et perpetuam elemosinam tres acras terre
cum pertinentiis suis in campo de Meriton quas acras Nicolaus Roc
aliquando tenuit de me ad firmam ; videlicet unam acram super Stonhearst et unam acram super Gerdendole et unam acram super Fulberwe habend. et tenend. prædicte domui et predictis fratribus et successoribus suis libere quiete integre pacifice et honorifice inperpetuum,
in puram et perpetuam elemosinam.   Ego itaque predictus Robertus*

An. MCXCVIII. 9, 10. Richard I.

Preceptum fuit Emmæ de Pori quod wa-
rantizet Joh. Morell 1 hidam terræ cum
pertin. in Borkestall quam tenet et de ea
clamat tenere sicut illam quam Lupellus de
Brai cujus hæres ipsa est dedit Rad'o Morell cum filia sua in maritagio cujus hæres
ipse est, &c. Will'us de Pori positus loco
Emmæ matris suæ defendit quod Lupellus de Brai nunquam dedit terram illam in
maritagio Rob'to Morell, et dicit quod
mater sua dirationavit terram de Acle versus Will'um Basset, ad quam terra de Ho-
lewell pertinet et quod nunquam feoffati
fuerunt predecessores sui per ablatores suos
et inde ponit super jurat. patriæ, &c. dies
dat. &c. Placita x. Ric. I.

<hr>

[m] Regist. Sandford, MS. in Musæo Bib. Bod.

et heredes mei warantizabimus predicte domui et predictis fratribus et successoribus suis totas predictas acras cum pertinentiis suis contra omnes homines mares et feminas et acquietabimus et defendemus ab omnibus servitiis prædictis acris cum pertinentiis suis provenientibus. Ita tamen quod predicta Christiana uxor mea nullum jus vel clameum in predictis acris ratione dotis suæ post decessum meum sibi possit vendicare. Hanc autem cartam fideliter et sine dolo tenendam predicta Maria pro se affidavit. Ut igitur hec omnia prescripta et prediuisa firma et stabilia in perpetuum maneant hoc presens scriptum sigilli mei impressione roboravi. Hiis testibus; Domino Radulpho de Cestreton milite, domino Hamundo de Sancta Fide, Johanne filio Nigelli, Johanne de...... Petro de Wendelingburgh, A. de Mercot, Nicolao Roc Joh. Roc, et aliis.

The same person at another time gave to the same religious use one messuage and half a yard land in Meritone, in this form of donation [n]

Sciant, &c. quod ego Robertus filius Simonis de Meriton dedi et concessi et hac presenti carta confirmavi Deo et beatæ Mariæ et fratribus militiæ Templi Salvatoris in liberam puram et perpetuam elemosinam pro animabus antecessorum et successorum meorum illud mesuagium et illam dimidiam virgate terre quam Thom. Pollard quondam de me tenuit in villa de Meriton* cum omnibus pertinentiis suis infra villam et extra habend. et tenend. predictis fratribus et eorum successoribus et assignatis suis in puram et perpetuam elemosinam libere et quiete bene et pacifice et integre in boscis in planis in pratis et pasturis et in omnibus libertatibus et liberis consuetudinibus infra villam

---

* *Ricardus rex Angliæ, &c. Sciatis me concessisse fratribus militiæ Templi Salomonis in Anglia quietantium de essartis in terris subscriptis scil.* MM *acras terre in Walliis et* XL *acras in Salopscire et apud Bolewode et de* X *acris in Oxfordscir apud Meriton et de* XL *acris in eodem comitatu quas ipsi assartaverunt de foresta nostra de Scottore inter ipsam forestam et Coveleia et de* VII *acris in Northantonscir apud Bradenden et de* CC *acris in Bedfordsir apud Sarnebroke, et de* VII *acris in Huntingdonsir apud Oggir et de* XL *acris in Barksir apud Bickleshham.*

[n] Regist. Sandford, MS. in Museo Bib. Bod.

et extra cum libero introitu et exitu. Ego vero predictus Robertus et hæredes mei predictis fratribus et eorum successoribus et assignatis prædictum messuagium et dimidiam virgate terre cum omnibus perti- nentiis suis contra omnes homines et feminas Judeos et Christianos warantizabimus et de omni servitio exactione consuetudine sectis curie auxiliis querelis et demandis acquietabimus et defendemus et quare volo quod hec mea donatio concessio warantizatio rata et stabilis in perpe- tuum permaneat presentem cartam impressione sigilli mei corrobo- ravi. Hiis testibus; domino Radulpho de Cestreton, Johanne filio Nigelli, Johanne le Poure de Cherleton, S. le Poure de Otindon, Wal- tero clerico, et aliis.

There was now a trial between Gerard de Camvill lord of the ma- nor of Midlington, and the prioress of Ambresbury; the said Gerard claiming the pasture of Avintun called Thornton, which belonged to the manor of Avintun, of which Richard de Camvill was seized in fee in the time of king Henry: the prioress pleaded that the said pas- turage belonged to the village of Kenetby [o].

<h3 style="text-align:center">An. MCXCIX. 10. Richard I. 1. K. John.</h3>

King Richard dying this year on the sixth of April was succeeded by his brother John, which change much raised the interest of Gil- bert Basset lord of Burcester, and Gerard Camvill lord of Midleton, who had both been great adherers to earl John.

Thomas de S. Walery lord of Ambrosden was indebted to the new king one hundred and seventy marks for the relief of his barony; as appears from the accounts of Jeffery Savage, deputy of Hugh de Nevil sheriff of this county [p].

A relief was by Norman custom a fine paid by feudatory tenants to the principal lord, whether of the barons to the king, or of the in ferior vassals to the barons, upon the first accession to such rights and honors. By the law of William the Conqueror the relief of a baron consisted in horse and arms, and things of that nature; but

---

[o] R. Dods. MS. vol. 97. f. 1.   [p] Ibid. MS. Rot. Pip. vol. 14. p. 26.

upon the assize of arms made an. 27. of Henry the Second, every man's arms were to be preserved for his heir, and then was the relief made payable in money, which yet was not set in certain sums, till the grand charter of this prince after reduced them to a standing rate[q].

Soon after the coronation, which was May the twenty-seventh, there was a scutage tax imposed of two marks on every knight's fee; the speedy collection of which is entered in this year's accounts of the sheriff.

Gerardus de Campvil regi comp. de ii *marc. de scut.* 1 *mil.* &c.[r] The king in his first year confirmed several grants to the church of St. Maries de Parco *alias* Notley abbey in Crendon, founded by Walter Giffard duke of Buckingham; and farther grants them yearly two load of wood out of his adjoining forest of Bernwood.

Concessimus etiam eisdem canonicis duas bigas singulis annis euntes et redeuntes in foresta de Bernwud pro bosco ad focum eorum per visum forestariorum a Pascha usque ad festum Omnium Sanctorum exceptis xv. *diebus ante festum S. Johannis Baptistæ et* xv. *post*[s].

Thomas de Verdon died this year in Ireland, and left widow Eustace daughter of Gilbert Basset[t]. The king gave livery and seizin to Gilbert Basset of the manor of Scandeford, which had belonged to Walter Dunstanvil his uncle, and was the marriage right of Alice his mother, for which, in the preceding reign, he had sued in the king's court: and also now granted to the said Gilbert and Egeline his wife, a market in their manor of Strafford, to be held on Sunday in every week[u]. For markets and fairs were often kept upon the Sundays, till in time the abuse appeared worthy reformation. By a clause writ of the king in the second of Henry the Third, the market of Bercamstede, which used to be kept on Sunday, was transferred to Monday[x]: and within the same year the markets of Brack-

[q] W. Dugd. MS. et Coke's Instit. part 1. f. 76. part 2. f. 7.   [r] R. Dods. MS. Rot. Pip.   [s] Mon. Ang. tom. 2. p. 155.   [t] Dugd. Bar. tom. 1. p. 472.   [u] R. Dods. MS. vol. 80. p. 5.   [x] Ibid. vol. 33. f. 32.

ley and Walingford were altered from Sunday to week-days by like special writ [y].

An. MCC. 1, 2. K. *John.*

When William king of Scots did homage to king John at Lincoln, November 22, among the barons present at this solemnity were Gilbert Basset baron of Hedingdon, lord of Burcester, &c. with Thomas and Alan his brothers, and Gerard de Camvil lord of Midleton [z]. Gilbert Basset was now sheriff of Oxon. and Berks. and in his accounts it appears, that Robert de Piselee was indebted to the king sixty marks and one horse or palfry, to be reconciled to the king, and to enjoy in peace Alice de Chesterton, whom he had married without licence from the king [a]

The meaning of this is, that every virgin or widow, possessed of lands held *in capite* from the crown, could not dispose herself in marriage without licence first obtained from her supreme lord. Whereas Robert de Piselee, without any such application for the king's consent, had married Alice de Chesterton, a rich heiress to lands of that tenure; by which he had incurred the king's displeasure, and must have lost his wife's lands, if he had not by this fine made his peace.

Gilbert de Basset had one only daughter and heir Eustace, who, in the beginning of the reign of Richard the First, was married to Thomas de Verdon baron of Alton in Staffordshire, and lord of the manor of Heth in this county; who died in Ireland *an.* 1199. Upon which, in this year, Gerard de Camvill lord of Midleton gave a thousand pounds to the king for the guardianship of his widow with her lands, and liberty to dispose of her in marriage to Richard his son [b].

The arms of S. Walery were two lions passant, as in a seal ap-

---

[y] Prynne, Collect. tom. 3. p. 40.   [z] R. de Hoved. p. 811.   [a] R. Dods. MS. Rot. Pip. Oxon.   [b] Ibid. Linc.

pending to a charter of Thomas de S. Walery, for the soul of Bernard his father, dated 1200 [c].

Reginald earl of Bologne and Dammartin, lord of the manors of Merton and Pidington, procured from the king a charter for a fair once a year at his village of Norton (now Cold-Norton) in this county, for three days, *viz.* on the feast of Simon and Jude, and two days following [d]. And at Cheping-Norton, William Fitz-Alan the third, lord of this manor, in the sixth of king John obtained a charter for a yearly fair [e]. Hugh bishop of Lincoln, just after his return from Rome, died at the old Temple in London on the first of December; whose body was removed to Lincoln, and there carried in procession in presence of two kings, three archbishops, and a great resort of nobility and clergy [f]. He was canonized at Rome *an.* 1220, and his festival observed on the fifteenth of November [g].

An. MCCI.   2, 3. K. John.

Gilbert Basset lord of Burcester nigh this time provided, that his body should be buried in the priory of Burcester, of his own foundation; and to that end gave to those monks all the land which he had bought of Baldwin de Munz in the village of Kirtlington, as also two mills in Kirtlington, paying yearly to the monks of Aulney in Normandy eleven shillings, and to the heirs of Ingeram two shillings for all service.

Sciant præsentes et futuri quod ego Gilbertus Basset dedi et concessi et præsenti charta mea confirmavi Deo et ecclesiæ beatæ Mariæ et sanctæ Edburgæ virginis de Burcester et canonicis ibidem Deo servientibus pro salute. animæ meæ et antecessorum et successorum meorum cum corpore meo ibidem sepeliendo totam terram meam quam emi de Baldewino de Munz in villa de Kertlington cum omnibus pertinentiis suis tam in homagiis quam in aliis servitiis sine ullo retinemento ad me vel hæredes meos pertinente: habendam et tenendam dic-

[c] R. Dods. MS. vol. 20. p. 58.   [d] Ibid. vol. 67. f. 1.   [e] Dugd. Bar. tom. 1. p. 311. b.
[f] R. de Diceto, p. 708.   [g] Mat. West, sub an. 1200.

*tis canonicis in perpetuum in liberam et perpetuam elemosinam libere
et quiete pacifice et integre intra villam et extra, in pratis, pascuis, et
pasturis, boscis et planis cum omnibus libertatibus ad dictam terram
pertinentibus faciendo inde servitium capitali domino fœdi quantum
pertinet ad illud tenementum.   Dedi etiam dictis canonicis duo molendina mea de Kertlington cum omnibus pertinentiis suis sectis et liberis consuetudinibus in viis et planis et semitis cum omnibus libertatibus ad dicta molendina pertinentibus infra villam et extra, ita libere
quiete et plene sicut ea liberius melius et quietius tenui in manu mea.
Reddendo inde annuatim monachis de Alneto undecim solidos et hæredibus Hyngerami duos solidos pro omni servitio.   Et ut hæc mea donatio concessio et præsentis chartæ meæ confirmatio prædictæ terræ et
dictorum molendinorum cum eorum pertinentiis perpetuæ firmitatis
robur obtineat præsenti scripto sigillum meum apposui.   Hiis testibus ·
dominis Rogero de Danteseye, Johanne Luvel, Ada de Peryton, Rogero de Aumary, Gilberto Braci, Radulfo de Cesterton, Philippo de
Wythull, Ada de Gayl, Johanne de Brai, Willielmo de Sudeford, et
multis aliis* [b].*

This manor of Kirtlington, in the nineteenth of Henry the Third,
was granted by the king to Gilbert Basset baron of Wicomb, nephew
to this Gilbert, son of his younger brother Alan, which manor had
formerly belonged to John Humetz constable of Normandy [i]

The king had this year a scutage of two marks for every knight's
fee of such as had his licence to stay at home, upon his passing into
Normandy; on which occasion Amory son of Robert lord of the
manor of Bucknell paid for four fees, Robert de Chesterton for two
fees, Stephen de Hampton one fee, Thomas de S. Walery ten fees.
But Gilbert Basset lord of Burcester, who attended the king, had a
writ of *quietus* for his seven knight's fees within the honor of Walingford [k]. These seven fees consisted of the manors of Coleham
and Uxbrigge, com. Mid. Picheleshorne, in com. Buck. Burncestre,

---

[b] Ex Orig. penes D. Guil. Glynne, Baronettum.   [i] Dugd. Bar. tom. 1. p. 384. a.   [k] R.
Dods. MS. vol. 47. f. 90.

Stratton and Wrechwike, com. Oxon. Ardyngton, com. Berks. and
Compton, in com. Wilts[1].

Reginald Dammartin earl of Bologne (in right of Ida his wife, the
daughter of Henry duke of Lorain by Maud his wife, daughter of
Matthew earl of Bologne by Mary his wife, the second daughter of
king Stephen) confirmed the foundation of the priory of Cold-Norton made by William Fitz-Alan the second[m], (who died[n] about the
nineteenth of Henry the Second,) and gave to it additional endowments, by this charter.

*Reginaldus comes Boloniæ et Ida ejus uxor Boloniæ comitissa ad
quos præsens scriptum pervenerit salutem.   Sciatis nos concessisse et
hac præsenti carta confirmasse domui hospital. de Northona et canonicis ibidem Deo servientibus et S. Mariæ virgini et beato Johanni
Evangelistæ atque S. Egidio pro animabus parentum et antecessorum
nostrorum videlicet comitis Matthei et Mariæ comitissæ et Alberici
comitis Dam. Martini et Matildis comitissæ ejusdem uxoris et pro
animabus nostris et hæredum nostrorum in puram et perpetuam elemosinam trecentas acras et quadraginta octo et dimidiam terræ quas
inde dictæ domui et canonicis ibi Deo servientibus nostri dederunt antecessores.   Et etiam manerium domus sicut sedet et constitutum est.
Licet autem tot acras terræ cum manerio sæpe dictis domui et canonicis nostri non dedissent antecessores, nos domui et canonicis manerium et predictas acras terræ ex dono nostro dedimus et concessimus et
carta nostra confirmavimus.   Ut hæc autem donatio stabilis et firma
permaneat præsentem paginam sigillis nostris dignam duximus roborari.   Non hoc autem prætermittendum est quod domus illa de nostra
donatione est et nos-ibi priorem apponere debemus.   Actum An. Domini* MCCI.   *Hiis testibus; Radulpho fratre nostro, Radulpho de
Claro-Monte, Nevilone de Senlio, Engeramo de Hesdino, Rogero de
Oeli, Willielmo de Bray, Rogero de Burtona, et pluribus aliis*[o]

Which charter, with the concessions of many other benefactors,

[l] Chartular. de Borstalle inter tit. de Standelfe et Gathampton.   [m] Mon. Ang. tom. 3.
p. 55. a.   [n] Dugd. Bar. tom. 1. p. 314. a.   [o] Regist. Coll. Æn. Nas. Oxon. MS. p. 17.
et Mon. Ang. tom. 3. p. 1. p. 55. b.

was confirmed at Woodstock by king Henry the Third in the thirteenth of his reign [p].

An. MCCII. 3, 4. K. John.

The king granted to Gerard de Camvill, lord of the castle an dmanor of Midleton, two markets to be held for two days in each week, one at Sutton in com. Linc. and the other at Midleton in com. Oxon. by these letters patent.

Johannes Dei gratia rex Angliæ, &c. Archiepiscopis, &c. salutem. Sciatis nos concessisse dilecto nostro Gerardo de Kanvill quod habeat duo mercata per duos dies duratura in qualibet septimana, unam scilicet apud Sutton in Hoyland, et aliam apud Midlinton, &c. Datum anno regni nostri tertio. Testibus, Willielmo Mareschallo comite Pembroke, Roberto de Harecourt, Guarino filio Geroldi, Willielmo de Pratellis, &c. [q]

About the same time Gerard de Camvill confirmed the donation, made to the church of St. Mary's and the nuns in Clerkenwell, of one mark of yearly rent from the mills of Hildriksham, given by his sister Maud, the relict of William de Ros, for the souls of the said William her husband, William de Ros her son, and Beatrice her daughter [r].

Thomas de S. Walery lord of the manor of Ambrosden confirmed to the abbot and monks of Tame, eight acres of land in the village of Stoke, which Peter de Talemasch sen. and Richard his son had given to them, as also one perch granted by Peter de Talemasch jun. son of the said Richard; *Testibus Radulpho de Harenge, &c.* [s]; which Ralph de Harenge was steward of this barony of S. Walery [t].

An. MCCIII. 4, 5. K. John.

Ralph abbot of Wells dying this year was succeeded by John abbot of Notley in this neighbourhood [u].

---

[p] Mon. Ang. tom. 2. p. 275. b.　[q] MS. Eliæ Ashmole in Musæo Ashmol.　[r] Regist. de Clerkenwell, MS.　[s] Ex Libro de Tame, MS.　[t] Mon. Ang. tom. 1. p. 486. b.　[u] Annal. Waverl. sub an.

The king gave to Walter Borstard *, who served in his chapel, the manor of Bruhull (now Brill), paying yearly the old service, with addition of forty shillings a year, and the duty of keeping the king's houses at Brill; by this form of donation.

Johannes Dei gratia rex Angliæ, dominus Hiberniæ, &c. Omnibus fidelibus suis salutem. Sciatis nos dedisse et concessisse et præsenti charta nostra confirmasse Waltero Borstard servienti de capella nostra manerium nostrum de Bruhull cum omnibus pertinentiis suis ad fœdi firmam tenendam sibi et hæredibus suis de nobis et hæredibus nostris reddendo inde annuatim antiquam firmam et de incremento XL*. *pro omni servitio. Et ipse custodiet domus nostras de Bruhull sine liberatione. Quare volumus et firmiter præcipimus quod prædictus Walterus et hæredes sui habeant et teneant prædictum manerium de Bruhull cum omnibus pertinentiis suis ad fœdi firmam per prædictum servitium bene et in pace libere quiete integre plenarie et honorifice in omnibus locis et rebus cum omnibus libertatibus et liberis consuetudinibus ad manerium illud pertinentibus sicut prædictum est. Datum per manus Cicestrensis electi apud Merleberg* XXIII. *die Aprilis, anno regni nostri quinto* ˣ.

This tenure was in soccage, not in knights service; for this reason, because this manor was an ancient demesne of the kings of England, and at the general survey was found to have been in the hands of Edward the Confessor, from whom no tenant held by military service ʸ

The doomsday tenure was in this form.   *Brunhell fuit manerium*

---

* *Joh'es Dei gratia rex Angliæ, &c. Sciatis nos dedisse et confirmasse Waltero Buistard servienti nostro Borestall quod est membrum manerii nostri de Bruell cum omnibus pertin. suis in feodi firmam habend. sibi et heredibus suis de nobis et heredibus nostris* pro quatuor libris per ann. pro omni servitio. Concessimus etiam custodiam domuum nostrarum Oxon. cum liberationibus et omnibus aliis ad custodiam illam pertinentibus,—habend. sibi et heredibus suis imperpetuum. Quare volo, &c.

ˣ R. Dods. MS. vol. 25. p. 38.   ʸ H. Spelm. Codex Legum, MS. sub Gul. I.

Edwardi regis. Tunc xx. *hidæ se defendebant; semper terra est* xxv. *carucat. In dominio sunt* iii. *Ibi* xx. *villani cum* xiii. *bordariis; habent* xvi. *carucatas, et adhuc quinque possunt fieri . . . . . . et* i. *molendinum de* x. *solidis, pratum* xx. *carucat. Silva* cc. *porc. inter totum reddit per annum* xxxviii. *libras de albo argento et pro foresta* xii. *libras ursas et pensatas. Tempore regis Edwardi reddebat* xviii. *libras ad numerum.*

Brunhell was the manor of king Edward. Then twenty hides were taxed. The land was always twenty-five carucates. In demesne are three. There are twenty villains with thirteen borderers; they have sixteen carucates, and there may be yet five more.. ... There is one mill of ten shillings rent, a meadow of twenty carucates. Wood for two hundred hogs. In the whole it pays yearly thirty-eight pounds of white silver, (*i. e.* the pure metal before it is coined or stamped,) and for the forest twelve pounds burnt and weighed, (*i. e.* melted down.) In the time of king Edward it paid eighteen pounds in number, (*i. e.* in ready money.)

Gilbert Basset, lord of Burcester and founder of that priory, died this year, leaving one only daughter Eustace, late widow of Thomas de Verdon, now wife of Richard de Camvill. His next surviving brother was Thomas Basset, to whom the king, by writ dated August the second this year, gave his brother's lordship of Hedingdon, to be held by the service of one knight's fee and twenty pounds yearly : x^l. at Michaelmas, and x^l. at Easter. The manor of Burcester and other lands passed to Richard de Camvil in right of his wife.

Thomas de S. Walery lord of Ambrosden confirmed to the church of St. Mary's and nuns in Stodly the site of their house, and half a hide of land in Horton which his father Bernard had given, and further bestows on them free pasnage or mast feeding for their hogs at Stodly, and provides that the prioress shall be alway elected by the approbation of him and his heirs, and come to their court, and do fealty to them. *Hiis testibus ; Milone capellano, Bernardo capellano, Augustino capellano, Radulfo Harenge tunc temporis seneschallo, Wil-*

*lielmo de Friencurt, Philippo de Francer, Roberto de Chetewode, Ra-
dulfo filio Galfridi de Horton, Otewio de Estall, Willielmo filio Nicholai de Lega, Nicholao de Folebroke, et aliis* [z]

An. MCCIV.   5, 6. K. John.

The king meeting his parliament at Oxford confirmed a charter of
Henry the Second, with the addition of other grants to the abbey of
Bruer in the forest of Whichwode, and recites, *Ex dono Willielmi
filii Rici terras in territorio de Midleton quas eis dedit et concessit* [a].

William Fitz-Nigel lord of Borstall and forester of Bernwood died
this year, and by Mabile his wife left son and heir John Fitz-Nigel,
who paid ten marks to the king at Brill for enjoyment of his father's
office, and for liberty to marry at his own pleasure.   At the same
time Walter Borstard was indebted one hundred shillings and one
hundred capons for possession of the manor of Brill lately granted
to him ; both which particulars are thus entered in the sheriff's accompts.

Bukingeham et Bedefordscir.

G. filius Petri. Rob. de Braibroc pro eo regi computat.

Johannes filius Willielmi filii Nigelli debet x. *marcas pro habendo
officio quod pater suus habuit apud Bruhull et unde saitus fuit die quo
obiit et per sic quod ipse non maritetur nisi ad voluntatem suam.*

Walterus Buistard debet c[t]. *et* c. *capones pro habendo manerio de
Bruhull cum pertinentiis ad feodum firmum sibi et hæredibus suis de
rege et hæredibus suis reddendo inde antiquam firmam de* XL[t]. *annuatim
pro omni servitio et demanda et pro custodiendis domibus regis ibidem* [b].

Richard son of Gerard de Camvill of Midleton, having married
Eustace daughter of Gilbert Basset and widow of Thomas de Verdon, did in right of his wife claim the whole estate of Thomas de Ver
don then in possession of Nicolas his brother; and, after a trial in
the king's court, it was now determined that Nicolas de Verdon

---

[*] Mon. Ang. tom. 1. p. 486.   [a] R. Dods. MS. vol. 21. f. 59.   [b] Ibid. Rot. Pip. vol. 14.
p. 94.

should restore to the said Eustace as a reasonable dowry, the two manors of Farnham in Bucks. and Heth in Oxfordshire.

Finis inter Ricardum de Camvil et.Eustaciam uxorem ejus petentes et Nicolaum de Verdon tenentem de rationabili dote ipsius Eustach. quam ipsa clamat versus eundem Nicolaum de omnibus tenementis quæ fuerunt Thomæ de Verdon quondam viri sui.—Idem hic recognovit et concessit eidem Richardo et Eustac. manerium de Farnham in com. Buck. et manerium de Heth in com. Oxon [c].

The said Gerard de Camvill had now from the king a special license to hunt the hare, fox, and wild-cat throughout all the king's forests [d].

In this sixth of king John died Ralph Foliot, who had given the church of Fretwell in this county to the canons of St. Frideswide in Oxford [e]. And within the same year the king directed a precept to the sheriff of Oxon. that without delay he should give to Wido de Diva seizin of all his goods and chattels within his liberties, except the castle of Dadington, which the king would keep in his hands; as also the manor of Dadington, which the king gave to Thomas Basset baron of Hedingdon, who granted it with his daughter Alice in marriage to William Malet baron of Curi in com. Som. [f] : who being in arms against the king in the seventeenth of king John, this manor was by the king given back to the said Thomas Basset [g].

An. MCCV. 6, 7. K. John.

Richard son of Gerard de Camvill of Midleton castle having married Eustace daughter of Gilbert Basset, now gave two thousand marks and ten palfries to the king, for livery of her father's inheritance, excepting what the king laid claim to in the manor of Stoke.

Linc. Oblata VII. *Joan.*

Richardus de Camvill dat duo millia marcas et decem palefridos pro habenda hæreditate quæ fuit Gilberti Basset unde idem Gilbertus obiit

---

[c] Dugd. MS. A. 2. p. 448.   [d] Dugd. Bar. tom. 1. p. 627. b.   [e] Ibid. p. 679. b.   [f] R. Dod. MS. vol. 103. f. 8.   [g] Dugd. Bar. tom. 1. p. 111. b.

seisitus salvo domino regi quod ipse vendicat in manerio de Stoke, et mandatum est, &c. [h]

From hence Mr. Dugdale has inferred that Gilbert Basset died in this seventh of king John[i], which indeed is a mistake. He died in the fifth of John, before his barony of Hedingdon was given to his brother Thomas; but the reason why the livery of his lands to his daughter and heir was deferred to this year was her minority, she coming now to full age. By this means Richard de Camvill became lord of the manor of Burcester, and patron of the priory. His father Gerard de Camvill as copartner with Fulk de Oyri and others, in consideration of three hundred marks fine to the king, obtained license for measuring the whole marsh betwixt the waters of Spalding and Tid in the county of Lincoln[k].

William Mareschall earl of Pembrook held *in capite* from the king the honor of Giffard in the county of Bucks. of which honor the head or chief seat was at Crendon, com. Bucks.

Com. Buck. Willielmus Mareschallus comes de Pembroke habet ibidem capitalem honorem, scilicet honorem Giffard, caput illius honoris Crendon tenet de domino rege[l].

Within this year Thomas de S. Walery, lord of Ambrosden, confirmed to the church of St. Mary's and the monks of Bitlesden all his land in Dodford, for the salvation of his own soul, and that of Edela his wife, and Avoris his mother, and Annora his daughter, and Reginald and Bernard his brothers[m].

An. MCCV. 6, 7. K. John.
Oxon. Kertlinton. terra illa valet de redditu assiso VIII[l]. v[s]. I[d]. exceptis operibus, et si opera fuerunt posita ad diem valet x[l]. II[s]. VIII[d]. Ex rot. de terris Normannorum. anno 6. Joh'ıs. m. 3.

The king at Brill this year, from whence he directed his letters to Meiler Fitz-Henry, justiciary of Ireland. Teste meipso apud Brehul vicesimo die Decembris. Claus. 7. Joh. Append. to Dr. Brady's Hist. of England, p. 1651.

[h] W. Dugd. MS. B. p. 315.   [i] Dugd. Bar. tom. 1. p. 383.   [k] Ibid. p. 627. b.   [l] Testa de Nevil, MS.   [m] R. Dods. MS. vol. 105. f. 60.

An. MCCVI. 7, 8. K. *John.*

In the sheriff's accompts, Thomas de S. Walery lord of Ambrosden appears indebted to the king ten marks and nine shillings in arrear for the scutage tax imposed at Oxford, 1204 [n].

The king granted to William Basset, son and heir of John son of Osmund Basset, one knight's fee in Okelee, which Osmund held by the gift of Brien Fitz-count lord of the honor of Walingford.

Rex concessit Willielmo Basset filio et hæredi Johannis Basset filii Osmundi Basset fœdum unius militis cum pertinentiis in Okelee quod prædictus Osmundus habuit ex dono Briani filii comitis et præterea quartam partem in Ispeden quam idem Osmundus habuit ex dono prædicti Briani [o].

In the accompts of Thomas Basset sheriff of Oxon. and Berks. it appears that the abbot of Egnesham owed one palfry for the having a trial by a jury of twelve men of the neighbourhood of Erdinton, to determine whether two carucates of land in Erdinton were the lay fee of Thomas de S. Walery, or the frank almoigne of the said abbey.

Abbas de Egnesham debet I. *palefridum pro habenda recognitione duodecem legalium hominum de vicineto de Erdinton utrum duæ carucatæ terræ cum pertinentiis in Erdinton sunt laicum fœdum Thomæ de S. Walerico vel libera elemosina pertinens ad abbatiam suam* [p].

Note, there was always money or some other valuable consideration paid to the king for leave to have a trial or judgment in any controversy. *And this* (says a good [q] antiquary) *may be the reason why Glanvil so very often in his treatise of the Laws and Customs of England hath these words,* Petens ac quærens perquirit breve, *The demandant or plaintiff purchases a writ. Hence* (says he) *it is probable at first came the present usage of paying* 6[s]. 8[d]. *where the debt is* 40[l]. 10[s]. *where the debt is* 100[l]. *and so upwards in suits for money due*

[n] R. Dods. MS. Rot. Pip.   [o] Ibid. vol. 4. p. 91.   [p] Ibid. Rot. Pip.   [q] Dr. Brady, Hist. Engl. p. 209.

upon bond. But it is certain, this was owing to king Alfred, who, when he had settled his courts of judicature, to prevent the arbitrary delays of justice, did order, that, without petitioning leave from the king, writs of citation should be granted to the plaintiff to fix the day of trial, and secure the appearance of the other party [r].

This judicial reference to twelve men was a custom that obtained among the northern nations : a good author [s] attributes the institution of it to Regner Lodbrog ; by whose appointment all controversies should be decided by the judgment of twelve chief men, who at first acted not only as a jury, but as judges : when time and the confusion of our Saxon governments had made this practice obsolete, king Alfred revived it with this alteration, that in every action twelve legal or free men of the neighbourhood should make their inquest into the matter of fact, and report it upon oath to the thane or lay nobleman and the bishop, (who were to be assessors in the county court, till their jurisdiction was separated upon the conquest of William the First,) or to the other justices itinerary commissioned by the king, by any of which judges no penal sentence could be given without an agreement of the jury in their verdict : and therefore when one Cadwin a justiciary, in the trial of Hackwy for his life, upon the dissent of three of the twelve, had substituted three other who joined in returning of him guilty ; king Alfred had the said Cadwin hanged for perverting this course of justice [t]

In Easter term the trial between Richard de Camvill and Eustace his wife and prior of Keingworth, for the right of the said church of Keingworth, was put off *sine die*, because the said Richard de Camvill was now in the king's service [u]. In Michaelmas term was a trial on the gift of the church of Minstre* in this county to the monks of Ivry in France, by Maud the wife of William Lovell [x]

* One half of the profits of the church of Minstre appropriated to the convent of Ivry ; the other moiety was the endowment of the parochial priest. Ex regist. Linc.

[r] Alfredi vita, l. 2. cap. 16.   [s] Sax. Gram. l. 9.   [t] Miroir de Justices, cap. 5.   [u] R. Dods. MS. vol. 97. f. 30.   [x] Ibid. f. 31.

An. MCCVII.   8, 9. K. *John.*

Reginald de Dammartin earl of Bologne adhering to the king of
France, was disseized of his fee in the manors of Merton and Pidington and his other possessions in England; but within this year he
came over, made his submission and did his homage to the king at
Lambeth, upon condition he should make no covenant or contract
with the king of France without leave of the king of England : upon
which terms he was restored to his estate[y].

Thomas de S. Walery, by charter dated August 1207, gave to the
nunnery of Stodley, of his father's foundation, three shillings a year
rent in Beckley; and by another charter he gave to the said nuns, in
every week, one carriage of dead fuel in his wood of Horton.

*Occurrit alia charta de tribus solidatis redditus in Bekeley eisdem
monialibus concessis per Thomam de Sancto Walerico data mense
Augusti, An. Dom. MCCVII. hoc est anno nono R. Joannis.   Unde colligendum erit Bernardum de Sancto Walerico patrem Thomæ vixisse
tempore Henrici secundi.*

*In alia charta Tho. de S. Walerico pro salute animæ suæ et Edelæ
uxoris suæ concedit eisdem monialibus qualibet septimana unam car-
rectam ligni mortui in bosco suo de Horton per visum forestarii sui
ejusdem nemoris[z].*

In this same year he confirmed his father's foundation of Godstow

An. MCVII. 8, 9. K. John.
Rex presentat Tho. de Twyford ad eccl'iam de Twyford et mittit presentat.
suum archid'o Buck. ut admittat eum. Rot.
pat. 8. Joh. Oxon. Term. Mich. ann. VIII.
R. Joh.

Jurati veniunt recognoscere utrum una
virgata terræ cum pertin. in Langeton sit
libera elemosyna pertinens ad eccl'iam de

Berencestr an laicum feodum pertinens ad
baroniam abb'is de Westmin. qui venit et
dicit quod assisa non debet inde procedere,
quia beatus rex Edwardus dedit terram illam eccl'iæ de Westmin. et carta sua confirmavit quam ostendit, et quoniam constat
q'd elemosyna est, eunt ad curiam chris-
tianam, et ibi fit placitum inter eos inde.
Placita temp. R. Joh'is, anno 7. rot. 15.

y R. Dods. MS. vol. 80. p. 39.   z Mon. Ang. tom. 1. p. 487.

or Lieu-Dieu in France, with consent of Edela his wife and Allanore his daughter[a]. To which abbey, on marriage of Allanore de S. Walery with Robert earl of Dreux, many of this family were benefactors. Allanore countess of Dreux gave some rents at St. Albine near Diep, an. 1241. Robert earl of Dreux confirmed their fee at Basinvol, an. 1270. John earl of Dreux confirmed their possessions at Gamaches, an. 1290. Again, an. 1330, John earl of Dreux ratified the charter of Robert his brother, dated an. 1311, wherein Robert had confirmed the grant of Beatrix countess of Montfort his grandmother[b].

Egeline the widow of Gilbert Basset sued now for a larger dowry out of the lands of her deceased husband: whereupon in Easter term, the tenth of king John, an inquisition was made into the estate which he died possessed of.

Termino paschæ Rot. 8. in dorso Oxon. Mid. Sur. Buck. Berks.

Extenta terrarum Gilberti Basset in com. prædictis, viz. manerium de Ardinton quod Richardus de Camvill et Egelina uxor ejus tenent. redditus in Walingford, villa de Helemere in com. Buck. Coleham cum Oxebrig membro ejus in com. Mid. maneria de Stoke et Bernecestre in com. Oxon. manerium de Scandeford quod fuit Walteri de Dunstanvill et per regem datum Gilberto Basset; Egelina de Courtney petit dotem de his terris[c].

William Basset had this year a farther confirmation of one knight's fee in Okelee.

Confirmatio Willielmi Basset filii et hæredis Johannis Basset filii Osmundi Basset de 1. fœdo militis cum pertinentiis in Okelee quod prædictus Osmundus tenuit ex dono Briani filii comitis[d]

The king's patent letters for this grant run thus. *Johannes Dei gratia, &c. Sciatis nos concessisse, &c. Willielmo Basset filio et hæredi Johannis Basset filii Osmundi Basset fœdum 1. mil. cum pertinentiis in Okelee quod prædictus Osmundus habuit ex dono Briani filii comitis et præterea quartam partem 1. fœdi mil. in Ipseden quam idem*

---

[a] W. Dugd. f. 1. p. 69. et Neustria Pia, p. 893.   [b] Ibid. p. 891.   [c] R. Dods. MS. vol. 97. p. 37.   [d] W. Dugd. MS. vol. H. p. 96.

Osmundus habuit ex dono prædicti Briani habendam et tenendam sibi et hæredibus suis in perpetuum sicut carta prædicti Briani et confirmationes H. avi regis Hen. patris nostri rationabiliter testantur. Concessimus et confirmavimus eidem Willielmo et hæredibus suis procreatis de Cecilia de Dunstanvil quondam uxore sua villam de Menelida cum pertinentiis suis quam Alanus de Dunstanvil pater ipsius Ceciliæ dedit ad se maritandam, &c. Datum xxvi. *Februarii* [e]

King John was at Woodstock * in this ninth of his reign, where, on the fifth day of August, he confirmed several donations to the abbey of Neth in the county of Glamorgan [f].

An. mccviii.   9, 10.   K. John.

The king's refusal to admit Stephen Langton to be archbishop of Canterbury occasioned a great quarrel between him and the pope, which by degrees was so inflamed, that March 22d the bishops executed the orders of the pope, and interdicted the whole kingdom; whereon all ecclesiastic offices were to cease, except confession, the eucharist to dying persons, and the baptism of infants. Upon this the king seized all the lands and goods of those religious persons who denied to perform divine service; and, within this diocese of Lincoln, committed all the said seizures to William de Cornhull archdeacon of Huntindon, and Gerard de Camvill lord of Midleton castle; and sent out this precept.

Rex omnibus de episcopatu Lincoln. clericis et laicis salutem. Sciatis quod a die Lunæ proxima ante ...... Pascha commisimus W. de Cornhull archidiacono Huntingdon et Gerardo de Camvile omnes terras et res abbatum et priorum et omnium religiosorum et etiam clericorum de episcopatu Lincolniæ qui divina extunc celebrare noluerint,

---

* He confirmed a donation to William de Barry of Lande in Ireland, dat. per manum H. de Well. archidiaconi Wellensis apud Wudestock octavo die Novembris anno regni nostri nono. Appen. to Dr. Brady's Hist. of Eng. p. 166.

[e] Dods. MS. vol. 53. f. 13.   [f] Mon. Ang. tom. 1. p. 119. b.

*et mandamus vobis quod eis extunc sicut ballivis nostris sitis inten-
dentes, &c.* [g]

This Gerard de Camvill was now one of the king's justices itinerant in the county of Lincoln, with Robert de Aumari lord of Buck
nell [h]. Thomas de Fekenham, being possessed of a part of the manor
of Brill, paid to the king five marks and one palfry, for a lawful inquest whether his part of the manor ought to partake of the waste of
Brill by right of common in the said manor; to which common it
was objected he had no right.

Rob. de Braibroc vic. com. Buck. et Bedf.

*Thomas de Fekenham debet R. v. marcas et i. palefridum sic quod
inquisitio fiat utrum membrum illud de manerio de Bruhull quod
idem Thomas tenet debeat participare de vasto manerii de Bruhull
ratione communæ ejusdem manerii in qua communa nihil habet ut
dicunt* [i].

In the night of Epiphany was born to the king a son called Ri
chard, after lord of the manor of Ambrosden, &c. [k]

An. MCCIX. 10, 11. K. John.

Thomas de S. Walery lord of the manor of Ambrosden having incurred the king's displeasure, and been disseized of all his lands, was
glad this year to make his peace by a composition of one thousand
marks to the king.

Oxon. vic. Tom. Basset.

*Thomas de Sancto Walerico R. de M. marcas pro habenda benevo-
lentia regis et pro habendis terris suis unde dissaitus fuit illa occasione* [l].

While the king had seized this barony into his hands, the whole or
most part of it was committed to Robert de Braibroc, so called from
his chief seat in Northamptonshire, the son of Ingebald by Albreda,
one of the daughters and heirs to Ivo Newmarch [m]

---

[g] Prynne, Collect. tom. 2. p. 255.　[h] Dugd. Orig. Jurid. sub an.　[i] R. Dods. Rot.
Pip. 1. vol. 14. p. 158.　[k] W. Dugd. MS. vol. M. p. 31.　[l] R. Dods. MS. Rot. Pip. vol.
14. p. 170.　[m] R. Dods. MS. vol. 108. f. 20.

In this or the preceding year Richard de Camvill and Eustace his wife, for the health of their own souls and of Richard their son, gave to the canons of Berncester all the tithe hay of their demesne in the villages of Berncester, Stratton, and Wrechwic for pure and perpetual alms.

Omnibus sanctæ matris ecclesiæ filiis ad quos præsens scriptum pervenerit Ricardus de Camvill et Eustacia uxor ejus salutem in Domino. Noverit universitas vestra nos divinæ pietatis intuitu et pro animarum nostrarum salute et pro anima Ricardi filii nostri et pro animabus omnium antecessorum nostrorum dedisse et concessisse et hac præsenti charta nostra confirmasse Deo et ecclesiæ sanctæ Mariæ et sanctæ Edburgæ de Bernecestra et canonicis ibidem Deo servientibus totam decimam fœni nostri de dominico nostro in villa de Berncestre et in villa de Stratton et in villa de Wrechewic in puram et perpetuam elemosinam de nobis et hæredibus nostris libere et quiete et integre in perpetuum percipiendam habendam et tenendam. Et ut hæc nostra donatio firma sit et stabilis eam præsenti scripto et sigillorum nostrorum appositione roboravimus. Testibus hiis; Thoma Basset, Alano Basset, Roberto Aumari, Roberto et Radulfo filiis ejus, Roberto filio Aumari, Petro Blundo, Otuelo de Insula, Henrico de Audeli, Genteschiv Paupere, Henrico de Rokebi, Roberto de Rokebi fratre ejus, Radulfo de Marchamel, Roberto de Bakepuz, magistro Laurentio, et multis aliis [n].

To the original parchment are two seals appending: on the first the impress of a horse with this inscription, ✠ Sigillum Ricardi de Canvill; on the other a woman erect with a branch in her right hand, and this inscription, ✠ Sigillum Eustaciæ Basset. About the same time one of the witnesses Genteschive Povre of Ottendun gave to the monks of Tame five acres of land in the said village of Ottendun [o].

An. MCCX. 11, 12. K. John.

Egeline widow of Gilbert Basset claimed the manor of Wrechwic

[n] Ex Orig. penes hon. D. Guil. Glynne, Bar.   [o] Ex libro de Tame, MS.

for part of her dowry against Richard de Camvill and Eustace his wife, who were indebted now to the king one mark to obtain leave for a new trial for this their freehold of Wrechwic.

Oxenefordscire Tom. Basset Vic. Nova Oblata.

Ricardus de Camvil et Eustacia uxor ejus debent i. *marcam pro habenda recognitione novæ assisæ de libero tenemento suo Wrechwic versus Egelinam de Curtenai.*

The issue of the trial seems to have been this, that Richard Camvil and Eustace his wife now quitted that moiety of the manor of Wrechwic, which Gilbert Basset had given in marriage with the said Eustace his daughter to her first husband Thomas de Verdon; and that Egeline de Courtney entered upon this with the other half of the said manor of Wrechwic, which her husband Gilbert Basset had reserved to himself: which latter half part in her free tenure she gave to the priory of Burcester, by this form of donation in parchment, with seal appending, but obliterate.

Universis sanctæ matris ecclesiæ filiis, ad quos præsens scriptum pervenerit, Egelina de Courtnai nobilis matrona salutem in Domino. Universitati vestræ notificetur me dedisse et concessisse et hac præsenti charta mea confirmasse Deo et ecclesiæ sanctæ Mariæ et sanctæ Edburgæ de Burncestre et canonicis ibidem Deo servientibus pro anima domini mei Gilberti Basset et pro anima filii mei Thomæ Basset et pro anima Richardi de Camvill filii Eustaciæ Basset filiæ meæ et pro animabus antecessorum nostrorum dimidiam partem terræ dotis meæ in manerio meo de Wrechwic cum toto bosco de Gravenhull scilicet illam medietatem de Wrechwic plenariam cum omnibus pertinentiis suis, quam prædictus Gilbertus Basset bonæ memoriæ sibi retinuit eo tempore quo prædictam Eustachiam Basset cum reliqua medietate de Wrechwic Thomæ de Verdon maritavit, habendam et tenendam libere et pacifice et quiete ab omnibus servitiis et exactionibus et consuetudinibus mihi pertinentibus. Et ego Egelina de Courtnai prædictam medietatem de Wrechewic cum omnibus pertinentiis suis prædictis canonicis de Burcestre warrantizabo contra omnes homines. Et ut hæc mea donatio firma et stabilis et inconcussa perseveret sigilli mei appo-

sitione hoc præsens scriptum confirmavi. Hiis testibus; Richardo de
Camvil, Eustacia Basset uxore ipsius, Thoma Basset, Alano Basset,
Roberto de Aumari, Roberto filio ejus, Radulfo de Aumari clerico,
Radulfo de Marchehamel, Roberto de Rokebi, Roberto de Bakepuz,
Roberto et magistro Laurentio clericis, et multis aliis [p]

There is another original exact duplicate, the seal whereof has the
impress of a Turk's head, the inscription not legible.

Thomas de S. Walery, at the request of Edela his wife and his chief
tenants, confirmed to the abbey of Oseney all their possessions within
his barony, within which were included two hides of land in Arncot
in the parish of Ambrosden.

Sciant præsentes et futuri quod ego Thomas de S. Walerico consilio
et petitione Edelæ uxoris meæ et proborum hominum meorum concessi
et hac charta mea confirmavi, &c. ecclesiæ S. Mariæ de Oseney et
canonicis ibidem Deo servientibus omnes possessiones de fœdo meo ad
ecclesiam S. Georgii quæ in castello de Oxeneford sita est pertinentes
tam de dominicis meis quam de tenuris hominum meorum, &c. [q]

In this twelfth of king John an inquisition was taken through England of the several tenures of estates from the crown, by which it appears that John Fitz-Nigel knight held one hide of land in Borstall,
called Dere-hide, by the service of being the king's forester in the
royal forest of Bernwood [r]

A forester was such an office as is now a wood-rieve, or in a park
a keeper. There were the king's foresters, who supervised a whole
royal forest by deputation from the king, who had great authority
and profits. And there were the foresters of the barons and knights,
tenants *in capite* of the king, who had lands or woods within the
bounds of any forest. Their respective office is set down in the precepts concerning forests by justices itinerant, an. 1195.

Rex præcipit quod omnes illi qui boscos habent intra metas forestæ
domini regis ponant idoneos forestarios in boscis suis de quibus fo-

p Ex Orig. penes hon. D. Guil. Glynne, Baronettum.   q Regist. Osen. MS. p. 83.
r R. Dods. MS. vol. 47. p. 129.

restariis ipsi quorum bosci fuerint sint plegii vel tales inveniant plegios idoneos qui possint emendare si forestarii in aliquo forisfecerint, quod domino regi pertineat. Item præcipit quod sui forestarii curam capiant super forestarios militum et aliorum, &c. [s]

Henry de Stafford held now the third part of a knight's fee in Bucknell.

Oxon. Henric. de Stafford in Bukenhull 3. part. fœd. [t]

An. MCCXI. 12, 13. K. John.

Gerard de Camvill of Midleton castle held now three carucates of land in Merston and Dedington in this county [u].

Reginald de Dammartin earl of Bologne being deprived of his earldom and all his lands in France, came over into England, and was kindly received by king John, to whom he did homage and fealty, receiving from him 300l. a year, part of which was the former estate of this family in the fee of Pidington and Merton. He was now a great favourite of king John, and intrusted with the command of the English fleet against the French, in joint commission with William Longspe earl of Salisbury [x]

In this or the following year Richard de Camvill and Eustace Bas-

An. MCCXI. 12, 13. K. John.

Universis S. matris eccl'iæ filiis ad quos præsens scriptum pervenerit, frater R. prior de Osneya H. decanus Oxon. salutem in Domino. Noverit universitas vestra controversiam quæ inter dom. H. abbatem et conventum Abendon ex una parte et magistrum Eustachium rectorem ecclesiæ de Cestreton ex altera parte super quibusdam decimis provenientibus, quæ de XL acris quæ sitæ sunt in brucrio de Cestreton quas Galfredus de S. Mauro tenet de feodo Willi-elmi de Legha senioris in Cestreton authoritate domini papæ Innocentii tertii in præsentia nostra vertebatur, magistro Alardo rectore scholarum conjudice nostro se per literas suas sufficienter excusante tali fine concordiæ sopitam fuisse, &c. facta est hæc compositio coram nobis in ecclesia B. Mariæ incrastino Inventionis S. Crucis, pontificatus d'ni papæ Innocentii anno 13. (i. e. 1211.) Ex Cartular. cœnob. Abbendon. MS. citat. apud Hist. et Antiq. Oxon. l. 2. p. 388.

[s] R. Hoved. p. 455. et Manwood of Forest Laws, cap. 21. §. 4.   [t] R. Dods. MS. vol. 47. p. 157.   [u] Ibid. vol. 4. p. 18.   [x] Tho. Walsing. sub an.

set his wife, for the sake of their own souls and of their ancestors and successors, gave to Robert prior of Berncester and the canons of that church, one messuage in the late tenure of Walter de Crockewell, with all appertenances, in pure and perpetual alms.

Universis sanctæ matris ecclesiæ filiis Richardus de Camvilla et Eustachia Basset uxor ejus salutem. Noverit universitas vestra nos pietatis intuitu pro salute animæ nostræ et antecessorum nostrorum et successorum nostrorum concessisse et confirmasse Deo et ecclesiæ sanctæ Edburgæ virginis de Berencester et domino Roberto priori et canonicis ibidem Deo servientibus unum messuagium scilicet illud quod tenuit Walterus de Crockwell in puram et perpetuam elemosinam cum omnibus pertinentiis suis tenendam de nobis et hæredibus nostris libere et quiete ab omni sæculari servitio et exactione. Nos vero et hæredes nostri prædictum messuagium cum omnibus pertinentiis suis eidem priori et canonicis ecclesiæ beatæ Edburgæ de Berncester contra omnes homines et fæminas warrantizabimus. Et ut hæc nostra donatio rata et inconcussa permaneat præsentem chartam sigillorum nostrorum appositione corroboravimus. Hiis testibus; Willielmo de Chauwarces, Thoma Britone, Henrico de Rokebi, Ric. de Horton, Roberto de Rokebi, magistro Willielmo cementario, Rob. de Baduit, Johanne Squier, et multis aliis[y].

An. mccxii. 13, 14. K. John.

In the latter end of the thirteenth of king John an inquisition was taken of the honor of S. Walery, of which Beckley was the head, and Ambrosden a member, in which the tenants are thus recounted: *Petrus Talemasche, Radulphus filius Galfridi, Stephanus de Fretwell, Milisent de Freisenvil, Robertus de Aumari, Ricardus D'aumari, Robertus de Burton, Fulco de Baiocis, Ricardus de Turstelod, Walterus de Bononia, Reginaldus de S. Walcrico, Bernardus de Areines, Radulphus Purcell, Robertus de Gent, Hugo de Wotenhull, Walterus Foliot, Cecilia de Arewell, Willielmus de Esses, &c.*[z] And at the

[y] Ex Orig. penes hon. D. Guil. Glynne, Bar.   [z] R. Dods. MS. vol. 47. f. 146.

same time an inquisition was taken of the honor of Walingford, by which it was found that Richard de Camvill of Midleton held seven knight's fees within the said honor of the inheritance of his wife, *viz.* Burcester, Wrechwic, Stratton, &c. lately the estate of Gil bert Basset [a].

James le Bret, lord of Bigenhull within the parish of Burcester, by consent of his wife Amable, gave to the priory of St. Edburg in Burcester four acres of meadow in Gore near the Ham (*i. e.* the house or piece of land) of Gilbert, by this charter.

Sciant præsentes et futuri quod ego Jacobus le Bret assensu uxoris meæ Amable et hæredum meorum dedi et concessi Deo et ecclesiæ S. Edburgæ de Berncester et priori et canonicis ibidem Deo servientibus pro anima patris mei et matris meæ et pro animabus antecessorum meorum et successorum meorum quatuor acras prati in Gore juxta Hamam Gilberti libere et quiete ab omni sæculari servitio in puram et perpetuam elemosinam. Has prædictas quatuor acras ego et hæredes mei warantizabimus prædictæ ecclesiæ contra omnes homines et fæminas in perpetuum. Et ut hæc donatio rata et inconcussa permaneat hanc præsentem chartam meam sigilli mei attestatione corroboravi. Hiis testibus; Roberto D'aumari, Roberto D'aumari filio ejus, Waltero Bret, Thoma Britun, Ricardo de Hortone, Roberto de Piselei, Hamundo de Sancta Fide, Thoma Gulifred, Radulfo clerico, Willielmo Palmero, et multis aliis [b]

To the original parchment is a fair seal appending, with the impress of a branch, and two turtle doves sitting opposite and billing, a device seemingly designed for an emblem of conjugal affection, with this inscribed, ✠ Sigillum Jacobi Le Brut Ama.

The prioress and nuns of Merkyate in com. Bedf. granted to Hervey prior of Burcester two selions or ridges of land in Hodesham, in exchange for one acre nearer to their land in Nyhenaker, and half an acre of meadow nigh to their meadow called Gilberts-ham, by mutual indenture, of which one part was in this form.

---

[a] R. Dods. MS. vol. 47. f. 146.   [b] Ex. Orig. penes D. W. Glynne, Baronettum.

Omnibus Christi fidelibus has literas visuris Johanna priorissa sanctæ Trinitatis de Bosco et ejusdem loci conventus salutem in Domino. Noveritis quod nos dedimus et concessimus et præsenti charta nostra confirmavimus Hervico priori de Berncester et ejusdem loci canonicis duos seliones in Hodesham qui jacent juxta rivulum extra curiam dictorum canonicorum habendos et tenendos dictis canonicis in perpetuum in eschambio unius acræ terræ in Burncestre propinquioris terræ nostræ in Nyhenaker et dimidiæ acræ prati propinquioris prato nostro quod vocatur Gileberdsham. Et in hujus rei testimonium huic scripto in modum chyrographi confecto vicissim sigilla nostra apposuimus. Hiis testibus; domino Rogero de Aumari, domino Roberto Purcell, domino Hamundo de S. Fide, militibus; Philippo de Wappele, Walhamoth Paupere, Gilberto de Sancta Fide, et multis aliis [c].

An. MC CXIII. 1415. K. *John*

Thomas de S. Walery, by adhering to the pope and the French interest, had again highly offended the king, who on this occasion sent a precept to the sheriff of this county, with orders for putting in some discreet steward to take care of his lands and chattels, commanding the sheriff to summon him to appear before the king on the day after St. John Baptist, there to answer to such things as should be charged against him.

Rex vic. Oxon. salutem. Præcipimus tibi quod ponas aliquem discretum hominem de tuis in terra Thomæ comitis de Sancto Walerico in balliva tua ad videndum quod nihil inde amoveatur. Et summone ibidem per bonos summonitores eundem Thomam quod sit coram nobis in crastino S. Johannis Baptistæ responsurus ad hoc quod ei proponetur. Teste meipso apud Roffam nono Junii an. reg. 15 [d].

The next day the king sent a precept to Ralph Hareng, seneschal of the honor of S. Walery, requiring him to assign to Gerard, son of Gerard de Rodes, land to the value of twenty pound out of the said estate. *Rex Radulpho Hareng salutem. Mandamus vobis quod statim*

---

[c] Ex Autog. penes D. W. Glynne, Bar.   [d] R. Dods. MS. vol. 97.

visis literis istis assignetis Gerardo filio Gerardi de Rodes viginti li-
bratas terræ de terra quæ fuit Thomæ de Sancto Walerico. Teste rege
x. Jun.*

Maurice de Gaunt, son of Robert the son of Robert Fitz-harding,
covenanted to serve the king at his own charge with twenty knights,
himself accounted one, for one whole year, in consideration he might
marry Maud the daughter of Henry de Oily, who gave him with his
said daughter the manor of Weston, now Weston on the Green[f].

Walter Borstard granted to Sir John Fitz-Nigel, lord of Borstall
and forester of Bernwood, half a hide of land in Borstall, and ten
acres in Brill, &c. by this deed.

Sciant præsentes et futuri quod ego Walterus Borstard dedi con
cessi et præsenti charta mea confirmavi Johanni filio Nigelli de Bor-
stall pro homagio et servitio suo totam illam dimidiam hidam terræ
cum pertinentiis in Borstalle unde messuagium et croftæ jacent juxta
messuagium Roberti filii Levre quod idem Robertus aliquo tempore
tenuit. Et præterea totam illam virgatam terræ et dimidiam cum per-
tinentiis suis in Borstall unde messuagium et croftæ jacent inter cu-
riam prædicti Johannis et curiam quæ fuit Gilberti filii Herialdi, et
prædictas illas decem acras terræ cum pertinentiis in Brehull quas
Reginaldus de la Penne tenuit et prædictus illas tres acras terræ cum
pertinentiis in Brehull unde Sampson le Poter tenuit unam et Walte-
rus le Poter aliam, et tertiam quæ vocatur le Heye et croftam Radul-
phi forestarii quantum se extendit, &c. reddendo nobis annuatim pro
prædicta dimidia hida terræ cum pertinentiis in Borstalle decem soli-
dos, et pro prædicta virgata terræ et dimidia de Borstalle septem so-
lidos et sex denarios, et pro prædictis decem acris terræ in Brehull
duos solidos, et pro prædicto assarto unum denarium, &c. Et pro hac
mea donatione confirmatione et warantia dedit mihi prædictus Johan-
nes in guersuma quadraginta solidos sterlingorum. Hiis testibus;
Fulcone filio Ricardi, Thoma filio Galfridi, Roberto de Valour, Hu-
gone de la Haie, Willielmo de Ikeford, Galfrido de S. Martino, Hen-

---

[e] R. Dods. MS. vol. 68. f. 103. Claus. 15. John. [f] R. Dods. Rot. Fin. MS.

rico de S. Andrea, Willielmo Gardyn, Richardo de Grenevil, Ada filio Petri, Helia Anglico, et aliis.

The said Walter Borstard, by another charter, granted to Sir John Fitz-Nigel half a hide of land in Borstall, for the yearly rent of ten shillings sterling, and one mark of silver in hand. *Hii sunt testes ; dominus Johannes abbas de Nutele, Willielmus de Ikeford, Thomas de S. Andrea, Willielmus frater suus, Robertus persona de Merston, Willielmus Carbonel, Ricardus Ferebraz, Nicholaus de Adulakeston, Thomas le Franceys, et multi alii* [g].

<h2 style="text-align:center">An. MCCXIV. 15, 16. K. John.</h2>

Gerard de Camvill of Midleton died this year or the last, and left by Nichola his wife Richard his sole heir, by marriage lord of Burcester, who had now livery of Midleton castle in Oxfordshire, as part of his inheritance by descent from his father [h]. The king's precept to the sheriff of the county to deliver him possession bears date January the fifteenth.

Rex vic. Oxon. salutem. Sciatis quod reddidimus Ricardo de Camvill castrum de Midleton quod fuit Gerardi de Camvill patris sui : et ipsi Richardo hæreditarie contingit. Et ideo mandamus, &c. Teste meipso, &c. decimo quinto Jan. [i]

The said Gerard de Camvill and Nichola de Haya his wife had given to the monastery of Combe, of his father's foundation, one hundred shillings to keep his anniversary there for ever [k]

Before this year died Egeline de Courtney, widow of Gilbert Basset, and mother of Eustace wife of Richard Camvill ; and the lands she held in dowry fell to the said Richard and Eustace his wife, who thereupon confirmed the donation made by Egeline their mother of one half of the manor of Wrechwic to the prior and canons of Burcester, in this form.

Omnibus sanctæ matris ecclesiæ filiis, ad quos præsens scriptum

---

[g] Cartular. de Borstall, MS. f. 111. [h] W. Dugd. Bar. tom. 1. p. 627. [i] W. Dugd. Analecta ex Rot. MS. C. 1. p. 5. et R. Dods. MS. vol. 53. p. 7. [k] Dugd. Antiq. War. p. 146. a.

pervenerit, Richardus de Camvilla et Eustacia Basset uxor ejus salutem in Domino.   Noverit universitas vestra nos divinæ pietatis intuitu et pro animabus antecessorum nostrorum et pro anima Ricardi de Camvill filii nostri dedisse et concessisse et hac præsenti charta confirmasse Deo et ecclesiæ S. Mariæ et S. Edburgæ de Burnecestria et canonicis ibidem Deo servientibus, illam medietatem manerii de Wrechwic quam Gilbertus Basset sibi retinuit eo tempore quo Eustaciam filiam suam de altera medietate maritavit cum toto bosco de Gravenhull in puram et perpetuam elemosinam habendam et tenendam in perpetuum eisdem canonicis de nobis et de hæredibus nostris libere et quiete pacifice et honorifice in bosco et in plano pratis et pascuis viis et semitis aquis et mariscis et locis omnibus et omnibus libertatibus et liberis consuetudinibus ad prædictam terram pertinentibus ab omni servitio et exactione sæculari liberam et quietam.   Et ego Richardus de Camvill et Eustacia uxor mea et hæredes nostri warantizabimus prædictam terram cum prædicto bosco de Gravenhull et cum omnibus sibi pertinentibus prædictis canonicis de Burncester contra omnes gentes.   Ut autem hæc nostra donatio et confirmatio perpetuum firmitatis robur optineat eam præsenti scripto et sigillis nostris appositis communivimus.   Testibus his; Roberto de Aumari, Roberto filio ejus, Radulfo filio ejusdem clerico, Roberto filio Amarici, Otvelo de Insula, Henrico de Audeli, Henrico Rokebi, Roberto de Rokebi fratre suo, Radulfo de Marchamel. Roberto de Bakepuz, Gentischiv Paupere, Hub. de Midlington, et aliis multis.

To this original deed in parchment there be two seals appending whole and fairly impressed; on the first, the effigies of a horse without rider and this inscription, ✠ SIGILLUM RICARDI DE CAMVILL. The other is a larger oblong oval with impress of a woman erect

An. MCCXIV. 15, 16. K. John.
Anno 6. Hug. Well. D. ep'us concessit priori et conventui de Bernecestr 5 marc. ann. de eccl'ia de parva Messenden. Rex concessit Rad'o de Nevill eccl'iam de Lute-

gareshall dat. per manum ipsius Rad'i. 6. Maii. anno reg. 16. Joh. Eodem die rex concessit eidem Rad'o de Nevill eccl'iam de Stratton.

holding a branch in her right hand and this inscription, + SIGIL-
LUM EUSTACIÆ BASSET [1].

For a further benefaction to the priory of Burcester, the said Ri
chard de Camvill, by will and consent of Eustace his wife, gave to
Robert Clerk for his homage and service one virgate of land in the
village of Berncester, late in the occupation of Robert Ball, to hold
for the yearly rent of one pound of cummin, on condition the said
Robert Clerk or his heirs, should find one lamp before the altar
of St. Nicholas in the greater church of St. Mary and St. Edburg
of Berncester, to burn every night entirely, and every day during
divine service, and at canonical hours, for the health of the souls
of him and his wife, and Gilbert Basset, and Richard Camvill their
son.

*Sciant præsentes et futuri quod ego Ricardus de Camvill de volun-
tate et assensu Eustaciæ Basset uxoris meæ dedi et concessi et hac
præsenti charta mea confirmavi Roberto Clerico pro homagio et pro
servitio suo unam virgatam terræ in villa de Bernecester cum omnibus
suis pertinentiis, illam videlicet virgatam terræ quam Robertus Ball
tenuit habendam et tenendam sibi et hæredibus suis de me et meis hæredibus libere et quiete integre honorifice hæreditarie in perpetuum,
reddendo inde mihi vel hæredibus meis annuatim unam libram cumini
in festo natalis Domini pro omni servitio vel exactione sæculari ad me
vel ad hæredes meos spectante salvo domini regis servitio ad tantam
scilicet terram pertinente. Ita tamen quod prædictus Robertus Clericus vel hæredes sui invenient lampadem unam ante altare Sancti Nicolai in majori ecclesia Sanctæ Mariæ et Sanctæ Edburgæ de Bernecester in perpetuum pro nostrarum salute animarum et pro anima
Gilberti Basset et pro anima Ricardi filii nostri qualibet nocte totaliter et quolibet die dum divina celebrantur, et ad horas canonicales
ardentem. Et ego Ricardus de Camvill et hæredes mihi warantizabimus prædictam virgatam terræ cum omnibus suis pertinentiis præ-*

---

[1] Ex Orig. penes hon. D. Guil. Glynne, Bar.

fato Roberto Clerico et hæredibus suis contra omnes gentes. Et ut hæc mea donatio concessio et confirmatio rata sit et firma eam præsenti scripto et sigillo meo eidem apposito roboravi. Testibus his; Roberto de Aumari, Roberto et Radulpho filiis ejus, Genteschiv Paupere, Radulpho Ivans et Hugone fratre ejus, Ada capellano, Henrico de Rokebi, et Roberto de Rokebi fratre ejus, Rad. de Marchamel, Roberto de Bakepuz, Abraham capellano, magistro Gilberto, Roberto clerico, Waltero cemitario, magistro Laurentio, et multis aliis [m]

To this script in parchment were two seals appending, of which the first is broken off, the other is the same stamp and inscription with the former of Eustace Basset.

They did by another charter confirm to the priory of Burcester their manor of Wrechwic and wood of Gravenhull, with the additional gift of a certain pasture called Coubrugge; to the original are two seals appending, with the same impress and inscription [n].

The king in this sixteenth of his reign by letters patent granted to Maurice de Gant, lord of the manor of Weston, the manor of Barew with all its appertenances to hold for life, as granted to Eva his sister [o].

King John was defeated in the battle of Bovines in Artoise in France, where Reginald Dammartin, earl of Bologne, lord of the fee of Pidington and Merton, was taken prisoner by the French king, and thrust into a strong tower in Perone in Picardy, laden with irons and chained to a great piece of timber [p]. King John brought off one prisoner Robert son of Robert earl of Dreux, (who by marriage became soon after lord of the manor of Ambrosden, &c.) for whom in exchange the French king released the earl of Salisbury [q]. But before king John would set at liberty the said Robert, he sent letters to the archbishop of Canterbury and the rest of the bishops and temporal lords, letting them know that because Robert was son to the earl

---

[m] Ex Autographo penes D. W. Glynne, Baronettum.   [n] Ex Orig. ibid.   [o] R. Dods. MS. vol. 53. f. 21.   [p] Brady, Hist. p. 493.   [q] W. Dugd. MS. vol. M. p. 9.

of *Dreux*, kinsman to the king of France, therefore he would not exchange him without their advice[r].

An. MCCXV.   16, 17.   *K. John.*

This year died * Richard de Camvill lord of Midle*t*on castle, and of Burcester, &c. leaving by Eustace his wife one only daughter and heir Idonea.   Before his death he confirmed to the abbey of Oseney one messuage with its other buildings in Erdinton, and gave to the monks free liberty to collect the tithes of his demesnes in Erdinton and Burcester, as had been granted to the chapel of St. George's, by Robert de Oily sen.

Sciant præsentes et futuri quod ego Ricardus de Camvilla dedi et concessi et hac præsenti charta mea confirmavi Deo et ecclesiæ S. Mariæ de Osen. et canonicis ibid Deo servientibus pro salute mea, &c. unum messuagium cum suis ædificiis in villa mea de Erdinton, &c. Concessi etiam prædictis canonicis quod libere et sine ulla vexatione possint congregare decimas suas quas habent de dominicis meis de Erdinton et de Burncestre.   Ita quod nec ego nec hæredes meis prædictis canonicis aliquam super prædictas decimas inferemus molestiam, &c. [s]

Mr. Dugdale[t] attributes this donation to Richard de Camvill sen. in the reign of Henry the Second: but it must needs be meant of this his grandson who was the first of that family, who had any right in Erdington and Burcester his wife's inheritance.   The same author is guilty of another mistake in reporting Richard de Camvill jun. to have lived beyond the second of Henry the Third; whereas he must

* The said Richard de Camvil and Eustace his wife confirmed to the abbey of Reading the grant which her father Gilbert Basset had made of a demesne meadow in Endentun com. Berks, and common pasturage of twenty-four oxen or other cattle, according to the original concession recited p. 133.   Cartular. abbat. Radinges. MS. f. LVIII.

[r] Dugd. Bar. tom. 1. p. 176. a.   [s] Regist. Osen. MS. f. 141.   [t] Dugd. Bar. tom. 9. p. 627.

needs have been dead this year, when the wardship of his daughter was committed to William Longspe earl of Salisbury, with liberty of disposing her in marriage to William his eldest son, with all the inheritance that came by her mother; viz. the estate of Gilbert Basset. And to this effect a precept was now directed to the sheriff.

Mand. est vic. Oxon. et Berks. quod habere faciant W. com. Sarum. maritagium filiæ Ricardi de Camvill genitæ de Eustachia quæ fuit filia Gilberti Basset uxoris ipsius Richardi ad opus Willielmi sui primogeniti de Ela comitissa Sar. cum tota hæreditate sua contingente ipsam filiam ejusdem Ricardi in balliva sua ex parte matris suæ [u].

This part of the county was now the passage between the king at Oxford and the barons at Brackley, where, after some messages sent and ineffectually returned, the barons declared for open war.

Maurice de Gaunt, taking part with the rebellious barons, his lands were seized and given to Philip de Albini, excepting Weston in this neighbourhood, and Beverston in com. Gloc. [x]

On the same occasion John Fitz-Robert lord of Clavering in Essex was disseized of his lands, and his manor of * Ainho, com. Northampt. was committed to Thomas de S. Walery, lord of the manor

---

* Terra Goisfridi de Mannevile in Sutone hundr.

Goisfridus de Mannevile tenet de rege Aienho. Ibi sunt iii hidæ et quint. par. unius hidæ. Terra est viii carucat. De hac terra est hida et quinta pars unius hidæ in d'nio; et ibi tres carucat, et viii servi et xxiii villani et ix bordarii cum v car. Ibi molin. de x solidis, et xx acri prati. Valuit vi lib. Modo viii lib. Algar tenuit T. R. E. Ex Lib. Domesd.

William E. of Essex, temp. H. 2. granted the whole village of Ainho to his aunt Adelicia de Essex, which her husband Roger Fitz-Richard settled on her in exchange for Gunton her first dowry. R. Dods. Collect. MS. vol. 90. f. 108.

Walterus de Plessetis fuit rector ecclesiæ de Aynho, an. 1322. Reg. Baldock ep'i Lond. f. 51.

Permutatio inter Joh. Edyngton, rectorem eccl'iæ de Aynho Linc. dioc. et Joh. Priklove, rectorem eccl'iæ de Wodelanferrere Lond. dioc. Reg. Braybrok ep'i Lond.

Aynho habet feriam in vigilia, in die, et in crastino S. Jacobi ap'li concessam fratribus hospitalis D. Jacobi de Ainho. Teste Rege. 10 Jun. 9 Joh.

---

[u] W. Dugd. MS. vol. B. 1. p. 29.   [x] Dugd. Bar. tom. 1. p. 412.

of Ambrosden, who continued faithful to the king's interest[y]. William Mallet baron of Curi was disseized for the like offence; several of his lands were given to Hugh de Vivion, and the manor of Ded ington in com. Oxon. restored to Thomas Basset baron of Hedington, by this precept. *Rex vicecomiti Oxon. salutem. Scias quod con cessimus Thomæ Basset terram de Dedinton cum pertinentiis quam dederat Willielmo Malet in maritagio cum filia sua. Et ideo præcipimus, &c. Teste rege apud Roffam* x. *Novem*[z]. From the same place on November the sixth, a like precept was directed to the sheriff of this county to restore to Ralph de Montibus his land in Kirtlinton[a]. And Reginald earl of Bologne, lord of the fee of Merton and Pidington, had a grant from the king of the manors of Kirkton and Dunham[b].

An. MCCXVI. 17, 18. K. John. 1. Henry III.

About this time James Bret, lord of the manor of Bigenhull in the parish of Burcester, with consent of his wife, gave to Richard prior of Burcester and the canons of that convent, a certain meadow of his demesne called Kinsitheam, for the soul of his father Walter Bret and of his ancestors and successors.

Sciant præsentes et futuri quod ego Jacobus Bret consensu et assensu Amable uxoris meæ dedi et præsenti charta mea confirmavi Deo et ecclesiæ Sanctæ Edburgæ de *Berncester *et R. priori ejusdem loci et*

An. MCCXVI. 17, 18. K. John. 1. Hen. III.

Sententia inter abb'em et conventum Osney et W. de Scto Maxentio rectorem de Mixeburi de duabus partibus decimarum 13 acrarum in Mixeburi spectant. ad ecclesiam Seti Georgii castelli Oxon. 1216. Ex cron. Osen. fol. 154. Bib. Cotton. Vitellius. E. 15.

* E rotulo Hug. Well. de ordinationibus

vicariarum ordinatarum auctoritate concilii:

Eccl'ia de Berencestr valet xx marc. et amplius. Vicarius habebit pro stipendiis suis et capellani sui et cl'icorum suorum xl sol. annuatim in certis portionibus assignandis, et ipse et capellanus ejus et el'ici sui habebunt victum suum de prioratu eisdem capellanis et cl'icis competentem, et

y Dugd. Bar. tom. 1. p. 107.　z R. Dods. MS. vol. 103. f. 41.　a Ibid.　b Ibid. vol. 97. f. 125.

canonicis ibidem Deo servientibus quoddam pratum dominii mei quod vo-
catur Kinsitheam integre et plenarie sine aliqua diminutione pro anima
patris mei Walteri Bret et antecessorum et successorum meorum in li-
beram et puram et perpetuam elemosinam et quietam ab omni sæculari
servitio et ex omnibus consuetudinibus et exactionibus et querelis mihi
et hæredibus meis pertinentibus; hanc prædictam liberam donationem
meam ego Jacobus Bret et hæredes mei warantizabimus Deo et jam
dictæ ecclesiæ et R. præfato priori et prædictis canonicis contra om-
nes homines et fœminas imperpetuum. Hiis testibus; Thoma Basset,
Alano Basset, Ricardo de Turs. Roberto Damari, Roberto Damari
filio ejus, Otvelo dë Insula, Genteschive Paupere, Roberto de Piselee,
Johanne filio Willielmo de Curtlinton, Ingelramo de Curtlinton, Rob.
de Badinton, et multis aliis.

To the original parchment is a seal appending with the impress of
a stalk or branch with two birds sitting opposite, and the inscription
of ✠ SIGILLUM JACOBI BRET [c].

The sheriff of this county was commanded to restore to Robert
Mauduit and Alan de Bocland, knights, full seisin of their lands in
the manor of Dedington, which Wido de Diva had granted them to
hold in fee [d]

The king a little before his death committed the estate of Thomas
de S. Walery lord of Ambrosden to Ralph Harengod, to keep for the
use of the said Thomas.

R. vic. Oxon. Scias quod commisimus Radulpho de Harengod to-
tam terram T. de S. Walerico cum omnibus pertinentiis suis custodien-

habebit fenum et prebendam ad equum
unum de prioratu, et oblationes suas, scil.
unum denarium pro corpore presenti et
unum denarium pro sponsalibus et unum
denarium pro purificatione cum integer denarius obvenerit; et in die natali Dni 3 denarios et in die Paschæ 2 denar. et in duobus aliis principalibus festis unum dena-

rium; habebit etiam confessiones suas et
secundum legatum usque ad sex denarios;
si quod supererit, canonici et vicarius dimi-
diabunt; habebit insuper incensum competentem extra prioratum et canonici omnia
onera ejusdem eccl'ie sustinabunt preter
onus parochiale.

c Ex Orig. penes hon. D. Guil. Glynne, Bar.   d Rog. Dods. MS. vol. 103. f. 49.

dam ad opus ipsius Thomæ. T. R. 13. *Aug. eodem modo vice-com.*
Northan. Berks. Bucks. and Bedf. et constabulario de Waling-
ford^e

Nigh this time Thomas de S. Walery confirmed the donation
made by his father of Wlgaricot (now Wolvercot) to the nunnery of
Godstow, by this charter.

Noverint præsentes et futuri quod ego Thomas de S. Walerico in-
tuitu pietatis et caritatis et pro salute animæ meæ et Edelæ uxoris
meæ et Avor. matris meæ et omnium antecessorum meorum concessi et
præsenti charta confirmavi donum illud quod Bernardus bonæ memoriæ
vir pater meus fecit nobili Henrico Anglorum regi filio Matildis illus-
tris imperatricis de Wlgaricot libere et pacifice quiete et honorifice te-
nendam cum omnibus pertinentiis suis in perpetuum sicut charta præ-
fati Bernardi patris mei super hoc ipso dono testatur. Concessi etiam
et præsenti scripto confirmavi Deo et ecclesiæ beati Johannis Baptistæ
de Godestow et sanctimonialibus ibidem Deo servientibus hoc ipsum
donum quod prænominatus Henricus rex filius Matildis illustris im-
peratricis fecit prætaxatis sanctimonialibus de prænominata villa de
Wlgaricot tenendam et in pace possidendam cum universis pertinentiis
suis in perpetuum sicut charta sæpedicti domini Henrici regis Angliæ
testatur. Et ut hæc mea concessio et confirmatio firmiter conservetur
præsentem chartam sigillo meo confirmare dignum duxi. Hiis testi-
bus; Radulfo Harenge Seneschallo meo, Walone de Cumberay, Ber-
nardo Malecter juvene, Willielmo de Westbiri militibus, Engram ca-
pellano, Willielmo de Pichecot, Willielmo clerico, persona de Am-
bresdon^f.

Alan Basset baron of Wicomb, brother of Gilbert late lord of the
manors of Midleton and Burcester, had a grant from the king of the
lordship of Menstre in this county, which had been given in dowry
to the daughter of *t*his Alan by John Lovel, from which family this
place had the appellation of Menstre-Lovel^g

---

^e W. Dugd. MS. vol. B. 1. p. 35.   ^f Regist. S. Frides. MS. carta 526. et Mon. Ang.
tom. 1. p. 527.   ^g Dugd. Bar. tom. 1. p. 383.

October the nineteenth the king died at Newerk, and his son Henry the Third began his reign[h].

<h3 style="text-align:center">An. MCCXVII. 1, 2. *Henry III.*</h3>

A mandate was sent to the sheriff of this county to restore to the abbot and monks of Westminster their manor of Islep near Oxford, of which they had been disseized by king John on a false report of the abbot's death[i]. A like precept was directed to give * Thomas de S. Walery possession of the lands of his brother Henry, of which he had been disseized upon occasion of the barons war.

Mand. est vic. Oxon. quod seisinam habere faciat Thomæ de Sancto Walerico terræ Henrici fratris sui in balliva sua quantum inde habuit ante guerram et disseisitus est occasione ipsius guerræ, &c.[k]

Which Henry de S. Walery on August the fifteenth had seizin of his lands in Fulbroc com. Oxon. Northon and Sutton com. Hunt. and Henton com. Berks. at which village he procured a market on every Wednesday, by the king's licence dated the twenty-third of September, 2. Hen. III.[l]

Nichola widow of Gerard de Camvill having been a martial woman, and stoutly adhering to king John, had in the eighteenth of that king the sherivalty of Lincoln committed to her; and had it now continued to her, with livery of the manors of Cherleton and Henxterugge, whereof the family had been dispossessed by Hubert de Burgh justiciary of England[m].

Nigh this time Robert Fitz-Michael, in consideration of one mark in silver, and the yearly rent of one pound of cummin at Easter,

---

* Hen. II. dedit manerium de Erdinton Bernardo de Scto Walerico, et post eum Thomas de Seto Walerico tenuit dictum manerium, quo defuncto circa principium regis Hen. III. translata est per filium suum hereditas ad Rob. com. Drocarum, qui Rob. seisinam suam perdidit omnium quæ habebat in Anglia. MS. Cotton. de cartis Egnesham.

[h] Mat. West. sub an.   [i] R. Dods. MS. vol. 53. f. 48.   [k] W. Dugd. MS. vol. B. 1. p. 38.   [l] Ibid.   [m] Dugd. Bar. tom. 1. p. 598.

granted to the church of St. Edburg in Burcester and the monks of that convent, two acres of land in Buricroft beyond the priory court lying between the land of Nicholas son of Harold, and the land of John Godard.

Sciant præsentes et futuri quod ego Robertus filius Michaelis pro salute animæ meæ et pro animabus antecessorum et successorum meorum dedi et concessi et præsenti charta mea confirmavi Deo et ecclesiæ beatæ Mariæ et Sanctæ Edburgæ virginis de Bernecestria et canonicis ibidem Deo servientibus in liberam et perpetuam eleemosinam duas acras terræ in Buricroft extra curiam dictorum canonicorum, scilicet illas duas acras quæ jacent inter terram Nicholai filii Haraldi et terram Johannis Godard cum omnibus pertinentiis suis tenendas et habendas dictas duas acras terræ dictis canonicis imperpetuum de me

Anno 9. Hug. Well. 1217.

Will. de Butell cl'icus ad eccl. de Cottesford ad pres. Abb. de Becc. Arch. Oxon.

Gervas de Pavely cl'icus ad eccl. de Mudelington ad coll. ep'i ad petitionem Willi Lungespe com. Sarum et R. abb'is de Barling inter quos vertebatur contentio super advocationem.

Ric. de Widehai cl'icus ad eccl. de Sulthorn ad pres. abb'is et conv. de Eignesham de voluntate R. de Mortuomari militis dicentis se jus habere patronatus in ead. eccl'ia. Salva pensione centum sol. mon. de Eignesham, inquisitione facta per I. archid'um Oxon.

Jacobus de Solariis cl'icus ad eccl. de Estreleg ad pres. Radi de Saucey mil. salvis eccl'ie de Helsop primo legato de parochianis de Estrelegh decedentibus, qui quidem parochiani apud Helsop debent sepeliri, et 4 sol. quos singulis annis cecl'ia de Helsop percipit de eccl'ia de Esterlegh no-

mine subjectionis. Mandat. archid. Oxon. ad inducend.

Rad. Bloet ad eccl. de Eawelm ad pres. d'næ Aldæ Bloet matris ejus. Mand. A. Oxon.

Galfridus de Croppery cl'icus ad medietatem eccl'ie de Heyford auctoritate concilii. Mandat. Archid. Oxon.

Mattheus capellanus de Cudington ordinatus ad vicariam iii or (sic) marcarum in cecl'ia de Cudington de consensu patroni et personæ. Mand. A. Oxon.

Mag'r Rob'tus mag'ri Roberti nepotis d'ni N. Tusculan. ep'i ad eccl. de Langetun ad pres. abb. et conv. Westm. Archid. Oxon.

H. de Launton capellanus ad capellam de Baldindon ad pres. Petri de la Mara. Inquis. facta per abb'em de Dorcestr, salva matrici eccl. de Dorkecestr pensione unius libræ incensi.

a Ex Orig. penes D. Guil. Glynne, Bar.

*et hæredibus me*is *bene et in pace reddendo inde annuatim mihi et hæredibus me*is *unam libram c*imin*i ad* Pascha *pro omn*i *servitio et exactione ad me vel ad hæredes me*os *pertinente. Et ego dictus Robertus et hæredes mei dicta*s *dua*s *acras terræ cum pertinentiis* su*is dicti*s *canonici*s *contra omne*s *hom*ine*s et fœmina*s *per prædictum servitium imperpetuum warantizabimus. Pro hac autem donatione concessione et chartæ meæ confirmatione prædicti can*onici *dederunt mihi unam marcam argenti. Et ut · hæc mea donat*io *concessio et chartæ meæ confirmatio firma et stabilis in posterum permaneat præsenti* scri*pto* sig*illum meum apposui. Hiis testibus ; dom*ino *Roberto Daumari, Genteschive Paupere, Radulfo de Cestreton, Johanne filio Willielmi, Waltero filio Dru, Walhamot Paupere, Roberto de Badinton, Rad. Franceis, Petro de Wendlebure, et multi*s *aliis* [n].

To the original is a seal appending, bearing a star between two crescents, with this inscription, S. ROBERTI FILII MICHAELIS.

There is another original script in parchment that runs in the same words, and has the same seal affixed, only with some different witnesses, *Johanne filio Willielmi de Kertlinton, Roberto cler*ico*, Nicholao camerario, et multi*s *aliis.*

Soon after this, the same person added two acres of land in Fort-furlung and Crocwell-furlung, and with the two former gave them freely to the said canons, by the service of one penny yearly.

*Sciant præsentes et futur*i *quod ego Robertus filius Michaelis de Burncester ded*i *concess*i *et hac præsenti charta mea confirmavi pro salute animæ meæ et pro animabu*s *antecessorum et successorum meorum Deo et ecclesiæ beatæ Mariæ et* S. *Edburgæ Burncester et canonicis ibidem Deo servientibus, quatuo*r *acras terræ meæ in Burncester quarum duæ jacent in Buricroft extra curiam dictorum canonicorum* inter *terram Nicholai filii Haraldi et terram Johann*is *Godard et una in Fortfurlung* inter *terram Rob. Petith et terram Willielmi le May una in Crocwell-furlung quæ jacet ad puttam inter terram Johannis le* P*almer et terram quam Walterus filius Rogeri tenuit*

---

[n] Ex Orig. penes D. Guil. Glynne, Bar.

*habendam et tenendam prædictas quatuor acras cum suis pertinentiis
in liberam et perpetuam eleemosinam dictis canonicis et eorum succes
soribus imperpetuum de me et hæredibus meis libere quiete et in pace
sine aliqua conditione exactione et demanda sæculari per liberum servitium unius denarii annuatim mihi et hæredibus. meis ad Pascha pro
omnibus servitiis persolvendi.* Et ego dictus Robertus et hæredes mei
prænominatas quatuor acras cum suis pertinentiis dictis canonicis et
eorum successoribus contra omnes homines et fœminas per prædictum
servitium imperpetuum warantizabimus defendemus et acquietabimus.
Et ut hæc mea donatio concessio et chartæ meæ confirmatio rata et stabilis in posterum permaneat præsenti scripto sigillum meum apposui.
Hiis testibus; domino Rob. Daumari, Genteschive Paupere, Rad. de
Cestreton, Johanne filio Willielmi de Kurtlington, Waltero Dru, Walhamoth Paupere, Rob. de Badinton, Petro de 'Wendlebure, et multis
aliis* [o].*

To the original is the same seal appending.

An. MCCXVIII. 2, 3. *Henry III.*

In the sheriff's accompts for this year it appears, that William earl
of Salisbury paid the arrears of two marks for one knight's fee, with
the custody of the daughter and heir of Richard de Camvill [p].

Alexander king of Scotland came to Northampton, and there did
homage to king Henry, for the county of Huntendon and other
lands held by his predecessors, by which means he became lord of
the fee of Pidington and Merton [q].

Nigh this time James le Bret, for a farther benefaction to the priory
of Burncester, gave to them five acres of his land in demesne in
Crocwell-furlung, with a marsh called Crocwell-moor, and four sei-
lons or ridges of land called Buttes reaching to Eldeford, to make
there a bercherie or sheep-cote, &c.

Sciant præsentes et futuri quod ego Jacobus le Bret assensu uxoris

---

* Ex Orig. penes D. W. Glynne, Baronettum.   P R. Dods. Rot. Pip. MS. vol. 15. p. 9.
q Chron. dé Mailros, sub an.

meæ Amable et hæredum meorum dedi et concessi Deo et ecclesiæ S. Edburgæ de Burncester et priori et canonicis ibidem Deo servientibus pro anima patris mei et matris meæ et pro animabus omnium antecessorum et successorum meorum quinque acras terræ de dominio meo in Crocwell-furlung propinquiores viæ cum marisco integro qui vocatur Crocwell-moor quantum ad me pertinet et de incremento quatuor seilones terræ qui vocantur Buttes et extendunt se ad Eldeford cum libertate rivuli quantum ad me pertinet ad faciendam berkeriam sive quicquid eis melius placuerit facere, tenendos de me et hæredibus meis libere et quiete ab omni sæculari servitio ad me vel ad hæredes meos pertinente in puram et perpetuam eleemosinam in viis et planis in aquis et molendinis et in omnibus aliis locis. Has prædictas quinque acras cum quatuor seilonibus et marisco ego et hæredes mei warantizabimus prædictæ ecclesiæ versus omnes homines et fæminas in perpetuum. Et si ego vel'hæredes mei prædictam terram cum marisco prædictæ ecclesiæ warantizare non potuimus ego et hæredes mei eschambium faciemus sæpe dictæ ecclesiæ ad valentiam prædictæ terræ et marisci. Ut autem hæc donatio rata et inconcussa permaneat hanc præsentem chartam meam sigilli mei attestatione corroboravi. Hiis testibus; Gilberto Basset, Roberto Damari, Roberto Damari filio ejus, Thoma Brutun, Ric. de Hart, Waltero Bret, Hamundo de Sancta Fide, &c.[r]

10. Hug. Well.

Andreas cl'icus ad eccl. de Wotton ad pres. A. comitisse Sarum. Mandat. A. Archid'o Oxon.

Fordunus capellanus ad vicar. eccl'ie de Kirtlington ad pres. abb'is et conv. de Alneto. Mand. Archid'o Oxon. ib.

Mag'r Rob. Bacun ad mediet. eccl'ie de Heiford quam Lucas cl'icus tenuit ad pres. abb. et conv. de Egnesham. Inquis. facta per A. Archid. Oxon. ib. 10 Hug. Well.

Gervas de Pavely cl'icus ad eccl. de Mudelington ad coll. ep'i ad petitionem Will. Lungespe com. Sarum. et R. abb'is de Barling inter quos vertebatur contentio de advocatione. ib. 10. Hug. Well.

Eustachius de Godervil cl'icus ad eccl. de Wendlebir ad pres. Walteri de Godervil milit. ratione eustod. terr. et hered. Galfridi de Pevelly salva annua 1. marc. prestatione de ead. eccl. per ipsum cl'icum ecclie de Cestreton facienda. A. Oxon.

[r] Ex Orig. penes D. Guil. Glynne, Bar.

To the original parchment appends a seal with the same impress and inscription with that *sub an.* 1216.

By letters patent dated in October, Nichola de Hay widow of Gerard, and mother of Richard de Camvill late lord of Midleton, had the custody of the castle of Lincoln again delivered to her[s]. One of her family was Robert de Hay rector of * Sulthorn, (now Souldern, com. Oxon.) who, in this reign of Henry the Third, claiming from the abbot and convent of Oseney a certain measure of corn for their demesne of Mixbury, and fourpence yearly for their demesne of Fulwell, by virtue of the old custom called Chirchscete, did by

* *Omnibus—A.* prior de *Brakele et T.* rector *eccl'ie* de *Eyno* salut. *Cum causa quæ vertebatur inter W. rectorem eccl'iæ* de *Sulthorn ex una* parte *et Steph. de Fretewell ex alia super quadam hida terræ ad eccl'iam pertinente* predictam, *quæ dicitur Chercheyd de Sulthorn, dictus Steph. per biennium fuit excommunicatus, antequam sententiæ papali obediret, tunc tandem per cartam suam reddidit* dictam terram *rectori eccl'iæ de Sulthorn.* Cartul. Egnesham, f. 147.

Hugo ep'us Linc. confirmat Roberto abb'i Egnesham et conv. eccl'ias et pensiones ex eisdem——eccl'iam de Sulthorn et in ea pensionem duarum marcarum argenti. ib. f. 16.

Willelmus de Wares nepos Rob'ti abb'is de Egnesham (qui fuit abb. 1. Joh. 3. Joh. 7. Joh.) admissus ad vicariam perpetuam de Sulthorn salva annua pensione centum solidorum abb'i et conv. de Egnesham. Temp. Hugonis ep'i Linc. Cartular. Egnesham. MS.

Contentio inter Rob. de Haia rectorem eccl'ie de Sulthorn et abbatem de Osney

super unam acram frumenti annuatim de dominico suo de Mixburi et 4 denariis de dominico suo de Fulwel tanquam ex antiquo eccl'ie de Sulthorn debitos ratione cujusdam consuetudinis quæ Anglice vocatur Chirchesset ita quievit assensu abbatis et conventus de Egnesham patroni dietæ eccl'ie. Abbas et conven. Osen. dederunt rectori de Sulthorn centum solidos ad comparandum certum redditum ad valentiam v solidorum eccl'ie sue de Sulthorn ab eadem perpetuo percipiend. in meliorationem d'ete eccl'ie, et d'ctus rector de Sulthorn renunciavit omne jus super dictam acram et quatuor denarios annuos inperpetuum. Testibus d'no Warino capellano d'ni Lincoln. ep'i. d'no W. de Winchecumb canon. Linc. Ex cronico Osneiensi, fol. 121. Bib. Cotton. Vitellius. E. 15.

Placita super advocatione eccl. de Sulthorn. Rie'us de Gravesend ep'us Linc. contulit illam eccl'iam Galfrido de Stokes. Eccl'ia valet 20 marc. Cartul. Egnesham. MS. f. 122.

[s] R. Dods. MS. vol. 53. f. 57.

consent of the abbot and convent of Egnesham, who were patrons of the said church of Sulthorn, agree to receive an annual pension of five shillings in full satisfaction for the said corn and money[t].

Richard brother of the young king, who in the preceding year had been made governor of Chilham castle in Kent, obtained now a grant from the king of the honor of Walingford, by which he became lord of the fee of Burcester, &c.[u] In the accompts of the sheriff, Reginald earl of Bologne answered for lands in Bampton. Petronilla wife of Jeffery Fleccar paid fifty shillings for a mill in Hedingdon, called Kings-milne. Thomas Basset answered for forty-two pounds ten shillings in Hedingdon, and twenty pounds for the fee farm of the said barony[x].

Within * this year one thing is worthy notice, because (I think) not observed by any historian. The young king at Oxford on March the thirtieth issued out his precept to the sheriff of this and other counties, to take care that all Jews within their respective liberties should bear upon their upper garments, whenever they went abroad, a badge of two white tablets on their breast made of linen cloth or parchment, that by this token they might be distinguished from Christians[y]

An. MCCXIX. 3, 4. *Henry III.*

William Mareschall earl of Pembroke departed this life at Caversham in this county, in which place he gave to the chapel of our Lady all that ground which the canons of Nutley had built upon for

---

* Hugo ep'us Linc. concessit priori et conventui de Berncestr 5 marc. annuas de eccl'ia de parva Messenden anno pont. sui 6. Rot. Hug. Well.

Mandatum est vic. Oxon. q'd faciat habere P. Winton. ep'o singulis septimanis unum mercatum per diem Lunæ apud manerium suum de Edburgebur ita q'd non sit ad nocumentum vicinorum mercatorum. T. com. apud Bannebir. xxvi. die Julii. Claus. 2. H. III. p. 1. m. 3.

[t] Regist. Osen. MS. f. 118.   [u] Dugd. Bar. tom. 1. p. 761. b.   [x] R. Dods. MS. vol. 89. [y] Ibid. vol. 53. f. 50.

themselves near the gate thereof, with fifteen acres of land lying westwards of the church.   By his death the manors of Mersh, Crendon, Ludgarshale, and patronage of the abbey of Nutley, passed to William his eldest son and heir [z]

In this year died Thomas de S. Walery, lord of the manors of Becklee, Horton, Ambrosden, and the whole barony of his name. He left one only daughter and heir * Allanora, who subscribed among other witnesses to a deed of William de Breosa jun. cited from the register of Dore abbey [a]·   She married Robert earl of Dreux, a French peer, who had now livery of all the lands in England of her inheritance, viz. Beckley, Ambrosden, &c. [b]   Which earl was of the royal blood of France by this descent.   The fourth son of king Lewis the Gros (who died 1137) was Robert de France earl of Dreux, who married Agnes countess of Brenne, an. 1153, by whom he had five sons and one daughter : his eldest son was Robert surnamed The Young, who married Yoland the eldest daughter of Raoul lord of Couci, by whom his eldest son and heir was this Robert the third, surnamed Gastabled, who took to wife the said Allanore daughter and sole heir of Thomas de S. Walery [c].

Nigh this time Isabel daughter of Hugh Gargat of Caversfield, (vulgo Casefield,) in her pure widowhood gave to the church of St. Mary's and St. Edburg in Burcester and the canons thereof, part of a croft which lay near the court of the said canons, (the other part of the said croft being before given by Muriel her sister,) on condition the said canons should receive her and her mother into the prayers of their house for ever ; and when they should depart this

---

* Rex vic. Middlesex. salutem.   Scias quod reddidimus Rob'to de Droc. et Annoræ uxori ejus terram suam in Anglia, quæ ipsam Annoram hereditarie contingit ex parte Thomæ de Scto Walerico patris sui, et unde idem Thomas seisitus fuit die quo obiit. T. com. apud Westm. xiii. Feb. Claus. 3. Hen. III. p. 1. m. 11.

---

[z] Dugd. Bar. tom. 1. p. 602.   [a] Vincent on Brook, Her. p. 666.   [b] Dugd. Bar. tom. 1. p. 455.   [c] Du Tillet, Recueil de Roys de France, p. 27.

life, their names should be inscribed in the martyrology of that convent, &c.

Sciant præsentes et futuri quod ego Isabele filia Hugonis Gargat de Kaversfeld in pura viduitate mea dedi et concessi et præsenti charta confirmavi Deo et ecclesiæ beatæ Mariæ et Sanctæ Edburgæ de Burncester et canonicis ibidem Deo servientibus pro salute animæ meæ et animarum patris et matris meæ et antecessorum et successorum meorum totam meam partem illius croftæ quæ jacet juxta curiam dictorum canonicorum de qua crofta dicti canonici habent alteram partem ex dono Murielæ sororis meæ tenendam et habendam dictis canonicis imperpetuum in liberam puram et perpetuam eleemosinam liberam ab omni exactione sæculari et quietam, excepto uno selione forinseco illius croftæ versus austrum ad faciendam quandam viam mihi et hæredibus meis et hominibus meis ad introitum et exitum cum averiis meis et suis. Ego vero Isabele et hæredes mei prædictam croftam debemus warantizare prædictis canonicis imperpetuum contra omnes homines et fæminas. Dicti vero canonici receperunt me et dominam matrem meam specialiter in orationibus suis et suffragiis domus suæ in perpetuum. Et cum de hac vita migraverimus facient nomina nostra scribi in martirologio suo. Et ut hæc mea donatio concessio et chartæ hujus confirmatio et warantizatio firma et stabilis in perpetuum permaneat presentem chartam sigilli mei appositione corroboravi. Hiis testibus; domino Roberto de Aumari, Roberto de Insula, Roberto Purcell, Widone de Haya, Hamundo de Sancta Fide, militibus. Rogero de Mixebury, Jordano de Eyford, Roberto de Burncester, capellanis. Rogero de Cudlenton, Symone Grosso, Widone de Kaversfeld, Rogero clerico, Petro de Wendlebure, Roberto clerico, Johanne de Weston, Johanne armigero, Nicolao camerario, et multis aliis.

To the original parchment a fair seal appends with the impress of a bird regardant, with this inscription, ✠ Sigillum Ysabele Gargat[d]

---

xi. Hug. Wells. Archid. Oxon.
Adam cl'icus nepos magistri Gilberti de
Scto Albano ad eccl. de Feringford ad coll.
ep'i auctoritate concilii.

[d] Ex Orig. penes hon. D. Guil. Glynne, Baronettum.

Sybil de Kaversfeld, widow of Hugh de Gargat and mother of the
said Isabel, did after confirm to the canons of Burcester one virgate
of land in the village of Stratton, which Isabel Gargat her daughter
in her widowhood had given for the maintenance of one canon in
the said church for ever.

*Sciant præsentes et futuri quod ego Sybilla de Kaversfeld quondam
uxor Hugonis Gargat in pura viduitate et libera potestate mea concessi et præsenti charta mea confirmavi Deo et ecclesiæ beatæ Mariæ
et Sanctæ Edburgæ virginis de Burncestria et canonicis ibidem Deo
servientibus pro salute animæ meæ et animarum patris mei et matris
meæ et Hugonis Gargat quondam viri mei et antecessorum et successorum meorum donationem unius virgatæ terræ in villa de Stratton
cum omnibus pertinentiis suis quam Ysabel Gargat filia mea in ligia
viduitate et libera potestate sua illis dedit in auxilium ad sustentandum unum canonicum in ecclesia de Burncestria in perpetuum; illius
scilicet virgatæ terræ quam Walterus persona aliquando tenuit cum
toto messuagio habendam et tenendam dictis canonicis imperpetuum in
liberam puram et perpetuam eleemosinam sicut charta Ysabel filiæ meæ
quam prædicti cononici habent testatur. Et ut hæc mea concessio et
chartæ hujus confirmatio et warantizatio firma et stabilis in posterum
permaneat præsenti scripto sigillum meum apposui. Hiis testibus;
domino Roberto de Aumari, Galfrido Geboyn, Roberto de la Haya
tunc vice-com. Oxon. Widone filio Roberti, Roberto de Insula, Hamone
de Sancta Fide, Roberto de Badinton, Petro de Wendlebyre, Johanne
de Weston clerico, Roberto clerico, Johanne armigero, Nicholao camerario, et multis aliis* e.*

To the original is a seal appending oval, with impress of a woman
in religious habit with a branch in her right hand, inscribed ✠ Sigillum Sibillæ Gargate.

Yoland de Coucy countess dowager of Dreux, mother of Robert
earl of Dreux, lord of the manor of Ambrosden, &c. had fifteen shillings yearly rent given to her by her said son, which she granted to
the Benedictine abbey of Brueil, by this charter.

e Ex Orig. penes hon. D. Guil. Glynne, Bar.

Ego Yolendis comitissa Branæ notum facio universis præsentes li-
teras inspecturis quod charissimus filius meus Robertus comes Dro-
censis et dominus S. *Walerici ad preces meas mihi dedit quindecem so-*
lidos censuales sitos in censu Reginaldi Burgonis singulis annis requi
rendos in festo S. *Remigii, dictos autem nummos assensu et voluntate*
Roberti filii mei pro remedio charissimi domini mei Roberti comitis
Drocensis et Branæ et meæ antecessorum meorum et liberorum meorum
concessi in perpetuam eleemosynam ecclesiæ S. *Johannis de Brolio cu-*
jus abbas et conventus charitatis intuitu ad preces meas mihi fideliter
concesserunt quod singulis annis post obitum meum anniversarium so-
lenniter celebrabunt.   Hanc eleemosynam dicto modo factam voluit
concessit et laudavit dictus charissimus filius meus Robertus comes
Drocensis &c. quod ut ratum &c. præsentem paginam sigillorum nos-
trorum robore confirmavimus.   Actum anno gratiæ MCCXIX. *mense*
Martio[f]

In a council of bishops held this year in Oxford, a blasphemous
impostor, that assumed the name and pretended to the wounds of our
blessed Saviour, was condemned and crucified at Abberbury (now
Adderbury) com. Oxon[g].

An. MCCXX.   4, 5. *Henry III.*

Maurice de Gaunt held the manor of Weston in free marriage
with Maud daughter of Henry de Oily, for which manor the said
Henry gave one thousand two hundred marks.

Mauritius de Gant habet manerium de Weston in liberum marita-
gium cum Matilda uxore sua filia Henrici de Oyli pro quo manerio
dedit prædictus Henricus M.CC. *marcas*[h].

Which Maud now dying without issue, her father claimed the ma
nor of Weston to be restored to him: and in Michaelmas term

An. MCCXX. 12. Hug. Well. Hug. de   pres. abb. et conv. Westm.
Glaston. cl'icus ad eccl. de Ighteslep ad

[f] Neustria Pia, p. 787. [g] Hen. de Knyghton, p. 2430. [h] R. Dods. MS. vol. 90. p. 138.

was a trial for the said manor consisting of five carucates of land ; but the issue was a confirmation of it to the husband Maurice de Gaunt [i]

Robert earl of *Dreux*, lord of the barony of S. Walery, confirmed to the abbey of Oseney the gift made by his wife's father Thomas de S. Walery of the whole manor of Mixbury, excepting the advowson of the church, and some other exceptions.

Sciant, &c. quod ego Robertus comes Drocarum pro salute mea et A. uxoris meæ et hæredum meorum concessi confirmavi Deo et ecclesiæ S. Mariæ de Osen. &c. totum manerium de Mixbury quod habent dono Tho. S. Walerici in liberam puram et perpetuam eleemosinam cum capitali curia, &c. excepta ecclesiæ advocatione, &c. scripto et sigilli mei appositione confirmavi [k].

Maud the widow of William de Courtney, son of Reginald de Courtney, father of Egeline Courtney, wife of Gilbert Basset, claimed one carucate of land in Wodsdon against the prior of Burcester, who pleaded a title of frank-almoigne to it. And the trial was at Westminster in the octaves of St. Hilary.

Placita apud Westmin. in octabis S. Hilarii 4. *H. III. Buck. Matildis de Courtnai versus priorem de Burncester unam carucatam terræ in Wottesdon ex dotatione Reginaldi de Courtnai.* Prior *dicit quod ipsa est de potestate, &c.* [l]

This manor of Wodsdon with Hillesdon in the same county was part of the estate of which Edward Courtney earl of Devon died possessed an. 1419. and seems to have continued to the last heir of this noble family Edward, who died without issue at Padua, an. 1556 [m].

There was now an agreement between William de Ros and Sibil de Caversfield (Casefield) and Muriel her daughter, by which Sibil and Muriel did remit to the said William de Ros the lands which

---

[i] R. Dods. MS. vol. 42. p. 136.　[k] Regist. Osen. MS. p. 289.　[l] R. Dods. MS. vol. 42. p. 131.　[m] Dugd. Bar. tom. 1. p. 641.

lately belonged to Hugh Gargat in the village of Warminton, to maintain the children which he' had by the said Muriel [n], dated 4. *H. III.* apud Oxon.

An. MCCXXI.   5, 6. *Henry III.*

The king having by judgment in his temporal court recovered the church of Oakley from the prior and canons of St. Frideswide's in Oxford, they, not willing to stand the verdict, procured letters from the pope, appointing delegates to examine the cause and give a new determination of it.   Which method was thought so prejudicial to the king's court, crown, and dignity, that a memorable prohibition was issued out against them [o].   And within this year the king in exercise of his right presented to the church of Oakley with its appertenances, i. *e.* the chapels of Brill and Borstall [p].   But pope Honorius the Third was so zealous in defence of the convent's title and supposed rights of holy church, that, in the third, fifth, and sixth years of his pontificate, he sent over three several bulls to assert the claim of the priory of St. Frideswide to the said church of Oakley, against all appeals and prohibitions of the king [q].

William Longspe earl of Salisbury having the wardship of Idonea de Camvill (yet a minor, the wife of William his son) had thereby the custody of her estate in Midleton, Burcester, &c.   This year there was a dispute between the said earl and the abbot of Barlings about

An. MCCXXI. 13. Hug. Well.
Wibertus cl'icus ad eccl. de Mixebir ad pres. nobilis viri R. com. Drucarum.

Rad'us quondam officialis archid'i Oxon. ad eccl. de Sumerton ad pres. f'ris Jordani procuratoris domus S'eti Thome Martyris dē Acon, cujus advocationem Rob. Arsic dicte domui dedit et concessit admissus est; salvo jure domui de Medleia si contigerit quod de consensu d'ni ep'i et cap'li Linc. et abb'is et conv. de Fiscanno matricis eccl'ie loci fundetur cui domui de Medleia dicta domus de Acon ad sustentationem fratrum ejusd. loci dictam eccl'iam concessit.

the right of patronage to the church of Midleton, and during the
controversy the bishop of Lincoln conferred the said rectory, saving
the right of both competitors [r].

William de Godervill being guardian of the heir of Jeffery de Pavelly by that title of patronage did now present to the church of
Wendleburie [s]. The said Jeffery de Pavelly was the son of Robert,
and in the first of king John paid a fine of fourscore pounds and one
hundred shillings for livery of his lands. In the fourth of king John
he paid for four knight's fees in Northamptonshire: and in the fifth
of king John gave one mark for an assize or trial of Mort d'Ancestor
between him and Agnes the wife of William de Rutington, concerning three bovates of land in Rutington [t]. The heir in minority, which
he now left, was Robert de Pavelly the third. The head of this family was Reginald de Pavelly, who founded the abbey of Lisle-Dieu
in the diocese of Rhemes, an. 1187, and had his anniversary there observed Oct. 29 [u]

An. MCCXXII. 6, 7. Henry III.

Thomas de Camvill priest, nephew of Gerard de Camvill of Midleton, laid claim to the advowson of the church of Godingdon, to
which his mother had presented Eustace de Faucomberg, now bishop of London, and after her death he gave the right of patronage
to the nunnery of Alveston. So as this Michaelmas term was a trial
in the King's Bench between the said Thomas de Camvill and the
abbess of Alvestone.

*Assisa pro advocatione ecclesiæ de Gedendon clamatæ per Thomam
de Camvill versus Abb'issam de Alvestow qui venit et concedit quod mater prædicti Thomæ Cristiana præsentavit ultimo Eustachium de Fau-
cumberge modo episc. Lond. et post mortem Christianæ illam dedit Deo
et Sanctæ Mariæ et canon. de Alvestowe in elemosinam. Et Thomas
dedit ci ecclesiam Sanctæ Trinitatis de Tudendon in elemosinam con-*

---

[r] Dods. MS. vol. 107. p. 7.   [s] Ibid. p. 1.   [t] Thoroton, Antiq. of Noting. p. 65. a.
[u] Neustria Pia, p. 885.

firmatam per episcopum. Thomas dicit quod ecclesiam illam antequam ei dedit, nec cartam illam dedit nec fecit ; abb'issa dicit quod sigillum illud suum est, et sic profert probare per testes vel jur. proprie circa Bedford [x]

While a suit was depending for the right of patronage, the presentation was made by the bishop of the diocese : accordingly Hugh bishop of Lincoln presented to the said rectory of Godington [y]

William archdeacon of London being guardian to the heir of Robert de Chesterton knight, presented to the rectory of Chesterton saving the right of vicarage which Ralph de Besaciis had in the said parish.

Archid. Oxon. 14. Hug. Wells*, Willielmus archid. London. ratione terræ et hæredis Roberti de Cesterton in manu sua existentium præsent. ad ecclesiam de Cesterton salva vicaria Ranulfi de Besaciis quam habet in eadem [z].

About this time Walter son of Hugh le Franchele of Bigenhull granted and confirmed to Godfry son of Roger le Bere and Margery sister of the said Walter, one messuage and curtilage with one acre of land in the village and fields of Bigenhull and Burncester, which messuage and curtilage were on the croft opposite to his house; and of the land one half acre lay in Hocstede, between the land of Henry par la Custume and the land of Maud the relict of James de Bigenhull, and the other half acre lay upon Nuzerdenselond between the land of Thomas son of William the steward, and the land of John son of Gilbert, for the yearly rent of twelve pence, and paying twenty shillings in hand.

---

* Willelmus de Paris clericus ad eccl. de Cestreton ad pres. Will'i archid. London. ratione terr. et hæred. Rob. de Cestreton in manu sua existent. per mortem mag'ri G. de Barry proximo rectoris ejusdem eccl'iæ ; salva perpetua vicaria mag'ri Ranulphi de Besaciis quam habet in eadem, totam dictam eccl'iam—quoad vixent, te-

nebit nomine vicariæ suæ, reddendo inde dicto Will'o de Paris 5 marc. et dimid. nomine pensionis. Rot. Hug. Well. pont. 14.

An. MCCXXII. 11. Hug. Wells.

Rogerus de Turbelvill ad eccl. de Ottenden ad pres. Gentichiv le Pover, &c. Kal. Octob.

* R. Dods. MS. vol. 12. p. 142.   y Ibid. vol. 107. p. 41.   z Ib.

Sciant *præsentes et futuri quod ego Walterus filius Hugoni le Fran-*
chele de Bigenhull dedi conce*ssi et hac præsenti charta mea confirmavi*
Godefrido filio Rogeri de Bere *et* Marger. *sorori meæ unum messua-*
gium cum uno curtilagio et unam acram terræ cum pertinentiis in
villa et in campis de Bigenhull et de Burncester scilicet *illud messua-*
gium cum curthylagio quod jacet super croftam meam contra domum
meam, et prædictum messuagium et curthylagium continet in latitu
dine tantum quantum croftum meum continet, et in longitudine tan
tum quantum messuagium et curthylagium Hugonis de Nova domo
continet, et una dimidia acra jacet in Hocstedè inter terram Henrici
par le custume et terram Johannis filii Gilberti. *Habendum et tenen-*
dum dictum messuagium et curthilagium terræ cum pertinentiis de me
et hæredibus meis prædictis Godefrido et Margeriæ et hæredibus
eorum vel assignatis eorum vel cuicunque et quomodocunque dictum mes-
suagium et curthilagium dare vendere vel assignare voluerint in quo-
cunque statu sint exceptis viris Religiosis et Judæis libere quiete bene
in pace et jure hæreditario in omnibus aysiamentis infra villam et ex-
tra ad dictum messuagium et curthilagium et ad dictam terram perti-
nentibus. Reddendo inde annuatim mihi et hæredibus meis, &c. duo-
decim denarios ad duos anni terminos, &c. Et dederunt mihi viginti
solidos argenti præ manibus in gersumam, &c. Hiis testibus; do-
mino Waltero de Langle, Johanne filio Willielmi de Curthlinton, Si-
mone Germayn de Bigenhull, Willielmo Nigro de eadem, Johanne de
la Forde, Willielmo Fowe de Cestreton, Roberto Sabern de Burnces-
tes, et multis aliis [a].

A controversy depending between Henry abbot of St. Peter's in
Glocester and the prior of St. Oswald, was by pope Honorius referred to the abbot and prior of Thame, and the abbot of Nutley, by
whose arbitration a peace was now made between them [b]

At or before this time Thomas Brito gave to the church of St. Edburg of Burncester, and R. Prior and the convent thereof for the
souls of Gilbert Basset and his wife Egeline de Courtnai, &c. ten acres

---

[a] Ex Orig. penes D. Guil. Glynne, Baronettum.   [b] Ex Ghartul. S. Pet. Gloces. MS.

of land in the field of Magendune, seven acres of which lay between the land of William Wind and William Petre, and three acres in Endepethe, and two acres of meadow in Lillesei.

Universis sanctæ matris ecclesiæ filiis ad quos præsens scriptum pervenerit Thomas Brito æternam in Domino salutem. Universitati vestræ notificetur me dedisse et concessisse et hac præsenti charta sigillo meo munita confirmasse Deo et ecclesiæ S. Edburgæ de Burncester et R. priori et conventui ejusdem loci pro animabus G. Basset nobilis viri et uxoris suæ E. de Courtnai et pro salute animæ meæ et animarum patris mei et matris meæ et parentum et amicorum meorum decem acras terræ in campo de Magendune scilicet septem acras quæ jacent inter terram Willielmi Wind et terram Willielmi Petri juxta ripam et tres acras in Endepethe et duas acras prati in Lillesei, habendas et tenendas de me et hæredibus meis in puram et perpetuam elemosinam libere et quiete cum omnibus libertatibus ad prædictam terram pertinentibus salvo domino regi servitio. Et sciendum est quod ego Thomas Brito et hæredes mei prædictas acras terræ et prati præfatis priori et conventui versus omnes homines et fæminas imperpetuum warantizabimus. Hiis *testibus;* Henrico vicario de *Wanetinge,* Everardo *capellano,* Alano Basset, *Thoma de Mascci, Thoma de Edburgebiri,* Ricardo de *Chalkelei,* Everardo de Grave, Henrico de Grave, Symone de Bore*well, Willielmo de Pavilli, et mult*is aliis [c]

To the original parchment is a seal appending with the impress of a lion passant, with this inscription, SIGILLUM TOME BRITUN.

The abbot of Egnesham presented a clerk to the church of Stoke, and the bishop of Lincoln by lapse to the church of Feringford[d].

An. MCCXXIII. 7, 8. *Henry III.*

In the seventh of Henry the Third William Mareschal earl of Pembroke marched with great forces into Wales, and fought a battle with Leoline prince of that country, and totally routed his whole

[c] Ex Orig. MS. penes D. Guil. Glynne, Bar.   [d] Dodsworth, Extract. e Regist. Eccles. Line.

army; for which good service he had a scutage of all his tenants in
several counties, among others of those in Mersh, Ludgareshall
Crendon, &c. [c]

About this time Osbert de Hameleden lord of the manor of Watlington would have detained the tithes of his own demesnes in Wat-
cumb within the said parish, which had been given to the abbey of
Oseney; of which complaint was made to the pope, who commissioned three delegates, S. abbot of Tame, H. abbot of Egnesham,
and R. prior of Burcester, to hear and determine the cause, who
prevailed with the said Osbert to acknowledge and confirm the right
of the abbey, by this charter.

*Sciant omnes sanctæ matris ecclesiæ filii quod ego Osbertus de Ha-
melden autoritate literarum domini papæ Honorii tertii ad abb. et
conven. de Osen. Oxon. coram S. abbc. de Thame et H. et R. de Egnesham et de Burncester prioribus judicibus a domino papa delegatis
super decimas de toto dominico meo de Watccumb sibi præstandis quæ
sitæ sunt intra limites parochialis ecclesiæ suæ de Watlinton virorum
prudentium usus consilio pro salute animæ meæ et antecessorum et successorum meorum coram præfatis judicibus constitutis decimas ad cc
clesiam præfatam de jure spectare plene recognovi, &c.* [f]

This year September the eleventh, a court was held at Wheatley
for the hundred of Bolendon before Jeffery le Curteys, where the
deeds and charters of the abbey of Oseney were produced and read,
and by the knights and freemen of the jury it was agreed, that the
said abbey had a right to all weyf and stray within their several lands
that belonged to the church of St. George's, as also the assize of
cloth, bread, and beer, and all royal privileges except the trial of rob-
bery and murder : upon which recognition of their right the said abbey had delivered to them the stray within their two hides of land in
Arncot, two hogs, and five pigs, &c.

*Anno ab incarnatione Domini 1123, mense septimo, xi. die mensis ad
hundredum de Bolendon apud Wateles coram Galfrido le Curteys suitæ*

---

[c] Dugd. Bar. tom. 1. p. 603.   [f] Regist. Osen. MS. p. 134.

ad 'hundredum ad declarandas libertates ad ecclesiam S. Georgii *pertinentes in'pleno hundredo auditæ* sunt *chartæ libertatum quas habemus
de regibus et ab omnibus qui testes* sunt *approbatæ maxime cum....
Tho. Basset vel Hugo Pluggeys quicquid habent in mane*rio *de Hedindon concessæ fuerint libertates istæ et recognitum est a militibus et liber*is *hominibus ibidem existentibus videlicet de Mattheo de Bikeston
Nicholao le Butler, Waltero de Gersindon, Gilberto de Hyda, Willielmo de Leukenor clerico, Simone de Waltham tunc seneschallo domini Johann*is *de S. Johanne, Widone de Wateles et ab omnibu*s *qui
ibi aderant quod ad nos spectat le Gwayf, &c. in te*rris *nostris ad ecclesiam* S. Georgii *pertinentibus ubicunque* sunt *inventa et etiam
emendatio panni pan*is *et cervisiæ et quicquid reg*is *est excepto murdredo et latrocinio probato prout chartæ nostræ testantur. Ita et
statim redditum' est nob*is *de Gwayf de Ernicot scilicet* II. *porc. cum
v. porcellis et apud Covele* I. *ov*is *cum agno suo, et omnia attachia-
menta hominum nostrorum et pleg. suorum habenda quieta clamata
sunt* [g].

This same year being the fifteenth of *H*ugo Wells bishop of Lincoln, the abbey of Egnesham presented to the church of *Mereton
by the right of patronage bestowed on them by David king of
Scots [h].   ,

At *t*his time a controversy depending between William Fitz-Richard priest, who seems to have had the king's title, and the prior
and canons of St. Frideswide about right of presentation to the
church of Oakley in this neighbourhood, a prohibition was sent by
the pope to his legate the bishop of Norwich elect.

...... *Norwicensi.electo camerario nostro apostolicæ sed*is *legato salutem et apost. benedictionem. Ex liter*is *abbatis de S. Albano intel-
leximus quod causa quæ inter priorem et canonicos S. Frideswidæ ex
una parte et W. filium Richardi clericum dioc. Lincoln. ex altera ver-*

* xv. Hug. Well.   riton ad pres. abb. et conv. de Egne-
Hug. Salvage subdiac. ad eccl. de Me-   sham.

g Regist. Osen. p. 107.   h Dods. Collect. Rot. Linc. MS. vol. 107. p. 12.

*titur super ecclesiam de Accleia quam ad se pertinere idem prior et ca-
nonici et a dicto W. injuste detineri proponunt eis commisimus fine
canonico determinandum, &c.* i

An. MCCXXIV. 8, 9. *Henry III.*

The king in June this year was at his court of Brill in this neighbourhood, and thence dated a patent to Thomas de Cyrencester for
the castle and honor of Berkamsted [k].

Genteschive le Povre, lord of the manor of Ottindon and patron of
the church, presented a clerk this year.

16. *Hug. Wells archid. Oxon. VIII. kal. Octob. Gentesch. le Povre
præsentat ad ecclesiam de Ottindon* [l]

In the tax imposed this year by the parliament at Northampton,
Robert earl of Dreux lord of the manor of Ambrosden answered for
ten knight's fees, being the whole barony of St. Walery. *Oxenfordscire, Falkesius de Breantee vic. Rob. de Droos de x. feod.* [m]

The abbot of Oseney presented to the vicarage of the church of
Chesterton.

*Archid. Oxon. 16. Hug. Wells. abbas de Osenci pt. ad vicariam ec-
clesiæ de Chesterton* [n].   "   r

William de Breante held during the king's pleasure the manor of
Kirtlington com. Oxon. which had been the land of Wido de Dive [o]:
and was now committed to Thomas Basset baron of Hedendon by
this precept to the sheriff. *Rex vice-com. Oxon. salutem. Scias quod
commisimus Thomæ Basset manerium de Kirtlington quæ est terra
Normannorum ad se sustentandum. Ideo præcipimus, &c. Teste rege* [p].

An. MCCXXIV. 8, 9. Henry III.
Abbas et conv. de Messenden presentant
ad vicariam de Caversfeld ordinatam per
dominum ep'um auctoritate Concilii. Rot.

Hug. Wells. anno 16.
16. Hug. Well. Henr. capellanus ad perpet. vicar. eccl. de Cestreton ad pres. abb.
et conv. Osen.

[i] MS. James. in Bib. Bod. vol. 26. p. 145.   [k] W. Dugd. MS. vol. C. p. 26.   [l] R. Dods.
MS vol. 107. p. 42.   [m] Ibid. vol. 15. p. 58.   [n] Ibid. vol. 107. f. 42.   [o] Ibid. vol. 53. f.
73.   [p] Ibid. vol. 103. f. 100.

The manor of Wodsdon in com. Bucks. held in dowry by Maud de Courtney after the death of Reginald her husband, was now on her death delivered to Robert de Courtney grandson of the said Reginald, by this precept to the sheriff of that county.

Rex vice-com. Bucks. &c. salutem. Præcipimus tibi quod sine dilatione plenam seisinam habere facias Roberto de Courtney de manerio de Wotesdon cum pertinentiis quod Matilda de Courtney tenuit in dotem post mortem Reginaldi viri sui avi prædicti Roberti cujus hæres est. Teste rege [q].

Ralph Fitz-Robert presented a clerk to the church of Erdolveslei, (now Ardly,) and the bishop of Lincoln to the church of Godington com. Oxon. [r] Robert de Aumari (or D'amory) lord of the manor of Bucknell, was in this year one of the justices itinerant in the county of Oxford [s].

An. MCCXXV. 9, 10. *Henry III.*

Henry de Oily son of Henry de Oily confirmed to the abbey of Oseney several donations in his manor of Weston, one virgate of land on which stood the mansion house of the canons, &c.

Ego Henricus filius Henrici, &c. in Weston hydam et dimidiam et tres virgatas de villenagio scilicet virgatam ubi mansio canonicorum est. Item virgatam quam Robertus tenet et virgatam quam Herbertus tenet et tres virgatas de dominico cum prato et omnibus pascuis meis pasturam pro bobus et ovibus et porcis suis communem cum meis [t].

An. MCCXXV. 9, 10. Henry III.

Barthol. de Bedawind .c^apell^{an}. ad perpet. vicariam in cecl'ia de Fretewell auctoritate Concilii ordinatam; consistit autem dicta vicaria in omnibus obventionibus altaris et in omnibus minutis x'mis totius parochiæ et in x'mis bladi et feni et omnibus aliis x'mis provenientibus de 3 virgatis terræ in eadem villa, scil. quas Ric. fil. Rad'i tenet, et in uno crofto cum messuagio in prato adjacente. Rot. Hug. Well. ann. 17.

[q] R. Dods. MS. vol. 103. f. 99.   [r] Ex Regist. Lincoln.   [s] Dugd. Orig. Jurid. sub an. Regist. Osen. p. 16.

The prior* of Burcester presented a clerk to the vicarage of the
said town ^v

In the accompts of the sheriff of Wiltshire, it appears that William
Longspe † earl of Salisbury was indebted to the king seven hundred
twenty-nine pounds three shillings and fourpence, and sixteen palfries for his custody of Idonea de Camvill and her manors of Burcester and Midlinton : and in arrears for the fine, which Richard de
Camvill should have paid for possession of his father's inheritance,
three hundred marks.

*Wiltescir. computus, &c. Willielmus comes Sarisb. debet pro hærede
Ricardi de Camvill* DCC. *et* XXIX^l. III^s. IV^d. *et* XVI. *palefridos et pro habendis terris quæ fuerant Giraldi patris sui* CCC. *marc* ^x

Henry de S. Walery, brother of Thomas late lord of the manor of
Ambrosden, &c. at a trial before the itinerant judges in com. Buck.

* An. 17. Hug. Well. Rob. de Sparke-
ford capellan. ad perpet. vicariam eccl'ie de
Berencestr per nos auctoritate Concilii ordinatam ad pres. prioris et conv. de Berencestr

† Hoc est testamentum Will'i Lungspe
com. Sarum. factum in media XL^{ma} ab incarnat. D'ni anno MCCXXV, quum disposi-
tum et provisum fuit q'd idem comes iret in
Wascon. in servitio d'ni regis; scil.

*Inprimis—Ego Will'us Longspe comes Sa-
rum assignavi quod debitum quod debui d'no
regi post ultimum compotum meum eodem
anno coram baronibus de scaccario apud
Westm. reddatur d'no regi de exitibus custo-
diarum mearum.—Item, Ego assignavi ad
edificationem domus Loci Dei ordinis Chartus.
omnes proventus custodie terre heredis Ric'i
de Campvill unde modo sum seisitus usque*

*ad plenam ætatem heredis mei.—Item, as-
signavi domui Sctæ Mariæ de Bentherond
capellam meam ferialem quam mecum ferre
consuevi preter dietas duas fialas de argento
sunt cum magna capella ut predictum est;
et assignavi eidem domui libram meum qui
vocatur Portchois; Item eidem domui assignavi* XX *vaccas.* CCC *oves matrices, et centum
multones. Item, assignavi domui de Bernecestr* CC *bidentes matrices,* X *vaceas, et* VIII
*boves. Hujus testamenti mei executores con-
stitui ven. pres. Cant. ar'epum; Bath. Linc.
Sar. ep'os; W. Mar. com. Pembroc. W. de
Wand. decan. Sarum. et mag'rum Edmundum thesaurarium Sarum. eccl'iæ ad conser-
vand. et consulend. et ut firmiter assistant
executioni dicti testamenti constitui—Adam
de Alta Ripa mil. et J. Bovet cl'icum.* Claus.
9. Hen. III. m. 19. dorso.

^u R. Dods. MS. vol. 107. p. 42.   ^x W. Dugd. MS. vol. 20. f. 15. Rot. Scac.

lost his lands in the said county by default to the king, because his attorney had not personally appeared in the court after four days admonition; but would have pleaded for an *essonium de malo lecti*[y], i. e. upon sickness of the party summoned attested in the open court for four days successively, the judges shall then appoint four knights to attend the sick person, and see him depute an attorney to appear for him. Which plea was now overruled by the judges, because no attorney could have an attorney, as no proctor could have a proctor, i. e. no representative could be represented by another. Upon which *Henry* de S. Walery was judged in default, and his lands taken into the king's hands[z].

The proctor of the religious house of St. Thomas the martyr of Acon presented a clerk to the church of Somerton, com. Oxon. the advowson of which was given to the said house by Robert de Arsic[a].

An. MCCXXVI.   10, 11.   *Henry III.*

Thomas le Frankleyn, son of Simon le Frankleyn of Borstall, granted to Sir John Fitz-Nigel and his heirs half a hide of land in Borstall, in consideration of thirty marks of silver paid in hand, and due service to the lord of the fee. *Hiis testibus; Johanne de* Esses, *Milone de Brehull, Roberto Ferebraz, Willielmo de Brehull, Radulpho Pynne, Nicholao le Burn, Elia Megrym, et aliis*[b]. After which the said Thomas le Frankleyn granted to the said Sir John Fitz-Nigel one piece of land in Borstall containing eight perches and a half in length, and three perches and three feet in breadth: and another piece of land between the new and old course of the river, for the yearly rent of one penny. *Hiis testibus; Willielmo filio Simonis de Brehull, Petro fratre ejus, Nigello de Bosco, Huberto le Turnur, Bartholomeo le Turnur, Radulpho filio Willielmi de Brehull, Helia Segrym, Roberto Avis, Johanne le Turner, et aliis*[c]. After the death of the said Thomas le Frankleyn, Margaret his relict did re-

<hr/>

[y] Braeton.   [z] Hengham Magna cap. 1.   [a] Ex Regist. Lincoln.   [b] Chartular. de Borstal, MS. f. 111.   [c] Ibid.

lease and quit claim to the said Sir John Fitz-Nigel, all her right in
the premises in consideration of twenty shillings in hand, to which
writing she put the seal of Gerard de Wyzeri, because she had herself no proper seal. *Hiis testibus ; domino Johanne filio Nigelli jun.
Gerardo de Wyzeri, et Eustachio de Grevenhull, militibus ; Johanne
Ferebraz, Nigello Travers, Nigello de Bosco, Thoma Brun, et aliis* [d].

William Longspe earl of Salisbury, who had the wardship of Idonea de Camvill, and had married her to his eldest son, died, on the
nones of March, an. 122⅖ ; and, by his last will made in the middle
of lent, he assigned all the profits of the land of the said heir of Richard de Camvill for the building of a Carthusian monastery, called
God's House, till his own heir should come of age.

*Ex testamento Willielmi Longspe facto media quadragesima. Ego
assignavi ad ædificationem domus Loci Dei ordinis Carthusiensis omnes proventus custodiæ terræ hæredis Ricardi de Camvill unde modo
seisitus sum usque ad plenam ætatem hæredis mei* [e].

The said William earl of Sarum, beside the custody of the heir and
lands of Richard de Camvill, had also the custody of the lands of
William de Vescy, and of the heir and lands of Hugh le Bigod [f]

Margaret, daughter and heir to Warine
Fitz-Gerold, having married Baldwin de
Redvers eldest son of William earl of Devon, and upon his death taking to her second husband Fulk de Breant, who died
9. Henry III. shee the said Margaret after
the year 1229 granted this charter to the
nuns of Clerkenwell for a yearly rent out of
her mannors of Newnham and Heyford Warine in this county. *Omnibus, &c. Marga-
rita de Redveria salutem. Noveritis me dedisse in ligea potestate et pura viduitate mea
pro salute animæ meæ et patris mei et matris
meæ et Baldwyni filii mei promogeniti et*

*aliorum puerorum meorum Deo et beatæ Ma-
riæ et monialibus de Clerkenwell quinquaginta solidos quieti redditus in auxilium ad
vestiendum conventum ejusdem loci unde eisdem teneor de testamento Aliciæ de Churcy
matris meæ annuatim percipiend. viz. in manerio meo de Newenham, et in manerio meo
de Heyford. Testibus, Rogero London ep'o,
d'no Gilberto de Bolebec, Willielmo de Bercamstede, &c.* Ashmole MS.

18. Hug.Well. Gilbertus de Wiginton capellan. ad vicar. eccl. de Wathlingetun per
privationem Andreæ capellani propter in-
continentiam ad pres. abb. et conv. Osen.

[d] Chartular. de Borstall, MS.   [e] Mon. Aug. tom. 2. p. 931.   [f] R. Dods. MS. vol. 80.
p. 239.

William de Longspe, son and heir of William earl of Salisbury, had married Idonea de Camvill daughter of Richard de Camvill, and had now livery of all the lands of her father's inheritance, *viz.* Burcester, Midleton, &c. having paid his fine to the king [g].

The king's precept was directed to the sheriff of Oxon. to certify that William de Longspe earl of Salisbury had been in person in the expedition made into Wales, 7. Henry III. and therefore the scutage should not be collected from his son for those lands which belonged to Richard de Camvill.

R. Vic. Oxon. salutem. Sciatis quod W. Longspe quondam comes Sarum fuit nobiscum in exercitu nostro Muntgumery. Et ideo tibi præcipimus quod de scutagio quod per summon. Scacc. exigis a Willielmo Longspe filio et hærede ipsius comitis pro exercitu illo de fœdis militum quæ ipse comes habuit in custodia cum filia et hærede Ricardi de Camvill quam prædictus Willielmus Longspe duxit in uxorem pacem ei habere permittas. Teste R. 21. Septemb. [h]

Another mandate was sent to the sheriff to remit the ox which he required of William Longspe for delivery of his wife's inheritance by her father.

Mandat. est vic. Oxon. quod de bove quem exigit a Willielmo Longspe pro scisina terræ quæ fuit Ricardi de Camvill cujus filiam et hæredem duxit in uxorem ei facienda pacem habere facias, &c. [i]

An. MCCXXVI. 10, 11. Hen. III.

* *Ego Henricus de Oyli pro salute* (sic) *et meorum dedi eccl'iæ S. Mariæ de Oseney totum monerium meum de Weston, &c. Facta autem fuit hæc carta apud Oseney, anno ab incarnatione Domini 1226; hiis testibus, Johanne de Scto Joh'e, Roberto de la Hay tunc vice com. Oxon. Will'o de Hampton, Rogero de Bray, Wydone filio Roberti, Will'o de Levekuor, &c.* Reg. Osen.

Carta domini Rogeri de Aumari de manerio de Weston concesso canonicis de Osen. Finis inde factus an. 45. Hen. III. *Ib.*

Ego Johannes filius Rogeri de Scto Johanne remisi pro me et hæredibus meis Thomæ Bacun et haredibus suis pro homagio et servitio suo totum jus quod habui in omnibus terris et tenementis et uno molendino aquatico in Weston, &c. Ib.

g R. Dods. MS. vol. 53. f. 87. and Dugd. Bur. tom. 1. p. 628.   h W. Dugd. Analecta MS. B. 1. p. 315.   i W. Dugd. Collect. Rot. et Fin. MS. B. 1. p. 326.

Ela countess of Sarum, widow of the said earl, did within *this* year present a clerk to the church of Wotton, com. Oxon. [k]

The abbey of Oseney presented now to the vicarages of Chesterton, Kidlington, and Watlington [l]. Which church of Watlington was given to them in the reign of king Henry the First by Halenad de Bidun, with one yard land of his demesne in that parish [m]. Genteschive le Povre within this year presented a clerk to the church of Ottindon, and three years before had with Emma de Podus his wife, presented to the church of Tackley [n]

Hugh de Nevill had now livery of the manor of Brill.

Hugo de Nevill habet seisinam de Brehull in com. Bucks. [o]

Robert earl of Dreux, lord of the honor of St. Walery, *i. e.* the manors of Ambrosden, Horton, Beckley, &c. and Allanore his wife, gave to the nuns of Stodley the church of Beckley.

Robertus comes Drocarum et dominus de Sancto Walerico et Allanora uxor ejusdem comitis filia et hæres Thomæ de Sancto Walerico conced. eisdem monialibus ecclesiam de Beckleia. Datum an. Dom. MCCXXVI. *mense Decembris* [p].

By an inquisition now taken at Oseney, it appears that the king had this year confirmed to the said abbey the donation made by Henry de Oily of his capital messuage wood and mill in Weston, with Bencroft, Grascroft, Hegcroft, &c. [q]

Walter le Povre, son of Genteschive lord of the manor of Otindon, was this year one of the justices itinerant for the county of Oxford [r].

An. MCCXXVII. 11, 12. *Henry III.*

Philip de Albini, sheriff of the county of Berks, had the honor of Walingford committed to his custody, and had thereby the rents and services of the manor of Burcester [s]

---

[k] Rog. Dods. MS. vol. 107. f. 1.   [l] Dugd. Bar. tom. 1. p. 599.   [m] Regist. Linc.
[n] R. Dods. MS. vol. 107. p. 42.   [o] Ibid. vol. 53. p. 88.   [p] Mon. Ang. tom. 1. p. 487.
[q] Regist. Osen. MS. p. 316.   [r] Dugd. Chron. ser. sub an.   [s] Dugd. Bar. tom. 1. p. 116. b.

Nigh this time Walter son of Richard de Kirtlington released and
quit claimed to the canons of Burcester all right and title to a new
mill on the other side of the Cherwell adjoining to an old mill, with a
parcel of willows, with free pontage or passage over the river, as also
one parcel of land near to the said mill containing in length twenty-
four feet toward the north, and seventeen feet in breadth toward the
west side of the mill in pure and perpetual alms.

*Omnibus Christi fidelibus has literas visuris Walterus filius Ri-
chardi de Kertlington salutem.   Noverit universitas vestra me pro salute animæ meæ patris mei et matris meæ antecessorum et successorum
meorum dedisse concessisse quietum clamasse et præsenti charta mea
confirmasse pro me et hæredibus meis Deo et ecclesiæ beatæ Mariæ et
S. Edburgæ virginis de Burncestria et canonicis ibidem Deo servientibus totum jus quod habui vel aliquo modo habere potui in novo molendino super fundo meo ex alia parte de Charwelle juncto veteri molendino de Kertlinton cum quadam particula saliceti quæ de fœdo meo
est.   Concessi etiam dictis canonicis quod habeant pontem liberum ultra aquam ad bladum cariandum et alia quæ viderint sibi expedire
cum quadrigis et equis ad prædictum molendinum cum libero exitu
et introitu.   Dedi etiam dictis canonicis quandam particulam terræ
meæ propinquiorem dicto molendino continentem in longitudine a ripa
aquæ viginti et quatuor pedes versus borealem partem et a situ dicti
molendini versus occidentalem partem in latitudine decem et septem
pedes et extra gablum molendini octo pedes in latitudine ad liberum
iter suum habendum ad stagnum suum emendandum et reparandum
cum opus fuerit et ad faciendum de dicto stagno quicquid melius viderint eis expedire : salvo mihi et hæredibus meis herbagio dicti stagni*

19. Hug. Well. Mag'r Will. de Button
subdiac. ad vicar. de Bureford ad pres. ab-
b'is et conv. de Keinesham; consistit autem ipsa vicaria in tota terra matricis eccl'ie et capelle de Fulebroc cum mesuag.
ad vicar. pertinente et in omnibus aliis tam
ad matricem quam ad dictam capellam pertinentibus exceptis omnibus et solis x'mis
garbarum cum capitali manso matricis eccl'ie.

Mag'r Helyas de Glovernia subdiac. ad
eccl. de Witteneya ad pres. Mag'ri Barthol.
Winton et Luci Surrei archid'oni procura-
torum ep'i Winton. ib. an. 19.

et herbagio ex altera parte aquæ quantum aliquis homo pro profundi-
tate aquæ poterit metere, habendam et tenendam dictis canonicis im-
perpetuum in liberam puram et perpetuam eleemosinam. Ego vero
dictus Walterus et hæredes mei omnia prænominata dictis canonicis
contra omnes homines et fœminas imperpetuum warantizabimus. Et
ut hæc mea donatio concessio quieta clamatio et chartæ meæ confirma-
tio rata et stabilis imperpetuum permaneat præsenti scripto sigillum
meum apposui. Hiis testibus; domino Philippo de Witthulle, Johanne
de Bigehull, Thoma de la Hayn, Philippo de Wapeleg, Mattheo de
Kertlinton, Ligero ejusdem villano, Johanne filio Willielmi, Willielmo
filio Benedicti, Widone Harengs, Willielmo filio Durandi, et aliis[t].

Robert earl of Dreux in right of his wife baron of S. Walery, and
lord of the manor of Ambrosden, presented to the church of North-
Leigh com. Oxon.[u]　The said Robert with Peter earl of Britain surnamed Mauclerk his brother, and other princes of the blood, conspired against the administration of Blanch queen regent of France,
widow of Lewis the Eighth, and mother of Lewis the Ninth[x], who
prudently won over the said Robert earl of Dreux by the gift of
several lands in Normandy, by charter dated in July 1227[y].　Upon
which reconciliation, the earl of Britanny, seeing himself deserted by
his brother, invited the king of England to come over and recover
Normandy lost by his father king John.　But before any such design could be effected, the said earl of Britain submitted himself to
king Lewis, who took his homage, and received him into favour at
request of his brother the earl of Dreux, who, during these contests
in France, had all his lands in England seized by the king, by which
means the manor of Ambrosden and the whole honor of S. Walery
were now in the king's hands; and Decemb. the fifth, the king presented to one moiety of the church of Rollesham, com. Oxon.　*Ra-*
tione terræ Walteri de Fontibus quæ est de fœdo Roberti comitis de
Dreux in manu sua existente[z].

---

[t] Ex Orig. penes hon. D. Guil. Glynne, baronettum.　[u] Ex Regist. Linc.　[x] Du
Tillet Recueil des Roys de France, p. 38.　[y] Ib. p. 45.　[z] Ex Regist. Linc.

William Longspe, late earl of Sarum, had given on St. Magdalen's day 1222, his manor of Hethrop in this county, there to found a monastery of the Carthusian order; but, these monks representing it to be an inconvenient place, Ela relict of the said earl translated them in this year to Henton in com. Wilts. [a]

On July the thirteenth William, son and heir of William son of Helias, did his homage, and paid one hundred shillings for his relief of one knight's fee in Oakley, held of the honor of Walingford [b]. Within this year the abbot of Missenden presented a clerk to the church of Kaversfeld, (now Casefield,) nigh Burcester, as also to the church of Chalfhunt, com. Bucks. And the abbot of Egnesham to the church of Meriton com. Oxon. [c]

Reginald Dammartin, earl of Bologne, lately deceased, had his estate in England seized by the king, within which estate was included the fee of Pidington and Merton. Upon a meeting of the barons at Northampton in August, the king gave all his mother's jointure to his brother Richard, with all the lands that belonged to the earl of Britain in England, which were lately the earl of Bologne's [d]. Within the same year Isolda de Do had livery of the manor of Wrastlingworth, (now Wrestingworth in Bedf.) part of the estate of Reginald late earl of Bologne, and of the manor of Pidington which belonged to the said earl.

Oxon. Isolda de Do habet maner. Wrastlingworth quod fuit com. Bolon. (i. e. Reginaldi) ad se sustendandam in servitio regis quamdiu &c. et seisinam Bedf. Eodem modo scribitur vic. de Oxon. pro eadem de manerio de Pedinton quod fuit ejusdem com. [c]

In the seventeenth of this reign the king gave the manor of Dun ham (lately belonging to this Reginald de Dammartin earl of Bologne) to Ralph son of Nicholas, till such time as the king should restore it to the heir of the said Reginald, and upon such restitution the king should make full compensation in wards and escheats to the said Ralph.

[a] E. Chron. MS. apud Jo. Lelandi Collect. tom. 2. p. 311.   [b] R. Dods. MS. vol 68. f. 109.   [c] Ex Regist. Linc.   [d] Brady, Hist. p. 511.   [c] R. Dods. MS. vol. 53. p. 98.

Henricus Dei gratia rex Angliæ dominus Hibern. dux Normanniæ Aquitaniæ et comes Andegaviæ archiepiscopis episcopis abbatibus prioribus comitibus baronibus, justit. vice-com. præpositis, ministris, et omnibus ballivis et fidelibus suis salutem. Sciatis nos concessisse dilecto et fideli nostro Radulpho filio Nicolai manerium de Dunham cum pertinentiis suis quod fuit comitis Boloniæ habendum et tenendum eidem Radulpho et hæredibus suis de nobis et hæredibus nostris adeo libere quiete et integre cum omnibus pertinentiis et libertatibus et liberis consuetudinibus ad manerium illud pertinentibus sicut Reginaldus de Dammartin quondam comes Boloniæ illud tenuit in manu sua donec hæredi ipsius comitis illud reddidimus per voluntatem nostram vel per pacem. Ita ut quod nec nos nec hæredes nostri prædictum Radulphum vel hæredes suos dittachiemus vel disseisiri faciemus de prædicto manerio vel ejus pertinentiis nisi illud reddidimus hæredi prædicti com. sicut prædictum est. Et si forte illud reddidimus nos vel hæredes nostri faciemus eidem Radulpho vel hæredibus suis competens escambium in wardis et escheatis ad valentiam prædicti manerii. Hiis testibus; venerabili patre Petro Winton. episcopo, Stephano de Segrave justic. Angliæ, Petro de Rivall, Roberto Passewell, Godefrido de Craucumbe, Johanne filio Philippi, Galfrido dispensario, et aliis. Datum per manum venerabilis patris Radulphi Cicestr. episcopi, cancell. nostri apud Westm. quarto die Maii anno regni nostri decimo septimo [f]

The said Reginald Dammartin earl of Bologne had a brother Simon Dammartin earl of Ponthieu, by marriage with Mary daughter and heir of William earl of Ponthieu and Alix his wife, daughter of king Lewis the young; which Simon had a daughter and heir Joan, second wife to Ferdinand the third king of Castile, whose daughter Eleanor was wife of our king Edward the First [g].

An. MCCXXVIII. 12, 13. Henry III.

Richard de Prestecote knight presented to the church of Blechingdon [h].

---

[f] Orig. MS. Pergam. cum sigillo appendente in Mus. Ashmol. diplom.   [g] Du Tillet Recueil de Roy, p. 50.   [h] R. Dods. MS. vol. 107. f. 44.

The king sent a mandate to the sheriff of Cambridgeshire dated
May the twenty-fourth, to take into the king's hands all the land
which was of the inheritance of Idonea de Camvill wife of William
de Longspe, which William earl of Salisbury, guardian of the said
Idonea, had committed to Roger de Askynny for his support[i].

Nigh this time died Robert earl of Dreux lately disseized of the
barony of St. Walery, and thereby of the manor of Ambrosden, &c.
leaving Allanora or Eleanor his widow, who, after married to Henry
lord of Sully in France, and dying in that kingdom, was buried with
her first husband the earl of Dreux in the abbey of Brenne. They
left issue three sons, John, Robert, and Peter; and one daughter
Yoland de Dreux wife of Hugo the fourth of that name duke of
Bourgogne. The eldest, John, succeeded in his father's honors, earl
of Dreux and of Brenne, lord of St. Walery in Normandy, who
married Mary of Bourbon, third daughter of Archibald the great
lord of Bourbon, by whom he had two sons and one daughter[k].

Before this time there arose a controversy between Alan Basset
baron of Wycomb and the convent of Burcester, concerning the advowson of the church of Compton, (called from that family Compton-
Basset,) in com. Wilts. which church had been given to the said
priory by the founder Gilbert Basset. The difference was referred
to Hugh bishop of Lincoln, and Josceline bishop of Bath and Wells,
by whose arbitration it was determined, that the bishop of Sarum
and his successors should have the right of advowson of the said
church, and should successively present a clerk to all tithes and other
dues, excepting two parts of the tithe of corn within the said parish,
and one croft which lay near the house of the incumbent, and one
acre of meadow near to the said croft, all which should remain as a
perpetual endowment to the prior and convent of Burcester. The
form of composition runs thus.

*Omnibus Christi fidelibus ad quos præsens scriptum pervenerit Hugo
Lincoln. et Jocelinus Bathon. Dei gratia episcopi salutem in Domino.
Noveritis quod cum controversia orta esset inter nobilem virum Alanum*

i R. Dods. MS. vol. 56. f. 38.   k Du Tillet Recueil de Roys de France, p. 27.

Basset et priorem et canonicos de Burncester super ecclesiam de Cump-
ton, tam dictus Alanus quam prior et canonici insuper et venerabilis
frater dominus Ricardus Sarum episcopus et Willielmus decanus et
capitulum Sarum in hoc consenserunt et ordinationi nostræ pure et ab-
solute se subjecerunt, ratum et sancitum habituri quicquid de dicta ec
clesia et ejus proventibus ordinaremus. Nos itaque habita delibera
tione et requisito prudentium virorum consilio de prædicta ecclesia de
Cumpton et ejus proventibus ordinavimus in hunc modum. Videlicet,
quod prædictus episcopus Sarum et ejus successores habebunt in per-
petuum advocationem prædictæ ecclesiæ de Cumpton cum omni jure
advocationis eidem ecclesiæ pertinente. Ita quidem quod prædictus
episcopus Sarum et ejus successores conferent in perpetuum cui vo-
luerint idoneæ personæ tertiam partem decimarum garbarum totius
parochiæ de Cumpton et omnes minutas decimas quæ de jure debentur
eidem ecclesiæ et omnes obventiones altaris et cemiterii prædictæ ec-
clesiæ et totam terram et curiam quæ fuit personæ illius ecclesiæ cum
omnibus libertatibus et liberis consuetudinibus ad prædictam ecclesiam
et terram illius pertinentibus. Præter duas partes decimarum gar-
barum prædictæ parochiæ et croftam quæ jacet juxta curiam per-
sonæ et unam acram prati vicinam eidem croftæ. Quas duas partes
decimarum garbarum et croftam et acram prati integre habebunt in
perpetuum dicti prior et canonici nomine perpetui beneficii absque omni
onere ordinario, extraordinariis oneribus inter personam qui pro tem-
pore fuerit et priorem et canonicos prædictos partiendis. De consensu
etiam dicti prioris et canonicorum providimus quod de terra quæ fuit
personæ, persona qui pro tempore fuerit decimas non dabit. Siquid
vero in hac ordinatione nostra obscurum fuerit vel minus plene decla-
ratum, illud de consensu partium nobis reservavimus declarandum.
Hanc autem ordinationem nostram partibus commendavimus et ipsa ab
eis gratanter fuit accepta. In cujus rei robur et testimonium tam
sigillis nostris quam sigillis memorati episcopi Sarum et capituli et
prædictorum Alani et prioris et canonicorum fecimus presens scriptum
communiri. Valete[1]

---

[1] Ex Orig. penes D. Guil. Glynne, Bar.

To this original deed in parchment there have been five seals appending, of which the first is tore off, the second has the fair impress
of a bishop in mitre and robes, with a crosier in his left hand, and
his right hand extended with this inscription, JOCELINUS DEI GRA-
TIA BATHONIENSIS EPISCOPUS ; on the reverse a bishop on his knees
praying to the images of saints with this inscription, HII TIBI PA-
TRONI SINT JOCELINE BONI. The third seal has the effigies of a
bishop in the same ornaments, with this inscription, RICARDUS DEI
GRATIA SA. EPISCOPUS, and on the reverse the angel's salutation of
the virgin, with a bishop praying and this inscription, AVE MARIA
GRATIA PLENA DOMINUS TECUM. On the third seal is impressed
the arms of Alan Basset, Undie, with this inscription, SIGILLUM
ALANI BASSET. The first paternal coat of this family had been
Undie gold and red, which Undie was much varied by several
branches of the family, and this Alan Basset differed the device of
Undie into white and blue, from whom the Sandfords descending
assumed the same mark, and now Browning beareth it as being descended from an heir of Sandford[m]. The fourth seal which was that
of the convent * of Burcester is broke off.

An. MCCXXIX.   13, 14. *Henry III.*

By an inspeximus this year into the several donations made to the

* Philippa one of the three daughters
and heirs unto Thomas Basset of Hedingdon was the second wife of Henry E. of
Warwick, who dying 13. Hen. III. his countess gave one hundred marks to the king
that she might not be compelled to marry,
but live a widow as long as she pleased or
marry whom she liked best, provided he
were a loyal subject to the king. Whereupon she took to husband the same year
one Richard Siward, who proved a turbulent spirited man, being, as Mat. Par. saith,
" vir martius ab adolescentia." She was a

benefactress to the canons of Berencester,
vulgo Bissiter, and in her full widowhead
gave them VII[s]. yearly rent, issuing out of
certain lands in Studley, com. Warwic, to
find one lamp continually burning before
the altar of St. John Baptist in the conventual ch. of Berencester, for the health of
her soul and all her ancestors and children's souls. When she died I do not find,
but at Berencester she lieth buried in the
monastery there of her father's foundation.
Dugd. Warwic. p. 306.

[m] Sir W. Dugd. Ancient Usage, &c. p. 22.

abbey of Oseney with confirmation of them, it appears that Roger St. John of Stanton did remit and quit claim (as his father had before done) to a mill and five virgates of land in Weston adjoining to Burcester, called Simeon's land, &c.

. *Ac etiam de illa remissione, &c. quas præfatus Johannes pater suus (i. e. Joh. de S. Johanne) eidem ecclesiæ et canonicis fecit de uno molendino et quinque virgatis terræ cum omnibus eorum pertinentiis in villa de Weston extra Burncester quæ vocatur Simeon's land et de molendino in Odes-Barton, &c.* [n]

Dugdale in his baronage attributes this confirmation to John the son of this Roger, but it was apparently done by Roger son of John [o]. Upon the disseizure and death of Robert earl of Dreux the custody of his lands in England, which he held in right of his wife, was now committed to Richard earl of Cornwall, the king's brother, who accounted for ten fees the whole barony of St. Walery [p] : who by that right presented to a moiety of the church of Rollesham, and the year following to the church of Horspath.

21. *Hug. Wells. R. comes Pictav. et Cornub. ratione terrarum Roberti com. Drocarum præsent. ad medietatem ecclesiæ de * Rollesham et anno sequente eadem ratione ad ecclesiam de Horspath* [q].

---

* 21. Hug. Wells. Robert de Esthall subdiac. ad medietat. eccl'ie de Rollesham ad pres. R. com. Pictav. et Cornub. ratione terrarum com. Drocarum in manu sua existentium eo quod Lucianus ultimus rector ejusd. beneficium aliud admisit cum cura.

NORTH-ASTON COM. OXON.

Omnibus Xti fidelibus Hugo Dei grat. Linc. ep'us salutem. Noverit universitas vestra nos ad presentationem prioris et conv. de Bradenestoke patronorum eccl'iæ de Northeston dilectum in Xto filium Reginaldum ca-

pellanum ad perpetuam ipsius eccl'iæ vicariam admisisse, ipsumque in ea vicarium perpetuum instituisse cum onere ministrandi personaliter in eadem. Consistit autem ipsa vicaria in toto alteragio et in manso et domibus ad ipsam eccl'iam pertin. cum VI *acris terræ jacentibus juxta Caldewelle in campo orientali et in medietate decimarum de Nedecote de terra Will'i Busyn et Arnaldi de Nedecote, et decimis molendinorum duorum Simonis Gambon, et inveniet vicarius clericum et luminaria competentia in eccl'ia et solvet omnia sinodalia salvis in omnibus epis-*

---

[n] W. Dug. MS. N. p. 31.　　[o] Dugd. Bar. tom. 1. p. 539.　　[p] R. Dods. Collect. Rot. Pip. vol. 15. p. 120.　　[q] R. Dods. MS. vol. 107. p. 43.

The other moiety of the church of Rollesham was in the patronage of Walter de Fontibus.

In October, Henry earl of Britain came over into England and did homage to the king; upon which he was restored to all rights in England, and seems thereby reinstated in the manor of Pidington and lands in Merton [r].

Warine Basset, a younger son of Alan Basset baron of Wycomb, laid claim to the manor of Mersh and advowson of the church, late in possession of William Mareschall earl of Pembroke, who gave them to the abbey of Gesting, and there was now a trial for right of presentation, which by the king's letters was declared to belong to the said abbey.

21. *Hug. Wells. Abbas de Grestenge p. ad eccl'iam de Merse. L'ræ regis. H. Dei gra. &c. epo. Linc. salutem. Ostensum est nobis ex parte abbatis de Gestenge q'd cum ipse teneat manerium de Mershe cum ad vocatione eccl'ie, &c. quod manerium Warinus Basset et Katerina uxor ejus petunt in cur. nostra, &c. Clericus abbatis præsentatur, &c.* [s]

---

copalibus consuetudinibus et Lincoln. eccl'iæ dignitate quod ut perpetuam oblineat firmitatem presens scriptum sigillo nostro duximus apponendum. Hiis test. magistris Will. de Benningwod, Ric. de Wendover. Will. de Winchcomb. Dat. per manum nostram apud Dorkecestr. kal. Dec. pont. nostri xxi. Ex registro prioratus de Bradenestoke. Bib. Cotton. Vitell. A. 11. fol. 123.

Ecclesia de Northeston concessa priori Bradenestok per W. de Estun, et Osbertum filium ejus, temp. Rob'ti ep'i Linc. et Rob'ti archid. Oxon. Ib. f. 85.

Contentio inter priorem Braden. et Simonem molendinarium de Northeston super decimis, 1226. Ib. f. 124.

Conventio super decimis in eccl'iis North-

eston et Dunstywe facta non. Maii, 1229. Ib. fol. 125.

Ecclesiæ de Northeston, Lynham et Wilcote concessa priori et conv. de Braden. per Clementem pap. 4[tum] id. Mart. pont 1. Ib. f. 125.

Carta de terris in Northeston. Ib. f. 157.

Will. Tryvet dominus de Northeston temp. Galfridi prioris de Braden. circa 46. Hen. III. Ib. f. 159.

Controversia tempore Honor. 3tii papæ pont. 6. inter Galfridum rectorem eccl'iæ de Stepeleston et priorem de Braden. super medietate decimarum garbarum de Nuthcote. Ib. f. 160.

---

[r] Brady, Hist. p. 513.   [s] R. Dods. MS. vol. 107. p. 36.

About this time Alice the daughter of Thomas Basset (brother of Gilbert Basset founder of the priory of Burcester) the widow of William Malet baron of Curi-Malet in com. Som. holding in dowry the manor of Dedington in this county, which she had in frank marriage from her father, gave some of those lands in Dedington to her nephew Gilbert Basset (son of Alan Basset her younger brother) baron of Wicomb, who after gave them to the priory of Burcester. Her original deed of grant is preserved, with some part decayed.

.... *di et concessi et hac presenti charta* .... *suo dimidiam virgatum terre quam Will.* .. *antea donaverat ei; que est de libero martagio in Dadinton. Prœterea dedi ei unam virgatam terre quam Thomas Basseth pater meus dedit ei, quam scilicet Willielmus Ploth tenuit in Dadinton illi et heredibus suis habendas et tenendas de me et heredibus meis in feodo et hœreditate libere quiete plene et integre reddendo inde annuatim mihi et heredibus meis unam libram cymini ad festum S. Michael. pro omni servicio, salvo servicio regali; et ego Aliz predicta et heredes mei warantizabimus predictas terras cum omnibus pertinenciis suis scilicet in bosco et plano in viis et semitis et in omnibus libertatibus et liberis consuetudinibus ad predictas terras pertinentibus predicto Gileberto et heredibus suis contra omnes homines, et quia volo quod omnia predicta sicut prediuisa sunt firma et stabilia permaneant hoc scriptum sigillo meo confirmavi. Hiis testibus; Roberto de Eston, Alexandro de Midlecumb, Rob. de Chauz, Rob. de Orton, et multis aliis*[r]*.

The king confirmed to the priory of St. Frideswide in Oxford all their possessions which they held by the gift of Reginald de S. Walery, formerly lord of the manor of Ambrosden, consisting of the village of Kniton in com. Berks, &c. [u] Within this same year the prior of S. Frideswide presented a clerk to the church of * Fretwell, com. Oxon. [x]

---

* Fulco de Banvill concessit eccl'iæ Scti   in perpetuam elemosinam quas pater suus
Olavi de Fretewell x acras terræ et dimid.   Fulco dederat eis. Testibus Will'o de

[r] Ex Autographo inter Collec. R. Dods. MS. vol. 76. f. 106.   [u] R. Dods. MS. vol. 80.
f. 175.   [x] Ex Regist. Linc.

An. mccxxx.   14, 15.   *Henry III.*

Maurice de Gaunt, who by marriage with the daughter of Henry
de Oily became possessed of the manor of Weston, died this year,
when by deed bearing date at Portsmouth he had given to the king
his said manor of Weston, with Beverston and Albricton ʸ.

About this time Walter Ingeram gave to the church of St. Mary
and St. Edburg in Burncester a certain plot of ground reaching in
length from Hoosford to the mill of Kirtlington on the west side toward the bank of Charwell to the metes and bounds by him assigned,
with full liberty to the canons of that priory to give, sell, or otherwise
assign, to dig, plant trees, or convert to any use, &c. in this form of
donation.

*Omnibus Christi fidelibus ad quos præsens scriptum pervenerit Wal-
terus Yngeram de Kirtlintona salutem in Domino sempiternam. Noverit universitas vestra me pro salute animæ meæ 'et animabus patris
mei et matris meæ parentum meorum dedisse concessisse quietum clamasse et hac præsenti charta mea confirmasse pro me et hæredibus
meis Deo et ecclesiæ beatæ Mariæ et S. Edburgæ virginis de Burncester et canonicis ibidem Deo servientibus et imperpetuum servituris*

Scto Amando et aliis. Ex Cartular. S.
Frideswidæ in Coll. C. C. Oxon. Cart. 469.
   21. Hug. Wells.
   Helicus de Risebergh capellanus ad eccl.
de Horspath ad pres. R. com. Pictav. et
Cornub. ratione terrarum Rob. com. Drocarum in manu sua.
   Nichol. de Anna subdiac. ad eccl. de Bek-
kel ad pres. prioriss. et conv. de Stodley.
ib.
   22. Hug. Wells. John de Crakhall coll.
per ep'um auctoritate concilii ad eccl. de
Sumerton. Notand. quod dicta eccl'ia cepit
vacare die lunæ prox. post exalt. Scte Cru-

cis anno prox. preterito ; presentavit autem
Eustachius de Greinvil mag'rum Robertum
nepotem suum die ven. prox. post festum
S. Dionysii prox. sequ. et fuit collata dicto
J. 5. id. apr. sequentis mane.
   22. Hug. Wells. Rob. de Haya ad eccl.
de Sulthorn ad pres. abb. et conv. de Egnesham. Rob. de Wenlingbery post presentato ad eand. juri suo renunciente—salva
d'nis abb'i et conventui ann. cent. sol. pensione de eadem.
   Ric. de Herdewic subdine. ad eccl. de Ble-
cheston ad pres. Rici de Prestecot. mil.

ʸ Dugd. Bar. tom. 1. p. 402.

totam illam placiam quæ se extendit in longitudine de Hooseford us-
que ad molendinum de Kertlinton ex parte occidentali juxta ripam
de Charwell usque ad metas et abundas ibidem per me concessas et
appositas in puram et perpetuam eleemosinam salva mihi pastura dictæ
placiæ ad metendum vel pascendum habendam et tenendam de me et
hæredibus meis vel assignatis dictam placiam supradictis canonicis et
eorum successoribus vel cuicunque et quomodocunque dictam placiam
dare vendere vel assignare voluerint. Ita quod dictam placiam fodere
vel in ea fossam facere salices vel alias arbores ad libitum suum ibidem
plantare possint et omnia alia facere quæ sibi viderint expedire. Præ-
terea concessi eisdem liberam viam ultra pasturam meam de quadrario
suo usque ad prædictam ripam ad stagnum dicti molendini emendan-
dum quomodocunque voluerint. Ego vero dictus Walterus et hæredes
mei vel assignati dictam placiam ac liberam viam ut prædictum est in
puram et perpetuam eleemosinam dictis canonicis et eorum successori-
bus versus omnes homines et fœminas warantizabimus acquietabimus
imperpetuum et defendemus. Et ut hæc mea donatio concessio ac
præsentis chartæ confirmatio rata et stabilis imperpetuum permaneat
presenti scripto sigillum meum apposui. Hiis testibus ; Johanne filio
Willielmi de Kirtlinton, Petro de Hanynton, Johanne de Kodesford,
Adam de Mareny, Adam de Northbroke, de eadem et aliis[z].

To the original in parchment is a seal appending, bearing a rose
with this inscription, ✠ S. Waltri Yngeram.

John Nevil married Hawise daughter of Robert Courtney, and had
with her in frank marriage lands to the value of twenty-one pounds
per an. out of the manor of Wotesdon, com. Buck. to be allotted by
a jury of twelve neighbouring inhabitants [a].

The following inquisition was taken at Brill relating to the manor
of Borstall and the custody of the forest of Bernwood, the hereditary
tenure of John Fitz-Nigel.

Inquisitio capta apud Brehull die Jovis proxime post festum S. Gre
gorii papæ anno regni regis Henrici filii regis Johannis quartodecimo

---

[z] Ex Orig. penes D. Guil. Glynne, Bar.   [a] R. Dods. MS. vol. 42. p. 148.

coram Roberto de Fonte seniore tunc forestario intra pontem Oxon. et Staunford ad eadem assignato per ipsum regem de jure hæreditario tenuræ Johannis filii Nigelli de foresta de Bernewode per sacramentum domini Walteri de Upton, Johannis Graundon viridarii, Adæ filii Petri et Bartholomæi le Venor et omnium regardatorum et agistatorum forestæ prædictæ qui dicunt per sacramentum suum quod Johannes filius Nigelli tenet unam hidam terræ arabilis quæ vocatur le Derhyde per serjantiam custodiendi forestam de Bernewode necnon solvendi annuatim pro terra prædicta x^s. *et pro foresta prædicta* XL^s. *et dicunt etiam quod idem Johannes debet habere feodum in bosco domini regis videlicet attachiamentum de spinis de bosco suo et de bosco qui vento prostituitur et pannagium et clamutiones et indictationes si quæ fuerint videlicet de viridi et venatione. Et dicunt quod prædictus Johannes et antecessores sui a tempore quo non extat memoria habuerunt in dominico bosco domini regis* husebote *et* heybote *pro custodia dictæ forestæ. In cujus rei testimonium, &c.* [b]

An. MCCXXXI. 15, 16. *Henry III.*

Robert de Pavelly presented a rector to the church of Wendlebury, and the prior of Burcester a vicar to the church of Newton.

Archid. Oxon. 23. H. Wells. Robertus de Pavilly pt. ad ecclesiam de Wendlebur. prior de Berencester pt. ad ecclesiam de Newton [c]

In Trinity term there was a trial upon the promise of money in

---

* 23. Hug. Wells. 1231. Galfridus de Lestr subdiac. ad eccl. de Wendlebur ad pres. Rob. de Pavilly.

Joh. de Coleham capellan. ad vicar. eccl'ie de Berncestr ad pres. prioris et conv. ejusd. per resign. Rob'ti. 24. Hug. Well.

Steph. de Newton capellan. ad eccl. de Newenton ad pres. prioris et conv. de Berencestr.

Mag'r Adam de Senestan ad eccl. de Hetha ad pres. prioris et conv. de Kenillew. ib.

Rob. de Kingeton subdiac. ad illam medietat. in eccl'ia de Rollesham quam Rob. de Esthall tenuit (in dioc. Roff. de novo beneficiatus) ad pres. Walt. de Fontibus.

---

[b] Ex Chartular. de Borstall, MS. penes hon. Joh. Aubrey, Bar.   [c] R. Dods. MS. vol. 107. p. 41.

consideration of a marriage in this county, in which cause the prior of Burcester was delegated a judge.

...... *Ad idem facit quod habetis de termino S. Trinitatis anno regni H. 15. in com. Oxon. et unde prior de Burncestre fuit judex* [d]

The manor of Charlton, passing to Gerard de Camvill of Midleton by his wife Nichola de Hay, one of the daughters and heirs of Richard de Hay, was now in possession of William de Longspe in right of Idonea de Camvill his wife. It had been held in dowry by the said Nichola widow of Gerard de Camvill, and now at her death descended to her grand-daughter Idonea, whose husband William de Longspe did now homage for it, holding it by the service of two knight's fees.

Rex cepit homagium Willielmi de Lungespe de terris quas Nic'a de Haya tenuit in dotem in Cherleton et Henstrug de honore de Camel qui Idoneam uxorem ipsius Will'i filiam et hæredem Ric. de Camvill jure contingit hereditar, &c. Tenetur per servitium duorum feodorum mil [e].

The said William de Longspe and Idonea de Camvill his wife had lands granted now jointly to them in Sutton and Clyve in com. Northamp. [f]

This Idonea de Camvill is by great mistake called Ida de Camyle and Idonia Candol, in some transcript of records by Mr. Vincent [g]

It seems to have been on this occasion, that there was a trial at Westminster, wherein the said William Longspe and Idonea his wife were defendants, and would have stopped the process because the said William was under age; but the action being laid on account of his wife who was of full age, their plea was overruled, and is by Bracton cited for a president in this form. *Si vir tenens fuerit infra ætatem et uxor plenæ ætatis cum implacitati fuerint, non remanebit Loquela sine die propter minorem ætatem viri, sive nupta sit ante impetrationem Brevis vel post. Quia mulier implacitata jure suo si propter minorem ætatem viri posset differre judicium, ita posset quæ-*

---

[d] Bracton, lib. 5. cap. 10.   [e] R. Dods. Collect. Fin. MS. vol. 56. p. 5.   [f] Dugd. Bar. tom. 1. p. 118.   [g] Vincent, Correct. of Brook. p. 466.

libet mulier in fraudem nubere viro minori cum participes haberet vel non quod esset iniquum, et de hac re &c. in rotulo de termino S. Hilarii apud Westmon. anno regis Henrici 15. *in com. Northamp. de Willielmo Longspe minore et Idonea uxore ejus majore* [h]

Gilbert Basset, brother and heir of Thomas Basset, did homage to the king for the manor of Kirtlinton, com. Oxon.[i] The king now granted to Henry le Tyes the manor of Grendon, com. Bucks. which lately belonged to Robert de Tybovil[k]. Which Henry about this time held Shireburne, com. Oxon. by the grant of Richard earl of Cornwall, which was part of the barony of Robert earl of Dreux[l].

Which Richard earl of Cornwall, brother to the king, having the forfeited estate of Robert earl of Dreux delivered into his custody, an. 1229, had now a full grant of it from his royal brother: a copy of the charter of donation dated the 15. Hen. III. is preserved by W. Dugdale[m]. Upon this the said earl Richard enjoyed the whole barony of St. Walery in this county, and was thereby lord of Aikeley, Ambrosden, &c. which two particular places are mentioned as including the whole, (one being the head of the barony, and the other a chief manor) in a memorandum inserted by R. Dodsworth. *Henr. tertius concessit Richardo comiti Cornub. M. de Aikeley et Amberesden in C. Oxon. quæ fuerunt Rob. Dryweis quondam ducis Lotharingiæ* [n].

This same year August 10th, the king granted his said brother the honor of Walingford with the manor of Watlington, &c. at the service of three knight's fees.

Henricus tertius decimo die Augusti an. regni ejusdem xv. *per chartam suam dedit Ricardo comiti Pictaviæ et Cornubiæ fratri suo honorem Walingford cum castro et omnibus pertin. suis cum M. de Watlington, &c. per servitium feodorum trium militum* [o].

William Mareschall earl of Pembroke, whose sister Isabel was first

[h] Bracton, l. 5. f. 123.   [i] R. Dods. MS. vol. 55. f. 49.   [k] Ib. vol. 80. p. 115.   [l] Dugd. Bar. tom. 2. p. 21. b.   [m] W. Dugd. MS. E. 2. p. 76.   [n] R. Dods. MS. vol. 20. p. 30.
[o] W. Dugd. MS. B. 1. p. 124.

the wife of Gilbert de Clare earl of Glocester, after of Richard earl of Cornwall, died without issue, and was buried in the new Temple at London, the 18. calends of May, whereby his adjoining manors of Mersh and Ludgarshale passed to Richard Mareschall his next brother [p].

An. mccxxxii. 16, 17. Henry III.

Richard earl of Cornwall confirmed to the abbey of Oseney the village of Mixbury, which Thomas de St. Walery had given to them.

Omnibus ad quos, &c. Ricardus comes Pictaviæ et Cornubiæ salutem. Noverit universitas vestra nos confirmasse, &c. ecclesiæ S. Mariæ de Osenei, &c. totam terram cum pertinentiis quam ei dedit Thom. de S. Walerico de Mixbury salvis nobis et hæredibus nostris advocatione ecclesiæ ejusdem villæ et servitio quod de nobis tenetur de terra quæ fuit Wydonis de Hareines in eadem villa et insuper concessimus et confirmavimus pro nobis et hæredibus nostris eidem eeclesiæ et canonicis in perpetuum * usum Francipleg de tota villa de Mixbury et de tenentibus Henrici Purcell de Niwenton de feod. Mixbury quem habere consueverunt. In cujus rei testimonium præsenti scripto sigillum nostrum apposuimus. Hiis testibus, &c. [q]

He had this year committed to him the custody of the castles of Brembre and Cnappe, till William heir of John Braose, a baron on the marches of Wales, should arrive to his full age [r].

Henry de Oily, the second baron of Hooknorton, died within this year, and was buried before the great altar in the church of Oseney [s]. He left two sisters heirs, of which Margery the elder was the wife of

---

25. Hug. Wells.
Rad. de Wulvele. subdiac. ad eccl. de Feringeford ad pres. Will'i Buzun ratione Margarete uxoris sue, qui recuperavit pres.

suam versus priorem de Coges, Eustach. de Greinvill et Joh. ux. ejus, Thomam de Hay et Alex. uxorem ejus.

* *Visum.*

---

[p] Dugd. Bar. tom. 1. p. 603. a.   [q] Regist. Osen. MS. p. 290.   [r] Dugd. Bar. tom. 1. p. 420. a.   [s] Tabula Annal. Oseneie. Cœnob. apud J. Lelandum.

Henry earl of Warwick, who had issue by her Thomas earl of Warwick, who in the 17. of Henry III. paid one hundred pounds and and two palfries for a relief of his said uncle's lands[t].

Almaric de St. Amand obtained a grant of the manor of Bloxham in this county, and two years after was made governor of St. Briavil castle in com. Gloucester, and warden of the forest of Dene, and sheriff of Herefordshire, and governor of Hereford castle[u].

An. MCCXXXIII. 17, 18. *Henry III.*

Wido de Areines gave to the abbey of Oseney all his land in Mixbury, being six virgates in villanage with his villains, and the suits and services of four virgates with homage, &c.

Sciant, &c. quod ego Wido de Areines dedi et concessi, &c. ecclesiæ beatæ Mariæ de Osenei et canonicis totam terram meam de Mixbury cum pertinent. suis in liberam et perpetuam eleemosinam scilicet 6. virgatas terræ de villenagio cum villanis et eorum sectis et servitiis quatuor virgatarum terræ cum homagiis, &c. quas quatuor virgatas terræ Thomas Clericus aliquando libere tenuit, &c.[x]

This donation was ratified by Richard earl of Cornwall lord of the fee.

Omnibus Christi fidelibus, &c. Ricardus comes Cornubiæ et Pictaviæ salutem in Domino. Noverit universitas vestra nos pro nobis et hæredibus nostris ratam habere donationem quam Wido de Areines fecit abbati et conventui de Osenei de terra sua quam habuit in villa de Mixbury quæ terra quandoquidem consuevit facere sectam ad curiam nostram de North Osenei hanc sectam, &c. relaxamus in perpetuum[y]

A mandate was sent to Peter de Rievall sheriff of Bucks. and Bedf. to give seisin to Hubert de Burg of the manors of Aspele and Henlawe, which he held by the gift of Reginald de S. Walery[z].

Alan Basset baron of Wycomb died this year leaving son and heir

[t] Dugd. Bar. tom. 1. p. 161. a. [u] Ibid. tom. 2. p. 19. b. [x] Regist. Osen. MS. p. 290. [y] Ibid. [z] R. Dods. MS. vol. 103. f. 161.

Gilbert Basset, who, with Richard Siward and other great men, took
part with Richard earl Mareschall in his contentions with the king,
for which all the lands of the said Gilbert Basset and Richard Siward
within this same year were wasted, and their castles and houses demolished by the power of Richard earl of Cornwall. Upon which
about Christmas, Richard Siward, to revenge those injuries, took with
him a tumultuous mob, and destroyed several manors of the said earl
of Cornwall in these parts, among which the manor of Ambrosden
did probably then suffer; which so far provoked the earl, that though
in the following year, on the death of Richard earl Mareschall, all his
abettors were restored to the king's favor, yet the said Richard Siward to decline the anger of the said earl was obliged to retire into
Scotland, and there wait till a peace should be made for him[a].

The said Alan Basset baron of Wycomb was a younger brother of
Gilbert Basset of Hedingdon, from whom he obtained the lordship
of Compton nigh Cheping-Norton in this county: at his death he
left by will two hundred marks to the University of Oxford for the
maintenance of two chaplains, and made the prior and convent of
Burcester his executors, who purchased three carucates of land in
Arncote in the parish of Ambrosden, with a wood in the said village,
out of the rents whereof they obliged themselves to pay eight marks
yearly at two equal payments, for support of two chaplains or scholars residing within the University of Oxford, who should pray for
the souls of the said Alan Basset and his wife, and should on every
special festival add a Placebo and Dirige to be after composed for
that purpose. This wood and land (thus purchased by the priory,
and charged with the provision for two scholars) was called and still
retains the name of Prior's Hill, from which wood four load of fuel
was yearly allowed the vicar of Burcester, by a composition made
an. 1754. *Vicarius habeat quatuor bigatas lignorum pro focalibus de
silva prioris vocat. Prior's Woode. apud Arncote*[b]: for which there is

[a] Tho. Wikes, sub an. [b] Transcrip. decret. Cancel. penes Tho. Shewring, A. M.
vicar. Burces.

now an annual pension paid to the said vicar. The [c]author of the
Antiquities of Oxford places the history of this benefaction under the
year 1243, which must needs be incongruous : for Alan Basset died
in this year, 1232; and that author cites the story from the register
of Hugh Wallis bishop of Lincoln, which could extend no further
than this year.

It is most likely that at this time began the *Scholæ Burcestrienses*,
the schools belonging to the priory of Burcester, when that convent
being thus obliged to maintain two scholars did hire a tenement of
the abbey of Oseney, called Hastyng, lying in School Street, on the
north side of St. Mary's nigh the schools belonging to University
college, for which they paid to the said abbey a yearly rent, and employed it to this use for the instruction and residence of scholars.
*Scholæ Burcestrienses ad prioratum Burcestriensem vel Biscestriensem
in comitatu Oxoniensi locatum spectabant. Sitæ erant in tenemento
quodam scholis ad collegium Universitatis pertinentibus ad boream adjacente ; pendebat vero inde possessor per manus Ballivi prædicti prioratus monasterio Osneiensi annuam pecuniæ summam. In Osneien-
sium rentalibus domus Hastyng aliquando vocatur : unde colligendum
videtur, quod eo nomine quispiam vel ipsam domum dicto prioratui, vel
saltem pensionem quam dixi exinde redeuntem Osneiensibus detulit
tempore Hen. III. Quorum tamen in rentalibus scholarum prædictarum infrequentem admodum et fortuitam, ut ita loquar, mentionem
reperio* [d].*

It was then customary for the religious to have schools that bore
the name of their respective order. Thus the Augustine schools, one
of divinity, another of philosophy, in which latter the disputing of
bachelors has yet continued the name to the exercise of Augustines.
The Benedictine schools for theology, the Carmelite schools for divinity and philosophy in the parish of St. Mary Magdalene. The
Franciscan schools, &c. And there were schools appropriated to the
benefit of particular religious houses, as the Dorchester schools, the

[c] Ant. a. Wood, Antiq. Un. l. 1. p. 92.   [d] Ant. a Wood, Antiq. Oxon. l. 2. p. 8.

Eynsham schools, the schools of St. Frideswide, of Littlemore, of
Oseney, of Stodley, &c.   The monks of Glocester had Glocester
convent in Oxford; the monks of Pershore in Worcester had an
apartment for their novices in that house, &c.ᶜ   So the young
monks of Westminster, of Canterbury, of Durham, of St. Albans,
&c.ᶠ   The convent of Burcester were more especially obliged to provide for the education of students in the University, as they were of
the Augustine order, who had this particular charge incumbent on
them.   In a general chapter held in the parish church of Chesthunt,
A. D. 1331, strict commands were given for maintaining scholars in
some University, as had been before decreed in their statutes made at
Northampton, Huntingdon, and Dunstaple.   In another chapter at
Northampton, A. D. 1359, it was ordained that every prelate (i. e.
abbot or prior) should send one out of every twenty of the canons to
reside and study in the University : and if any prelate should neglect
this duty, he should pay ten pounds for every year's omission.   Again,
in a general chapter, 1362, there is a solemnity appointed for the
electing of canons to be sent out for students in the University, and
the election time fixed about the feast of St. Margaret.   In a chapter at Oseney, held A. D. 1443, William Westkar, professor of divinity,
stood up and recited the names of those prelates, and had the allotted
fines imposed on them : as a catalogue of the persons and their respective sums does shew.   And in a chapter convened at the monastery of St. James's nigh Northampton, A. D. 1446, the visitors of
the respective archdeaconries made their returns of those abbots and
priors who had defaulted.   When, at the solicitation of the aforesaid
William Westkar, the king sent a preceptory letter, directed 𝕿𝖔 𝖔𝖚𝖗
𝖙𝖗𝖚𝖘𝖙𝖞 𝖆𝖓𝖉 𝖜𝖊𝖑𝖑-𝖇𝖊𝖑𝖔𝖇𝖊𝖉 𝖎𝖓 𝕲𝖔𝖉 𝖆𝖑𝖑 𝖙𝖍𝖊 𝖕𝖗𝖊𝖘𝖎𝖉𝖊𝖓𝖙𝖎𝖟, 𝖕𝖗𝖊𝖑𝖆𝖙𝖊𝖘 𝖆𝖓𝖉 𝖕𝖗𝖔𝖈𝖚=
𝖗𝖆𝖙𝖔𝖗𝖘 𝖔𝖋 𝖈𝖍𝖆𝖓𝖔𝖓𝖘 𝖗𝖊𝖌𝖚𝖑𝖊𝖗𝖊𝖘 𝖔𝖋 𝖙𝖍𝖊 𝖔𝖗𝖉𝖗𝖊 𝖔𝖋 𝕾𝖊𝖞𝖓𝖙 𝕬𝖚𝖘𝖙𝖊𝖓 𝖔𝖋 𝖙𝖍𝖞𝖘 𝖔𝖚𝖗
𝖗𝖊𝖆𝖑𝖒.   Wherein he grants their 𝖘𝖚𝖕𝖕𝖑𝖎𝖈𝖆𝖙𝖎𝖔𝖓 𝖋𝖔𝖗 𝖙𝖍𝖊 𝖒𝖔𝖗𝖊 𝖍𝖔𝖓𝖊𝖘𝖙𝖎𝖊
𝖆𝖓𝖉 𝖕𝖊𝖗𝖋𝖊𝖈𝖙𝖎𝖔𝖓 𝖔𝖋 𝖙𝖍𝖊 𝖘𝖆𝖎𝖉 𝖔𝖗𝖉𝖗𝖊, 𝖙𝖔 𝖍𝖆𝖇𝖊 𝖙𝖍𝖊 𝖕𝖑𝖆𝖈𝖊 𝖆𝖓𝖉 𝖌𝖗𝖔𝖜𝖓𝖉 𝖜𝖍𝖊𝖗𝖊
𝖙𝖍𝖊𝖞 𝖒𝖞𝖙𝖍 𝖒𝖆𝖐𝖊 𝖆 𝖈𝖔𝖑𝖊𝖌𝖊 𝖓𝖆𝖒𝖊𝖉 𝖔𝖋 𝖔𝖚𝖗 𝖇𝖑𝖊𝖘𝖘𝖊𝖉 𝖑𝖆𝖉𝖞.   And he orders

---

ᶜ Wood, Athen. Oxon. p. 577.   ᶠ Ibid. p. 595.

a levy of the multes taxed and limited for absence of scholars. But this project failing of one general college, they still continued the care of providing for particular scholars; and in the next chapter convened at Oseney, A. D. 1449, inquiry and complaint was to be again made of all abbots and priors that did not maintain students in Oxford or Cambridge. By rules sent from pope Benedict in the fifth of his pontificate to the abbot of Thornton and prior of Kirkham, to be observed within the dioceses of York and Lincoln, the pensions for such students are expressed, sixty pounds yearly to a master in divinity, to a bachelor, fifty, to a scholar or student in divinity forty, to a doctor of canon law fifty, to a bachelor or scholar in civil law thirty-five[g].

So in the acts and constitutions of the chapters of the Benedictine order, there be frequent provisions for scholars to be maintained one out of twenty monks at the University, with inquiries into such defaults, and penalties imposed for them[h]. They had a prior of students to govern all the novices of their order at Oxford and Cambridge; where they had a doctor in each faculty of divinity and canon law, under whom their inceptors were to commence at the public charge of their respective monastery[i]. The general colleges for this order were Glocester in Oxford, and Monks college (now Magdalene) in Cambridge[k].

To this commendable practice we owe the imitation of it by our first reformers. Among the injunctions of Edward the Sixth, A. D. 1547, it is provided that *every parson, vicar, clerk, or beneficed man having yearly to dispend in benefices and other promotions of the church an c[l]. shall give competent exhibition to one scholar, and for so many c[l]. more as he may dispend, to so many scholars more shall he give like exhibition*[l]. This inquiry is among archbishop Cranmer's articles of visitation in the 2d of Edward the Sixth, and bishop Rid-

---

[g] Capitula Gen. Ord. S. Aug. MS. in Mus. Bib. Bod.   [h] Reynerus de Benedict. Ang. Append. p. 107, 199, &c.   [i] Ibid. p. 131.   [k] Ibid. p. 207.   [l] Sparrow's Collect. p. 5, &c.

ley's articles, an. 1550. And by the injunctions of queen Elizabeth, A. D. 1559, the rate of allowance is specified, *Every parson, vicar, clerk, or beneficed man, having yearly to dispend in benefices and other promotions of the church an hundred pounds, shall give* 3¹. 6ˢ. 8ᵈ. *in exhibition to one scholar in either of the Universities, &c.* We are uncertain how well these orders were then obeyed, but we are sure the charity has now failed.

An. MCCXXXIV. 18, 19. *Henry III.*

The prioress of Stodley presented a clerk to the church of Beckley, reserving to herself a yearly pension of ten marks. Eustace de * Grenevill presented Robert de Grenevill his nephew to the church of Somerton : and Sir Richard de Prestecote, knight, presented to the church of Blechesdon ᵐ

William de Longspe in right of his wife, lord of the manor of Burcester, made the canons of that priory a more ample endowment by a confirmation and additional gifts of all his land in Wrechwic, his wood of Gravenhull, his pasture called Coubregge, with pasturage for fifty-two yearlings at Erdington, by this charter.

*Sciant præsentes et futur*i *quod ego Willielmus Longspe ded*i *et concess*i *et hac charta mea confirmavi Deo et ecclesiæ beatæ Mariæ et*

---

* Willielmus de Grenevil preb. de Halgeton in eccl'ia de Suthwell per mortem Tho. de Bruton, Dec. 29, 1269. Ex regist. Walt. Giffard. Ebor.

An. ᴀCCXXXIV. 18, 19. Henry III.

Mandatum est Joh'i de Nevill quod permittat abb'em de Thame habere agistamentum suum in foresta de Brehull, sicut habere debet per libertates quas rex communiter concessit in regno suo per cartam suam. Claus. 19. Hen. III.

In ipsis præterea diebus natilitiis bellum contra regem et suos consiliarios graviter accenditur. Nam Ricardus Sward con-junctis sibi cæteris exulibus terras Richardi comitis Cornubiæ fratris regis non longe a Brehulle sitas cum ædificiis et frugibus ac bobus in bostaribus, caballis quoque in stabulis, necnon gregibus in caulis, incendio tradiderunt. Mat. Par. sub. an. 1234, p. 394. This must be meant of the manor of Ambrosden, which was the nearest to Brill of any part of the estate of the said Richard E. of Cornwall.

ᵐ Regist. Linc.

Sanctæ Edburgæ de Berencestria et canonicis ibidem Deo servientibus &c. totam terram quam habui in Wrecheroych cum omnibus pertinenciis cum villanis et eorum sequelis et catallis cum bosco de Gravenhull cum pertinenciis et quadam cultura, quæ vocatur Coubregge cum pertinenciis et pasturam ad quinquaginta bidentes apud Erdintone cum dominicis bidentibus meis ibidem pascendis habendam et tenendam de me et hæredibus meis dictis canonicis et eorum successoribus in liberam puram et perpetuam elemosinam libere, quiete, integre et pacifice in bosco et plano viis et semitis, pratis, pascuis et pasturis cum omnibus dominicis terris et bosco pertinentibus quieta de me et hæredibus meis ab omnibus serviciis sectis consuetudinibus et demandis mihi et hæredibus meis pertinentibus. Et ego Willielmus Longspeye et hæredes mei prædicta terras et boscum cum villanis et eorum sequelis una cum prædicta pastura de Erdintone dictis canonicis et eorum successoribus contra omnes homines et fœminas inperpetuum warantizabimus. Ut autem hæc mea donacio, concessio et chartæ meæ confirmacio perpetuæ firmitatis robur obtineant præsentem chartam sigilli mei impressione et virorum fide dignorum testimonio roboravi. Hiis testibus; domino Stephano Longespeye, Jacobo de Aldedeleghe, Philippo Basset, Radulpho de Cesterton, Willielmo de Meauling, Richardo de Mundevill, militibus; Philippo de Wappelle, Roberto de Hoult, Roberto de Monasterio de Buckhull, Johanne Foucher, et aliis"[n].

The original is in the custody of Sir William Glynne, Bar. and has a seal appending with his arms on an embossed shield, six lions rampant, and on the reverse a long sword sheathed.

William Buzin in right of his wife presented to the church of * Feringeford (now Fringford) com. Oxon. the advowson of which

---

* Rectores eccl'iæ de Feringford.

Rob. de Hoketon, cap. pres. per dom. Rob. de Grey mil. ad eccl. de Feringford per mort. Tho. de Idemeston, 7. id. Jun. pont. 12. i. e. 1219. Reg. de Sutton.

Adam clericus nepos mag'ri Gilberti de Scto Albano ad eccl. de Feringford ad coll. ep'i auctoritate concilii. Rot. Hug. Wells. pont. 11. i. e. anno 1219.

Rad. de Wulvel subdiac. ad eccl. de Fe_

n Mon. Ang. tom. 2. p. 284.

the said William Buzin and Margery had recovered in the king's court against the prior of Coges, and Eustace de Grenevil and Joan his wife, and Thomas de Hay and Alice his wife[o]

John Frankland of Mixbury gave to the church of Oseney one acre of arable land in the east-field of Fulwell, lying in the ground called le Eley; as also one acre of arable land in the west-field of Fulwell, of which one half acre lay toward la Link and extended over Buringeswey, the other half acre in a ground called la Hangride; by two several charters.

Sciant præsentes et futuri quod ego Johannes Frankland de Mixbury dedi et concessi Deo et ecclesiæ beatæ Mariæ de Osenei unam acram terræ meæ arabilis in campo orientali de Fulewell jacentem in illa cultura, quæ vocatur le Ely, intra terram dictorum abbatis et canonicorum ex omni parte, &c.

Sciant præsentes et futuri quod ego Johannes Frankland de Mixbury dedi et concessi Deo et ecclesiæ beatæ Mariæ de Osenei unam acram terræ meæ arabilis in campo occidentali de Fulewell cum pertinentiis suis quæ sic jacet videlicet una dimidia acra jacet in cultura quæ vocatur la Hangide, &c.[p]

The king was at Oxford in June, where he gave this remarkable mandate to reform the discipline of that place.

Mandatum est majori et ballivis Oxon. quod per totam villam Oxon. clamari faciant quod omnes publices meretrices et concubinæ clericorum infra octo dies post hunc clamorem factum exeant villam Oxon. Ita quod nulla in dicta villa remaneat post terminum illum et si aliqua forte remaneat vel de novo in villam veniat post terminum illum ad ibi manendum per concilium cancellarii Oxon. vel magistri Ro-

ringford ad pres. Will. Buzun ratione Margar. uxoris suæ, qui recuperavit presentationem suam versus priorem de Coges, Eustach. de Greinvill et Joh. uxorem ejus, Tho. de Haya et Alex. uxorem ejus. Rot.

Hug. Well. an. 25.

Nich. de Runnes subd. ad eccl. de Ferigeford ad pres. Will. Buzun laici. Rot. Rob. Grosthead, anno 5. (1239.)

[o] Ex. Regist. Linc.   [p] Regist. Osen. MS. p. 290.

berti Grosseteste vel fratris Roberti Bacun capiantur et in prisona regis mittantur donec rex aliud inde preceperit, firmiter etiam prohibere faciant super gravem forisfacturam regis nequis de prædicta villa alicui hujusmodi meretrici vel concubinæ clericorum si forte aliqua vice veniat in villam, &c. T. R. apud Oxon. xxii. *die Junii* q.

Though the barony of St. Walery, the estate of Robert earl of Dreux forfeited to the crown, was first the custody and after the property of Richard earl of Cornwall; yet some part of the said barony (the manor of Horton, &c.) was allotted for a dowry to Alla nor widow of earl Robert, who this year confirmed a donation of her deceased husband's to the nuns of Stodley.—*Donationem præcedentem (nempe factam an.* 1226.) *post obitum mariti Allanora comitissa Drocarum et domina de Sancto Walerico eisdem monialibus confirmavit an. Dom.* mccxxxiv. *mense Augusti* r.

This Allanor de S. Walery was after married to Henry lord of Sully, and dying without children was buried with her first husband in the abbey of Brenne s.

An. mccxxxv.   19, 20. *Henry III.*

About this time Thomas Raynall gave to the abbey of Oseney two acres of arable land in the common field of Weston, of which one acre lay in Cornhull nigh the demesnes of the canons called Eldesfield, one rood in Flexlond extending toward Litlemore and Longforland, half an acre upon Rughill extending upon a ground called Stockling.

Sciant præsentes et futuri quod ego Thomas Raynall, &c. concessi ecclesiæ S. Mariæ · de Osenci et canonicis ibidem Deo servientibus duas acras terræ arabilis in campo de Weston de quibus una acra jacet

1. Rob. Grosthead.
Rob. Makerel subdiac. ad eccl. de Parva Missenden ad pres. prioris et conv. de Ber-

necestr salvis dictis priori et conv. 5. ann. marc.

q R. Dods. MS. vol. 103. f. 168.   r Mon. Ang. tom. 1. p. 187.   s Dugd. Bar. tom. 1. p. 455.

in Cornhulle juxta dominicum dictorum canonicorum quod vocatur Eldesfield et una roda jacet in Flexlond et se extendit in Litlemore et in Long-forland, &c. et una dimidia acra jacet super Rughulle et extendit supra culturam quæ vocatur Stockling [t].

The king, residing at his manor of Woodstock in this county, did from thence issue out his precept to John de Nevil, dated November the seventh, wherein he requires him, that notwithstanding his late command of seizing and keeping for the king's use all hogs that came for pannage and agistment within any of his forests and parks within his bailiwic, he should permit Robert Bishop of Lincoln and Ralph de Warewill to have their hogs run in the adjoining forest of Bernwood, discharging them from all trespass, and releasing their said hogs [u].

By which it does appear that John de Nevil of Brill was then one of the four agistors for the forest of Bernwood, whose office obliged them to take care of the feeding of hogs within the king's demesne woods, from Holy-rood day to forty days after Michaelmas, and to take pannage, which was one farthing, for the agistment of each hog: and that the bishop of Lincoln and Ralph de Warewill had liberty of agisting their hogs, either because they had woods of their own within the bounds of the forest, or else had express charters of acquitment from pannage [x].

The king at Westminster, November the thirteenth, gave to his brother Richard earl of Cornwall, lord of the manor of Ambrosden, &c. all the amercements in the circuit of William de Ralegh and other itinerant judges in the counties of Bedford and Bucks. imposed on them, who held of his honor of Walingford; as also all amercements in the circuit of the judges in the county of Rutland, commanding the barons of his exchequer to enroll the said donation, sending his precept to the sheriffs of Bedf. and Bucks. that without delay they should raise and pay the said amercements to the earl,

---

[t] Regist. Osen. MS. p. 317.   [u] R. Dods. MS. vol. 75. f. 114.   [x] Manwood of Forest Laws, cap. 12.

with a precept to the itinerant judges for the county, that under their seals they should issue writs to the sheriff of Rutland, for collecting the said amercements. And lastly directing another precept to the said sheriff to pay in the amercements so collected [y].

Within the same year the king granted to him the castle and honor of Knareburg in Yorkshire [z]. Hugh bishop of Lincoln died on the sixth of the ides of February, and was succeeded by Robert Grosthead, consecrated at Reading by Edmund archbishop of Canterbury [a]. The king spent a great part of this year at Woodstock, where on July the twenty-fourth he confirmed the endowments of the nunnery of Tarente in com. Dorset [b]. And on November the third he ratified the charters and privileges of the priory of Daventre in com. Northamp. [c]

An. MCCXXXVI. 20, 21. *Henry III.*

Richard Vintner of Brackly and Aldrede his wife claimed one virgate of land in Mixbury held by the abbey of Oseney, for which there was now a trial before the justices itinerant; and the issue was, that the said Richard and his wife, in consideration of thirty shillings received by them, did for ever quit claim to the said land.

Hæc est finalis concordia facta in curia domini regis die Mercurii proximo post festum S. Margaretæ an. reg. regis Henrici filii regis Johannis vicesimo coram Ran. abbate, Rob. de Lexinton, Oliverio de Vallibus, Joh. de Aulicote, et Willielmo de S. Edmundo, justic. itin. et aliis domini regis fidelibus tunc ibi præsentibus inter Richardum Vinetarium de Brachelle et Aldredam uxorem ejus petentem et Johannem abbatem de Osenei tenentem de una virgata ferræ cum pertinentiis in Mixebury, unde placitum fuit inter eos in eadem curia scilicet quod

2. Rob. Grosthead.
Rogerus subdiac. nepos nobilis viri R. com. Pictav. et Cornub. presentatus per eundem ad eccl. de Frothigham. Inquis. facta per W. archid. Stow.

y R. Dods. MS. vol. 75. f. 113.   z Ibid. vol. 123. f. 88.   a Matt. West. sub i.
b Mon. Ang. tom. 1. p. 888. b.   c Ibid. p. 673. a.

*prædicti Richardus et Aldreda remiserunt et quiete clamaverunt de se
et hæredibus ipsius Aldredæ prædicto abbati et successoribus suis et
ecclesiæ suæ de Osenei totum jus et clam. quod habuerunt in tota prædicta terra in perpetuum et pro hac eorum remissione quieta clamatione et concordia idem abbas dedit prædictis Richardo et Aldredæ
xxx. solidos sterling* [d]*

Nigh this time Richard de Bigod of Merston gave to the canons of
Nutley in Crendon the running of forty hogs in his wood.

*Ego Richardus le Bigod de Merston dedi canonicis de Nuttele 40.
porcos in bosco meo, &c. Testibus, domino Hugone de Angens, &c.* [e]

The abbot of Grostein presented a clerk to the neighbouring
church of Mersh [f].

The prior of Berncester presented to the church of Little-Missenden in the archdeaconry of Bucks. And Henry de S. Faith, prior of
Nottele in Crendon, was elected abbot of the said house, license being first obtained from the earl of Pembroke patron [g]

An. MCCXXXVII.   21, 22. Henry III.

Now or before this time Robert son of Robert de Amory confirmed to the abbey of Oseney the donation of one hide of land in

3. Hen. Grosthead.

Rad'us de Well subdiac. ad eccl. de Finemere ad pres. abb. et conv. S. Augustini
Bristol.

Rob. de Esthall subdiac. ad eccl. de
Stokbasset ad pres. R. com. Pictav. et Cornub. 5. cal. Jun.

Walt. de Cotes capellanus ad eccl. de
Stokes Thalesmarch ad pres. ven. viri W.
de Wburn archid'i Riehm.

*Omnibus ... Noverit un. v'ra nos auctori-
tate Gregorii pape noni abb'em et conv. de Abbendon in eccl. de Cudesdon canonice rectores*

*instituisse ipsosque in corporalem possessi-
onem ipsius eccl'ie induci fecisse salva vicaria
per dilectum filium mag'rum R. de Weseham
archid'um Oxon. in eadem taxata; dat. 18.
kal. Jun. pont. tertio.*

Taxatio vicarie sequitur.

Rogerus subd. nepos comitis Pictav. et
Cornub. ad eccl. de Frodingham ad pres.
R. com. Pictav. et Gornuh. ad eccl. de Fro-
dingham in archid. Stow ad pres. R. com.
Pictav. et Gornuh. (sic) ratione honoris de
Kirketon in manu sua existentis.

[d] Regist. Osen. MS. p. 280.   [e] W. Dugd. MS. vol. 74. p. 73.   [f] R. Dods. MS. vol.
107. p. 71.   [g] Ib. f. 71. and 74.

Chestreton, in consideration of thirty shillings to himself and one be-
zantine to his brother.

*Notum sit fidelibus S. ecclesiæ quod ego Robertus filius Roberti filii
Amarici, &c. confirmo donationem quam fecit Amphridus filius Roberti
de Oxon. ecclesiæ S. Mariæ de Osenei de una hida terræ in Cestre-
tona cujus duas virgatas tenuerunt Hemingus filius Siward et Nicholaus duas vero tenent Willielmus mercator et Osmundus filius Willielmi quas cum progenie sua concedo prædictæ ecclesiæ hanc hidam
concedo pro quinta parte servitii unius militis* III. *den. erga capitalem
dominum ita ut quando ego terram meam quietam habuero, prædicta
ecclesia eandem quietanciam habeat. In recognitione hujus donationis
dedit mihi prænominata ecclesia* XXX. *sol. et fratri meo unum bezan-
tium*[h].

An. MCCXXXVIII. 22, 23. Henry III.

The king was at Woodstock about the feast of St. Matthew, where
a pretended priest feigning himself mad got in by night at a window
of the king and queen's bedchamber with an intent of murder; but
a discovery and noise being made by a devout and noble woman,
Margaret Byset, the fellow was apprehended and tore in pieces by
horses at Coventry[i], or at Oxford[k].

Richard * earl of Cornwall, lord of the manor of Ambrosden, &c.
presented a clerk to the church of North-Luffenham in the archdeaconry of Northampton[l]: and was now esteemed the protector of

---

* An. 4. Rob. Grosthead. Nich. de Anna
subd. ad eccl. de Ambresdon ad pres. R.
com. Pictav. et Gornuh. dispensatum ei per
legatum ut eccl'iam alteram obtinere possit
habent. curam animarum una cum eccl. de
Beckel. Rot. Grosthead.

An. 5. Rob. Grosthead. Rob. de Anna ad
vicar. de Ambresdon ad pres. Nich'i de An-

na rectoris ejusd. de voluntate et assensu R.
com. Pictav. et Cornub. admissus.

4. pont Rob. Grosthead.

Ric. de Poklinton capellan. ad eccl. de
Merihthon ad pres. abb. et conv. de Egnesham.

Will. de Sulthorn subdiac. ad eccl. de
Ardulfel ad pres. Guidonis fil. Rob'ti.

---

[h] Regist. Osen. MS. p. 327.   [i] Mat. West. sub an.   [k] Cron. Tho. Wikes, sub an.

the whole nation from the oppressions of Rome, as this high character is given him by our best historian. *Et sperabatur certissime tunc
quod ipse comes Richardus esset liberaturus terram tam a Romanorum
quam aliorum alienigenarum misera qua premebatur servitute: et omnes a puero usque ad hominem senem crebras in ipsum benedictiones
congesserunt* [m].

Within this year Walter de Erugas, preceptor of the hospital of the
Knights of Jerusalem, presented to the church of Lutegareshale (now
Ludgarsall) in the archdeaconry of Bucks. The exemplary bishop
now visited this archdeaconry of Oxford; and at Dorchester, on
the ides of May, he granted the liberty of a chapel within the parish of Eston com. Bucks. to William de Clinton patron of the said
church [n].

At which time historians speak of a solemn dedication of several
churches in the diocese of Lincoln [o], and particularly in this county
of Oxford, by Robert Grosthead bishop of Lincoln, and William
Brewer bishop of Exeter. There is an epistle from Robert Grosthead to the archdeacon of Lincoln, wherein he warns him to give
notice to the rectors of all churches to provide for consecration :
since, according to the canons of a late council held at London,
every church unconsecrated was to have a solemn consecration within
two years following [p]. The epistle is undated, but the subject of it
seems to fix it to 1236.

The church of Chesterton seems to have been now consecrated,
when Roger de Gunelade knight gave to this church of St. Mary's
in Chesterton, for the endowment of it at the dedication, one acre
upon Fundeshulle, and one acre upon Rugge. At the same time
William son of Fulk de Chesterton, for the soul of Denise his wife
and Agnes his daughter, gave to the said church for endowment part
of a meadow which belonged to his fee in Blakemore.

Sciant præsentes et futuri quod ego Rogerus miles filius Richardi de

---

[l] Regist. Linc.   [m] Mat. Par. edit. Wats, p. 467.   [n] R. Dods. MS. vol. 107. f. 74.
[o] Mat. West. sub an.   [p] Append. ad Fasciculum, p. 340.

Gunelade dedi et concessi Deo et ecclesiæ beatæ Mariæ de Cestreton nomine dotis ad ejusdem ecclesiæ dedicationem per consensum hæredis mei Nicholai unam acram super Fundeshulle et unam acram terræ super Rugge in puram et perpetuam eleemosinam [q].

Willielmus filius Fulconis de Cestreton, &c. Sciatis me concessisse pro anima Dionysiæ uxoris meæ et pro anima Agnetis filiæ meæ Deo et ecclesiæ beatæ Mariæ de Cestreton nomine dotis ad ejusdem ecclesiæ dedicationem totam partem prati quod pertinet ad feodum meum in Blakemore [r].

For farther endowment of the said church of Chestreton, Bardulf son of Roger Bardulf, gave for a mansion house to the incumbent one messuage with a croft belonging to it, which Ralph the miller held, and his whole meadow in demesne in Blakemore: and confirmed to the said church the gift of his tenants of all they had in common in Blakemore, which was his fee.

Sciant præsentes et futuri quod ego Bardulfus filius Rogeri Bardulf dedi et concessi et hac præsenti charta mea confirmavi pro salute mea et meorum et pro anima fratris mei Rogeri et omnium antecessorum meorum et successorum Deo et ecclesiæ beatæ Mariæ de Cestreton nomine dotis ad ejusdem ecclesiæ dedicationem messuagium cum crofta eidem messuagio pertinente quod Radulphus molendinarius tenuit et totum pratum meum dominicum in Blakemore. Præterea concessi et confirmavi donum hominum meorum prædictæ ecclesiæ, videlicet totum pratum quod habent in communi in prædicto prato de Blakemore quod ad fœdum meum pertinet. Et ut hæc concessio et confirmatio robur firmitatis obtineat in perpetuum præsentis scripti munimine et sigilli mei appositione roboravi. Hiis testibus, &c. [s]

The same person gave to the said church the additional endowment of three acres of arable land of his demesnes lying between Wadewell and Small-Weye.

Sciant præsentes et futuri quod ego Bardulfus de Cestreton pro salute animæ meæ et pro salute animarum patris et matris meæ et om-

[q] Regist. Osen. p. 101.　　[r] Ibid.　　[s] Ibid. p. 62.

*nium parentum meorum dedi et concessi et præsenti charta confirmavi
Deo et ecclesiæ S. Mariæ de Cestreton tres acras terræ arabilis de dominico meo, quæ simul jacent inter Wadewell et Small-Weye et se extendunt ad orientem et occidentem habendas et tenendas in pace libere
et quiete in liberam puram et perpetuam eleemosinam in perpetuum.
Et ego Bardulfus et hæredes mei dictas tres acras cum pertinentiis
Deo et ecclesiæ prædictæ warantizabimus in perpetuum. In hujus rei
testimonium præsenti scripto sigillum meum apposui. Hiis testibus, &c.*[t]

No church could be legally consecrated without such allotment of
house and glebe generally made by the lord of the manor, who
thereby became patron of the church. Other persons at the time of
dedication often contributed small portions of ground, which is the
reason why in many parishes the glebe is not only distant from the
manor, but lies in remote divided parcels.

An. MCCXXXIX. 23, 24. *Henry III.*

On the eighteenth cal. of February, Isabel wife of Richard earl of
Cornwall died in childbirth at his manor of Berkhamstede, and was
buried in the abbey of Beaulieu [u].

Soon after the dedication of the church of Chesterton, there was
an agreement made between the abbot and convent of Glocester, to
whom the tithes had been given by Robert de Oily, and the abbot
and convent of Oseney, to whom several donations had been made
within the said parish of Chesterton, that the abbot and convent of
Glocester should convey to the abbey of Oseney their right of all the
tithes within the demesnes of Bardulf de Chesterton, *viz.* two parts of
the tithes of the said demesnes in consideration of half a mark of silver to be paid yearly by the church of Oseney on the festival of St.
Michael at Aldeswirth.

*Notum sit præsentibus et futuris quod ita convenit inter H. abbatem
et convent. S. Petri Glowecestr. et G. abbatem et conventum S. Mariæ
de Osenei videlicet quod dicti abbas et conventus Glowcestr. crediderint*

t Regist. Osen. p. 101.   u Dugd. Bar. tom. 1. p. 211.

*ad perpetuam firmam omnes decimationes ad se spectantes in dominico
Bardulfi de Cestreton prædictis abbati et conventui Osenei videlicet
duas partes omnis decimationis dicti domin*ici *pro dimidia marca argenti annuatim ab ecclesia de* Osenci *in festo* S. *Michaelis apud Aldeswirth sibi solvenda. Ut autem ista conventio rata et inconcussa perpetuo permaneat præsentis scripti serie et utriusque monasterii* sigilli
*testimonio una cum sigillis abbatum diviso inter eos chirographo con-
firmata est* [x].

In this fifth year * of Robert Grosthead bishop of Lincoln, Robert
prior of Burcester died, and the convent having obtained leave of
their patron William Longspe, (here called earl of Salisbury, and so
entitled by Mat. Paris, though he never had the legal title,) they
elected Hervey one of their canons into the said vacant honor.

5. *Rob. Grosthead, archid. Oxon. Herveius canonicus de Burnecestr.
petita et obtenta licentia elegendi a com. Sar. a conventu ejusdem domus vacantis per mortem Roberti prioris in priorem electus* [y].

It is indeed true that the title of earl of Salisbury here given to
William Longspe is a complimental error, that honor being not
ascribed to him in any authentic record; and the reason (which has
escaped Mr. Dugdale) must be this. His father William earl of Salisbury, in the latter end of his life, went out of the realm without
the king's leave; for which offence his castle, town, and earldom
of Salisbury were seized and retained in the crown, as appeared by
an inquisition taken in the 15. Ed. III. [r]

---

* Anno 5. Rob. Grosthead ep'i Linc. Frater Herveus canonicus de Bernecestr obtenta licentia eligendi a com. Sarum. a conventu ejusd. domus vacantis per mort. fris
Rob. quondam prioris ibidem in priorem
electus admissus est.

5. Rob. Grosthead.
Nich. de Runnes subdiac. ad eccl. de Ferigeford ad pres. Will'i Busam laici.
Mag'r Reginaldus de Welleford subd. ad
eccl. de Godinton ad pres. abbatisse et
conv. de Elnestowe per resign. Will'i de
Husseburn.

[x] Regist. Osen. p. 102.   [y] R. Dods. MS. vol. 107. p. 78.   [r] Ashmole MS. Notat. XI.
p. 71.

Almaric de S. Amand of Grendon in com. Buck. was in such high esteem at court, that upon the christening of prince Edward by Otto the pope's legate, he then stood one of his godfathers at the font[a].

An. MCCXL. 24, 25. Henry III.

In this year, the day after St. Martin's, Richard earl of Cornwall, lord of the manor of Ambrosden, took an oath at Northampton with many other barons for an expedition to the Holy Land[b]; and com mending himself to the prayers of all the religious in England, he took ship and arrived safe at Acon, where within two days he made public proclamation that no one of what nation soever should return home for want of money: which when the Saracens heard, they were so much afraid of the prudence and power of this earl, that this ter ror soon brought peace to the Christian world[c].

The prior of Burcester by right of patronage presented to the church of Little-Missenden in the county of Bucks[d]

Nigh this time Bardulf de Chesterton, knight, gave to the church of Oseney the tenement and park which his grandmother Margery held in dowry within the parish of Chesterton, and another tenement with appertenances in the said village, which William le Noreys held in villanage: as also two virgates of arable land in the fields of Ches terton held by William le Noreys and Richard Boc, containing four score and ten acres, in this form of donation.

Sciant præsentes et futuri quod ego Bardulfus filius et hæres Ro geri filii Bardulfi de Cestreton in Hennemers dedi et concessi et hac præsenti charta mea confirmavi Deo et ecclesiæ S. Mariæ de Osenei et Willielmo abbati et canonicis ibidem Deo servientibus illud tenementum cum vivario et aliis pertin. quod Margeria avia mea tenuit in dotem in dicta Cestreton et aliud tenementum cum pertin. in eadem villa quod Willielmus le Noreys aliquando tenuit in villenagio. Item dedi et concessi duas virgatas terræ arabilis in campis de dicta Cestreton quas

---

[a] Dugd. Bar. tom. 2. p. 19. b.   [b] Mat. Par. edit. Wats, p. 516.   [c] Mat. West. sub an.
[d] R. Dods. MS. vol. 107. p. 72.

quidem duas virgatas terræ Willielmus le Norcys et Richardus Boc aliquando tenuerunt et continent quatuor viginti et decem acras de terra arabili[c].

Soon after the said Sir Bardulf de Chesterton died, leaving son and heir Ralph de Chesterton knight.

About the same time Miles Balistar of Brill granted to Richard Toluse, for sixteen shillings received in hand, one acre of arable land in the field of Brill lying in Berecumbe, between the demesne land of the king, and an acre of Richard Burgoyn called Wodacre, and reaching to Thamwelle, for the service of one penny rent yearly at Michaelmas.

Sciant præsentes et futuri quod ego Milo Balistarius de Brehull dedi et concessi et hac præsenti charta mea confirmavi Richardo Toluse pro homagio et servitio suo et pro sexdecem solidis quos mihi dedit præ manibus in gersuma unam acram terræ meæ arabilis in campo de Brehull jacentem in Berecumbe intra dominicam terram domini regis et acram Richardi Burgoyn quæ vocatur le Wodacre et extendit in Thamwelle, habendam et tenendam de me et hæredibus meis vel assignatis sibi et heredibus suis, &c. reddendo inde annuatim mihi et hæredibus meis vel meis assignatis unum denarium ad festum S. Michaelis, &c. Salvo servitio domini regis forinseco ad tantam terram pertinente de eodem feodo in eadem villa, &c. Huic præsenti chartæ sigillum meum apposui. Hiis testibus ; Johanne filio Nigelli, Johanne Morel, Willielmi de Brehull, Nigello de Bosco, Huberto venatore, Radulfo filio Willielmi, Bartho. venatore, Richardo Burgoyn, Richardo de Thornberg, Willielmo de Angulo, Richardo de Brehull clerico, et aliis[f].

To the original parchment a seal appends with the impress of a cross-bow, a device agreable to his name with this inscription, ✠ S. Milis Balistar.

Hugh de Plessets, a Norman by birth and a domestic servant in the king's court, who took to wife Christian the daughter and heir of

---

c Regist. Osen. MS. p. 101.   f Ex Orig. penes hon. D. Guil. Glynne, Bar.

Hugh de Sanford by Joan his wife, was now sheriff of the county of Oxford, and nigh this time had a grant from Robert abbot of Missenden and that convent of all their land in Musewell in the manor of Pidington within the parish of Ambrosden, for the yearly rent of two marks, and twenty marks in hand, by this deed of conveyance.

Omnibus Christi fidelibus præsens scriptum visuris vel audituris Robertus abbas de Missenden et ejusdem loci conventus salutem in Domino. Noverit universitas vestra nos dedisse et concessisse et hac præsenti charta nostra confirmasse domino Johanni de Plesseto et hæredibus suis pro homagio et servitio suo totam terram de Musewell cum omnibus pertin. suis habendam et tenendam de nobis et successoribus nostris sibi et hæredibus suis libere et quiete reddendo inde annuatim nobis et successoribus nostris ipse et hæredes sui duas marcas argenti ad duos terminos scilicet ad festum sancti Michaelis unam marcam et ad festum S. Mariæ in Martio unam marcam pro omni consuetudine servitio et exactione sæculari sicut nos unquam prædictam terram liberius et plenius tenuimus et possedimus; salvis ecclesiæ nostræ de Missenden prædictæ terræ decimis ad capellam de Musewell spectantibus, et siqua sunt alia ad dictam capellam spectantia quæ laico retinere non licet. Prædictus etiam Johannes et hæredes sui prædictum redditum ad prædictos terminos per aliquem de suis apud Messenden facient deportari et nobis ibidem persolvi. Pro hac autem donatione et confirmatione prædictus Johannes dedit nobis viginti marcas in guersumam. Et nos et successores nostri prædictam terram cum pertinentiis suis sicut prædictum est prædicto Johanni et hæredibus suis contra omnes gentes warantizabimus acquietabimus et defen-

6 Rob. Grosthead.

Mag'r Joh. de Westona subd. ad eccl. de Cherlton ad pres. prioris de War. Mandat. J. archid'o Oxon.

Rog. capellan. ad eccl. de Ardulfel ad pres. Guidonis fil. Rob'ti, mil.

Valentin. de Cestretou subdiac. ad eccl.

de Parva Missenden ad pres. prioris et conv. de Berencestr.

Warinus de Dyve subd. ad eccl. de Lutingarshal ad pres. prioris Hosp. Jerus. in Angl. testibus d'no J. archid'o Oxon. J. de Dyharn canon. Linc. mag'ris G. de Weseham, &c. dat. 17. kal. Nov. pont. 7.

demus sicut ejusdem terræ feoffatores, &c. Ut autem hæc nostra donatio et confirmatio firma sit et stabilis imperpetuum præsens scriptum sigilli nostri appositione roboravimus. Hiis testibus; domino Willielmo de Kantilupo, domino Bertramo de Croil, domino Amaurico de S. Amando, domino Druy de Barentun, Rogero de Missenden, Willielmo de Blakewell, Rogero de Wynterwell, Willielmo de Harewod præposito de Noers, et aliis [s]*

An. MCCXLI.   25, 26. *Henry III.*

William Longspe, lord of the manors of Burcester and Midlington, granted to his brother Stephen Longspe the whole manor of Sutton nigh Banbury, with the hundred pertaining to the said manor, reserving to himself and heirs a certain meadow in Sideham, which his tenants of Midlington used to mow: but so as the said Stephen and his lawful heirs should be obliged to maintain the said meadow, and find all necessary provisions of meat and drink for the said tenants of Midlington on the day wherein they mowed the said meadow, &c.

Sciant præsentes et futuri quod ego Willielmus Lungespe dedi et concessi et hac præsenti charta mea confirmavi Stephano Lungespe fratri meo pro homagio et servitio suo totum manerium meum de Sutton juxta Bannebir' cum hundredo ad dictum manerium pertinente et omnibus pertinentiis suis retento mihi et hæredibus meis quodam prato in Sideham quod homines mei de Medelinton solebant falcare. Ita tamen quod dictus Stephanus et ejus hæredes de uxore sibi legitime desponsata procreati dictum pratum salvo custodire tenentur et 25. hominibus de Medelinton necessaria sicut suis homini-

Ipsis quoque dichus orta est gravis discordia inter dominum regem et episcopum Lincolniensem eo quod quidam regis clericus, prudens et fidelis, Johannes nomine, cognomento Mansel in possessionem ecclesiæ de Thame regis favore et auxilio missus est ratione provisionis a domino papa impetratæ, &c. M. Par. p. 570.

---

s Ex Chartular. de Borstall MS. sub tit. Musewell f. 31.

*bus propriis die quo falcatur pratum illud in cibo et potu inve-
nire tenentur, &c.* [h]

This year in a tournament held at Ware, Gilbert Mareschal earl
of Pembroke falling from his saddle and hanging by the stirrup was
so dragged and bruised, that he died the same evening on the fifth
of the cal. of July; before his death, for the health of his own soul
and of Margaret his wife, he had given to the neighbour canons of
Nutley all the tithes of his fishing belonging to the manor of Caversham, with all the tithes of his mills at Caversham, as also all his
lands called Chibenhurst, and a rent of xvi*. yearly for the maintenance of two lamps burning night and day in the chapel of our
lady at Caversham, for the health of his soul and the soul of earl Richard his brother [i].

There was now a final agreement made between William Paynant
plaintiff and the abbot of Oseney defendant in the king's court at
Oxford, concerning sixteen acres of land with their appertenances in
Weston : whereby the said abbot granted to William Paynant common pasturage for his cattle in several places within the said parish
of Weston.

*Hæc est finalis concordia facta in curia domini regis apud Oxon. in
die paschatis in tres septimanas anno regni regis Henrici filii regis
Joann. xxv. inter Will. Paynant petentem et Johannem abbatem de
Osenci tenentem de sexdecem acris terræ cum pertinentiis in Weston
scilicet quod prædictus abbas concessit prædicto Willielmo communem
pasturam ad averia sua in omnibus locis subscriptis scilicet in Forlowe-
denemede et in Uuerforlond et in Nether-forlond et in Brades-forlond
et in minori Long-forlond sicut cultura de Long-forlond jacet juxta
Forlowe inter villam de Weston et Forlowe et in Cornhulle et in
Rhughulle et in Ballethorn, &c.* [k]

The king constituted Sir Ralph de Chesterton and other knights
commissioners to inspect all the castles within this county, and to

[h] Extract from Sir Christ. Hatton's Book of Seals. MS. R. Dods. vol. 90. p. 121. [i] Dugd.
Bar. tom. 1. p. 60. [k] Regist. Osen. MS. p. 319.

take care for the necessary repair of them by this precept to the sheriff, the like orders being sent through all other counties.

Rex vic. Oxon. salutem. Præcipimus tibi quod per Bardulphum de Cestreton, Symonem de Lekenore, Johannem de Elsefeld, et Gilbertum de la Bryde, videri facias omnes defectus singulorum castrorum et pro quanto poterunt illi defectus emendari quanta poteris festinatione distincte et aperte per literas sigillo suo et sigillis prædictorum militum signatas nos certificare non omittas, &c. Teste rege apud Merleberge xxv. *die Jan.*[l]

Alanore countess dowager of **Dreux**, whose late husband had forfeited the barony of St. Walery in this county, (held in right of his said wife daughter and heir of Thomas de S. Walery,) gave to the abbey of Lieu-Dieu in Normandy some rents at St. Albins near Deep, by charter dated in this year 1241.[m] The king was at Woodstock, and, on February the twenty-eighth, there confirmed the several donations made to the priory of Alencester, com. Warwic[n].

At the beginning of the year Richard earl of Cornwall, lord of Ambrosden, &c. took again the crusado for the Holy Land[o]. At a parliament this spring at Reading he took his solemn leave of the nobles, who greatly importuned his stay, and thus expostulated with him. *Cur nos comes spes post regem unica deseris? aut cui nos desolatos relinquis? Invadent nos in absentia tua alienigenæ rapaces, &c.*[p]

At Whitsuntide he took ship from Dover, attended by William Longspe lord of Burcester and Midlington. Before his voyage he presented a clerk to the church of Ambrosden[q].

Within this year died Almaric de St. Amand of Grendon in com. Buck. having just before his death presented a clerk to the church of Grendon[r]: leaving Ralph his son and heir, who at this time paid twenty-five pounds for the moiety of the lands of Joan de Beauchamp, one of the coheirs to the barony of Cainho[s].

---

[l] R. Dods. MS. vol. 109. f. 77.   [m] Neustria Pia, p. 893.   [n] Mon. Aug. tom. 1. p. 173. b.   [o] Histor. Ang. Script. tom. 2. p. 44.   [p] Mat. Par. edit. Wats, p. 536.
[q] R. Dods. MS. vol. 107. p. 79.   [r] Regist. Linc.   [s] Dugd. Bar. tom 2. p. 20. a.

Nigh this time Sir John Fitz-Nigel lord of Borstal and forester of Bernwood died, leaving issue by Isolda his wife John Fitz-Nigel jun. who succeeded to the honor, estate, and office of his father [t].

An. MCCXLII. 26, 27. Henry III.

Richard earl of Cornwall, being safely arrived at the Holy Land, accepted of a truce with the souldan of Babylon, on condition all the French prisoners should be released, the city of Jerusalem and adjoining parts should be free from molestation, with other ho nourable articles [u].

On the Saturday *post gulam Augusti,* after August the first, the feast of St. Peter *ad vincula,* an inquisition was taken of the manor of Brehull.

Extenta manerii domini regis de Brehull facta die sabbati post gulam Augusti regni regis Henrici filii regis Johannis XXVI. *inter alia sic continetur. Jurati dicunt, &c. Præterea dominus rex habet unum boscum qui vocatur Ixhull et est pastura inter separalia quæ possit sustinere* XXIV. *animalia sicuti boves vaccas et equas pro pastura cujuslibet animalis* IV[d]. *Item in communi pastura domini regis ad placitum suum fiat sicuti equi boves vaccæ porci capræ et oves sustinere qual. boscum Luxhull, le Vitwood, Hildesdene et pastura de Lechemede, de Paunshale, Luewyveslade et boscum de Malcumbe et Arnegrove appendunt dicto manerio de Brehull ad itinerationem Roberti Passelewe Richardi de Wrotham et sociorum suorum et valet in pannagio et aliis per an.* L[s]. *Item Johannes filius Nigelli tenet le de Hyde libere pro* X[s]. *et ballivam pro* XL[s]. *Item dicunt quod quadraginta octo tenentes*

---

8. Rob. Grosthead.
Jordanus cl'icus prioris de Ware subdiac. ad eccl. de Cherleton ad pres. N. prioris de War salvis Rogero fil. d'ni Rogeri com. Winton cl'ico x. mare. annuis quamdiu in habitu clericali honeste se gesserit et uxo-

rem non duxerit nec habitum religiosum susceperit, nec aliud beneficium ecclesiasticum adeptus fuerit.
Mag'r Reginaldus de Welleford ad eccl. de Godindon ad pres. abb'is et conv. de Alnestow. Non. Aug. pont. 8.

[t] Regist. Borstall. MS. penes D. Joh. Aubrey Bar. [u] Mat. West. sub an.

tenent octodecem virgatas terræ integræ et triginta duas virgatas terræ et debet quælibet virgata terræ redditum per an. v'. *Præterea quinque dies de consuetudine videlicet per unum diem fœnum levare et per tres in autumpno metere, &c. Dominus de Ludgershale tenet unam portionem terræ in capite de domino rege infra curiam suam unde reddit curiæ de Brehull* xxx^d. *per an. et faciet sectam curiæ et homines sui reddent pannagium dicto manerio cum agistamentum acciderit, &c.* [x]

About this time William Longspe, lord of Burcester, granted and confirmed to Valentine Clerk all that he had in lands, rents, and mills of the tenure of Richard de Berton at Loffreford in the manor of Standeford, which the said Richard had granted to him, to be held by the said Valentine for the yearly rent of one pair of guilt spurs or sixpence at Whitsuntide, &c.

Sciant præsentes et futuri quod ego Willielmus Lonspe dedi concessi et præsenti charta mea confirmavi Valentino Clerico pro homagio et servitio suo quicquid habui vel habere potui in terris redditibus et molendinis quæ sunt de tenura Richardi de Berton apud Loffreford in manerio de Standford quæ idem Richardus mihi concessit et per chartam suam remisit cum omnibus pertinentiis suis valoribus et aysiamentis habenda et tenenda dicto Valentino et hæredibus suis vel assignatis suis de me et hæredibus meis libere quiete hæreditarie et in perpetuum reddendo inde annuatim unum par calcariorum deauratorum vel sex denarios ad Pentecosten pro omnibus servitiis consuetudinibus sectis omnium curiarum et demandis ad me vel ad hæredes meos pertinentibus salvo forinseco servitio dominorum. Hanc autem donationem concessionem et chartæ meæ confirmationem tenemur ego et hæredes mei prædicto Valentino et hæredibus vel assignatis suis warantizare defendere et acquietare versus omnes gentes in perpetuum per prædictum servitium. Et ut hæc mea donatio concessio et chartæ meæ confirmatio ratæ et stabiles in posterum perseverent præsentem chartam sigilli mei munimine roboravi. Hiis testibus; dominis Bra-

---

[x] Chartul. de Borstall. MS. sub tit. Brehull. f. 11.'

denstoke et Bernecestre prioribus, dominis Stephano et Richardo de Longspe fratribus meis, Henrico et Mathia de Mara, Radulfo de Aungeis, Alano Pagano, Thoma Makerel, et aliis[y].

Of these brothers of William Longspe, Stephen, when he had been seneschal of Gascoigne and justice of Ireland, came at last to the title of earl of Ulster, and Richard was a canon in the church of Salisbury.

Soon after the said William Longspe granted and confirmed to Valentine son of William one half virgate of land in Holeme, called Smitheslond, and arable land called Beckeruge-wrothehegg, and a little meadow called Auker-plot, to hold for the yearly rent of one penny.

Sciant præsentes et futuri quod ego Willielmus Longspeie dedi concessi et præsenti charta mea confirmavi Valentino filio Willielmi pro homagio et servitio suo unam dimidiam virgatam terræ in Holeme quæ vocatur Smitheslond cum omnibus pertinentiis suis.... ..cum terra arabili quæ vocatur Beckeruge-wrothehegg cum omnibus pertinentiis suis cum libero introitu et exitu ad dictum pratellum quacunque hora voluerint, habendam et tenendam Valentino et hæredibus suis de me et hæredibus meis libere quiete integre et hæreditarie in perpetuum. Reddendo inde annuatim ipse et hæredes sui mihi et hæredibus meis unum denarium die S. Michaelis et fraternitati hospitalis Jerusalem pro me et uxore mea et hæredibus meis quinque denarios pro omnibus servitiis consuetudinibus sectis et demandis ad me vel ad hæredes meos pertinentibus salvo forinseco servitio quantum pertinet ad dimidiam virgatam terræ in eodem manerio. Et ego Willielmus et hæredes mei dicto Valentino et hæredibus suis dictam terram. . et pratellum cum omnibus suis pertinentiis contra omnes gentes in perpetuum warantizabimus. Ut autem hæc mea donatio concessio confirmatio et warantizatio firma et stabilis perseveret in posterum præsentem chartam sigilli mei munimine roboravi. Hiis testibus; dominis Steph. Longspe, Gaufrido de Lucy, Roberto Dover, Ricardo Longspe, Rogero de Layburn,

---

[y] Ex Orig. confirmat. W. Longspe tertii apud D. Guil. Glynne.

Henrico et Mathia de Mara militibus, Radulfo de Aungeis, Thoma Makerel clerico, Alano Pagano, et aliis[z].

After this William Longspe and Idonea his wife granted and con firmed to the said Valentine son of William Clerk all the land which Jeffery son of Roger Steward of Holeme held in the said Holeme, and all the land which Ernald Pilly held in the said village, with pannage or free running in time of mast for twenty hogs in their woods of Holeme, and in their wood of Esserugge, paying yearly one besantine or two shillings in money. Hiis *testibus ; dominis Everardo le Tyeis, Henrico de Mara, Ricardo de Longspe, Rogero de Leyburn, militibus. Michaele de Sancto Albano, Waltero Mauncel, Thom. de Wandover, Tho. Mauncel, Thom. Makerel, et aliis*[a].

There was a fourth grant of the said William Longspe to the said Valentine, under the year 1248.

This year June the twenty-sixth died Thomas earl of Warwick, and left surviving his widow Ela sister of William Longspe, who had the manors of Hokenorton and Bradam in this county assigned for her dowry, and was after married to Philip Basset. This noble lady was *so great a friend to the University of Oxford, that she caused a common chest to be made, and did put into it two hundred and twenty marks : out of which such as were poor scholars might upon security at any time borrow something gratis for supply of their wants ; in consideration whereof the University were obliged to celebrate certain masses every year in St. Mary's church. Which chest was in being in king Edward the Fourth's time, and called by the name of Warwick chest.* She died very aged an. 1300, 28th of Edw. 1. and (says Leland) being a woman of very great riches and nobility with buried at the hedde of the tumbe of henry Dilly in Oseney church under a very fair flat marble in the habit of a Nones graven yn a coper plate[b].

An. MCCXLIII. 27, 28. *Henry III.*

In this year Richard earl of Cornwall returned from his expedition

---

z Ex orig. confirmat.   a Ibid.   b Jo. Lel. Itin. 4to. MS. vol. 2. p. 10.

to the Holy Land full of glory, and was honourably met at Dover by the king and queen[c]: and on St. Clement's day was married with great solemnity at Westminster to Senchia daughter of Beatrix countess of Provence, and sister to two queens of England and France[c]. Wikes reports the wedding to have been kept at Walingford on St. Cecile's day : the Waverly annals make the nuptial feast [d] to have been first held in the king's great hall at Westminster, at which Mat. Paris represents no less than thirty thousand dishes.

About Michaelmas the king required scutage three marks, as Mat. Paris reports, others say twenty shillings, of every knight's fee. At which time Roger de Amory, lord of the manor of Bucknell, was charged for three knight's fees; but producing a charter of Henry de Oilly releasing to Ralph d'Amory one knight's fee, he was by judgment of the barons acquitted for two fees, and the third to be required of the heirs of Henry de Oily.

Term Mich. 27. Hen. III. Bedef. Buck.

Mem. quod Rogerus de Aumeri protulit cartam Henrici de Oilli in hæc verba. Henricus de Olleio constabularius regis omnibus hominibus suis et amicis Francis et Anglis salutem. Notum sit vobis quod ego Henricus Oilli condono Radulfo de Aumary seruitium unius militis illi et heredibus suis de seruitiis trium militum que mihi debebat et nominatim pro seruitio quod mihi fecit. Quare volo et firmiter præcipio

Anno 9. Rob. Grosthead.

Walterus de Cherlebir capell. ad vicar. eccl'ie de Bernecestr ad pres. prioris et conv. de Bernecestr.

Eod. anno. R. de Burton capellan. ad vicar. eccl. de Bernecestr ad pres. prioris et conv. de Bernecestr.

Rad. Grosset subdiac. prepositus Augustens. ad eccl. de Wytteneya ad pres. regis ratione ep'atus Winton. vacantis. Prior et conv. S. Fridesyde presentant ad vicar.

eccl'ie de Fretewell.

Will. de Bernecestr capellan. ad eccl. de Wivelescote ad pres. d'ni J. de Arsie per resign. Will. de Rading custodis ejusd.

Mich. de Wuburne subd. ad eccl. de Langeton ad pres. abb. et conv. Westm.

Mag'r Joh. de Cheham ad eccl. de Buckehull ad pres. Rog. de Almarico mil.

Will. de Seto Eadmundo ad eccl. de Sulthorn. 2. id. Apr. pont. 9.

---

[c] Math. Par.   [d] Mat. West. sub an.

quatinus Radulphus et heredes sui sint quieti de prædicto seruitio de
me et heredibus meis in perpetuum, et pro hac etiam concessione dedit
mihi centum solidos.   Test. abbate de Osneia et aliis contentis in
charta.   Et ideo consideratum est per barones quod idem Rogerus re-
spondeat tantum scutagium pro duobus feodis militum et quod rex ca-
piat se ad heredes ejusdem Henrici de tertio feodo [e].

John de Plessets, who held Musewell in Pidington in fee from the
abbey of Missenden, by the king's earnest intercession obtained to
wife Margery widow of John Mareschal, sister and heir of Thomas
earl of Warwick, by which means in 31. of Henry III. he had the
title of earl of Warwick, and came now to the possession of Hokenorton and Kidlington held from the king by barony [f].

Before the end of this year the king passing over to France was
attended by Richard earl of Cornwall and William Longspe, who
were both engaged in the famous battle of Xantoigne, where a glorious victory fell to the English [g].

An. MCCXLIV.   28, 29. Henry III.

Thomas Basset brother of Gilbert Basset, and successor to him in
the barony of Hedingdon, had committed to his custody, in the 6th
of John, Henry eldest son and heir of Waleran earl of Warwick,
which young earl Henry first married Margery the eldest daughter
and one of the heirs of Henry de Oily baron of Hokenorton, and she
dying, he after took for his second wife Philippa, eldest of the three
daughters and heirs of his guardian Thomas Basset, and departing
this life 13. Henry III. left Philippa his surviving widow, who after
married to Richard Siward, from whom she was divorced, and did
now in her pure widowhood give to the church of St. Mary's and
St. Edburg, and the canons of Burcester, all her right in seven shillings yearly rent which Roger of Stodley paid for a tenement he had
in Stodley, on condition the said canons for the health of her soul

---

[e] R. Dods. e Rot. Scac. MS. vol. 29. p. 43.   [f] Dugd. Bar. tom. 1. p. 772.   [g] Mat.
Paris sub an.

and her ancestors' and children's souls, should find one lamp alway
burning before the altar of St. John Baptist in the said conventual
church of Burcester; in which she was after buried.

    *Sciant, &c. quod ego Philippa Basset comitissa Warewick in libera
viduitate et ligea potestate mea dedi, &c. pro salute mea et omnium
antecessorum meorum necnon et puerorum meorum Deo et ecclesiæ
beatæ virginis Mariæ et Sanctæ Edburgæ virginis de Berencestre et
canonicis ibidem Deo servientibus totum jus, &c. in* VII. *solidis annui
redditus quem Rogerus de Stodleya mihi annuatim reddere solebat de
tenemento quod de me tenuit in Stodleya cum omnibus pertinentiis suis
habend. &c. dictis canonicis et eorum successoribus in perpetuum libere, &c. Ita tamen quod dicti canonici pro salute animæ meæ et omnium antecessorum meorum et puerorum meorum unam lampadem
semper ardentem coram altari beati Joh. Baptistæ in ecclesia conven-
tuali de Berencester in perpetuum inveniant, &c. Hiis testibus; domino Philippo Basset, domino Hugone Dispensatore, domino Jac. de
Aldithle, domino Willielmo de Bingham, domino Ric. de Henton, domino Willielmo de Horton, domino Willielmo de Calne, Gilberto de
Ridches, Willielmo Spilsman, &c.* [h]

    It is pity so great a compiler of these matters, Sir William Dug-
dale, should twice miserably confound the circumstance of this story:
not only in his baronage of England, where mistakes are too frequent; but in his antiquities of Warwickshire, the most exact of all
his labours, he gives the same imperfect account. *Philippa countess
of Warwick, in her pure widowhood gave to the canons of Berencester*
(vulgo *Bissiter*) *in com. Buck.* VII[s]. *yearly rent issuing out of certain
lands in Studly within this county,* (com. War.) *to find one lamp, &c.
When she died I do not find; but at Berencester she lyeth buried in the
monastery there of her father's foundation* [i]

    In which relation, it is no less false that Bisseter is in com. Buck.
than that Stodley is in com. War. when it is certainly meant of

---

[h] Guil. Dugd. MS. Transcrip. ex cartis in officio armorum.   [i] Antiq. Warw. p. 306.
et Baronage, vol. 1. p. 72.

Stodley in Horton, nigh adjoining. Nor can the monastery by any title be called of her father's foundation, when it was her uncle only that built and endowed it; nor did her father enjoy the manor or any part of the fee whereon it stood.

Roger de Amory, lord of the manor of Bucknell and patron of the church, presented a clerk to that rectory[k].

The vigilant and exemplary bishop of Lincoln did now again visit this archdeaconry of Oxford, and from Dorchester 13. cal. Octob. 1244, granted a chapel to Roger de Hida within his mansion house in the parish of Whitchurch in this county[l].

At the feast of Ascension this year an agreement by mutual inden ture was made between William prior of Pothele or Poghele in Berk shire and the convent of the said place on the one hand, and Ralph de Chesterton, knight, on the other. That whereas Thomas de Mazcey lord of the manor of Westbatterton had given the said ma nor to the priory of Poghele, by the service of one knight's fee to the capital lord, to be paid at the death of every prior, which manor was now in possession of Sir Ralph de Chesterton, he the said Ralph should confirm the gift, and the priors successively perform the service.

Sciant universi quod anno regni regis Henrici filii R. Joh. xxviii. *ad Ascensionem Domini inter W. priorem de Pothele et ejusdem loci conventum ex una parte et Radulfum de Cestreton ex altera ita con-*

An. 10. Rob. Grosthead.

Rob. de Byrton capellan. ad vicar. eccl. de Berencestr ad pres. prioris et conv. de Berencestr. Testibus mag'ris N. Tessun; W. de Pok; Th. de Aylesbir; Ric. de Pok, capellanis St. de Castell. dat. 4. non. Octob. pont. 10.

Joh. Pockebroc subd. ad eccl. de Blechesdon ad pres. R. de Prestekole.

Mag'r Simon de Stantede subd. ad eccl. de

Langeton ad pres. abb. et conv. de Westm. per resign. Mich. de Wuburne.

Phil. de Eya subd. ad eccl. de Henle ad pres. R. com. Cornuh.

Galfridus de Leominstre capellan. ad vicar. de Fretewell ad pres. prioris et conv. s'ete Frideswide. 4. kal. Octob. pont. 10.

Guido de Dalude subd. ad eccl. de Hamelhamstede ad pres. R. com. Pictav. et Cornub.

[k] R. Dods. MS. vol. 107. p. 78.   [l] Ibid. p. 79.

venit; videlicet quod de cætero quolibet priore de Pothele amoto vel defuncto quilibet successor amoti vel defuncti debet sine contradictione dicto Radulfo et hæredibus suis ut capitalibus dominis de Westbatter ton servitium pertinens ad feodum unius militis pro eadem terra secun dum tenorem chartæ domini Thomæ de Mazcey quam dicti prior et conventus habent de ipsa terra : quam quidem chartam dictus Radulphus pro se et hæredibus suis verbo ad verbum prædictis priori et conventui confirmavit. Nec poterunt dictus Radulphus vel hæredes sui amplius quam ibi exprimitur exigere, nec aliquis prior dicti loci valebit contra hoc venire. In cujus rei testimonium hoc scriptum cyrographatum hinc inde sigillis partium roboratur. Hiis testibus; Sampsone Folioth, Radulfo de Bingedon, Radulfo filio Alani, Ric. de Durneford, Petro de Muribi, Elia Clerico, Willielmo de Hac, Rob. de Pothele, Ric. de Estwode, Adam de Middleton, et aliis [m].*

To the original indenture is the seal of the convent of Poghele, impressed with a monk in religious habit treading on a dragon or fiery serpent; the inscription obliterated.

This donation of Westbatterton to the priory of Poghele in Berks. is recited in the confirmation of Hen. III. *an. reg.* 32. *De dono Thomæ de Mazcey totam terram quam tenuit in Westbaterton sine ullo retenemento* [n].

Soon after this the said Ralph de Chesterton, knight, gave to the priory of Burcester all his right and claim in the said service of one knight's fee in the village of Bettreton, payable at the death of every respective prior of Pothele.

Omnibus Christi fidelibus hoc præsens scriptum visuris vel audituris dominus Radulfus de Cestreton miles salutem in Domino sempiternam. Noverit universitas vestra me pro salute animæ meæ et animarum patris mei et matris meæ et filiorum meorum antecessorum et successorum meorum dedisse concessisse et hac præsenti charta mea confirmasse Deo et ecclesiæ beatæ Mariæ et sanctæ Edburgæ virginis de Burncester et canonicis ibidem Deo servientibus et in perpetuum servituris

---

[m] Ex Orig. penes D. Guil. Glynne, Bar.   [n] Mon. Ang. tom. 2. p. 266.

*in liberam puram et perpetuam eleemosinam totum jus et clamium quod
habui vel quoquo modo habere potui in redditu et servitio unius feodi
militaris in villa de Betreton cum omnibus pertinentiis suis in quibus
prior et domus de Pothelee mihi et hæredibus meis tenebantur, videlicet quotienscunque aliquis prior in dicto prioratu de Pothele mortuus
fuit vel amotus per cartam dictæ domus centum solidi sterlingorum ut
prædictum est mihi et hæredibus meis reddendi sunt, quam scilicet
cartam dicti canonici de Burncestre habent de dono meo habendam et
tenendam de me et hæredibus meis dictis canonicis et eorum successoribus ut prædictum est in liberam puram et perpetuam eleemosinam
salvo mihi et hæredibus meis forinseco servitio inde debito et consueto.
Ut hæc autem mea donatio concessio et chartæ meæ confirmatio rata et
stabilis in perpetuum permaneat præsenti scripto sigillum meum
apposui.   Hiis testibus; dominis Nicholao de Cyfrewast, Nicholao
de Henrede, Richardo de eadem, Richardo Paupere militibus; Elya
de Rokeby, Willielmo de Speholt, Roberto de Eton, et aliis*[o].*

To the original is affixed a seal, with an inscription, that seems to
be the mitre of a bishop, with this inscription, SIGILLUM RADULFI
DE CESTRETON.

The king at Westminster, October the fifth, committed to Richard
earl of Cornwall and baron of St. Walery the manor of Bensington
com. Oxon. with the hundred and all appertenance; sending a mandate to the sheriff to give him seisin of it[p].   At the same time the
king directed this mandate to the barons of the exchequer relating
to the said earl.

*Mandatum est baronibus de scaccario quod inquisitionem faciant si
terra illa in Parva Weledon (in com. Northampt.) de qua per summo-
nitionem scaccarii exigitur a Richardo de Punchardon* xl*s. et quam
Richardus comes Cornubiæ cui rex dedit honorem* S. Walerici *dedit*

An. 11. Rob. Grosthead.   de Heyford Warin ad pres. d'ne Margerie
M.g'r Joh. de Brudiport subd. ad eccl.   de Redveriis com. de Insula.

[o] Ex Orig. penes D. Guil. Glynne, Bar.   [p] R. Dods. MS. vol. 109. f. 12.

eidem Ricardo sit de prædicto honore vel non ; et si Robertus de Braybrock tempore quo idem honor fuit in manu domini Joannis regis eandem terram tenuit ad firmam de concessione ipsius regis de prædicto honore pro XL. *solidis annuis ad scaccarium reddendis. Et si per inquisitionem illam inquirere poterint quod prædicta terra sit de honore prædicto et quod prefatus comes eam dederit prædicto Ricardo postquam rex honorem illum eidem comiti dederat, et quod præfatus Robertus terram illam tenuit de concessione præfati regis de honore prædicto pro prædictis* XL'. *dum idem honor extitit in manu sua et non alia ratione tunc tam ipsum comitem quam ipsum Ricardum ab exactione* XL'. *prædictorum in perpetuum quietos esse faciat. Teste rege*[q].

An. MCCXLV. 29, 30. *Henry III.*

By a council at London three weeks after Candlemas a grant was made the king of twenty shillings on every knight's fee, for the marriage of his eldest daughter; one half to be paid at Easter, the other at Michaelmas. At the collection of which, William Longspe paid 20'. for his one fee in Midlington; Richard earl of Cornwall 10[l]. for ten fees in his barony of St. Walery; the prior of Burcester three marks, &c.[r]

Richard earl of Cornwall sent now one thousand pounds by the knights hospitalers for the relief and assistance of travellers and pil-

An. MCCLV. 29, 30. Hen. III.
Rogerus de Weseham, deeanus ecclesiæ Lincolniensis (rector ecclesiæ de Aillesbiria) electus est et subrogatus in episcopum Cestrensem. Episcopus igitur Lincolniensis ecclesiam de Aillesbiria, quam ex multo tempore desideraverat a decanatu Lincolniensi (eo quod credebat decanum ex ejus ubertate cornua audaciæ assumentem, contra episcopum Lincolniensem recalcitare) radicitus sequestrare et abalienare; statim et in continenti ipsam magistro Roberto de Marisco contulit, non sine magno et multo ecclesiæ suæ præjudicio, ut multis videbatur, et injuria; cum a tempore cujus non extat memoria decanatui Lincolniensi semper dignoscitur adhæsisse. Mat. Paris sub an. 1245. p. 660, 661.

q R. Dods. MS. vol. 109. f. 20.   r R. Dods. Collect. Rot. Pip. vol. 15. p. 235.

grims in the Holy Land [s]: and at Christmas entertained at Walingford the king, the queen, and nobility. At which time he presented to the church of Hamel-Hampsted in the archdeaconry of Huntingdon [t]. And April 22. the same year, the king granted to him the manor of Mere with all appertenances, that he might there found a religious house of what order he pleased [u]. The king now confirmed to Walter de Grey, son of Robert de Grey, nephew of * William archbishop of York, all his lands in Coges given by the said archbishop, and of the gift of Stephen, son of Henry Simeon and Joan daughter of Robert Arsic his wife, all those lands in Somerton, Northbrooke, Frettwell, and Neuton-Purcell, and all the right which he had in the dowry of Margery de Verun, in the manor of Fairingford, (i. e. Fringford,) with the advowson of that church [x].

About this time William Longspe, by right earl of Salisbury, though he had never possession of that earldom, lord of the manors of Burcester and Midlington, gave to the priory of Burcester a certain pasture land called Heescroft, lying on the west side of the highway leading to Wrechwich as far as the bridge, with the whole meadow ground adjoining, to enclose and convert at their pleasure ; as also his whole right and title in a mill which Robert Puff held of him, saving to himself and heirs the free grinding of corn for their own family ; as also a messuage in Crocwell, for which the said canons used to pay yearly fifteen pence : in consideration of all which the canons did remit to him and his heirs sixty shillings yearly rent, which they had in the mill of Wivesly.

Sciant *præsentes et futuri quod ego Willielmus Lungspe dedi et concessi et præsenti charta mea confirmavi Deo et ecclesiæ beatæ Mariæ et sanctæ Edburgæ virginis de Berencester et canonicis ibidem Deo servientibus totam culturam terræ meæ quæ vocatur Heescroft quæ ja-*

* Walter.

[s] Mat. Par. sub an.　[t] R. Dods. MS. vol. 107. f. 81.　[u] Ib. vol. 80. f. 131.　[x] Ibid.

cet ex occidentali parte regalis viæ qua itur versus Wrechwich usque ad pontem cum toto prato meo dominico intra dictam culturam et aquam adjacentem ad claudendam et faciendam quicquid inde dictis canonicis placuerit. Præterea dedi et concessi dictis canonicis quicquid habui vel habere potui in molendino quod Robertus Puff de me tenuit cum omnibus pertinentiis suis et sectis et cum omnibus libertatibus ad dictum molendinum pertinentibus salva mihi et hæredibus meis molitura libera familiæ nostræ quieta in dicto molendino sicut ego et antecessores mei solebamus in tempore dicti Roberti et antecessorum suorum. Præterea concessi eisdem quoddam messuagium de Crocwell unde dicti canonici solebant reddere annuatim mihi quindecem denarios. Hæc omnia concessi dictis canonicis habend. et tenend. in perpetuum de me et hæredibus meis in liberam et perpetuam eleemosinam et omnimodo quietam. Et ego dictus Willielmus Lungespe et hæredes mei dictam culturam et omnia alia prænominata dictis canonicis versus omnes gentes debemus warantizare. Pro hac autem donatione et concessione et chartæ meæ confirmatione et warantizatione prædicti canonici concesserunt et quietum clamaverunt mihi et hæredibus meis sexaginta solidatos redditus quos habebant in molendino de Wivelslya ex donatione magistri Galfr. Geboyn et concessione mea. Et ut hæc mea donatio et concessio et chartæ meæ confirmatio et warantizatio rata et stabilis in posterum permaneat, præsenti scripto sigillum meum apposui. Hiis testibus; domino Nicholao Malens, domino Ricardo Lungespe, Henrico de la Mare, Johanne de Muel militibus; Stephano Lungespe, Rogero de London seneschallo, Rad. de Funceis, Willielmo Fuckeram, Alano Pagano, Thoma persona de Holem. Rogero de Derreford, Ricardo de Sutton, Willielmo de Prestewod, Walhameth Paupere, Roberto de Firefont, Roberto Clerico, et multis aliis.

To the original parchment a seal appends with the arms of that family, six lions rampant, and this inscription, ✠ SIGILLUM WILLI LUNGESPE⁷

---

⁷ Ex Orig. penes D. Guil. Glynne, Bar.

An. MCCXLVI. 30, 31. *Henry III.*

William de Hampton (now Hampton Poyle) lord of that manor then valued at 8*l.* 14*s. per an.* died this year, and the following inquisition was made by a jury of neighbouring inhabitants.

Inquisitio facta per Walterum Philbert, Willielmum Juvenem de Weston, Petrum de Wendlebury, Galfr. le Brocher, Adam clericum de Blechesdon, Willielmum de Weston, Walterum le Werres, Walterum le Otheslar, Willielmum Juvenem de Hampton, Jo. Gilbert, Rogerum clericum de Wendlebury, et Willielmum Such, quantum terræ Willielmus de Hampton tenuit de domino rege in capite in com. Oxon. et per quod servitium et quantum terra ista valeat per an. et quis propinquior hæres ejus sit. Qui jur. dicunt quod prædictus Willielmus tenuit manerium de Hampton quod val. per an. octo libr. et quatuordecim solid. pro quo manerio una cum manerio de Welewe in com. Sutht. quod nunc tenent monachi de Con. Scti Ed'ri fecit domino regi servitium feodi unius militis. Dicunt etiam quod Stephanus Filing ejus propinquior ejus hæres est [z]

Richard earl of Cornwall and William de Longspe were by the king's writ acquitted from their payment of the aid imposed the last year.

Oxon. Vic. Alanus de Farnham.

Isti sunt quieti per breve.

Willielmus de Lungespee de 1. *feod. Gerardi de Camvill in Midlington.*

12. Rob. Grosthead.

Girardus de Farann˙ subd. ad eccl. de Horspad ad pres. R. com. Cornub. et Pictav.

. . . . . . ad eccl. de Henle ad pres. R. com. Cornub. et Pictav. per resign. Ph. de Eya.

An. MCCXLVI. 30, 31. Hen. III.

Abb. Osency presentat (R. tunc ep'o Linc.) Hugonem capellanum ad eccl'iam de Sunereford vacantem per mortem Alexandri de Sunereford thesaurarii S'eti Pauli London, et personæ eccl'iæ de Sunereford. Dat. die Omnium S'etorum, 1246. Ex cronico Oseneiensi, fol. 198. Bib. Cotton. Vitellius. E. 15.

z R. Dods. Extract. Escheat. MS. vol. 93. p. 1.

Com. Ric. fr. R. de x. *feod. Thom. de* S. *Walerico*[a].

These parts must be now concerned in the scrutiny made by the bishop of Lincoln, who, at the instigation of the predicants and minors, commanded his archdeacons and rural deans to make strict inquisition of the lives and manners of all nobility and commonalty within their precincts ; which was thought such a grievance, that on complaint the king stopped the proceedings[b].

Ralph de St. Amand of Grendon in com. Bucks. died this year, and left Almaric his son and heir under age, whose wardship, with the benefit of his marriage, was obtained by Paylyn Peyvre an active man of that age[c].

An. MCCXLVII. 31, 32. *Henry* III.

William Longspe lord of Burcester and Midlington, &c. having again taken upon him the cross, in order to another pilgrimage to the Holy Land, came to Rome, and spake thus to the pope; *Sir, you see that I am signed with the cross, and am on my journey with the king of France to fight in this pilgrimage. My name is great and of note, viz. William Longspe, but my estate is slender ; for the king of England, my kinsman and liege lord, has deprived me of the title of earl, and of that estate. But this he did judiciously, and not in*

An. 13. Rob. Grosthead.

Phil. de Eya subd. ad eccl. de Ambresdon ad pres. R. com. Cornub.

D'n's Aldemarus frater d'ni regis ad eccl. de Dadinton (ad pres. d'ni Rad'i Hareng ratione terre Alicie uxoris sue viventis et in manu sue existentis) per mort. Ranulfi Briton.

Job'es de Stanton subdiac. ad eccl. de Finemere ad pres. abb'is et conv. S. Augustini Bristol.

Lauren. Espur subd. ad eccl. de Heyford

ad pres. d'ne Margerie de Riperiis vacant. per ingressum magr'i J. de Brideport ult. rectoris.

Joh. de Axebrug subd. ad eccl. de Finemere ad pres. abb'is et conv. S. Augustini Bristol.

Nich. de Anna subd. ad eccl. de Beckelegh ad pres. priorisse de Stodley.

Mag'r Tho. de Hangrave diac. ad vicar. eccl'ie de Cuddesden ad pres. abb'is et conv. de Abbendon.

[a] R. Dods. MS. vol. 14. p. 246.   [b] Brady, Hist. p. 597.   [c] Dugd. Bar. tom. 2. p. 20. a.

displeasure, or by the impulse of his will; therefore I do not blame him for it. Howbeit I am necessitated to have recourse to your holiness *for favour, desiring your assistance in this distress.* We see here *that earl Richard (of Cornwall) who though he is not signed with the cross, yet through the especial grace of your holiness, he hath got very much money from those who are signed.* And therefore I, who am *signed and in want, do intreat the like favour.* The pope taking into consideration the elegancy of his speaking, the efficacy of his reasons, and the comeliness of his person, granted to him in part what he desired. Whereupon he received above a thousand marks from those who had been signed[d]; though he did not begin his expedition till about two years after[e].

In the sheriff's accounts of this year, it appears that the manor of Pidington, the late possession of Godfrey de Craucumb, was now escheated to the king, and Hugh de Garget answered for the revenues of it.

Oxon. Alanus de Farnham Vic.

Hugo Gergot de ...... exitibus manerii de Pidington quod fuit Godefridi de Craucumb[f].

Richard earl of Cornwall presented this year to the churches of Ambrosden, Horspath, and Brightwell[g].

This earl on June the 17th caused the church of Beaulieu, a Cistertian abbey of his father king John's foundation, to be consecrated by William bishop of Winchester, at which ceremony he entertained the king and queen and their children, with many nobles: from which place he carried twenty monks and ten convert brethren to stock his new abbey of Heyles nigh Winchcomb in Glocest.[h] the foundation of which was begun in the preceding year, to accomplish a vow which he had made in danger of shipwreck[i].

An. MCCXLVIII. 32, 33. Henry III.

Audomar the king's brother was presented to the church of Da-

d Dugd. Bar. tom 1. p. 178.　e Mat. Par.　f R. Dods. MS. vol. 15. p. 270　* Ibid. vol. 107. p. 79.　h Annal. Waverl. sub an.　i Mon. Ang. tom. 1. p 928

VOL. I.

dington com. Oxon. by Ralph Harenge, who had the advowson in
right of Alice his wife [k]. Within the same year the prioress of Stodley presented to the church of Beckley [l].

About this time William son of John Flerd de Chesterton in Henemarsh gave to the church of Oseney his whole claim and title to
one messuage with a croft and garden and other appertenances,
which he held from that convent, in a hamlet called Brokend, by
the service of twelve pence *per an.*

Sciant præsentes et futuri quod ego Willielmus filius Johannis Flerd
de Cestreton in Henemers dedi et concessi, &c. ecclesiæ S. Mariæ de
Oseney illud messuagium cum crofto et gardino et aliis pertinentiis
quod de eis et eorum ecclesia tenui in hameleto quod vocatur Brokend
per servitium duodecem denariorum, &c. [m]

In the purparty now assigned to William de Valence and Joan his
wife one of the heirs of Walter Mareschal earl of Pembroke, was the
knight's service which John Morell held of the said earl in Grendon
com. Bucks. and the knight's service which Paulin Peyvre held of
the said earl in Chilton, and the service which Hamo de S. Faith
held in the said village of Chilton [n].

The latter end of this year in March William Longspe, lord of
the manor of Burcester, granted and confirmed to Valentine son of
William Clerk one messuage late in possession of Matthew Dean in
Holemer, and all the land in the late tenure of John de Cross on
the east part of that messuage, and one croft enclosed in the west
part of that messuage, and all the arable land between the said
messuage, and the land late in possession of Jeffery le Sleye and
Colesmannesriding, &c. for the yearly rent of two shillings and sixpence.

Sciant præsentes et futuri quod ego Willielmus Lungespie dedi et

---

14. Rob. Grosthead.   don ad pres. d'ni B. com. Cornub.
Walterus de Stok diac. ad eccl. de Gren-

---

[k] Ex. Regist. Linc.   [l] Ibid.   [m] Ex Regist. Osen.   [n] Rog. Dods. MS. vol. 108.
f. 59.

concessi et præsenti charta mea confirmavi Valentino filio Willielmi Clerici pro homagio et servitio suo quicquid habui vel habere potui vel in posterum habere potero in messuagio cum pertinentiis quod fuit quondam Matthei Decani in Holemer et in tota terra quæ fuit Johannis de Cruce in orientali parte dicti messuagii et in una crofta clausa in occidentali parte dicti messuágii et in tota terra arabili inter dictum messuagium et terram quæ fuit quondam Galfridi le Sleye et Colesmannesriding et in tota terra cum pertinentiis quam Alanus Payen aliquando tenuit in dominico inter præfatum messuagium et croftas prædictas et terram Gilberti Lichfot ex parte boreali præfati messuagii et in tota terra cum pertinentiis quam idem Alanus habuit de terra Sebeth cum duabus peciis ,...... dictæ terræ pertinentibus salvo tamen Alano Payen ad vitam ipsius Alani tantum libertate pannagii porcorum et busche in charta Matthei Decani contenta quæ libertas post decessum præfati Alani dicto Valentino et hæredibus suis sive assignatis solute et quiete sine alicujus clamio remanebit. Præterea dedi et concessi præfato Valentino hæredibus et assignatis suis homagium et totum servitium quod Alanus Payen mihi facere debuit et consuevit de terris et tenementis quæ de me tenuit vel tenere debuit in dicta villa de Holemer. Habendam et tenendam dicto Valentino Clerico et hæredibus suis sive assignatis, &c. reddendo inde annuatim duos solidos et sex denarios scilicet ad annunciationem beatæ Mariæ virginis quindecem denarios et ad festum Sancti Michaelis quindecem denarios, &c. Et ut hæc mea concessio warantia defensio et acquietatio et chartæ meæ confirmatio rata et inconcussa in posterum perseverent, præsentem chartam sigilli mei munimine roboravi. Hiis testibus; dominis Henrico et Matthia de Mara fratribus, Johanne de Barantino, Radulfo de Aungies, Roberto Mauncel militibus; Michaele Mauncel, Tho. Mauncel, Roberto et Henrico de Kingeshide, Thom. de Wardovre et aliis. Datum mense Martii anno gratiæ millesimo ducentesimo quadragesimo octavo et regni regis Henri fil. Regis Johannis tricesimo tertio °.

See the confirmation of this and other precedent grants to

° Ex Orig. confirmat. penes D. Guil. Glynne, Bar.

the said Valentine Clerk by William Longspe 'the third, son of William, under the year 1254. On the death of Walter, abbot of Hide nigh Winchester, Roger de S. Walery succeeded to that honor [p].

An. MCCXLIX. 33, 34. Henry III.

The king reduced to great wants borrowed large sums of his brother Richard earl of Cornwall, and caused new money to be coined in most cities and large towns, out of which he fully repaid his brother, and gave him one half of the profits of coinage, which made him immensely rich [q]. Within which year the said earl presented to the church of Grendon in the archdeaconry of Bucks [r].

The manor of Pidington within the parish of Ambrosden being now in the custody of Hugh Gargate, the tenants of the 'said manor were discharged from a tax of sixteen pounds and half a mark by the king's mandate to the sheriff.

Claus. 33. *Hen.* III. *Rex illas* XVI. *libras et dimidium marcæ ad quas homines qui fuerint Godefridi de Craucumbe in Pydinton, &c. nuper talliati fuerunt assignavit ponendas per visum Hugonis Gargate custodis prædictorum maneriorum in* 'prædictis maneriis instaurandis. *Et mandatum est vice-comiti Oxon. quod homines de prædicto manerio de Pydinton pro prædicto tallagio de cetero non distringat. Teste rege apud Westminstr.* ix. *die Maii* [s].

Nigh this time Philip Basset baron of Wycomb, son of Alan Basset, gave to the church of St. Edburg of Berencestre and the canons, sixteen acres of arable land and one acre of meadow in the fields of Berencestre, with four messuages in the said village for per-

Ann. 15. Rob. Grosthead.   tewell ad pres. R. com. Cornub. mand.
Rob. capellanus ad eccl. de Cestreton ad   R. archid'o Oxon.
pres. d'ni Rad'i de Cestreton mil.   Mag'r Alex. de Capuan ad eccl. de Hors-
Henr. de Eston capellan. ad eccl. de Brit-   path ad pres. R. com. Cornub.

p Annal. Eccles. Winton. apud Whart. Ang. Sac. pars 1. p. 309.   q Chron. Tho. Wilkes sub an.   r R. Dods. MS. vol. 107. f. 73.   s Ibid. vol. 108. f. 78.

petual alms, excepting a certain reserved rent to the lords of the demesne, in this form of donation.

Omnibus Christi fidelibus ad quos præsens scriptum pervenerit Philippus Basset salutem in Domino. Noveritis nos dedisse concessisse et hoc præsenti scripto nostro confirmasse pro salute animæ nostræ et animarum antecessorum nostrorum Deo et beatæ Mariæ et ecclesiæ S. Edburgæ de Berencester et canonicis ibidem Deo servientibus sexdecem acras terræ arabilis et unam acram prati in campis de Berencester una cum quatuor messuagiis in eadem villa cum pertinentiis quæ habuimus in villa de Berencester. Habenda et tenenda sibi et successoribus suis de nobis et hæredibus nostris in puram et perpetuam eleemosinam quietam et solutam ab omni sæculari servitio curiarum sectis et omnibus aliis demandis. Salvo redditu inde debito nomine nostro et hæredum nostrorum per dictos religiosos reddendo. Nos vero et hæredes nostri dictam terram et prædictam acram prati cum prædictis messuagiis contra omnes homines et fæminas warantizabimus acquietabimus et defendemus in perpetuum. In cujus rei testimonium huic scripto sigillum nostrum fecimus apponi. Hiis testibus; dominis Willielmo de Insula, Radulfo de Cestreton, Thoma de Breale militibus; Philippo de Wappeley, Rogero de Codesford, Widone de Turresme, Alano de Turresme, et aliis[1].

To the original in parchment is a seal appending with the arms of this family, undie, white, and blue, and this inscription SIGILLUM PHILIPPI BASSET.

There is another original confirmation of these lands, in the same form and with the same witnesses, this only alteration. *Salvis capitalibus dominis feodorum illorum servitiis quæ de dictis terra prato et messuagiis debentur: quæ servitia dicti viri religiosi et eorum successores pro nobis et hæredibus nostris facere tenentur, prout chartæ originales quas dicti viri religiosi habent de feoffatoribus per traditionem nostram plenius important, &c.*

To this confirming charter a seal appends with the same arms on

---

[1] Ex Orig. penes D. Guil. Glynne, Bar.

a shield with a crescent over it, to shew this is the younger family to
that of Hedendon, or to denote this Philip to be the younger brother
of Fouke, now dean of York, from whom a large estate soon after
devolved to this Philip.

Adomar de Lezignian, brother to king Henry and parson of the
church of Dedington com. Oxon. had the custody of the lands of
Thurstan Despenser, whose widow Lucia had the manor of Ewelm in
this county assigned for her maintenance till her dowry should be
set forth, the marriage of the heir being granted to Paulin Peyvre of
Chilton, com. Bucks [u].

An. MCCL. 34, 35. Henry III.

William Longspe, lord of Burcester and Midlington, in the month
of July with several nobles under his command, went over and joined
with the army of the king of France in an expedition to the Holy
Land, where by many valiant exploits he purchased the French
envy, and his own glory: taking a strong tower near to Alexandria,
and surprising the merchandize and provisions of the enemy [x]

This year Sir Ralph de Chesterton, knight, presented a clerk to
the church of Chesterton [y].

Richard earl of Cornwall did again present to the vacant churches
of Ambrosden and * Brightwell [z]. And in April he took ship for
France with Senchia his countess and Henry his eldest son, passing
through that kingdom with forty knights attending him, with such

---

* Rectores eccl'iæ de Brightwell com.
Oxon.

D'nus Joh. Porter p'b'r pres. per Joh.
Fortescu pro corpore d'ni regis militem ac
gardianum et custodem Joh'is Stoner filii et
hæredis Will. Stoner militis nuper defuncti
ratione minoris ætatis dieti Joh'is ad eccl.
de Bryghtwell Linc. dioc. per mort. mag'ri

Rob. More. 8. Feb. 1496. Reg. Smith, ep'i
Linc.

Mag'r Nich'as Bradbridge, A. M. p'b'r
pres. per Adrianum Fortescu et Annam
uxorem ejus filiam et hæredem Will'i Stoner
mil. defuncti ad eccl'iam de Bawdewyn
Bryghtwell per mort. d'ni Joh'is Porter.
30. Jul. 1502. ib.

[u] Dugd. Bar. tom. 1. p. 389.   [x] Mat. Par. p. 783, &c.   [y] R. Dods. MS. vol. 107.
p. 79.   [z] Ibid.

splendid equipage, that the French admired and envied the glorious
shew. When he came to Lions before Rogation-week the pope received him there with great honor, and dined at the same table with
him[a]. About Michaelmas he returned into England, and at Christmas his countess was delivered of a son at Berkamsted, whom the
archbishop of Canterbury baptized by the name of Edmund, in honour of St. Edmund archbishop[b]. Alice de Craucumb, a sister in
the nunnery of Stodley, was elected prioress of the said house; licence of electing being first asked and obtained from Richard earl of
Cornwall patron[c].

Robert Grosthead bishop of Lincoln, attended by the archdeacon
of Oxford, went over to the pope to answer the appeal of the
Knights Templars and other religious, who would have been exempted from his jurisdiction, and by their money bought so much
of the pope's favour, that the poor bishop came home with disap-
pointment[d]. But how much the religion and good discipline of
these parts were secured by the vigilance of this exemplary diocesan,
appears from the declaration that he himself now made before the
pope and cardinals, wherein he told them, that upon his first consecration he considered himself to be a bishop and pastor of souls, and
therefore thought it necessary, (lest the blood of his flock should in
the last judgment be required at his hands,) with all diligence as the
Scripture advises and commands, to visit the sheep committed to
him. For which reason he began a circuit of visitation in his diocese through each respective archdeaconry, and in each of them

---

Anno 16. Rob. Grosthead.

Mag'r Will. de Mara diac. ad eccl. de
Ottendon ad pres. prioris et conv. de Berencestr; commissa est ei cecl'ia sub titulo commendo donec ep'us revocaverit,
ep'o tunc agente in transmarinis.

Valentinus de Dorsetta subd. ad eccl. de

Middelington ad pres. abb. et conv. de Barling.

Will. de Rowell ad eccl. de Weston ad
pres. d'ni Wydonis fil. Rob'ti militis.

Joh. ——— capellan. ad eccl. de Newe-
ton ad pres. prioris et conv. de Berencestr.
per resign. Steph'i rectoris ejusd.

---

[a] Mat. West. sub an.   [b] Ibid.   [c] Regist. Linc.   [d] Mat. West. sub an.

through the several rural deaneries, causing the clergy of every deanery in order to meet at a certain time and place, who should give notice to the people to appear on the same day with their children to be confirmed, and to hear the word of God, and to confess. In which assemblies of the clergy and people, he himself did often preach to the clergy, and a friar predicant or minor to the laity; after which four of the friars heard confessions and enjoined penance: and when the children were confirmed on that and the following day, then he and his clergy applied themselves to the inquisition, correction, and reformation of abuses, &c. [e]

An. MCCLI. 35, 36. *Henry III.*

In a battle of the Saracens and Christians between Damieta and Kairo, William Longspe behaving himself with the greatest bravery, after he had killed above one hundred of the enemy with his own hand, was there slain, and two years after his body was brought to Acres and buried in the church of St. Cross. The men of miracles report that his noble mother Ela, abbess of Lacock, saw his soul entering the heavens: which story is remembered by M. *Paris,* and thus delivered in the register of Lacock.

Gulielmus Longspe secundus qui viriliter contra hostes Christi *in* Terra Sancta *dimicans ibidem pro nomine Jesu contumeliam patiens vi-*

An. MCCLI. 35, 36. Henry III.
Compositio inter abbatem de Oseney et rectorem de Mixbury qui tunc fuit Johannes cancellar. Ebor. Testibus, Joh'e archid. Cornub. Rog. archid. Exon. Will. cancellar. Well. Acta Parisiis 1251, die Martis proxima ante Pascha. Ex cronico Osneiensi, fol. 91. Bib. Cotton. Vitellius, E. 15.
Carta Tho. de Walerico de toto manerio suo de Mixbury salvo jure suo patronatus

eccl'ie sibi et heredibus remanente. Hec carta confirmatur per Joh'em regem. Chron. Osen. Vitell. E. f. 134.
17. Rob. Grosthead.
Joh. de Gnatteshul capellan. ad vicar. eccl. de Cudesdon ad pres. abbis et conv. de Abbendon.
Rog. de Bocking capellan. ad eccl. de Heyford ad pontem ad pres. Ric'i de Hanred laici.

[e] Whart. Ang. Sac. tom. 2. p. 347.

tam temporalem finiens in Christo sine fine victurus, ut fertur, athleta Dei ad cœli palatium A. D. 1249, *ascendit, cujus animam Domina Ela mater ipsius tunc existens abbatissa de Lacock vidit cœlos pene-trantem in stallo suo et coram cæteris sororibus denunciavit* [f]

This date of 1249, can be applied only to his first expedition ; that his death was in 1250, all historians agree [g].

He left Idonea his widow, and William his son and heir : after his death the king seized all his lands.; but in October this same year re-stored the manors of Burcester and Midlington to the said widow Idonea as her rightful dowry, with what other lands were her proper inheritance from her father Richard de Camvill, and she doing her homage had livery of them.

Idonea quæ fuit uxor Willielmi Lungspe fecit regi quod facere de-buit pro seisina habenda de terris quæ sunt de hæreditate sua propria quas rex cepit in manum suam post mortem prædicti Willielmi. Et mandatum est, &c. T. R. 14. *Octob. &c.* [h]

On the death of Richard de Prestcote an inquisition was made in these parts by Peter de Wendlebury and other jurors, who upon oath reported, that the said Richard held two hides of land in the village of Blechesdon of Richard de Greynvil, *viz.* one hide in serjeantry from the king by the service of carrying one shield of brawn before the king when he hunted in the forest of Whichwood : and one other hide by the service of the fourth part of one knight's fee of the fee of Henry Bagot, the value of each hide forty shillings : and that Walter de Prestcote was the next heir of the said Richard, then twenty-four years of age [i].

When Richard earl of Cornwall had expended ten thousand marks in finishing the monastery of Hales com. Gloc. he had the church solemnly dedicated to St. Mary on the ninth of November [k], in pre-sence of the king and queen, and thirteen bishops, and most of the barons, with above three hundred knights, whom he entertained with

---

[f] Cit. e Mon. Ang. tom. 2. p. 311.   [g] Mat. Par. Mat. West. Tho. Wikes, &c. sub an.
[h] W. Dugd. MS. B. p. 76.   [i] R. Dods. MS. vol. 93. f. 8.   [k] Mon. Ang. tom. 1. p. 210.

incredible state and plenty, letting fall this generous and devout expression, *I wish it had pleased God that all my great expences in my
castle of Walingford had been as wisely and soberly employed*[l]. After
the whole solemnity was over, he gave the monks one thousand
marks to purchase lands or build houses: and the king by charter
settled on them the yearly rent of twenty pounds[m]

Nigh this time Henry de Merch of the town of Mersh in this
neighbourhood, gave the advowson of the church of Stibenton (now
Steventon) in com. Bedf. to the abbey of Thorney, which his son
Eustace de Mersh after confirmed[n]

Aymer de Lezignian by the mother's side brother of the king,
having been lately presented to the church of Dedington com. Oxon.
being not above twenty-three years of age, was by the king's importunity elected bishop of Winchester, and confirmed by the pope[o], and
by him consecrated, an. 1260, with great opposition of the barons,
who represented him to the pope as one that had disturbed the kingdom, and infatuated the king and prince[p].

An. MCCLII. 36, 37. *Henry* III.

By letters patent dated May 31, the king granted to Richard earl
of Cornwall the manors of Okeham com. Rut. and Lechlade com.
Gloc. which had belonged to Isabel de Mortimer, to hold to the
said earl and his heirs begotten on the body of Senchia his wife: and
by another charter granted to him and his heirs by the said lady, a
weekly market on Monday at the said manor of Okeham[q]. John
de Grendon canon of Nutley com. Buck. was elected abbot of the
said house, licence being first asked and obtained from Simon Mont
fort patron[r].

18. Rob. Grosthead.   leslep ad pres. abb'is et conventus Westm.
Walt. de Tudinton subd. ad eccl. de Ys-

---

[l] Mat. Par. sub an.   [m] Annal. Waver. sub an.   [n] W. Dugd. MS. B. p. 76.   [o] Annal. Waverl. sub an.   [p] Whart. Ang. Sacra. pars 1. p. 310.   [q] R. Dods. MS. vol. 80.
p. 169.   [r] Ib. vol. 107. f. 74.

About the fifth of Hen. III. there had been a dispute between William Longspe earl of Salisbury and the abbot of Barlings, upon the right of patronage to the church of Midlinton, which being now again void, the abbot of Barlings presented to it[s]

William Longspe son and heir of William Longspe and Idonea his wife, upon the death of his mother had livery of her estate of Midlington, paying for his relief fifty shillings.

Oxon. Nicholaus de Henred, Vice-Com.

Willielmus Lungespe filius et hæres Idoneæ quæ fuit uxor Willielmi Lungespe l[s]. *pro relevio suo de terris quas prædicta Idonea tenuit de rege in capite*[t].

Upon which he did his homage to the king on October the 19th.

R. cepit homagium Willielmi de Longspe filii et hæredis Idoneæ, quæ fuit uxor Willielmi de Longspe de omnibus terris quas ipsa Idonea tenuit de R. in capite in com. Oxon. et l[s]. *pro relevio, et* l[s]. *pro relevio in com. Buck. T. R. &c. 19. Octob.*[u]

There was after in an. 1256, a new claim of a greater relief to be paid by the said William Longspe, and it was referred to the barons who adjudged that his mother Idonea holding from the king *in capite* two baronies, one of Nichola de Hay in Lincolnshire, the other of Gerard de Camvill in this county, he should answer to the king for the said baronies the sum of two hundred pounds.

Memorand. quod in originali de an. xxxvi. *Hen. III. continetur quod rex cepit homagium Willielmi Longespeye de omnibus terris quæ fuerunt ipsius Idoneæ, &c. prædicta Idonea tenuit de rege in capite duas baronias viz. baroniam quæ fuit Nicholai de la Haye in com. Lincoln. et baroniam quæ fuit Gerardi de Kaunvile in com. Oxon.... et ideo consideratum est per barones quod prædictus Willielmus respondeat domino regi de ducentis libris pro relevio suo de prædictis baroniis: et non de* l[s]. *sicut continetur in prædicto originali*[x].

The adjoining manor of Ludgarshall had been held in dowry by

[s] R. Dods. MS. vol. 107. f. 79. [t] Rot. Pip. Extrac. R. Dods. [u] W. Dugd. Collec.
Rot. Fin. vol. B. 1. MS. p. 311. [x] R. Dods. MS. vol. 29. p. 83.

Sibil de Huntingfield, by whose death or marriage without the king's consent it was escheated to the crown, and Thomas Maunsell the king's escheator for that county did for this year's profits account to the king thirty-five shillings.

Buckingham et Bedford.

Alex. de Hammeden Vic.

Thomas Maunsel escaetor regis in com. Buk.——*de manerio de Lutegaresall quod* Sib*illa de Huntingfeld tenuit in dotem; sicut comp. regi* xxxv[s].[y]

The king this year granted the hermitage of Brill to the canons of * Chetwood[z], to find a chaplain of their own order to serve in the chapel of St. Wereburg at the hermitage of Brill, and another chaplain to serve in the chapel of his court at Brill[a]; by this charter.

Henricus Dei gratia rex Angliæ, &c. omnibus ad quos præsentes literæ pervenerint salutem. Sciatis quod concessimus priori et canonicis de Chetwode pro nobis et hæredibus nostris heremitorium S. Werburgæ de Brehull cum pertinentiis tenendum et habendum eisdem

* *Omnibus &c. Robertus &c. auctoritate pontificali concedimus quod apud Chetwode in fundo d'ni Rad'i de Norwic construatur et edificetur eccl'ia Canonicorum Regularium ordinis beati Augustini. dat.* 17. *cal. Decemb. pont.* 10. *Rot. Rob. Grosthead.* (1246.)

Fr. Tho. de Haneworth canonicus de Thurgarton ad regimen prioratus de Chetwode admissus per d'num Rad'um de Norwic. ib. anno. 10.

Rob. de Walthon capellanus presentatus per d'num Rad'um de Chetwode mil. ad heremitagium et capellam s'etorum martyrum Steph'i et Laurentii per M. archid. Buck. et in ea custos perpetuus canonice institutus; dictum heremitagium fundatum

est per d'num Rob. militem quondam d'num de Chetwode ad celebrand. ibidem divina pro anima et animabus antecess. et success. suorum, qui dictum locum postmodum optinuit dedicari, vulgariter autem locus ille a laicis Hermitag nuncupatur propter solitudinem, non quod heremita aliquis aliquo tempore ibidem solebat conversari. Capellanus vero ibidem deserviens in seculari habitu cum honesta familia sua ibidem vivere debet; habet etiam annuatim xx[ti·] iiii[or·] acras terræ ad seminandum, et duæ marcæ annuæ et oblationes et obventiones quæ proveniunt ibidem die S. Laurentii quæ est . . . . x[s]. ib. anno 12.

[y] R. Dods. MS. vol. 15. p. 304.   [z] W. Dugd. MS. O. p. 219.   [a] Mon. Ang. vol. 2. p. 339.

priori et canonicis et eorum successoribus in perpetuum sicut Ricardus de Brehull capellanus illud tenuit. Ita quidem quod inveniant singu- lis diebus duos capellanos divina celebrantes unum scilicet in eodem heremitorio et alium in capella nostra de Brehull sicut fieri consuevit. In cujus rei testimonium has literas nostras fieri fecimus patentes. Teste meipso apud Brueram IIII^{to} *die Novembris anno regni nos- tri* XXXVI^{to}. [b]

Four years after, the king gave them another charter already pub- lished [c], wherein he recites, that having before granted them one ca- rucate of land within the manor of Brehull to find a chaplain at the hermitage of St. Werburg, and fifty shillings yearly to find another chaplain of their own order at his court of Brill, having complaint made that the prior and canons were much damnified in their said land, by the trespass of deer and other forest beasts; he therefore gives them leave to enclose all the arable ground belonging to the said carucate of land, with the grant of five cart-loads of brushwood to maintain their fences, and one dead oak yearly for firing. *T. rege apud S. Albanum* XXVI. *die Februarii anno regni* XL^{mo}.

One Albert, clerk and notary to the pope, was now sent by his master into England to offer the kingdom of Arabia to Richard earl of Cornwall, who prudently required security from his holiness by the delivery of some castles or other pledges, to which Albert de- murred till he had got a great many benefices in England, and then repassed the Alps, bringing such an answer to the pope as stopped all farther proceedings [d].

An. MCCLIII. 37, 38. *Henry* III.

James de Aldithley, (alias Audley,) baron of Aldithley in Staff. had a grant from the king of free warren in all his demesne lands,

An. MCCLIII. 37, 38. Hen. III. Adam de Eston cl'icus regis pres. per re- gem ad eccl'iam de Yslep. 22. Mar. Pat. 37. H. 3. m. 14. Lit. dirig. ep'o Linc.

[b] Regist. Borstall. sub tit. Brehull. f. 129. [c] Mon. Aug. tom. 2. p. 337. b. [d] Mat. West. sub an.

and among others in Stratton (now Stratton Audley) and Whert-
wyke or Wretchwike.

*Rex &c. Sciatis nos concessisse, &c. dilecto, &c. Jacobo de Aldith-
leg quod ipse et hæredes sui habeant liberam warrenam in omnibus
dominicis terris suis—Strattone et Wrechwyke in com. Oxon. &c. T.
R. 16. Nov.*[e]

The privilege of free warren was this, that within such liberty no
person should hunt or destroy the game of hare, coney, partridge, or
pheasant, without the leave of him to whom the said privilege was
granted, under the forfeiture of ten pounds [f].

The manor of Stratton and half that of Wretchwyke came to the
said James baron of Audley in frank marriage with Ela his wife, a
daughter of William Longspe, which though not observed by Dugdale[g] in the history of these families, does appear from an inquisition
taken 8. Edw. I. after the death of the said baron [h]

The arms of Aldithley, who were a branch of the family of Verdon, was frette distinguished with a canton, and thereon a cross pate ;
but this James lord Aldithley bore only gules a frette or.

The king passing over to Gascoign committed the custody of his
whole kingdom to our Richard earl of Cornwall and Walter de Grey
archbishop of York [i]. Which earl Richard granted to the monks of
Okeburn, a release of suite and service within his honor of Walingford, which charter has a seal appending, being an impress of the said
earl armed on horseback, with a lion rampant crowned on his sur-
coat, inscribed *Sigillum Richardi Comitis Cornubiæ* [k]

Religion and ecclesiastical discipline suffered much in these parts
by the death of the excellent diocesan Robert Grosthead, who departed this life at Buckden, Nov. 8.[l]

An. MCCLIV. 38, 39. *Henry III.*

William Longspe, lord of the manors of Burcester and Midling-

---

[e] W. Dugd. MS. vol. E. 2. p. 80.   [f] Ib. MS. vol. H. p. 233.   [g] Dugd. Bar. tom. 1.
p. 176. and 747.   [h] Rot. Pip.   [i] Chron. Tho. Wikes, sub an.   [k] Mon. Ang. tom. 1.
p. 583.   [l] Whart. Ang. Sac. tom. 2. p. 342.

ton, married Maud the daughter of Walter baron de Clifford and Margaret his wife, and had with her in frank marriage the manor of Culminton in Shropshire, to the grant of which one of the wit nesses is Hervey prior of Burcester. *Hiis testibus; domino Herveo priore de Berncester, dominis Rog. de Clifford, Jacobo de Aldith ley, &c.*[m]

This Maud surviving her said husband was after married to John Giffard of Brimsfield in Glocestershire: who, an. 1283, founded a cell in Oxford (now Glocester Hall) for thirteen monks chose from the convent of Glocester of the Benedictine order, who were to pray for the souls of him and of Maud Longspe formerly his wife[n].

About this time William Longspe confirmed the several grants made by William his father to Valentine Clerk of lands in Holemer, which are mentioned under the years 1242, and 1248.

Omnibus Christi fidelibus ad quos præsens scriptum pervenerit Willielmus Longspei tertius salutem, noveritis me cartas Willielmi Longspei patris mei et Idoneæ matris meæ inspexisse in hæc verba, &c. Has autem donationes concessiones et cartarum confirmationes ratas habemus pro me et hæredibus meis et eas præsentis scripti munimine et sigilli mei impressione roboravi. Hiis testibus; dominis Ricardo Longspei, Hugone de Foresta, Radulfo de Aungics militibus; Willielmo de Bellocampo, Richardo de Wyggesby, Roberto de Harkel, Walkelmo de Rosey, Thoma Gulafr. et aliis[o].

To the original deed of confirmation is a seal appending, with the impress of a gantlet, and this inscription, ✠ SIGILLUM WILLI LUNGESPIE. But the more common seal of William de Longespie was a sword pendant between two Saracens heads.

The pope now granted to the king the tenth of all spirituals for three years, which occasioned a taxation of all ecclesiastical revenues to be made through every diocese in England, by Walter bishop of Norwich delegated by the pope to this office[p]. The present valu-

---

[m] W. Dugd. MS. vol. L. p. 41.   [n] Annal. Wigorn. sub an. 1283, and Mon. Ang.
[o] Ex Orig. penes Hon D. Guil. Glynne.   [p] Annal. Burton, p. 331.

ation of Ambrosden, Burcester, and other adjoining churches, is to be seen under the other taxation made an. 1291.

An. MCCLV. 39, 40. Henry III.

This year there was an aid granted to the king of scutage or forty shillings on every knight's fee, for the making prince Edward a knight; upon which Richard earl of Cornwall paid twenty pounds for his ten fees of the barony of St. Walery, and William de Longspe forty shillings for one fee of Gerard de Camvill in Midlington.

> *Oxon. Vic. Nicholaus de Henred de* i. *dim. an.*
>
> *Johannes de Turbervill de ult. dim. an.*
>
> *Auxilium regi concess. ad primog. fil. suum mil. faciend. sc. de quo-libet feodo* XL'.
>
> *Com. Ric. fr. reg.* xx¹. *de* x. *feod. Tho. de S. Walerico.*
>
> *Willielmus de Lungespe reg. comp.* XL'. *de* 1. *feod. Gerardi de Kan-vil in Midlington* q.

There was this year a design to assart (*i. e.* to grub and enclose) three acres of land in the forest of Bernwood upon a plain called Fernhurst, between Brill and Pidington; of which complaint being made, an inquisition was taken by a jury of twelve legal freemen, who returned their verdict that it would be a great prejudice to the forest, especially in the time of fawning or the fence month, which was fifteen days before Midsummer, and fifteen days after ʳ; and a stoppage

.An. MCCLV. 39, 40. Hen. III˙

Rex dedit priori de Chetwode unam ca-rucatam terræ in Brehul ad inveniendum unum capellanum sui ordinis ad deserviend. cape llæS'ctæ Wereburgæ apud Heremito-rium de Brehul et 50 sol. ann. ad inve-niend. alium capellan. ejusd. ordinis ad de-serviend. capellæ curiæ nostræ de Brehull et dedit licentiam includendi eam. 2G.

Feb. Pat. 40. H. III. m. 15.

Rex ... omnibus ... Sciatis quod si contin-gat Rad'um de Norwico electum in ar'e'pa-tum Dublin confirmari tunc dilectum con-sanguineum nostrum Ernaldum de Bovis-vill ad eccl. de Brehull quam idem'Rad'us tenet de dono n'ro presentabimus. dat. 5. *Maii.* Pat. 40. Hen. III. m. 13.

q Rot. Fin. inter Collect. R. Dods. MS. vol. 15. p. 325.   ʳ Manwood of Forest Laws, cap. 13.

to the highway between the king's manor of Brehull and Pidington, and no less damage to the inhabitants in their rights· and privileges within the said forest, &c.

Hæc est inquisitio facta per duodecim liberos et legales jurat. de foresta Bernewod per præceptum domini regis. Dicunt quod foret dampnum et valde nocumentum foreste si tres acre assarte essent in quadam plana quæ vocatur Fernhurst in foresta de Bernwod in com. Oxon. Ad dampnum verteretur foresta quia ille locus est in uno acriori loco totius foreste quia si essent assartate, bestie amitterent procursus suos ad transversum foreste: item ille locus est magis et maximus excercitus bestiarum tocius foreste.· Preterea gentes et malefactores quererent inde causam et citius ad forestam accederent ad malefaciendum tam tempore fennacionis quam alio tempore. Item alta via et generalis inter Brehull et Pidinton maneria domini regis omnino esset astopata. Item homines illorum maneriorum penitus amitterent clamia sua in dicta foresta quod quidem verteretur ad maximum dampnum. Isti sunt per quos dicta inquisitio facta fuit, Alanus de Tingwike de Acle, &c. [s]

The Jews at Lincoln, Aug. 1. had crucified a boy of nine years of age called Hugh, (made for this a saint and martyr,) for which barbarous impiety the principal actors and some other prisoners were in a council at Reading condemned to a sharp and ignominious death; but with immense sums of money they bribed the favour of Richard earl of Cornwall, whose power did deliver and protect them [t].

An. MCCLVI.   40, 41. Henry III.

Upon the death of William king of the Romans the electors, who resolved to make the best market of their votes, sent away John de Atneis into England with proposals to * Richard earl of Cornwall,

---

* Litera Ric'i in regem Romanorum electi Johanni Messenensi archiepiscopo de rege Bohemiæ in electionem suam consen-   tiente; dat. apud Walingford xi kal. Feb. 1257. Rymer 1. 618.

[s] R. Dods. MS. vol. 93. p. 12.   [t] Burton. Annal. p. 313.

that upon good terms of money, they would elect him to that kingdom.   Upon which motion, the earl sent over his trusty friends Richard earl of Glocester and John Maunsell to compound with the
electors, who agreed with the archbishop of Mentz for eight thousand Colegn marks, with the archbishop of Colegn for twelve thousand Colegn marks; with the duke of Bavaria for eighteen thousand
marks sterling, computing each mark at twelve shillings; and with
some of the other electors for eight thousand Colegn marks.   Upon
which compact he was chosen king of Almagne or the Romans, on St.
Hilary day at Frankfort [u].

Almaric de St. Amand (son of Ralph who died 30. Henry III.)
having been in ward to Paulin Peyvre, and in 37. Henry III. to John
Grey, made now proof of his full age, and obtained the king's precept to the sheriffs of Bucks. Oxon. &c. for livery of his lands, among
which were the manors of Bloxham, com. Oxon. and Grendon, com.
Bucks. where was his capital seat [x].   At the feast of Assumption of
the Virgin Mary the king came to Woodstock, and invited thither
Alexander king of Scots and most of the English nobility, whom he
entertained there with great variety and pomp [y].

William Longspe, lord of the manors of Burcester and Midlington, had lately in Gascoign treated with Edmund Lacy upon a marriage between Henry eldest son of the said Edmund, and Margaret
eldest daughter and heir of the said William : and now on the Friday
before Christmas-day they came to a full agreement, that the said
William Longspe should give Margaret his daughter and heir to
Henry son of Edmund Lacy, and in frank marriage with her the
manors of Burncester and Midlington : and the said Edmund should
grant to Margaret, in case she should outlive her husband, a dowry
of the manors of Skippeys and Scales.

An. gratiæ MCCLVI. *die veneris proxima ante natalem Domini circa
horam diei primam facta est hæc conventio inter dominum Edmundum
de Lacy ex una parte et dominum Willielmum Longespe ex altera.   Et*

---

[u] Chron. Tho. Wikes, sub. an.   [x] Dugd. Bar. tom. 2. p. 20. a.   [y] Mat. West. sub an.

quia prælocutum fuerat in Vasconia, super maritagio Henrici filii et hæredis dicti Edmundi et Margaretæ filiæ et hæredis dicti Willielmi dicto die ex consensu partium completum est: ita videlicet quod dictus Willielmus Longespe dedit et concessit Henrico filio dicti Edmundi Margaretam filiam suam et hæredem et cum ipsa in libero maritagio maneria sua de Burnecestere et Middeltone cum omnibus homagiis redditibus serviciis et consuetudinibus et omnibus aliis pertinentiis sine aliquo retinimento. Et dictus Edmundus dedit et concessit dictæ Margaretæ toto tempore vitæ suæ ad ipsam dotandam, si humanitus de ipso Henrico contigerit, maneria sua de Skyppeys et Scales, cum omnibus homagiis redditibus serviciis consuetudinibus et omnibus aliis pertinentiis. Et ut hoc maritagium cum donationibus concessionibus dictarum terrarum et præsenti conventione ut superius dictum est robur firmitatis obtineant, &c. Hiis testibus; dominis Jacobo de Audele, Galfrido de Bellocampo, Ricardo de Mundevill, Roberto de Andeseker, Willielmo de Bellocampo, Roberto de S. Andrea, Johanne Beke, Hugone de Foresta, militibus; Ricardo Gubiun, Henrico de Braytost, &c. [z]

On December 23, the king at Merton confirmed the said contract with this farther proviso, that if the said Henry should die before the marriage consummate, that then John his younger brother should take to wife the said Margaret.

Rex, &c. cum inter dilectos &c. Edmundum de Lacy et Willielmum Longespe sit conventum super matrimonio contrahendo inter Henricum primogenitum filium et heredem ipsius Edmundi et Margaretam primogenitam filium et heredem dicti Willielmi: ita quidem quod si idem Henricus antequam matrimonium inter ipsum et dictam Margaretam contrahatur in fata concesserit Johannes junior filius dicti Edmundi eidem Margarete matrimonialiter copuletur. Nos conventionem, &c. ratam habentes, &c. T. R. apud Merton 23. Dece. [a]

On the ninth of February following, the said Edmund Lacy paid to the king a fine of ten marks for his royal assent and confirmation of this match.

---

[z] Guil. Dugd. Collect. MS. vol. L. p. 18.   [a] W. Dugd. MS. vol. C. 1. p. 66.

Edmundus de Lacy finem fecit cum rege pro x. *marc. auri pro habenda concessione et confirmatione regis super matrimonio contrahendo
inter Henricum primogenitum filium et hæredem ipsius Edmundi et
Margaretam primogenitam filiam et hæredem Willielmi de Longspe,
&c. ·T. R. 9. Feb.* [b]

The said William Longspe by Maud his wife had one other
younger daughter Catharine, after married to Nicholas de Aldithley
baron, who died in 27. Edw. I. in which year the said Catharine upon
the death of Maud her mother widow of John Giffard of Brimesfield,
was found to be coheir to her, and had for a share of her mother's
inheritance (as daughter and coheir to Walter de Clifford) the castle
of Thlandevry, &c. in Wales [c].

An. MCCLVII. 41, 42. Henry III.

William Longspe died this year, as also Edmund Lacy on Magdalen day, July 21. upon which Henry de Lacy husband of Margaret Longspe succeeded to the estate of both : but being a minor
was in ward to the king; and his wife in custody of the queen.

Richard earl of Cornwall, lord of the manors of Ambrosden, Beckley, &c. having been elected king of the Romans in the preceding
year, the archbishop of Cologne, the bishop of Liege, the bishop of
Utrecht, the earl of Holland, and other nobles, came over to conduct him to his new kingdom : upon which he set sail at Yarmouth
April 29. with forty-eight ships, and May the fifth arrived at Dort
in Holland, thence to Aquisgrane, where on Ascension-day May the
seventeenth, he was solemnly crowned, with Senchia his lady empress, by Conrade archbishop of Cologne [d].   An account of his voyage and coronation is given in a letter from himself to prince Edward, dated from Aquisgrane May 18. [e]

Before his voyage he gave to the priory of Knaresburg, com. Ebor.
the chapel of St. Robert in Knaresburg, and the advowson of the

<hr>

[b] W. Dugd. Collect. Rot. Fin. MS. vol. S. 251.   [c] Dugd. A. 1. p. 177. and Bar. vol. 1.
p. 748.   [d] Chron. Tho. Wikes, sub. an.   [e] Annal. Mon. Burton, p. 376.

church of Hamstwait, &c. *Hiis testibus; dominis Willielmo de Ros, Johanne de Stotevill, Willielmo de Ireby, Willielmo de Turnival, Ricardo de Turri, Johanne filio Thomæ, Rogero de Aumary, militibus. Dominis Philippo le Eya, Willielmo Blundell, Roberto de Kynton, clericis, et aliis. Dat. Londoniis decimo die Aprilis anno gratiæ* MCCLVII[f].

Maud the widow of William Longspe promising on oath not to marry without the king's leave had a dowry assigned to her, upon which Richard Longspe brother to the deceased William, who had the reversion of the manors of Scandeford, Erdintone, and Charltone, entered into recognizance, that if the said Maud should claim a dowry in those manors, he would warrant such a dowry, without charge or trouble to the queen who had the wardship of Margaret daughter and heir of the said William.

Term. S. Hilar. 41. Hen. III. Recognitio Richardi Longespee. Idem Richardus recognovit quod si contingat Matilde que fuit uxor Willielmi Longespeye petere dotem suam in maneriis de Scandeforde, Erdintone et Corletone, idem Ricardus warantizabit ei dictam dotem: ita quod domina regina que est custos heredis predicti Willielmi non teneatur ad warantizandum predictam dotem[g].

John Morell of Adingrave granted in this year to John Fitz-Nigel of Borstall and Isolda his wife, four acres of arable land, and the third part of half an acre in the fields of Acley, as also a meadow in Adingrave called Wolveds-ham, &c. for the yearly rent of one pound of cloves at Easter, and ten marks in hand. *Hiis testibus; domino Thoma de Valeyns, domino Willielmo filio Eliæ, Waltero de Burg, Petro Carbonel, Henrico de Beaufort, Willielmo de Grenevill, Wal-*

---

1. Ric. Gravesend.

Gilbertus de Leyre subd. ad eccl. de Meriton vac. per mort. d'ni R. de Pokeli ad pres. abb. et conv. de Egnesham.

Gerardus de Feys archid'us Leodien. pres.

per d'num Ric'um Romanorum regem ad eccl. de Frothingham in archid. Stow vac. per resign. ven. pres. d'ni Rogeri Cov. et Lich. ep'i. mandat. archid'o Stow. an. 1. Ric. Gravesend.

[f] R. Dods. MS. et Mon. Ang. tom. 2. p. 831.   [g] Ibid. vol. 29. p. 86.

tero le Chevaler de Cherdesle, Thoma de S. Andrea, Willielmo Golie,
Waltero de Horton, Hugone filio Philippi de Wynchendon, Willielmo
de Buktot, Philippo de Herull, Willielmo le Venur, Roberto filio Alani
de Acley, et aliis apud Borstall [h]

James Aldithley, baron and lord of the manors of Stratton and
Wretchwike, having attended Richard earl of Cornwall in his coronation at Aquisgrane, returned about Michaelmas into England with
Henry eldest son of the said Richard, and hearing the Welch in his
absence had made divers incursions upon his lands on their borders,
he marched down, entered their territories, and did great execution
on them, by the help of some Almain horse which he brought over
with him [i]. In this expedition against the Welsh, among the knights
and esquires sent by the abbot of St. Albans, were John de le Mersh
and Richard de Birencester [k].

An. MCCLVIII. 42, 43. *Henry III.*

Our Richard king of the Romans having his treasure this year
computed, was found able to expend a hundred marks a day for ten
years, besides his standing revenues in England and Almaign [l]. While
he was in England he had prudently governed all state affairs; but
the seditious barons took advantage of his absence, and meeting at
Oxford about the feast of St. Barnabas, they bound themselves in
five articles, much to the diminution of the royal dignity: and when
Richard king of the Romans was at St. Omers in his return for England, he was met by some of that party, and forbid to pass on to
England, till he had taken an oath for observance of those Oxford
articles; nor could he proceed till he had taken his oath so to do as
soon as he should arrive in England; which he accordingly performed
at Canterbury, having landed at Dover, January the twenty-eighth,
and entered London with great joy February the first [m]

---

[h] E. Chartular. de Borstall. f. 7.   [i] D. Powell, Hist. of Wales, p. 323.   [k] Ex Chartular. Abbatiæ S. Alban. in R. Dods. MS. vol. 78. f. 102.   [l] Mat. Par. p. 942.   [m] Chron.
Tho. Wikes, sub an.

Within this first year of Richard Gravesend bishop of Lincoln*,
Margaret de Lacy, countess of Lincoln and Pembroke, first the wife of
John Lacy earl of Lincoln, and now widow of Walter Mareschal earl
of Pembroke, presented to the chapel of St. Ann on the bridge at
Caversham, com. Oxon. and to the church of Little-Steping in the
archdeaconry of Lincoln [n]

Maud the only daughter and heir of Reginald earl of Dammartin
(who was lord of the manors of Merton and Pidington) and Ida
countess of Bologne his wife, died this year without issue, having
been first married to Philip of France son to king Philip and Mary de
Meranie, by whom she had one daughter Joan that died without
issue; and secondly to Alphonso afterwards king of Portugal. Upon
her decease the earldom of Dammartin fell not to Matthew the eldest[o], but to Reginald the second son of John lord of Trie and
Moucy, by Alice his wife, daughter of the said Reginald and Ida[p]

The king being informed that his haven of Rumenale (alias Rom-
ney) in Kent, was in danger of being destroyed by stoppage of the
river Newenden, had sent into those parts Nicholas de Handlo, soon
after lord of Borstall. And when no effectual care was taken, the
king, by another precept, dated at Oxford June 21. commanded the
said Nicholas de Handlo again to repair thither in person with the
sheriff of Kent, and twenty-four knights to examine and settle that
matter[q].

* Margareta de Lacy comitissa Lincoln.
et Pembrok. omnibus ballivis et fidelibus suis
salutem. Sciatis quod ratam habeo et gra-
tam concessionem et quietantiam, quam dilectus filius Ricardus de Clara com. Glouc.
et Hertford fiat abbati et monachis Radinge
de xxxii denaratis annui redditus et de secta
curiæ de tenementis quæ idem abbas et monachi habent in Kaversham. Quare volo et

concedo quod prædicti abbas et monachi prædicta tenementa sua habeant et teneant libere et quiete secundum tenorem cartæ quam
modo habent de prædicto comite, et in hujus
rei testimonium has literas nostras dictis abbati et monachis concessimus patentes; dat.
tertia die Martii anno regni regis Henrici
filii regis Johannis xxxi. Cartular. Radinges. MS. f. lxxiii. a.

[n] R. Dods. MS. vol. 107. f. 117.   [o] Du Chesne, l'Histoire de la Maison de Dreux, l. 1.
ch. 4.   [p] Du Fresne, Observations sur l'Histoire de S. Lovys, p. 42.   [q] Dugd. History
of Fens, p. 14.

An. MCCLIX. 43, 44. *Henry III.*

In the late election of a king of the Romans, four of the electors dissented from the choice of earl Richard, and the archbishop of Cologne now declared for the king of Spain, who on this frivolous pretence appealed to Rome, where, while money made the cause depending, Richard king of the Romans sent a letter to pope Alexander for justice against the king of Spain, a copy of which letter with the pope's answer is delivered in the Burton annals [r]

King Richard on the eighteenth of June sailed over to Almaign, and after a progress through his kingdom returned October 24. [s] And nigh this time gave to the monks of Thame one virgate of land and two knight's fees with their appertenances in Stoke-Talmasche [t].

King Henry by charter dated at Westminster, August the fourth, granted to the prior and canons of Chetwood com. Buck. a certain assart or ground newly grubbed, containing about 21. acres, in lieu of fifty shillings yearly paid from the exchequer to enable them to maintain a constant chaplain to officiate in the chapel of the king's court at Brehull [u].

An. MCCLX. 44, 45. *Henry III.*

In a trial this summer before the justices itinerant at Bedford about the manor of Aspele in this county, it appeared that Reginald de S. Walery, once lord of Ambrosden, had sold the said manor to Hubert de Burgh; and that Wido or Guy, father of the said Reginald, had claimed the whole barony of Bedford from Simon de Beauchamp, who compounded with him for that manor, being a part of the said barony.

2. Ric. Gravesend.	3. Ric. Gravesend.
Rogerus capellan. ad vicar. eccl. de Ccs- treton vac. per resign. Everardi ad pres. abb. et conv. Osen.	Walt. subd. ad eccl. de Somerton vac. per mort. d'ni Joh'is de Crakehale ad pres. Walteri de Gray mil.

[r] An. Mon. Burt. p. 425, 427. [s] Chron. Tho. Wikes, sub an. [t] Mon. Ang. tom. I. p. 803. a. [u] Chartular. de Borstall. MS. f. 130.

*Bedf. jurati dicunt quod Reginaldus de S. Walerico vendidit mane-
rium de Aspele Huberto de Burgho. Dicunt etiam quod Wido de S.
Walerico pater dicti Reginaldi implacitavit Simonem de Bellocampo
de tota baronia de Bedford et pro pace habenda dedit dictus Simon
dicto Wydoni et hæredibus suis manerium de Aspele quod fuit de dicta
baronia, &c.* [x]

In Michaelmas term at Buckingham was a trial for certain lands
in Mersh held of Robert Bryan, wherein the jury found that Giles
Lisle held them from William de Beauchamp senior, by knight's service, who came to seize them as part of his wardship, because the
heirs of the said Giles were under age [y].

Upon the death of Frederic the emperor, the pope claimed the
kingdom of Sicily, Apulia, and Calabria, as the patrimony of St.
Peter, and had offered them to earl Richard before his election to
the kingdom of Almaign, upon whose refusal the pope conferred it
upon Edmund the second son of Henry the Third, obliging the king
to pay one hundred fifty thousand five hundred and forty marks of
silver. Which sum the king being unable to discharge, the pope
imposed it as a fine on the English monasteries [z].

Richard king of the Romans (who this year presented to the church
of Frothingham in the archdeaconry of Stowe) having occasion to
visit Rome upon his own and the king's urgent affairs, the king issued
out one writ to impower him to tax all his tenants, and another to
his several tenants to grant him liberal aid and contribution toward
his expences in this expedition: both which writs are preserved in
Prynn's collection [a].

Upon a breach of truce by Lewelin prince of Wales, Henry baron
Aldithley, lord of Stratton and Wretchwike, being one of the lord
marchers of Wales, was commanded to hasten into those parts, with
all the power he could raise, for preventing farther mischief from
those ill neighbours [b]. In which year he was again constituted go-

[x] W. Dugd. MS. vol. A. 1. p. 130.   [y] R. Dods. MS. vol. 42. p. 106.   [z] Chron. Tho.
Wikes, sub an.   [a] W. Prynne, Collect. tom. 2. p. 997.   [b] Dugd. Bar. tom. 1. p. 747.

vernor of the castles of Salop and Bruges : he was also this year appointed one of the justices itinerant for the counties of Oxon. and Berks[c].

An. MCCLXI. 45, 46. *Henry III.*

Roger de Aumorie (alias D'amory) son of Robert de Aumorie claimed the manor of Weston and advowson of the church from the abbey of Oseney, to whom the said manor was given by Henry de Oily baron of Hokenorton. The controversy was referred to our Richard king of the Romans, who at his house in Beckley (the head of his barony of St. Walery, whereof Ambrosden was a member) made this composition between Richard abbot of Oseney and the convent on the one part, and Roger de Amory on the other ; that the said abbot and convent should pay to Roger de Amory three hundred marks sterling, and in consideration thereof the said Roger should quit claim to that whole estate which was computed at two knight's fees.

Memorandum quod die Veneris proximo post festum sancti Nicholai anno regni regis Henrici filii regis Joannis XLV. *apud Beckle coram serenissimo domino Ricardo Romanorum rege semper Augusto facta est concordia inter venerabilem Richardum abbatem et conventum Osenei ex una parte et dominum Rogerum de Amory ex altera videlicet quod dicti abbas et conventus dabunt dicto Rogero* CCC. *marcas sterlingorum et incipient solvere* C. *marcas ad pascha primo sequens et quod residuæ ducentæ marcæ solventur eidem intra tres annos proxime sequentes post pascha prioratum apud Osenei. Idem quoque Rogerus pro se et hæredibus suis in perpetuum remisit eidem abbati et conventui totum jus et clamium quod habuit vel aliquo modo habere potuit in duobus feodis militum cum pertinentiis in Weston unde eos implacitavit in curia domini regis per breve de recto, et prosecutum est quousque dictus abbas et conventus posuerunt se super magnam assisam ; convenit igitur inter eos quod supradictæ concordiæ servabitur*

---

[c] Dugd. Chron. ser. sub an.

AMBROSDEN, BURCESTER, &c. 363

chirographum in curia domini regis ante solutionem primæ pacationis. In cujus rei testimonium dominus rex huic memorando sigillum suum cum sigillo dicti Rogeri fecit apponi [d] Upon which agreement Roger de Amory did release and quit claim for himself and heirs, to the church of St. Mary's in Oseney, the whole manor of Weston nigh Blechesdon, with the advowson of the church and all other appertenances, in this form.

Sciant præsentes et futuri quod ego Rogerus de Amory filius et hæ- res Roberti de Amory remisi et quietum clamavi de me et hæredibus meis Deo et ecclesiæ S. Mariæ de Osenei et canonicis ibidem Deo ser- vientibus et eorum successoribus totum manerium de Weston juxta Blechesdon integrum cum advocatione ecclesiæ et cum omnibus perti- nentiis suis, &c. [e]

The said Roger de Amory sold to William son of Richard de Ox- ford, one virgate of land in Chesterton [f].

Toward the end of this year, upon the death of the prior of Chet- wood, the canons, having first obtained licence from the king their patron, chose John sub-prior of Burcester, (by way of postulation,) to be prior of Chetwood.

4. *Ricardi de Gravesend; frater Johannes supprior Berncestr a ca- nonicis de Chetewod petita prius licencia a domino rege patrono suo eligendi et optenta in priorem de Chetwod postulatur* [g].

November the ninth died Senchia wife of Richard king of the Ro- mans [h]. About Candlemas there was a parliament held at London, where the king and barons referred their differences to the arbitra- tion of the king of France, and our king of the Romans [i].

About this time Robert Clerk senior of Burcester, with the con-

An. MCCLXI. 45, 46. Henry III.

Robertus de Cantia habet literas regis de present. ad eccl'iam de Adberbyr (Adder-

bury) vacant. ad donat. regis ratione ep'a- tus Winton. vac. Literæ direct. Linc. ep'o. 20. Dec. Pat. 45. Hen. III.

[d] Regist. Osen. MS. p. 316. et R. Dods. MS. vol. 39. f. 96. Wikes sub an. [i] Ibid.

[e] Ibid. Regist. p. 317. [f] Excerpta ex Regist. Osen. [g] R. Dods. MS. vol. 107. p. 110. [h] Chron. Tho.

3 A 2

sent of Maud his wife and Robert his son and heir, granted and confirmed to Robert le Taillur for his homage and service a camera or small enclosure with its appertenances in the village of Berncester, nigh a messuage which Juliana Culyn formerly held with a plat of ground, &c. for the yearly rent of twelve pence, in consideration of twenty shillings sterling paid in hand, &c.

Sciant præsentes et futuri quod ego Robertus de Berncester senior Clericus assensu et bona voluntate Matildæ uxoris meæ et Roberti Clerici filii et hæredis mei dedi concessi et hac præsenti charta mea confirmavi Roberto le Taillur pro homagio et servitio suo quandam cameram cum pertinentiis in villa de Berncester juxta messuagium quod Juliana Culyn quondam tenuit in eadem villa cum quadam placia terræ quæ extendit unum ...... in plateam juxta eandem cameram quam placiam dicta Juliana aliquando tenuit cùm dicta camera. Ha benda et tenenda de me et hæredibus meis dicto Roberto et hæredibus suis vel cuicunque dictam cameram cum placia terræ dare legare ven dere invadiare vel assignare voluerit libere quiete bene et in pace in tegre et pacifice reddendo inde annuatim mihi et hæredibus meis dictus Robertus et hæredes sui vel sui assignati duodecim denarios et ad duos terminos anni scilicet ad festum S. Michaelis sex denarios et ad fes tum beatæ Mariæ in Martio sex denarios pro omni servitio consuetu dine demanda et exactione sæculari ad me vel ad hæredes meos perti nente. Et si ita contigerit quod dictus Robertus le Taillur vel hære des sui dictam cameram cum placia vendere voluerint licebit dicto Roberto Clerico vel hæredibus suis leviori pretio quam aliquis alius dictam habere cameram cum placia. Ego vero Robertus Clericus et hæredes mei dictam cameram cum placia dicto Roberto et hæredibus suis vel suis assignatis contra omnes homines et fæminas per prædictum servitium in perpetuum warantizabimus et defendemus. Pro hac autem donatione concessione et chartæ hujus confirmatione et warantizatione dedit mihi dictus Robertus præ manibus viginti solidos sterlingorum. Et ut hæc mea donatio concessio chartæ meæ confirmatio et warantizatio perpetuæ firmitatis robur optineat hanc præsentem chartam sigilli mei impressione roboravi. Hiis testibus; Philippo de

Wappel, Walhemoth Paupere, Johanne le Paumer, Gilberto de Lang-
ton, Roberto Michel de Berncester, Thom. Forsterlyng, Jacobo Coco,
Roberto de Bukehull, Thom. filio Germani de Bigehull, et multis
aliis [k].

To the original parchment is a seal appending bearing a flower
de luce, with this inscription, ✠ SIGILLUM ROBERTI CLERICI.

The ancient punishment of felons within the borough of Walingford was not hanging, but dismembering, or the loss of eyes and
stones; as appears by this memorable record cited by Mr. Selden,
45. Hen. III. *Berks. coram Gilberto de Preston et sociis suis in*
oct. purif. B. Mariæ Rot. 29. The jurors of the borough of Walingford give in *quod nullus de natione istius burgi pro quocunque facto*
quod fecerit debet suspendi, imo secundum consuetudinem istius burgi
debet oculis et testiculis privari, et tali libertate usi sunt a tempore quo
non extat memoria, and so they say one Benedict Hervey was lately so
punished.   *Et quæsiti juratores si tali libertate usi sunt, dicunt quod*
a tempore Henrici avi domini regis nunc usi fuerunt eadem libertate
per cartam ejusdem D. regis quam eis fecit per quam eis concessit om-
nes libertates quas civitas Winton. habet [l].

An. MCCLXII.   46, 47. *Henry III.*

On May the first William Fitz-Elias knight, granted to Alice
daughter of Simon de Maydwell six virgates of land in * Oakle, with
heybote and housebote in his demesne woods of Oakle, &c. by this
charter.

Sciant præsentes et futuri quod ego Willielmus filius Eliæ miles
dedi, &c. Aliciæ filiæ Simonis de Maydwell, &c. sex virgatas terræ
cum omnibus suis pertinentiis quas Elias frater meus dedit Simoni de
Maydwell patri dictæ Aliciæ in villa de Ackle, &c. concessi etiam
prædictæ Aliciæ heybotum et housbotum in dominicis boscis meis de

* This rather Oakle in North'tonshire.

k Ex Orig. penes Hon. D. Guil. Glynne.   l Selden's Notes upon Hengham, p. 153.

Acle et ad faciendas porchorias suas in boscis prædictis ubi sibi pla-
cuerit et ad habendos porcos suos quietos de pannagio &c. reddendo
inde annuatim &c. unam libram piperis vel sex denarios ad Natale Do-
mini, &c. Hiis testibus ; domino Nicholao de Turry, domino Roberto
de Brues, domino Ada de Greynvill, domino Willielmo de Englefield
justitiario domini regis, domino Thoma de Waloniis, domino Simone
de S. Licio, domino Eustachio de Greynvill, et aliis ; dat. apud Neu-
port Paynell, kalend. Maii anno regni Henrici filii regis Johannis qua-
dragesimo sexto [m]

There were twenty marks eight shillings and sixpence in arrears
due to the king for pannage or running of hogs in the forest of Brill
in the fourteenth of this reign; and the dispute was, whether it ought
to be paid by one William de Montacute guardian of William son
and heir of William de Ichford,. or by another William de Montacute lord of the manor of Aston.   By an inspection into the exchequer rolls, the first William was charged with the payment, and
the other acquitted.

Buck. pro rege debit : an. reg. Hen. 46. Quia constat per inspec-
tionem rotulorum de scaccario quod Willielmus de Monteacuto custos
Willielmi filii et heredis Willielmi de Icheforde et alii nominati in brevi
debent regi xx. marc. viii[s]. vi[d]. de padnagio foreste regis de Brohull
de anno regis xiv. et non Willielmus de Monte acuto qui nunc tenet
manerium de Astone.   Mandatum est vicecom. quod eidem Willielmo
pacem, &c. et distringat alios in brevi contentos heredes vel tenentes
terras eorum ad reddendas regi portiones ipsos contingentes de pre-
dictis denariis, &c. [n]

During this year Richard king of the Romans was guarantee between king Henry and his barons, and in a new parliament at London, within a fortnight after Easter, it was provided that four knights
out of every county should be returned to the said Richard king of
Almaign, who should choose out one of each county to be sheriff
for the first part of the year till Michaelmas, and for the remainder of

[m] Chartular. Borstall. p. 86.   [n] R. Dods. MS. vol. 29. p. 103.

the year the king should appoint whom he pleased. So great was the confidence of king and people in this prince, who June the twenty-sixth sailed over to his kingdom of Almaign °, and returned the tenth of February following. Before this voyage he presented to the church of Pelham in the archdeaconry of Stow ᴾ.

An. MCCLXIII. 47, 48. Henry III.

Margery sister and heir of Thomas Beauchamp earl of Warwick (whose mother was Margery eldest daughter and heir of Henry de Oily baron of Hokenorton) married John de Plesset, who in her right became earl of Warwick. He died February the twenty-sixth, and was buried in the quire of Missenden abbey in com. Buck. After his death by inquisition it appeared, that with Hokenorton, Kidlington, ʼand Bradham held by barony, he was also possessed of the manor of Musewell within the hamlet of Pidington in the parish of Ambrosden, held from the abbey of Missenden.

Jur. dicunt quod Johannes de Plessetis quondam comes de Warwico ten. man. de Okenardton una cum maneriis de Kedlinton et Bradeham pro servitio unius baroniæ. Et Hugo de Plessetis est filius, item tenet manerium de Musewell de abbate de Mussenden ᑫ.

His son Hugh de Plesset in April next ensuing doing his homage had livery of the manors of Hokenorton, Kidlington, &c. paying for his relief one hundred pounds in 48. Hen. III. ʳ

In the great rebellion which broke out on pretence of the king's violation of the provisions made at Oxford, managed chiefly by Simon Montfort earl of Leicester, and Gilbert Clare earl of Glocester, Richard king of the Romans adhered faithfully to his royal brother; for which the London mob marched out with infinite numbers to his manor of Thistleworth, where they pulled up the park pales, burnt all the buildings, and carried away the moveables; and then return-

---

° Chron. Tho. Wikes, sub an.   ᴾ R. Dods. MS. vol. 107. f. 97.   ᑫ W. Dugd. MS. vol. A. 1. p. 132.   ʳ Dugd. Bar. tom 1. p. 773.

ing fell upon his house in Westminster, and there committed all the outrage that could be acted by the madness of the people [s].

James de Aldithley, baron and lord of Stratton and Wretchwike, stood also so firm to the king in these troubles, that the rebellious barons seized on all his castles and lands in the counties of Salop and Stafford [t]. He was now constituted justice of Ireland, for which office in 10. Edw. I. the king acknowledged himself indebted to his heirs 1288[l]. 5[s]. 10[d].

In this year Roger d'Amory, knight, presented to the church of Bucknell, in which parish he resided [u].

Hugh le Povre of Ottindon com. Oxon. gave this charter to the nunnery of Acornbiri or Cornbiri com. Heref.

Sciant præsentes et futuri quod ego Hugo le Poer filius Oteweli le Poer dedi &c. Deo et beatæ Mariæ et priorissæ de Cornebiri et monialibus, &c. pro salute anime mee et Giliane uxoris mee &c. duodecim solidos et tres denarios annui redditus &c. in Barewe in parochia de Orleslen &c. Testibus, Ada de Bosco, Warino de Grendon, &c. [x]

About this time William de Baluthon granted and confirmed to Thomas de Creschlond and Alice his wife, eight acres of arable land with one acre and one rod of meadow in the fields of Lutegarshale, of which the particular boundings are so expressed as to be good authority for the ancient names of lands in that common field.

Sciant præsentes et futuri quod ego Willielmus de Baluthon dedi concessi et hac præsenti carta mea confirmavi Thomæ de Creschelond et Aliciæ uxori suæ octo acras terræ meæ arabilis cum una acra et

---

<table>
<tr><td>1263. Ann. 5. Ric'i Gravesend.</td><td>4. id. Jun. 1263.</td></tr>
<tr><td>Andreas cl'icus d'ni regis Aleman. subd. ad eccl. de Mixebiry vacant. per consecrationem mag'ri J. de Exon. ep'i Winton. ult. rectoris ejusd. ad pres. ejusd. d'ni regis.</td><td>Phil. de Eya subd. ad eccl. de Chalegrave vacantem per hoc quod mag'r Walterus ultimus rector ejusd. est in ep'um Exon. electus et consecratus ad pres. regis Aleman.</td></tr>
</table>

---

[s] Chron. Tho. Wikes, sub an.   [t] Dugd. Bar. tom. 1. p. 747. b.   [u] R. Dods. MS. vol. 107. p. 117.   [x] Ib. vol. 63. f. 84.

una roda prati in campis de Lutegarshale unde una dimidiæ acræ jacet super Coston juxta terram Johannis de Broncthon: una dimidia acræ jacet super Uferlong juxta terram domini de Lutegarshale una dimidia acræ jacet apud le Portweye juxta terram Walteri ad Portam. una dimidia acra in le Brutine juxta terram Galfrid. filii Hugonis. una dimid. acræ jacet apud Dylingshame juxta terram Johannis de Broncthon: una roda jacet apud Tusfurlung juxta terram Nicholai le Grey: una roda jacet apud Pusfurlong juxta terram Galfridi filii Hugonis: duæ rodæ simul jacent dimid. acr. apud Redgath juxta terram Galfridi filii Hugonis, una dimid. acra jacet apud Gilberdeshull juxta terram Galfridi filii Hugonis, una dimid. acra jacet apud le Cornforlong juxta terram Nicholi le Grey, una dimid. acra jacet super Bracforlong in Costone juxta terram Galfridi filii Hugonis, una dimid. acræ super Crouforlong juxta terram Galfridi filii Hugonis, una dimid. acræ jacet apud le Greneweye juxta terram Johannis de Brouton, una acra jacet apud Redforlong juxta terram Walteri ad Portam, una dimid. acra apud Medlungforlong juxta terram Galfridi filii Hugonis: una roda prati jacet in Longdale in Westmode juxta pratum Radulphi le Sergaunt, una roda in Mordale juxta pratum rectoris ecclesiæ de Lutegarshale: una roda in Longdale in More juxta pratum ejusdem rectoris: una roda prati jacet in Blakenheg juxta pratum ejusdem rectoris, una roda prati in Linlongesdale juxta pratum prædicti rectoris. Habenda et tenenda omnes terras et prata prædicta de me et hæredibus meis et meis assignatis dictis Thomæ et Aliciæ uxori suæ et hæredibus suis et suis assignatis et cuicunque dare vendere invadiare assignare seu in testamento legare voluerint, libere quiete bene et in pace integre honorifice et hæreditarie, cum omnibus suis pertinentiis libertatibus et liberis consuetudinibus ad dictam terram in omnibus locis tam infra villam Lutegarshale quam extra spectantibus: reddendo inde annuatim mihi et hæredibus meis et meis assignatis ipsi et hæredes sui et sui assignati unam rosam ad festum S. Johannis Baptistæ pro omnibus servitiis demandis auxiliis curiæ sectis, suettis, releviis, escaetis, tallagiis, soccagiis et pro omnibus sæcularibus exactionibus et terrenis demandis quæ a dicta terra exigi poterint vel vindicari. Et ego vero prædictus Willielmus et hæredes mei et mei assignati dictam terram et dictum pratum cum omnibus pertinentiis suis dicto Thomæ et Aliciæ et eorum hæredibus et assignatis contra omnes homines mares et fæminas warantizabimus defendemus et ab omni servitio et terrena demanda ut prædictum est per servitium prænominatum acquietabimus in perpetuum. Et ut hæc mea donatio concessio warantia et chartæ meæ confirmatio rata et inconcussa et stabilis sine dolo permaneat in perpetuum hanc chartam sigilli mei impressione corroboravi. Hiis testibus; Waltero de S. Andrea, Thom. de Echecote, Joh. de Greynvill de Wattone, Waltero Golye, Martino de Greynvill, Radulfo le Staunton de Lutegarshale, Johanne de Broucthon, David de la More, Willielmo Mott, Johanne Meyet, Elia Clerico et aliis[γ]

A label appending with seal broken off.

An. MCCLXIV. 48, 49. *Henry III.*

In April Richard king of the Romans attended his royal brother in the march of an army to Northampton, and assisted much in the siege and taking of that town defended by Simon Montfort, junior. And on May the fourteenth commanded the body of the king's army at the fatal battle of Lewes in Sussex, where, after an entire defeat by the barons forces, the king and he were both taken prisoners. His lands were all seized by the victorious earl of Leicester, himself and younger son Edmund imprisoned, and his elder son Henry (with prince Edward eldest son to king Henry) forced to surrender to the earl of Leicester, as a pledge for keeping the oath extorted from the king.

One of our histories, that makes a partial defence of Montfort,

An. MCCLXIV. 48, 49. Henry III.
Rex omnibus &c. salutem. Sciatis quod ι eu. patri R. Coventr. et Lichf. ep'o et mag'ro Nich'o archid'o Norfolc. plenam et lib. dedi- *mus potestatem ad tractand. apud Brackele in presentia Joh'is de Valencia militis et nuncii regis Franc. T. R. apud Oxon. 20' Mart.* Rymer 1. 784.

[γ] Ex Orig. pergam. penes D. W. Glynne, Bar.

brings a scandalous report on Richard king of the Romans, that he run from this battle and hid himself in a windmill, where he was caught and ridiculed by some of the pursuing barons : and after five months captivity redeemed himself for seventeen thousand pounds sterling, and five thousand pounds in gold [z]. It is certain Gilbert Clare earl of Glocester desired this rich prisoner for the benefit of ransom, and so much resented the denial made by the sons of Montfort, that he deserted the barons party; contrived the prince's escape, and commanded the body of the royal army in the battle of Evesham. [a]

Roger de St. John, lord of Staunton, slain in the battle of Evesham, had confirmed to the canons of Oseney that gift which his father had made to them of a mill and five yards land in Weston near Burcester, called Simeon's land. He likewise confirmed the grant of the church of Great Barton, with the chapels of Sandford and Ledwell [b].

James de Aldithley, lord of Stratton and Wretchwick, having been sent by the king to repress the outrages of the Welch, and having defeated Lewelin prince of Wales, joined with the earl of Glocester, and made a loyal attempt to rescue his captived prince [c]

An. MCCLXV. 49, 50. *Henry III.*

The prior of Ware, being proctor of the abbey of St. Ebrulf in Normandy, presented to the church of Charlton on Otmoore, which church was impropriated to the said abbey.

1264. Ann. 7. Ric'i Gravesend.
Rogerus de Amary subd. ad eccl. de Buckehull vac. per resignat. d'ni J. Glasguensis ep'i ad pres. . . . . . de Amary patris sui.

1264. Rog. de Capella subd. ad eccl. de Wytefeld vac. per mort. d'ni Ric'i de Ros ad pres. d'ni regis Aleman. ratione terrarum et hered. d'ni Henr. de Wytefeld, sabbato 4[or.] temporum ante natale d'ni.

[z] Chron. Maïlros, sub an.   [a] Mat. Par.   [b] Dugd. Bar. tom. 1. p. 539.   [c] Mat. Par sub an.

Archid. Oxon. 9. Ric. Gravesend ; prior de Ware procurator abbatis sancti Ebrulfi in Anglia præsentat ad ecclesiam de Cherlton [d].

After the battle of Evesham, fought on August the fifth, wherein prince Edward entirely defeated the barons army, with the death of the leader Simon Montfort, our Richard king of the Romans was released by Simon Montfort jun. from his imprisonment in the castle of Kenilworth, and on September the ninth came to his castle of Walingford, where he was gladly received by his friends and tenants of these parts [e].

At Christmas following Simon Montfort the younger submitted himself to the king on such terms as should be made by our Richard king of the Romans, the pope's legate, and Philip Basset, who determined that he should deliver the castle of Kenilworth to the king, depart the kingdom, and receive 500. marks *per an.* out of the exchequer [f].

Richard king of the Romans, lord of the manor of Ambrosden, &c. now founded a nunnery of the Benedictine order, dedicated to St. Mary at Burnham com. Buck. and endowed it with the manor of Burnham and the advowson of that church: with several lands in the manor of Chippeham, &c. *Hiis testibus; Henrico illustri rege Angliæ fratre nostro ; domino Edwardo primo ejusdem regis genito nepote nostro ; dominis W. Bathon. cancellario Angliæ, R. Lincoln. et R. Coventren. et Lichfelden episcopis, Henrico et Edmundo filiis nostris, Philippo Basset, Willielmo de Huntercumbe, Willielmo de Wyndlesore, Ricardo de Oxeye, Philippo de Covele, et aliis. Dat.*

Ann. 8. 1265.

Mag'r Will. de Flecton pres. per procuratorem abb. et conv. Scti Ebrulfi ad eccl. de Cherlton super Ottemor vac. per mort. Jordani; inquis. facta per R. archid. Oxon. 1265. Magister Thedisius de Camilla pres. per d'num regem Aleman. ad eccl. de

Frothingham in archid. Stow per mortem cujusdam archid'i de Alemannia ult. rectoris ejusd. admiss. 8. kal. Mart. dispens. q'd esset in minoribus ordinibus.

Andr. de Byham subd. ad eccl. de Stok vac. per resign. mag'ri Bartholomei ad pres. abb. et conv. Egnesham. 3. non. Jun. 1265.

[d] R. Dods. MS. vol. 107. p. 118. [e] Chron. Tho. Wikes, sub an. [f] Mat. Par. sub an

apud Cippeham decimo octavo die Aprilis indictione nona anno domini millesimo ducentecimo sexagesimo sexto, regni vero nostri anno nono[g]*

Margery de Eston was elected the first prioress, and the church of Burnham was soon after appropriated to the use of those sisters[h]

Nigh this time Robert Pufph, a miller in Burcester, gave to John his younger son one acre of land in the field of Burcester, lying between the two ways which lead toward Battehulle, and bounded with the land of Maud de Clyfford and Robert Redwy, to him and his heirs to dispose of at pleasure except to religious men, and to pay yearly one penny at Michaelmas.

Sciant præsentes et futuri quod ego Robertus Pufph molendinarius de Berencester dedi concessi et hac præsenti charta mea confirmavi Johanni minori filio meo pro servitio suo unam acram terræ meæ in campo de Berencester, illam videlicet quæ jacet inter duas vias quæ extendunt versus Batehull et jacet inter terram dominæ Matildæ Clyfford et terram Roberti Redwy. Habenda et tenenda dictam acram terræ de me et hæredibus meis sibi et hæredibus suis vel suis assignatis vel cuicunque dictam acram terræ dare vendere legare vel assignare voluerit in quocunque statu sit exceptis viris religiosis libere quiete bene et in pace cum omnibus aysiamentis infra villam et extra ad dictam acram terræ spectantibus: reddendo inde annuatim mihi et hæredibus meis dictus Johannes et hæredes sui vel sui assignati unum denarium argenti ad festum S. Michaelis pro omnibus servitiis querelis consuetudinibus et demandis sæcularibus et pro omnibus rebus quæ modo sunt vel unquam contingere possunt. Et ego prædictus Robertus et hæredes mei dictam acram terræ prænominato Johanni et hæredibus suis vel suis assignatis per prædicturum servitium contra omnes homines et fæminas in perpetuum warantizabimus acquietabimus et defendemus. Et ut hæc mea donatio concessio et præsentis chartæ meæ confirmatio rata et stabilis permaneat præsentem chartam hanc sigilli mei impressione roboravi. Hiis testibus; Helya Carectario, Willielmo Molendi-

g Mon. Ang. tom. 1. p. 531. b.   h R. Dods. MS. vol. 107. f. 111.

nario, Simone Germayn, Willielmo Nigro, Johanne de la Forae, Ro-
berto Sebern, Willielmo Germayn de Bigehull, et multis aliis[i].

To the original parchment a seal appends with the impression of a
spicate figure, intended possibly for a sheaf or ear of corn, with this
inscription in oval margin, S. ROBERTI PUFPH.

An. MCCLXVI.   50, 51. *Henry III.*

This year the prior of Burcester presented to the vicarage of Little-
Missenden in Bucks[k], and the prioress of Stodley to the vicarage of
Ilmer in the said county[l]

An inquisition was now taken at Brill relating to the manor of Borstall and the custody of the forest of Bernwood, then in the hereditary tenure of Sir John Fitz-Nigel knight.

Inquisitio capta apud Brehull die Jovis proxime post festum S. Gre-
gorii papæ anno regni regis Henrici filii regis Johannis quinquage-
simo coram Hugone de Golevingham tunc seneschallo forestæ regis
intra pontem Oxford et Stanford ad eadem assignato per ipsum regem
et consilium de jure hæreditario tenuræ Johannis filii Nigelli militis
de foresta de Bernwode per sacramentam domini Walteri de Upton,
Johannis de Grendon Viridarii, Bartholomei le Venour, Johannis Py-
dington, Willielmi de Boys, Johannis Rosson, et omnium regardatorum
et agistatorum forestæ prædictæ, qui dicunt per sacramentum suum quod
prædictus Johannes filius Nigelli tenet de rege unam hidam terræ ara-
bilis in Borstalle vocatam le Dere hide cum uno bosco vocato Hullwode
per magnam serjantiam custodiendi forestam de Bernwode nec non
solvendi domino regi annuatim pro terra prædicta x[s]. *et pro terra fo-*
resta XL[s]. *videlicet ad festum sancti Michaelis archangeli et annun-*
tiationis beatæ Mariæ per æquales portiones per manus seneschalli fo-
restæ inter pontem Oxon. et Stamford qui pro tempore fuerit videlicet
pro proficuis ten. de eadem balliva quæ ad ipsum regem debent perti-

---

[i] Ex Orig. penes D. W. Glynne, Bar.   [k] R. Dods. MS. vol. 107. p. 112.   [l] Ibid.

*nere, exceptis indictationibus siquæ fuerint scilicet de viridi et vena-
tione. Et dicunt etiam quod Willielmus filius Nigelli pater prædicti
Johannis per chartam feoffamenti adquisivit sibi et hæredibus suis de
Fulcone de Lisuris et Willielmo de Lisuris prædictam terram et ballivam de Bernewode reddendo eis et hæredibus eorum eandem firmam
scilicet pro terra prædicta x'. et pro foresta prædicta xl'. qui quidem
Fulco et Willielmus nullum jus habuerunt in prædicta terra nec balliva
sed prædictus Willielmus filius Nigelli et antecessores sui tenuerunt dictas terram et ballivam de domino rege ante tempus conquest. Angliæ
per unum cornu quod est charta prædictæ forestæ. Et dicunt etiam
quod prædictis Johannes filius Nigelli et antecessores sui a tempore
quo non extat memoria solebant habere in bosco domini regis housbote
et heybote cum omnibus feodis forestario pertinentibus secundum assisam forestæ. In cujus rei testimonium sigilla sua apposuerunt. Dat.
die et anno supradictis* [m].*

All the adjoining parishes in this county were commanded to send
out four or five men, according to the bigness of them, to meet at
Oxford within three weeks after Easter, and thence to march to the
castle of Kenilworth, where the garrison refused to submit; and
though besieged by the prince, and after by the king, they would not
surrender till about St. Lucy's day [n]. When the king was resolved
to go himself in person, Osbert Giffard carried in to him the *posse
comitatus* of Oxfordshire, who with banners and ensigns displayed
marched to the castle, and environed it on the morrow after St. John
Baptist.

While the king was at Northampton, he sent messengers to Simon
Montfort with an army to demand surrender of the castle of Kenilworth: whereupon he submitted himself to the pope's legate, Richard king of Almaign, and Philip Basset, who brought him to
Northampton, where in the king's presence the king of Almaign gave
him thanks for his life, ingeniously acknowledging that he himself
had been murdered at Kenilworth shortly after the battle of Eve-

[m] Ex Chartular de Borstal. f. 11.   [n] Annal. Waverl. sub an.

sham, had not this Simon prevented it.   It was proposed that the
said Simon should surrender the castle, but the soldiers within utterly
refused to yield it up.

The king gave a charter of confirmation to the abbey of Oseney
dated at Westminster, Jan. 23. wherein are recited these gifts of Robert de Oily ....*dedit duas hidas in Ernecote cum bosco et aliis pertinentiis ....duas partes decime de Blechesdona, de Weston, de Berin-
cestr cum Wrechewike, Bukenhull, &c.* °*

An. MCCLXVII.   51, 52. Henry III.

Stephen de Hampton held half a knight's fee in Burcester, who
died this year, and left Alice his daughter and heir fifteen years of
age, married to Walter de la Poyle, which family gave name to
Hampton-Poyle [p]

After his death an inquisition was taken that begins thus :

*Oxon. Jur. dicunt quod Stephanus de Hampton ten. maner. de
Hampton.   Item dicunt quod idem Stephanus ten. dimid. feod. 1. mil.
in Burchester, &c.* [q]

Gilbert Clare earl of Glocester, under a pretence of loyalty, got
with an army into London about Palm-Sunday, and then set up for
a restorer of the disinherited barons, and maintained the city against
the king, who after a long siege had his forces so much weakened, that
they must have broke up, if our Richard king of the Romans had not
supplied them with money and provisions : till on June the fifteenth,
by mediation of him and Henry his eldest son, the earl was reconciled
to the king, and the city surrendered [r]

In pursuance of the inquisition taken the former year, the king
confirmed to Sir John Fitz-Nigel his hide of land in Borstall, and the
custody of the forest of Bernwood, by this charter.

*Henricus Dei gratia, &c.   Omnibus &c.   Quia accepimus per inqui-
sitionem quam per custodem forestæ nostræ inter pontem Oxford et*

° W. Dugd. MS. vol. N. p. 28.   p R. Dods. MS. vol. 40. p. 107.   q Ibid.   r Chron.
Tho. Wikes, sub an.

Stanford fieri fecimus quod Johannes filius Nigelli de nobis tenere debet in capite jure hæreditario ballivam forestæ nostræ de Bernwood videlicet a Stoneford usque ad aquam quæ vocatur le Burie quæ currit inter Steplè-Claydon et Padbury et unam hidam terræ in Borstall quæ vocatur le Derehyde reddendo inde nobis quinquaginta solidos per annum, et nihilominus custodiet forestam prædictam quam quidem ballivam idem Johannes et antecessores sui tenuerunt de nobis et antecessoribus nostris ante conquestum Angliæ. Volumus et concedimus pro nobis et hæredibus nostris quantum in nobis est quod idem Johannes et hæredes sui habeant et tencant ballivam forestæ prædictæ sicut ipse et antecessores sui ballivam prædictam tenuerunt temporibus retroactis faciendo nobis et hæredibus nostris omnia servitia quæ ad nos pertinent. In cujus rei testimonium has literas nostras fieri fecimus patentes. Teste meipso apud . . . . . tertio die Decembris. Anno regni nostri quinquagesimo primo[*]

Richard king of the Romans, lord of the manor of Ambrosden, now presented to the church of Hepham in the archdeaconry of Stow, and to the church of North-Luffenham in the archdeaconry of Northampton[t].

Nigh this time Robert Pufph miller in Burcester granted to Isabel his daughter one acre of land in the field of Burcester which lay upon Wowelond, between the land of Henry Lacy on the one side, and the land lately of Maud de Clifford on the other, and reached to the way leading toward Stratton, to pay one penny yearly rent. In consideration whereof the said Robert received six shillings in hand, &c.

Sciant præsentes et futuri quod ego Robertus Pufph molendinarius de Berncester dedi concessi et hac præsenti charta mea confirmavi Ysabellæ filiæ meæ pro servitio suo unam acram terræ meæ in campo de Berncester illam videlicet quæ jacet super Wowelond inter terram domini Henrici de Lacy ex una parte et terram quæ fuit Matildæ de

---

[*] Ex Cartular. de Borstall. f. 11.   [t] R. Dods. MS. vol. 107. f. 97. 101.

Clifford ex altera et extendit se ad viam quæ ducit versus Stratton. Habendam et tenendam dictam acram terræ de me et hæredibus meis vel meis assignatis dictæ Ysabellæ et hæredibus suis vel suis assignatis vel cuicunque vel quandocunque dictam acram terræ dare vendere legare vel assignare voluerit in quocunque statu sit libere quiete bene et in pace in planis et pascuis pratis et omnibus aliis tantæ terræ adjacentibus jure hæreditario in perpetuum. Reddendo inde annuatim mihi et hæredibus meis dicta Ysabella et hæredes sui vel sui assignati unum denarium ad nativitatem S. Johannis Baptistæ pro omnibus servitiis, &c. Pro hac autem donatione concessione et præsentis chartæ meæ confirmatione dedit dicta Ysabella prænominato Roberto sex solidos argenti præ manibus in gersumam. Et ut hæc mea donatio concessio et præsentis chartæ meæ confirmatio et warantizatio rata et stabilis imperpetuum permaneat, præsentem chartam hanc sigilli mei impressione roboravi. Hiis testibus; Roberto Clerico de Berncester, Helya Carectario, Roberto Scissore, Johanne Calduse, Willielmo Molendinario, Simone Germayn de Bigehulle, Roberto Michel de Berncester, et multis aliis [u]

An. MCCLXVIII. 52, 53. *Henry III.*

There was now by the king's assent an aid imposed on the inhabitants of Ambrosden, and all other tenants of Richard king of the Romans, to raise the money he had expended for his redemption when a prisoner to Montfort's party[x]. And this illustrious prince (*detersa jam captivitatis ignominia*) sailed over again to his kingdom of Almaign, and there married Beatrix niece to the archbishop of Cologn, on June 16. and on August the third arrived at Dover, where the nobility with great honor received him.

John Peyvre lord of the manor of Chilton left heir a minor granted in ward to the queen, whose bailiffs were ejected out of the manor of Chilton, and the young heir stole away by some of the earl of Glo-

---

[u] Ex Orig. penes hon. D. Guil. Glynne, Bar.   [x] R. Dods. MS. vol. 29. p. 120.

cester's tenants: upon which at a trial in Westminster there was a
precept issued out to the sheriff of Bucks. to go to the said earl's
manor of Crendon, and there arrest the said persons, &c.

Westmin. Term. Pasch. Buk. Rot. 4.

Alianora regina Anglie op. se versus plures de raptu heredis Jo-
hannis Peyure qui tenuit de rege in capite apud manerium Johannis de
Chilton concess. regine. Et defend. ejecerunt ballivos regine de ma-
nerio de Chilton in R. contemptum : unde preceptum fuit vic. Buk.
quod accedat ad manerium comitis Glovernie de Crendon et cap'et de-
fend. quod e'ent coram rege ubicunque, &c. y

Henry Lacy earl of Lincoln and Salisbury, till now in ward to the
king, coming to full age did homage with Margaret his wife, and had
livery of all the lands whereof her father William Longspe died possessed, *viz.* the manors of Burcester and Midlington, &c. z

Upon the death of the prior of Burcester, William de Quainton,
one of the canons, was elected his successor, with leave first obtained
of Henry de Lacy earl of Sarum patron of the said convent a. And
John de Glocester was now chosen abbot of Nuttle, licence of electing being first obtained from Gilbert de Clare earl of Glocester and
Hertford then patron of the said abbey b. Sir Osbert Giffard, knight,
presented Sir John Waleran clerk to the church of Dedington com.
Oxon. c

About the same time Robert Clerk of Burcester granted and confirmed to Adam Burgeys of Wendlebury, one house and curtilage or
spot of ground in Burcester which Maud his sister held of him, to
pay yearly to him and his heirs one pound of cumin at Michaelmas,

1268. Ann. 11. Ric'i Gravesend.
Ric. de Compton capellan. pres. per
abb'em et conv. de Osen. ad vicar. eccl.
de Cestreton vac. per resign. Rog. non.

Novemb.
Mag'r Jacobus de portu cl'icus pres. per
priorem et conv. de Kenilwortha ad eccl. de
Hethe. 6. kal. Aug. 1268.

y R. Dods. MS. vol. 42. p. 92.   z Dugd. Bar. tom. 1. p. 103.   a R. Dods. MS. vol.
107. p. 118.   b Ibid. f. 112.   c Ibid. f. 117.

in consideration whereof the said Adam Burgeys paid him five marks in hand.

Sciant præsentes et futuri quod ego Robertus Clericus de Berncester dedi concessi et hac præsenti charta mea confirmavi Adæ Burgeys de Wendleburie pro servitio suo unam domum curtilagium cum pertinentiis suis in villa de Burncester illam scilicet quam Matildis soror mea de me aliquando tenuit in eadem villa de Burncester habenda et tenenda de me et hæredibus meis sibi et hæredibus suis vel suis assignatis vel cuicunque dare legare vel assignare voluerit tam in ægritudine quam in sanitate sine ullo retinemento reddendo inde annuatim mihi et hæredibus meis ipse et hæredes sui vel sui assignati unam libram cymini ad festum Sancti Michaelis pro omnibus servitiis consue tudinibus curiarum sectis wardis releviis escaetis herietis et omnibus aliis sæcularibus demandis. Ego vero prædictus Robertus et hæredes mei prædictam domum curtilagium cum omnibus pertinentiis suis contra omnes homines et fæminas Judæos et Christianos pro prædicto servitio warantizabimus acquietabimus et in perpetuum defendemus prædicto Adæ et hæredibus suis vel suis assignatis. Pro hac autem donatione concessione et præsentis chartæ meæ confirmatione, dedit mihi prædictus Adam quinque marcas præ manibus in gersuma. Et ut hæc mea donatio concessio et præsentis chartæ meæ confirmatio perpetuæ firmitatis robur obtineat præsentem chartam sigilli mei impressione roboravi. Hiis testibus; dominis Henrico de Boeles, Johanne filio Wydonis militibus. Johanne filio Willielmi de Kertlinton, Roberto Jordan de eadem, Johanne de Boleme, Willielmo filio Rogeri de Wendlinbury, Nicholao de Berkeswelle de Stratton, Johanne de la Forde de Burncester, Roberto Sebern de eadem, Hugone Carectario, Hugone Clerico, Hugone Scissore, Johanne Fabro, Johanne de Bigehulle, Johanne Puff, Simone Germeyn de Bigehulle, et aliis [d].

Isabel de Fortibus daughter of Baldwin earl of Devon, widow of William de Fortibus earl of Albemarle, having now livery of the Isle of Wight, and being sole heir to the earldom of Devon by the death

[d] Ex Orig. penes D. W. Glynne, Bar.

of Baldwin (the fifth of that name) her brother without issue, being possessed of the lordship of Heyford-Warin in this county, she granted a charter of confirmation to the priory of St. Edburg in Burcester of five quarters of bread corn given to them by Maud de Chesny her great grandmother, to make hosts or consecrated bread, out of her said manor of Heyford-Warin.

Sciant &c. quod ego Isabella (de Fortibus comitissa Albemarlie et Devon. ac domina Insule) pro salute anime mee et animarum antecessorum et successorum meorum concessi, &c. ecclesie beate Marie et Sancte Edburge virginis de Burnecestr et priori et canonicis, &c. quinque quarteria frumenti que habent de dono Matildis de Chesneto proavie mee ad hostias faciendas in domo predicta de manerio meo de Hayford-Waryn, &c. Testibus dominis Johanne de Sancta Elena, Ri cardo Asseton, Rogero de Insula militibus [e].

See this confirmed by Sir Robert L'isle lord of the manor of Heyford-Waryn, sub an. 16. Ed. III.

James baron Aldithley lord of Stratton and Wrechwike, having been constantly engaged in martial expeditions, began now in his declining years to enter upon acts of devotion : accordingly this year he went on pilgrimage to James of Compostella in Spain; and to the Holy Land in 54. Hen. III. [f]

There was at this time a great difference between John earl of Warren and Henry Lacy lord of Burcester touching a certain pasture, upon which they raised what forces they could, resolving to fight for it. But the king upon notice forbad such riotous meeting, and commanded his judges to compose the matter, who, upon inquiry by oaths of the country, adjudged the right to Henry Lacy [g]. This pasture must have been nigh to Crendon the manor of the said earl of Warren, by descent from Walter Mareschal earl of Pembroke.

An. MCCLXIX.   53, 54. *Henry III.*

The Augustine friars that came into England an. 1251, and soon

---

[e] Ex evidentiis Willielmi L'isle de Wilburham in Com. Cantab. inter Collectanea R. Dods. MS. vol. 130. f. 9.   [f] Dugd. Bar. tom. 1. p. 748. a.   [g] Mat. West. sub an.

after to Oxford, were there first settled by Sir John Handlo, knight, soon after lord of Borstall, who purchased land to build their convent. The donation was in the preceding year confirmed by the king[h]. Thus it is represented by the Oxford historiographer, who gives him the title of knight, and fixes him at Borstall, whereas it is certain, he had not yet that honor nor that seat, nor were the first charters of Hen. III. procured by any interest of John de Handlo, who was no benefactor to them till the latter end of Ed. I.

A great difference between prince Edward and Gilbert Clare earl of Glocester was referred to the arbitration of Richard king of the Romans, who on June the twenty-sixth drew up articles for their mutual agreement: that the said earl should accompany the prince in his expedition to the Holy Land, &c. for performance of which the earl delivered to the king of the Romans his two castles of Tunbridge in Kent, and Henly in this county[i].

Prince Edward from Portsmouth began his voyage to the Holy Land, leaving his two sons by consent of Parliament in custody of Richard king of the Romans, to be educated by him in their father's absence[k].

Before this time William de Borstall, chaplain, granted to Sir John Fitz-Nigel one toft of land in Borstall, for the yearly rent of three shillings. *Hiis testibus; Willielmo Welet, Roberto Ferebraz, Helia Segrym, Radulpho filio Simonis de Borstall, Roberto filio Aviciæ, Johanne de Thomele, Willielmo de Tyngewike et aliis*[l].

This yearly rent of three shillings was about this time remitted to Sir John Fitz-Nigel by William son of Simon le Frankleyn of Borstall, chaplain. *Hiis testibus; Helia Segrym, Thoma Brun, Roberto*

1269. Vacante prioratu de Bernecestre per resign. f'ris Reginaldi petita licentia ab Henr. de Lacy patrona ejusd. Walterus de Quendon electus est, admiss. 16. kal. Jun. Rot. Ric'i Gravesend, anno 12.

Will. de Wyltesier capell. pres. per priorem de Ware procuratorem abb. et conv. S'cti Ebrulfi ad eccl. de Cherleton vac. per mort. mag'ri Willi. 3. kal. Apr. 1269.

---

[h] Wood, Antiq. Oxon. l. 1. p. 115.　　[i] Chron. Tho. Wikes, sub an.　　[k] Ibid.　　[l] Ex Chartular. de Borstall. penes D. Joh. Aubrey, Bar. f. 4.

Avis, Johanne de Murrell, Radulpho filio Simonis, Roberto Fere-
braz, &c. [m]

An. MCCLXX.   54, 55. *Henry III.*

Alice the widow of Edmund Lacy earl of Lincoln had a grant
from the king in the 42d year of his reign of the custody of her husband's land, and the guardianship of Henry his son and heir, who
coming to age, and having livery of his estate in the 53d of this
king, she now paid as a fine for these profits by her received, the
sum of three thousand seven hundred fifty-four pounds fourteen shillings eightpence, to be employed in the new structure of the abbey
of Westminster.

Rex &c. Sciatis &c. quod dilecta nobis Alesia de Lacy liberavit per
præceptum nostrum custodi operationum nostrarum Westm. pro XI. *an.*
viz. ab an. regni nostri 42. ad 53. tria millia et septingentas, et quin-
quaginta et quatuor libras XVIII. *sol.* VIII[d]. *de fine suo quem nobiscum*
fecit pro habenda custodia terrarum et hæred. Edm. de Lacy defuncti.
6. Novemb. &c. [n]

John earl of Warren and Surrey, lord of the manor of Crendon in
Bucks. did by special instrument dated at his said manor of Crendon
oblige himself to come to prince Edward into the king's court, and
stand to the judgment of it for an offence by him committed against
Sir Alan la Zouch and Sir Roger his son at Westminster, for which
misdemeanor a fine of ten thousand marks was laid upon him [o].

An. MCCLXX. 5 4, 55. Hen. III.
Henricus rex commisit Waltero Giffard
ep'o. Bath et Well. (demum arch. Ebor.)
castrum suum Oxon. cum prato et molendinis et maneria de Brehull et Pydington per
terminum septem annorum reddendo annuatim pro manerio de Brehull triginta libras et pro Pydington 20 libras et proventus de castro apud Oxon. et molendino et
pratis cedant ad munitionem castri adversus hostes.   Rex pro sumptibus et expensis
dicti Walteri Giffard ratione turbationum
regni pardonat ei pro omnibus arreragiis
per totum tempus. Dat. apud Wynton. 25.
Dec. regni nostri 55[to.] Ex regist. Wal. Giffard, arch. Ebor. fol. 77.

[m] Ex Chartular. de Borstall. penes D. Joh. Aubrey, Bar. f. 4.   [n] W. Dugd. MS. C. p. 28.
[o] Dugd. Bar. tom. 1. p. 78. b.

Richard king of the Romans sent a writ to the bailiffs and stewards of his honor of Knaresburgh, to protect and defend the Cistertian abbey of that town in their possession of the church of Stavely which he had given to them, &c. *Dat. apud Knaresburg* VII. *Septemb. regni nostri anno quinto decimo* [p].

About this time Hamo de Gattone granted and confirmed to Richard de la Vache one messuage and all the land and meadow, and all villains and their tenements, &c. in the village of Wrechwike, which descended to him by the death of Hamo de Gattone his uncle, to be held for the service of one penny yearly at Michaelmas, and to the capital lords of the fee one penny or one pair of gloves to the value of a penny. For which grant the said Hamo de Gattone received the full sum of one hundred pounds sterling.

Sciant præsentes et futuri quod ego Hamo de Gattone dedi et concessi et hac præsenti charta mea confirmavi Ricardo de la Vache pro homagio et servitio suo unum messuagium et totam terram et pratum cum omnibus villanis et eorum tenementis et sequelis una cum communis pasturis et cæteris omnibus pertinentiis in villa de Wrechwike, quæ mihi descenderunt per mortem domini Hamonis de Gattone avunculi mei. Habenda et tenenda prædicto Ricardo et hæredibus suis vel suis assignatis solvendo unum denarium ad festum Sancti Michaelis super eundem feodum et capitalibus dominis illius feodi unum denarium vel unum par cyrothecarum de pretio unius denarii ad prædictum dominum super eundem feodum pro me et hæredibus meis pro omnibus servitiis consuetudinibus exactionibus auxiliis querelis wardis maritagiis sectis curiarum universarum et omnibus servitiis tam domini regis quam aliorum quorumcunque dominorum et omnibus aliis sæcularibus demandis quæ de prædictis tenementis poterint in posterum exigi vel haberi. Et ego prædictus Hamo et hæredes mei vel mei assignati præ-

A. D. 1270. Londini circa pentecosten factus est dominus rex Alemaniæ seneschallus et custos totius Angliæ, quoniam dominus Edwardus versus Terram Sanctam profecturus erat. Ex cron. vetusto MS.

dicto Ricardo et hæredibus suis vel suis assignatis omnia prædicta terras et tenementa cum omnibus suis pertin. sicut prædictum est contra omnes Christianos et Judæos per prædictum servitium warantizabimus acquietabimus et in perpetuum defendemus. Pro hac autem donatione concessione warantia et hujus chartæ meæ confirmatione dedit mihi prædictus Ricardus centum libras sterlingorum præ manibus integram summam. In cujus rei testimonium præsentem chartam sigilli mei impressione roboravi. Hiis testibus; dominis Roberto Malet, Johanne de Cheyni, Philippo Muredent, militibus; Johanne le Waleis, Thom. de S. Andrea, Galfrido de Sancto Martino, magistro Waltero de la Mare, Willielmo de Huckote, Waltero fratre ejus, Ricardo de Cantilupo, Willielmo de Falehame, Johanne de Overe, et aliis [q].

There was a trial this year in Easter term at Westminster, by which it appeared that William de Longspe, father of Margaret wife of Henry de Lacy, was seized in fee of the third part of two parts of the manor of Erdinton in com. Berks. which third part James de Aldithley of Stratton-Audley and Ela his wife did now enjoy [r].

An. MCCLXXI.   55, 56. *Henry III.*

This year March the thirteenth at Viterbo in Italy, Simon de Montfort and Guy his brother murdered Henry eldest son of Richard king of the Romans, whereby the inheritance of Ambrosden fell the next year to his younger brother Edmund. There is a Latin epistle from Charles king of Sicily to prince Edward, giving an account of this assassination, dated from Viterbo, &c. [s] Upon whose death his brother Edmund, then in Syria, returned back into England, and was joyfully received by his father [t].

The body of the said Henry murdered at Viterbo was brought to London May the fifth, his heart was preserved at Westminster, and the remainder of his body buried at his father's monastery of Hales [u].

About this time John St. John baron of Stanton remitted and quit

q Ex Orig. MS. penes D. Guil. Glynne, Bar.   r R. Dods. MS. vol. 42. f. 96. b.   s Cod. MS. Bodl. 91. f. 141.   t Chron. Tho. Wikes, sub an.   u Ibid.

claimed to Thomas Bacon of Rousham all right and title to five virgates of arable land, eight acres of meadow, and one mill in Weston,
which the said Thomas confirmed to the abbey of Oseney.

*Sciant præsentes et futuri quod ego Joannes filius Rogeri de S.
Joanne concessi remissi et omnino quietum clamavi pro me et hæredibus
meis Thomæ Bacun et hæredibus suis pro homagio et servitio suo totum jus et clamium quod habui vel habere potui in omnibus terris et
tenementis et uno molendino in Weston, &c.*

*Sciant præsentes et futuri quod ego Thomas Bacun de Rousham dedi
concessi et hac presenti charta mea confirmavi Deo et ecclesiæ S. Mariæ
de Osen. et Willielmo abbati v. virgatas terræ arabilis et octo acras
prati et unum molendinum cum pertin. in Weston, &c.* [x]

About St. Andrew's day died [y] Philip Basset baron of Wycomb,
and was buried at Stanley, who had been a benefactor to the priory
of Burcester of his ancestor's foundation, giving several lands by this
charter.

*Sciant præsentes et futuri quod ego Philippus Basset miles pro sa-
lute animæ meæ et animarum patris et matris meæ et animæ Fulconis
Basset quondam Londinensis episcopi fratris mei et animarum omnium
antecessorum meorum dedi concessi et hac præsenti charta mea confirmavi Deo et ecclesiæ beatæ Mariæ et S. Edburgæ virginis de Berencestria et canonicis ibidem Deo servientibus et in perpetuum servituris
in liberam puram et perpetuam elemosinam omnes terras et tenementa
cum pertinentiis quæ habui in Cliftone et Heentone et Dadyngtone in
comitatu Oxoniæ de dono domini Rogeri de Stampford, et omnes terras et tenementa cum pertinentiis quæ habui in Grymesbury in parochia de Bannebyri in comitatu Northamptoniæ de dono prædicti domini Rogeri habendas et tenendas de me et hæredibus meis prædictis
canonicis et eorum successoribus ibidem Deo servientibus et imperpetuum servituris in liberam puram et perpetuam elemosinam omnes
prædictas terras et tenementa cum homagiis redditibus servitiis releviis*

---

[x] Regist. Osen. MS. p. 319.   [y] Annal. Waverl. sub an. et Annal. Eccles. Wigorn.
sub an.

escaetis messuagiis terris pratis pasturis boscis molendinis stagnis vi-
variis aquis haiis fossatis liberis introitibus et exitibus et cum omnibus
aliis ad easdem terras et tenementa pertinentibus vel quoquo modo per-
tinere valentibus, libere quiete bene in pace et omnino integre absque
ullo retenemento.　Et ego dictus Philippus et hæredes mei warantiza
bimus defendemus et acquietabimus omnes prædictas terras et tene-
menta cum omnibus suis pertinentiis prædictis canonicis et eorum suc-
cessoribus ibidem Deo servientibus et in perpetuum servituris in li-
beram puram et perpetuam elemosinam contra omnes gentes.　Et ut
hæc mea donatio concessio et præsentis chartæ mea confirmatio et wa-
rantizatio mea firmum robur optineant imperpetuum præsenti scripto
sigillum meum apposui.　Hiis testibus; dominis Nicholao de Yat-
ingden, Thoma de Hederne, Richardo de Rulg, Rogero de Avmari,
Radulfo de Cestertone, Rogero de Lenne, Alano de Rumalii, militi-
bus, &c. [z]

The said Philip Basset had sold the manor of Sulthorn (now Souldern) to Ralph de Bray for forty marks of silver[a].　He died possessed of the manors of Kertlington, Chefield, and Hunington, com.
Oxon.[b] which, with the manors of Haselee, Ascote, and Peryton,
passed to Roger le Bigod earl of Norfolk and mareschal of England,
who had married Aliva the sole daughter and heir of the said Philip
Basset[c].

December the twelfth, Richard king of the Romans at his castle of
Berkamsted was taken with violent fits of the palsy, to the loss of his
tongue, and often of his senses; and continued in such desperate
condition till his death in April following.

Maud Longspe, widow of William Longspe, mother of Margaret
wife of Henry de Lacy earl of Lincoln and lord of the manor of
Burcester, &c. by letters this year made a grievous complaint to the
king, that John Giffard baron had taken her by force from her manor house at Kaneford, and carried her to his castle of Brimesfield,

[z] Mon. Ang. tom. 2. p. 284.　[a] R. Dods. MS. vol. 42. f. 101.　[b] Dugd. Bar. tom. 1.
p. 385.　[c] R. Dods. MS. vol. 82. f. 10. b.

and there kept her in restraint. He being thereupon sent for by the king, and told what was informed against him, denied the charge, saying, he took her not thence against her will: and tendered to the king a fine of three hundred marks for marrying her without his li_cence : of which the king accepted, upon condition that she made no farther complaint [d].

John Morel of Adyngrave having sold to John Fitz-Nigel jun. of Borstall one messuage and one hundred acres of land in the village and fields of Adyngrave and Crendon, &c. gave this letter of attorney to deliver possession.

Omnibus Christi fidelibus præsentes literas visuris vel audituris Johannes Morell de Adyngrave salutem in Domino sempiternam. Noverit universitas vestra me constituisse Sampsonem de Adingrave attornatum meum ad ponendum Johannem filium Nigelli jun. de Borstall nomine meo in seisina de omnibus terris et tenementis quæ habui in villa de Adingrave quæ quidem tenementa cum pertinentiis eidem Johanni filio Johannis filii Nigelli per chartam meam dedi tenenda sibi et hæredibus suis et assignatis in perpetuum. In cujus rei testimonium has literas meas fieri feci patentes. Dat. apud Brehull die S. Gregorii papæ anno regni regis Henrici filii regis Johannis quinquagesimo quinto. Valete [e].

In the year following Agnes Mildenhale, the widow of John Morell, did release and quit claim the said premises. *Hiis testibus ; domino Eustachio de Grenevill, Johanne filio Nigelli, Henrico de Grenevill, Johanne de Grenevill, Roberto de Sulgrave, Hugone de Winchindon, Nigello de Boys, et aliis. Dat. apud Brehull die Sabbati proxime ante festum S. Barnabæ apost. an. R. Ed. 1. [f]*

An. MCCLXXII. 56, 57. *Henry III.* 1. *Edw. I.*

Richard king of the Romans after his long paralytic illness died April the second at Berkamsted, his heart was preserved in the friar minor's church at Oxford, and his body interred in his own Cistertian

[d] Dugd. Bar. tom. 1. p. 500.   [e] Chartular. de Borstall. f. 12.   [f] Ibid.

abbey of Hales. He had been so great a patron of Walter de Merton, that this munificent prelate an. 1274. founded his college in Oxford, *pro salute animarum Henrici quondam regis Angliæ nec non Germani sui Ricardi Romanorum regis inclyti et hæredum suorum.* After his death on Wednesday before Palm-Sunday, an inquisition was taken of his lands in these parts, and it was returned upon oath, that the manors of Beckley, Ambrosden, Blackthorn within the said parish, and Willarston within the parish of Mixbury, were held by barony of the honor of St. Walery, that the advowsons of the churches of Beckley and Ambrosden belonged to the said manors, and the advowson of the church of Mixbury to the manor of Willarston; (and indeed it was seldom seen that the possession of the manor and patronage of the church were in several hands, before the perpetual advowsons were given to the monks;) that Simon St. Liz held one knight's fee of the said king of Almaign, that William le Brun and Robert de Fretwell held of him seven knight's fees in the village of Horton, that the said earl held the manor of Henly in this county, that his son Edmund was next heir, and on the feast day of S. Stephen last past was of the age of twenty-two years.

Extent. terrarum et tenement. domini regis Alman. de maneriis de Beckele et Ambredon et Blakethurn et Willarston, facta die Mercurii prox. ante festum Palmarum per Henricum de Canda &c. Qui dicunt super sacramentum suum quod maneria de Bekele, Ambreden, Blakethurn et Willarston tenebantur per baroniam de honore Sancti Walerici. Advocatio ecclesie de pertinet ad manerium de Beckele, Ambredon advocatio ecclesie spectat ad manerium. Et quod advocatio ecclesiæ de Mixebury pertinet ad manerium de Willarston. Dicunt etiam quod Simon de Sancto Licco tenet unum feodum militis de predicto rege Aleman. et Willielmus le Brun et Robertus de Fretvelle te-

---

nuerunt in villa de Horton VII. *feoda militum de dicto domino rege.*
Et dominus Edmundus est filius dicti domini R. Aleman. et heres suus
proximus et fuit ad festum Sancti Stephani anno preterito de etate
XXII. *annorum. Idem tenet man. de Henle in com. Oxon.* ⁱ

This Willarston in the parish of Mixbury seems to have been so
called from its situation nigh some noted well or spring. So Wyln-
hale, formerly wrote Wylenhale, is guessed to be so named from the
wells or springs in several parts; *willas* and *willon* in old English
were wells ʰ.

On the Friday before Palm-Sunday this inquisition was taken relating to the honor of Walingford.

Extenta domini regis Aleman. de burgo suo de Walingford in com.
Barock. facta die veneris prox. ante dominicam Palmarum anno regni
regis Henrici filii Johannis LXIᵗᵒ. *coram domino Fulcone de Rucote, &c.*
per sacramentum XII. *virorum videlicet Roberti de Lauchis, &c. qui*
dicunt per sacramentum suum quod dictus rex Aleman. tenuit dictum
burgum in capite de domino rege Anglie cum advocacionibus ecclesia
rum in dicto burgo quarum ecclesia Omnium Sanctorum valet cˢ. *ec-*
clesia S. Petri valet XLˢ. *et ecclesia Michaelis valet .. . Edmundus*
heres de etatis XXII. *annorum et amplius* ⁱ.

April 28. Edmund earl of Cornwall did his homage to the king and
had possession of his father's large inheritance. *Rex cepit homagium*
Edmundi filii et hæredis Ricardi regis Alemanniæ R. fratris defuncti.
28. *Apr.* Du Tillet by great mistake makes Edmund to have been
the elder brother of Henry, slain in Italy ᵏ.

About Michaelmas he married Margaret sister to Gilbert earl of
Glocester, and on the feast of St. Edward October the thirteenth, he
was knighted by the king with Henry de Lacy lord of Burcester,
who then received the earldom of Lincoln to that of Salisbury, which
in his wife's right he before enjoyed ¹.

ᵍ R. Dods. MS. vol. 64. p. 38. and Dugd. MS. vol. A. 2. p. 140.   ʰ Dugd. Antiq.
Warw. p. 149.   ⁱ R. Dods. MS. vol. 64. f. 38.   ᵏ Du Tillet, Recueil de Roys, p. 5·
¹ R. Dods. MS. vol. 46. p. 158.

November 16. died Henry the Third king of England. December
the seventh, Edmund earl of Cornwall brought his new bride to Walingford, and kept there a magnificent feast for the barons and great
men[m].

In this year James lord Audley broke his neck[n], and left Ela
daughter of William Longspe his widow in possession of Stratton,
and one half part of the manor of Wrechwick which her father had
given in marriage with her : which moiety of Wrechwick she gave to
the priory of Burcester, who before enjoyed the other half of the
said manor by the gift of Egeline de Courtney, and confirmation of
Richard de Camvill and Eustace his wife[o]; so as now the prior and
canons became possessed of the whole manor of Wretchwick and
Gravenhull-wood. The donation of Ela de Audley widow was thus.

Sciant præsentes et futuri quod ego Ela de Audithel quondam uxor
preclaræ memoriæ domini Jacobi de Audithel defuncti in pura vi
duitate ligia potestate et mera voluntate mea dedi concessi et hac præ
senti charta mea confirmavi Deo et ecclesiæ sanctæ Mariæ et S. Ed-
burgæ virginis de Berncester et canonicis ibidem Deo servientibus et
imperpetuum servituris pro salute animæ meæ et animæ domini Ja-
cobi de Audithel quondam domini mei prædicti et animarum patris
et matris meæ et antecessorum et successorum meorum in liberam et
puram et perpetuam eleemosinam totam terram meam quam habui vel
quoquo modo habere potui in villa de Wrechwick in com. Oxon. de
dono patris mei domini Willielmi Longspe cum messuagiis villanagiis
redditibus pratis pasturis liberis consuetudinibus et omnibus aliis per-
tinentiis ad dictam terram pertinentibus. Habenda et tenenda dictam
terram de me et hæredibus meis vel assignatis prædictis canonicis et
eorum successoribus libere quiete integre bene et in pace in liberam
puram et perpetuam eleemosinam ut prædictum est cum omnibus perti-
nentiis prænominatis quietam et solutam ab omnibus servitiis consue-
tudinibus curiarum sectis et sæcularibus demandis. Ego vero dicta
Ela et hæredes mei vel assignati totam prædictam terram cum omni-

[m] Chron. Tho. Wikes, sub an.   [n] Ibid.   [o] Dugd. Bar. tom 1. p. 748.

bus pertinentiis in liberam puram et perpetuam elemosinam sicut præ-dictum est versus omnes mortales in perpetuum warantizabimus acquie-tabimus et defendemus. Ut hæc autem mea donatio concessio et præ-sentis chartæ meæ confirmatio rata stabilis in perpetuum permaneat præsenti scripto sigillum meum apposui. Hiis testibus; dominis Rog. de Almari, Waltero de Langel, Ricardo de Povre, militibus; Ada le Gait, Willielmo de Avener, Johanne le Balimer, Willielmo la Megre, Roberto Clerico de Berncester, et aliis[p].

On the original parchment is a seal appending with the figure of a woman erect, bearing in one hand the arms of Audley, frette, and in the other the arms of Longspe, six lions rampant with this inscription, ✠ SIGILLUM ELE DE ALDITHLEG.

:An. MCCLXXIII. 1, 2. *Edward I.*

In a late trial William de L'isle had recovered the right of presentation to the church of Chesterton against John le Bret, and then conveyed his full right of patronage to Edmund earl of Cornwall, who now presented to the said church of Chesterton.

Archid. Oxon. 16. Ric. de Gravesend. Nobilis vir dominus Ed-mundus comes Cornub. presentat ad ecclesiam de Cestreton. Per breve regis patet quod Willielmus de Insula recuperavit presentationem suam ad ecclesiam de magna Cesterton versus Johannem le Bret et idem Wil-lielmus de Insula remisit totum jus suum quod habuit in advocatione dicte ecclesie dicto comiti et heredibus[q]

Within the same year the said earl of Cornwall presented to the church of * Munton in the archdeaconry of Northampton, and being patron of the abbey of Burnham did now grant licence of election to those sisters, who chose Maud de Dorkcestre abbess[r]. Henry de Lacy earl of Lincoln presented to the church of Wadanhawe in the archdeaconry of Northampton[s].

* Manton.

p Ex Orig. penes Hon. D. W. Glynne, Bar.　　q R. Dods. Extract. e. Reg. Linc. vol. 107. p. 119.　r Ib. f. 113.　s Ib. f. 103.

By inquisition taken this year, it appeared that Gilbert Clare earl of Glocester had seized one half of a knight's fee in Ludgarshall, which John de Trayly held of him, and that the said John de Trayly late lord of Ludgarshall held of the king *in capite* one plot of ground valued at 7^d. *per an.* and left heir Walter his son aged twenty-two years.

Bucks. Jur. dicunt quod comes Gloverniæ seisivit dimid. fcod. mil. in Ludgarshall quod dictus Johannes de Trayly de eo tenuit. Item jur. dicunt quod Johannes de Trayly quondam dominus de Ludgarshall tenuit de domino rege in capite unam placeam terræ quæ valet vii^d *per an.*[t]

Reginald bishop suffragan of * Glocester was substituted by Richard bishop of Lincoln to visit these parts of the diocese of Lincoln, and to consecrate new churches. On June the eighth he consecrated the church of Weston on the Green, dedicated to the Virgin Mary, to St. James the Apostle, and St. Nicholas the Confessor, devoting three altars in the said church to these respective saints, and ordaining that whosoever should make some oblation to any of the said altars, should for such devotion and offering have twenty days indulgence. Which grant runs thus.

Omnibus Christi fidelibus ad quos præsens scriptum pervenerit Reginaldus miseratione divina + Glovensis episcopus salutem in Domino

16. Ric. Gravesend. 1273.

Will. de Burencestr capellanus pres. per priorem et conv. de Burencestr ad vicar. eccl. de Burencestr vac. per mort. Rob'ti de Eylesbir. Non. Mart. mandat. J. archid'o Oxon.

Will. de Deen subd. pres. per nobilem virum d'num Edm. com. Cornub. ad eccl. de Cestreton vac. per mort. Rob. de Anna. 2 Non. Jun. pont. 16. 1274.

Mag'r Nich. de Bokelaunde subd. pres.

per d'num N. ep'um Winton ad eccl. de Eadburgbir vac. per mag'rum J. de Magdenestam archid'um Oxon. cui d'n's ep'us commisit vices suas. ib.

* Cloyne in Ireland.

+ *Clonensis*, in Hibernia.

R. Clonensis ep'us vice R. Linc. ep'i dedicavit eccl. de Elsefeld. 7. id. Jul. 1273.

Ordinatio vicarie de Ellesfeld facta fuit 15. cal. Feb. 1295. Lib. S. Fridesw.

Eccl'ia de magna Barthon dedicatur per

[t] R. Dods. MS. vol. 41. p. 3.

sempiternam. Cupientes ut altaria B. Mariæ semper virginis, B. Ja-
cobi apostoli, et Sancti Nicholai confessoris quæ sexto id. Junii an.
Dom. M.CC.LXIII. *vice venerabilis patris Ricardi Dei gratia Linc. epi-*
scopi in parochiali ecclesia de Westona ejusdem dioc. dedicavimus, con-
gruis honoribus frequententur, de Dei omnipotentis misericordia B.
Mariæ semper virginis, B. Jacobi et S. Nicholai omnibusque sancto-
rum meritis confidentes, omnibus vero contritis et confessis qui dicta
altaria singulis annis in præcipuis festivitatibus causa devotionis visi-
taverint et aliquid de bonis sanctis et Deo collatis subsidium charitatis
contulerint scilicet ad altare B. Mariæ 20. dies ad altare B. Jacobi
20. dies et totidem ad altare S. Nicholai de injuncta sibi penitentia
misericorditer relaxamus, dummodo loci diocesani hanc nostram ratam
habuerint indulgentiam. In cujus rei testimonium præsentibus literis
sigillum nostrum duximus apponendum. Dat. apud Weston die et anno
prænominatis [u].

That this church was meant of Weston on the Green appears from
the being recorded among the charts and donations of this parish to
the abbey of Oseney, with this note.

Memorandum quod abbas de Osenei habet totum manerium de
Weston de dono Henrici de Olleio ultimi cum visu Franciplegii et om-
nibus aliis pertinen. et habent insuper ibidem liberam warrenam de
concessione regis Henrici.

The same bishop in this circuit on the first day of June consecrated the church of Stane (now Stone) in com. Bucks. dedicated to
St. John Baptist, with forty days remission of penance to all that
should visit the church, and make some offering on the anniversary
of dedication. On July the fifth the church of St. Mary's at Water-
Piry with forty days indulgence, &c. Which church was given by
William son of William son of Helon, with consent of his wife

Reginaldum ep'um Clonensem vice et auctoritate Ri'ci Linc. ep'i XI. kal. Jul. 1273.
Reg. Osney, MS.

Eccl'ia de Waterpiry consecratur per
Reginald. Clonensem ep'um. 3. Non. Jul.
1273. ib. f. 120.

Reg. Osen. MS.

Emma daughter of Fulk Lovel, to the abbey of Oseney; confirmed to the said abbey by Emma in her pure widowhood, at the beginning of Hen. III.ˣ On July the sixth the chapel of Foresthulle dedicated to St. Nicholas the Confessor, &c. On July the twelfth the chapel of St. Martin's in Sandford belonging to the parish of Great-Barton, &c.

Edmund earl of Cornwall paid his relief for possession of his father's estate, of which a fair part was the barony of St. Walery in this county.

Oxon. Nova Oblata.

*Edm. de Alem. filius et hæres Ricardi quondam regis Alem...... de relevio suo de omnibus terris et tenementis quæ præfatus Ricardus tenuit in capite die quo obiit sicut captum in orig. LVI. R. Hen.*ʸ

An. MCCLXXIV. 2, 3. *Edward I.*

The abbot of Barlings presented a clerk to the church of Midlington ᶻ. On the octaves of Epiphany, Alesia de Lacy confirmed to John Sampson the grant made to him by Andrew le Gramere of the mills of Aberford in the county of York, dated with a seal appending bearing three wheat-sheafs ᵃ.

Ela widow of James baron Audley, did now again renounce all claim and title to two carucates of land with their appertenances in the manor of Wrechwick, which were given with her in marriage and remained to her in dowry, which she had about two years, since given to the prior and canons of Burcester.

Omnibus sanctæ matris ecclesiæ filiis præsens scriptum visuris vel

---

Rex universis.—Noveritis nos mutuo recepisse a dilecto consanguineo n'ro Edmundo comite Cornubie duo millia marcarum Thome Bek custodi garderobe n're die martis prox.

post festum Omn. S'ctorum anno regni n'ri secundo apud Northampton per manus Egidii de Audenarde liberaturum quam pecuniam solvere tenemur. T. R. apud Northampton. 2. Ed. I. 1274. Rymer. 2. p. 41.

ˣ R. Dods. MS. vol. 39. f. 97.   ʸ R. Dods. Extract. Rot. Pip. vol. 16. p. 3.   ᶻ R. Dods MS. vol. 107. p. 119.   ᵃ Ibid. vol. 154. f. 112.

3 E 2

*audituris Ela de Aldithleia quondam uxor Jacobi de Aldithleia salu-
tem in Domino sempiternam. Noverit universitas vestra quod ego in
libera viduitate mea et ligea potestate pro salute animæ et pro anima
Jacobi quondam viri mei concessi remisi et absolute quietum clamavi
pro me et hæredibus meis et assignatis omnibus et singulis Deo et ecclesiæ beatæ Mariæ et Sanctæ Edburgæ virginis de Berncester et canonicis ibidem Deo servientibus et in perpetuum servituris totum jus et
clamium quod habui vel aliquo modo habere potui in duabus carucatis
terræ cum pertinentiis suis in villa de Wrechwick in parochia de Berncester quas habui de dono domini Willielmi Longspei patris mei in
liberum maritagium in puram et perpetuam eleemosinam. Ita quod
nec ego nec hæredes mei vel assignati mei in prædicta terra cum pertinentiis seu earum parte aliquod jus vel clamium de cætero exigere
habere vel vendicare poterimus : et si fecimus, tenore præsentium illud
clamium irritum fore et inane fatemur et protestamur. Hanc autem
concessionem quietam clamationem et remissionem prædictis religiosis
contra omnes gentes warantizabimus acquietabimus et in perpetuum
defendemus. In cujus rei testimonium hoc præsens scriptum sigilli mei
impressione roboravi. Hiis testibus ; dominis Rogero de Aumari, Roberto filio ejus, Johanne filio Widonis, Roberto Malet, Johanne Carbonel, Ricardo Paupere, militibus. Johanne Blundo de Codesford,
Waltero de Crokesford, et multis aliis. Datum apud Stratton anno
regni regis Ed. secundo [b].*

To the original parchment is a seal appending with the same impress as that to her former deed, *sub. an.* 1272.

There is another original chart of confirmation, and full release

1274. 6. kal. Mart. ad preces d'ni R. ep'i
Rofens. commendavit d'nus ep'us eccl. de
Newenham mag'ro Petro de Abendon ad
ipsam presentato et habuit literam paten-
tem in forma consueta remota clausula usque ad sue beneplacitum voluntatis que in
prima concessione commende sibi facte de
eadem erat expressa.

Hen. de Skerling subd. pres. per abba-
tiss. et conv. de Alnistow ad eccl. de Godington vac. per resign. mag'ri Joh. de Fra-
visham. 10. kal. Apr.

[b] Ex Orig. penes hon. vir. D. Guil. Glynne, Bar.

to the same effect. *Hiis testibus; dominis Rogero et Roberto de Aumary, Johanne filio Wydonis, Roberto Malet, Johanne Carbonel. Henrico de Noeles, militibus. Johanne le Blund de Codesford, Johanne Hugone de eadem, Johanne de Boleme, Johanne de la Forde, et aliis*[c].

John de Grenevill, son of William de Grenevill of Chilton, granted and confirmed to John Fitz-Nigel jun. of Borstall, one messuage with a croft in the demesne of Adingrave, in consideration of one hundred shillings sterling. *Hiis testibus; domino Roberto Malet, Johanne Carbonel, Petro de Chalons, mil. Willielmo le Venur, Ricardo de Warnadeston, Henrico de Grenevill, Osberto de Culverdon, Johanne le Chivaler, Johanne de Brok, et aliis. Actum die Jovis proxime ante festum apostolorum Simonis et Judæ anno gratiæ* MCC. *septuagesimo quarto*[d].

Ralph son of Simon Frankleyn of Borstall had granted to John Fitz-Nigel jun. two roods of land in the field of Borstall for the yearly rent of one penny. *Hiis testibus; Waltero de Horton, Nigello de Boys de Brehull, Thoma Brun de Borstall, &c.* And Robert Frankleyn of Borstall granted half an acre of arable land in the field of Borstall for the yearly rent of one halfpenny. *Hiis testibus; Waltero de Horton, Nigello de Boys de Brehull, Thoma Brun de Borstall, &c.* The said Robert Frankleyn now granted to John Fitz-Nigel jun. half an acre of land in Midlehurst-furlong in the field of Borstall, for the rent of one rose on St. John Baptist's day, and half a mark of silver in hand. *Hiis testibus; Waltero de Horton, Thoma Brun de Borstall, Willielmo de Herford de eadem, Nigello de Boys de Brehull, Roberto Tulusa de eadem, Johanne Ferebraz, et aliis. Actum die Sabbati proxime post festum apostolorum Petri et Pauli anno regni domini Edw. secundo*[e]

John de Verdon, lord of the manor of Heth in this county, died on the twelfth of the calends of November 1274, leaving issue Theobald his son and heir, who in the following year doing his homage,

c Ex Orig. ibid.   d Ex Chartular. de Borstall. f. 19.   e Ib. f. 8.

and paying one hundred pounds for his relief, had livery of the said
manor of Heth, and all other his father's lands[f].

An. MCCLXXV. 3, 4. Edward I.

Within this third of Ed. I. an inquisition was taken in the city of
Lincoln concerning the custody of that castle, which because it relates not only to Henry de Lacy, now lord of the manors of Burcester and Midlington, but to the progenitors of his wife by whom
those manors came, and to Gerard de Camvill once lord of Midleton castle, and Nichola de Hay an eminent lady, all formerly concerned in these parts, it will be proper to recite it.

3. *Ed. I. Inquisitio facta per* XII. *fideles civitatis Linc. juratos co-*
ram dominis Willielmo de S. Omero et Warino de Chaucumbe justic.
domini regis ad hoc assignatos.

Dicunt quod castrum Lincoln. fuit quondam in manibus R. Ricardi
et postea in manu R. Johannis fratris ejusdem Ricardi et illud tenuit
in dominico una cum civitate Linc. et tunc idem Joh. rex tradidit cus-
todiam illius cuidam qui vocabatur Gerardus de Camvilla qui despon-
saverat dominam Nicholaam de la Hay qui idem tenuit dum vixit per

1275. Joh. Farnys subd. pres. per f'rem
W. priorem de Wara ad eccl. de Cherleton
super Ottemor vac. per mort. Will'i. 13. kal.
Maii anno 17. Ric'i Gravesend.

Eod. anno 1275. Henr. de Pavely pres-
b'r pres. per dominum Rob'tum Pavely mil.
ad eccl. de Wendlingbir vac. per mort ma-
g'ri Will'i. 2. Non. Nov. inquis. facta per
W. archid'um Oxon.

Will. de Caneford p'b'r pres. per abb. et
conv. de Barling ad eccl. de Midlington
vac. per mort. Valentine. 3. id. Jul. ib.

1275. 18. Ric'i Gravesend. Mag'r Will.
de Dunham p'b'r pres. per abb. et conv. de

Egnisham ad medietat. eccl. de Heyford
ad pont. vac. per mort. mag'ri Rob. de London. 9. kal. Dec.

Joh. de Audinardo ordinatus subdiac. 2.
kal. Mart. pont. 18. et in eccl'ia de Merse
in archidi'atu Buck. cujus custodiam jam-
diu tenuit rector canonice institutus ejusdem custodiam prius habuit d'nus Egidius
de Audinardo.

Joh. de Audinardo subdiac. 1277. pont.
19. Ric'i Gravesend. pres. per proc. prioris
et conv. Grestein ad eccl. de Merse. 13.
cal. Maii.

[f] Dugd. Bar. tom. 1. p. 473.

voluntatem domini regis et post decessum ejusdem Gerardi dicta do-
mina Nichola de la Hay tenuit idem ad voluntatem R. Johannis in
tempore guerre et in tempore pacis et post guerram accidit quod
dictus Johannes rex venit ad Linc. et dicta domina N. exivit ad por-
tam orientalem castri portans claves castri in manu sua et obviavit
dicto domino regi et obtulit ei claves tanquam domino et dixit quod
esset mulier magne etatis et quod multos labores et anxietates in dicto
castro sustinuerat et amplius talia non poterat sustinere. Et dictus
Johannes rex dulciter dixit, sustineatis si placeat adhuc, et ita habuit
custodiam castri toto tempore vite Johannis R. et post decessum Joh.
R. illa domina habuit custodiam illius in tempore R. H. patris regis
qui nunc est, sed per quot annos in temp. R. H. ignoramus. Et tunc
translatavit se dicta domina Nicholaa usque ad Swaneton et ibi obiit.
Et dominus H. rex tunc tradidit custodiam illius castri cuidam qui
vocabatur Philippus de Lascels et ille habuit custodiam per tres annos
vel plus et post ipsum Philippum quidam qui vocabatur Walterus de
Everwic habuit custodiam pro voluntate domini R. H. sed per quot
annos ignoramus : et postea accidit quod Willielmus de Longspe qui
obiit in Terra Sancta venit ad dominum R. H. et exoravit voluntatem
regis quod poterit perhendinare in dicto castro quum venturus esset
apud Lincoln et dominus H. rex concessit et perhendinare et custodiam
castri et sic tenuit per voluntatem regis : et post eum dominus Williel-
mus Longspe fil. ejus idem tenuit per voluntatem regis et post eum do-
minus Henricus de Lacy qui nunc est idem tenuit per concessionem
quam dominus rex H. pater domini regis nunc fecit Willielmo Longspe
antecessori uxoris predicti Henrici [g].

Sir Robert de Pavely, knight, presented to the church of Wendlebury [h].

About this time Henry vicar of Weston on the Green gave to the
monastery of Oseney the yearly rent of twelve shillings, in the village
of Weston and the fields of Blechesdon, for a pietance or over-com-
mons on the anniversary of his death, as also six acres of land with

g R. Dods. MS. vol. 89. f. 51.　　h Ib. vol. 107. p. 119.

meadows and appertenances in the fields of Blechesdon, &c. in this form of donation.

Sciant præsentes et futuri quod ego Henricus vicarius de Weston dedi et concessi et per chartam meam confirmavi Deo et ecclesiæ S. Mariæ de Osen. et canonicis in ea Deo servientibus annuum redditum XII. *sol. in villa de Weston quos percipere solebam annuatim videlicet de Gilberto de Weston* III. *sol. et* X. *denar. pro duabus acris terræ et dimid. in campis de Blechesdon et uno messuagio juxta cæmiterium ecclesiæ de Weston quæ de me tenet et de Reginaldo Pelipar* XVI. *denar. pro tribus rodis et una roda prati in campis de Blechesdon et uno messuagio juxta cæmiterium ecclesiæ de Weston et de Ada molendinario* IV. *sol. pro messuagio quod de me tenet in Weston et de Thoma de Mudlinton* II. *sol. pro messuagio quod de me tenet in Weston et pro terris quas idem Ada et Thomas de me tenent in campis de Blechesdon quos quidem quatuor solidos et duo solidos de tenementis prædictorum Adæ et Thomæ attornavi ad unam pietantiam faciendam in conventu Osneiensi annuatim in perpetuum in die anniversar. mei obitus pro anima mea. Dedi insuper et concessi prædictis ecclesiæ et canonicis* IV. *acras terræ cum pratis et pertin. suis in campis de Blechesdon quarum una acra jacet in cultura quæ vocatur Chippesen, alia jacet in cultura quæ vocatur Fenacre et jacet juxta terram abbatis de Godstow et tertia acra jacet in eadem cultura juxta le Forthodrove et extendit se in Hilleden et jacet juxta terram Rogeri d'Amory et quarta acra jacet in cultura quæ vocatur Renmeda et jacet juxta terram Ricardi Picun et quicquid in omnibus prædictis habui vel habere potui sine ullo retinemento* [i]

Margery Clement, one of the sisters in the nunnery of Stodley, was elected prioress of that house, by leave first obtained of Edmund earl of Cornwall patron.

18. *R. Gravesend; soror Margeria Clement electa in priorissam prioratus de Stodley petita prius et obtenta licentia eligendi a domino Ed. com. Cornub. dictæ domus de Stodley patrono* [k].

i Regist. Osen. MS. p. 321.   k R. Dods. MS. vol. 107. p. 120.

Nigh this time John Pufph, son of Robert Pufph miller in Burcester, granted to the prior and canons of that town all his right in one acre of arable land lying in a certain ground called Brodelond in the common field of Burcester, in consideration whereof the said prior and canons released to him and Muriel his wife twelve-pence yearly out of ten shillings annual rent due to the said convent.

Sciant præsentes et futuri quod ego Johannes Pufph de Berncester dedi et concessi et quietum clamavi pro me et hæredibus meis viris religiosis priori et conventui de Berncester totum jus et clamium quod habui vel aliquo modo habere potui in una acra terræ meæ arabilis quæ jacet in quadam cultura quæ vocatur le Brodelond in campo de Berncester habenda et tenenda prædictis religiosis et corum successoribus, &c. Pro hac autem donatione concessione quieta clamatione prædicti prior et conventus concesserunt et relaxaverunt pro se et successoribus suis mihi et Muriellæ uxori meæ duodecim denarios annuatim de decem solidis redditus quos sibi tenebant annuatim. Et ut hæc mea donatio concessio et quieta clamatio perpetuæ firmitatis robur obtineant præsenti chartæ sigillum meum apposui. Hiis testibus; Adam le Gayt, Willielmo le Megre, Johanne de Cotesford, Johanne filio Willielmi de Kertlington, Ricardo de Caune de eadem, Willielmo Paute, Roberto Clerico de Berncester, et aliis[1].

Nigh this time Henry Fitz-Gilbert of Borstall granted to John Fitz-Nigel jun. two roods of land in the field of Borstall for the yearly rent of one penny. *Hiis testibus; Waltero de Horton, Nigello de Boys de Brehull, Ricardo Taluse de eadem, Thoma Brun de Borstalle, Willielmo de Hereford de eadem, Johanne del Brok de Northmerston clerico, et aliis.* And William son of Nigel son of Peter le Myra of Borstall, granted to John, son of John Fitz-Nigel, all that messuage with its appertenances which Simon son of Baldwyn sometimes held of the abbot of Missenden in the village of Borstall, paying the yearly rent of one pound of cloves, and one mark of silver in hand. *Hiis testibus; domino Roberto Malet, domino Jo-*

[1] Ex Orig. penes D. Guil. Glynne, Bar.

hanne Carbonel, Henrico de Benson, Waltero le Chevaler, Galfrido de Wermenhal, Johanne de Esses, Waltero de Horton, Johanne Morell, Thoma de S. Andrea, Johanne de Broughton, Rogero le Serjant de Lutegarshall, Richardo de Halethon de eadem, et aliis [m].

In a court roll of the tenures and possessions of the abbey of Wo-born made this year, 3. Edw. I. it appears that the said abbot held in the lower Swanborn, four hides and a half of the honor of Brehull, by means of the heir of Braybrook, who held of the heirs of Henry de Clinton, and they of the king [n].

About this time Richard de Culne and Christina his wife released and quit claimed to the prior and convent of Burncester, all the right and claim which they had in two shillings yearly rent due from the said convent for one of their water-mills in Kertlinton, on the north bank of Cherwell. This was the chiefage, or lord's rent, which the convent bought off for twenty shillings.

Sciant præsentes et futuri quod ego Ricardus de Culne et Christina uxor mea unanimi assensu et plena voluntate dedimus concessimus re-misimus et præsenti scripto quietum clamavimus pro nobis et hæredi-bus nostris quiete et absolute religiosis viris priori et conventui de Burncester et eorum successoribus in liberam puram et perpetuam elec-mosinam totum jus et clamium quod habuimus vel quoquo modo habere potuimus in duobus solidis argenti annui redditus quos ab eis peteba-mus de uno molendino aquatico quod prædicti religiosi tenent in villa de Kertlinton et situm est ex parte boreali ripæ de Cherwelle de qui-bus etiam placitum motum fuit inter dictos religiosos et nos in com. Oxon. Habenda et tenenda dictos duos solidos annui redditus prædictis religiosis et eorum successoribus de nobis et hæredibus nostris ut præ-dictum est in perpetuum: pro hac autem donatione concessione remis-sione et quieta clamatione dederunt prædicti religiosi nobis viginti so-lidos sterlingorum præ manibus. Et nos prædictus Ricardus et Chris-tina uxor mea prædictos duos solidos argenti et hæredes nostri præ-dictos duos solidos annui redditus prædictis priori et conventui et

[m] Ex Chartul. de Borstall. f. 9.   [n] R. Dods. MS. vol. 67. p. 13.

eorum successoribus warant. &c.   In cujus rei testimonium nos præd. Ricardus et Christina hanc præsentem chartam sigillorum nostrorum muniminibus roboravimus.   Hiis testibus ; Adam de Gaii, Willielmo le Megre, Willielmo la Avener, Johanne filio Willielmi de Kertlinton, Johanne de Codesford, Waltero de Croxford, Willielmo Povre, et aliis °.*

To the original parchment two seals append, one impressed with a bird, the other with a stag, the inscriptions defaced.

An. MCCLXXVI.   4, 5. *Edward I.*

In this year's accounts of Richard de Holebrook, steward of the king's demesnes, there are receipts for the manor of Brill, *quod fuit antiquum dominicum regis* [p]

Nigh this time William Pyll of Oxford gave to the religious nuns of Stodley his house, called a school, between his own house on the north and the house of Lawrence Kepeharm on the south, in the parish of St. Mary's.

Sciant præsentes et futuri quod ego Willielmus Pylla de Oxon. dedi et concessi, &c.   Deo et B. Mariæ et domui de Stodley et sanctimonialibus ejusdem loci unam domum meam cum pertinentiis quæ dicitur schola quæ domus sita est inter gabulam tenementi mei ex parte boreali et gabulam tenementi Laurentii Kepeharm ex parte australi in parochia B. Mariæ virginis, &c. [q]

This house was after called the Stodley schools, and brought half a mark yearly rent to the said nunnery, as appears by inquisition of the sixth and seventh of Edw. I.

1276. Joh. de Burton p'b'r pres. per Walt. de la Peville ad eccl. de Hampton ad pontem vac. per mort. Rogeri. 9. kal. Oct. 19. Ric'i Gravesend.

1276. An. 20. Ric. Gravesend. Galfri-

dus de Crekelade p'b'r pres. per f'rem Rob. procuratorem Becci in Angl. ad eccl. de Cotesford vac. per mort. Rocelini. 11. kal. Jun.

° Ex Orig. penes D. W. Glynne, Bar.   [p] R. Dods. Extract. Rot. Pip. MS. vol. 16. p. 24.   [q] Ant. a Wood, Antiq. Oxon. l. 2. p. 13.

3 F 2

Sampson de Adingrave and Mary his wife granted and confirmed to John Fitz-Nigel jun. of Borstall, one messuage with a croft adjoining in the village of Adingrave, with sixteen acres and a half of arable land lying in several places in the fields of Adingrave and Acley. *Hiis testibus; Thoma de S. Andrea in Essendon, Waltero de Horton in eadem, Willielmo Colie in eadem, Johanne de Grenevil in Chilton, Henrico de Grenevil in eadem, magistro Waltero de Bidindon in Adingrave, Nicholao le Brun in Acley, Nigello Travers in eadem, Nigello de Bosco in Brehull, Johanne Ferebraz in eadem, et multis aliis. Datum apud Brehull die S. Luciæ anno regni regis Edwardi quarto*[r]. In the summer following this final agreement was made in the king's court at Westminster. *Hæc est finalis concordia facta in curia domini regis apud Westminster a die S. Johannis Baptistæ in quindecem dies anno regni regis Edwardi filii regis Henrici quarto coram magistro Rogero de Seyton, magistro Radulpho de Feringham, Thoma Weylond, Johanne de Lovetoft et Rogero de Leys, justit. et aliis domini regis fidelibus tunc ibi præsentibus inter Johannem filium Nigelli quer. et Samson. de Adingrave et Mariam uxorem ejus deforc. de uno messuagio triginta et sex acris terræ et dimidia et uno denario redditus cum pertin. in Adingrave et Acley unde placitum conventionis sum. fuit inter eos in eadem curia. Scilicet quod prædicti Samson et Maria recognoscunt prædictum tenementum cum pertin. esse jus ipsius Johannis et illud ei reddiderunt in eadem curia et remiserunt et quietum clamaverunt de se et hæredibus ipsius Mariæ prædicto Johanni et hæredibus suis in perpetuum. Et pro hac recognitione fine et concordia idem Johannes dedit prædictis Samson et Mariæ centum solidos sterlingorum*[s].

Edmund earl of Cornwall presented to the church of Leir in the archdeaconry of Leicester, in right of the custody of the lands and heir of Henry de Hastings, the advowson of which church he recovered in the king's court against John son of William de Leyra[t].

---

[r] Ex Chartular de Borstall. f. 13.   [s] Ibid. f. 15.   [t] R. Dods. MS. vol. 107. f. 109.

An. MCCLXXVII. 5, 6. *Edward I.*

I find preserved in a long slip of parchment a register for this year of the receipts and dues of the priory of Burcester, given in by their respective stewards, and by their other officers, granger, cook, sacrist, and bursars, before the supprior, William de Thornberg, Walter de Oxon, and Stephen de Oxon, deputed auditors : whereby it appears by the bursar's accounts, that their receipts did exceed their expences 25^l. 6^s. 5^d. *ob.*

The title is this, *Registrum priorat. Berncester de anno R. R. E. quinto.*

The names of those places for which their stewards accounted are Clifton, Sutton, Caversfield, Westkote, Arnkote, Beaumund; and their officers that accounted are *grangiarius, coquarius, sacristarius, bursarius.*

For an instance of the rest, I shall transcribe only the first account, that of Clifton, with that of Arnkote within my parish of Ambrosden, and the concluding accounts of the bursars.

CLIFTON.

Md. quod die proxima post festum Sancti Michaelis anno reg. E. sexto computavit Johannes Cunon præpositus de Clifton de manerio de Clifton de omnibus receptis et expensis per ipsum factis ab in-crastino Sancti Michaelis anno reg. E. quinto usque festum Sancti Martini evangelistæ anno prædicto et ab eodem die et anno computat Johannes Willard præpositus de Clifton modo prædicto usque in crastinum Sancti Michaelis anno reg. E. sexto coram dominis . . . . suppriore. Willielmo de Thornberg, Waltero de Oxon. Steph. de Oxon. auditoribus deputatis. Et omnibus computatis et rite allocatis tenetur Johannes Willard domui in XVIII^s. IV^d. *et remanet in granario* V. *quarteria et dimidium frumenti.* IV. *boves,* VI. *mutilones, et sex africanæ fæminæ,*

1277. Litera regis de lite inter Edmun-   Alemanniæ. Rymer, 11. p. 87.
dum com. Cornub. et Beatricem reginam

II. *pullani fœmini*, VIII. *boves*, XI. *vaccœ*, I. *bovett. mas.* IV. *boviculœ fem.* V. *vituli*, LX. *casei.*

ARNEKOTE.

Md. quod die et anno supradictis computat Walterus de Gaung ser-
viens de Arnikote coram aud. &c. de omnibus receptis et expensis per
ipsum factis in dicto manerio ab in-crastino Sancti Michaelis an. reg.
Ed. vᵗᵒ. *usque ad diem lunœ proxime post festum Sancti Swithini anno*
prœdicto et ab eodem festo die et an. comp. Johannes de Coless eodem
modo usque ad in-crastinum SanctiMichaelis an. reg. E. vrᵗᵒ. *et sic*
omnibus computatis et allocatis tenetur dictus Johannes domui in vrˢ.
vrrᵈ. *ob. quad. et rem. in granario frumenti quarterium, brasii* VIII.
quarteria, v. *et dim. pisarum et de instauramento* III. *jumenta*, III.
pulli masculi, I. *fœm.* XVI. *boves*, I. *bovett.* I. *juvencus*, II. *bovitil. masc.*
II. *sues*, XIV. *porci*, V. *capones.* I. *gallus*, IX. *gallinœ*, V. *pullani.*

BURSAR.

Md. quod die et anno supradictis computaverunt fratres Radulfus
de Meriton et Stephanus de Oxon. de bursar. domus Berncester coram
auditor, &c. de omnibus receptis et expensis per ipsos factis in dicto of-
ficio a festo Sancti Michaelis an. reg. E. vᵗᵒ. *usque ad idem festum an.*
reg. E. vrᵗᵒ. *et sic continuandum usque ad festum Nicholai an. reg. E.*
vrᵗᵒ. *et sic omnibus computatis et rite allocatis excedunt expensas re-*
cépta xxvˡ. vrˢ. vᵈ. *ob.* ᵘ

On the Wednesday after St. James's-day, in this fifth of Edw. I.
by indenture dated at Missenden, Richard de la Vache granted and
confirmed to Walter prior of Berncester, and to the convent of the
said place, all the land, meadow, &c. which he held by the gift of
Hamo de Gattone in the village of Wrechwike, paying yearly to him
and his heirs five marks and a half, and in default of payment it
should be lawful for the said Richard and his heirs to distrain the

---

ᵘ Ex Orig. penes hon. D. Guil. Glynne, Bar.

goods and chattels on all the lands of that convent in Wrechwike, as well on that fee which they before held, as on that which was now granted.

Sciant præsentes et futuri quod ego Ricardus de la Vache dedi concessi et hac præsenti charta mea confirmavi Waltero priori de Berncestria et ejusdem loci conventui et eorum successoribus totam terram illam pratum et villanos cum villanagiis omnibus catallis et tota sequela ipsorum quæ habui ex dono domini Hamonis de Gattons in villa de Wrechwike cum omnibus libertatibus et pertinentiis suis. Habenda et tenenda de me et hæredibus meis vel meis assignatis prædictam terram pratum et villanos, &c. reddendo annuatim mihi et hæredibus vel quibuscunque meis assignatis prædicti prior et conventus et eorum successores quinque marcas et dimid. videlicet ad festum beatæ Mariæ in martio triginta sex solidos et octo denarios, &c. et capitalibus dominis feodi unum denarium pro omnibus servitiis consuetudinibus exactionibus et omnibus sæcularibus demandis. Et ego Ricardus de la Vache et hæredes mei dictam terram &c. warantizabimus &c. Et si predictos priorem et conventum vel eorum successores prædictum redditum in parte vel in toto terminis præscriptis solvendo cessare contigerit, volunt prædicti prior et conventus &c. quod liceat prædicto Ricardo &c. prædictos priorem &c. per omnia bona sua &c. in omnibus terra de Wrechwike &c. distringere &c. In cujus rei testimonium præsenti chartæ in modum cyrographi confectæ partes alternatim sigilla sua apposuerunt. Hiis testibus; dominis Rogero de Aumari, Roberto Malet de Langleye, Johanne Carbonel, Willielmo Tryvet, Johanne de Cheyne, Roberto de Aumari, Johanne Heyrmit, militibus. Johanne le Waleys, et aliis. Dat. apud Messenden die Mercurii proxime post festum S. Jacobi anno regni R. Edwardi quinto [x]*.*

To the original indenture a seal appends with the impress of three lions rampant, with this inscription, ✠ Sigill Ricardi De La Vache.

The arms of this family were gules, three lions argent, with a label, cheque, or and azure [y]

---

[x] Ex Orig. penes D. Guil. Glynne, Bar.   [y] R. Dods. MS. vol. 35. f. 104.

The same grant was recited and confirmed by Richard de la Vache in another charter dated at Chalfhunt, in the octaves of the Assumption of the virgin Mary, 5. Edw. I. [z]

Osbert vicar of the church of Merton was prosecuted by Thomas le Camvill and Elizabeth his wife, for proceeding in a cause before the ecclesiastical court against the king's prohibition. Whether this be meant of the vicar of Merton next adjoining to Ambrosden, or of Merston near Oxford, is not so plain [a].

Henry Lacy, in right of his wife Margaret lord of Burcester and Midlington, had now livery of the profits which his ancestors received in right of the earldom of Lincoln, with all arrears from the time he was by king Hen. III. girt with the sword of that earldom [b]: for which the king issued out this clause writ to the treasurer and barons of his exchequer. *Rex thesaurario et baronibus suis de scaccario et camerariis suis salutem. Mandamus vobis quod dilecto et fideli nostro Henrico de Lacy com. Linc. faciatis habere feodum suum quod percipere debet et antecessores sui in com. Linc. percipere consueverunt ad scaccarium prædictum nomine comitatus una cum arreragiis suis a die quo dictus comes arma militaria a domino H. rege patre nostro cepit*

An. MCCLXXVII. 5, 6. Edw. I.

Ricardus Linc. ep'us religiosis viris abb'i et conv. de Hegles, ord. Cisterc. salut. Cum nobilis vir d'n's Edmundus com Cornub. cujus predecessores domum vestram fundaverunt et bonis propriis dotaverunt divine pietatis intuitu numerum monachorum ad augmentum divini cultus augeri desiderans in eadem nobis humilime supplicaverit ut de Hamelhamstede et de Northle n're dioc. eccl'ias cum capellis de Bovendone et Slaverdene dicte eccl'ie de Hamelhamstede spectantibus, quarum advocationes vobis liberaliter concessit ut adjec-

tione decem monachorum vestri conventus sacer numerus amplietur, domui v're appropriare curaremus—prescriptas eccl'ias vobis et succ. v'ris in pios et proprios usus —concedimus—salvis archid'o Hunt. 5. sol. annuis pro eccl'ia de Hemelhamstede et archid'o Oxon. 4. sol. ann. de eccl'ia de Northle — pro recompensatione juris sequestri sui in eisdem. dat. 7 kal. Mart. 1277. pont. 20.

Joh. Linc. ep'us confirmat 6. id. Jun. 1303. Ordinatio vic. de Northle sequitur. Reg. Dalderby.

---

[z] Ex Autog. penes D. W. Glynne, Bar.   [a] W. Prynne, Histor. Col. tom. 3. p. 1217.
[b] Dugd. Bar. tom. i. p. 104.   [c] R. Dods. MS. vol. 110. p. 79.

et cinctus fuit gladio comitatus illius. T. R. apud Westm' IV. *die Maii* [c].

Under this year, in the register of Egnesham, are recorded the pensions paid to the said abbey out of some churches in the deanery of Burcester. *An.* MCCLXXVII. *decan. de Berncester.* *Abbas de Egnesham percipit in Heyford - Warin* VIII'. *inde decim.* IX[d]. *In Heyford ad pontem de annua pensione* XX'. *inde decim.* II. *sol. Item de pensione ecclesiæ de Sulthorn* c. *sol. inde decim.* x. *sol. Item de decima in Berncester* XII'. *inde decim.* XII[d]. [d]

On the vigil of St. Luke the Evangelist died Beatrix de Famestaiz, the relict of Richard king of the Romans, and was buried in the house of the Frier-minors in Oxford [e].

AD. MCCLXXVIII. 6, 7. *Edward I.*

Edmund earl of Cornwall lord of Ambrosden founded the chapel of St. Nicholas in his castle of Walingford, and endowed it with 40[l]. *per an.* in Wareberrewe and Shillingford for the maintenance of a master, five chaplains, six clerks, and four cofferers: the charter of foundation is preserved by the industrious Mr. Dodsworth [f].

In the scutage for the king's expedition into Wales assessed at forty shillings the knight's fee, our Edmund earl of Cornwall paid twenty pounds for his ten knight's fees of the barony of S. Walery; and Henry Lacy earl of Lincoln forty shillings for one knight's fee in Midlinton.

Oxonia Scutagium Wallie. Scuto assesso ad XL'
Edm. com. Cornub. heres com. Ric. f'ris R. H. XX[l]. *de* x. *feod. Thom. de S'co Walerico.*
Willi'us Lungespe XL'. *de* 1. *feodo Gerardi de Camvill in Midlington* [g].

An. MCCLXXVIII. 6. 7. Edw. I.
1278. Will. de Brampton subd. pres. per
d'num Rog. de Insula mil. ad mediet. eccl.

de Heyford vac. per mort. Will'i. 6. kal.
Martii. 21. Ric'i Gravesend.

c R. Dods. MS. vol. 110. f. 79.   d Regist. Egnesham, MS. p. 2.   e Ex Chron. MS. apud J. Lel. Collectan. tom. 2. p. 341.   f R. Dods. MS. vol. 130. f. 126.   g R. Dods. MS. Rot. Pip. vol. 16. f. 48.

One B. de Berincester, a monk of Egnesham, had a mind to change his station, and enter into some more strict order of religion, which desire was granted by special charter running thus.

Omnibus Christi fidelibus ad quos præsentes literæ pervenerint I. miseratione divina abbas de Egnesham et ejusdem loci conventus salutem in Domino. Cum dilectus nobis in Christo frater B. de Birencester commonachus noster instinctu Spiritus Sancti ad arctiorem religionem firmiter convolare proposuit ut asserit. Nos unanimi consensu eidem instanter petenti condescendentes licentiam concessimus specialem dummodo introitum suum, &c. In cujus rei testimonium sigilla nostra præsenti chartæ sunt appensa. Dat. apud Egnesham die lunæ proxime post festum apostolorum Petri et Pauli, A. D. m.cc.lxxviii[h]

The king at Woodstock in February sent a prohibition relating to some tithes within the demesnes of Edmund earl of Cornwall[i]: who in this year presented to the church of Sautresdon in the archdeaconry of Bucks[k]

Thomas Pech, son of William Buttok of Horspath, with consent of Agnes his wife, daughter of John Morell, had granted and confirmed several lands in Adingrave and Acley to Sir John Fitz-Nigel of Borstall, for which this fine was now passed in the king's court at Westminster.

Hæc est finalis concordia facta in curia domini regis apud Westminster a die S. Johannis Baptistæ in quindecem dies anno regni regis Edwardi filii regis Henrici sexto coram magistris Rogero de Leyton, Thoma Weylond, Johanne de Lovetot et Rogero de Leye justit. et aliis domini regis fidelibus tunc ibi præsentibus inter Johannem filium Nigelli quer. et Thomam Pech et Agnetem uxorem ejus deforc. de uno messuagio duobus croftis et una virgata terræ cum pertin. in Ardingrave et Acley unde placitum conventionis sumptum fuit inter eos in eadem curia scilicet quod prædictus Thomas et Agnes recogn. prædictum tenementum cum pertinentiis esse jus ipsius Johannis et illud ei

---

[h] Regist. Egnes. MS.   [i] Seld. Hist. of Tithes, p. 356. 357.   [k] R. Dods. MS. vol. 107. f. 113.

reddiderunt in eadem curia et remiserunt et quieta clamaverunt de se et hæredibus ipsius Agnetis prædicto Johanni et hæredibus suis in perpetuum. Et pro hac recognitione fine et concordia idem Johannes concessit pro se et hæredibus suis quod ipsi de cætero reddent singulis annis prædictis Thomæ et Agneti tota vita utriusque ipsarum Thomæ et Agnetis tria quarteria frumenti tria quarteria avenarum et unum quarterium fabarum ad duos terminos scilicet medietatem in quindena S. Michaelis et aliam medietatem ad festum beatæ Mariæ in Martio: et post mortem utriusque ipsorum Thomæ et Agnetis idem Johannes et hæredes sui erunt quieti de solutione prædicti bladi in perpetuum[1].

An. MCCLXXIX. 7, 8. *Edward I.*

Richard king of the Romans at his death had left provision for three secular priests to pray for his soul: his son and heir Edmund earl of Cornwall having a greater opinion of the regulars, would have that office for his father performed by six Cistertian monks, to which purpose he built and endowed the monastery of Reuley, de Loco Regali, in the north suburbs of Oxford, sometime called North-Oseney.

Edmundus com. Cornubiæ fundavit Oxon. monasterium Cister. monachorum ea intentione videlicet ut pro tribus sacerdotibus secularibus quos pater ejus Ric. pro anima sua divina voluit celebrare, sex monachi de quibus magne confidebat Deum devotius exorarent[m].

This citation of Dugdale was from the annals of the church of

1279. 22. Ric'i Gravesend. Tho. de Capella subd. pres. per d'num regem ad eccl. de Blechesdon vac. per mort. Joh'is.

Miracula multa Deus ostendit in capella de Abendon, quam Edmundus comes Cor-

nubiæ præcedenti anno admonitus in somnis ædificavit in loco, ubi B. Edmundus confessor communem accepit nativitatem. Annal. Wigorn. Whartoni Ang. Sac. P. 1. p. 510.

[1] Ex Chartul. de Borstall. penes D. Joh. Aubrey, Bar.   [m] W. Dugd. Analect. e. MS. Chron. vol. M. p. 34.

Worcester, since printed, where this foundation is recorded under the year 1281 [n].

When he founded this convent, he excepted within the limits of the said house ground sufficient to hold his court for his honor of St. Walery [o].

The said earl in his charter of foundation gave them his whole manor of Erdington, with his mills in Kersinton or Gersingdon, two parks, and his whole wood in Netlebed, (in which manor Oliver de Standford in 27. Edw. I. held some land *per serjantiam espicurnantiæ cancellaria domini regis*, by the office of spigurnel or sealer of the king's writs in Chancery [p],) all his land in the village of Willauston or Willarston in the parish of Mixbury, with sixty shillings yearly rent paid by the monks of Tame out of Stoke-Talmach. This abbey was augmented by the Cistertian abbey of Pynn in Poictiers, who resigned to this new foundation all their lands in England, for the yearly rent of three marks [q].

To prove the corruption of this age in excessive pluralities, we may note that in this year Bogo de Clare, rector of St. Peter's in the East, Oxon. was presented by the earl of Glocester to the church of Wyston in the county of Northampt. and obtained leave to hold it with one church in Ireland, and fourteen other churches in England, all which benefices were valued at 228[l]. 6[s]. 8[d]. [r]

Sir Hugh de Plessets, baron of Hokenorton and Kidlington, com. Oxon. holding Mussewell within the parish of Ambrosden from the abbey of Missenden com. Bucks. did now grant to John Fitz-Nigel jun. one carucate of land in Mussewell within the forest of Bernwood, with a mill, closes, commons, &c. by this charter.

Sciant præsentes et futuri quod ego Hugo de Plessetis dedi et concessi et præsenti charta mea confirmavi Johanni filio Nigelli de Borstall juniori pro homagio et servitio unum messuagium et unam carucatam

[n] Annal. Eccles. Wigorn. in Whartoni Anglia Sac. pars 1.　• R. Dods. MS. vol. 39. f. 96.　[p] Blount, Ant. Ten. p. 72.　[q] Mon. Ang. tom. 1. p. 935.　[r] R. Dods. MS. vol. 107. f. 133.

terræ cum pertinentiis in Mussewell infra forestam de Bernewode cum molendino clausis et omnibus communibus viis semitis pratis pasturis pascuis et omnibus aliis rebus et pertinentiis ad prædictam terram quo-cunque modo pertinentibus sine aliquo retinemento habendum et tenen dum omnia prædicta tenementa cum omnibus pertinentiis suis de me et hæredibus meis vel assignatis libere quiete et hæreditarie in perpetuum, reddendo inde annuatim mihi et hæredibus meis duas marcas argenti ad duos anni terminos : videlicet in festo annuntiationis beatæ Mariæ unam marcam et ad festum S. Michaelis unam marcam pro omnibus servitiis curiarum sectis auxiliis herietis et omnibus consuetudinibus exactionibus et demandis ad me et hæredes meos vel ad prædicta tene-menta quocunque modo pertinentibus. Et ego prædictus Hugo et hæ-redes mei vel assignati omnia prædicta tenementa cum omnibus per-tinentiis suis contra omnes gentes per prædicta servitia warantiza-bimus acquietabimus et defendemus in perpetuum. Et pro hac mea donatione concessione warantia acquietantia et defensione et præsentis chartæ confirmatione dedit mihi prædictus Johannes quinquaginta marcas argenti præ manibus. Et quia volo quod omnia prædicta firma et stabilia in perpetuum permaneant, præsentem chartam sigilli mei im-pressione roboravi. Hiis testibus ; domino Roberto Malet, domino Jo-hanne Carbonel, domino Ricardo le Povre, domino Willielmo le Povre, militibus ; Johanne filio Nigelli seniore, Thoma de S. Andrea, Ricardo de Bellofago, Waltero de Horton, Philippo Munekan, Johanne de Grenevill, Nicholao de Brun, Galfrido de Burton, Nigello de Bosco, Nigello Travers, et aliis. Datum in festo circumcisionis Domini anno regni regis Edwardi filii regis Henrici septimo .*

This land in Mussewell had been demised by the said Sir Hugh de Plessets to Sir Richard le Povre, knight, during his life, who for a valuable consideration had quitted his interest for his said term of life, and a farther confirmation was made of it to John Fitz-Nigel jun. by this second charter.

Universis præsentes literas visuris vel audituris dominus Hugo de Plessetis miles salutem in Domino. Cum dimiserimus domino Ricardo

---

le Povre militi terram nostram de Mussewell in foresta de Bernewode cum omnibus pertinentiis suis ad terminum vitæ suæ, et nos eidem Ricardo satisfecimus de termino suo, qui nobis plenam seisinam fecit die lunæ proxime post circumcisionem Domini anno regni regis Edwardi septimo : et nos prædictam terram cum omnibus pertinentiis suis integraliter Johanni filio Nigelli juniori de Borstall dedimus et charta nostra confirmavimus secundum tenorem chartæ nostræ quam de nobis habet solvendo nobis et hæredibus sive assignatis nostris duas marcas argenti annuatim, videlicet ad festum beatæ Mariæ in Martio unam marcam et ad festum S. Michaelis unam marcam. Volumus et concedimus pro nobis et hæredibus vel assignatis nostris quod dictus Johannes filius Nigelli distringat vel dampna habeat seu expensas per dom. abbatem de Missenden vel successores suos vel de quibuscunque aliis pro prædictis duabus marcis temporibus præteritis vel futuris terminis prædictis non solutis : et quod nos vel quicunque tenent seu tenuerint terras nostras de Missenden, Witham, Cudlinton, vel aliquas alias terras nostras sive fuerint hæredes nostri sive assignati satisfacient dicto Johanni et hæredibus suis et assignatis de dictis dampnis et expensis siquas habent vel habuerint secundum quod simplici eorum verbo monstrare poterint sive aliquo alio genere probationis. Et quod quilibet justitiarius vice-comes vel ballivus nos et hæredes et assignatos nostros distringere possint per bona nostra mobilia et immobilia et hominum nostrorum et difforciationem tenere quousque dicto Johanni et hæredibus sive suis assignatis plenarie fuerit satisfactum de dictis dampnis et expensis ut prædictum est. In cujus rei testimonium has literas meas dicto Johanni et hæredibus suis vel assignatis fieri fecimus patentes. Hiis testibus ; domino Roberto Malet, domino Johanne Carbonel, domino Petro de Calivis, domino Willielmo le Povre, Galfrido de Burton, Johanne filio Nigelli sen. Ricardo de Bellofago, Johanne de Grenevill, Willielmo de S. Audoeno, Waltero de Horton, Nicholao le Brun, et aliis. Dat. apud Cudelinton die Sabbati proxime post Epiphaniam Domini anno regni regis supradicto[t]

After which, the said Sir Hugh de Plessets released the yearly rent

---

[t] Ex Chartular de Borstall. MS. f. 32.

of two marks, and reserved only the acknowledgment of one clove to be paid at Missenden on Christmas-day.

Omnibus &c. Hugo de Plessetis miles &c. Concessimus Johanni filio Nigelli de Borstall &c. unum messuagium et unam carucatam terræ cum pertin. infra forestam de Bernwode in quodam loco qui vocatur Mussewell, &c. reddendo inde annuatim duas marcas argenti, &c. reddendo inde mihi et hæredibus meis unum clavum gariophyli tantum apud Messenden ad Natale Domini, &c. Hiis testibus; domino Roberto Malet, domino Johanne Carbonel, domino Willielmo le Povre, domino Waltero de Withull, Johanne filio Nigelli seniore, Galfrido de Burton, Thoma de S. Andrea, Henrico Dimmok, Willielmo le Mare, &c. Hoc scriptum factum fuit in festo S. Dionysii anno regni regis Edwardi filii regis Henrici septimo [u].

On the Monday after New-year's day, Sir Richard Povre, knight, in consideration of twenty marks of silver, had remitted and quit claimed all his right to the said messuage and one carucate of land in Musewell, by this deed.

Universis, &c. Ricardus Povre miles salutem. Sciatis me quietum clamasse Johanni filio Nigelli de Borstall juniori totum jus et clamium quod habui vel habere potui in uno messuagio cum una carucata terræ quæ vocatur Musewell, &c. Pro hac autem remissione, &c. dedit mihi prædictus Johannes quadraginta marcas argenti præ manibus, &c. Hiis testibus ; domino Willielmo le Povre, Galfrido de Burton, Johanne filio Nigelli de Borstall, Willielmo de S. Owen, Ricardo de Beufo, Nicholao le Brun de Acley, Waltero de Horton, Roberto Tulus, et multis aliis. Dat apud Musewell die lunæ proxime post festum circumcisionis Domini anno regni regis Edwardi septimo [x].

An. MCCLXXX. 8, 9. Edward I.

Edmund earl of Cornwall farther endowed his collegiate chapel within his castle of Walingford, thus noted in the travels of Jo. Le land. 𝔗𝔥𝔢𝔯𝔢 𝔦𝔰 𝔞 𝔠𝔬𝔩𝔩𝔢𝔤𝔦𝔞𝔱𝔢 𝔠𝔥𝔞𝔭𝔢𝔩 𝔢𝔪𝔬𝔫𝔤 𝔱𝔥𝔢 𝔟𝔲𝔦𝔩𝔡𝔦𝔫𝔤𝔰 𝔴𝔦𝔱𝔥𝔶𝔫 𝔱𝔥𝔢

---

[u] Ex Chartular. de Borstall. MS. f. 33.   [x] Ib.

3 ꝺike, Eꝺmunꝺ erle of Cornewale sunne to Richarꝺ king of the Romains was the first founꝺer anꝺ enꝺower of this college.—By the patents anꝺ ꝺonations of Eꝺmunꝺe erle of Cornwaul anꝺ lorꝺ of the honor of Wallingeforꝺ, ther wer 14 paroch chirches in Walingforꝺ [y]

A frequent place of residence to the said earl and his father was the capital seat of the honor of St. Walery, at Beckley, on the north side upon the hill where a stone pigeon-house now stands, and where are visible remains of the foundations of that palace. This town of Beckley had a reputation for the relicks of St. Donanwerdh, (I suppose,) a British saint, as I find entered among the collections of Leland:

  S. Brenwaldus apud Bamptonam.
  S. Donnanuerdh apud Beckeleiam.
  S. Romwaldus apud Bukingham [z].

June the second, the said Edmund earl of Cornwall granted to his servant John de le Russe two pieces of meadow lying near the Thames, called Portires Eytes, for the yearly rent of one rose to be paid in the castle of Walingford on Midsummer-day, by this charter.

Noverint universi fideles quod Edmundus comes Cornubiæ dedit concessit et hoc præsenti scripto suo confirmavit dilecto servienti suo Johanni de la Russe duas placias prati quæ jacent prope Thamisiam quæ vocatur Portires-Eytes, &c. reddendo inde annuatim prædicto Edmundo comiti et hæredibus suis unam rosam in festo nativitatis beati Johannis Baptistæ in castro de Walingford pro omni servitio exactione et demanda. In cujus rei testimonium præsenti scripto bi-, partito tam dictus Edmundus comes quam dictus Johannes sigilla sua apponi fecerunt. Hiis testibus; domino Russel tunc seneschallo honoris de Walingford, Statio Clement, Johanne de Louches, Johanne Balistario, Henrico Yvone, et aliis. Dat. apud London. secundo die Junii anno regni regis Edwardi octavo [a]

The manor of Godington in this neighbourhood, the late posses-

---

[y] Lel. Itin. vol. 2. p. 12, 13. [z] Lel. Collectan. MS. tom. 2. p. 369. [a] Ex Chartul. Borstall. sub titulo Clapcote, f. 29.

sion of Robert de Camvill, falling into the Queen's hands, was by
her given to Wido Ferrers and his heirs.

*Alianora regina uxor regis concessit Guidoni Ferrar p. servit. totum
manerium de Godindon quod fuit domini Roberti de Camvill in com.
Oxon. tenend. dict. Guidoni et hæredibus. Dat. per reginam 2. Feb.
8. Ed. I.*[b]

Nigh this time Alice de Langley, widow, granted and confirmed
to Thomas, son of Matthew of Berncester, for his service and homage one plot of land in the village of Berncester, which plot of
ground lay near to the messuage of Nicholas ad Fontem, and contained in breadth fifty-two feet, and in length the same dimension
with the messuage and curtilage of William Carpenter, with full liberty to give or sell the said plot to any persons except to the Religious and the Jews; reserving the suit and service of her court and
mill of Bigenhull, with the toll of corn and malt; paying two shillings yearly rent, and half a mark in hand.

*Sciant præsentes et futuri quod ego Alicia de Langley in libera vi-
duitate dedi concessi et hac præsenti charta mea confirmavi Thomæ
filio Matthæi de Berncester pro servitio suo et homagio unam placiam
terræ in villa de Berncester videlicet placiam illam quæ jacet juxta
messuagium Nicholai ad Fontem et dicta placia terræ continet in latitudine quinquaginta duos pedes et in longitudine tantum quantum messuagium et curtilagium Willielmi Carpentarii continet, habendum et
tenendum de me et hæredibus meis dictam placiam terræ dicto Thomæ
et hæredibus suis vel cuicunque dictam placiam terræ vendere dare vel
assignare voluerint, exceptis viris Religiosis et Judæis, libere et quiete
bene et in pace cum omnibus libertatibus et liberis consuetudinibus ad*

An. MCCLXXX. 8, 9. Edward I.

Memorandum quod Hugo de Plessetis anno
regni regis Edwardi nono dedit manerium
de Hedindon quod olim spectabat Thomæ

Basset domino regi, de quo manerio abbas
de Oseney per cartam Matildis imperatricis
XII. sol annuatim percipere consuevit. Reg.
Osen.

[b] R. Dods. MS. vol. 67. f. 369. qu.

dictam placiam pertinentibus intra villam et extra.   Salva mihi et hæ-
redibus meis secta curiæ et molendini mei de Bigenhulle cum omni-
modo blado et brasio, reddendo inde annuatim mihi et hæredibus meis
vel meis assignatis dictus Thomas et hæredes sui seu assignati duos
solidos ad quatuor anni terminos : scilicet ad natale Domini sex dena-
rios ad pascha sex denarios, ad festum S. Johannis Baptistæ sex de-
narios, pro omnibus servitiis consuetudinibus exactionibus et sæcula-
ribus demandis ad me vel hæredes meos pertinentibus salva secta curiæ
et molendini.   Ego vero Alicia et hæredes mei dictam placiam terræ
dicto Thomæ et hæredibus suis vel suis assignatis prout dictum est
contra omnes homines et fœminas per prædictum servitium warantiza-
bimus acquietabimus et in perpetuum defendemus.   Pro hac autem do-
natione concessione et chartæ meæ confirmatione dedit mihi dictus
Thomas dimid. marc. præ manibus integ. summam.   Et hæc mea do-
natio concessio et chartæ meæ confirmatio ut rata et stabilis in perpe-
tuum permaneat hanc præsentem chartam sigilli mei impressione robo
ravi.   Hiis testibus ; domino priore Waltero de Berncester, Roberto
Clerico de eadem, Roberto Hebern de eadem, Johanne de Bigenhulle
de eadem, Simone de Bigenhulle, Willielmo Magistro de eadem, Hu-
gone de la Newehus de eadem, et multis aliis [c].

Within this year 1280, the first of Oliver Sutton bishop of Lincoln, the proctor of the prior and convent of Longvil in France,
of the Cluniac order, presented to the churches of Newton-Long-
vil and Ackele in com. Bucks [d].   And Edmund earl of Cornwall
presented to the church of Rollesham, (now Rowsham [e];) and in
the same year, Henry earl of Lincoln, lord of the manor of Burcester, presented to the church of Thoresby in the archdeaconry of
Lincoln; and in the third year of Oliver Sutton, to the church of
Winceby, and in the fifth, to the church of Wadington in the same
archdeaconry [f].

---

[c] Ex Orig. penes hon. D. W. Glynne, Bar.   [d] R. Dods. MS. vol. 107. f. 140.   [e] Ib.
f. 144.   [f] Ib. f. 126, et 128.

An. MCCLXXXI. 9, 10. *Edward I.*

The abbey of Rewley begun by Edmund earl of Cornwall in 1279, was now finished, and furnished with monks from the abbey of Tame, and the church dedicated to the Virgin Mary on the eleventh of December, by Robert bishop of Bath and Wells.

Dominus Edvardus comes Cornubiæ fundavit novam abbatiam ordinis cistertiensis apud Oxoniam et monachos de Thama ibidem introduxit et contulit eisdem prima donatione manerium de Erdintone, et locum abbatiæ fecit dedicari 3. idus Decembris a venerabili prælato domino Roberto Burnel Bathoniensi et Wellensi episcopo [g]

In this year Walter prior of Burcester, under a title to wood and land in Arncote within this parish of Ambrosden, had caused Thomas de Meriton, one of his canons, to make an *in-hoc* in the fallow common-field belonging to both Arncot's in Muckle-croft, near the court or mansion-house of the said prior, on the east side in Nether-Arncote; by which means William abbot of Oseney (which abbey had two hides of land in the said Arncote) complained that he was thereby damnified in the common-pasture of the said field, upon which it was put to the inquiry and arbitration of some neighbours; upon whose verdict it was agreed, that the prior of Burcester should never hereafter make any such *in-hoc* without the consent of the abbot of Oseney; and that the said abbot of Oseney, of his mere liberality, should allow to the said prior the crop of that croft for this turn.

Noverint universi quod cum anno regni regis Edwardi IX. Frater Walterus prior Berncestriæ per fratrem Thomam de Meriton fieri fecit quoddam in-hoc *in campo waretabili utriusque Ernicote in Mucklecroft sub curia ejusdem prioris ex parte Orientali in Nether-Ernicote per quod Frater Willielmus abbas Osen. dicebat se de communi pastura ibidem disseisiri. Idem prior facto inde per vicinos diligenti scrutinio certioratus per eosdem de dicto* in-hoc *ad nocumentum et gravamen*

seu impedimentum utriusque partis abbatis et prioris et suorum tenent.
in iisdem Ernicots facto et idcirco idem prior pro se et suis tenentibus
de dicta villa dicto abbati concedit quod de cæterc nullum in-hoc *ibidem*
faciet sine assensu dicti abbatis et idem abbas ex mera liberalitate sua
croppum de dicta crofta præfato priori instanter concessit pro hac vice.
In cujus rei testimonium partes præsenti scripto in modum chirographi
confecto altrinsecus sigilla sua apposuerunt. Hiis testibus, &c. [h]

This word *in-hoc,* or *hinhoke,* (called at this day in the north *in-*
tok,) is not explained in any glossary which I have yet seen; but
from this description it seems to have been the making an enclosure
in some part of a common-field that lies fallow, and thereby depriving the inhabitants of their right of commoning. This sense of the
word seems confirmed by a like instance in this country.

Die Veneris proxime post festum S. Bernardi Apostoli xxiii. *Ed. filii*
Ed. Rogerus abbas de Bruera et ejusdem loci conventus salutem. No-
verit universitas vestra nos fecisse quoddam Hinhokium in campo de
Dunthrop sine assensu et voluntate prioris et conventus de Cold-Norton
unde dictus prior et conventus se senserint ex hoc non modicum gra-
vari existimantes illud fieri in præjudicium et exhæredationem domus
suæ; unde quorundam fratrum et aliorum amicorum fretus consilio
prædictum inhokium *volunt depascere. Nos vero lite omnimoda ab-*
sorpta pacem inivimus sub hac forma, videlicet quod nos concedimus
dicto priori et conventui pro pastura sua infra dictam culturam fruc-
tus decimæ acræ in longum et latum pro hac vice. Protestamur etiam
nos de cætero nunquam tale quid attemptare in' præjudicium et grava-
men dictæ domus de Norton nisi prius nobis constiterit de dictorum
prioris et conventus mera voluntate et communi assensu [i].

Emma Segrym of Borstall, in her pure widowhood, confirmed to
Robert Coysyn of Borstall one half acre of arable land in the field of
Arnegrove at Gosehulle, for the yearly rent of one farthing, and one
mark of silver in hand. *Hiis testibus; Johanne Welshe, Johanne*
de Clare, Hugone Richards, Johanne Segrym, Roberto de Hereford,

---

[h] Reg. Osen. MS. p. 328.　　[i] Ex Regist. Coll. Æn. Nas. Oxon. MS. p. 25.

Willielmo Broun, et aliis. Dat. apud Borstall die Sabbati in vigilia apostolorum Philippi et Jacobi anno regni regis Edwardi decimo [k]

At this time Roger de Moubray, a potent northern baron, entailed all his lordships of Thresk, Kirby-Malesart, Burton in Lonesdale, Hovingham, Melton-Moubray, Eppeworth, and the whole isle of Axholme, upon the heirs of his own body lawfully begotten, and for default of such issue upon Henry de Lacy earl of Lincoln and his heirs[1]: but there happened no such default of heirs. Sir Almaric de S. Amand, knight, presented to the church of Grendon com. and Archid. Bucks[m]: whose ancestors had given to the abbey of Godstow twenty-five acres in Blechesdon *ad seminandum,* to sow yearly, and as many *ad waretandum,* to lie fallow [n]

An. MCCLXXXII.   10, 11. *Edward I.*

Henry de Lacy earl of Lincoln, lord of Burcester and Midlington in right of his wife Margaret Longspe, had by his said wife a son called Edmund de Lacy, (contracted to Maud daughter and heir of Patric de Chamworth, which Maud was after married to Hugh Despenser,) who died young without heir. The said Henry had another son named John, who in minority came to an unfortunate end, so as there remained only one daughter, Alice, born this year, who being presumptive heir to her father, was at nine years of age espoused to Thomas son and heir of Edmund earl of Lancaster, brother to the king: to whom in right of this his wife came the manors of Burcester and Midlington, in 5. Ed. II.

This match and conveyance being not clearly stated in Dugdale's Baronage, I will here transcribe the more exact history.

Henrici de Lacy secundi comitis Lincolniæ filius fuit Edmundus de Lacy junior, qui natus est de Margareta filia Willielmi de Longspey, cui rex Edwardus ipso anno dedit maritagium Matildæ puellæ quinquennis, filiæ et hæredis Patricii de Chanworth, quam genuit de filia

k Ex Regist. Coll. Æn. Nas. Oxon. MS. p. 25.   l Dugd. Bar. tom. 1. p. 325. b.   m R. Dods. MS. vol. 107. f. 141.   n Mon. Ang. tom. 1. p. 525.

Willielmi de Bello Campo comitis de Warwyk, quam postea duxit uxorem Hugo Dispenser. Iste itaque Edmundus dominus et filius Henrici de Lacy statim juvenis est defunctus, nullo post' se relicto hærede de corpore suo procreato. Dictus igitur Henricus comes Lincolniæ de præfata Margareta uxore sua genuit alium filium nomine Johannem et filiam unam nomine Alesyam, sed Johannes iste priusquam annos nubiles attigisset, super turrem quandam in castro de Pontefracto incaute discurrens lapsus est ultra muros et in terram collisus et confractus protinus expiravit, nullum post se sui corporis relinquens hæredem. Prædicta igitur Alesia, filia et hæres dicti Henrici de Lacy, IX. ætatis suæ anno desponsata fuit Thomæ de Lancastria filio et hæredi Edmundi comitis Lancastriæ fratris ejusdem domini regis Edwardi[o].

The said Henry earl of Lincoln was in the expedition made this year into Wales; and upon the recognition made at Rothelan of the services pertaining to the king, he acknowledged seven knight's fees and a half to be due from him for his own inheritance, and that of Margaret his wife[p].

In this third year of Oliver Sutton bishop of Lincoln, Edmund earl of Cornwall presented to the church of Henly[q]. As also John the son of Wido, knight, presented to the church of Ardulvele, (now Ardly,) and the year following to the church of Weston; I suppose Weston by Thame[r]. And Sir William le Povre, knight, to the church of * Otingdon.

Baldwin son of Roger de Tingewike granted and confirmed to Sir John Fitz-Nigel, jun. all his lands in the fields of Acley of the fee of Adingrave, for two and twenty marks sterling in hand. *Hiis testibus; Roberto Malet, Johanne Carbonel, Ricardo de Arches, milit. Johanne filio Nigelli seniore, Nicho le Brun de Acley, Roberto Tulus, Nigello Travers, Thoma Brun, et aliis. Dat. apud Borstall die Mar*

---

* Rectores ecli'æ de Oddington.   de Ottindon ad pres. Gentechiv le Povcr.
Rogerus de Turbelvill subdiac. ad eccl.   8. cal. Octob. Rob. Hug. Well. pont. 14.

[o] E. Cod. MS. in Bib. Cot. citat. in Mon. Ang. tom. 2. p. 187.   [p] Dugd. Bar. tom. 1. p. 104.   [q] R. Dods. MS. vol. 107. p. 144.   [r] Ib. p. 145.

tis proxime post festum S. Luciæ Virginis. Anno regni regis Edwardi filii regis Henrici decimo [s].
The said Baldwin de Tingewike granted to the said John Fitz-Nigel, seven acres of land in Brehull and Acley. *Hiis testibus; Johanne filio Nigelli de Borstall, Thoma de S. Andrea de Essedon, Roberto Tulus, Nigello Travers tum firmario de Brehull, Nicholao de Brun de Acley, Johanne Ferebraz de Brehull, Nigello de Boys de eadem, Simone de S. Audomar, Thoma Brun de Borstall, Roberto Aleyn de Acley, et aliis. Dat. die Mercurii in festo nativitatis S. Johannis Baptistæ. Anno regni regis Edwardi filii regis Henrici decimo* [t].

An. MCCLXXXIII. 11, 12. *Edward I.*

Edmund earl of Cornwall now founded the first college for the order of the Bonhommes at Esserugge, Asherugge, now Ashridge in com. Bucks, to which this church of Ambrosden * was soon after

* An. MCCLXXXIII. 11, 12. Edw. I.
Carta dicti Edmundi Comitis Cornubiæ de Maneriis de Cestretone et Ambresdone.

Sciant præsentes et futuri, quod nos Edmundus claræ memoriæ Ricardi Regis Alemanniæ filius, et comes Cornubiæ dedimus, concessimus, et hac præsenti cartâ nostra confirmavimus, pro salute animæ nostræ, et animarum antecessorum et successorum nostrorum, Deo ac beatæ Mariæ, ac fratri Ricardo rectori ecclesiæ de Esserugge, in honore preciosi sanguinis Jesu Christi fundatæ, et fratribus suis ibidem Deo servientibus et imperpetuum servituris maneria nostra de Cestretone et Ambresdone in com. Oxon. cum advocationibus ecclesiarum eorundem maneriorum, simul cum homagiis ac omnibus serviciis liberorum tenentium, et hæredum suorum, una cum villanis, coterellis, eorum catallis,

serviciis, sectis et sequelis, et omnibus suis ubicunq; pertinentibus absq; ullo retenemento: habendum et tenendum prædicta maneria cum advocationibus ecclesiarum ad eadem maneria spectantibus simul cum homagio et omnibus serviciis omnium liberorum tenentium et hæredum suorum, una cum omnibus villanis, coterellis, et eorum catallis, serviciis, sectis et sequelis omnimodis et eorum ubiq; pertinentibus, et omnibus libertatibus, et liberis consuetudinibus, quibus nos vel antecessores nostri in eisdem maneriis, et advocationibus prædictis ullo tempore utebantur, adeo libere, sicut nos vel successores nostri prædicta maneria et advocationes ecclesiarum prædictarum unquam melius vel liberius tenuimus prædictis rectori et fratribus suis ecclesiæ de Esserugge prædicta et eorum successoribus de nobis et hæredibus nostris in liberam, puram et perpe-

[s] Ex Chartular. de Borstall. MS. f. 22.   [t] Ibid. f. 23.

impropriated. Jo. Leland has thus entered it among his Collect. *Edmundus comes Cornubiæ fundavit domum de Assheruge anno D.* 1283 [u]. And among his travels, (wherein really he was but a superficial observer,) he leaves this short mention of it: 𝕮𝖍𝖊 𝖍𝖔𝖚𝖘𝖊 𝖔𝖋 𝕭𝖔𝖓𝖊𝖍𝖔𝖒𝖊𝖘 𝖈𝖆𝖚𝖑𝖑𝖎𝖉 𝕬𝖘𝖘𝖈𝖍𝖊𝖗𝖚𝖌𝖊 𝖔𝖋 𝖙𝖍𝖊 𝖋𝖚𝖓𝖉𝖆𝖙𝖎𝖔𝖓 𝖔𝖋 𝕰𝖉𝖒𝖚𝖓𝖉𝖊 𝖊𝖗𝖑𝖊 𝖔𝖋 𝕮𝖔𝖗𝖓𝖊𝖜𝖆𝖑𝖊, 𝖆𝖓𝖉 𝖔𝖜𝖓𝖊𝖗 𝖔𝖋 𝕭𝖊𝖗𝖈𝖐𝖍𝖆𝖒𝖘𝖙𝖊𝖉𝖊 𝕮𝖆𝖘𝖙𝖊𝖑 𝖎𝖘 𝖆𝖇𝖔𝖚𝖙 𝖆 𝖒𝖎𝖑𝖊 𝖔𝖋 [x]. The foundation is thus recorded by Harpsfield: *Conditum est in hac diœcesi (nempe Lincoln.) ab Edmundo Richardi comitis fratrisque Henrici regis filio cœnobium quod Assheruggium dicitur prope Berchaustedium pagum, distantem a Londino circiter viginti quinque millia passuum. Quod et portione sanguinis dominici ornavit. Dicuntur cœnobitæ, et revera multi nomini suo respondebant, boni homines* [y]. This fable of Christ's blood, which profited much that house, is told at large by Hollinshead: Edmund the son and heir

tuam elemosinam sine ullo retenemento nostri seu hæredum nostrorum, sive ministrorum nostrorum quorumcunq; ita quod cedente vel decedente rectore ecclesiæ de Esserugge prædictd, quod nos vel hæredes nostri, seu ministri nostri, seu hæredum nostrorum nullatenus habeamus ingressum in prædictus maneriis, seu advocationibus ecclesiarum prædictarum, sive in aliquibus suis pertinentiis quicquam nos intromittamus, tempore vacationis, quo carebunt rectore: sed semper in manibus ipsorum fratrum, tam tempore vacationis quàm aliis temporibus remaneant, nec statum suum in aliquo mutent.

Volumus etiam et concedimus, pro nobis et hæredibus nostris, quod prædictus rector et fratres sui, et eorum successores, et etiam eorum tenentes, in omnibus burgis et villatis nostris, et etiam in singulis nundinis et mercatis nostris libere valeant emere et vendere,

omnes mercandisas absq; ullo theloneto, seu stallagio, nobis vel hæredibus nostris, seu aliquibus ministris nostris inde præstando. Et nos prædictus Edmundus et hæredes nostri omnia prædicta in formâ superius expressâ prædictis rectori et fratribus suis prædictis, et eorum successoribus contra omnes Christianos et Judæos, sicut nostram liberam, puram et perpetuam elemosinam warantizabimus, acquietabimus, et imperpetuum defendemus. Et ut hæc nostra donatio, concessio, et præsentis cartæ nostræ confirmatio perpetuæ robur firmitatis optineant, eam sigilli nostri impressione duximus roborandam. Hiis testibus; dominis Johanne de Gatesdene, Edmundo de Wedon, Henrico de Motisbrok, Reginaldo de Botereaus, Johanne Neinmuth Militibus, Radulpho de Mareschall, &c. Mon. Ang. vol. 3. p. 69.

[u] Lel. Collectan. MS. tom. 2. f. 286.   [x] Ib. Itin. tom. 1. f. 121.   [y] Hist. Angl. eccles. p. 480.

of Richard earl of Cornwall, who was second son to King John, being with his father in Germany, where, "beholding the relikes and " other precious monuments of the ancient emperors, he espied a " box of gold, by the inscription whereof he perceived (as the opi- " nion of men then gave) that therein was conteined a portion of " the bloud of our Saviour. He therefore being desirous to have " some part thereof, so intreated him that had the keeping of it, " that he obteined his desire, and brought it over with him into Eng- " land, bestowing a third part thereof, after his father's deceasse, in " the abbeie of Hailes, as it were to adorne and inrich the same, bi- " cause that therein both his father and mother were buried; and the other two parts he did reserve in his own custodie, till at length, " mooved upon such devotion as was then used, he founded an abbeie " a little from his manor of Bercamsted, which abbeie was named " Ashrug, in the which he placed the moonks of the order of Bon- " hommes, being the first that ever had beene seene of that order in " England; and herewith he also assigned the two other parts of that " bloud to the same abbeie. Whereupon followed great resort of " people to those two places, induced thereunto by a certeine blind de- " votion[z]." This was not the first import of that wonderful treasure, if we believe the stories of that religion, which tell us, that Joseph of Arimathea brought into Britain two silver vessels filled with the blood of our Saviour: which by his order were buried in his tomb. And to King Henry III. a crystal containing a portion of the same blood was sent from the master of the Temple at Jerusalem, attested with the seals of the patriarch: which treasure, on the day of St. Edward's trans- lation, the king committed to his church of St. Peter's in Westmin- ster, and obtained from the bishops then present, the indulgence of six years and one hundred sixteen days, to all that should come to pay a visit and veneration to that sacred relic[a]. So Mat. Paris, *sub an.* 1249, tells us, the king summoned his nobles and prelates to cele- brate the feast of St. Edward in St. Peter's church, where a chief

---

[z] Hollins. Hen. 3. sub an. 1272.   [a] Mat. West, sub an. 1217.

motive was *pro veneratione sancti sanguinis Christi nuper adepti.*
How prodigal in such pretences, see W. Prynne's Hist. Col. tom. 2.
p. 715. But of many instances we must not omit, that among the
relics in the abbey of Fescamp in Normandy is pretended to be the
true blood of Christ, as preserved by Nicodemus when he took the
body from the cross, given to the said abbey by William duke of
Normandy, buried by his son Duke Richard, and again discovered
an. 1171, and attended with infinite miracles [b]. This cheat was
winked at in the times of ignorance, but at the Reformation discovered and exposed; as the relation is given by J. Speed: " Ash-
" ridge in great repute for the blood (supposed out of Christ's sides)
" brought out of Germany by Henry the eldest son of Richard king
" of the Romans and earl of Cornwall, whereunto resorted great con-
" course of people for devotion and adoration thereof. But when
" the sunshine of the gospel had pierced thorow such clouds of
" darkness, it was perceived apparently to be only honey clarified
" and coloured with saffron, as was shewed at Paul's cross by the bi-
" shop of Rochester, 24. February, 1538 [c]."

The veneration paid to this relic inclined many to bequeath their
bodies to be buried in the church of Ashrugge, to the great advantage of these brethren. So Sir Thomas Bryan, knight, chief justice,
by his will made Feb. 7, 1495, and proved Decemb. 11, 1500. So
Sir Thomas Denham, knight, of Ethrop in Bucks, by will made
Sept. 18, and proved Feb. 13, 1519. So his son Sir John Denham,
knight, by will proved Octob. 30, 1535 [d].

These Bonhommes followed the rules of St. Austin. I think there
were but two more convents of them in England, one at Erdington
in Wilts, founded by W. de Erdindon bishop of Wint.; the other at
Bristol, founded by Henry de Gaunt, a priest, which society Leland
in his Itin. calls the Gaunts, *alias* the Bonhommes.

As to the name Ashridge, it is no doubt from a hill set with ashes,

[b] Neustria Pia, p. 258.   [c] J. Speed, Theat. of Brit. in Bucks.   [d] R. Dods. Extract.
[e] Regist. Prærog.

the old word was *Aescrugge, Rugge,* as after *Ridge,* signifying a
hill, or steep place, and the Ashen-tree being first *Aesc,* as after
Ashche, &c. In Walsingham's account of the death of Edmund earl
of Cornwall at this convent of his own foundation, the place is called
Assherngger ; but in this, as in infinite other parts of that edition, the
foreign printers mistook the copy [e].

In this fourth year of Oliver Sutton bishop of Lincoln, our Ed-
mund earl of Cornwall presented to the churches of Beckley and
Mixbury [f]; and to the church of Helmeswell in the archdeaconry of
Stowe; and to the church of Wystaneston in the archdeaconry of
Leicester, by reason of the custody of the land and heir of Henry de
Hastings; and *an.* 1285, by the same title to the church of Schaker-
ston [g].

By an inquisition this year in the county of Bucks, it was found
Almaric de St. Amand the day he died held the manor of Crendon
and the advowson of the church from Edmund earl of Cornwall, as
also the manor of Bloxham in the county of Oxon. from the said earl,
and left Guido his son and heir aged 17 [b]

King Edward, having now entirely subdued the Welsh, gave the
land of Denbigh to Henry Lacy earl of Lincoln, lord of Burcester,
&c. who thereupon began to build the town of Denbigh, which he
walled in, and made a castle within it ; in the front whereof was his
statue in long robes. And anciently prayers were made every Sunday in St. Hillarie's chapel there for Lacy and Percy [i]. Which said
earl, Aug. 25, gave the chapel of St. Nicholas in Pontfract to the
abbey of St. John de Pontfract [k].

An. MCCLXXXIV.   12, 13. *Edward I.*

There was at this time a chart of Oliver Sutton bishop of Lincoln
reciting the ordination of vicarages, in all those parishes which were

e Tho. Walsing. &c. Francof. 1603. p. 78.   f R. Dods. MS. vol. 107. p. 144.   g Ib.
p. 139.   h R. Dods. MS. vol. 44. p. 131.   i Dugd. Bar. tom. 1. p. 104.   k R. Dods.
MS. vol. 117. p. 19.

impropriated to the abbey of Oseney, made by Hugh Wells one of
his predecessors, which ordination because it immediately relates to
the churches of Weston, Chesterton, Heyford-Warin, &c. shall be
here transcribed, to acquaint us what allowance that age afforded to
the vicars, even beyond the portion now allotted to them. "For
" every vicar presented by the said abbot and convent, and insti-
" tuted by the bishop, was to have two marks yearly for his clothes,
" every second * legacy to the value of sixpence, and one half of it,
" if beyond that value: and out of all oblations to the altar at every
" mass one penny, if the oblations were worth a penny: and what-
" soever else by devotion of the faithful should be reasonably con-
" ferred upon him. As also a sufficient exhibition of victuals at the
" table of the canons whenever they staid within his parish: and the
" canons should find a clerk to serve him and obey him, who should
" take an oath of fidelity to the vicar, saving his fealty to the said
" canons, who should likewise find a boy to wait upon him, and
" maintain the boy in all expences. And when the canons were not
" resident, then the clerk, who as before appointed should attend
" the vicar, was to have the key of the canons' house, therein to pro-
" vide for the diet of the vicar sufficiently and honourably. The ca-
" nons should farther furnish the said vicar with a horse, whenever
" he had occasion to travel upon the concerns of the convent or
" the church: and should finally bear all burdens, i. e. first-fruits,
" tenths, procurations, and all taxes whatsoever."

*Universis sanctæ matris ecclesiæ filiis ad quos præsentes literæ per-
venerint Oliverus permissione divina Linc. episcopus. salutem in Domino sempiternam. Noverit universitas vestra ex inspecto registro
bonæ memoriæ quondam domini H. prædecessoris nostri super ordinationibus vicariarum in nostra diœcesi per eundem authoritate concilii
ordinatarum, compertum est vicarias dilectorum filiorum abbatis et
conventus Osen. per eundem fuisse ordinatas sub hac forma. In omnibus ecclesiis quas abbas et canonici Osen. tenent in propriis usibus tam*

---

* Mortuary.

in archidiaconatu Oxon'. quam in aliis archidiaconatibus Lincoln. dioc. ubi vicariæ non fuerint prius ordinatæ per episcopum de consensu ipsorum per dom. Linc. episcopum H. secundum authoritatem concilii provisum est in hunc modum. Vicarius per abbatem et conventum Osen. præsentandus et instituendus ab episcopo habebit nomine perpetuæ vicariæ suæ ad vestitum suum duas marcas per annum : habebit secundum legatum ad valentiam vi. *denariorum, et quod ultra sex denarios fuerit inter ipsum et canonicos dimidiabitur : habebit etiam de oblationibus ad altare provenientibus unum denarium, missale quoties celebraverit, et denarius provenerit, et quicquid ex devotione fidelium et rationabiliter fuerit collatum. Item habebit sufficientem exhibitionem sicut canonici quoad victualia in mensa canonicorum ubi canonici moram faciunt. Canonici vero clericum ci et ecclesiæ ministerio et ejus obsequio devotum invenient qui juramentum fidelitatis ipsi vicario præstabit salva fide dictorum canonicorum qui et ipsi vicario similiter garconem invenient ipsius obsequio-deputatum quos in omnibus suis expensis procurabunt. Ubi autem non fuerint canonici residentes, clericus qui ut supra dictum est expensis eorum procurabitur clavem eorum deferet in domo eorum et curam· habebit liberam, ut per ipsum vicario sufficienter in victualibus et · honorifice omnia ministrentur. Canonici et eidem vicario equum invenient quotiens pro negotiis eorum et ecclesiæ fuerit profecturus tam ad capitula quam ad alia ; necnon et omnia onera singularia ecclesiarum sustinebunt. In cujus rei testimonium sigillum nostrum præsentibus est appensum. Datum apud Luddington. anno Domini millesimo ducentesimo octogesimo quarto et pontificatus nostri quinto*[1].

In this fifth year of Oliver Sutton bishop of Lincoln, Edmund earl of Cornwall presented a rector to the church of * Ambrosden [m]. And

---

* Mag'r Joh. de Mollesworth pres. per dom. Edm. com. Cornub. ad eccl. de North Luffenham vac. per hoc quod mag'r Walterus de Cornubia ultimus rector ejusdem eccli'am de Ambresdon curam animarum habentem recepit titulo institutionis.admiss. 13 kal. Mart. 1281. exeunte. Rot. Ol. Sutton ep'i Linc.

[1] Regist. Osen. MS.   [m] R. Dods. MS. vol. 107. f. 141.

within the said year Lora de Cantia was elected prioress of the abbey
of Merkyate, or St. Trinity de Bosco, by leave first obtained from
the dean and chapter of Paul's in London[n].

Robert Aleyn of Acley granted to Sir John Fitz-Nigel of Borstall
two acres of arable land in the field of Acley for the yearly rent of
one pound of cloves at Easter. *Hiis testibus; domino Johanne filio
Nigelli, Roberto Malet, Johanne Carbonel, Eustachio de Grenevill,
milit. Nicholao de Brun de Acley, Nigello Travers, Petro de Rupell
de Wotton, Johanne de Rupell fratre suo, Thoma Brun de Borstall, et
aliis. Dat. apud Musewell, vicesimo octavo die Martii, anno regni regis Edwardi filii regis Henrici duodecimo et anno ab Incarnat. Domini millesimo ducentesimo octogesimo quarto[o].*

An. MCCLXXXV. 13, 14. Edward I.

This year the king by charter confirmed the donation made to
the priory of Oseney, by Richard de Camvill lord of Burcester, .
*quod libere et sine ulla vexatione possint congregare decimas suas quas
habent de dominicis suis de Erdinton et de Bernecestre[p].* By the same
or another *inspeximus* of the same year, there is a confirmation of
their lands in Chesterton.... *Necnon donationem, &c. quas Bardulphus filius et heres Rogeri filii Bardulphi de Cestreton in Henemers
per cartam suam fecit ecclesie predicte de illo tenemento cum edificiis vivariis croftis et aliis pertinentiis quod Margeria avia sua tenuit
in dotem in dicta Cesterton. Et de alio tenemento cum edificiis, &c.
quod Willielmus le Noreys aliquando tenuit in eadem villa. Donationem insuper, &c. quas idem Bardulphus, &c. fecit, &c. de duabus virgatis terre arabilis in campis de dicta Cesterton[q].*

In this year the structure of the college of Ashrugge being finished,
it was endowed by charter of the founder Edmund earl of Cornwall.

Sciant præsentes et futuri quod nos Edmundus claræ memoriæ Ri-

---

[n] R. Dods. MS. vol. 107. f. 143.   [o] Ex Chartular. de Borstall. MS. penes Joh. Aubrey, Bar.   [p] Mon. Ang. tom. 2. p. 112.   [q] Guil. Dugd. MS. vol. N. p. 32.

cardi regis Alemanniæ filius et comes Cornubiæ dedimus concessimus et hac præsenti carta nostra confirmavimus pro nobis et hæredibus nostris Deo et beatæ Mariæ ac rectori bonorum virorum fratrum ecclesiæ in honorem prætiosi sanguinis Jesu Christi apud Esserugge fundatæ, &c.[r]

This same year the said earl had from the king a charter of free warren in his neighbouring manors of Great Chesterton and Little Chesterton[s]

Nigh this time the abbot of Oseney being challenged for fees and

An. ʌ CCLXXXV. 13, 14. Edw. I.

Universis ad quos presentes literæ pervenerint Will'us de Luda salutem in D'no. Noveritis me in festo annuntiationis beatæ Mariæ anno regni regis Edwardi XIIII. *concessisse d'no Waltero Trailli militi quod si idem d'nus Walterus vel heredes sui solverint mihi et heredibus meis centum viginti et octo libras bonorum et legalium sterlingorum apud Novum Templum de Londo:n in festo S. Mich'is in anno subsequenti, tunc ego predictus Will'us de Luda vel hæredes mei reddemus cartam feoffamenti de manerio de Lutegareshule in com. Buck. prefato d'no Waltero vel heredibus suis et bonam quietam clamantiam de jure hereditatis per considerationem curie d'ni regis faciemus; et si contingat dictum d'num Walterum in solutione dicte pecunie deficere termino et loco supradictis tunc ipse d'nus Walterus concedit et vult quod nichil sibi vel heredibus suis valeat ista concessio nec mihi nec heredibus meis in aliquo noccat; et scialis q'd dictus d'nus Walterus concessit mihi dicto Will'o et heredibus meis dictum manerium de Lutegareshule cum omnibus pertin. suis infra villam et extra sine*

aliquo retenemento habend. et tenend. ad terminum vite mee reddendo inde per annum dicto d'no Waltero et heredibus suis quadraginta libras. Et quia ego prenotatus Will'us totum firmum quadraginta librarum predicto d'no Waltero pre manibus solvi de decem annis et dimidio predictum manerium cum suis pertin. quiet. a solutione quadraginta librarum annuatim a festo Pasche anno regni regis Edwardi quarto decimo usque ad terminum dictorum decem annorum et dimidii plenarie completorum remanebit michi heredibus et assignatis meis vel executoribus si de me humanitus contingat. Et sciendum est, quod dictus d'nus Walterus et heredes sui vel assignati totum manerium prediction cum pertin. suis michi et heredibus meis vel assignatis warantizabunt et defendent et contra omnes acquietabunt. In cujus rei testimonium ego dictus Will'us et predictus.d'nus Walterus huic scripto bipartito sigilla nostra alternatim apposuimus. Dat. apud Weston. nono decimo die mensis Febr. anno D'ni MCC. *octuagesimo quinto. Ex libro Placitorum temp.* Ed. I. et Edw. II. MS. olim penes Edw. Coke mil. Justitiar. de Baneo.

r Mon. Ang. tom. 2. p. 344.   s Dugd. Bar. tom. 1. p. 765.

military service in the tenure of lands given to that abbey, he pleaded exemption to several parts of their estate, and among others to their two hides of land in Arncot within the parish of Ambrosden, for which was claimed half a knight's fee, whereas he pleaded it to be not included within the barony of St. Walery, but an antecedent gift of Robert de Oilly, whose charter the abbot produced confirmed by Henry the IIId.

Qualiter extincta sunt feoda domini abbatis quæ ab ipso petita sunt patebit inferius. Abbas de Osen. respondet quantum ad unum feodum in Forest-hulle et dimid. feod. in Ernicota ab ipso petita quod non sunt de honore S. Walerici et profert chartam Rob. de Oleio cum confirmatione regis Henrici patris domini regis qui nunc est : videlicet tres hidas in Walton cum terra in Twenti acres duas hidas in Ernicote et terram de Wotton et terram de Foresthulle et de Barton in puram et perpetuam eleemosinam. Item dicit de dimid. feod. in North Osen. quod illud habet per chartam et confirmationem regis in puram et perpetuam eleemosinam. Et residuum quod habet de honore Sancti Walerici tenetur de abbate Regalis Loci per assignat. com. per soccagium : et non habentur ibidem nisi tria cotagia. Item dicit de tribus feodi in Mixbiry quod tenet illa feoda pro dimidio feodi per chartam Thomæ de S. Walerico et Guidonis de Arraniis et per confirmationem domini regis Alemanniæ. Abbas de Oseneia tenet diversa tenementa in North-Osen. et Walton quæ consueverunt respondere pro uno feodo et negat. Item abbas tenet dimid. feodi in Wotton, in Forest-hulle unum feodum, in Ernicote dimid. feodi quæ quidem fuerunt Willielmi de Areysnes et nescit. Item tenet dimid. feodi in parva Hampton, quod fuit Rob. de Gay quod negat, &c. [t]

On the second of January, an. 128⅘. Henry de Lacy earl of Lincoln, constable of Chester, lord of the manor of Burcester, confirmed to that convent the charter of Gilbert Basset, by which they had granted to them the pasturage of three draughts, or team of oxen,

t Regist. Osen. MS. p. 107.

and one load of fuel out of Bernwode. As also a charter of William Longspe, whereby they had a mill late in possession of Robert Puff, reserving a freedom of toll for his own corn, &c.

Henry de Lascy conte de Nichole e conestre de Cestr. seignuir de Rosse e de Rewennok a tuzke cest escrit verrunt ou ovront saluz en deu. Come miseoms regarde la chartre le sire Gilberd Basset fist au priur e au covent de Bernecestr par la quele il lur grante e done pasture a treis caruces de boefs a pestre e pasturer en queu leu entre boefs meme cely sire Gilberd ou ses heirs pasturassent. Et a ceo le un Charette de bosche ke vendrett a son maner de Bernecestre hors de son bois de Bernewode. Ea avoins regarde de la chartre sire William Longspe par la quele il done e grante as devant dit prior e covent tut le droit e le cleim ke il out avon au avoir peut en le molin que jadis fut a Roberd Puff suigvant a la priore ou tute la syute de les tenant de meime la ville au tut ses autres franchises e purtenances a luy e a sa franche meenee franche monture e le molim avant dit. Nus pur deu et pur salu de nostre alme e pur le salu de nos ancestres e nos heirs avoins grante et pur cette nostre esscrit conferme pur nus e pur nus heirs as devant dit prior e covent en franche et perpetuele aumosne pasture a treis caruces des boefs a pestre e pasturer en queu leu nos demesnes boefs ou de nos heirs pessent e pasturent hors du clos de nostre court de Bernecestre. Ea coe avons grante e conferme pur nus e pur nus heirs as devant dit prior e covent ke quel hovre ke nus ou nus heirs seroins carier busche hors de nostre boys de Berrewode jeskes a nostre maner de Bernecestr ke nostre forester livre as devant dit prior a covent la une charette en meme le boys. E estre ceo avoins grante et conferme pur nus e pur nos heirs as devant dit prior e covent syute de tus nos tenant de nostre maner avant dit du blè cressant e meme la ville suave a nus et nus heirs franche mouture e tus le molins les devent dit prior e covent en Bernecester pur nus e pur nostre franche meenee. E voluns ke si nul de nos tenant de la ville avant dit seu ataint ke il carie au face carier son ble ou son brees pur moudre alurs ke as molins le prior ke il doigne a nus e a nos heirs deus sols pur le trespasse. E as devant dit le prior e covent cette mouture de tant de *ble sul ne sett par aperte de faute ke eus ne peussent moudre as molins le prior. E volans e grantans pur nus e pur nos heirs ke tus se grante de cet escrit scent fermement gardes e maintenue sauns nul amenusement a tus jours. E a plus grand seurte de ceste chose nus e la devant dit prior e covent a ces escrit cirografer chaungablement avoins mis nus seeus. A cc tesmoignes, monsire Robert le fil Roger, monsire Roger de Trompinton, monsire Willame le . . . . . . monsire Baudewyn de Maners, monsire Willame de Stopham, monsire Wachlin de Ardeme Chevalers, Willame de Hany clerk, e autres. don a Bernecestre le secund jour de Januer, lan du rey Edward fil au rey Henri quatorizime* [u].*

To the original appends a large seal with the impress of the earl on horseback in armour, with sword drawn in his right hand, and a shield on his left bearing his coat, a lion rampant coronet. On the reverse his arms again, with inscription obliterate.

The said earl now ratified by charter dated at Holton the grant of a place called Ruddegate, made by Henry Torbeck and Elena his wife to the canons of Burscough in com. Lanc. with caution that one leper within his lordship of Widenes should thenceforth be admitted and maintained in that priory; and that mass should be there yearly celebrated at Easter, and that they should register in their martyrology and canon his name and the name of Margaret his wife [x].

Alice widow of Edmund, mother of Henry de Lacy earl of Lincoln, at the request of the said earl her son, confirmed the gift which Robert de Tylly made to the convent of Nostel, of one toft and croft in the village of Gomersale, and the advowson of the church of Byrstal in com. Ebor. by this deed.

Noverint universi quod nos Alesya de Lascy ad instantiam delecti filii nostri domini Henrici de Lascy com. Linc. et constabularii Cestriæ ra tum habemus et stabile donum quod Robertus de Tylly fecit priori et con' ventui de Sancto Oswaldo de Nostel de uno tofto et crofto quod Jordanus Mareschallus de dicto Roberto tenuit in villa de Gomersale et de advo

---

u Ex Orig. penes hon. D. Guil. Glynne, Bar.   x Mon. Ang. tom. 2. p. 307.

*catione ecclesiæ de Byrstall cum suis pertinentiis et eisdem priori et
conventui in dictum toftum et in advocationem dictæ ecclesiæ liberum
ingressum concedimus.   In cujus rei testimonium has literas nostras
eisdem fecimus patentes.   Dat. apud Rowelle v. Id. Feb. an. Domini*
MCCLXXX. *quinto* [y].

The same donation was confirmed by Henry de Lacy earl of Lincoln, by another charter dated Feb. the seventeenth [z].

Within this year, being the sixth of Oliver Sutton bishop of Lincoln, Edmund earl of Cornwall presented to the church of Chalgrave in this county [a].

Ela countess of Warwick having had the manors of Hokenorton and Bradam, com. Oxon. assigned for her dowry in 26. Hen. III. was now found to hold the said manor of Hokenorton of the king *in
capite, per serjantiam scindendi coram domino rege die natalis Domini et habere cultellum domini regis de quo scindit* [b].

An. MCCLXXXVI.   14, 15.   Edward I.

Amory de St. Amand, knight, held the manor of Crendon nigh adjoining, in the county of Bucks, and the advowson of the said church, from Edmund earl of Cornwall; as appears by inquisition taken this year.

*Jur. dic. quod Almaricus de S. Amando habuit maner. de Crendon
in com. Buck. et advocationem ecclesiæ dicti manerii de com. Cornub.
extent. man. de Sarney in com. Glouc. quod fuit dicti Almarici* [c].

Jordan de Morton in this neighbourhood paid twenty marks, as a fine to the king, for taking to wife without the king's licence Maud the widow of John le Mersh, who held land *in capite* [d].

The king passing over to France in the latter end of June, committed the custody of his kingdom to our parochial lord Edmund earl of Cornwall [e]: who, in this seventh of Oliver Sutton, presented

---

. [y] R. Dods. MS. vol. 95. f. 77.   [z] Ib.   [a] Ib. vol. 107. p. 144.   [b] Blount, Ancient
Tenures, p. 73.   [c] Dods. MS. vol. 44. f. 131.   [d] Ex Rot. Pip.   [e] Annal. Waverl. sub an.

3 K 2

to the church of Blunham in the archdeaconry of Bedford, and to
the chapel within the castle of Okeham, com. Rut. void by the death
of William Dixi the last chaplain [f]. Henry de Lacy earl of Lincoln
presented to the vicarage of one half of the church of St. Dennys of
Kirkeby near Lafford, in the archdeaconry of Lincoln, by reason of
the custody of the lands and heir of Sir Thomas de Frampton [g]. And
his lady mother Alice de Lacy, by deputation from her son, presented to the church of Wivelyngham [h]. The said earl of Lincoln
now confirmed the gift of Robert de Tylly to the priory of Nostel in
com. Ebor. of lands in Gomersale, and the advowson of Byrstal confirmed by Alice his mother, in another charter dated at Rowel, 5. Id.
Feb. 1285 [i].

An. MCCLXXXVII.   15, 16. Edward I.

It appears from the accounts of the exchequer, that in the second
scutage of Wales, assessed at 40ˢ. the knight's fee, and this year collected, Edmund earl of Cornwall paid twenty pounds for ten fees of
Thomas de S. Walery; and William Longspe paid forty shillings for
one fee of Gerard de Camvill in Midlington [k].

In the king's absence, the Welsh, under the conduct of Resamere-
duth broke into rebellion, and committed great spoils in the borders
of England, against whom Edmund earl of Cornwall marched with a
very numerous army, pursued them to their mountainous retreats
and castles; and, after a peace made by mediation of the earl of Gloucester, returned about Michaelmas [l].

Isabel widow of Robert and mother of Baldwin de Tingewick, did
quit claim to the land sold by her said son to Sir John Fitz-Nigel.
*Hiis testibus; domino Rogero Extraneo, domino Petro de Louch, do-
mino Simone de Blesworth rectore ecclesiæ de Thrapton, Roberto Gre-*

---

[f] R. Dods. MS. vol. 107. f. 136. 143.   [g] Ib. f. 129.   [h] Ib. f. 132.   [i] Ex Chartul. de
Nostell. R. Dods. MS. vol. 138. f. 33.   [k] Ib. Rot. Pip. MS. vol. 16. f. 117.   [l] Chron.
Thom. Wikes, sub an.

leny de Islep, Willielmo de Horton clerico, et aliis. Dat. apud North-ampton die Dominica proxime ante festum annuntiationis Dominicæ anno regni regis Edwardi quinto decimo [m].

Richard son of Henry de Portreve of Brehull, granted and confirmed to John Fitz-Nigel, jun. all his lands and possessions within the village of Brehull and without, which he had by inheritance of his father, in consideration of forty shillings paid in hand. *Hiis testibus; domino Roberto de Cary, domino Johanne filio Nigelli patre, domino Johanne Carbonel, domino Eustachio de Grenevil de Chilton, Waltero de S. Andrea, Willielmo de S. Audoeno, Johanne le Brun, Thoma de Adingrave, et aliis. Dat. apud Schabinton die S. Silvestri anno regni regis Edwardi quinto decimo* [n].

The day following Agnes widow of Henry le Portreve, in consideration of three shillings paid in hand, released and quit claimed all her right in the premises. *Hiis testibus; Nigello Travers, Roberto Tuluse, Nigello de Bosco, Petro de Penna, Willielmo Pomerey, Ricardo filio Radulphi Pymme, et aliis. Dat. apud Brehull in crastino S. Silvestri, anno regni regis Edwardi quinto decimo* [o].

In this eighth of Oliver Sutton, Henry de Lacy earl of Lincoln presented to the church of Halton in the archdeaconry of Stow, master Robert de Lascy chaplain [p]. And within the same year this agreement was made between the said earl of Lincoln and the abbey of Kirkstall.

Conventio die Sabbati proxime post festum S. Lucæ Evangelistæ an. Dom. 1287. Ita convenit inter religiosum virum Hugonem abbatem de Kirkestall, Cistert. ord. Ebor. dioc. et nobilem virum dom. Hen. de Lacy com. Linc. &c. quod cum abbas pro se et conventu suo et corum successoribus, remiserit et quietum clamaverit præfato comiti et hæredibus suis in perpetuum omnes terras tenementa et redditus quos habuerunt et tenuerunt de prædicto com. et antecess. suis in Akerington, Clyvacher, et Hunnecotes in com. Lancast. et in la Rondehay, Secroft,

---

[m] Ex Chartular. de Borstall. f. xxiv. [n] Ib. f. ix. [o] Ib. f. x. [p] R. Dod. MS. vol. 107. p. 132.

*et Schadewell in com. Ebor. &c. præfatus comes recognovit et concessit
pro se et hæredibus suis solvere singulis annis in perpetuum dictis ab-
bati`et conventui, &c.* 50. *marcas sterlingorum percipiend. in Scaccario
ipsius com. de Pontefract ad duos anni terminos, &c. et pro prædictis
terris, &c. in com. Ebor.* 30. *marcas, &c.* Hiis *testibus ; venerabilibus
patribus E. Bathon. et Well. ep. &c. D. Johanne de Vescy, Ottone de
Grandisono, Johanne, de S. Johanne, Willielmo de Latymer, Johanne
de Boun, &c. Dat. ut supra. Confirmatio regis dat. apud Sanctum
Seuerum* 27. *die Octob. an. regni* 15.[q]

In the year 1297, on the feast of Simon and Jude, Henry Lacy
earl of Lincoln gave bond to the said abbot and convent for one
hundred and fifty pounds sterling, to be paid in Midlent, for five
years arrears of rent for those lands in Lancashire, and another bond
for two hundred pounds for arrears of rent for the other lands in
Yorkshire[r].

An. MCCLXXXVIII. 16, 17. Edward I.

The king at Langley, April the seventeenth, confirmed the charter of Edmund earl of Cornwall to his fraternity of Bonhommes at
Asherugge[s]. Before the end of this year, Edmund earl of Cornwall
farther endowed his said monastery of Asherugge with our manor of
Ambrosden and the manor of Chesterton nigh adjoining, with the
advowson of both churches, and made them and their tenants toll
and stallage free in all fairs and markets within the liberties of him
and his successors, by this form of donation.

*Sciant præsentes et futuri quod nos Edmundus claræ memoriæ Ri-
cardi regis Alemanniæ filius et comes Cornubiæ dedimus concessimus
et hac præsenti charta nostra confirmavimus pro salute animæ nostræ et
animarum antecessorum et successorum nostrorum Deo ac beatæ Mariæ
ac fratri Ricardo rectori ecclesiæ de Esserugge in honore preciosi sanguinis Jesu Christi fundatæ et fratribus suis ibidem Deo servientibus et
imperpetuum servituris maneria nostra de Cestretone et Ambrosdone in*

<hr>

[q] R. Dods. MS. vol. 116. f. 10.　　[r] Ib. f. 12.　　[s] Mon. Ang. tom. 2. p. 344.

com. Oxon. cum advocationibus ecclesiarum eorundem maneriorum simul cum homagiis e omnibus serviciis liberorum tenentium et hæredum suorum una cum villanis, coterellis, eorum catallis, serviciis, sectis et sequelis, et omnibus suis ubicunque pertinentibus absque ullo retenemento. Habendum et tenendum prædicta maneria cum advocationibus ecclesiarum ad eadem maneria spectantibus simul cum homagio et omnibus serviciis omnium liberorum tenentium et hæredum suorum una cum omnibus villanis, coterellis, et eorum catallis, serviciis, sectis et sequelis omnimodis et corum ubique pertinentibus, et omnibus libertatibus et liberis consuetudinibus quibus nos vel antecessores nostri in eisdem maneriis et advocationibus, &c. ecclesiarum prædictarum unquam melius vel liberius tenuimus prædictis rectori et fratribus suis ecclesiæ de Esserugge prædicta et eorum successoribus de nobis et hæredibus nostris in liberam puram et perpetuam elemosinam sine ullo retenemento nostri seu hæredum nostrorum sive ministrorum nostrorum quorumcunque. Ita quod cedente vel decedente rectore ecclesiæ de Esserugge prædicta quod nos vel hæredes nostri vel ministri nostri seu hæredum nostrorum nullatenus habeamus ingressum in prædictis maneriis seu advocationibus ecclesiarum prædictarum sive in aliquibus suis pertinentiis quicquam nos intromittamus tempore vacationis quo carebunt rectore, sed semper in manibus ipsorum fratrum, tam tempore vacationis, quam aliis temporibus remaneant, ne statum suum in aliquo mutent. Volumus etiam et concedimus pro nobis et hæredibus nostris quod prædictus rector et fratres sui et corum successores, et etiam eorum tenentes in omnibus burgis et villatis nostris, et etiam in singulis nundinis et mercatis nostris libere valeant emere et vendere omnes mercandisas absque ullo theloneto, seu stallagio, &c. nobis vel hæredibus nostris inde præstando. Et nos prædictus Edmundus et hæredes nostri omnia prædicta in forma superius expressa prædictis rectori et fratribus suis prædictis, et eorum successoribus contra omnes Christianos et Judæos, sicut nostram liberam puram et perpetuam elemosinam warantizabimus, acquietabimus et in perpetuum defendemus. Et ut hæc nostra donatio concessio et præsentis cartæ nostræ confirmatio perpetuæ robur firmitatis optineant cam sigilli nostri impressione duximus roborandam. Hiis testi-

bus; dominis Johanne de Gatesdenc, Edmundo de Wedon, Henrico de Motisbrok, Reginaldo de Botereaus, Johanne Neinmuth, militibus; Radulfo de Mareschall, &c. [t]

We may here observe, that Edmund earl of Cornwall designed no part of the revenues of this church of Ambrosden should be converted to the use of his new convent, which he had in lay fees sufficiently endowed. But he only trusts them with the presentation of a clerk, on a charitable opinion, that these Good-men would better execute the right of patronage, and more incorruptly provide an able incumbent: but too many guardians have embezzled a trust to their own proper use. So these holy brethren, without any regard to the donor's intention, soon resolved the inheritance should be theirs: and therefore purchasing a deed of gift from the pope, (who like the tempter in the wilderness offered what he had no right to bestow,) they quickly made themselves the perpetual rector. And indeed in this manner was the illegitimate birth of most impropriations; the lay patrons devoutly (and, as they thought innocently) resigned their right of presentation to religious houses, and they by their interest and money procured from the popes an annexion of the tithes to themselves, with an arbitrary portion, or a poor settled reserve, to a servant of theirs, whom they should call a vicar.

In this year began a new taxation of the value of all churches upon this occasion: the pope had the first-fruits and tenths of all spiritual preferments in England. For the more easy collecting of them there had been a general taxation of them made by Walter de Suthfield bishop of Norwich, by command of pope Innocent the Fourth, who had granted the tenths to king Henry III. for three years. This tax-. ation was done *an.* 1254, by appointing the rural dean and three rectors or vicars in every deanery, who upon oath were to certify the just estimate of all church revenues [u]. This was an oppression to the clergy; but it was soon made more grievous: for when the pope had again granted the tenths to the king for three years, the king in the

[t] Mon. Ang. tom. 3. p. 69.   [u] Annal. Burton. sub an.

fifty-third of his reign, an. 1269, for a compensation to what they fell short of the due value, made the clergy pay within those three the tenths of four years [x]. And now at this time the tenths were granted to king Edward by his Holiness, as an aid toward his expedition to the holy land: that they might be gathered to the full extent of them, the pope appointed two principal collectors, Richard bishop of Winchester, and Oliver bishop of Lincoln [y]; who in every diocese were to appoint their deputies and assistants. In this diocese of Lincoln the delegated collectors were the abbot of Oseney, and the prior of St. Catherines in Lincoln; of whom the former was to collect the counties of Oxford, Bucks, Northampt. Bedford, and Huntingdon, and the prior the residue of the diocese, during five years. And in every deanery new taxers were commissioned, who in every dignity and cure exceeded the former computation, to the great burden of the clergy. The inquisition began this year [z]; but the return was not fully made till the year 1291, under which year shall be given the taxation of these parts.

The king in this sixteenth of his reign gave to Henry Lacy earl of Lincoln, and lord of the manor of Burcester, &c. the Black-friars' old house in Holborn, upon their removal to a new church and house built near Baynard's castle [a]. In this ninth of Oliver Sutton, Edmund earl of Cornwall presented to the church of Stoke-Basset in the archdeaconry of Oxford [b].

Within this year died Sir John Fitz-Nigel, sen. of Borstall, leaving issue Sir John Fitz-Nigel, jun. his son and heir: some time before his death he was summoned into the king's court at Westminster, to shew by what warrant he claimed the view of Frankplege of his tenants in Borstall, of which suit the issue is thus delivered.

Johannes filius Nigelli sen. summonitus fuit ad respondendum domino regi de placito quo warranto clamat habere visum Franciplegii de te-

[x] Chron. Tho. Wikes, sub an.   [y] Ib.   [z] W. Dugd. Analecta e Chron. Antiq. MS. vol. M. 2. p. 108.   [a] Stow's Survey of London, p. 443.   [b] R. Dods. MS. vol. 107. f. 116.

nentibus suis in Borstall qui ad dominum regem et coronam suam per-
tinet.' Et Johannes per attornatum suum venit et dicit quod anteces-
sores sui feofati fuerant per prædictum dominum regem de quodam
tenemento quod vocatur Derhyde ubi habet manerium suum et tenentes
qui veniunt ad visum suum, et dicit quod pro tenemento illo et pro
visu illo reddit per annum domino regi decem solidos qui soluti sunt
ad Scaccarium per manus seneschalli de foresta, et dicit quod ipse et
antecessores sui a tempore quo non extat memoria extiterunt seisiti de
prædicto visu, et quod ita sit, petit quod inquiratur. Et Gilbertus de
Thornton qui sequitur pro rege dicit, quod Franciplegium est quædam
libertas regia mere spectans ad coronam et dignitatem domini regis
contra quam longa seisina valere non debet, unde petit judicium.
Postea autem die S. Michaelis in xv. *dies anno reg. Ed.* xiv. *venit*
prædictus Johannes per attornatum suum et dicit quod est capitalis
forestarius de feodo, et dicit quod reddit quadraginta solidos per an.
domino regi pro prædicta balliva et decem solidos pro habendo visu
Franciplegii de tenentibus suis, et quod ipse et omnes forestarii qui
tenuerunt prædictam hidam terræ semper habuerunt visum Franci-
plegii et requisitus si habeat furcas sive alia judicialia dicit quod non.
Et super hoc datus est ei dies a die Paschæ in xv. *dies in Scaccario, ad*
quem diem venit prædictus Johannes per attornatum suum, et datus
est ei dies a die S. Michaelis in xv. *dies, deinde datus est ei dies a die*
Paschæ in xv. *dies. Ad quem diem testatum est quod obiit et nihil ad*
præsens[c].

An. MCCLXXXIX. 17, 18. *Edward I.*

Many miracles are said to have been now observed in a chapel at
Abingdon, which our Edmund earl of Cornwall had built in the preceding year over the place where Edmund the confessor archbishop
of Canterbury was born[d]

In this year the tenth of Oliver Sutton bishop of Lincoln, the king

---

[c] Ex Chartul. de Borstall. f. 7.   [d] Annal. Wigorn. sub an.

presented to the church of Oakley, with the chapels of Brill and
Borstall[e]. And William de Thornberg, one of the canons of Burcester, was elected prior of the said convent; a licence for choosing
being first obtained from Henry de Lacy earl of Lincoln, patron of
the said house[f]. William, one of the monks of Nuttle, was elected
abbot of that convent; leave for choosing being first asked and obtained from the lady Maud de Mortimer, whom they thought their
patroness, though the earl of Gloucester claimed that right[g].

Upon the late death of Sir John Fitz-Nigel, senior, of Borstall,
this inquisition was made of the extent of his lands and tenements.

*Extenta terrarum et tenementorum quæ fuerunt domini Johannis
filii Nigelli defuncti in villa de Borstall in com. Buck. facta ibidem
die dominica proxime post annuntiationem beatæ Mariæ anno regni
regis Edwardi* XVII. *qui dicunt per sacramentum suum quod capitale
messuagium valet per an. cum tota inclausa* II[s]. *et non plus, salva reprisa
domorum et aliarum officinarum. Dicunt etiam quod est ibidem una
hida terræ quæ vocatur Derhyde et continet in se* LX. *acras terræ arabilis et valet quælibet acra per annum* III[d]. *summa* XV[s]. *et certus visus
valet per an.* II[s]. *et reddit domino regi pro prædicta hida et certo visu*
X[s]. *et est ibidem quædam placca prati quæ vocatur Quethenelkell et
valet per an.* VI[d]. *dicunt etiam quod sunt ibidem in dominico in villa
de Borstall Brehull et Acle* VI. *virgatæ terræ arabilis, &c. et valet
quælibet acra per an.* III[d]. *summa* XXV[s]. IV[d]. *ob. q. reddendo domino
regi ad manerium suum de Brehull* XLVIII[s]. V[d]. *faciendo etiam domino
regi ad manerium suum de Brehull servitium cum uno homine pro*

An. ᴋCCLXXXIX. 17, 18. Edward I.
  D'n's rex mandavit vic. Oxon. per breve
suum q'd attachiaret Joh'em ep'um Winton, Philippum de Hoyvill, et magistrum
Will'um personam eccl'iæ de Witteneye
ministros predicti ep'i ita q'd haberet cor-
pora corum coram ipso d'no rege et ejus
consilio ad parliamentum suum post Pas-

cha anno regni sui octavo decimo ad respondend. ipsi d'no regi de quibusdam trans-
gressionibus—in boscis et chaccis ipsius
ep'i ut in venatione capta et assartis—predictus ep'us profert cartam — preceptum
q'd predictus cp'us eat sine die. Ex placitis Parliam. 18. Ed. I.

    [e] R. Dods. MS. vol. 107. f. 142.   [f] Ib. f. 146.   [g] Ib. f. 112.

qualibet virgata terræ vel opera per unum diem, summa operationum
XXXIII. *et dimid. et valent per totum* III*. IV*ᵈ*. ob. Dicunt etiam quod*
sunt ibidem III. *acræ terræ et dimid. et* I. *roda, et valet quælibet acra*
per an. III*ᵈ*. et tenentur de Nicholao de Esses. Et sunt ibidem* XV.
acræ terræ et valet quælibet acra per annum III*ᵈ*. summa* III*. IX*ᵈ*. et*
tenentur de hæredibus Willielmi filii Eliæ, et sunt ibidem in Hikeford
VI. *acræ terræ, et valet quælibet acra* III*ᵈ*. summa* XVIII*. et tenentur*
de Johanne de Accrue. dicunt etiam quod sunt ibidem de redditu assis.
I.X*. scilicet ad festum S. Michaelis et ad festum S. Thomæ apostoli*
et ad annunt. beatæ Mariæ et ad festum S. Johannes Baptistæ per
æquales portiones. Dicunt etiam quod balliva forestæ de Bernewode
valet per annum XLII*. et tenetur in capite de domino rege, dicunt*
etiam quod Johannes filius prædicti Johannis est propinquior hæres
ejus plenæ ætatis et miles ʰ

An. MCCXC. 18, 19. *Edward I.*

Henry de Lacy earl of Lincoln and lord of the manors of Burcester and Midlington, by writ from the king, was allowed to give seventy acres of land and ten shillings yearly rent in Saxton within the

An. MCCXC. 18, 19. Edw. I.
Pat. 18. E. 1. Licentia regis concessa Edmundo com. Cornub. ut det terras rectori
et fratribus domus de Asherugge in honore
preciosi sanguinis Jhesu Christi fundate.
28. Jul. m. 12.

He (Edmund earl of Cornwall) was cited
in the king's palace at Westminst. to appear before the archbishop of Cant. for
which the persons who served the citation
were imprisoned. Ang. Sac. Pars. 1. p. 402.

Mag'r Phil. de Heddeshovere pres. per
dom. Edm. com. Cornuh. ad eccl. de Bekkele quia mag'r Ric. de Sottewell institutus
fuit in eccl. de Frothingham. 15 kal. Apr.
pont. 11. i. æ. 1290. Reg. Ol. Sutton.

Rog. de Bikkerwik subd. pres. per Edm.
com. Cornub. ad eccl. de Stoke-basset vac.
quia idem Rog. non fit p'b'r infra annum.
5. kal. Aug. pont. 11.—iterum presentatus
et admissus, 8. Id. Dec. pont 12.

Simon de Wellis cl'ic. ad mediet. eccl'ie
de Heyford ad pontem per mort. mag'ri W.
ad pres. abb. et conv. de Egnesham x. kal.
Jan. pont. 11.

Rob. Trevet diac. pres. per Tho. de Gardino ad eccl. de Sumerton vac. per mortem
Walt. de Cotes. 5. kal. Feb. pont. 11.

Mag'r Rob. Bakun pres. per d'num Adam
le Despenser mil. ad eccl. de Ewelm vac.
per mort. Ingerami. 16. kal. Apr. pont. 11.

ʰ Ex Chartular. de Borstall. MS. f. 99.

county of York, to a chaplain who should celebrate divine service in the chapel of the Virgin Mary of Saxton, which land was held from the king *in capite*[i]

In the eleventh of Oliver Sutton, Edmund earl of Cornwall presented to the church of Frothingham, in the archdeaconry of Stowe[k], and to the churches of Stoke-Basset and Beckle, in this county[l]; and an. 13, to the church of All Saints of Helmeswell, in the archdeaconry of Stowe, and to the church of Rollesham, in this county.

Walter de la Hale and Juliana his wife, granted to John Fitz-Nigel of Borstal part of a curtilage and two furlongs of arable land, for the payment of one penny yearly to the king at his manor of Brehull. *Hiis testibus; Johanne le Brun de Acley, Nigello Travers, Johanne Ferebraz, Nigello de Boys, Willielmo Ulewyn, Johanne Segrym, Ricardo Elys, Willielmo filio Willielmi, Hugone filio Nigelli, Thoma Brun et tota curia de Brehull*[m].

An. MCCXCI.   19, 20.   *Edward I.*

The general taxation * of church dignities and benefices was this year completed and registered : the abbot of Oseney and prior of St. Catherines, appointed collectors for this diocese of Lincoln, deputed Ralph rector of Wotton, and Richard rector of Gilling to be taxers in the archdeaconries of Oxford, Bedford, and Bucks, excepting the deanery of Rotland.

Of this register there is one copy in parchment MS. folio in the Bodleian Library, that formerly belonged to Sir Henry Spelman. It has only this general title, LIBER TAXATIONUM OMNIUM BENEFICIORUM IN ANGLIA. In the first page there is a quære, whether not composed in 20. of Edw. I. when the bishops of Winchester and Lincoln were commissioned to tax all benefices throughout all Eng-

* On occasion of the pope's granting the king the tenth of all spiritualities for six years *in subsidium Terræ Sanctæ.*

[i] R. Dods. MS. vol. 44. f. 162.   [k] Ib. vol. 107. f. 153.   [l] Ib. f. 163.   [m] Ex Chartul. de Borstall. f. 5.

land? In a small loose paper in the said book there is a memoran
dum by an unknown hand, that the church in Garlek-Hyth in Ar
chid. Lond. which was built in the reign of Edw. II. by Richard Ro-
thering sheriff of London, is here valued at seven marks, which ar-
gues this taxation to have been after that of Edw. I. *viz.* in that of
Edward the IIId's reign. But this is a poor ignorant surmise, as if
there could be no church in Garlek-Hyth till that sheriff built a new
one, or as if it was then first made a distinct parish. When collated
with other copies of this year's taxation, it appears one of the tran-
scripts of them. There is one more ancient record of it in MS. in
the Bodleian Library, wherein the account of this diocese of Lincoln
bears this inscription. *Taxatio spiritualitatis in dioc. Lincoln. per
Radulphum et Ricardum de Morton et de Willing ecclesiarum rectores
sub reverend. patribus O. Dei gratia Linc. et J. Wynton. episcopis
taxatoribus principalibus a domino Nicholao pp.* IIII. *deputatis una cum
incremento per retaxationem a supradictis patribus sanctis an. Dom.*
MCCLXXXXI. There is endorsed on the said book, " This manuscript
" was written an. 1291. Nicholas IV. being pope about the 19.'Ed. I."
Tho. Walsingham refers it to the preceding year, because then pre-
paring. *Circa idem tempus jubente papa Nicholao taxatæ sunt ecclesiæ Anglicanæ secundum verum valorem et extunc cessavit taxatio
Norwicensis per Innocentium quartum prius facta* [n]. And Tho. Wikes
attributes it to the year 1292, because then possibly was the first collection by those new rates. Most of the historians complain of it as
a grievous exaction. There is another transcript of great part 'of it
preserved by the most industrious Mr. Roger Dodsworth, among his
Collections, vol. 86.

A specimen of Ambrosden, Burcester, and neighbouring churches
shall be here given, with their difference from the * old taxation by
the bishop of Norwich, now annulled.

---

* The Norwich taxation was by Walter   1245. deceased 1257. to whom P. Innocent
de Suthfeld bishop of Norwich, consecrat.   IVth, upon giving the tenth of all eccl. be-

[n] Tho. Walsing. inter Ang. Script. a Cambdeno edit. p. 44.

ARCHID. OXON.

DECANATUS *de* CUDESDON.

	verus valor	Norwycens.
Ecclesia de AMBRESDON	XL. *marc.*	XXX. *marc.*
Ecclesia de MERTON *deducta pensione*	XVII. *marc.* X^s.	XV. *marc.*
Pensio abbatis EYNESHAM *in eadem*	XXX^s.	

DECANATUS *de* BURNCESTRE.

Ecclesia de BURNCESTRE *deducta*	verus valor	Norwycens.
porcione	XVIII. *marc.*	XV. *marc.*
Porcio abb'is de ALNETO *in eadem*	II. *marc*	
Porcio abb'is de OSENEY *in eadem*	XL^s	
Porcio abb'is de EYNESHAM *in eadem*	.XII^s.	
Ecclesia de WESTON	XIV. *marc.*	XII. *marc.*
Ecclesia de CHERLETON *deducta porcione*	XXX. *marc.*	XX. *marc.*
Pensio prioris de WARE *in eadem*	III. *marc.*	
Ecclesia de WENDELEBURY	X. *marc. et dimid.*	IX. *marc.*
Ecclesia de CESTERTON	XVI. *marc.*	XII. *marc.*
Ecclesia de LANGTON	XII. *marc.*	IV. *marc.*
Ecclesia de GODINTON	VI. *marc. et dimid.*	IV. *marc.*
Ecclesia de MIDELINTON	XV. *marc.*	VIII. *marc.*
Ecclesia de BIKENHULLE *deducta porcione*	XV. *marc.*	XI. *marc.*
Porcio abb'is de OSENEY *in eadem*	X^s	
Ecclesia de BLECHESDON *deducta porcione*	XV. *marc.*	XXX. *marc.*
Porcio abbatis de OSENEY *in eadem*	X^s	

There were at this time twenty-seven churches in the deanery of Burcester, their valuation CCLXVIII^l. XV^s. IV^d.

<hr>

nefices to the king for three years, sent a command to take the valuation, which was done in every deanery by the dean and three of the rural chapter, an. 1254. Vid. Whart. Ang. Sac. vol. 1. p. 411.

Within this year Edmund earl of Cornwall gave several lands and tenements in the parish of St. Peter's East, Oxford, to the brothers of the Holy Trinity within that city : for which and other charities he had the title of *summus religiosorum patronus* [o]

Within the twelfth of Oliver Sutton bishop of Lincoln, Richard de Amory, knight, presented a clerk to the church of Bukenhull [p] · and Sır Almaric de S. Amand to the church of Alrinton. A new prioress was now elected in the nunnery of Stodley, leave being first asked and obtained from the patron Edmund earl of Cornwall [q] · Alice de Lacy, mother of Henry earl of Lincoln, in right of her dowry, presented to two parts of the church of Clipston in the archdeaconry of Northampton [r]. And within this same year Alice de Lacy, sole daughter and heir of Henry earl of Lincoln, at nine years of age, was married to Thomas eldest son and heir of Edmund earl of Lancaster.

John de Verdon lord of the manor of Heth in this county, was arraigned for treason and divers other misdemeanors at Bergavenny,

---

An. MCCXCI. 19, 20. Edward I.

Radulfus de Hengham diaconus ad presentationem Edmundi com. Cornub. ratione custodiæ terrarum Joh'is Wake institutus ad eccl'iam de Middelton. x. kal. Aug. 1291. resignat. 1293. Ex regist. Joh'is Romane arch. Ebor.

Ithelus de Kayrwrt subd. pres. per Ric. de Aumori ad eccl. de Brikkenhill vac. per mort. Rog. de Aumori. 4. id. Maii. pont. 12. R. Sutton.

Rob. de Hoketon cap. pres. per d'num Rob. de Grey mil. ad eccl. de Feringford per mort. Tho. de Idemeston. 7. id. Jun. pont. 12.

Mag'r Hug. de Thurleby pres. per abb.

et conv. de Egnesham ad eccl. de Heyford per ingress. Simonis de Welles in ord. fratrum predicatorum. 10. kal. Sept. pont. 12.

Mag'r Will. de Chaddeleshunt repres. per priorem et conv. de Kenilworth ad eccl. de Hethe vac. quia idem Will'us non fuit p'b'r infra annum; admiss. 7. id. Octob. pont. 12.

Otto de Dune Amenay p'b'r pres. per proc. abb'is et conv. de Becco Herlewini ad eccl. de Cottesford per cess. Joh'is de Cusantia. 17. kal. Jan. pont. 12.

D'n's Edm. de Maydestan p'b'r pres. per T. ep'um Winton. ad eccl. de Abberbury vac. per mort. mag'ri Nich'i. 4. non. Feb. pont. 12.

---

[o] Ant. a Wood. Antiq. Un. Ox. l. 1. p. 133. f. 163.   [r] Ib.

[p] R. Dods. MS. vol. 107. f. 163.   [q] Ib.

before the king and his council; and upon full hearing had judgment to be committed to prison, as also to forfeit all his royalties in the lands of Ewyas Lacy. But the king, taking into consideration the good services of his ancestors done to himself and his progenitors, and because he acknowledged his offence, and submitted himself, granted, that after his death his heirs should enjoy those privileges; and, for five hundred marks fine, freed him of his imprisonment[s].

Richard Pigeon of Borstall granted to John Pipett of Borstall, two acres of land in the field of Borstall, of which one half acre lay at Smeth-weye, and one rood at Wodewell, and one half acre near Fauleshoe, and one rood in Coppidthorne, and one rood in Redforlong, and one rood in Cornforlong. *Hiis testibus; Nigello Travers, Hugone filio Nigelli de Brehull, Johanne Ferebraz, Johanne Segrym, Roberto Baudreyt, Johanne Brun, et multis aliis. Dat. apud Borstall die Martis proxime post festum S. Johannis Baptistæ anno regni regis Edwardi decimo nono*[t]

An. MCCXCII. 20, 21. *Edward I.*

The king sent a precept to the sheriff of Bucks in behalf of an inhabitant or native of the parish of Ambrosden, John de Prydington, for a prohibition against William vicar of the church of Little-Brickhill, who had prosecuted the said John de Prydington in the ecclesiastical court, upon a cause that was not within the cognizance of it[u].

Henry Lacy earl of Lincoln was now sent ambassador to the king of France, to treat concerning the restraint of such pirates as robbed the English merchants[x].

An. MCCXCII. 20, 21. Edw. I.   vac. per resign. Will'i de Chaddeleshunt.
Henr. de Dunton cap. pres. per priorem   5. non. Oct. pont. 13.
et conv. de Kenilworth ad eccl. de Hethe

[s] Dugd. Bar. tom. 1. p. 473, b.   [t] Ex Chartul. de Borstall, MS. penes D. Joh. Aubrey, Bar. [u] W. Prynne, Hist. Col. tom. 3. p. 477.   [x] Dugd. Bar. tom. 1. p. 101. a.

In this thirteenth of Oliver Sutton, Edmund earl of Cornwall presented to the church of Manton in the archdeaconry of Northampton [y].

Within this year died Hugh de Plessets baron of Hokenorton, who had demised his land of Musewell in the parish of Ambrosden to John Fitz-Nigel of Borstall: he left issue Hugh his son and heir, twenty-five years of age, who doing his homage had livery of the said barony of Hokenorton, within which was the adjoining manor of Chesterton, which was held from his father by Sir Bardulf de Chesterton for half a knight's fee: the tenure of which manor, and the services of under-tenants, appear from a court roll of the hundred of Chadlinton taken in the beginning of Edw. I.

Jurat. dicunt quod Bardulphus de Cestreton tenet manerium de Cestreton de Hugone de Plessetis tanquam pertinentiam ad manerium suum de Hokenorton pro dimidio feodo militis, et tenet in dominico suo in eodem manerio II. *carucatas terre cum pertinentiis, et valent per annum* CVI[s]. VIII[d]...... *Johannes Propositus tenet* I. *virgatam terre operabilis et debet opera, &c. quæ valent quolibet anno* XIII[s]. IV[d]. *ob. q. ..... Bardulphus de Fraxino tenet tantum terre per idem servicium. ..... Henricus de Fretorn tenet de predicto Bardulpho* I. *croftam.. Willielmus de Barton tenet* I. *virgatam terre. ..... Summa tocius valoris* XI[l]. XIII[s]. X[d]. *..... Dicunt quod idem Bardulphus de Cesterton debet sectam ad hundredum de Chadelinton de tribus septimanis in tres septimanas et ad duos magnos comit. et debet* V[d]. *de ward penie ad festum S. Martini, et* VIII[s]. *de turno vice-comitis et cum vice-comes tenet turnos suos in predicto hundredo idem Bardulphus mittet ibi unum de suis ad petendam libertatem suam et habebit, nec ipse nec homines sui venient ibi, et ballivi com. Glouc. venient quolibet anno semel ad tenendum visum Franciplegii in eodem manerio et asportabunt omnia amerciamenta inde proveniencia et* IV[s]. *de certo visus ejusdem, summa* XII[s]. V[d]. *..... Et dicunt quod abbas de Oseney tenet ecclesiam ejusdem manerii in proprios usus sct nesciunt quo wa-*

ranto, et III. *virgatas terre..... Dicunt quod abbas de Eynesham te_ net in eodem manerio* XVI. *virgatas terre de Hugone de Plessetis tan_ quam pertinen. ad manerium suum de Hokenorton pro quart. feodi mi_ litis de quibus Nicholaus le Wyld tenet* I. *virgatam terre &c. summa* VII[s]. VI[d]. *ob*[z].

This Hugh de Plessets had taken to wife Isabel the third daughter of John de Ripariis, cousin and one of the heirs to Philippa Basset countess of Warwick, and for the purparty of his said wife had the manor of Hedindon, with the hundred of Bolendon, and the hun_

An. MCCXCII. 20, 21. Edw. I.
Cum abbas Regalis Loci Oxon. coram Thoma de Weyland et sociis suis nuper justitiariis domini regis de banco placitasset ep'um Linc. de averiis ipsius abbatis captis et injuste detentis—et idem ep'us advocasset captionem et detentionem averiorum predicti abbatis juste, &c. pro eo q'd abbas de Egnesham de eodem ep'o tenet manerium de Erdington in quo averia predicta capta fuerunt per servitium duorum feodorum militis de quo predecessores sui ep'i a tempore quo non extat memoria fuerunt in seisina per manus predecessorum predicti abbatis de Enesham: et super hoc predictus abbas Loci Regalis dixisset quod ipse habet quoddam breve pendens in curia regis versus- com. Cornub. de hoc, quod idem com. Cornub. acquietet ipsum de servitio quod prefatus ep'us ab eo exigebat de predicto manerio: et unde idem com. qui medius est inter eos ipsum abb'em acquietare debuit; et quia idem com. porrexit cartam D. H. regis patris D. regis nunc quæ testabatur q'd idem dominus H. rex concessit Ricardo com. Pictavie et Cornub. patri predicti com. predictum manerium si-

mul cum aliis terris et tenementis quæ fuerunt Roberti Drews in Anglia, et dixit quod ratione illius cartæ non potuit sine d'no rege respondere. Tandem in crastino purificationis anno vicesimo dictum est attornato predicti com. quod de loquela predicta inde quietus recederet quoad tunc salvo jure cujuslibet.—Placit. Parl. 20. Edw. I.

1292. pont. 13. Ol. Sutton. Mag'r Joh. de Deneby presb. pres. per abb'em et conv. de Westminstre ad eccl. de Langeton vac. per mort. mag'ri Rob. Baret. 2. non. Octob.

Rog. de Kivelingworth pres. per abb. et conv. de Egnesham ad eccl. de Meriton vac. per resign. mag'ri Rob. de Kivelingworth. 18. kal. Feb. pont. 13.

Indulgentia xx. dierum concessa orantibus pro anima quondam mag'ri Nich'i de Bocland rectoris eccl'ie de Abberbiri cujus corpus in cimiterio dicte eccl'ie tumulatus. 12. kal. Jun. pont. 13. Ol. Sutton. Memorand. Ol. Sutton. f. 58.

Mag'r Alex. de Quappelad cl'ic. pres. per abb. et conv. de Egnesham ad mediet. eccl. de Heyford ad pont. per mort. mag'ri Hug. de Thurleby. 13. kal. Jan. pont. 13. Ol. Sutton.

[z] R. Dods. MS. vol. 114. f. 177.

dred lying without the north gate of Oxford[a]. Which Hugh de
Plessets in 5. Edw. I. was impleaded by the men of Hedington for
depriving and abridging them of their ancient customs and privileges
within the said manor, and in the king's court at Westminster this
memorable composition was made.

*Noverint universi præsentes et futuri quod cum homines de manerio
de Hedingdon quod est de antiquo dominico coronæ Angliæ, Hugonem
de Plesseys dominum ejusdem manerii in curia domini regis Edwardi filii regis Henrici anno regni ejusdem regis Edwardi quinto
coram eodem domino rege implectassent pro eo quod idem Hugo ab
eisdem hominibus alias consuetudines et alia servitia exigebat quam
facere deberent vel temporibus quibus dictum manerium in manibus
regum Angliæ extiterat facere consueverunt.   Tandem dicto placito
inter dictum Hugonem et eosdem homines quiescendo convenit in hunc
modum, videlicet quod prædictus Hugo concessit pro se et hæredibus
suis quod omnes homines terram tenentes in prædicto manerio de cætero habeant et teneant terras suas in eodem manerio per eandem firmam per quam eas prius tenere consueverunt, videlicet quælibet virgata terræ quæ pro decem solidis tenere consueverit de cætero pro decem solidis teneatur et quæ pro octo solidis tenebatur pro octo solidis
teneatur, et quæ pro quinque solidis pro quinque teneatur, et qui pro
minore firma terram suam tenuerit illam pro eadem firma teneat, et
qui minus tenuerit de una virgata minus det et hoc secundum modum
tenuræ suæ terræ illius et secundum quantitatem tenementi sui.   Præ
terea cum eas eorundem hominum integram virgatam terræ tenens de-
cesserit hæres ejus per duplicationem sui redditus annualis et per quatuor solidos terminum ultra relevabit et qui minus tenuerit de una virgata ultra redditum suum duplicatum minus det secundum quantitatem tenementi sui.   Item præfati homines facient singulis annis præfato Hugoni et hæredibus suis pro qualibet virgata terræ sexdecem
operationes videlicet una die inter festum S. Michaelis et natale Do-*

[a] Dugd. Bar. tom. 1. p. 774.

mini illi qui carúcas habuerunt arabunt terram domini in dicto mane-
rio eodem modo et in tantum quo terram propriam absque fictione
arare deberent, et alia die in eodem termino tam illi quam alii ejusdem
manerii solos equos habentes terram domini ibidem herciabunt et per
duos dies in quadragesima similiter arabunt et herciabunt et uno die
postea sarculabunt blada domini ibidem et per duos dies prata domini
falcabunt tertio vero die herbam ibi falcatam vertent et fœnum ibi le-
vabunt et quinto die fœnum illud cariabunt usque ad curiam prædicti
manerii de Hedingdon illi videlicet qui carectas habuerunt et qui ca-
rectas non habuerunt venient cum furcis suis ad dictum fœnum levan-
dum et thassandum, et pro falcatione et aliis supradictis circa dictum
fœnum modo prædicto appositis seu apponendis solventur eisdem homi-
nibus de denariis domini singulis annis proximo die quo falcare incipient
quinque solidi.   Item uno die warectabunt terram domini prout decet
ad unum diem cum carucis suis et quilibet eorum animalia habens me-
tet in autumpno unam acram bladi de blado domini ibidem sumptibus
propriis et pro hiis ultimis duabus operationibus iidem homines com
munam ubique habebunt in dominicis pasturis domini, exceptis pasturis
et aliis locis ejusdem domini qui tempore confectionis istius scripti
claudebantur et aliis pasturis suis iidem homines hactenus communicare
nullatenus consueverunt.   Tribus autem diebus in autumpno metent
blada domini sumptibus ejusdem domini primo scilicet die cum omni-
bus famulis suis exceptis uxoribus et pastoribus suis et illa die come-
dent iidem homines et omnes dicti messores cum domino ad nonam et
præfati homines et non messores eadem die cum domino cœnabunt et
aliis diebus duobus pro singulis virgatis singulos homines ad metendum
invenient et hoc ad sumptus domini.   Ita quod diebus illis comedent
dicti messores cum domino ad nonam.   Item uno die cariabunt blada
domini ibidem scilicet qui carectas habuerint et qui carectas non ha-
buerint adjuvabunt ad thessandum bladum et uno die colligent nuces
nomine domini in bosco qui vocatur Stowode.   Item facient sectam cu-
riæ domini de Hedingdon de sex septimanis, et si breve domini regis
in dicta curia attachietur tunc sectam illam facient de tribus septima-
nis in tres septimanas et ad præfatam curiam singulis annis inter fes-

*tum S. Michaelis et S. Martini venient cum toto ac pleno dyteno sicut
hactenus facere consueverunt et omnes prisones qui infra dictum manerium de Hedingdon capientur sumptibus propriis custodient. Et sciendum quod si homines prædicti filias suas extra libertatem dicti manerii maritare voluerint dabunt domino pro qualibet filia sic maritata
duos solidos et hoc pro catallis extra libertatem dicti manerii cum ipsa
remotis, et si infra libertatem ejusdem manerii eas maritaverint nihil
dabunt pro maritagiis earundem. Præterea sciendum quod quoties
contigerit aliquem prædictorum hominum pro aliquo delicto quoque
modo amerciari in eadem curia per pares suos et non per alios amer-
cientur et hoc secundum modum delicti. Concessit etiam præfatus
Hugo pro se et hæredibus suis quibuscunque quod præfati homines et
eorum hæredes omnia et singula quæ infra dictum manerium de jure
hæreditario habere debeant de cætero habeant et utantur, et quod alia
servitia non facient quam prædicta. Pro præmissis vero concessionibus eisdem hominibus factis et pro omnibus aliis quæ ab eis quoquo
modo exigi potuerint per præfatum Hugonem vel hæredes suos extra
servitia prænominata concesserunt præfati homines pro se et hæredibus et quibuscunque successoribus suis singulis annis die Omnium Sanctorum tres marcas, et quotiens dominus rex suos dominicos talliare contigerit dabunt prædicto Hugoni et hæredibus suis quinque marcas: et
dictus Hugo concessit pro se et hæredibus suis quod iidem homines
quieti sint de tallagio pro eisdem. Et ut omnia et singula præmissa
præfatus hominibus et eorum hæredibus rata et inconcussa perpetuis
temporibus permaneant, dictus Hugo pro se et hæredibus suis præsenti
scripto sigillum suum apposuit et dicti homines præmissas conventiones
in rotulis placitorum domini regis de anno supradicto ad majorem securitatem inrotulari procurarunt* [b].*

These rights and privileges were confirmed to the tenants of Hedingdon by king Edw. III. at Westminster, Octob. 20. *regni* 29. The
same grants were renewed and ratified by Sir Richard d'Amory lord
of the manor of Hedingdon, 31. Edw. III. and again confirmed by

---

[b] Ex Regist. Borstall. penes D. Joh. Aubrey, Bar.

king Richard II. at Oxford, Octob. 4. *regni* 16.[c] Before the death
of Hugh de Plessets, sen. this fine was passed between him and Sir
John Fitz-Nigel, jun. of Borstall, in relation to the land of Musewell
within the parish of Ambrosden.

Hæc est finalis concordia facta in curia dom. regis apud West-
minster in Octab. S. Martini anno regni regis Edwardi filii regis
Henrici vicesimo coram Thoma Weylond, Johanne de Lovetot, Rogero
de Leycestre, et Willielmo de Burtone, justitiariis domini regis fideli-
bus tunc ibi præsentibus inter Johannem filium Nigelli, jun. quer. et
Hugonem de Plessetis deforc. de uno messuagio una carucata terræ et
uno molendino cum pertinentiis in Musewell unde placitum conven-
tionis sumptum fuit inter eos in eadem curia: scilicet quod prædictus
Hugo recognovit prædictum tenementum cum pertinentiis esse jus ip-
sius Johannis ut illud quod idem Johannes habet de dono prædicti Hu-
gonis habend. et tenend. eidem Johanni et hæredibus suis de prædicto
Hugone et hæredibus suis imperpetuum reddendo inde annuatim unum
clavum cariophili ad natale Domini pro omni servitio consuetudine et
exactione: et prædictus Hugo et hæredes sui warantizabunt acquie-
tabunt et defendent eidem Johanni et hæredibus suis prædicta tene-
menta cum pertinentiis suis per prædictum servitium contra omnes ho-
mines imperpetuum. Et pro hac recognitione warantia acquietantia
fine et concordia idem Johannes dedit prædicto Hugoni unum spura-
rium aureum[d].

An. MCCXCIII. 21, 22. *Edward I.*

An inquisition was now made whether the abbot of Rewley
(founded by Edmund earl of Cornwall) owed service to the county
court at Oxford, or to the king's court of the hundred of Poghedele,
(now Ploughly;) and return was made that he owed no suit or service
to either, because he had no lands in this county but the manors of
Erdinton (now Yarnton) and Willarston, and the site of the abbey,

---

[c] Ex Regist. Borstall. penes D. Joh. Aubrey, Bar.   [d] Ib. f. 33.

which were of the honour of St. Walery, with two coppices of wood in Netlebed; and eight virgates of land, with twenty acres of meadow and their appurtenances in Wendlebury, which were of the fee of Amory de St. Amand [e].

Henry Lacy earl of Lincoln attended the king with his army into Wales, where, not far from the earl's town and castle of Denbigh, the English received a great repulse. After the earl's return, in consideration of his good service, the king granted to him a special charter for fairs and markets in several of his lordships. Among other, a market on the Monday every week at his manor of Midlington adjoining to Burcester, and a fair there yearly on the eve and day of St. Thomas the martyr. This martial earl was in this same year in the expedition made into Gascoign [f].

Edmund earl of Cornwall gave lands to Walter de Cornwall his base brother [g].

Within this year 1293, Thomas Brent gave to the abbey of Oseney all the tithe of his demesne lands in Heyford Warin, at which time Simon was parson of that church [h].

Placit. Parl. 21. Edw. I.

Et quia predictus Will. de Cherington cognovit quod litera citatoria coram officiali de arcubus London perrexit Ric'o de Glocestre persone eccl'ie de Chepingnorton in eccl. S. Trin. apud Cantuar. ubi tunc fuit curia regis et infra hospitium d'ni regis dictum est eidem mag'ro Will'o quod non recedat a curia prius quam dominus rex super hoc sibi direxit voluntatem suam.

Edmund earl of Cornwall gave several tenements in the parish of St. Peter's in the East, Oxford, to the master and brothers of the Holy Trinity, and founded there a chaple or chauntry for five capellanes to pray for his soul.—Hiis testibus; d'no Ricardo de Cornubia, fratre nostro, &c. dat. apud Beckele in festo decollationis S. Joh. Bapt. anno regni reg. Edwardi XXI. Hist. et Antiq. Un. Oxon. l. 1. p. 133.

Ric. de Scireburn capellan. pres. per d'num Hen. Thyes mil. ad capellam de Oke vac. per mort. Joh. de Draycote. kal. Jul. pont. 14. Ol. Sutton.

Pat. 21. Edw. I. Rex concedit Henrico fil. Nigelli licentiam quod ipse 1 toftum et 38 acras terre in Lacheford dare possit abb'i et conv. de Thame et succ. suis. 10. Nov.

[e] Mon. Ang. tom. 1. p. 936.　　[f] Dugd. Bar. tom. 1. p. 104. b.　　[g] MS. Ashmol. 844.
f 1.　　[h] Collectanea W. Wirley de Monast. Osneiæ et S. Frideswidæ, Oxon. MS. Wood. F. 16. p. 5.

An. mccxciv. 22, 23. *Edward I.*

The king being now a second year engaged in a war with France, several of the clergy and religious made their contributions, to whom for acknowledgment and reward the king granted particular protections. Among others, Ralph de Mertival rector of Ambrosden, having assisted the king with half the profits of his benefice, received a special protection in this form.

Rex capitaneo marinariorum et eisdem marinariis vice comitibus et omnibus ballivis et fidelibus, &c. ad quos, &c. salutem. Cum dilectus nobis magister Radulfus de Mirtivall persona ecclesiæ de Ambrosden medietatem beneficii, &c. nobis in subsidium nostrum de anno præsenti juxta taxationem ultimo inde factam liberaliter concesserit et gratanter. Nos ejusdem Radulphi quieti et tranquillitati ex hac causa libencius providere volentes suscepimus in protectionem et defensionem nostram specialem præfatum Radulphum et singulos de prædicto Radulpho homines terras res redditus et omnes possessiones ejusdem, &c. In cujus, &c. has literas fieri fecimus patentes per prædictum annum duraturas. Teste rege apud Westm. 18. die. Octob.[i]

A protection in the same form was granted to the prior and convent of Burcester[k]. Another to the rector and brethren of Ash rugge[l]. As also to Thomas de Capella parson of Blechesdon; to Richard de Pyryte parson of Chinnor; and to Giles Filliol parson of the churches of * Ardeleye, Rybinghale, Great Ockle and Little Ockle.

This payment of half their revenues is in the writs of protection

* Rectores de Ardeley.
Will. de Sulthorn subdec. ad eccl'iam de Ardulfel ad pres. Guidon. fil. Roberti. Rot. Rob. Grosthead. an. 4. (1238.)
Joh. de Schulton cl'ic. pres. per dom. Joh. fil. Guidonis mil. ad eccl. de Ardele

vac. per hoc quod Roger de Schulton institutus fuit in eccl. de Croulton. 3. Id. Jul. 1300. Reg. Dalderby. pont. 1.
An. mccxciv. 22, 23. Edw. I.
Pat. 22. Edw. I. m. 6. Magister Rad'us de Martivall persona eccl'ie de Ambresdon

i W. Prynne, Hist. Collect. tom. 3. p. 592.   k Ib. p. 589.   l Ib. p. 594. et Reyneri Append. ad Apostolat. Benedict. in Anglia, p. 66.

represented as a liberal and free concession and contribution : when indeed it was an imposition and levy which they could not resist. For, on the nineteenth of September, the king convened an assembly of bishops, archdeacons, abbots, and proctors of the clergy, where against their will they granted the king one half of their yearly profits. And such orders were issued out upon it, that whoever contradicted this exaction, should be dealt with as enemies to the king and nation [m]. The same proportion of one entire half of all revenues was given to Henry VIII. by convocation, an. 1523 [n]. It seems probable that some of the most poor, or the most stout of the clergy, were unwilling to bear this burden ; but others, that could make a virtue of necessity, appeared forward and zealous in it, and to them the protections were given as a distinguishing mark of favour.

About this time a perambulation of the forest of Bernwood was made, and the limits of it returned upon oath, in this form.

Juratores dicunt quod foresta de Bernewode incipit apud Gosachrehend que extendit in rivulum que vocatur Thame streme inter campum de Thomeley et campum de Wormehale includendo forestam ex parte dextra per omnes bandas et metas subscriptas et excludendo extra forestam ex parte sinistra totum residuum et sic usque inter Shiremen inter campum de Thomeley et Wormehale et sic usque Brodwey et sic usque Brechey et sic usque fossatum Oteweysdyches Scrobbes per le Gotecote et sic per le Hollowey usque Menemersh et sic usque le Hok de Okewode versus Shortrudingsend et sic usque Denebroke et sic usque Suthewelleringe et sic usque Salfcroftestyle et sic usque Wy de crouche ad

hab. lit. de protect. per 1. ann. duratur. T.R. apud Westm. 18. Octob.

Edm. fil. Bernardi habet lit. reg. ad pres. ad 3[tiam] partem eccl'iæ de Wottesdon per mort. Rad'i fil. Bernardi nuper rectoris ejusd. et ad donationem regis spectant. ratione custodiæ terrarum et hæredis Hug. de

Courtenay defuncti. 16. Nov. Pat. 23. Ed. I. m. 1.

Will. de Rogate habet lit. reg. de pres. ad portionem in eccl'ia de Wotesdon per resign. Edmundi fil. Bernardi ratione custodiæ terrarum et hæred. Hug. de Curtenay defuncti. 17. Apr. 25. Ed. I.

[m] Annal. Eccles. Wigorn. sub an.   [n] Burnet, Hist. of Reform. par. 1. p. 21.

*Schyreine et sic usque Northcrofts et sic usque Oddestaple et sic usque
Stonput et sic per fossatum usque Merelalake et sic usque Garcroft
abbatisse de Godestowe et sic per fossatum montis Hurnlake et sic usque Croftwellend et sic usque Ernecotehath per fossatum et sic usque
Moleshe et sic usque Corbynsnede et sic inter boscum Alani Plunkenet et boscum Johannis filii Nigelli usque Holwodebroke et sic per
hayiam de Longelondsend et sic usque le Hoke versus le Frereslosne et
sic usque Risiford inter dominicum regis et Alani Plunkenet et sic
usque Brendelegh inter campum de Pydington et sic usque Stonford
et sic usque Hethencburne inter Akemannestrete inter devisas com.
Oxon. et Buck.*[o]

Robert Grey of Rotherfield in this county had the barony of Coges near Whitney, by the gift of his uncle Walter de Grey archbishop of York, who had it from Joan daughter and coheir of Robert de Arsik, and from Thomas de Haya and Alexandra his wife,
sister to the said Joan. Which Robert de Grey, having married
Avice daughter of William St. Liz, died about this time, possessed of
the moiety of the manors of Somerton, Feryngford, and Herdwyke
in this county, part of the said barony held by the service of keeping
Dover castle[p]

In a trial this year, it was determined that Henry Lacy earl of
Lincoln and Margaret his wife had a free market in their manor of
Colham, and a yearly fair at Woxbridge, com. Mid. which was a
member of Colham, and had been the estate of Richard Camvill[q].
The said earl, considering he had no issue of his body but Alice his
daughter, at the king's request, did, on the feast of Simon and Jude,
at Westminster, pass a fine to settle the reversion of his whole estate
on Edmund earl of Lancaster and his heirs[r].

The king had given the manor of Pidington in the parish of Ambrosden to Alan de Plugenet, who, having done great service in several wars, did now receive command to attend the king at Portsmouth

---

o Collectanea W. Wyrley, ut supra, f. 9. b.   p Dugd. Bar. tom. 1. p. 723. a.   q R.
Dods. MS. vol. 119. p. 21.   r MS. Ashmol. num. 814.

upon the first of September, well fitted with horse and arms, thence
to sail with him into Gascoign. This manor of Pidington had been
given or confirmed to the monastery of St. Frideswide in Oxford, by
Malcolm king of Scots and earl of Huntingdon, whose charter of donation being omitted in the year MCLIX. shall be here inserted.

*Malcolmus rex Scotorum dapifero suo de Huntingdon et omnibus
probis hominibus suis tocius honoris Francis et Anglis salutem. Sciatis
me dedisse Domino et S. Mariæ et Frideswidæ Oxon. et canonicis ibidem
D'no servientibus in liberam et perpetuam elemosinam villam de Pydington in Oxfordscyre pro salute mea et fratrum meorum et pro anima
avi mei et patris mei et omnium parentum in sustentationem canoni
corum in perpetuum. Ita scilicet ut Johanna filia . . . . . . Basset dictam villam in vita sua teneat et servicium inde debitum canonicis predictis reddat, post decessum ejus canonicis remaneat in perpetuam possessionem et puram elemosinam cum omnibus libertatibus &c. Testibus; Herberto episcopo Glasc. apud Grasguer*.*

Which grant was confirmed by Henry II. king of England, and by
Thomas archbishop of Canterbury [t].

An. MCCXCV. 23, 24. *Edward I.*

April the seventeenth, Hugh son of Elyas Carter of Burcester,
granted and confirmed to Robert Clerk of Berencester, one buttery,
and garret or room over it, in the village of Berncester, situate between
the house where he dwelt and the entrance which led to the hall of
the said Robert, extending in breadth along the highway toward
the church-yard of the parish church of Berencester, to hold free and
without reserve of rent or service for ever, in consideration of which
the said Robert Clerk gave two marks sterling in hand, &c.

*Sciant præsentes et futuri quod ego Hugo filius Eliæ Carectarii de
Berencester dedi et concessi et hac præsenti charta mea confirmavi et
omnino pro me et hæredibus meis et assignatis quietum clamavi Roberto Clerico de Berencester unum cellarium et unum solarium in villa*

de Berencester, videlicet illud cellarium et illud solarium quæ sita sunt intra domum meam quam ego inhabito et introitum qui ducit ad aulam prædicti Roberti et extendit se in latitudine juxta altam stratam versus cœmiterium ecclesiæ parochialis de Berencestr. Habend. et tenend. dictum cellarium et dictum solarium cum fundo et cum muris et cum libero introitu et exitu et cum omnibus aliis pertinentiis et aysiamentis prædicto Roberto et hæredibus suis et assignatis quibuscunque libere quiete integre bene et in pace et hæreditarie in perpetuum sine ullo retenemento mei vel hæredum meorum et sine omnimodo servitio inde perveniente ad nos quocunque modo pertinente. Pro hac autem donatione concessione et præsentis chartæ meæ confirmatione dedit mihi prædictus Robertus duas marcas sterlingorum præ manibus in gersumam. Et ego prædictus Hugo et hæredes mei et assignati prædictum cellarium et solarium cum fundo et cum muris et cum libero introitu et exitu et cum omnibus aliis pertinentiis et aysiamentis ut prædictum est prædicto Roberto et hæredibus suis et assignatis quibuscunque contra omnes homines et fœminas warantizabimus acquietabimus et in perpetuum defendemus. Et ut hæc mea donatio concessio et præsentis chartæ meæ confirmatio rata et stabilis in perpetuum permaneat præsentem chartam hanc sigilli mei impressione roboravi. Hiis testibus; Magistro Ricardo de Wendlebury, Johanne de Cotesford, Ricardo de Caune, Simone Germayn de Bygenhull, Johanne Ateford de Berncester, et aliis. Datum et actum apud Berncester quinto decimo kalend. Maii. anno regni regis Edwardi vicesimo tertio[u].

An. MCCXCV. 23, 24. Edw. I.

A. ep'us Dunelm. concessit Edm. com. Cornub. manerium suum de Hoveden per 6. annos pro 4500 marc. sterling. Rex confirmat. 24. Apr. Pat. 24. Edw. I.

Pat. 24. Edw. I. Joh. de Hastyng de licentia regis dat priori et conv. de Stodley advocationem eccl'ie de Aston Cantelua habend. sibi et succ. in perpetuum in escambium 13. librat. terre cum pertin. in predicta villa de Aston quas idem prior et conventus tenent de eodem Joh'e in lib. et perpet. elemos. 15. Nov.

Rob. de la Kerveyl cl'ic. pres. per d'num Rog. de Insula mil. ad mediet. eccl'ie de Heyford ad pontem vac. per hoc quod Will. de Brampton ult. rector ejusd. institutus fuit in aliud beneficium. 5. kal. Jun. pont. 16.

Will. de Luda cl'icus pres. per abb. et conv. de Barlinges ad eccl. de Middelington vac. per mort. mag'ri Petri Durandi. 16. kal. Jan. pont. 16. Ol. Sutton.

[u] Ex Orig. penes hon. D. Guil. Glynne, Bar.

John Segrym, son of William, granted to John Fitz-Nigel of Borstall one messuage in the village of Borstall, which Walter May for
merly held, yielding due service to the capital lord of the fee, and
paying twenty shillings in hand. *Hiis testibus ; Johanne le Brun,
Johanne Ferebraz, Thoma Brun de Borstall, Johanne filio Roberti
Segrym, Ricardo Elys, Waltero de la Hale, et aliis. Dat. apud Borstall die Sabbati proxime post festum S. Petri in cathedra. Anno regni
regis Edwardi vicessimo tertio* [x].

In this year William de magna Rollendright, perpetual vicar of
Elsfield, near Oxford, entered an action against the prior of St. Frideswide for keeping in their hands the whole right of the said church
of Elsfield. William son of William de Stratford, with consent of
Benet his wife and William his son, had given to the said priory the
fifth part of the village of Elsfield, and afterward his whole possessions in that manor ; excepting one messuage which he gave to the
nunnery of Stodley, which Petronilla prioress of that house let in
firm to Simon de Coleham [y]

Henry Lacy earl of Lincoln had been the preceding year in the
expedition into France with Edmund earl of Lancaster, then general, and went now in the other expedition into Britanny under the
said earl of Lancaster [z] ; with twenty-six bannerets, seven hundred
esquires, &c.: where the said earl of Lancaster dying about Whitsuntide, the earl of Lincoln was made general of the English, and
his son-in-law Thomas succeeded to the earldom of Lancaster [a]. The
said earl presented to the churches of Swaneton and Kirkeby in the
archdeaconry of Lincoln [b]

Within this year was a trial for the right of patronage of the
church of * Hameldon in com. Buck. between Edmund earl of Corn-

---

*Rectores eccl'iæ de Hameldon com. Buck.   Guivonem Fayrfax ad eccl. de Hameldon,
Nicholaus Bateman clericus pres. per   7. Jun. 1432. qui jus habet presentandi vir-

x Ex Chartular. de Borstall. MS. f. vi.   y Collectanea W. Wyrley, MS. Wood, F. 16.
f. 9. b.   z Dugd. Bar. tom. 1. p. 104. b.   a Hen. Knyghton, p. 2508.   b R. Dods.
MS. vol. 107. f. 151.

wall and * Margaret his wife on the one part, and Gilbert de Clare earl of Glocester on the other: the title was adjudged to the earl of Cornwall in right of his wife; whereupon his clerk was now instituted

tute cujusdam feofamenti in manerio de Hameldon una cum advocat. ejusdem. Reg. W. Gray. ep'i Linc.

Mag'r Ricardus Tone decretorum doctor pres. per Guidonem Fayrfax ad eccl. de Hameldon per resign. Nich'i Bateman. 12. Jun. 1434. ib.

Tho. Bladesmyth presbyter pres. per Guidonem Fayrfax armig. ad eccl. de Hamylden per resign. mag'ri Ric'i Tone decr. doctoris. 12. Maii 1435. ib.

* Margaret relict of Edmund E. of Cornwall died at her manor of Kirkton com. Linc. and left executors of her goods John de Capella (soon after rector of Amersden) and Peter de Bresse, and executor of her will M. Rich. de Clare, who were cited to give an account of their trust by the prior of Burcester, and the official of the archdeacon of Oxford, who were delegated commissioners for that purpose by John Bp. of Lincoln; to whom the rural dean of Kirkton made this report:

Reverende discrecionis viris domino priori Burcestre et domini .. archidiaconi Oxon. officiali venerabilis in Christo patris ac D. D. Johannis Dei gracia Lincoln. episcopi ad audienda raciocinia administracionis executorum testamenti domine Margarete de Clare quondam comitisse Cornub. et cetera facienda que in hac parte requiruntur agenda commissariis specialiter deputatis suus humillimus et devotus vicarius de Kyrketon obedienciam debitam et devotam cum omni reverencia et honore. Mandatum vestrum nuper recepi sub hac forma: prior de Burcestre et domini . archidiaconi Oxon

officialis venerabilis in Christo patris ac D. D. Johannis Dei gracia Lincoln. episcopi ad audienda raciocinia administracionis executorum testamenti domine Margarete de Clare comitisse Cornubie in bonis que in diocesi Lincoln. habuit dum vivebat et cetera facienda que in hac parte requiruntur agenda commissarii specialiter deputati discreto viro ......vicario de Kyrketon salutem in auctore salutis. Auctoritate qua fungimur in hac parte cujus copiam vobis transmittimus presentibus annexam vobis firmiter injungendo mandamus quatenus dom. Johannem de Capella et mag. Petrum de Brixia executores dicte domine Margarete in testamento ejusdem nominatos et mag. Ricardum de Clare executorem testamenti ejusdem auctoritate ordinaria deputatum in manerio quod dicta defuncta habuit apud Kyrketon sub districtu vestro ubi administrasse dicuntur ac etiam in ecclesia ejusdem puplice et solempniter citetur quod compareant coram nobis in ecclesia S. Michaelis ad portam borealem Oxon. secundo die juridico post festum S. Marie Magdalene proxime futurum testamentum dicte defuncte et inventarium bonorum omnium que ipsa in diocesi Lincoln. habuit dum vivebat et omnia munimenta administrationem eorundem occasione bonorum hujus contingencia exhibituri creditoribus ac legatariis ac ceteris quibuscunq; quibus occasione testamenti seu bonorum hujus in dioc. Lincoln. fuerint obnoxii in forma juris responsuri et compotum finalem de administracione sua in bonis supradictis per eosdem legitime facta reddituri, ulteriusque facturi et recepturi in hac parte cum continuacione et

in the said church [c]. The king presented to a third portion of the church of Wodesdon, by right of custody of the land and heir of Sir Hugh de Courtney, knight [d].

prorogacione dierum et locorum quod justicia suadebit in ecclesia et de Kyrketon supradicta et omnibus ecclesiis vestri decanatus quibus videbitur vobis expedire tribus diebus dominicis seu festivis proximis post recepcionem presencium intra missarum solempnia publice et solempniter denuncietis seu denunciari et publice proclamari faciatis quod si quis sit qui a dictis executoribus petere seu exigere voluerit quicquam dictis die et loco compareat suas peticiones et quodlibet interesse propositurus et prout jus exigit prolaturi et prosecuturi ulteriusque facturi et recepturi in hac parte quod hujus negocii qualitas poposcerint et natura et quid in premissis feceritis nos die et loco supradictis distincte et aperte certificetis per literas vestras patentes harum seriem continentes. Dat. apud Burcestre V. nonas Julii. an. Dom. MCCCXV°. *Quod quidem mandatum vestrum in omnibus reverenter et obedienter sum executus. In cujus rei testimonium sigillum decanatus de Kyrketon presentibus est appensum. Dat. apud Kyrketon* VII. *kal. Julii. anno supradicto.* MS. Bib. Bod. Digby. 154.

Adquietancia super Compotum.

Universis sancte matris ecclesie filiis pateat per presentes quod cum dominus Johannes de Capella et magister Petrus de Brixia executores testamenti domine Margarete de Clare comitisse Cornubie quibus administracio bonorum dicte defuncte in forma juris una cum adjutorio magistri R. de Clare fuerat concessa, ac magister R. de Clare dicti testamenti ut premittitur coadjutor ad reddendum

ratiocinium administracionis sue de bonis que dictu defuncta in dioc. Lincoln. habuit dum vivebat ad diem Jovis proximum post festum B. Marie Magdalene, an. Dom. MCCCXV°. *in ecclesia S. Michaelis ad portam borealem Oxon. coram nobis . . . . . . priore Burcestre et d'ni archidiaconi Oxon. officialem d'ni Johannis Dei gracia Lincoln. e'pi in hac parte commissariis specialiter deputatis fuissent evocati predictus Johannes personaliter et prefati magistri Petrus et Ricardus per magistrum Elyam de S. Albano procuratorem eorundem literatorie constitutum eisdem die et loco juxta citacionem per nos primitus sibi factam coram nobis comparentes et testamentum dicte defuncte inventarium omnium bonorum ejusdem que in dioc. Linc. habuit dum vivebat quod ad septingenta triginta tres libras, novem solidos, obolum et quadrantem se extendebat, et omnia munimenta administracionem eorundem in bonis supradictis contingencia plenarie exhibentes factis primitus juxta juris exigenciam proclamacionibus et denuntiacionibus creditoribus legatariis ac omnibus aliis quorum interesse poterat quovis modo quod dictis die et loco coram nobis comparerent suas petitiones et quodlibet interesse contra executores ac coadjutorem prenotatos proposituri et prout jus exegit probaturi et prosecuturi, ulteriusque facturi et recepturi in hac parte quod esset justum nullisque omnino comparentibus licet legitime preconizatis et in forma juris expectatis ceterisque juris solempniis omnibus et singulis que in hac parte requiruntur rite et legitime*

An. MCCXCVI.   24, 25. *Edward I.*

In this year Henry Lacy carl of Lincoln, on the feast of St. Ambrose, by licence from the king, had the abbot and convent of Stanlawe translated to Whalley, and placed in the monastery which he there built for them [e] : at which time the said earl was forty-seven years of age.

July the twenty-first, Sibilia daughter of Walter, son of the provost or steward of Pyrie, granted and quit claimed for ever to John, son of John Fitz-Nigel the bastard of Borstall, and his heirs or assigns, all her right and title in all the lands, meadows, and tenements which Eustace her brother lately held in fee and by hereditary right in the village and fields of Arncote within the parish of Ambrosden, in consideration of twenty shillings in silver paid in hand to the said Sibilia.

Sciant præsentes et futuri quod ego Sibilia filia Walteri filii præpositi de Pyria concessi et omnino quiete clamavi pro me et hæredibus meis vel assignatis in perpetuum Johanni filio Johannis filii Nigelli le bastard de Borstall et hæredibus suis vel assignatis totum jus et cla-

observatis compotum sue administracionis in forma juris reddiderunt finalem, et quia nos commissarii supradicti per fidelem calculacionem et exquisitam indagacionem pensatis hinc inde pensandis et allocatis allocandis invenimus executores et coadjutorem predictos tum in expensis funeris circa dictam defunctam &c. &c. in dicta dioc. contingentibus omnia bona dicte defuncte que in dicta dioc. habuit dum vivebat quorum summa superius plenius apparet et ultra ea viginti libras, III. solid. ob. q. fideliter expendidisse ac in eisdem bonis per omnia legitime administrasse, fidelitatem ac diligenciam eorundem in hac parte quam plurimum commendantes *ipsos ab administracione &c. auctoritate nobis in hac parte commissa absolvimus per decretum, eosque tenore presencium absolutos esse totaliter et quietos pronunciamus per presentes, potestate executoribus et coadjutori predictis allocacionem xx. lib. III. sol. ob. q. supradictam de bonis in alia diocesi existentibus ad dictam defunctam pertinentibus petendi et recipiendi per nos concessa ac etiam reservata. In quorum omnium testimonium nos prior Burcestre sigillum nostrum quo utimur et nos domini archidiaconi Oxon. officialis sigillum officii nostri presentibus apposuimus. Dat. die. et loco et an. D. supradictis.* MS. Bib. Bod. Digby. 151.

[e] Chron. abbatiæ de Stanlawe, R. Dods. MS. vol. 59. f. 133.

*mium quod habui vel aliquo modo habere potui in omnibus terris pratis
et tenementis quæ vel quas Eustachius frater meus quondam tenuit in
feodo et hæreditarie in villa et campis de Arnicote. Ita vero quod ego
dicta Sibilia nec hæredes mei nec mei assignati nec aliquis pro me vel
per me aliquod jus vel clamium in prædictis terris pratis et tenementis
de cætero exigere potuerimus vel vendicare. Pro hac autem concessione et mea perpetua quieta clamatione dedit mihi dictus Johannes viginti solidos argenti præ manibus integram summam. Et ut hæc mea
concessio et mea perpetua quieta clamatio rata et inconcussa permaneat
in perpetuum hanc præsentem chartam sigilli mei impressione roboravi.
Hiis testibus; domino Johanne filio Nigelli, Roberto Bell de Wodepirie, Waltero de Sancto Andrea, Thoma de Achecott, Waltero de
Staford, Rad. de Chelberge, Johanne de S. Andrea, Gilberto le Fui-
heler, Rogero Clerico, et aliis. Dat. apud Arnicote in crastino S.
Margaretæ virginis anno regni regis Edwardi vicessimo quarto.*

Appending a seal of green wax, impressed in oval form with the
head of a spear, and this inscription, S. SIBILIÆ DE PYRIA [f].

There had been one Emma de Pirie, wife of William son of He
lias, who confirmed her husband's grant of the church of Wormenhale in com. Buck. to the priory of St. Frideswide, to which it had
been given by William Fitz-Helias, and confirmed by Elias son of
Robert Fitz-Helias, and by Jeffery, another son of the said Robert,
with consent of Letitia his wife, and by William Fitz-Helias, with
consent of the foresaid Emma his wife, who likewise confirmed to
the said monastery one virgate of land and six acres, which Otwell
Lisle held and gave at the dedication of the church of Wormenhall [g].
There was one Adam de Pirie and Hamedon his son, who possessed houses and ground in the parish of All-Saints, Oxon. *temp.*
Hen. I. [h]

An. MCCXCVI.   sona eccl. de Sulthorn habet lit. protect.
Pat. 25. Edw. I. Joh. de Bernewell per-   2. Mart.

[f] Ex Orig. penes Joh. Coker, gen. de Burcester.   [g] W. Wyrley, MS.   [h] Regist.
Frideswydæ, MS. chartæ 165 et 474.

John de Weston in this neighbourhood, indebted to the king, was committed to the Fleet, from whence escaping, he was apprehended by one Henry de Oxford about Walingford, and sent to the Tower of London; but on satisfaction made was soon after released [i].

Juliana de la Hale, the widow of Walter de la Hale, released and quit claimed to Sir John Fitz-Nigel of Borstall, all her right in part of a curtilage and two furlongs of arable land, granted by her said husband and herself in the year 1290. *Hiis testibus; Johanne le Brun, Nigello Travers, Johanne Ferebraz, Nigello de Boys, Williel-mo Ulwyne, Johanne Segrym, Ricardo Elys, &c. et tota curia de Bre-hull. Dat. apud Borstall die Lunæ proxime post festum S. Hilarii. Anno regni regis Edwardi* xxiv[to]. [k]

Ichel de Kerwent, rector of the church of Bucknell, adjoining to Burcester, had refused to pay the tax imposed upon the clergy of one half of their revenues, an. 1291; for which contempt the abbot of Oseney, collector, complained to his diocesan the bishop of Lincoln, and when he persisted in his refusal, his church was put under an interdict. Upon which he sued the said abbot in the spiritual court. The abbot appealed to the king, who directed a precept to the sheriff of Oxon. requiring him forthwith to attach the body of the said Ichel de Kerewent, and carry him before a baron of the Exchequer, there to answer for the contempt and damage, and to make full satisfaction.

Rex vic. Oxon. salutem. Ex gravi querela abbatis de Osney unius collectorum subsidii, &c. a clero concessi in dioc. Linc. accepimus quod

16. kal. Octob. pont. 18. Ol. Sutton. Tho. de Capella resignavit eccl'iam de Ble-chedon quia institutus fuit in eccl'ia de Sevenak. Mem. Ol. Sutton, f. 175.

Mag'r Rob. de Kenelingworth cap. pres. per abb. et conv. de Egnesham ad eccl. de Meriton vac. per institut. Rogeri de Kene-lingworth in aliud beneficium. 7. id. Octob. pont. 17. Ol. Sutton.

Mag'r Rob. de Leyam cl'ic. pres. per abb. et conv. Westm. ad eccl. de Islep vac. per mort. Walt. de Tudington. 11. kal. Jan. pont. 17.

[i] Mem. in Scac. temp. Ed. I. MSS.   [k] Ex Chartul. de Borstall. f. 5.

3 O 2

*cum idem abbas Ychelum de Kerewent rectorem ecclesie de Bucking
hull ad solutionem ejusdem subsidii ecclesiam suam contingentis faciendam sepius monuisset et per cohercionem ecclesiasticam authoritati
diœcesani compulisset eandem ecclesiam interdicto tandem supponendo
pro eo quod huc usque inde satisfacere non curavit : idem Ychelus ipsum abbatem ea de causa jam in curia Christianitatis coram officiario
diœcesani prædicti trahit in placitum ipsum multipliciter ibidem in-
quietando in nostri contemptum manifestum et solutionis dicti subsidii
retardationem necnon predicti abbatis damnum non modicum que sustinere nolumus nec impuniter transire. Tibi precipimus quod ipsum
Ychelum attach. ita quod corpus ejus habeas coram baron. in crastino, &c. ad satisfaciendum nobis de dicto subsidio ecclesiam suam con
tingente de quo nondum satisfecit : et ad respondend. nobis et predicto
abbati de contemptu et damno predicto. Teste J. de Cobeham*[1].*

By an inquisition taken this year in the county of Bucks, the jurors found that William de Mortimer held the third part of the manor of Crendon, excepting the third part of the advowson of the abbey of Nottley, by the gift of Maud de Mortimer, which she made to
the said William and his heirs[m]. Sir William Mortimer, a knight
and stout soldier, was enfeoffed by Maud his mother, (daughter and
coheir of William de Braose of Brecknock, and widow of Roger lord
Mortimer of Wigmore,) of the third part of the manor of Crendon
in com. Buck. and dying without issue in 24. Ed. I. left Edmund lord
Mortimer of Wigmore his brother and heir[n].

An. MCCXCVII. 25, 26. *Edward I.*

The prior of Burcester had again a special writ of protection, of
which several were likewise granted to religious houses, and to many
parochial incumbents, among which were *Thomas de Capella persona
ecclesiarum de Blechesdon et Sevenak, Willielmus vicarius ecclesiæ de
Witteneya, magister Simon persona ecclesiæ de Heyford-Waryn*[o]

---

[1] Mem. in Scacc. edit. Serjeant Maynard, Lond. 1678. p. 38.   [m] R. Dods. MS. vol. 44.
p. 222.   [n] Dugd. Bar. tom. 1. p. 143. a.   [o] W. Prynne, Histor. Collect. tom. 3. p. 709.

The said Thomas de Capella was clerk in Chancery, and had a letter from the king to excuse his attendance at visitation in the 26. of
Edw. I.[p] But he seems now to have resigned his church of Blechesdon; for before the end of this eighteenth of Oliver Sutton, the said
church of Blechesdon was void, when Hugh Musegrave and Maud
his wife presented Richard Musegrave clerk; and Nicholas Trimenel
and Mabil his wife presented another clerk: but on a trial *de jure
patronatus*, the latter withdrew their presentation[q]. In the same
year Agatha de Oxon was elected prioress in the nunnery of Garinges, (now Goring,) com. Oxon. licence of choosing being first
asked and obtained from Edmund earl of Cornwall, who was patron
by no other title but that the said house was situate within his honour
of Walingford[r]. William de Druesvall had given one hide of land of
his proper fee in this village of Garinges to the abbey of Egnesham,
when he made his son a monk in that monastery. *Testes; Hugo
filius Ricardi, Ranulphus de Scisuris, Willielmus Boterel, Walterus
Foliot, Thomas Basset, Robertus Basset*[s]. This grant of William was
confirmed by his grandson and heir Thomas de Druesvall[t], who re
stored to the said abbey the common pasture, which they claimed, in

An. MCCXCVII. 25, 26. Edw. I.
Vacante eccl'ia de Blechesdon per resign.
Tho. de Capella, Ric. de Musegrave cl'icus
pres. per Hug'. de Musegrave et Matildem
uxorem ejus (qui recuperavit pres. contra
Nich. Trimenel et Mabiliam ux. ejus) admiss. 11. kal. Apr. pont. 18. Archid. Oxon.
Will. de Wrotham cl'icus habet lit. regis de pres. ad eccl'iam de Brehull ad donat. regis. Lit. dirig. e'po Linc. 7. Apr.
Pat. 26. Edw. I.
1297. Will. de Wrotcham pres. per reg.
ad eccl. de Acle cum Brehull per privati-

onem Ric'i de Luda. admiss. 2. kal. Jun.
pont. 19.
Vacante eccl'ia de Abberbir que est de
patronatu d'ni Winton. ep'i per mort. Edm.
de Magdenstan ultimi rectoris ejusdem in
itinere versus Romanam curiam decedentis
dominus Bonifacius Papa VIII. eand. eccl'iam cum omnibus suis juribus et pertinentiis Rob. de Magdenstan p'b'ro contulit et providit de illo per literas sub dato
id. Febr. pont. ejusd. pape tertio. Reg. Ol.
Sutton.

p W. Prynne, Histor. Collect. tom. 3. p. 789.   q R. Dods. MS. vol. 107. p. 161.   r Ib.
s Regist. de Egnesham. chart. 127.   t Ib. chart. 128.

the said village of Goring, and had possessed in the reign of Hen. I. which because he had for some time unjustly detained, therefore, to make them satisfaction and full restitution, he gave them *gravam juxta Eppelhangar et quandam insulam proximam ville de Stoches,* and the service which Adam de Wodecot did him, *pro dicta grava et insula*[u]. On account of this hide of land and right of common and tithes of them, frequent suits were long depending between the abbey of Egnesham and the nunnery of Goring.

Within this year died Roger de Coventry abbot of Oseney, and Walter de Lutegareshall was made guardian of the said abbey during the time of vacation. Upon the election of a new abbot, there was a remarkable trial, of which the cause and issue is thus recorded.

Abbas de Oseneya obiit anno regni regis Edwardi vicesimo quinto et ante restitutionem temporalium dictæ abbatiæ successori dicti abbatis dictæ domus electo factam, petiit escheator ad opus domini regis cupam et palefridum dicti abbatis defuncti et etiam lanas bidentum ejusdem abbatiæ de tempore vacationis abbatiæ prædictæ, per quod ad prosecutionem dicti electi super præmissis in concilio regio tertio die Julii anno prædicto apud Westmin. et examinatis causa et petitione eschaetoris supra cupa et palefrido et lanis prædictis mandatum est per prædictum consilium prædicto eschaetori quod a præfato electo cupam nec palefridum nec etiam lanas prædictas exigat vel exigi permittat. Unde dictis die et loco mandatum est Waltero de Lutegareshall custodi dictæ abbatiæ quod occasione dictorum cupæ palefridi et lanarum nichil exigat et securitatem prius inde sibi conventam dictis abbati et conventui ejusdem loci faciat liberari[x]

Hugh de Plessets, who held Musewell in the parish of Ambrosden, was now summoned to parliament among the barons of the realm[y]: and nigh this time granted to the church of St. Mary's in Oseney, free pannage, *housbute* and *heybute* in all his woods and

---

[u] Regist. de Egnesham. chart. 129.   [x] Chartul. de Oseney, f. 1. (nunc deest.)   [y] Dugd. Bar. tom. 1. p. 774.

parks. *Hiis testibus; Galfrido Arthor, Rogero de Amory, Fulcone de Oilly, Hugone de Tywe, Roberto filio Wydonis, Philippo de Hampton, Radulpho filio Radulphi, Rogero Testard, Rogero de Amory* [z]

Ichel de Kerewent, rector of Bucknell, being convicted of detaining the king's dues, for which he was impleaded in the court of Exchequer, the temporals of his living were now seized, and put into the hands of John de Burey, Gilbert de Buckenhull, chaplain, John de la March, chaplain, and eight other persons, who received the profits for two years; within which time the said rector made his submission and peace, and was restored to his properties, an. 1298 [a]

Juliana daughter of Richard Elys of Borstall, granted to John son of James Biffegod of Borstall one messuage and half a carucate of land by this charter.

Sciant præsentes et futuri quod ego Juliana filia Ricardi de Elys de Borstall pro servitio suo et quadraginta solidis sterlingorum præ manibus dedi, &c. Johanni filio Jacobi Biffegod de Borstall unum messuagium et unam dimidiam virgatam terræ, &c. quæ habui et tenui in feodo de domino rege in villa de Borstall, &c. reddendo et faciendo annuatim, &c. secundum consuetudinem manerii domini regis de Brehull, &c. Hiis testibus ; Nigello Travers, Johanne le Broun tunc Ballivo manerii domini regis de Brehull, Johanne Ferebraz, Helia de Brehull, Hugone filio Nigelli, &c. Dat. apud Brehull die Jovis proxime ante festum S. Joh. Bapt. anno regni regis Edwardi filii regis Henrici vicesimo quinto [b].

An. MCCXCVIII.   26, 27. Edward I.

By an inquisition taken this year in the neighbouring parts of the county of Bucks, the jurors found, that William late bishop of Ely died seized in his demesne as of fee, of the manor of Lotegarshale, (now Ludgarsal,) with all appertenances, one part of which he held of the king *in capite* as a member of the king's manor of Brehull,

---

[z] W. Wyrley, Collectanea MSS. ut supra.   [a] W. Prynne, Histor. Collect. tom. 3. p. 791.
[b] Ex Chartul. de Borstall, f. 91.

and the other part of the earl of Gloucester and Joan his wife: and that William Touchet and Isabel wife of Roger de Morteyn were next heirs to the said bishop[c].

This William Louth bishop of Ely was consecrated Oct. 1, 1290, and died in the beginning of this year, on the 25th, 27th, or 28th of March[d].

Edmund earl of Cornwall, in right of his honour of St. Walery, was possessed of some demesne land in Knyttington, in com. Berks, and his steward used to hold a court in that place, and had by custom been entertained at the charge of the prior of St. Frideswyde, to which monastery the said manor was given by Guy de St. Walery: which charge of reception the prior finding to be a burden, and the stewards pleading to be a custom, the said prior made his complaint to the earl, who sent his mandate to Simon de Grenhull steward of St. Walery, that he should make a special inquisition upon this matter, and return him the full and just account.

Edmundus comes Cornub. dilecto et fideli suo Simoni de Grenhull seneschallo honoris S. Walerici salutem. Monstravit nobis prior beatæ Frideswydæ Oxon. quod cum dominus Johannes de Diggeby dudum seneschallus noster Walingford et honoris prædicti ad manerium dicti prioris de Knyttington accessisset ad visum suum ibidem tenend. prout mos singulis annis existit, idem Johannes semel ex gratia et ad rogatum ipsius prioris ad sumptum etiam ipsius hospitabatur ibidem, quod

An. MCCXCVIII. 26, 27. Edw. I.

Will. de Blakethurn subd. pres. per d'num Laur. de Paveley milit. ad eccl. de Wenlingbury vac. per mort. Hen. de Pavely, admiss. 18. kal. Dec. pont. 19.

Mag'r Joh. le Flemeng cap. pres. per rectorem et f'res domus de Asserugge ad eccl. de Ambresdon vac. per mort. mag'ri Rad'i de Martivallis, admiss. 6. id. Dec. pont. 19.

Henr. de Exon. subd. pres. per Edm. com. Cornub. ad eccl. de Bekkele vac. per mort. mag'ri Phil. de Heddeslore. Inquis. facta per offic. W. archid'i Oxon. admiss. 6. kal. Feb. pont. 19.

Joh. de la Carneyle cl'icus pres. per d'num Joh. de Insula milit. ad medietat. eccl'ie de Heyford ad pont. vac. per mort. Rob. de la Carneyle. 13. kal. Jan. pont. 19.

[c] R. Dods. MS. vol. 44. p. 237.   [d] Histor. Elien. apud Wharton Ang. Sacr. p. 638.

quidem Johannes toto tempore suo, et ballivi sui cum ad dictum visum tenendum venissent dictum hospitium usurparint, quæ quidem hujus-modi usurpatio taliter introducta hucusque continuatur in non modi-cum dicti prioris et domus suæ gravamen ut dictum est. Et ideo vo-bis mandamus quod inquirentes super hujus plenius veritatem de eo prout invenitur nos reddatis certiores, ut ulterius ipsis quod juris fuerit et rationis fieri faciamus. Dat. apud Ashrigge. kal. Maii, an. regni R. Edwardi xxvi^o. ^c

On receipt of which precept, the steward caused a court for the honour of St. Walery to be held at North-Oseney, and there an inquisition was made upon the oath of twelve men, who gave their verdict, that the said manor of Knyttinton was formerly in the hands of Guy de St. Walery, who gave the said manor in frank almoign to the prior and canons of St. Frideswyde; and that one Peter de Asherugge, then steward of the honour of St. Walery, did appropriate the said manor to the honour of St. Walery, and held there a yearly court, levying twelve pence of the said village; and that the place of keeping the said court was upon an open green, within the said village, over against the house of Hugh de Gardin; and in rainy weather, by leave of the bailiff of the said prior, the steward held his court in the manor house of the prior, and sometime in the houses of the other tenants of the said prior, so as the steward had no right to houseroom or entertainment, or any other claim, but the sum of twelve pence from the said village: and in the time of John de Diggeby, formerly steward of the honour of St. Walery, John de Lukenor, then prior of St. Frideswyds, desired the said John de Diggeby to stay with him on the court day at his manor house, and there entertained him at his own charge; and for two following years the prior made the like invitation; after which the said John de Diggeby, for the whole time of his stewardship, had there his enter tainment by extortion, not by right.

Inquisitio facta fuit in plena curia de North-Osen. die Martis

c Regist. S. Frides. MS. carta 406. qu.

proxime post festum S. Botulphi an. regni regis Edwardi xxvi[to]. *co-*
ram -seneschallo S. Walerici per sacramentum Galfridi de Elfinton,
Walteri de Haysel de Cherewell, Johannis le Cumber de Pusye, Ri-
cardi de Houghton de Knyttinton, Willielmi le Cumber de Pusye, Wal-
teri Aleyn de Harewell, Willielmi de Aula de eadem, Henrici Wilard
de eadem, Hugonis Hucthild de eadem, Johannis de la Grave de Hen-
ton, Willielmi Payn de Knyttinton, Walteri Morin de Henton, qui
dicunt super sacramentum suum quod manerium de Knyttinton ali-
quando fuit in manibus Guidonis de S. Walerico et tunc temporis fuit
illud manerium spectans ad hundredum de Shryningham et idem Guido
dedit prædictum manerium in puram et perpetuam eleemosinam priori
Sanctæ Frideswydæ et ejusdem loci conventui. Et præterea venit
quidam Petrus de. Asherugg tunc seneschal. honoris S. Walerici, et
appropriavit dictum manerium ad honorem S. Walerici et ibidem te-
nuit unum visum per annum levando de eadem villat xii. *denarios de*
recto visu pro omnibus. Et fuit locus tenendi visum ibidem in qua-
dam viridi placea in villa de Knyttinton contra domum quandam Hu-
gonis de Gardino et in tempore pluvioso per licentiam ballivi prioris
aliquando seneschallus tenuit visum ibidem in curia prioris et ali-
quando in domibus aliorum tenentium in villa prædicta: ita quod se-
neschallus non habuit ibidem aliquod hospitium nec aliquod tectum nec
nisi tantum modo prædictos xii. *denarios pro recto visu, et dicunt pro*
tempore Johannis de Diggeby quondam seneschalli honoris S. Walerici
dominus S. Johannes de Leukenor tunc prior S. Frideswidæ supplica-
vit dictum Johannem de Diggeby morandum secum die visus ad mane-
rium suum de Knyttinton sumptibus ejusdem prioris impensis eidem
Johanni de Diggeby, et idem Johannes seneschallus venit ad manerium
prædictum et ad rogatum dicti prioris per duos annos et per dictos duos
annos toto tempore suo habuit hospitia sua ibidem per extortionem et
non de jure. In cujus rei testimonium præfati juratores huic inquisi-
tioni sigilla sua apposuerunt [f].

Upon which return of the jury, Edmund earl of Cornwall directed

[f] Regist. S. Frides. MS. carta 406. qu.

another precept to Simon de Grenhull, steward of his honour of Walingford, to refrain from such oppression of the said prior, &c. dated
July the fourth, 26. Edw. I. [g]

Within this nineteenth year of Oliver Sutton bishop of Lincoln,
Laurence de Pavely, knight, presented to the church of Wendle-
bury. John son of Guido, knight, presented to the church of
Weston, and the king to the church of Oakley, with the chapels of
Borstall and Brill [h].

By an inquisition taken this year in the county of Berks, it appears that Alan Plugenet, on the day whereon he died, held the manor of Pidington within the parish of Ambrosden, of the king, for one
knight's fee, and that Alan Plugenet was his son and heir [i]. This
Alan was descended from Hugh de Plugenet, who in the 2. Hen. II.
had lands given him in Hedingdon, com. Oxon. who, being a person
highly esteemed for wisdom and military knowledge, had been summoned to parliament among the barons of this realm, from the 23d
to the 25th Edw. I. He left Joan his wife surviving [k]. His ancestor
Hugh de Plugenet, with consent of Josceus his son, had granted to
the church of St. Frideswides common pasture in his manor of Hedingdon, and a ground in the said parish called Godenthecroft, and
thirty acres of arable land, and all tithe of his own demesnes and of
his tenants in Hedingdon and Merston, and the rent of Hakeling-
croft, to find one lamp in the church of Hedingdon [l]

When Hugh de Plessets in the ninth of Edw. I. surrendered to the
king this manor of Hedingdon, a reserve was expressly made of an
annual pension, 12[s]. per an. to the abbey of Oseney from the said
manor, which had been given for a prebend to the said conventual
church, which having been for some years detained by the said
Hugh de Plessets, he was sued for the arrears, and compelled to pay
them [m].

[g] Regist. S. Prides. MS. carta 410. qu.   [h] R. Dods. MS. vol. 107. f. 170.   [i] W. Dugd.
MS. vol. A. 1. p. 177.   [k] Dugd. Bar. tom. 2. p. 3.   [l] W. Wyrley, Collectanea MSS. in
Mus. Ashmol. ut supra.   [m] Chartular. de Oseney, f. xliv.

Ralph de Martival, rector of the church of * Ambrosden, died this year. The patronage being lately reposed in the hands of the rector and brethren of Asherugge, they presented a chaplain of their college, John le Fleming, who was admitted Novemb. 26. at Empingham, com. Rut. was instituted by proxy of John de Scalleby, priest, swore canonical obedience, and had a writ to the archdeacon of Oxford for induction.

> *Tempore domini Oliveri Sutton episcopi Lincoln. qui cœpit præesse in ecclesia catholica ibidem in anno Dom.* $M^{mo}.CC^{mo}.LXXX^{mo}$.
> *Ambrosden.*
>
> *Magister Johannes le Fleming capellanus præsentatus per rectorem et fratres domus de Asherugge ad ecclesiam de Ambresdon vacantem per mortem magistri Radulphi de Martuallis ultimi rectoris ejusdem, facta prius inquisitione per officialem archidiaconi Oxon. per quam, &c. ad dictam ecclesiam, et admissus VI. id. Decembris anno XIX. apud Empingham et rector in persona Johannis de Scalleby presbyteri procuratoris sui canonice institut. in eadem, juravitque episcopo canonicam obedientiam in forma consueta. Scriptum est dicto archidiacono vel ejus officiali quod, &c. et habeat literam de institutione patentem* [n]

Ichel de Kerewent, rector of Bucknell, toward the end of this year had made satisfaction for the king's tax, and reparation of damage to the abbot of Oseney, upon which the interdict on his church was taken off, and he was restored to the full enjoyment of his temporals; but those persons to whom the sequestration was committed

---

* Venit apud Nettleham, 9. kal. Nov. pont. 19. Mag'r Rogerus de Martivall archid'us Leycestr. presentatus per rectorem et fratres domus de Asserugge ad eccl'iam de Ambresdon vacantem per mortem mag'ri Rad'i de Martivall ultimi rectoris ejusd. et facta inquisitione per offic. W. archid. Oxon. per quem, &c. ep'us certa consideratione commisit dicto magistro Rogero custodiam sequestri ipsius ep'i in dicta eccl'ia de Ambresdon quousque eam duxerit revocandam. Rot. Oliv. de Sutton ep'i Linc. MS.

[n] Ex Regist. Linc. transcript per N. Thorold. Notar. Pub.

were unwilling to part with their stewardship: wherefore, to gain a repossession, the rector procured from the king a precept directed to the sheriff, being one of those writs which the lawyers have entitled, *de vi laica amovenda.*

Edvardus Dei gratia rex Angliæ, &c. vic. Oxon. salutem. Præcipimus tibi sicut alias tibi præcepimus quod ponas per vadium et salvos plegios Johannem de Burey, Gilbertum de Bukenhal capellanum, Johannem de la March capellanum, &c. quod sint coram justiciariis nostris apud Ebor. in Octab. S. Trinitatis ad respondend. tam nobis quam Ithael Skerwent personæ ecclesiæ de Bukenhull de placito quare cum ad requisitionem venerabilis patris O. Lincoln. episcopi pluries præcepimus quod omnem vim laicam quæ se tenet in ecclesia de Bukenhull quo minus idem episcopus officium suum spirituale ibidem exercere possit, sine dilatione amoveres ab eadem : et tu virtute illorum brevium nostrorum ad eandem ecclesiam pro vi prædicta amovenda pluries accesseris, prædicti Johannes, Gilbertus, Johannes, Walterus, &c. qui se vi laica in eadem ecclesia tenuerunt in adventu tuo ibidem se alibi transtulerunt, et confestim post discessum tuum ab ea, aggregatis sibi aliis malefactoribus se in eam vi armata iterato intruserunt, et bona et catalla prædicti Ithaci ad prædict. ecclesiam spectantia distraxerunt et consumpserunt et alia enormia intulerunt et in eadem ecclesia adhuc se tenent pristinam malitiam suam continuantes et ipsum Ithaclem indebite fatigantes in nostri contemptum manifestum et mandatorum nostrorum illusionem et ipsius Ithaelis dampnum gravamen et jacturam et contra pacem nostram. Et insuper prædict. episcopum officium suum spirituale ibidem exercere non permittunt. Nos igitur libertatem ecclesiasticam illæsam conservare et malitiæ prædictorum malefactorum in hac parte celeri juris remedio obviare: tibi præcipimus quod in propria persona tua accedas ad ecclesiam prædictam et omnem vim laicam quam ibidem inveneris absque mora amoveas ab eadem juxta tenorem mandati nostri prius inde directi et habeas ibi nomina plegiorum et hoc breve. Teste J. de Metingham apud Ebor. 3 die Februarii anno regni nostri vicesimo septimo.

In obedience to this precept, the sheriff in his own person went several times to the church of Bucknell; but those persons, as they had done before, still absented themselves, and, I suppose for fear of a worse issue, left quiet possession to the said rector. This return of the sheriff is endorsed on the said writ.

Accessi in propria persona mea ad ecclesiam de Bukenhull quam-pluries, et nullam Laicam vim in eadem inveni ullo tempore quo ibidem fui cum toto vicencto illo ad vim Laicam ab eadem renovandam[o].

An. mccxcix.   27, 28.   Edward I.

John Giffard baron of Brimsfield died 5. cal. June, when the estate which he possessed in right of Maud de Longspe, sometime his wife, was divided between Margaret countess of Lincoln, daughter of the said Maud, by William de Longspe her former husband, now thirty years of age; and Catharine Alianore and Maud her daughters, by the said John Giffard[p].

Walter de Ailesbury, a tenant of Edmund earl of Cornwall, was by the said earl constituted governor of the castle and honour of Walingford, and of the barony of St. Walery, by virtue of which his jurisdiction obtained in Burcester, Ambrosden, &c.[q]

There had been of late a controversy between the priory of Burcester and the convent of Asherugge, about a certain place or parcel of land in the common pasture near to Wrechwike, which difference was now composed between William de Thornberge prior of Burcester and his convent on the one part, and Ralph de Astone rector of Asherugge and his convent on the other; whereby it was agreed that the prior and his convent might appropriate and inclose three acres of common pasture in Blakethorn, (excepting meadow to be mowed,) in any such place as where the tenants of the priory and convent used to common.

Cum mota esset controversia inter fratrem Willielmum de Thornberge priorem de Burncester et ejusdem loci conventum ex parte una,

<hr>

o W. Prynne, Hist. Collect. tom. 3. p. 794.   p Dugd. Bar. tom. 1. p. 501.   q W. Dugd. Antiq. Warwic. p. 610.

et fratrem Radulfum de Astone rectorem de Asherugge et ejusdem loci conventum ex parte altera, super quadam placia in communi pastura juxta Wrechwike in comitatu Oxon. Tandem pro bono pacis habendo convenit inter eos in hac forma, videlicet quod prædictus rector et ejus conventus concesserunt pro se et successoribus suis quantum in ipsis est prædicto priori et eidem conventui quod possint sibi appropriare et includere pro voluntate sua tres acras prædictæ placiæ super qua·lis erat mota inter eos quæ jacet juxta separiam prædictorum prioris et conventus de Burncester habend. et tenend. prædictis priori et conventui et eorum successoribus imperpetuum sine contradictione seu impedimento ipsorum rectoris et conventus seu successorum suorum quorumcunque. Pro hac autem concessione et præsenti compositione habenda concesserunt prior et conventus de Burncester pro se et successoribus suis quantum in ipsis est dicto rectori de Asherugge et ejusdem loci conventui quod sibi possint appropriare et includere pro voluntate sua tres acras de communi pastura in Blakethorn in eodem com. ubicunque et quomodocunque sibi placuerit absque impedimento seu contradictione prædictorum prioris et conventus seu successorum suorum, dummodo talis appropriatio et inclusio non fiat in prato falcabili sed in tali loco ubi tenentes prædicti prioris et tenentes prædicti rectoris de Blakethorn omni tempore anni consueverunt communare seu communam clamare. Nec licebit de cætero præfatis priori et conventui de Burncester vel successoribus suis aliquo modo de prædicta communi pastura juxta Wrechwike plus includere vel sibi appropriare quam tres acras prænominatas sine voluntate et assensu prædictorum rectoris et conventus de Asherugge et eorum successorum, nec præfati rector et conventus de Asherugge nec eorum successores amplius quam tres acras includent vel sibi appropriabunt de communi pastura in Blakethorn ut predictum est sine expressa voluntate prædictorum prioris et conventus de Burncester vel successorum eorundem. Et ad hujus concessionis perpetuam memoriam partes prænominatæ huic scripto indentato sigilla capitulorum suorum hinc inde apposuerunt. Hiis testibus; dominis Ricardo de Aumari, Johanne filio Nigelli milite, magistro Ri-

*cardo de Wendlebury, Ricardo de Caunne, Rogero de Drayton, Wil-
lielmo Maunde, Johanne atte Chambre, et aliis. Dat. apud Asherugge
die Lunæ proxime post festum decollationis Johannis Baptistæ. Anno
regni regis Edwardi filio regis Henrici vicesimo septimo'.*

Roger Pejoun of Borstall granted to Isabel daughter of Thomas
Brown of Borstall, for due service and forty shillings in hand, one
messuage and half a virgate of land, held in fee from the king in the
village of Borstall. *Dat. apud Borstall die Mercurii proxime post
festum S. Petri qui dicitur ad vincula, anno regni regis Edwardi filii
regis Henrici vicesimo septimo. Hiis testibus; Nigello Travers, Johanne Ferebraz, Reginaldo filio Nigelli de Bosco, Hugone filio Nigelli, Ricardo Pymme, Johanne Broun, Ricardo Holay, &c.*[s]

Edmund earl of Cornwall gave to the nunnery of Stodley, whereof he was patron, one acre and a half of his waste in Horton,
to enlarge an enclosure of the said nuns. Dat. 1. Octob. an. R. E.
xxvii[t].

The arms of Edmund earl of Cornwall were field argent three
lions gules coronated in a black border charged with bezantines: why
he bore these arms different from the royal family, being the grandson of king John, see in Cambden[u].

Henry Lacy earl of Lincoln had a precept directed to him, requiring his attendance at York upon the feast day of St. Peter *ad
vincula,* to consult with the archbishop there, and divers other nobles, for manning of the king's castles in Scotland, and guarding of
the marches[x].

Sir John Fitz-Nigel of Borstall married Joan his only daughter
by Isabel his wife, to John son of Richard de Handlo of Borstall;

An. MCCXCIX. 27, 28. Edw. I.   de Fynemere vac. per mort. mag'ri Rad'i de
Joh. de Langeton cl'icus pres. per abb.   Oxon. 6. non. Octob. pont. 20.
et conv. s'cti Augustini de Bristol ad eccl.

[r] Ex Orig. MS. penes D. Guil. Glynne, Bar.   [s] Ex Chartular. de Borstall. MS. f. 91.
[t] Mon. Ang. tom. 1. p. 487.   [u] Cambden. Brit. in Danmon.   [x] Dugd. Bar. tom. 1. p. 105. a.

upon which match these following fines and infeoffments were made, to convey the estate of the said Sir John Fitz-Nigel to the said John de Handlo.

Edwardus Dei gratia, &c. Sciatis quod per finem quem Johannes filius Nigelli fecit nobiscum, &c. licentiam dedimus eidem Johanni quod de duabus bovatis terræ cum pertinentiis in Borstall et de balliva forestarii forestæ de Bernwode quæ de nobis tenentur in capite per serjantiam custodiendi forestam nostram prædictam, feoffare possit Robertum de Harwedon et licentiam dedimus eidem Roberto quod ipse habita inde plena seisina prædictam terram et ballivam cum pertinentiis præfato Johanni dare possit et concedere tenendum ad terminum vitæ ipsius Johannis, ita quod post decessum ipsius Johannis terra illa et balliva cum pertinentiis remaneant Johanni filio Ricardi de Hantlou et Johannæ filiæ Johannis filii Nigelli uxori ejus, &c. Et si contingat ipsos Johannem Hantlou et Johannam obire sine hæredibus, &c. tunc prædicta tenementa, &c. ad rectos hæredes ipsius Johannis filii Nigelli integre revertant, &c. Teste meipso apud Westm. tertio die Augusti anno regni vicesimo septimo[y].

. Sciant præsentes et futuri quod ego Johannes filius Nigelli dedi, &c. Roberto de Harwedon rectori ecclesiæ de Thingdone maneria mea de Borstall, Musewell, Adingrave, Acley, et Thomele, et totam ballivam meam forestariæ de Bernwode, &c. reddendo mihi dicto Johanni et assignatis meis ad totam vitam meam trescentas libras argenti per annum ad tres terminos subscriptos, scilicet ad festum S. Michaelis centum libras, et ad natale Domini centum libras, et ad festum S. Johannis Baptistæ centum libras, &c. Hiis testibus; domino Hugone le Dispenser justitiario forestæ citra Trentam, domino Johanne de Hastang, domino Henrico filio Nigelli, Johanne de Greynvill, Waltero de S. Andrea, Ada filio Petri, Nicholao de Esses, et aliis. Dat. apud Borstall xii. die Augusti anno regni regis Edwardi vicesimo septimo[z].

Johannes le Fitz-Nigel miles omnibus tenentibus suis de Adingrave, Acley et Thomele salutem. Quia feoffavimus dom. Robertum Harwe-

---

[y] Ex Chartul. de Borstall, MS. f. 33.   [z] Ib. f. 31.

don clericum de omnibus terris et tenementis quæ habui in Borstall, Musewell, Adingrave, Acley, et Thomele, una cum balliva mea fores-tariæ de Bernwode, &c. mando quod eidem Roberto de servitiis ves-tris, &c. de cætero sitis intendentes et respondentes. In cujus rei tes-timonium præsentes literas sigillo meo signatas eidem feci patentes. Dat. apud Borstall, &c.[a]

Sciant præsentes et futuri quod ego Robertus de Harwedon clericus concessi, &c. Johanni de Handlo et Johannæ uxori ejus maneria mea de Borstall, Musewell, Adingrave, Acley et Thomele, et totam ballivam meam forestæ de Bernwode, &c. et hæredibus de corporibus prædicto-rum Johannis et Johannæ legitime procreatis. Et si contingat quod prædicta Johanna uxor dicti Johannis sine hæredibus obierit, &c. tunc post decessum dicti Johannis de Handlo omnia prædicta, &c. ad rectos hæredes Johannis filii Nigelli plene et integre sine aliqua contradic-tione revertantur. Hiis testibus ; dominis Hugone le Despensar, Ri-cardo de Aumari, Johanne Peivre, Laurentio de Bluntesdon, Egidio de Insula, militibus; Johanne de Tingewike, Johanne de la Lude, Gil-berto de Gay, Ada filio Petri, et aliis. Datum apud Curtelington die Veneris proxime post festum S. Luciæ virginis, anno regni regis Ed-wardi vicesimo octavo[b].

The said Robert de Harwedon constituted Richard de Harington and Nicholas de Eshes, or either of them, to give possession to the said John de Handlo and Joan his wife, by letters of attorney dated at Curtlington, Decemb. 18. 28. Edw. I. And the said John de Handlo and Joan his wife appointed Richard de Staundon, clerk, their attorney, to take possession of the premises, by their letters pa-tent dated at Curtlington, on the Friday after St. Lucy's day, 28. Edw. I. After which Hugo le Despensar, justice of the forests on this side Trent, directed his letters to all the officers of the forest of

Pat. 28. Edw. I.   terr. et hered. Warini de Insula defuncti.
Walterus de Bedewind habet lit. de pres.   15. Jul. Lit. dirig. Linc. ep'o.
ad eccl. de Heyford Waryn ratione custod.

[a] Ex Chartul. de Borstall, f. 34   [b] Ibid.

Bernwode, to receive and acknowledge the said John de Handlo to be keeper of the said forest. *Dat. apud Minstre*, xiv. *die Decemb. anno regni regis Edwardi vicesimo octavo*[c].

Hugh, son of John Richards of Borstall, in 10. Edw. I. had granted to John de Handlo *unum furendellum prati in Bradmoor. Hiis testibus; Ricardo le Warde, Nicholao de Fraxino, Johanne de Adingrave, Willielmo Broun, et Roberto de Byrencestre. Dat. apud Borstall die Jovis proxime ante festum apostolorum Philippi et Jacobi, anno regni regis Edwardi decimo*[d].

An. mccc. 28, 29. Edward I.

Edmund earl of Cornwall had a grant from the king for free warren in his manors of Thonnoyk in Lincolnshire, and Esthall in this county[e]. He granted to William de Bereford and Margaret his wife a fishery in the Thames from Shillingford bridge * to the stream running from Yeldenebrigg between Bensyndon and Shillingford, which fishery was valued at half a mark yearly. *Datum apud Rutherfield decimo die Septembris anno regni regis Edwardi filii regis Henrici vicesimo octavo*[f]. He died at his convent of Asherugge on Saturday morning, Octob. 1; his bowels were immediately there buried; his heart and flesh were more solemnly interred January the twelfth, in presence of Edmund the king's son, Anthony de Beke bishop of Durham, Walter de Langton bishop of Chester, the earl of Warwick, and many others. After which his bones were carried to the abbey of Hales in Glocestershire, of his father's foundation, where a magnificent funeral was solemnized on the Thursday before Palm Sunday: which the king honoured with his own presence, and sent letters of invitation to the bishops of Hereford, Worcester, and Exon; to the abbots of Evesham, Teuksbury, Winchomb, Pershore, Egnesham, Cirencester, Osency, Stanly, Bordesley, Rewley, Glo-

* Vid. Rymer. 11. 865, 879.

c Ex Chartul. de Borstall, f. 34.   d Ibid.   e R. Dods. MS. vol. 67. f. 120.   f Ex Regist. Borstall. MS. f. 30.

3 Q 2

cester, Worcester, &c. desiring them to attend at the same place and
time to celebrate the said obsequies with greater honour. The form
of the letters was this :

Rex, &c. Salutem. Bonæ memoriæ Edmundo quondam comite Cor-
nubiæ consanguineo nostro, sicut domino placuit, nuper in patriam qua
iter est cunctis mortalibus generatis vocato : nos humationi corporis
ipsius in monasterio de Hailes die Jovis proxime ante dominicam in
ramis palmarum faciendæ proponimus domino concedente personaliter
interesse, benevolentiam vestram attente rogantes quatenus ob commune
humanitatis debitum ac nostri honorificentiam ad humationem prædic-
tam ejus una nobiscum cum devotione celebraturi exequias in præfatis
loco et termino concurratis, ut ex hoc divinam misericordiam valeatis
uberius promereri [g]

One of his monks made him this epitaph in the poetry of those
times.

> Cornubiæ comes et dominus mundusque beatus,
> Dicitur Edmundus de regum germine natus.
> Virtutis titulum trahit a probitate parentum,
> Et decus addit ei comitiva modesta clientum.
> Dapsilis in mensa, frugalia pabula præstans,
> Sacratas domini leges in pectore gestans.
> Protervos domitans ne Wallia prædominetur,
> Regis et absentis regnum ratione tuetur.
> Dulcis in elloquio, justus, pius atque benignus,
> Prudens consilio, regni moderamine dignus.
> Fraxinei dorsi per eum novus ordo virescit,
> Summa cœlicolæ nova messis in aggere crescit.
> Sumptibus Edmundi comitis locus ædificatur,
> Regius Oxoniæ, quo plebs studiosa moratur [h].

The sepulture of his heart at Asherugge was with the heart of
Thomas de Cantilupe, late bishop of Hereford, a holy confessor ; in
veneration of whose merits the said earl had prepared a repository

---

[g] Guil. Dugd. Analecta, MSS. vol. B. 1. p. 130.   [h] Ib. Collectanea ex diversis MSS.
vol. L. f. 17.

made with exquisite art on the north side of the choir of that conventual church, where the bishop's heart was some time preserved; but on this occasion was removed by the pope's authority, and with the earl's heart, the portion of Christ's blood, and other sacred relics, was committed to an apartment finely guilt, by the earl in his lifetime prepared for that use [i]

He died without legitimate issue; his honours and lands fell to the king, whom he had before declared his heir: in his treasury were found infinite sums of gold and silver, and great store of jewels [k]. Here I cannot but take notice of a great error in the register of St. Augustin's in Bristol, which reports, that Edmund earl of Cornwall left one daughter, Isabella, married to Maurice lord Berkley. This mistake was copied out by one Newlond, an abbot of St. Augustin's, who, in a fair pedigree of the family of Berkley, with a succession of their abbots intermixed, does so deliver it: as I remember to have seen among the records in Berkley castle, to which I had access by the favour of Mr. Robert Maundy, my kind countryman, an ingenious lover of these studies. This same authority imposed on the laborious Mr. Dodsworth, who to some of his collections has affixed this note. *Isabellam hanc fuisse filiam Edmundi filii regis Romanorum ex fide libri vetusti S. Augustini credimus, licet alii e familia Lusigniana, et uterina Henrici tertii sorore natam suspicantur. Neptem vero fuisse Henrici tertii docet charta in clausis Hen. III.* When the truth is, Isabel, the wife of Maurice the third lord Berkley, was the daughter of Gilbert Clare earl of Glocester, and so the niece, not the daughter of Edmund earl of Cornwall, who married Margaret sister of the said earl of Glocester. She was indeed grandmother to Ed. *I.* her mother being Joan de Acres the king's daughter. But when

An. MCCC. 28, 29. Edw. I.   Hethe vac. per mort. Hen. de Dunton. 6.
Mag'r Rob. de Picheford pres. per pri-   id. Apr. 1300. Reg. Dalderby.
orem et conv. de Kenilworth ad eccl. de

[i] Ad calcem lib. MS. de vita trium magorum in Bib. Bodl.   [k] Collect. ex vet. MSS.
Guil. Dugd. MS. vol. 39. f. 75.

Mr. Dodsworth represents her to be niece of Hen. III. he confounds her with Isabel, wife of Maurice the second lord Berkley, who was the daughter of Maurice de Creoun a baron in Linc. by Isabel his wife, daughter of Hugh le Brun earl of March, by Isabel widow of king John; so as this elder Isabel, lady Berkley, was indeed on the mother's side niece to king Hen. III.

Our said earl left Margaret his widow, to whom at Lincoln, in the year ensuing, the king allowed a dowry of five hundred pounds per an.[1]: for the payment of which several lordships were assigned, and among others the manor and town of Henly in this county.

The inquisition taken at his death, rehearsing the honours and manors of which he died possessed, is preserved among the collections of Mr. Dodsworth[m].

He left one base son, who, from his father's title, was called Richard Cornwall, knight; to whom his father gave the manor of East-Hall in Lye, (now Astol-Lye, within the hundred of Bampton in this county,) to hold to him and his heirs in fee tail. This Richard, by Joan his wife, had issue Sir Brian Cornwall, knight; which Brian took to wife Elizabeth, daughter to Brian de Brompton, knight, and had issue Edmund, Brian, and Peter: the said Edmund dying without issue, Brian Cornwall, knight, married Maud daughter of the lord Strange, and had issue John Cornwall, knight, Henry, Brian, Thomas, and Isabel. The said John Cornwall, knight, took to wife Elizabeth, daughter to John Wasteney, knight, by whom he had issue Elizabeth, daughter and heir, married to William Lichfield, knight, and had issue Elizabeth and Maud. The said Elizabeth was wife of Roger Corbet of Moreton, and died without issue. As also the said Maud, wife of John Wood, died without issue: by which means the said manor of Astol-Lye remained to Henry Cornwall, knight, who died without issue; then passed to Bryan, after to Thomas, who both died without issue: the said manor descending to Isabel their sister and sole heir, which Isabel married John Blount,

---

[1] Tho. Walsingham, sub an.   [m] MS. vol. 44. p. 255.

knight, and had issue John, who took to wife Alice daughter to Ry-
nar de la Beere, and had issue by her Humphrey Blount, knight;
upon whose death an inquisition was taken Octob. 31. 17. Ed. IV.
wherein the jurors returned upon oath, that the said Sir Humphrey
Blount at the day of his death held the manor of Astol-Lye in fee
from Edward prince of Wales, as part of the honour of the castle of
Walingford, for his homage and fealty only; that Thomas Blount his
son and heir was then of the age of twenty-one years[n].

This manor of Astol-Lye had formerly belonged to the family of
de Ivery, lords of Ambrosden, by one of whom the tithes were given
to the monks of Ivery in France: the profits and burden of the
vicar are recounted in a presentation made 11. Hug. Wells, an. 5.
Hen. III[o].

There had been a controversy of rights and profits between the
priory of Burcester and the abbey of Aulney in Normandy, which
was now composed on these terms: the convent of Burcester demised to the use of the convent of Aulney their prebendary church
of Sotton, with the chapel of Bokingham, and their respective manors, for the term of two years, at the rent of two hundred pounds.

Prior *et conventus de Bernecester dimiserunt Godvano Beke de Flo-
rentia et Stephano germano suo ecclesiam prebendalem de Sotton cum
capella de Bokingham et earum maneriis an. Dom. millesimo trecentesimo, in festo S. Hillarii ad terminum duorum annorum pro redditu
ducentarum librarum sterlingarum &c.*[p]

Within this year seems to have been an election of a new prior of
* Burcester, confirmed by their patron Henry Lacy, earl of Lincoln;

* Rogerus de Cottesford elect. prior de
Burncestr per cessionem fr'is Will'i de
Thornberg per licent. H. de Lacy patroni
ejusd. admissus die Martis prox. post festum S. Martini; pont. 1. Reg. Dalderby
ep'i Linc.

An. MCCC.

Vacante cecl'ia de Midelington per mort.

[n] W. Dugd. MS. vol. 39. f. 81.   [o] R. Dods. MS. vol. 107. f. 11.   [p] Mon. Ang
tom. 2. p. 1007. et R. Dods. MS. vol. 63. f. 109.

who, in the register of the diocese of Lincoln, in this first year of John
Dalderby, bishop, is thus mentioned in the abstracts of Mr. Dods-
worth : *Dominus Henricus de Lasey com. Linc. patronus prioratus de
Bernecester* [q].

The said Henry earl of Lincoln was now again in the wars of
Scotland; and within this same year was sent to the pope with Sir
Hugh Spenser from the king, to complain of divers injuries received
from the Scots.   He was now also made lieutenant of Gascoign [r].

Within this year Ela countess of Warwick died and was buried in
the conventual church of Oseney [s]. Sir John Fitz-Wido, knight, presented to the church of Ardley on the third of the ides of July [t].

Robert *Doily*, sen. had given two parts of the tithe of his demesnes
in Burcester to the chapel of St. George in his castle of Oxford,
and the secular canons which he there settled, which canons were
after dissolved, and their endowment converted to the abbey of
Oseney, built by Rob. *Doily*, jun. which abbey retained their right
and title to the said tithes till this year; when, to make up a controversy which had been long depending between the said abbey of
Oseney and the priory of Burcester concerning the premises, by
mutual indentures made on the tenth day of August, it was fully
agreed, that the abbot and convent of Oseney should for ever grant
the said tithes to the prior and convent of Burcester, and should receive the yearly rent of sixty shillings sterling, to be paid half yearly

Petri Durandi in Rom. curia decedentis
d'n's papa cand. eccl'iam contulit mag'ro
Ric. de Celleseye juris cononici professori
habitaque inter ipsum et Will. de Luda in
eadem cecl'ia ad pres. abb'is et conv. de
Barling institutum per ep'um Oliverum
tandem idem Will'us dictam eccl'iam re-

signavit. Id. Maii 1300. et Rie'us admiss.
est. 16. kal. Jan.
    Joh. de Schulton cl'icus pres. per d'num
Joh. fil. Guidonis mil. ad eccl. de Ardele
vac. per hoc quod Rogerus de Schulton institutus fuit in eccl'ia de Croulton. 3. id.
Jul. 1300. pont. 1. Joh. Dalderby.

q R. Dods. MS. vol. 107. f. 199.   r Ibid.   s Ex Tab. Annal. Oseneien. Cœnob. apud
Jo. Leland. tom. 2. p. 286.   t R. Dods. MS. vol. 107. p. 199.

by equal portions under the penalty of forty shillings; and farther to secure the said payment, the prior and convent did tie and oblige all their lands and tenements in Arncote, within the parish of Am brosden.

Hæe est conventio facta inter religiosos viros abbatem et conventum ecclesiæ beatæ Mariæ Oseney ex parte una et priorem et conventum Burncestriæ ex altera, videlicet quod cum dicti religiosi de Oseneye duas partes decimæ garbarum provenientium de dominico in Burn-cester quod comes Lincoln. et dictus prior nunc tenent in eadem legi-time assecuti fuissent ratione ecclesiæ Sancti Georgii in castro Oxon. eisdem canonicis appropriatæ ipsasque decimas a tempore cujus con-trarii memoria non existit pacifice possedissent ac super jure et posses-sione prædictarum decimarum tam per viam actionis quam per viam reconventionis inter prædictos abbatem et conventum ex parte una et priorem et conventum ex altera in consistorio Lincoln. aliquandiu li-tigatum fuisset, demum communibus amicis utriusque monasterii inter-venientibus pro utriusque monasterii quiete et ad utilitatem dicti mo-nasterii de Burncester notoriam lis conquievit in hunc modum, videli-cet quod iidem abbas et conventus Oseneye prædictus duas partes deci-marum prædictis priori et conventui de Burncestria ad perpetuam fir-mam concesserunt pro sexaginta solidis bonorum et legalium sterlingo-rum ab eisdem priore et conventu Berncestre prædictis abbati et con-ventui Oseneye apud Osceniam, videlicet medietatem in festo Sancti Michaelis Archangeli et aliam medietatem in festo annunciationis beatæ Mariæ virginis absque ulteriori dilatione pro dictis decimis singulis annis solvend. sub pæna quadraginta solidorum solvendorum abbati et conventui Oseneye quotiens iidem prior et conventus Burncestre in præ-dictorum sexaginta solidorum solutione terminis prædictis cessaverint. Et prædicti prior et conventus Burncestriæ omnia onera ordinaria et extraordinaria ac omnes prestationes ratione dictarum decimarum sive authoritate papali aut legatorum seu nuntiorum sedis apostolicæ aut aliorum quorumcunque ad hoc auctoritatem habentium quocunque no-mine censeantur imponenda semper sustinebunt. Ita quod solutio præ-dictorum sexaginta solidorum integraliter dictis religiosis Oseneye

*semper remaneat. Ad hæc autem omnia et singula fideliter obser-
vandu prædicti prior et conventus de Burncestre pro se et successoribus
suis coercioni et discretioni officialis domini Lincoln. episcopi vel cu-
juscunque alterius judicis quem prædicti abbas et conventus elegerint
se subjecerunt, quod possint eos et eorum successores per omnem censuram ecclesiasticam ad omnium et singulorum premissorum observa
tionem absque articuli seu libelli petitione et quocunque strepitu judi-
ciali compellere. Insuper nos prior et conventus Burncester volentes
firmam et plenam securitatem parari dictis religiosis Oseneye in hac
parte nos et successores nostros et omnia bona nostra et specialiter omnes terras et tenementa nostra in Erncote eisdem canonicis Oseneye
obligamus ad solutionem dictorum sexaginta solidorum ut præmittitur
in posterum fideliter faciendam. Ita quod si contingat nos in dicta
solutione dictis terminis et loco quod absit deficere, possint nos et successores nostros et prædictas omnes terras et tenementa nostra infra et
extra ad quorumcunque manus devenerint distringere ad solutionem
memoratam in forma præmissa fideliter faciendam et districtiones retinere quousque eisdem abbati et conventui et eorum successoribus de
prædicto redditu plenarie fuerit satisfactum una cum dampnis et expensis si quæ vel quas prædicti religiosi Oseneye sustinuerint occasione
prædicta, renuntiantes in hoc facto omnibus impellationibus super hoc
habitis, appellationibus, in integrum restitutioni, regiæ prohibitioni et
omni alii remedio juris canonici et civilis sibi competentibus et compe-
tituris quæ ipsis religiosis de Burncester poterint prodesse, ac eisdem
religiosis Oseney in hoc facto obesse. Inque omnium suprascriptorum
memoriam perpetuam et testimonium partes huic scripto indentato altrinsecus sigilla sua apposuerunt. Dat. apud Oseneiam* III. idus Augusti, anno Dom. M°. trecentesimo* [u].*

To the original indenture is appending the seal of the abbey of
Oseney, the virgin Mary sitting with our Saviour in her arms, and
underneath the impress of an ox. Their arms being azure two
bends or.

This year, June the sixteenth, John Puff, son of Robert Puff of

[u] Ex Orig. penes D. Guil. Glynne, Bar.

Burcester, granted to John Abbod of the said town one acre of arable land in the north field of Burcester, which he had by the gift of Robert his father, and which lay between the two ways that lead from Burcester toward Bukenhull, between the land of the earl of Lincoln and of Gilbert Attewelle, in consideration of twenty shillings, by the following deed.

Sciant præsentes et futuri quod ego Johannes Puff filius Roberti Puff de Burncester dedi concessi et hac præsenti charta mea confirmavi Johanni Abbod filio Thomæ Abbod de Burncester unam acram terræ arabilis in campo boreali de Burncester illam videlicet quam habui de dono prædicti Roberti patris mei et jacet inter duas vias quæ se extendunt de Burncester versus Bukenhulle inter terram dom. com. Linc. et terram Gilberti Attewelle habend. et tenend. dictam acram terræ prædicto Johanni et hæredibus suis et assignatis de capitalibus dominis feodi libere quiete bene et in pace et hæreditarie in perpetuum reddendo inde eisdem unum denarium annuatim in festo Sancti Michaelis pro omnibus servitiis forinsecis et intrinsecis curiarum sectis et omnibus sæcularibus demandis quæ aliquo modo poterint contingere vel exigi ratione dicti tenementi. Pro hac autem donatione concessione et præsentis chartæ confirmatione dedit mihi prædictus Johannes viginti solidos in gersuma : et ego prædictus Johannes et hæredes mei et assignati prædictam aeram terræ prædicto Johanni et hæredibus suis et assignatis per prædictum servitium contra omnes homines et fœminas warantizabimus acquietabimus et in perpetuum defendemus. In cujus rei testimonium hanc præsentem chartam meam sigilli mei impressione roboravi. Hiis testibus ; Willielmo Maunde, Rogero de Dreyton de Cestreton, Simone Germeyn, Nicholao le Blake de Bigenhulle, Roberto Clerico de Burncester, Johanne a la Forde, Johanne Fabro juniore de eadem, et aliis. Dat et act. apud Burncester sexto decimo die Junii, anno regni regis Edwardi vicesimo nono [x].

An. MCCCI.   29, 30.   Edward I.

This year died John le Fleming, rector of the church of Ambros-

[x] Ex Orig. penes Hon. D. Guil. Glynne, Bar.

3 R 2

den. The rector and convent of Ashrugge, who by the donation of
Edmund earl of Cornwall were undoubted patrons, presented John
de Capella, an acolyte or taper-bearer of their own convent: but the
fee of the manor of Ambrosden by the earl's death lapsing to the
king, it was pretended the patronage of the church was also in the
crown. Maurice de Pashelew, clerk, procured the king's title to the
church of Blakethorn, a hamlet in the parish of Ambrosden; a mistake that arose from the parsonage house and glebe lying within the
said hamlet of Blakethorn, to which hamlet the parochial church
could not be properly ascribed. Upon this double presentation the
bishop ordered the official of the archdeacon of Oxford to require an
inquisition upon the right of patronage from each of the presented
clerks : the said John de Capella returned his form of inquisition,
by which it appeared that the rector and convent of Asherugge had
undoubted right of presentation to the said church; and the said
Maurice de Pashelew desisted from his claim to the king's title. Upon
which, notification was given, that if any person could object against
the admission of John de Capella, he should appear and give his
reasons within a time limited before the bishop. But no one appearing, the said John de Capella was admitted rector of the church
of Ambrosden on the fifth of July at Snelleshale, and was there ca-
nonically instituted, with a precept to the archdeacon to give him
induction. Yet was the bishop and the law so tender of the king's
right, that the said new incumbent obliged himself by oath to a vo-

An. mccci. 29, 30. Edw. I.

Rex dilecto et fideli suo Waltero de
Glouc. escaetori suo eitra Trentam. Cum
venerabilis pater J. Lincoln. ep'us exami-
nato processu electionis nuper in eccl'ia de
Garinge de duabus monialibus ejusdem domus in discordia factæ alteram earundem
videl. Margeriam Neela quæ nobis extitit
presentata in priorissam domus illius cujus
advocatio per mortem bonæ memoriæ Edmundi quondam com. Cornubiæ consan-
guinei nostri ad manus nostras devenit præ-
fecerit sicut per literas patentes ipsius ep'i
nobis inde directas nobis constat, nos præ-
fectionem acceptantes cepimus fidelitatem
ipsius Margeriæ et temporalia domus prædictæ prout moris est restituimus eidem; et
ideo vobis mandamus quod eidem Margeriæ temporalia domus prædictæ liberatis in
forma prædicta. Teste rege apud Nettleham; 9. die Feb. Pat. 29. Edw. I. m. 29.

luntary resignation, if it could be proved, that the king had right of patronage to the said church of Ambrosden.

Tempore Johannis Dalderby olim episcopi Lincoln. qui cœpit præesse in ecclesia catholica ibidem in anno Dom. millesimo trecentesimo.

Vacante ecclesia de Ambresdon per mortem magistri Johannis le Fleming ultimi rectoris ejusdem. Rector et conventus de Asherugge Johannem de Capella acolytum, et dominus E. Dei gratia rex Angliæ Mauritium de Pissiaco clericum ad ecclesiam de Blakethorn quæ est hamelettum in parochia de Ambresdon episcopo præsentarunt; et licet scriptum fuisset officiali archidi. Oxon. pro inquisitione ad præsentat· hujus facienda, solus tamen dictus Johannes suam inquisitionem reportavit, et quia per candem et alias satis constitit de jure præsentandi ad candem ecclesiam dictis rectori et conventui competente, dictusque Mauritius præsentationem de ipso factam minime prosequebatur, licet per tempus non modicum expectatus fuisset, et etiam proclamatum extitisset, quod si quis contra dictum Johannem aliquid proponere vellet, quare ad dictam ecclesiam admitti non deberet, certo die sub dilatione congrua coram episcopo compareret, et proponeret in hac parte quiequid sibi de jure putaret competere: dictus Johannes ad dictam eccle siam de Ambresdon est admissus III. non. Julii anno secundo apud Snelleshale, et rector canonice institutus in eadem, juravitque episcopo canonicam obedientiam in forma consueta: scriptum est dicto archidiacono vel ejus officiali quod &c. Et est sciendum quod dictus Johannes post institutionem suam prædictam juravit tactis sacrosanctis evangeliis quod si contingeret dictum regem evincere jus patronatus ecclesiæ memoratæ, illam sine coactione aliqua resignaret y*

Upon inquisition on a writ called *ad quod dampnum*, in the county of York, the jurors found it would be no loss or prejudice to the king, if Alice de Lacy, the wife of Thomas earl of Lancaster, daughter of Henry Lacy earl of Lincoln, and heir to the manors of Bur-

---

* Admissus 3. non. Jul. 1301.

y Ex Regist. Lincoln. transcrip. et exam. per N. Thorold. et J. Walker, notar. pub.

cester and Midlington, should grant one messuage and four acres of land in Poterinton, to a chaplain that should celebrate divine service in the church of Berwyck, for the souls of the said Alice and Adam de Poterinton [z]

The king within this year presented to the church of * Beckle, as having the honour of St. Walery escheated to him. Henry de Lacy earl of Lincoln presented to the church of Northcotes, 6. id. Apr. and to the church of Wadington, 3. non. Maii, and to the church of Wynceby; all within the archdeaconry of Lincoln [a].

An. mcccii. 30, 31. Edward I.

In Hilary term the prior of Rufford was impleaded by John bishop of Lincoln for setting up a market in Hadenham, in com. Bucks, kept on Thursday, to the prejudice of the Tuesday's free market at Tame, com. Oxon. granted to Oliver late bishop of Lincoln; which being found a prejudice, the new market at Hadenham was put down [b]

William Bourward of Ocley granted to Sir John de Handlo lord of Borstall one cottage, with a curtilage, in the village of Borstall, and all the service of Henry Pipat, John Pipat, Emma Hobby, and John Steel of Arncote, and other servile tenants, in consideration of

---

* 1301. Jacobus de Berkhamsted subd. pres. ad eccl. de Bekkele vac. per resign. Hen. de Exon. ad pres. regis. 16. kal. Jun. pont. 2. Joh. Dalderby.

    An. mcccii. 30, 31. Edw. I.

1302. pont. 3. Joh. de Dalderby ep'i Linc. Andreas de Cottesford capellan. pres. per pr. et conv. de Burencestre ad vicariam eccl'ie de Burnecestre vac. per mort. Will'i de Kynton. 2. non. Mart.

Nich. de Harlawe acol. pres. per priorem et conv. de Burncestr ad eccl. de Newenton vac. per hoc quod Andreas ult. rector ejusd.

institutus fuit in vicaria de Burncestr. 7. kal. Apr. pont. 3.

    Walterus de Maydestan persona eccl'iæ de Bukenhale qui cum Waltero Coventr. et Lichfeld. ep'o profecturus est ad curiam Romanam, habet literas de protectione per biennium duraturas. T. R. apud Gildeford. 20. die Januar. Pat. 31. Ed. I. m. 4.

   . Petitio Will'i personæ de Lutegareshale in com. Buck. d'no regi in Parliamento porrecta. anno 30. Edw. I. Vid. Rileii Plac. Parl. p. 603.

---

[z] R. Dods. MS. 44. p. 274.   [a] Ib. vol. 107. f. 166.   [b] Ib. vol. 119. f. 101.

one mark in hand. *Hiis testibus ; Johanne Brun, Martino de le Ro-*
kalle, Ricardo le Warde, Nigello Travers, Thoma de Herford, et mul-
tis aliis[c].

Alice, widow of Henry Segrym of Borstall, granted to the said Sir
John de Handlo, *duas seliones,* two ridges of arable land in a field
called Southcroft, between the land of John Fitz-Nigel of Arncote on
the one side, and a croft of the said John Fitz-Nigel and Grascroft
on the other. *Hiis testibus ; Johanne le Brun, Martino de la Ro-*
kaylle, Ricardo le Warde, Thoma de Baukestoft, Nigello Travers,
Thoma de Herford, Ricardo de Luches, et multis aliis[d]

An. mcccIII. 31, 32. *Edward* I.

Walter le Povre, knight, paid a fine to the king, that he might
give the pasturage of eight oxen in his manor of * Odington to the
master and brethren of St. John's hospital without the east gate, Oxford[e].

An. mcccII. 31, 32. Edw. I.

Joh. Albon p'b'r pres. per priorem et
conv. de Burncestr ad eccl. de Neuton Purcell vac. per resign. Nich. de Herlawe. 8.
id. Mart. pont. 4.

* Rectores eccl'iæ de Ottingdon com. Oxon.

1250. Mag'r Will. de Mara diae. ad eccl.
de Ottindon ad pres. prior. et conv. de Bi-
rencestr. commissa est ei cecl'ia sub titulo
commendam donec ep'us revocaverit ; ep'o
tune agente in transmarinis. Rot. Rob.
Grosthead, anno 16.

D'n's Joh. de Wy presb. coll. ad eccl.
de Otyngdon super Ottemor vac. per mort.
Ric'i le l'ovre. kal. Oct. 1327. devoluta fuit
ad ep'um ob litem inter Walterum le Povre milit. et Walterum de Islep de jure
presentandi infra 6. menses non termina-

tam. Reg. Burgwersh.

Will. de Fordham, acol. pres. per Walt.
le Povre ad eccl. de Otyngdon super Ottemor vac. per resign. D. Joh. de Wy. kal.
Feb. 1329. Reg. Burgwersh.

Tho. Thame prior sive magister hospitalis S. Trinitatis de Langbrugg juxta Berk-
legh Wigorn. dioc. et magister Reginald
Povy, rector eccl'iæ de Ottingdon permutant ad pres. Rog. Power. 9. Apr. 1403.
Reg. Beaufort ep'i Linc.

Joh. Beek p'b'r pres. per Rog. Fovre de
Blechyngdon ad eccl. de Odyngton 17. Jan.
1412. Reg. Alnewyk.

Mag'r Will. Wagge, A.M. pres. per Tho.
Povre arm. ad eccl. de Otyndon per resign.
mag'ri Joh. Beek. 9. Jun. 1147. ih.

1150. 20. Mar. Mag. Joh. Halewey, A.M.
pres. per Rog. Povere armig. ad eccl. de

c Ex Chartul. de Borstall, f. 35.   d Ibid.   e R. Dods. MS. vol. 41. p. 311.

This family of Povre was descended from Roger Pauper, or Povre, son of Roger bishop of Salisbury, by Maud of Ramesbury, his harlot, in the reign of Hen. II.

Henry Lacy earl of Lincoln was now joined in commission with the bishop of Winchester and others, to treat of peace betwixt king Edward and Philip king of France[f].

Edmund lord Mortimer being mortally wounded in a battle with the Welsh at Buelt, and dying of his hurts in Wigmore castle, and being buried in that abbey; Margaret his widow, daughter of Sir William de Fendles, a Spaniard, and kinswoman to queen Elianore, among other large possessions allotted for her dowry, had the third part of the manor of Crendon in com. Bucks.[g]

Odyngton per resign. mag'ri Will'i Wagg. Reg. Lumley.

Mag'r Joh. Pavy, A. M. pres. per Rog. Power armig. ad eccl. de Odynton per resign. mag'ri Joh. Holwey. 13. Feb. 1459. Reg. Chedworth.

D'n's Oliver Sompneur p'b'r pres. per Rog. Power armig. ad eccl. de Odynton per mort. Mag'ri Joh. Pavy. 9. Nov. 1478. Reg. Rotherham.

1483. 22. Apr. Tho. Tempall. arm. ratione custodiæ Job'is Power filii et hered. Joh. Power presentavit mag'rum Will. Petyr utr. jur. Bacc. p'b'rum ad eccliam de Odyndon, per resign. mag'ri Oliveri Sompnour, qui acceptavit eccliam de Tackley. Reg. Russel.

Mag'r Tho. Randolf pres. per Joh. Lewysson et Eliz. uxor. ejus ad eccl. de Odyngton per resign. d'ni Will'i Fendyk. 16. Oct. 1487. ib.

Mag. Rad'us Hamsterley, A. M. p'b'r pres. per Joh'em Power de Bletingdon gen.

ad eccl'iam de Odyngton per resign. mag. Tho. Randolfe. 8. Maii 1499. Reg. Smith.

Mag'r Rob. Lawson, A. M. pres. per Joh. Power gen. ad eccl. de Oddington per resign. Mag'ri Rad'i Hamsterley, 4. Mart. 1507. Pensio annua x. mare. solvenda resignanti. ib.

Mag'r Edm. Horde deer. doctor pres. per Joh. Pecocke ad eccl. de Odyngton ratione advocationis sibi factæ per Joh. Power armig. per mort. mag'ri Roh'ti Lawson. 10. Jan. 1515. Reg. Alwater.

Mag. Joh. Leycestr pres. per Joh. Power ad eccl. de Odyngton per expressam professionem mag'ri Edmundi Horde deer. doctoris monasticæ religionis ea ratione vacant. apud Osen. 10. Maii 1520. juravit quod non dedit nec promisit aliquid nec aliquid pro illius promotione promittit seu dari novit, admissus est. ib.

1573. 8. Sept. Will. Davis cl'icus institutus in eccl'ia de Odyngton ad pres. Franc. Povre armig. Reg. Parker ar'ep'i Cant.

[f] Dugd. Bar. tom. 1. p. 105. a.   [g] Ib. p. 143. b.

About this time John de Charlton *super* Otmoor gave to the abbey of Oseney four shillings yearly rent, which Thomas Frankleyn used to pay him : this with consent of Maud his wife and Sibil his mother. After which, John son of the said John de Charlton and Christian his wife, gave to the said abbey that land in Hokenorton upon which stood the berchery or sheep-cote of John Sutton[h].

An. MCCCIV.   32, 33. Edward I.

The church of St. Mary's in Kurtlington (now Kirtlington) was appropriated to the Cistertian abbey of Aulney, within the diocese of Baieux in Normandy, by which means the said abbot and convent were possessed of the tithes of the demesne both of John de Langly and the prioress and convent of Merkyate, com. Bedf. in right of their cell within the territory of Berncester : which church of Kirtlington the abbot of Aulney did now demise and for ever grant to the prior and convent of Burcester for the yearly rent of forty shillings.

Universis sancte matris ecclesie filiis presentes literas visuris vel audituris. Pateat per presentes quod cum religiosi viri abbas et conventus de Alneto Baiocensis dyocesis ordinis Cisterciensis decimas garbarum provenientium de dominicis terris nunc domini Johannis de Langeleye et domine priorisse et conventus de cella infra territorium de Berencestria scituat. legitime fuissent assecuti racione ecclesie beate Marie de Kurtlyngton eisdem abbati et conventui de Alneto et eorum successoribus imperpetuum canonice appropriate, &c. Abbas de Alneto dimisit ecclesiam de Kurtlington priori et conventui de Berencestria ad perpetuam firmam reddendo inde quadraginta solidos per annum, &c. Datum decimo quarto Maii, anno MCCCIV.[i]

An. MCCCIV.   32, 33. Edw. 1.   Pat. 32. Ed. I. Joh. de Heyford cl'icus
1304. Joh. de Heyford cap. pres. per   habet lit. reg. de pres. ad eccl. de Heyford
regem ad eccl'iam de Heyford Warin vac.   Waryn ratione custod. terr. et hered. Wa-
per resign. Simonis de Heyford.   rini de Insula defuncti. 13. Apr.

h W. Wyrley, Collectanea MSS. in Mus. Ashmol.   i Mon. Ang. tom. 2. p. 1007. et
R. Dods. MS. vol. 63. p. 109. b.

Upon the original chart was endorsed the composition between the priors of Burcester and Aulney in Normandy with this title, *Contro-versia inter priorem de Bysseter et priorem de Alneto,* of which the form is recited sub an. 1300. This abbey of Aulney, in the diocese of Baieux, of the Cistertian order, was founded by Jordan de Say about the year MCXIII. rebuilt and endowed MCLV. by Richard de Humetz, constable to Hen. II. who married Agnes daughter and heir of the said Jordan de Say[k] : by whom he had a daughter called Agnes, married to Baldwin de Wake, to whom king John, in the eighth of his reign, granted she should hold the manor of Wichendon or Winchendon, com. Buck. *in capite,* which her father had given with her in marriage. Which Agnes, with consent of Baldwin de Wake her son and heir, gave to the canons of Nutley, for the health of the soul of Baldwin her husband, a certain messuage in the said manor of Winchendon[l]

Henry Lacy earl of Lincoln, with Margaret his wife, had lately given to the canons of Bromhall, in Berkshire, one hundred acres of his waste at Asserige : and in this year gave leave to the monks of Selby to have that ancient church-yard at Whitgift, which had been long before consecrated, thereon to build a church or chapel to the honour of St. Mary Magdalen, for the benefit of the inhabitants of Snaith [m]. *Datum apud Cliftonam juxta Eboracum die Jovis proxime ante festum apostolorum Simonis et Judæ, anno gratiæ* 1304[n].

An. MCCCV.   33, 34. Edward I.

Isabel, the widow of Sir John Fitz-Nigel, released and quit claimed to Sir John de Handlo and her daughter Joan his wife, all her right of dowry in the manors of Borstall, Oakle, &c. and to thir-teen marks of yearly rent.

Omnibus, &c. Isabella quæ fuit uxor domini Johannis filii Nigelli militis salutem in Domino. Noveritis me in plena viduitate mea &c.

---

[k] Neustria Pia. p. 760.   [l] Dugd. Bar. tom. 1. p. 631.   [m] Ibid. p. 105.   [n] Mon. Ang. tom. 1. p. 374. a.

remisisse et quietum clamasse Johanni de Handlo et Johannæ uxori ejus filiæ meæ &c. totum jus et clamium, &c. quod habui in maneriis de Borstall et Acle et Adingrave, et Musewell, Brehull, Thomele, et Claydon, nomine dotis, quod mihi competit vel competere poterit, &c. et totum jus &c. in tredecem marcis argenti annui redditus quæ mihi per dictum Johannem de Handlo pro dote mea dictorum maneriorum per quoddam scriptum mihi assignabantur, &c. Hiis testibus; domino Hugone le Despensar, domino R. de Burghasse, Georgio de Lanton, Thoma de Gore, Rogero de Stokenhesse, Thoma de Horton, Roberto de Leuknore, Nicholao de Esses, Ada de Paupere, Willielmo de Rufen. Dat. London. die Lunæ in vigilia purificationis beatæ Mariæ virginis. Anno regni regis Edwardi tricesimo tertio[o]

Within this year the king granted to Sir John Handlo several acres of waste in the forest of Bernwode by this charter.

Edwardus Dei gracia rex Anglie, &c. Omnibus ad quos presentes litere pervenerint salutem. Sciatis quod de vastis nostris in foresta nostra de Bernewode in com. Buk. dedimus et concessimus pro nobis et heredibus nostris dilecto et fideli nostro Johanni Handlo quadringenta unam acras et unam rodam et dimidiam pro perticis viginti pedum, videlicet decem et septem acras in quodam loco qui vocatur Merdescombe juxta Mosewell et centum acras in quadam placea que vocatur le Hallehull juxta Lutgershale et quinquaginta et novem acras

An. MCCCV. 33, 34. Edw. I.

Ad petitionem Joh'is de Segrave petentis de hoc quod Margeria quæ fuit uxor Hugonis de Plessetis cujus terrarum et heredis custodiam rex concessit eidem Johanni habeat ultra rationabilem dotem ipsam contingentem in manerio de Hoggenorton cxiv. acras terræ, &c. Ita responsum est, terræ in manum regis rescisientur et reextendantur. Rot. Parl. 33. Edw. I.

Ad petitionem abb'is et conventus de

Osceney petentium quod cum ipsi et predecessores sui habuerunt xii. sol. redditus in liberam elemosinam in manerio de Hedendon de dono Matildis imperatricis unde seisiti fuerunt quousque dominus rex predictum manerium dedit dominæ reginæ quæ nunc est quod rex percipere velit quod eis solvantur. Ita responsum est coram rege solvantur prout solvi consuevit; et super hoc habeant breve, &c. Rot. Parl. 33. Edw. I.

[o] Ex Chartul. de Borstall penes D. Joh. Aubrey, Bar.

3 S 2

*et dimidiam et rodam unam in quadam placca que vocatur Godstowe
wode et sexaginta et quinque acras et dimidiam et unam rodam in quadam placea que vocatur Lachemede et viginti acras et unam rodam
et dimidiam in quadam placca que vocatur la Wocche juxta Lutgarshale et centum et triginta et octo acras et dimidiam in placca quadam
que vocatur lez Cleres de Lutgarshale, habend. et tenend. de nobis et
heredibus nostris prefato Johanni et heredibus suis imperpetuum, reddendo inde nobis et heredibus nostris per annum ad festum nostrum S.
Michaelis per manus vicecomitis comitatus predicti qui pro tempore
fuerit centum solidos et quatuor denarios et unum obolum et unum
quadrantem &c. per dilectos et fideles nostros Walterum de Gloucestre
et Willielmum de Hardene ad predicta vasta arentanda nuper per nos
assignatos, &c.   Ita quod predictus Joannes et heredes sui predictas
quadringenta et unam acram et unam rodam et dimidiam vasti pro voluntate sua fossata et haya secundum assisam foreste includere et in
culturam redigere et eas sic inclusas et in culturam redactas tenere
possint, &c.   In cujus rei testimonium has literas nostras fieri fecimus
patentes.   Teste meipso apud Westm. decimo die Aprilis anno regni nostri tricesimo tercio [p].*

Within this same year, in Trinity term, was a trial for the right of
patronage to the church of * Souldern, now in the deanery of Burcester, which, to shew the state of that church and the course of law
in that age, deserves to be here inserted.

*Placita coram Radulpho de Hengham et sociis suis justitiariis do-
mini regis de Banco in termino S. Trinitatis, anno regni Ed. filii regis
Henrici* xxxiii.

*Thomas abbas de Egnesham per attornatum suum optulit se versus
Luciam quæ fuit uxor Thomæ de Leuknore et Petrum de Schevyndon
quod essent hic ad hunc diem audituri assisam ultimæ præsentationis,*

---

* *Ego Jordanus de Say pro anima filii Willielmi die quo eum sepulturæ apud Egne-sham tradidi eidem monasterio eccl'iam de* Sulethorn *concessi.   Testes Ranulfus filius meus &c.* Ex cart'ario de Egnesham. Bib. Cotton Claudius, A. 8. fol. 135.

[p] Ex Chartular. S. Frideswidæ penes decan. et capit. Ædis Christi, Oxon. p. 145.

qui idem Thomas in curia hic adramivit versus eos de advocatione ec-clesiæ de Soulthorn quæ vacat et cujus advocationem prædicti Lucia et Petrus ei deforc. et ipsi non veniunt ad hunc diem unde judicium assisæ capiatur versus eos per eorum defaltum, et recognitores dicunt super sacramentum suum quod prædictus Thomas tempore regis nunc et tempore pacis decem et septem annis elapsis ut verus patronus ejus-dem ecclesiæ ad eandem ecclesiam præsentavit quendam Johannem de Bernwell qui ad præsentationem suam fuit admissus et institutus in eadem, post cujus mortem prædicta ecclesia modo vacat. Requisiti de jure ipsius abbatis dicunt, quod tempore regis patris domini regis nunc vicesimo anno ejusdem regis H. levatus est quidam finis inter quendam Nicholaum quondam abbatem de Egnesham prædecessorem abbatis nunc et quandam Luciam de Arderne aviam prædictæ Luciæ per quem finem eadem Lucia recognovit advocationem illam esse jus præ-dictæ abbatiæ de Egnesham et post mortem cujusdam Gilberti abbatis prædecessoris abbatis nunc vacante prædicta abbatia quidam Richar-

An. MCCCV. 33, 34. Edw. I.

Pat. 34. Edw. I. Will. de Boresworth ha-bet lit. regis de pres. ad eccl. de Heyford Waryn ratione custod. terr. et hered. Tho. de Breaute. Lit. dirig. J. ep'o Line. 22. Febr.

Idem presentatur per reg. ad eandem ec-el'iam ratione custod. terr. et hered. Wa-rini de Insula defuncti. 22. Apr.

Rex venerabili in Xto Patri J. eadem gratia episcopo Linc. salutem. Licet nuper quibusdam de causis vobis madaverimus quod nos super vera valore ecclesiæ de Heyford Waryn vestræ dioc. ad quam Williclmum de Boresworth clericum vobis præsentaveramus, quantum videlicet vuleat per annum juxta ultimam taxationem de ecclesiis Anglicanis factum ratione decimæ earundem in subsi-dium Terræ Sanctæ nuper concessæ, nos red-deretis certiores et quod interim executioni præsentationis nostræ predictæ supersederetis,

de quo juxta tenorem dicti mandati nostri nos reddidistis certiores; vobis nichilominus mandamus quod executionem præsentationis nostræ quam vobis pro prædicto clerico nos-tro ad præsens mittimus prout ad vos pertinet fieri faciatis non obstante prædicto mandato nostro vobis de supersedendo executione pri-oris presentationis nostræ inde factæ vobis directæ. Teste rege apud Wynton. 12. die Maii. Claus. 34. Ed. I. m. 13.

Mag'r Simon de Well pres. per Tho. abb. et conv. de Eynesham ad eccl. de Sul-thorn per mort. Joh. de Bernewell kal. Jul. pont. 6. dictus abbas recuperavit pre-sentationem suam in curia regis versus Lu-ciam quæ fuit uxor Tho. de Leukenovre. Reg. Joh. Dalderby, pont. 5.

Joh. de Well acol. pres. per abb. et conv. de Egnesham ad eccl. de Stoke abbatis vac. per instit. Simonis de Well in eccl'ia de Sulthorn. 2. non. Aug. pont. 6.

dus de Gravesend quondam Lincoln. episcopus loci illius ordinarius et advocatus prædictæ abbatiæ contulit illam ecclesiam cuidam Galfrido de Stokes clerico suo qui fuit institutus in eadem, ac requisiti de collusione inter partes prælocuta contra statutum ac etiam de valore ejusdem ecclesiæ dicunt quod nulla est collusio inter partes inde prælocuta, &c. dicunt etiam quod ecclesia illa valet per an. viginti marcas et quod tempus semestre nondum elapsum est. Ideo concessum est quod prædictus Thomas abbas habeat breve episcopo Lincoln. quod ad præsentationem ipsius abbatis ad prædictam ecclesiam idoneam personam admittat, et quod idem abbas recuperet versus eos decem marcas pro damnis suis [q]*

An inquisition was taken at Oxford before Nicholas de Persch, sheriff of this county, on Saturday next before Easter-day, to inquire how the manor of Hedingdon was alienated from the crown. The jurors, Robert Neal of Pyrie, &c. returned upon oath, that Henry king of England, great grandfather to the present king, gave the said manor of Hedingdon, with the hundred of Bolendon, and the hundred without the north-gate of Oxford, to Thomas Basset and his heirs for ever, for his good service in divers wars, paying to the Exchequer the yearly rent of twenty pounds in silver. After him the said manor descended to Philippa, daughter of the said Thomas, as her purparty with Juliana her sister; which Philippa dying without heirs, the said manor passed to Isabella daughter of Juliana, by John de Ripariis, which Isabella married to Hugh de Plessets, which Hugh, after the death of his wife Isabella, made an exchange with the king for the manor of Compton; by which means the said manor of Hedingdon was now in the king's hands [r]. And the said Hugh de Plessets settled on Thomas his son and heir the manors of Kidlington, Hokenorton, and Missenden, in lieu of his right to the manor of Hedingdon, which he had given to the king.

Ego Hugo de Plessetis concedo quod maneria mea de Cudelinton, Hokenorton et Messenden quæ sunt de hereditate mea &c. remaneant

---

[q] Ex Chartul. de Borstall penes D. J. Aubrey, Bar.   [r] R. Dods. MS. vol. 64. f. 105.

post decessum meum Thome de Plessetis filio et heredi meo et heredibus suis pro jure suo manerii de Hedindon cum pertinentiis quod dedi domino meo regi Anglie et heredibus suis per chartam meam, &c. Testibus; dominis Johanne de Vescy, Ottone de Grandissono, Roberto de Tipetot, Stephano de Pencestre, &c. [s]

A native of this parish, Robert de Pydington, one of the brothers of the hospital of St. John's in Northampton, being with the master and others of the fraternity imprisoned on a precept of *capias excommunicatum;* he and the rest were now released upon request of the archbishop of Canterbury, because they had appealed to Rome [t].

Henry Lacy earl of Lincoln was sent over with the bishops of Litchfield and Worcester to the solemn inauguration of the pope at Lyons, and presented him with divers vessels of pure gold from the king [u]. After his return he proposed to found a college in Oxford for the maintenance of thirteen scholars, to whom he would give and assign the advowsons of the churches of Wadington, Wyvelingham, Thoresby, Buckeby, and Halton upon Trent: in order to which foundation the king issued out this precept.

Edwardus rex Angl. &c. Waltero de Gloucester escactori citra Trentam salutem. Mandamus vobis quod per sacramentum, &c. inquiratis si sit ad dampnum &c. si concedamus dilecto et fideli nostro Henrico de Lacy com. Linc. quod ipse advocaciones ecclesiarum de Wadinton, Wyvelingham, Thoresby, Buckeby, et Halton super Trentam que de nobis tenentur in capite dare possit et assignare tresdecem scholaribus in quadam domo in Oxon. per ipsum comitem de novo construenda commoraturis &c. Teste meipso apud Westmin. xviii. Octob. anno regni xxxiii. [x]

In pursuance of which mandate, the following inquisitions were taken.

North. Inquisitio capta apud Buckeby 10. Maii, anno regni Ed. 34. coram jurat. qui dicunt quod non est ad dampnum nec prejudicium

s R. Dods. MS. vol. 126. f. 92, b.   t W. Prynne, Histor. Collect. tom. 3. p. 1086.
u Dugd. Bar. tom. 1. p. 105. a.   x R. Dods. MS. vol. 108. f. 54.

regis nec aliorum si rex concedat Henrico de Lacy quod ipse advoca-
cionem ecclesie de Buckeby in com. North. dare possit et assignare tres-
decem scholaribus in quadam domo in Oxon. per ipsum comitem de novo
construenda commoraturis, &c. et quod ecclesia predicta valet per an.
xx. marcas, &c.

Inquisitio capta apud Linc. *die Martis in septimana Paschatis anno*
regni Ed. 34. *jurat. dicunt quod ecclesia de Wadyngton fuit de antiquo*
dominico regis et tenetur in capite de eodem et valet per an. xl. *libras.*
Ecclesia de Wyvelingham est de feodo Haye de hereditate Margarete
uxoris predicti comitis et tenetur de rege in capite et valet per annum
xx. libras. Ecclesia de Thoresby tenetur de domino rege in capite per
servitium militare et valet per annum xx. *libras. Ecclesia de Halton*
super Trentam tenetur de rege in capite et valet xl. *marcas: et dicunt*
quod si heres predicti comitis fuerit infra etatem et predicte ecclesie
illo tempore vacarent rex amitteret presentationes &c. et aliud damp-
num regi &c. non potest iminere [z]

On the 14. cal. Decemb. the said Henry earl of Lincoln presented
to the said church of Wyvelingham in the archdeaconry of Stow [a].

In Hilary term, Gilbert de Segreve, archdeacon of Oxford, having
his title declared null to the chapel of St. Mary's and All Saints in
York, appealed from the king's court to Rome, upon which he was
summoned to Westminster, and obliged to renounce his appeal by
oath, and to find sureties for appearing at the next parliament [b].

The keeper of the gaol in Oxford having in his custody one Alice
de Droys, condemned for felony, and reprieved for pregnancy, suffered her to go abroad under the guard of a servant: she making her
escape, the master was saved by benefit of clergy, but the servant
was hanged [c]

John de Handlo of Borstall in this neighbourhood, having attended the king in his wars in Scotland, had returned from that service without the king's leave: upon which the king sent his precept

[y] R. Dods. MS. vol. 108. f. 54. b.   [z] Ib. f. 55.   [a] Ib. vol. 107. f. 190.   [b] Ib. vol. 117.
f. 143.   [c] Ibid.

to the sheriff of Oxfordshire to seize into his hands the lands, goods, and chattels of the said John de Handlo within his liberties, for his contempt in deserting the king, &c. This related to the manor of Musewell in the parish of Ambrosden, Shippenhall, Chadlington, &c. [d]

About this time inquisition was made into the rents, services, and customs of all manors and other lands belonging to the bishop of Lincoln: upon which occasion is preserved an exact account of the manors of Banbury, Thame, and Dorchester, with all their appendages in this county: of which I will only set down the general rents.

Summa reddituum assis. de manerio forinseco Banbury cum molendinis forinsecis LIV[l]. XIV[s]. III[d]. *Item de incremento facto in dicto manerio* III[l]. XV[s]. IV[d]. *Item de molendinis in Banbury affirmat.* XXII[l] *Item de Burgo affirm.* XXIII[l]. *Item de hundreto affirm.* IX[l]. *summa totalis reddituum, &c.* CLXX[l]. IX[s]. *et* VII[d]. *Summa gallinarum in dicto manerio de* II. *assis.* CXVIII. *gallinæ.* Item de serjantia CXL. *gallinæ, et mille et* CCC. *ova.*

Summa reddituum assis. de burgagio in Thame LXXV[s]. *Item de novo incremento* VII[s]. IX[d]. *Summa reddituum assis. in manerio forinseco* XVIII[l]. XV[s]. *Et de Wudeway* IV[s]. *et* VII[d]. *Summa totius redditus assis. de Burgo et de manerio forinseco et Wudeway* XXII[l]. XIX[s]. I[d]

An. MCCCVI. 34, 35. Edw. I.
1306. Will'us de Boresworth acol. pres. per regem ratione custod. terr. et hered. d'ni Warini de Insula mil. defuncti ad eccl. de Heyford Warin tanquam vacant. quia Joh. de Crawel ultimo institutus in eadem per annum et amplius se absentavit ab ec-cl'ia predicta carceri per potestatem laicam tanquam predo et fur notorius extitit mancipatus, quem quidem carcerem idem J. latenter fregens et ad eccl'iam tanquam sibi

conscius confugiens ab ea temeritate sua recessit ac demum processu habito in foro ecclesiastico contra prefatum J. super premissis ex officio—tandem decretum amovendum—dictus Will. de Boresworth admissus est, 4. id. Decemb. pont. 7. Reg. Dalderby, Linc.

Mag'r Ric. de Abindon acol. pres. per abb. et conv. S. Augustini Bristol ad eccl. de Finnemere vac. per resign. Joh. de Langetou. 11. kal. Aug. pont. 7.

d W. Dugd. MS. vol. B. 1. p. 372.

Item de exitibus burgi xvii^l. iv^s. i^d. *ob. Summa totalis* lxiii^l. ii^s. iii^d.
ob. Summa gallinarum ibidem clxxiii. *gallinæ.*
Summa reddituum assis. in manerio *de Dorcestre* xlii^l. ix^s. iii^d.
Summa reddituum carucatariorum si fuerint ad firmam xxii^s. *Summa
reddit. porcariarum et bercarum si fuerint ad firmam* v^s. vi^d. *Item de
Wudeway* xxviii^s. *et de piscaria de Thamisia affirmata* xiii^s. iv^d.
Summa summarum totius redditus Wudeway et piscar. xlvi^l. i^d.
Summa gallinarum carucat. et cotar. cxiv. *gallinæ. Summa gallin.
habent in socag. si fuerint ad opus* lx. *gallin. Summa total. gallina-
rum* clxiv. *gallinæ.*

The whole revenue of the bishopric was thus computed.

*Summa totius redditus assis. in maneriis Linc. episcopi prænominat.
cum incrementis et burgis, molendinis, firmis, Wapentac. et* hundred.
affirmat. dccclxi^l. xiii^s. xi^d. *præter molendina illa quæ sunt in manu
episcopi quæ valuerunt* cclxxii^l. ix^s. vi^d. *anno sexto decimo confirmationis domini episcopi Hugonis secundi. Summa totius redd. prædicti
firmarum et valor molendinorum* mccccxxiv^l. iii^s. v^d. *Summa gallinarum in dictis maneriis* mmiii. *gallinæ. Summa ovorum in dictis
maneriis* mmmmlxxx. *et* xiii. *ova. Summa redditus de quo archidiaconi respondent episcopo Linc. per an.* ccxvi^l. xvi^s. viii^d. *Summa
summarum totius redditus firmarum et valorum molendinorum maneriorum Lincoln. episcopi et annui redditus archidiaconorum* mcccxxxi^l.
i^d.^{e}

Alan de Plugenet, lord of the manor of Pidington, having been in
the Scottish wars 28, 29, and 31. of Edw. I. was now at the feast of
Pentecost made a knight with prince Edward and many others, by
bathing and other ceremonies; and attending the prince this summer
into Scotland, continued there the following year^f

An. mcccvii. 35. *Edward* I. 1. *Edward.* II.

An inquisition was taken in these parts, whereby the jurors found

<hr/>

^{e} Ex Rental. Episc. Linc. MS. membran. penes D. D. T. Halton, archid. Oxon. ^{f} Dugd.
Bar. tom. 2. p. 3.

that Henry Tyeis at his death held the manors of Fretwell and Sherborn in this county, and that Henry his son and heir was twenty-two
years of age[g]. He had obtained the manor of Sherburne from Richard earl of Cornwall, and in 28. Edw. I. had a grant from the king
of free warren in his demesne lands in that parish.

In this eighth year of John de Dalderby bishop of Lincoln, William de la More, master of the order of the knights templars, on the
14th of July, presented a clerk to the church of Mersh[h]

The king upon his expedition to Scotland died at Burgh upon
Sands, near Carlisle, July the seventh. Henry Lacy earl of Lincoln was with the king upon his death-bed, and was one of those
whom that king desired to be good to his son, and not to permit
Piers de Gaveston to return into England. After the king's death
this earl, with Anthony Beck bishop of Durham, and divers others
of the barons, entered into a solemn association to defend king Edward the Second, and the rights of his crown, by special instrument
bearing date at Boleign, January 31. and the same year he was made
governor of Skipton castle, in com. Ebor[i]

On the Wednesday after Epiphany, 130[7]. all the knights templars
were seized and imprisoned, and their lands escheated to the king:
by which means the adjoining manor of Merton came into the king's
hands[k].

An. MCCCVII. 35. Edw. I.

Ad petitionem Hugonis de Courtenay
petentis terras et tenementa quæ Baldewy-
nus de Ryvere primus et heredes sui per-
quisiverunt in maneriis de Neweham et de
Upheyford in com. Oxon. de quibus quidem
tenementis Isabella de Fortibus comitissa
obiit seisita in dominico suo ut de feodo
unde idem Hugo est proximus heres—Ita
responsum est—Mittantur istæ petitiones
coram rege sub sigillo cane. in crastino
ascensionis—et mandetur per breve de cancel. vicecom. de Cantebr. Bedef. et Oxon.
quod premunire faciant matrem Roberti filii
et hæredis Warini de Insula infra ætatem et
in custodia regis existentis, &c. Rot. Parl.
35. Ed. I.

[g] R. Dods. MS. vol. 48. p. 8. [h] Ib. vol. 107. p. 204. [i] Dugd. Bar. tom. 1. p. 105. a.
[k] Mon. Ang. tom. 2. p. 519.

An. mcccviii.   1, 2. *Edward* II.

Thomas earl of Lancaster, son-in-law to Henry Lacy earl of Lincoln, had the stewardship of England, which had belonged to the
earldom of Leicester, granted to him and his heirs as freely and fully
as Simon de Montfort late earl of Leicester had held it, by letters
patent dated at Westminster, 9. May[1].

Sir John de Handlo of Borstall was made governor of St. Briavel's
castle in Glocestershire, and keeper of the forest of *Dene*[m]; and purchased from Philip Mymekan the bailiwick of the forest of Shotover
and Stowode, with all appertenances in the village of Hedingdon.
*Hiis testibus; Ricardo Daumari, Johanne de Elsefeld, Willielmo
de Scalebrook, et Henrico de Williamscot, militibus; Roberto de
Luches, Ricardo de Bere, Ricardo de Luches, Roberto Neal, Nicholao de Esshes, et aliis. Dat. London. die Jovis proxime post festum
S. Vincentii martyris. Anno regni regis Edwardi filii regis Ed. secundo*[n]

But for acquiring and entering upon the said bailiwick without the
king's licence, he was obliged to procure a royal pardon, granted in
this form.

*Edwardus Dei gratia rex Angliæ dominus Hiberniæ et dux Aqui-
taniæ, omnibus ad quos præsentes literæ pervenerint salutem. Sciatis
quod de gratia nostra speciali pardonavimus dilecto et fideli nostro Johanni de Handlo transgressionem quam fecit adquirendo sibi et hæredibus suis ballivam forestariæ forestarum nostrarum de Shotovre et
Stowode in com. Oxon. de Philippo Mymekan qui ballivam illam tenuit
de nobis in capite et eam ingrediendo nostra super hæc licentia non ob-*

<hr>

An. mcccviii. 1, 2. Edw. II.
Mag'r Rob. de Cisterna cap. pres. per rectorem et fratres domus de Asherigge ad

eccl. de Cestreton vac. per mort. Will'i de
Deen. Id. Jul. pont. 9. Joh. Dalderby.

[1] R. Dods. MS. vol. 106. *qu.*   [m] Dugd. Bar. tom. 2. p. 61. b.   [n] Ex Chartul. de
Borstall, MS. f. 44.

tenta. Teste meipso apud Westmin. vicesimo quinto die Feb. anno regni nostri secundo[o].

The Bonhommes of the convent of Ashrugge, to whom the presentation of this church of Ambrosden was given by Edmund earl of Cornwall, not content with the honour of patronage without the profit of the tithes, petitioned pope Clement the Fifth, that he would authorize the appropriation of the said church to their convent, and effectually begged or bought the pope's consent, given in letters missive dated in this third year of his pontificate, and recited in the bishop of Lincoln's licence, *sub an.* 1334. Thus at Rome began the sad abuse that yet wants a reformation.

Richard Midleton, alias *de media villa*, a Franciscan, entitled *doctor fundatissimus*, who now flourished in school divinity, was possibly a native of this neighbourhood; Fuller leaves it uncertain, whether he was born in Midleton-stony in Oxfordshire, or Midleton-Cheyney in Northamptonshire[p].

The manor of Ambrosden, with the rest of the honour of St. Walerie, was in the crown since the last escheat by the death of Edmund earl of Cornwall without heirs. But within this first year of his reign, the king made a grant in fee of the whole earldom of Cornwall, the honour of St. Walerie, with Beckley the capital manor, and all other members of it, the town and honour of Walingford, with the manors of Watlington and Bensington, and of all other lands which Edmund earl of Cornwall held at the time of his death, as well in reversion as possession, to Piers de Gaveston[q]: who soon after obtained a precept from the king to John de Clinton for livery of the castle of Walingford, the honour of St. Walerie, and the town of Cicester; and to John de Knockyn for livery of the manor of Watlington[r]

An. MCCCIX. 2, 3. Edward II.

In the beginning of 3. Edw. II. there was a trial at Craumarsh,

[o] Ex Chartul. de Borstall, MS. f. 44.   [p] Fuller, Ch. Hist. cent. 14. p. 94.   [q] Dugd. Bar. tom. 2. p. 42. b.   [r] Gul. Dugd. MS. B. 1. p. 112.

nigh Walingford, before G. de Leukenor and J. de Messington, between the prior of S. Frideswide in Oxford and Sir Hugh de Plessets, who held the fee of Musewell in Ambrosden; by which it did
appear that the said Sir Hugh de Plessets, and John son of Thomas
Philips, and John de Chandos, and Thomas Thursteyn, had unjustly
disseised the said prior of a free tenement in Hedington [*]

Richard d'Amory, knight, lord of the manor of Bucknel, and resident in his court or mansion-house in that parish, computed for
the lands of the knights templars escheated to the king within the
manors of Bradwell, Shilleford, Meriton, Covele, with its members,
viz. Brugshele, Gersingdune, and Horspath, Wernesgrave, Esyng-
done, with its members, viz. Littlemore and Oxon, Woodstoke, Hen-
syngton, Walecote, Blechesdon, &c. from the 20th of May, 1. Ed. II.
to Michaelmas following; and from thence to the 17th of Feb.
2. Ed. II. accounting forty shillings and ten pence for the rents of
vassals and cottagers, and twenty-two shillings and two pence for
the rent of three free tenants in Blechesdon, Fencote, and Hampton-
Gay. He likewise accounted from Michaelmas 2. Ed. II. to July 25.
3. Ed. II. twenty-four pounds six shillings two pence, for the manor
of Meriton; and thirty-one pounds two shillings for Couley [t].

Piers de Gaveston, by his new honours and extravagant favours
from the king, grew imperious, and despised the English nobles, who
so resented his intemperate carriage, that upon the day appointed
for the king's coronation, (the festival of St. Matthias,) they petitioned the king he might be removed; and when they saw it would
not be, they endeavoured to defer that solemnity, but in vain : for to
honour him yet further, the king gave him the crown of St. Edward

An. mcccix. 2, 3. Edw. II.   Joh. Dalderby.
Ric. de Ellesfeld acol. pres. per d'nam   Licentia regis concessa est rectori et
Joh'am de Gray relictam quondam d'ni   fr'ibus de Asherugg appropriandi sibi ec-
Rob. de Grey ad eccl. de Somerton vac. per   cl'iam de Ambresdon. 7. Sept. Pat. 3. Ed. II.
mort. Rob. Tryvet. Id. Mar. 1309. pont. 10.

W. Wyrley, Collectanea MSS. in Mus. Ashmol.   [t] R. Dods. MS.

the Confessor, to carry in that solemn procession [u]. After which, not able to contain himself within any bounds of prudence or moderation, he proclaimed a tournament, to be kept nigh his castle of Walingford; and thither brought so many foreign men at arms, that he most vilely insulted over all the English lords who came to that solemnity: among whom were Thomas earl of Lancaster, the earls of Pembroke, Hereford, Warren, &c. who were so offended at the affront put upon them, that they entered upon a common consult for satisfaction and revenge [x]

John de Verdon, lord of the manor of Heth in this county, having had summons to parliament among other barons, from 25. to 34. Ed. I. inclusive, departed this life at his castle of Alveton on Sunday the feast of St. Bartholomew the Apostle, whence his corpse was carried with great honour to the abbey of Croxden, and there interred on the fourth of the ides of October, leaving issue Theobald his son and heir [y].

An. MCCCX.   3, 4. Edward II.

That insolent favourite Piers de Gaveston having married Margaret second sister and co-heir to Gilbert de Clare of Glocester, had again the earldom of Cornwall, with all the honours and lands of Edmund late earl of Cornwall, granted to him and Margaret his wife, and to the heirs of their bodies lawfully begotten, by indentures dated Aug. 4.

An. MCCCX. 3, 4. Edw. II.
Ordinatio vicariæ de Ennestan cujus eccl'ia concessa est in proprios usus abb'is et conv. de Winchcumb, Waltero tunc abbate ejusd. Id. Oct. 1310.

Tho. de Stanton cap. pres. per procur. abb'is et conv. de Bek Herlewin ad eccl. de Cotesford vac. per mort. Ottonis. 7. kal. Dec. 1310.

Will. Vacce nepos mag'ri Will'i Vacce de Chambriaco per provis. papal. fit rector eccl'ie de Witney per resign. Will'i Vacce de Cambriaco in cur Rom. admiss. Id. Feb. 1310.

Pat. 4. Ed. II. Will. de Wrotham persona eccl'ie de Brehull habet lit. protect. 6. Octob.

Pat. 4. Ed. II. Galf de Welleford habet lit. reg. ad eccl. de Blechesdon, Linc. dioc. 20. Dec.

u Dugd. Bar. tom. 2. p. 42. b.   x Tho. Wal. sub an.   y Dugd. Bar. tom. 1. p. 473.

3. Ed. II.[z] Upon which he obtained several precepts to sundry persons, to make livery unto him of the lordships and lands thereto belonging.

Amory de St. Amand, knight, having been summoned to parlia ment from 28. Ed. 1. to 4. Ed. II. in this year died without issue, leaving John de St. Amand (guessed to have been a professor in the civil or canon law, being called *magister Johannes de S. Amando*) his next heir, who within the 4th of Ed. II. doing his fealty had livery of his lands[a]

The arms of this family of St. Amand were or, frette sable, with cheif sable, three piles or.

His manor of Grendon, nigh adjoining in com. Buck. was assigned for a dowry to Mary his widow[b]. Soon after his death an inquisition was taken, wherein the jurors found, that at the time of his death he held the said Grendon, with the advowson of the church of the manor of Beckley, which is the capital manor of the honour of St. Walerie, by the service of one bow of ebony and two arrows yearly, or sixteen pence in money[c]. Here I cannot but observe a mistake in the Natural History of Oxford, which makes the town of Hokenorton, in this county, to be the head of the barony of St. Waleries[d]: whereas that village was never in the hands of the family of St. Walerie, but remained to the Doyly's, and was the head of the barony of that name.

There was an inquisition taken in this year, July 19, in the neighbouring parish of Wendleburgh, wherein it appeared that Laurence de Preston held two knight's fees in Preston, Haklington, Horton, Pidington, Quenton, and Wotton; and that Gilbert de Elewell and Richard de Luterington held one knight's fee in Haclynton and Pidington[e].

Upon the king's advance toward Scotland, Henry Lacy earl of

[z] R. Dods. MS. vol. 35. f. 23.   [a] Dugd. Bar. tom. 2. p. 20. b.   [b] Gul. Dugd. MS. B. 1. p. 142.   [c] Ib. MS. A. 1. p. 177.   [d] Nat. Hist. Oxf. ch. 10. §. 130.   [e] R. Dods. MS. vol. 86. f. 120.

Lincoln, lord of the manor and patron of the priory of Burcester, was constituted governor of the realm in the king's absence[f]: and had the custody of the abbey of Kirkstall (founded by Henry de Lacy lord of Pontfract, there buried an. 1193. 5. Ric. I.) committed to him by the king to receive the profits and discharge the debts of that house, by these letters patent.

Edwardus Dei gratia Angliæ rex, &c. Cum abbathia de Kirkestall quæ de fundatione nostra existit accumulatis pœnis gravibus tanta prematurs arcina debitorum quod nisi per celere remedium succuratur vix poterit ab onere hujusmodi relevari : nos statui monachorum ejusdem domus providere cupientes domum illam recipimus in manum nostram, et eam dilecto et fideli nostro Henrico de Lacy comiti Lincoln. commisimus custodiendam &c. Teste meipso apud Westmin. xvi. die Novemb. an. regni nostri quarto[g]

The said earl being now sixty years of age fell into a sickness, and believing his death to be near, he sent for his son-in-law Thomas earl of Lancaster, and putting him in mind of the honours and riches which God had conferred upon him, and of his duty to pay the greater love and honour unto God, he spoke thus : " Seest thou " the Church of England, heretofore honourable and free, enslaved " by Romish oppressions, and the king's unjust exactions? Seest " thou the common people impoverished by tributes and taxes, and " from the condition of freemen reduced to slavery? Seest thou the " nobility, formerly venerable through the Christian world, now vili- " fied by aliens in their own native country? I therefore charge you, " in the name of Christ, to stand up like a man for the honour of " God and his church, and redemption of your country. Associate " yourself to that noble and prudent person Guy earl of Warwick, " when it shall be most proper to debate of the public affairs of the " kingdom, who is judicious in council and mature in judgment. " Fear not any opposers, who shall contest against you in the truth. " If you follow this my advice, you shall gain eternal honour[h]."

[f] Dugd. Bar. tom. 1. p. 105. a.   [g] R. Dods. MS. vol. 117. f. 14.   [h] Tho. Walsing. sub an. 1312. Cod. MS. in Bib. Cot. cit. in Mon. Ang. tom. 2. p. 189.

After which speech, he departed this life at his mansion-house, called Lincoln's-Inn, in the suburbs of London, (which he himself had built in that place, where part of the Black-friars' habitation anciently stood,) on the feast of St. Agatha, Feb. 5. 1310[i]. He was buried in the new work of St. Paul's church, betwixt our Lady's chapel and St. Dunstan's chapel; where a fair monument was raised for him with his effigies in armour, cross legged, as one professed for defence of the holy land against the infidels: which noble monument was defaced about the year 1598[k]. Sir William Dugdale imputes the time of this earl's death to the year 1312. 5. Ed. II. citing Walsingham for the authority of that date[l]. It is true, Tho. Walsingham under that year speaking of Thomas earl of Lancaster, takes thence occasion to report the dying speech of his father-in-law the earl of Lincoln; but he does not fix his death to that time. He left sole daughter and heir Alice wife of Thomas earl of Lancaster, who succeeded to all the honours and lands of his said father-in-law; and, by the addition of Lincoln and Salisbury, was now earl of five several counties[m]. Who paying his fine had livery of the castle of Denbigh, and all other the lands of her inheritance, his homage for them being performed in the next ensuing year, upon Thursday after the feast of St. Bartholomew, in the presence of divers bishops, earls, and barons, and other of the king's council, in a certain chamber within the house of the Friars preachers in London[n]

Presently after the death of the said earl, there was an inquisition taken in these parts, whereby the jurors found that Henry de Lacy late earl of Lincoln held at the time of his death the manor of Burncester, for the term of his life, by the law or courtesy of England, of the inheritance of Margaret his wife, formerly countess of Salisbury, as of the honour of Walingford, by military service: and that there were within the said manor one hundred and sixty acres of land: that the prior of Burncester held of the said Henry de Lacy earl of Lincoln the site of the said priory of Burncester, with four carucates

[i] Stow's Survey, 4to. p. 270.   [k] Dugd. Bar. tom. 1. p. 105. b.   [l] Tho. Walsing. sub an.   [m] Dugd. Bar. tom. 1. p. 780. a.   [n] Ibid.

of land, twenty acres of meadow, and one water-mill, with other appertenances, to the yearly value of forty pounds, with the church of
the said town to their proper use, to the value of thirty marks; with
the manor of Wretchwike, worth twenty pounds per ann. in pure and
perpetual alms: and that Alice, daughter of the foresaid Henry and
Margaret, which Henry earl of Lancaster had taken to wife, was the
nearest heir of the foresaid Henry and Margaret, of the age of twenty-
six years and upward.

Oxon. 4. Ed. II.

*Jur. dicunt quod Henricus de Lacy nuper comes Linc. tenuit die
quo obiit, manerium de Burncester ad terminum vite sue per legem
Anglie de hereditate Margarete uxoris sue quondam comitisse Sarum
ut de honore de Wallingford per servitium militare, et sunt ibidem c. et
LX. acre terre &c. Et dicunt quod prior de Burncestre tenuit de predicto Henrico de Lacy com. Linc. die quo obiit, scitum predicti prioratus de Burncester cum 4. carucatis terre, 20. acris prati et uno molendino aquatico cum aliis suis pertin. ibidem, que valent per an. XL.
libras, et cum ecclesia ejusdem ville in proprios usus quæ valet per an.
XXX. marcas, et cum manerio de Wrethewike quod valet per an. XX^l. in*
*puram et perpetuam elemosinam. Dicunt etiam quod Alesia filia pre-
dictorum Henr. et Margarete quam Thomas comes Lancast. duxit in
uxorem, est propinquior heres predicti Henrici et Margarete, et est etatis XXVI. annorum et amplius*[o].

There was nigh the same time another inquisition taken in the
county of Stafford, where the jury found that Henry Lacy late earl
of Lincoln held the manor of Burncester in the county of Oxon
of the inheritance of Margaret his wife. And that the prior of
Burncester held of the said earl the site of his priory, with four
carucates of land, six acres of meadow, one water-mill, with other
appertenances, to the value of forty pounds, and the church impropriated to the value of thirty marks, and the manor of Wretchwike
twenty-two pounds: and that the said earl held the manor of Mid-

o R. Dods. MS. vol. 89. f. 139.

3 U 2

lington in the said county of Oxford in demesne as in fee, being parcel of the honour of Pontfract. The same jurors report, that Wido
Ferre held of the said earl the manor of Godington for the fourth
part of one knight's fee : and that Alice wife of Thomas earl of Lancaster was next heir, aged twenty-eight years [p]

The said Henry earl of Lincoln, after the decease of his first wife
Margaret Longspe, had married Joan sister and heir of William
Martin: which Joan surviving the earl her husband, her marriage
was granted by the king to Ralph de Monthermer; but without his
licence, or the king's, she married to Nicholas de Aldithley, baron.
Whereupon the honour of Pontfract came to Alice, wife of Thomas
earl of Lancaster, by a precedent entail. By the said Nicholas, who
died 10. Ed. II. she had issue James, not fully three years of age at
his father's death [q]

An. MCCCXI.   4, 5. Edward II.

There was now a trial at law for the patronage of the church of
Blechesdon between the king as plaintiff, and Henry de la Wade,
John son of John de Croxford, Maud de Musgrave, and John le
Lou: on the calends of May, 1311, the eleventh of Joh. de Dalderby, the king recovered his right of presentation. Yet I find that
on the thirteenth of the calends of Apr. 1317, Thomas de Musgrave
presented a clerk to the church of Blechesdon then vacant [r]

The barons, not able to endure the haughty spirit of Piers de Gaveston earl of Cornwall, lord of the honours of St. Walerie and Walingford, in a parliament at London, prevailed with the king to banish him into Ireland; but on the dissolution of the parliament he

<hr>

An. MCCCXI. 4, 5. Edw. II.
    Galfridus de Welleford pres. per reg. ad
eccl. de Blechesdon vac. per mort. Ric'i de
Musegrave. kal. Maii 1311. pont. 11. Joh.
Dalderby.

Joh. de Aulton capellanus pres. per abb.
et conv. de Egnesham ad medietatem eccl'ie de Heyford ad pontem vac. per resign.
mag'ri Alex. de Juappelade. 17. kal. Jul.
1311.

[p] R. Dods. MS. vol. 48. p. 63.   [q] W. Dugd. MS. A. 1. p. 207. et Bar. tom. 1. p. 106.
et 748. b.   [r] R. Dods. MS. vol. 107. p. 201.

was from thence recalled, and met by the king at Chester. Upon his
return, and farther provocations given to the barons, they made their
bold address to the king, that unless he freed his court of this insolent earl, they would arm themselves against him as a perjured person. Upon which the earl abjured the realm, and went first into
France, after into Flanders; but presuming on his interest with the
king, soon returned to England, and obtained many new grants and
favours from his too indulgent master[s].

Thomas earl of Lancaster, in right of Alice his wife, sole daughter
and heir to Henry de Lacy earl of Lincoln, doing his fealty, had livery
of the castle of Denbigh, and all other the lands of her inheritance;
his homage for them being performed the next ensuing year, upon
Thursday after the feast of St. Bartholomew, in the presence of divers bishops, earls, and barons, and other of the king's council, in a
certain chamber within the house of the Friars preachers in London[t].

Alan Plokenet, or Plugenet, who was possessed of the manor of Pidington (detained from the monks of St. Frideswide) in 2. Ed. II.
had procured licence for a market every week upon the Friday, at
his manor of Kilpec com. Heref.; as also for a fair there yearly on
the eve and day of the assumption of our Lady, and two days follow
ing: and this year received summons to be at Roxburgh upon the
feast day of St. Peter *ad vincula, i. e.* Aug. 1. well fitted with horse
and arms to march against the Scots[u]

An. mcccxii. 5, 6. *Edward II.*

Richard Clifford, son and heir of John de Clifford, knight, released
to Margaret wife of Nicholas de Cryoll, and to Elizabeth de Paben-

An. mcccxii. 5, 6. Edw. II.
Andr. de la Hyda p'b'r pres. per pr. et
conv. de Kenilworth ad eccl. de Hethe vac.
per mort. Rob. de Picheford. 17. kal. Sept.
1312.

Rob. de Derlington acol. pres. per d'num

Edmund. Bacun mil. ad eccl. de Ewelm vac.
per mort. Rob. Bacun. 7. kal. Jan. 1312.

Joh. de Barton acol. pres. per abb. et
conv. de Egnesham ad mediet. eccl'ie de
Heyford ad pont. vac. per resign. Joh. de
Aulton. 16. kal. Apr. 1312. Reg. Dalderby.

[s] Dugd. Bar. tom. 2. p. 43. a.   [t] Ib. tom. 1. p. 780.   [u] Ib. tom. 2. p. 3. a.

ham all the right which by inheritance he could claim in any lands or tenements within the manor of Pudington in com. Oxon, *i. e.* Pidington in the parish of Ambrosden[x].

The king granted licence to Sir John de Handlo to fortify his mansion-house of Borstall with a wall of lime and stone; *i. e.* to make a castle of it.

Rex, &c. Licentiam dedimus Johanni de Handlo quod ipse mansum suum de Borstall juxta Brehull in com. Buck. muro de petra et calce firmare et kernellare possit. Teste rege apud Westmin. 12. *Sept.*[y]

Nicholas de Amory, lord of the manor of Bucknell, adjoining to Burcester, obtained from the king a charter of free warren in all his demesne lands within his manors of Bokenhall and Blechesdon in com. Oxon, and Thornbergh in com. Buck[z].

John de Bloxham accounted for the lands of the knights templars in the counties of Oxon and Berks, from Mich. 5. Ed. II. to Mich. 6. Ed. II. seven pounds nineteen shillings for Couley, with its members, Horspath, Brugeset, and Gersindon. As also one hundred fourteen shillings and two pence for Meriton[a].

William Hamlewyne of Brehull (now Brill) granted and demised to John Tulus of the same village one acre and an half of arable land in the field of Brehull, whereof one acre lay at le Frithvente, between the land of the prior of * Chetwood, and the land lately belonging to John Ferbaz; and the other half acre lay in Cocseteforlong, between the land lately of John Ferbaz, and the land which had belonged to Elias de Brehull, to hold by inheritance of the capital

---

* Placita pasch. anno 6. Edw. II.

Jurati dicunt quod prior de Chetwode et omnes antecessores sui locum vocatum *Priour assart* apud Brehull tanquam separale et inclusum tempore confectionis cartæ regis H. avi regis tenuerunt, et quod predictus Ric'us Prynne et alii qui se dicunt esse tenentes d'ni regis de manerio de Brehull et ibidem clamabant habere communam clausum prædictum fregerunt et herbam prædicti prioris ibidem depasti sunt cum averiis suis ad dampnum ipsius prioris xl[s].

---

[x] R. Dods. MS. vol. 41. f. 59. [y] W. Dugd. MS. C. p. 135. [z] Dugd. Bar. tom. 2. p. 100. a. [a] R. Dods. MS. vol. 35. f. 66.

lords of the fee by the usual service: in consideration whereof the said John Tulus paid twenty shillings and six pence into the hands of the said William Hamlewyne.

Sciant præsentes et futuri quod ego Willielmus Hamlewyne de Brehull dedi concessi et hac præsenti charta mea confirmavi Johanni Tulus de eadem villa unam acram et dimidiam terræ arabilis in campo de Brehull unde una acra jacet apud le Frithvente inter terram prioris de Chetwode ex parte una et terram quondam Johannis Ferbaz ex altera, et alia dimidia acra jacet apud le Cocseteforlong inter terram quondam Johannis Ferbaz ex parte una et terram quæ fuit Elyæ de Brehull ex altera, habend. et tenend. dictam acram et dimidiam terræ cum omnibus suis pertinentiis prædicto Johanni et hæredibus suis vel assignatis libere quiete bene et in pace jure hæreditario in perpetuum de capitalibus dominis feodi illius per servitia inde debita et de jure consueta pro omnibus aliis servitiis sæcularibus et cunctis terrenis demandis. Et ego vero dictus Willielmus et hæredes mei prædictam acram et dimidiam terræ cum pertinentiis præfato Johanni et hæredibus suis vel suis assignatis contra omnes homines et fœminas warantizabimus defendemus et acquietabimus in perpetuum: pro hac autem donatione concessione et præsentis chartæ meæ confirmatione dedit mihi prædictus Johannes viginti solidos et sex denarios præ manibus. Et ut hæc mea donatio concessio et præsentis chartæ confirmatio rata stabilis et inviolata permaneat in perpetuum huic præsenti chartæ sigillum meum apposui. Hiis testibus; Reginaldo de Boys, Henrico de Dadreshulle, Willielmo Pomeray, Ricardo Pymme, Thom. de Hereford, Willielmo Brown, Ricardo le Turner, et aliis. Datum apud Brehull die Lunæ proxime post Hokeday anno regni regis Edwardi filii regis Edwardi quinto[a].

In this year, says the historian, to relieve the oppression of holy mother church, and to recover the just liberties of the kingdom, Humphrey de Bohun earl of Hereford, Aymer de Valence earl of Pembroke, Guy de Beauchamp earl of Warwick, the earl of Arundel,

---

[b] Ex Orig. penes hon. D. Guil. Glynne, Bar,

and many other barons, adhered to Thomas earl of Lancaster, (lord
of the manors of Burcester and Midlington,) and chose him their
general, who by advice of the associated peers sent honourable messengers to the king, then at York, to entreat him he would deliver up
Piers de Gaveston earl of Cornwall, (lord of the fee of Burcester and
Ambrosden, and all other manors within the honours of Walingford
and St. Walerie,) or else, as had been before ordained, would command him to quit the realm. The king slighted this message, and
removed to Newcastle, toward which place the earl of Lancaster
marched with an army, not to do any injury to the king, but to get
judgment upon Piers de Gaveston. Upon this advance, the king
fled with his favourite to Tinemouth, and thence by ship to Scard-
burgh, commanding the garrison of that castle to receive the said
Piers de Gaveston, and protect him, while he himself went toward
Warwickshire[c]. The barons, after they had seized the horses left at
Newcastle, marched on to the siege of Scarburgh, from whence Thomas earl of Lancaster with some forces withdrew, to prevent scarcity
of provisions, and left the carrying on the siege to the earls of Pembroke and Warren; who so wearied out the garrison, that Piers de
Gaveston was forced to surrender himself, on condition of standing
to the judgment of the barons. The king, when he heard of this, desired liberty to speak with him, and that his life might be saved.
The earl of Pembroke persuaded the barons to comply with this request of the king, promising, under penalty of the loss of all his lands,
to keep him till such discourse with the king, and then to deliver
him to the barons. Upon which the rest of the barons committed
the said Piers de Gaveston to the custody of the earl of Pembroke,
who proposed to bring him to Walingford castle; and coming to
Dadington in com. Oxon, the earl committed him to some of his

---

Magister Wilhelmus de Boys, qui vivens   sorum apud Buttlesden ubi sepulturam ele-
nobilitatem suam probis moribus decoravit,   gerat crebris claruit miraculis. E cron. MS.
in morte quoque sua infra domum religio-   apud Joh. Leland. tom. 2. p. 300.

[c] Tho. Walsingham sub an.

guards, while he went to lodge with his lady in an adjacent village, (perhaps at his manor of Mersh in com. Buck.) The earl of Warwick having intelligence of this slender guard, came that night and took him away to his castle of Warwick; where after a consult whether they should carry him to the king, or put him to death, this latter was resolved upon: so they brought him out to a place called Blacklow, and there beheaded him, Jan. 19. The Friars preachers carried his body to Oxford, where it lay two years; and was thence by the king's order conveyed to Langley, where a convent was founded by the king for the health of the soul of that unhappy favourite. On his death the barony of St. Walerie reverted to the crown, when the king immediately granted it to his new creature Hugh Despenser senior; who accordingly obtained a charter for the manor and park of Beckley, to be held upon the same services as Edmund earl of Cornwall had performed for them [d].

An. MCCCXIII.   6, 7.   Edward II.

The king with a pompous retinue marched northward to the relief of the town of Berwick, besieged by the Scots; and sent this summons to Thomas earl of Lancaster, lord of the manor of Burcester, to attend him at Newcastle.

Rex dilecto consanguineo et fideli suo Thomæ com. Lanc. salutem. Licet nuper pro diversis negotiis nos et statum regni nostri tangentibus parliamentum nostrum apud Westmin. die Dominica in quindena pasch. proxime jam futuri proposuerimus tenere, &c. Quia tamen Robertus de Brus et sui complices inimici et rebelles nostri castra villas et fortalitia nostra ceperint, &c. et villam nostram de Berewico super Twed. obsidere, &c. nituntur, &c. pro repulsione corundem inimicorum ordinavimus esse apud Novum Castrum super Tynam die Dominica ab instanti die pasch. in tres septimanas, &c. Parliament. prædict. tenere non poterimus &c. vobis significavimus quod vos usque Westmon. venire nullatenus oportebit, &c. Vos affectuose requirimus et rogamus, &c.

[d] Dugd. Bar. tom. 1. p. 390. b.

equis et armis quanto decentius et potentius poteritis, &c. ad dictam villam de Novo Castro accedatis, &c. Teste rege apud Westmin. xxiv. *die Martis* [e].

An. mcccxiii. 6, 7. Edw. II.

Some parishioners of A. refused to pay an accustomed mortuary to the rector of the said church, who, complaining to the court of Christianity, obtained a mandate from the official of the archdeacon of Oxford to the dean of B. to goe to the said church of A. with a competent number of his rural clergy, and there admonish the said parishioners to pay those accustomed dues; and, upon their default, to excommunicate with bell, book, and candle. Though the following record has only the initial letters A. and B. yet I conclude "decanus de B." is the rural dean of Burcester, and "parochiani ecclesiæ de A." are the parishioners of the church of Ambresdon; because in the same manuscript there be several other instruments expressly relating to Burcester and Ambresdon, and few or none that refer to any other places.

Officialis Oxon. discreto viro decano de B. salutem in auctore salutis. Ad aures nostras nuper ascendente clamore pervenit, quod nonnulli parochiani ecclesie de A. in reprobum sensum conversi jura et libertates sancte ecclesie nequiter avertere pervertere infringere et perturbare per malitiam presumpserunt, et etiam presumunt in presenti mortuaria ad dictam ecclesiam de consuetudine laudabili debita ab ea conferendo in animarum suarum grave periculum et scandalum plurimorum. Subditos igitur nostros in culpam et errorem ex infirmitate prolapsos ne pereant ad viam salutis revocare cupientes vobis committimus et firmiter injungendo mandamus quatenus

ad ecclesiam de A. aliquo die Dominico seu festivo personaliter accedentes rectores et vicarios et capellanos parochiales in numero competenti vobiscum associantes vicinos si fuerit necesse in eadem ecclesia post lectum evangelium indicto silentio premissa secundum materie seriem informatione congrua omnes et singulos dicte ecclesie jura seu libertates infringentes seu perturbantes quovis modo seu mortuarium seu mortuaria ab eadem injuste ut premittitur auferentes vel ad eam pertinentia seu pertinens detinentes in genere publice moneatis quod ab hujusmodi presumptione et perturbatione de cetero penitus desistant, et que vel quod per eos fuerit vel fuerint ablata seu detenta dicte ecclesie cum omni festinatione qua poterint integre restituant ut tenentur. Alioquin omnes et singulos malefactores hujusmodi Deo odibiles et eis in premissis consentientes ac scienter faventes canonica monitione premissa in ecclesia de A. tribus diebus dominicis proximis post receptionem presentium intra missarum solempnia pulsatis campanis et candelis accensis in genere excommunicetis seu excommunicari per alios faciatis, et quod in premissis feceritis nos cum per partem rectoris ecclesie antedicte fueritis requisiti certificetis per literas patentes harum seriem continentes. Dat. apud Niweham, 2. id. Junii an. Dom. mccc. *tertio decimo.* Ex MS. in Bib. Bodl. Digby, 154.

Tho. Boteler de Bokenham capell. pres. per d'num Rob. de Insula mil. ad eccl'iam de Heyford Waryn vac. per resign. Will'i. 16. kal. Feb. 1313.

[e] R. Dods. MS. vol. 115. p. 28.

John de Handlo of Borstall was now in the wars of Scotland, being of the retinue of Hugh le Despensar. He had been in the same service in 4. Ed. II.

When the king in this expedition came to Berwick, he stayed there to receive all the barons and knights who owed to him military service; who all came except Thomas earl of Lancaster, (lord of the manors of Burcester and Midlington,) and the earls of Warren, Warwick, and Arundel, who refused to appear, because the king delayed to put in execution the articles for redress of grievances often petitioned for, and often granted [f].

Sir Theobald de Verdon, lord of the manor of Heth, was now constituted justice of Ireland, having likewise the lieutenancy of that realm, and the fee of five hundred pounds *per ann.* then granted to him. In which year Maud his wife, departing this world at his castle of Alveton, was honourably buried in the abbey church of Croxden, before the altar of St. Benedict, upon the feast of St. Dennis and his fellow martyrs; Thomas earl of Lancaster and many other nobles being present at her funeral [g]: which Thomas earl of Lancaster was this year godfather to Thomas eldest son and heir of Guy Beauchamp earl of Warwick, and at his christening gave to him a casket of gold with a bone of St. George [h].

One of his feudatory tenants, Adam de Banaster, after Michaelmas, *movens guerram contra dominum suum Thomam,* about the feast of St. Martin, was taken with William de Lee in a grange, where they had hid themselves, and was imprisoned and beheaded [i].

An. MCCCXIV. 7, 8. *Edward II.*

Sir Laurence de Pavely, knight, lord of the manor of Wendlebury, did this year, the fifteenth of John de Dalderby, present a clerk to the said church of Wendlebury on the 18th of the calends of May [k].

---

[f] Tho. Walsing. sub an.   [g] Dugd. Bar. tom. 1. p. 474.   [h] Ibid. p. 231.   [i] Henry de Knyghton sub an.   [k] R. Dods. MS. e Reg. Linc. vol. 107. p. 201.

3 x 2

And Sir Richard d'Amory of Bucknel, knight, on the 4th cal. of June presented to the church of Bix-Gibwyn in this county[1]

Many of the peers who were concerned in the fatal death of Piers de Gaveston earl of Cornwall, were obliged for that offence to purchase their pardon from the king; among whom Thomas earl of Lancaster, lord of the manor of Burcester, had his solemn pardon, dated Octob. 16[m].

John Abel, the king's escheator on this side Trent, had information that the abbot and convent of Oseney had appropriated to their house two virgates of land in Chesterton nigh adjoining, by the gift of Bardulf de Chesterton, without the king's licence, after the publishing the statute of Mortmain made 7. Ed. I. by which default the said land would have been forfeited to the king, the lord of the fee having made no claim within one year after the said alienation[n]. Upon which the abbot of Oseney appeared personally before the said escheator, and did assert that William abbot of Oseney, his predecessor, had obtained a gift of the said land before the publication of the said statute. For more perfect information, the said escheator directed his letters to John de Trillawe, requiring him to impannel a jury of the neighbouring inhabitants at a fixed time and place, to make a fuller inquisition within what year and in what manner the abbot and convent obtained those lands.

Johannes Abel escheator domini regis citra Trentam dilecto sibi in Christo Johanni de Trillawe salutem. Licet nuper accepimus per inquisitionem coram nobis factam quod abbas et conventus de Oseney ap-

An. MCCCXIV. 7, 8. Edw. II.
Joh. de Waure acol. pres. per abb. et conv. de Egnesham ad eccl. de Meriton vac. per resign. mag'ri Rob. de Kynelingworth. 7. id. Dec. 1314. Reg. Dalderby.

Steph'us de Marcham cap. pres. per rector. et conv. de Assherugge ad eccl. de Cestreton vac. per resign. mag'ri Rob. de Cisterna. Id. Feb. 1314.

[1] R. Dods. MS. e Reg. Linc. vol. 107. p. 201. [m] E Ashmole MS. notat. X. p. 151. [n] Stat. Mortmain in Pulton. p. 26.

*propriaverint sibi et domui sue duas virgatas terre in Chesterton de
Bardulfo de Chesterton post publicationem statuti de terris et tenementis ad manum mortuam non ponendis editi sine licentia regis:
quia cum idem abbas coram nobis personaliter constitutus asserit Willielmum abbatem predecessorem suum terram illam diu ante publicationem statuti predicti, et non post ut predictum est, adquisivisse: nos
volentes inde plenius certiorari assignavimus vos ad inquirendum per
sacramentum proborum et legalium hominum de visneto de Chesterton
per quos rei veritas melius sciri poterit et inquiri de quo vel de quibus
idem abbas et conventus terram illam acquisiverint et quo anno et quo
modo.   Et ideo vobis mandamus quod ad certos diem et locum quos ad
hoc provideritis inquisitionem illam faciatis in forma predicta et tam
distincte et apte factam nobis sub sigillo vestro &c.   Dat. London.
xxviii. die Januarii an. regni regis Ed. fil. Ed. octavo[o]*

To execute this precept John de Trillawe at Rollandright in com.
Ox. on Aug. 2. the Sunday after the feast of St. Peter *in cathedra*,
had an inquisition made upon the oaths of John le Myrye, Edmund
de Dene, Richard Onvylle, Richard Alleyn, John le Knyght, Nicholas de Cherlton, William Basset, John Attebourne, Nicholas le
Blount, Thomas Fouke, John Hereward, and John Herevyle, who
returned upon oath, that William abbot of Oseney, predecessor of
the present abbot, in the fourth year of Ed. I. had purchased to
himself and his successors two virgates of land in Chesterton, from
one Bardulf, son of Roger Bardulf, before the statute of Mortmain:
which verdict was given under the seals of the twelve jurors.

*Inquisitio capta coram Johanne de Trillawe ad hoc per dom. Johan-
nem Abel eschaetorem domini regis citra Trentam assignatum die Dominico in crastino S. Petri in cathedra. an. regni regis Edwardi filii
regis Edwardi octavo, per sacramentum Johannis le Myrye, Edmundi
de Dene, Ricardi Onvylle, Ricardi Aleyn, Johannis le Knyht, Nicholai de Cherlton, Willielmi Basset, Johannis Attebourne, Nicholai le
Blount, Tho. Fouke, Johannis Hereward, et Johannis Herevyle, ju-*

----

[o] Regist. Osen. MS. p. 102.

rat. qui dicunt super sacramentum suum quod quidam Williclmus quon-
dam abbas de Oseney predecessor abbatis qui nunc est an. reg. regis Ed-
wardi filii regis Hen. 4to. perquisivit sibi et successoribus suis duas vir-
gatas terre in Cestreton de quodam Bardulfo filio Rogeri Bardulf
ante statutum dom. regis editum et publicatum de terris et tenementis
ad manum mortuam non ponendis. In cujus rei testimonium predicti
jurati presentibus sigilla sua apposuerunt. Datum apud Rollendryht
magnam die et anno supradictis [P].

William Broun of Borstall granted to Sir John Handlo, knight, a
croft behind the church in Borstall, containing five selions or ridges
of land, for five marks of silver; and by another chart conveyed to
him his messuage, garden, and close, nigh the church-yard of the
said village, for five other marks of silver. *Dat. apud Borstall nono*
decimo die Maii anno regni regis Edwardi filii regis Ed. septimo.
Hiis testibus; dom. Willielmo de Berford juniore, Roberto filio Eliæ,
Johanne le Brun, Johanne Arches, Nicholao de Esses, Ricardo le
Warde, Willielmo de Draycote, et multis aliis [q].

On the morrow after Michaelmas day, 8. Edward II. John de
Wyithulle, son and heir of Sir Walter de Wyithulle, by deed dated
at Kirtlington, did release and quit claim to Hugh le Duke of
Wretchwike, within the parish of Burcester, all his right and claim
in eighteen perches of arable land in length, and four perches in
breadth, in the field of *Tackle, in a parcel of ground called Wyit-
standelf, to remain to the said Hugh and his heirs for ever.

Omnibus Christi fidelibus ad quorum notitiam præsentes literæ per-
venerint Johannes de Wyithulle filius et hæres quondam domini Wal-

---

* Rectores eccl'iæ de Tackley com. Oxon.
Mag'r Joh. Hulse jur. civ. bacc. p'b'r
pres. per Clementiam Newere relictam Jo-
h'is Newere gen. ad eccl. de Takley per
mort. d'ni Oliver. Somner. 17. Maii. 1499
Reg. Smith, ep'i London.

Mag'r Oliver Sompnour decr. bacc. pres.
per Ric. Harcourt mil. ad eccl. de Tacke-
ley per resign. mag. Will. Corte. 28. Mart.
1483. Idem Oliv. tunc resignavit eccl'iam
de Odyngton. Reg. Russel.

[P] Regist. Osen. MS. p. 102.   [q] Ex Chartul. de Borstall. MS. f. 60.

*teri de Wyithulle salutem in Domino.   Noveritis me relaxasse et quie-
tum clamasse pro me et hæredibus meis Hugoni le Duke de Wretchwike et hæredibus suis et assignatis totum jus et clamium quod habui
vel aliquo modo habere potui in octodecem perticis terræ arabilis in
longitudine et quatuor perticis in latitudine in campo de Takkele in
cultura quæ vocatur Wyithstandelf inter terram Walteri Waleys de
Takkele ex una parte et terram Galfridi Weel ex altera, quam quidem
terram dictus Hugo habet de dono Ysabellæ relictæ domini Walteri
de Wyithulle.   Ita quod nec ego Johannes nec hæredes vel assignati
mei nec aliquis nomine meo aliquod jus vel clamium in prædictam terram cum suis pertinentiis de cætero exigere vel vendicare potero vel
poterimus.   Præterea ego Johannes et hæredes et assignati mei prædictam terram cum suis pertinentiis prædicto Hugoni et hæredibus et
assignatis suis contra omnes gentes warantizabimus et in perpetuum
defendemus.   In cujus rei testimonium huic præsenti scripto sigillum
meum apposui.   Hiis testibus ; Hugone de Barton, Stephano de Wivle,
Henrico de Bowles, Thoma de Gay, Alano de Codesford, Roberto de
Park de Woodstock, Johanne a la Forde de Burncester, et aliis.   Dat.
apud Kurtlinton in crastino Sancti Michaelis an. reg. Edwardi filii
regis Edwardi octavo* [r].*

The precedent grant of Isabel relict of Sir Walter Wyithulle, dated
at Kurtlinton on the eve of the assumption of the Virgin Mary, is
preserved, and runs in the same style.

On the third of the nones of Feb. (*i. e.* Feb. 3.) 1315, Sir Theobald de Verdon, lord of the manor of Heth, wedded to his second
wife Elizabeth, the daughter of Gilbert de Clare earl of Glocester,
(by Joan of Acres, daughter of king Ed. I.) widow of Richard Burgh
earl of Ulster, the marriage being solemnized at Bristol [s].

An. MCCCXV.   8, 9.   *Edward II.*

A perambulation of the forest of Bernwode was now made, and the
limits of it were returned in this form of inquisition upon oath, which

---

deserves the greater remark, because it corrects the names of many places as delivered in the other inquisition, *sub an.* 22. Ed. I.

Juratores dicunt quod foresta de Bernwode incipit apud Gosacrehe-vede, et extendit in rivulum qui vocatur Thame inter campum de Thomele et campum de Wormenhale includendo forestam ex parte dextera per omnes bundas et metas subscriptas et excludendo extra fo-restam ex parte sinistra totum residuum et sic usque ad Shyremere inter Thomele et Wormenhale et sic usque Brodewey et sic usque le Breche et sic usque fossatum Oteweysdiches apud le Gatecote et sic per le Holeweye usque Menemersh et sic usque le Hoke de Okewode apud Shortrudyngesende et sic usque ad Sevebroke usque Southwelleryne et sic usque Southwelleheved et sic usque Chalkavestyle et sic usque Wodycrouche ad Shiremede et sic usque Northcroftsburne et sic usque Oddestaple et sic usque Stanneputts et sic per fossatum usque Mere-lake et sic usque le Grascroft abbatissæ de Godestowe et sic per fossa-tum usque Mous-hurnelake et sic usque Crofteswelleende et sic usque Ernicote-hach per fossatum et sic usque Moulesho et sic usque Corby-nesredle et sic inter boscum Alani Plokenet et boscum Johannis filii Nigelli usque Hullewodebroke et sic usque Yheutyndon inter boscum

An. MCCCXV. 8, 9. Edw. II.

Will. de Pavely acol. pres. per d'num Laur. de Pavely mil. ad eccl. de Wenling-bur. vac. per mortem Will'i de Blakethorn. 18. kal. Maii. 1315. Reg. Dalderby.

About this time one R. de C. being presented to the church of H. constituted John Chapell rector of Ambresdon his proctor, to take induction in his name.

Pateat universis per presentes quod ego R. de C. clericus ad ecclesiam de H. Linc. dioc. legitime presentatus in omnibus causis et ne-gociis personam meum qualitercunque tan-gentibus coram quibuscunque judicibus or. de-legatis vel eorum commissariis dilectum mihi in Christo J. de C. rectorem ecclesie de A. pre-dicte dioc. meum facio ordino et constituo procuratorem verum et legitimum per presen-tes dans eidem generalem et specialem po-testatem nomine meo agendi deferendi exci-piendi replicandi institucionem canonice com-plendam possessionem inductionemque pre-dicte ecclesie de H. meo nomine petendi nan-cissendi et recipiendi canonicam obedienciam ordinariis faciendi et super eadem jurandi necnon et aliud quodlibet genus liciti sacra-menti in animam prestandi et omnia alia fa-ciendi que per verum et legitimum procura-torem poterunt expediri appellandi appella-tiones prosequendi pro eodem vero rem ratam habendi et judicatum solvendi sub ypoteca rerum mearum promitto et cauciones expono. Ex MS. in Bib. Bodl. Digby, 154.

domini regis et boscum Alani Plokenet et sic usque Mousewelldyche et sic per hayam de Longelondsende et sic usque le Hoke apud le Fereslone et sic usque Rysiford inter boscum domini regis et Alani Plokenet et sic usque Brendeheyge inter campum de Pydington et Lotegarshale et sic usque Woundenmere inter com. Oxon. et Bucks. et sic usque Stodefeld et sic usque Hetheneburude inter Akeman-street inter divisas com. Oxon. et Bucks. et dicunt prædicti jurati quod boscus de Waterpurye est Roberti filii Eliæ, et boscus de Ledhale qui est Johannis Beaufou, et boscus de Horton qui est comitis Cornubiæ, et boscus de Wodepirie qui est Ricardi de Aumari, et boscus de Ernecote qui est comitis Lincolniæ et abbatis de Oseneye, et boscus de Nether-Ernecote qui est prioris de Burncester, et boscus de Pydington qui est Alani Plokenet, fuerunt afforestati post coronationem domini Henrici regis proavi domini regis nunc ad tale dampnum quod nec ipsi nec eorum antecessores seu prædecessores per tempus prædictum usque nunc nichil de boscis prædictis capere potuerunt nisi per liberationem forestarii et ejus forestariorum voluntatem, nec aliud proficuum de iisdem boscis percipere, sicut prius habere et facere consueverunt ante tempus coronationis domini Henrici regis prædicti absque attachiamento et impedimento forestarii prædicti [t].

The king at this time confirmed several grants to the abbey of Grestein in Normandy; and among others he recounts the concession, donation, and confirmation which John de Montacute made to the said abbot and convent of the manor of Merse with its appertenances in the county of Bucks, and of the advowson of the church of the said manor, and of one hide of land with its appertenances in the said village; as also the grant, remission, and confirmation, which Baldwin, son of Thomas de Haldeham and Isabel de Montacute, made to the said abbot and convent of the manor of Mersh [u].

This donor must be one of that family of Montacute, who were after earls of Salisbury, who had the manor of Aston-Clinton and other possessions in com. Buck. of whom the last earl Thomas Mon-

---

[t] Ex Chartul. de Borstall, MS. f. 113.   [u] Mon. Ang. tom. 2. p. 984.

tacute died 7. Hen. VI. and left widow Alice, daughter of Thomas
Chaucer, after married to William de la Pole earl of Suffolk. Dugdale in his Baronage mentions no one of this line named John till
after the time of this donation. I suppose by the confirmation of this
gift by Isabel de Montacute, we may infer the first grant to have
been made by her father, whom Dugdale[x] calls William; but he was
more probably John de Montacute, who died 31. Hen. III. and left
two daughters, Margery wife of William de Echingham, and this Isabel, after married (to Thomas de Audham, says Dugdale, but indeed)
to Baldwin son of Thomas de Audham.

Thomas earl of Lancaster, lord of the manors of Burcester and
Midlington, obtained a charter for a market every week upon the
Friday at his manor of Burton-Stather in com. Linc. and two fairs;
the one to begin on All-hallow eve, and to continue the next day
and thirteen days after; the other on the eve of the holy Trinity,
the day, and three days after: and in the following year had licence
to make a castle of his manor house at Dunstanburgh in com. Nor-
thumb.[y]

Alan de Plugenet, lord of the manor of Pidington, received a summons from the king to be at Newcastle-upon-Tyne on the festival of
the blessed Virgin's assumption, well fitted with horse and arms, to
march against the Scots. The first of this family who obtained from
Maud the empress the manor of Hedingdon, Hugh de Plugenet,
confirmed to the canons of St. Frideswide a certain island called
Langeney, by this charter.

*Sciant tam presentes quam futuri quod ego Hugo de Pluggenant
pro salute anime mee et pro anima Matildis imperatricis domine mee
et Henrici regis filii sui et Alani de Pluggenant filii mei et Emme
filie mee et pro animabus omnium antecessorum et successorum meorum dedi et concessi Deo et ecclesie S. Frideswide de Oxon. et canonicis ibidem Deo servientibus insulam quandam que vocatur Lan-
genia cum omnibus pertinenciis suis habend. et tenend. de me et here-*

[x] Dug. Bar. tom. 1. p. 644.   [y] Ib. p. 780. a.

dibus meis libere et quiete sicut predicti canonici illam tenuerunt tempore illo quo Matildis imperatrix manerium de Hedindon mihi pro homagio et servicio meo dedit, videlicet reddendo inde annuatim decem et octo solidos ad festum S. Michaelis pro omni servicio. Ut igitur hec donacio mea et concessio imperpetuum rata et inconcussa permaneat imperpetuum ipsam presentis scripti testimonio et sigilli mei apposicione roborari curavi. Hiis testibus .

John Lovel, lord of the manor of Tichmersh in com. Northam. and Mynster-Lovel in com. Oxon, died 8. Ed. II. leaving Maud his wife surviving, daughter and heir to Sir Philip Burnel, knight; which Maud, without the king's licence, took to her second husband John de Handlo, knight, of Borstall, who paid a fine of one hundred pounds to have the king's pardon for this transgression.

Rex, &c. Sciatis quod per finem c¹. quem dilectus et fidelis noster Johannes de Handlo fecit nobiscum pardonavimus ei transgressionem quam fecit ducendo in uxorem Matildam quæ fuit uxor Johannis Lovel de Tichemersh defuncti. Teste rege 20. Feb.[a]

Within this eighth of Ed. II. the king, by letters patent dated at Westminster, Jan. 7, granted to the said Sir John de Handlo fifty-six acres and half a rood (by the measure of twenty foot to a perch) of waste land within the forest of Bernwood; of which, twenty-eight acres and a half and one rood were in the king's demesne wood of Brehull, abutting upon a close in Lutegarshale, called le Wecche[b]. He had likewise the bailiwick and custody of the forest of Shotover and Stowode confirmed to him by another act of Philip Mymekan of Hedingdon. *Dat. apud Hedingdone die Mercurii proxime ante festum conversionis S. Pauli an. regni regis Edwardi filii regis Edw octavo. Hiis testibus; dominis Ricardo d'Amory, Willielmo de Bereford juniore, Johanne de la Mare militibus; Richardo de Luches, Johanne le Moigne, Roberto Neel, Thoma Elys, Johanne de Luches, de com. Oxon. Johanne le Brun, &c.*[c]

[z] Ex Chartul. S. Frideswydæ penes decan. et capit. Æd. Christi, Oxon.   [a] Gul. Dugd. MS. vol. B. 1. p. 377.   [b] Ex Chartul. de Borstall, MS. f. 38.   [c] Ibid. sub tit. Hedingdon. f. 40.

On the eleventh of the ides of May, the said Sir John de Handlo presented a clerk to the church of Beckley, the head of the barony of St. Walerie [d]; which was granted to him by his potent friend and relation Hugh Despenser, senior, who had obtained it from the king in 5. Edw. II.[e]: whose daughter Aliva was the wife, now the widow, of Edward Burnell, brother of Maud wife of the said Sir John Handlo.

An. MCCCXVI.   9, 10. *Edward II.*

Gilbert Clare earl of Gloucester being slain in the battle of Bannocksburne near Strivelin in Scotland, 7. Ed. II. left no issue male. Upon which, after two years expectance of a son to be born on the body of Maud his wife, (daughter of John de Burgh son to Richard earl of Ulster,) the great inheritance was shared among his three sisters; and Maud his widow had for her dowry an assignation of several manors, among which was the manor of Caversham in this county, with certain lands in Burford, Nether-Orton, and * Heyford *ad pontem*, with the hundred of Chadlington [f].

---

* Rectores eccl'iæ de Heyford ad Pontem com. Oxon.

Galfridus de Cropper clericus ad medietatem eccl'iæ de Heyford auctoritate concilii. Mandatum archid'o Oxon. Rot. Hug. Well. anno ut videtur, pont. 9. 1216.

Mag'r Robertus Bacun ad medietatem eccl. de Heiford quam Lucas clericus tenuit ad pres. abb. et conv. de Eynesham, inquisitione facta per J. archid. Oxon. Rot. Hug. Well. pont. 10.

Will. de Henred clericus ad mediet. eccl. de Heyford quæ fuit G. de Croppy ad pres. Ric. Henred fratris sui. Rot. Hug. Well. pont. 11.

Rob. de Turri subdiac. ad mediet. eccl.

de Hayford per resign. mag'ri Rob. ad pres. abb. et conv. de Eynsham. Rot. Hug. Well. pont. 18.

Sampson Brassard ad med. eccl'iæ de Heyford ad pres. Ric. de Hanred mil. Rot. Rob. Grosthead, anno 7.

Rog. de Bocking capellan. ad eccl. de Heyford ad pontem ad pres. Ric'i de Hanred laici. Rot. Rob'ti Grosthead, anno 17.

Mag'r Will. de Dunham presb'r pres. per abb. et conv. de Eynisham ad mediet. eccl. de Heyford ad pontem vac. per mort. mag'ri Rob. de London. 9. kal. dec. 1275. Rot. Ric. Gravesend. anno 18.

Will. de Brampton subdec. pres. per dom. Rog. de Insula ad mediet. eccl. de Heyford

---

[d] R. Dods. MS. vol. 107. f. 201.   [e] Dugd. Bar. tom. 1. 390. b.   [f] Ibid. p. 217.

Edward lord Burnel departed this life without issue, leaving Maud the wife of John de Handlo of Borstall, (before the wife of John Lovel,) his sister and heir, twenty-four years of age; upon which the said John de Handlo had livery of all his lands, doing his fealty, excepting such as Aliva widow of the said Edward held in dowry:

vac. per mort. Will'i, 16. kal. Mart. 1278. ib. anno 21.

Simon de Welles cl'icus admiss. ad medietatem eccl'iæ de Heyford ad pont. per mort. mag'ri W. ad pres. abb. et conv. Egnesham, x. kal. Jun. pont. 11. Ol. Sutton, i. e. 1290. Reg. Ol. Sutton ep'i Linc.

Mag'r Hugo de Thurleby pres. per abb. et conv. de Eynesham ad mediet. eccl'iæ de Heyford per ingress. Simonis de Welles in ord. fratr. Predicatorum, 10. kal. Sept. 1291. ib.

Mag. Alex. de Quappelud cl'icus pres. per abb. et conv. de Eynesham ad mediet. eccl. de Heyford ad pontem per mort. Hug. de Thurleby, 13. kal. Jan. pont. 13. i. e. 1292. ib.

Rob. de la Kerneyl cl'icus pres. per dom. Rog. de Insula milit. ad mediet. eccl'ie de Heyford ad pont. vac. per hoc, q'd Will. de Brampton ult. rector ejusd. institutus fuit in aliud beneficium, 5. kal. Jun. pont. 16. i. e. 1295. ib.

Joh. de la Curncyle cl'icus pres. per d'num Joh. de Insula mil. ad mediet. eccl. de Heyford ad pont. vac. per mort. Rob. de la Curneyle, 13. kal. Jan. pont. 19. i. e. 1298. ib.

Joh. de Aulton capell. pres. per abb. et conv. de Eynesham ad mediet. eccl. de Heyford ad pontem vac. per resign. mag'ri Alex. de Quappelode, 17. kal. Jul. 1311. Reg. Dalderby.

Joh. de Burton acol. pres. per abb. et conv. de Eynesham ad mediet. eccl. de Heyford ad pontem vac. per resign. Joh. de Aulton, 16. kal. Apr. 1312. Reg. Dalderby.

Hug. Moton clericus pres. per Joh. de Lyle ad med. eccl'iæ beatæ Mariæ virg. de Heyford ad pontem vac. per mort. Joh. de la Curnels, 7. id. Jan. 1320. Reg. Burgersh.

Will. de Balleby p'b'r pres. per abb. et conv. de Eynesham ad mediet. eccl'iæ de Heyford ad pontem vac. per resign. Nich'i de Impinton sub nomine permutationis quam idem Nich'us cum capella beati Thomæ de Pottokesherdwyk dictæ dioc. quam præfatus Will'us titulo institutionis prius tenuerat. admiss. 3. non. Octob. 1328. ib.

Tho. de Welleford acol. pres. per dom. Joh. de Insula milit. ad medietatem eccl. de Heyford ad pontem vac. per resign. Alani la Zouch, 2. kal. Jul. 1330.

Joh. de Stok acol. pres. per f'rem Joh. abb. de Eynesham et conv. ad mediet. eccl. de Heyford ad pontem vac. per mort. d'ni Will'i, 4. non. Sept. 1338. Reg. Burgwersh.

Joh'es Aleyn capellanus 1mæ cantariæ pro animabus regum et pontificum in eccl. cath. S. Pauli London. fundatæ et Joh'es Excestr. rector medietatis eccl'iæ de Heyford ad pontem ad pres. abb. et conv. de Eynesham permutarunt, 21. Aug. 1403. Reg. Repingdon ep'i Linc.

and the title of lord Burnel passed to the descendants of John de Handlo by her the said Maud [g]

Alice the relict of Philip Mymekan, in consideration of ten pounds received in hand, released and quit claimed to the said Sir John Handlo all her right to the lands and tenements in Hedingdon, which her husband had conveyed to him. *Hiis testibus; dominis Ricardo d'Amory, Ricardo de Bere, Ricardo de Luches militibus, Gilberto Wase, Nicholao de Fraxino, Roberto Neel, Johanne de Bradelee, et aliis. Dat. apud Oxon. die Veneris proxime post festum S. Scholasticæ virginis. an. regni regis Ed. filii Ed. nono*[h]. Nigh the same time he paid a fine to the king to obtain a pardon for entering upon the said one messuage and carucate of land held *in capite*[i]. In this same year Emme Segrym of Borstall, in her pure widowhood, granted to the said *Sir* John Handlo one piece of land in Borstall, containing in length three perches, and in breadth two perches four feet, in consideration of two shillings received in hand. *Hiis testibus; Johanne le Brun de Acle, Reginaldo de Bosco juniore de Brehull, Johanne le Welshe de Borstall, Johanne le Here, Johanne de Clere, Hugone Richards, Johanne Segrym, Willielmo Brun, et aliis. Dat. apud*

An. MCCCXVI. 9, 10. Edw. II.

Pat. 9. Ed. II. Carte Prioratus de Burncestr confirmantur per *inspeximus.* Carta Gilb'ti de Basset facta Joh'i priori de Burncestr temp. regis Hen. III. Phil. Basset fuit frater Fulconis ep'i Lond. m. 19.

Rob. de Hanlo cl'icus pres. per d'num Joh. de Hanlo milit. ad eccl. de Bekkele vac. per resign. Jacobi de Berkhampstede. 2. id. Maii. 1316. Reg. Dalderby.

Edmundus de Lodelawe p'b'r pres. per d'num de Hanlo mil. ad. eccl. de Bekkele

vac. per institut. Rob'ti de Hanlo in eccl'ia de Hasele. 3. id. Jul. 1318. cum consensu coadjutoris ep'i. ib.

Ric. de Gardinis acol. pres. per d'num Tho. de Gardinis milit. ad eccl. de Somerton vac. per instit. Ric'i de Elsefeld ult. rectoris ejusd. in eccl. de Rya Cicestr. dioc. 3. kal. Jul. 1316. pont. 17.

Mag'r Will. de Dalderby p'b'r pres. per abb. et conv. de Eynesham ad eccl'iam de Schulthorn vac. per resign. Simonis; admiss. 11. kal. Feb. 1316. ib.

[g] Dugd. Bar. tom. 2. p. 61.   [h] Ex Chartul. de Borstall, sub tit. Hedingdon, f. 46.
[i] Ib. f. 45.

Borstall die Dominica proxime post festum S. Barnabæ, anno regni regis Edwardi filii regis Edwardi nono [k].

John Fitz-Nigel of Arncot in Ambrosden, (commonly called le Bastard, a natural son of the late Sir John Fitz-Nigel of Borstall) granted to Sir John Handlo several lands and tenements, in consideration of twenty-five marks of silver received in hand. *Hiis testibus ; dominis Roberto le Luch, Roberto filio Eliæ, militibus, Johanne le Brun, Willielmo de Greycote, Ricardo le Warde, Nicholao de Fraxinis, et aliis. Dat. apud Borstall die Mercurii in vigilia ascensionis Domini, anno regni regis Ed. filii Ed. nono* [l].

By an inquisition taken in these parts it was found that Margery le Waleys held for the term of her life one messuage and three carucates of land at Stokfolts, in the parish of Oakle, com. Bucks, jointly with Adam de Montalt her late husband; and that Elizabeth, daughter of the aforesaid Adam de Montalt, aged eighteen years, was heir of the said Adam; and that the said Elizabeth, and Amicia daughter of Nicholas Trimnel, were heirs of the said Margery Waleys [m]

There had been a long contest for the patronage of this church of Oakle, with its chapels of Brehull and Borstall, between the kings of England and the prior and monks of St. Frideswide, till in 19. Ed. I. the right was adjudged to the latter, and the king gave them seisin by this precept to the sheriff of Bucks.

Rex vicecomiti Buck. salutem. Sciatis quod prior sancte Frideswide Oxon. in curia nostra coram nobis post consideracionem ejusdem curie nostre recuperavit adversus nos advocacionem ecclesie de Acleia cum capellis ad ecclesiam illam spectantibus et pertinenciis suis ut jus ecclesie sue S. Frideswide : et ideo tibi precipimus quod eidem priori de advocacione predicte ecclesie cum capellis ad ecclesiam illam spectantibus et aliis pertinenciis suis sine dilacione plenariam seisinam habere facias. Teste G. de Scrop apud Norwycum XXVIII. *die Januarii, anno regni nostri decimo nono* [n]

---

[k] Ex Chartul. de Borstall, sub tit. Borstall, f. 39.   [l] Ib. fol. 40.   [m] R. Dods. MS. vol. 48. p. 123.   [n] Ex Chartul. S. Frideswydæ penes decan. et capit. Oxon.

When the monks had formerly possession of the church, they had all profits appropriated to themselves, and appointed one of their own canons to officiate; but while the advowson was in the crown, a parson was presented and inducted to the whole benefice. As soon as the monks were repossessed of the advowson, they could not eject the present incumbent, but procured an order from the bishop of Lincoln, diocesan, that upon his death or cession they might again enter on their beloved appropriation.

Henricus permissione divina Lincolniensis episcopus dilectis in Christo filiis priori et conventui monasterii S. Frideswide Oxon. salutem graciam et benedictionem. Licet super appropriacione ecclesie de Acleye et capellis de Brehull et Borstall et Adingrave eidem ut asseritur pertinentibus et annexis tam diutina quam sumptuosa suborta fuerit questio, &c. Nos ex officii nostri debito omnem vobis facere justiciam volentes cum favore volumus juxta appropriacionem prefatam quandocunque cedente vel decedente rectore ipsius ecclesie nunc incumbente ecclesiam et ipsius possessionem propria auctoritate libere ingredi possitis et dictam ecclesiam cum suis capellis in usus proprios retinere et fructus percipere ex iisdem. Proviso tamen quod ecclesia per idoneum canonicum domus vestre predicte prout sede apostolice vobis est indultum et antiquitus extitit consuetum deseruiatur, qui quidem canonicus tanquam vicarius perpetuus a loci diocesano curam animarum eidem ecclesie imminentem recipiet et supportet absque eodem diocesano nullo modo amovendus, ut ab eadem congrue deseruiatur in divinis. Salvis etiam mihi omnibus episcopalibus consuetudinibus et Lincolniensis ecclesie dignitate. In cujus rei testimonium presentibus sigillum nostrum apposuimus [o].

Thomas earl of Lancaster, lord of the manors of Burcester and Midlington, granted to the monks of Whalley a place called Tocstath, with licence to translate their abbey to that place as of a more commodious situation, and to call it by the title of *Locus benedictus*

---

[o] Ex Chartul. S. Frideswydæ penes decan. et capit. Oxon.

de Tocstath, by charter dated *apud Whalley in festo S. Jacobi apostoli, anno Domini millesimo trecentesimo decimo sexto* [P].

An. MCCCXVII.   10, 11.   *Edward II.*

Richard d'Amory, knight, of Bucknell, had a grant from the king for the privilege of free warren at Bucknell, Blechesdon, Stoke de l'Isle, Wode-Piry, and Bix-Gibwyn in com. Oxon, and Mersh and Thornbergh, in com. Bucks [q].

An. MCCCXVII.   10, 11. Edw. II.

John Chapel, rector of Ambrosden, being indebted to Peter Cosin, merchant, in the sum of fifty-seven pounds, and upon prosecution at law, being found to have no temporals to satisfy the said debt, a precept was directed to the bishop of Lincoln to sequester his benefice on default of payment. The bishop directs his orders to the official of the archdeacon of Oxford, and the official to the rural dean of Burcester, to execute the said precept.

Officialis Oxon. discreto viro decano Burcestr. salutem in auctore salutis. Mandatum domini Johannis Dei gracia Linc. episcopi nuper recepimus sub hac forma. Johannes permissione divina Linc. episcopus dilecto in Christo filio officiali archidiaconi Oxon. salutem graciam et benedictionem. Literas domini regis recepimus sub hac forma; *Edwardus Dei gracia rex Anglie dominus Hibernie dux Aquitanie venerabili in Christo patri Johanni eadem gracia episcopo Linc. salutem. Mandamus vobis sicut pluries mandavimus quod venire faciatis coram justiciariis nostris apud Westmin. a die Pasche in tres septimanas de J. Capella personam ecclesie de Ambresdon clericum vestrum ad respondendum Petro Cosin mercatori de Malus de*

placito quod reddat quinquaginta et septem libras quas eidem debet et injuste detinet ut dicit et unde vic. nostri London. alias mandaverunt justiciariis nostris apud Westmin. quod predictus Johannes clericus est et non habet laicum feodum in balliva sua per ubi petet suum et sciatis quod nisi hoc mandatum nostrum plenius exequamini graviter ad vos capiemus et habeatis ibi hoc breve. T. W. de Berford apud Westmin. XVI. *die Novemb. anno regni nostro* Xmo. *Quocirca vobis sicut pluries in virtute obediencie et sub pena excommunicacionis majoris firmiter injungendo mandamus quatenus dicto Johanni in virtute obediencie et sub pena privacionis beneficii sui predicti districtius injungatis quod dictis die et loco compareat facturus quod tenor dicti mandati regis postulat et requirit, et ut nos dicto die et diebus sequentibus assignandis in dicto placito conservet indempnes, volumus quod ab eo exigatis et recipiatis ydoneam caucionem, quam si non presliterit bona sua ecclesiastica sequestretis et sub arcto sequestro vestro periculo custodiatis donec a nobis aliud inde habueritis in mandatis, contradicitores vobis et rebelles per censuram ecclesiasticam canonice compescendo et quid inde faceritis nos citra festum Pasche predicte certificetis per literas vestras pa-*

[P] Mon. Ang. tom. 1. p. 905. a.   [q] R. Dods. MS. vol. 56. p. 135.

William Broun of Borstall and Ivo Bardolfe quit claimed to Sir
John Handlo, knight, their right to two pence yearly rent due to
them from John Fitz-Nigel, bastard, of Arncot. *Hiis testibus ; Ricardo le Warde, Nicholao de Esshes, Johanne de Adingrave, Willielmo
Broun, Johanne le Welshe, Roberto de Herford. Dat. penultimo die
mensis Februarii, anno regni regis Edwardi filii regis Ed. decimo*[r].
At the same time Emma Segrym of Borstall, in her pure widowhood,
granted to Sir John Handlo seven pence yearly rent, due from the
said John Fitz-Nigel, bastard. *Hiis testibus ; Ricardo le Warde, &c.*[s]

April the twenty-second, the king granted to Isabel his queen the
castle and honour of Walingford, within which was the manor of
Burcester, as also the honour of St. Walerie, within which was the
manor of Ambrosden, to hold during life[t].

In this year the king at Walsingham confirmed the several donations made to the priory of Burcester by special charter[u].

Walter de Langley, lord of the manor of Bigenhull in the parish
of Burcester, in consideration of a sum of money, granted and demised to Robert le Clerk and Christian his wife, and to the longest
liver of them, all that part of a croft which lately belonged to John
Michel in the town of Burcester, paying twenty pence yearly rent.

*tentes harum seriem ac estimacionem bono-
rum plenius continentes. Dat. apud parcum
Stowe, kal. Marcii, consecracionis nostre
anno* xviimo. *Quocirca vobis sub pena superius contenta firmiter injungendo mandamus quatenus dictum mandatum in omnibus
suis articulis exequamini diligenter vice nostra ; et quod inde feceritis nos citra diem
Martis vel saltem in illo die Martis tempes-
tive certificetis distincte et aperte per literas
vestras patentes harum seriem et factum vestrum in premissis ac estimacionem bonorum*

*inventorum ibidem plenius continentes. Dat.
Oxon. kalend. Aprilis anno Domini* mcccxvii.
Ex MS. in Bibl. Bodl. Digby, 154.

Joh. fil. Joh'is de Cotesford p'b'r pres.
per proc. abb'is et conv. de Becco Herlewin ad eccl. de Cotesford vac. per resign. Tho. de Staunton. 11. kal. Jul. 1317.

Tho. de Croxford acol. pres. per Tho. de
Musgrave ad eccl. de Blechesdon vac. per
resign. Galfridi de Welleford. 13. kal. Apr.
1317.

[r] Ex Ghartul. de Borstall, MS. f. 41.
p. 138.   [u] Mon. Ang. tom. 2. p. 285.   [s] Ibid. f. 39.   [t] Guil. Dugd. MS. vol. C.

Dated at Bigenhull on the morrow after the feast of St. Michael, 10. Ed. II.

A tuz ceuls que cest escrit veut ou ovrut Walt. de Langley seigneur de Bigenhulle en la counte de Oxenford saluz en deu. Sachez moy aver donee grante et par cest escrit conferme a Robt. le Clerk de Berencestre et a Chrestiene sa femme toute cela place de la croufte que jadis estoit a Johan. Michel en la ville de Berencester que content en longure de la croufte que Robt. le fil. Robt. Barun tent. juskes a la croufte que Johannes Stephnes tent de moy en Berencester et en la tour del tenement le dyt Robert le Clerk jusques a la place de meismes la croufte que Alice Sebern tent. de moy selun ceo que le bounds en tour le dyt place purportent. A aver et tenir la dyt place de moy et mes heyrs et des mes assignes a le avant diz Robert et Christiene ou aucun de euls que plus longement vivra franchement quietement beu et en pees reddant de cel per an. dys deners a la feste de nativite, et dys deners a la feste de la nativite seint Johan. le Baptist pur toutes autres services et coustumes et demaundis et per ceo don et grant et confermement des cest escrit les avaunt dyt Robert et Chrestienne moy ay donnez un sume de argent avant mayn, &c. Ces tesmoynes; Henry de Bowelles, Johanne de la Forde, Johanne Abbot, Simone Germayn, Nicholao de Blakeacres. Done a Bigenhulle len demain de la Seynt Michel en lan du regn le roi Edward fil. le roy Edward dyseme[1].

To the original a seal appending with the arms of Langley, frette bordered with besants.

On the Monday before Ascension-day, Alice wife of Thomas earl of Lancaster, (by whom the manors of Burcester and Midlington came to the said earl,) at Cancford in Dorsetshire, was violently taken away by a certain knight of the family of John earl of Warren, there being many in the conspiracy; and (as was said) by the king's consent she was carried in triumph, and in contempt of the earl her husband, to the earl of Warren's castle of Rigate. In their passage among the hedges and woods between Haulton and Farnham, those

[1] Ex Orig. penes D. Guil. Glynne, Bar.

3 z 2

that conveyed her saw several banners and streamers, (the priests and people being then in a solemn procession round the fields,) upon which they were struck with a sudden terror; and thinking the earl or some of his retinue were come to rescue the lady, and revenge the affront, they left her and fled away: but when sensible of their mistake, they returned, and with them a person of a very mean stature, lame, and crook-backed, called Richard de St. Martin, who with wonderful impudence challenged the countess thus miserably insnared for his wife, openly protesting that he had known her carnally before she was married to the said earl, which she likewise freely acknowledged to be true : so as this lady, who through the whole course of her life had been reputed chaste and honourable, on a sudden turn of fortune must be proclaimed through the whole world for a lewd and infamous woman. The wretch who had thus got possession of her grew so insolent, as to presume in his pretended wife's name to claim in the king's court the earldoms of Lincoln and Salisbury, though with no effect[x].

This occasioned the divorce between the earl and his countess, which historians mention to have been some time before his death[y] And the earl of Lancaster, in a spirit of revenge, demolished the earl of Warren's castles of Sandal and Wakefeld, and wasted all his manors on the other side Trent[z].

This indignity gave so much farther provocation to Thomas earl of Lancaster, that when the king called a parliament in London to treat of the injuries done by the Scots, &c. he absented from it, as he had before done at Clarendon; for which he was publicly proclaimed an enemy to the king and kingdom[a]. The news whereof being brought to pope John the Twenty-second, he sent two cardinals his nuncios into England, to make up the breach between the king and the earl. And as the earl was marching into the northern parts against the Scots, a soldier was brought to him, who had a pa-

---

[x] Tho. Walsing. sub an.　　[y] MS. in Bib. Bod. James. vol. 27.　　[z] Ex Chron. Abb. S. Werburg. Cest. MS.　　[a] Tho. Wal. sub an.

per under the great seal, and letters under the privy seal, to authorize him to treat with the king of Scots about the death of the said
earl.   The soldier upon his own confession was drawn and hanged,
and his head set upon Pontfract castle: the earl keeping the cre-
dential papers for a proof of the conspiracy.   Upon which the people
of England were so convinced, that whereas they had before generally
despised the earl, upon this discovery they adhered to him, and were
very solicitous for his health and safety[b].

Sir Theobald de Verdon, lord of the manor of Heth, (who had
been summoned to parliament among the barons whilst his father
lived, *viz.* in 28. Ed. I. and afterward till 9. Ed. II. inclusive,) departed this life at his castle of Alveton, on Tuesday 6. calends of
Aug. and was buried in the abbey of Croxden upon the 13th of October following, Elizabeth his widow being then great with child, who
on the feast day of St. Benedict was delivered of a daughter, named
Isabel, which daughter was afterwards the wife of Henry lord Ferrers
of Groby, who thereby came to the possession of the said manor of
Heth[c].

An. MCCCXVIII.   11, 12. *Edward II.*

The two cardinals, who were sent over by the pope to reconcile
the king and Thomas earl of Lancaster, took up their residence at
Leicester, to which place came the king, queen, archbishop of Canterbury, and most other bishops; and on a day prefixed, Thomas

An. MCCCXVIII. 11, 12. Edw. II

Edmundus de Lodelawe p'b'r pres. per
d'num Joh. de Hanlo mil. ad eccl. de Beckele vac. per institutionem Rob'ti de Hanlo
in eccl. de Hasele. 3. id. Jul. 1318. cum
consensu coadjutoris ep'i.

Joh. de Wappinbir acol. pres. per Jo-
h'am relictam Guidonis le Fitzwith quæ
recuperavit presentat. suam versus Hugo-

nem de Plessetis ad eccl. de Ardele vac. per
dimissionem Joh. de Shulton ultimi rectoris; admiss. 18. kal. Jul. 1318. de consensu coadjutoris ep'i.

Joh. de Welleton acol. pres. per d'num
Rob. de Insula mil. ad eccl. de Heyford
Waryn vac. per mort. Tho. le Botiler ult.
rectoris. 4. non. Febr. 1318.

[b] Tho. Walsing. sub an.   [c] Dugd. Bar. tom. 1. p. 474.

earl of Lancaster marched with a pompous retinue of eighteen thousand men, and met the king at Syroches-Brigge, alias Sotes-Brigge, where the king and earl saluted each other, and to all appearance were made friends[c]. But the earl's concern in the death of Gaveston could never be forgiven, and his great aversion to the other favourites, the two Spencers, with his bold spirit of freedom that alway opposed every arbitrary action, made him hated by this less judicious prince, who only dissembled a peace till he could effect his revenge.

Toward the expedition to be now made into Scotland, this earl had command to raise two thousand foot well armed out of his lands and fees; and to bring them to the king at Newcastle within one month after the feast of the nativity of St. John Baptist. In order whereto, he retained by indenture Sir Hugh Menill, knight, for the term of his whole life, to assist him in the wars of England, Ireland, Scotland, and Wales, with three men at arms well mounted, armed, and arrayed; covenanting to allow him harness for his own body, and recompense for what arms and horses should be lost during the war in his service; as also apparel and saddles, livery of hay and oats for his horses, and the like wages for so many grooms as he gave to his other *bas-chevaliers*, knights bachelors: and in times of peace, upon his going to parliament or elsewhere, livery of hay and oats for four horses, and wages for the like number of grooms, with an annuity of ten marks. He likewise retained Sir John de Ewre, knight, to serve him with ten men at arms in time of war, whereof three to be knights, allowing them bouch of court, with livery of hay, oats, horseshoes and nails, as other bannerets usually had: and in time of peace, attending him to parliament, or other assemblies, with all his knights in livery, to have diet in his hall, as also hay, oats, horseshoes and nails, for eight and twenty horses, and wages for as many grooms; with livery of wine and candles for his chamber. And when

[c] Hen. Knyghton, sub an.

he should come himself with one knight, then to have bouch of court, with hay and oats for seven horses, wages for so many grooms and livery of wine and candles for his chamber [f].

Within this same year the said earl granted licence to the convent of Spalding, of which he was patron, to choose a prior of the said house, on the 7th cal. of Feb.; and in the same nineteenth of John Dalderby, bishop of Lincoln, there was a trial *de jure patronatus*, of the church of Ardele near Burcester, between Sir Hugh de Plessets and Joan the relict of Wido le Fitz-Wythe: to the latter of which the right of advowson was adjudged; and her clerk was instituted and inducted to the said church on the fifteenth of July [g].

William Broun of Borstall granted to Sir John Handlo a certain meadow in the said village. *Hiis testibus; Ricardo le Warde, Nicholao de Esshes, Johanne Neel, Johanne le Welshe, Johanne Broun, Johanne Clere, Thoma le Porter, et aliis. Datum apud Borstall die Sabbathi proxime ante festum nativitatis S. Johannis Baptistæ, anno regni regis Ed. filii regis Ed. undecimo* [h]. And within the same year, John son and heir of John Broun of Borstall granted to the said Sir John Handlo one acre of arable land in Tounfurlong, within the common field of Borstall. *Dat. apud Borstall die Martis proxime ante festum translationis beati Thomæ martyris, anno regni regis Ed. filii regis Ed. undecimo* [i].

An. MCCCXIX.   12, 13. *Edward II.*

William de Paumes granted to Thomas earl of Lancaster the homage and all the services which John son and heir of John de Broghton held of him, by reason of the manors of Broghton and Newinton near Banbury in this county, by the following charter.

Sachent touz gens que Ieo William de Paumes Seigneur de Naborne ay donne a noble homme mons. Thomas counte de Lancastre et de Leycestre seneschal Angleterre le homage et tout les services que John fils

---

[f] El. Ashmole, MS.   [g] R. Dods. MS. vol. 107. f. 187. b.   [h] Ex Chartular. de Borstall.
MS. f. 40.   [i] Ib. f. 41.

et heir John de Broghton et ses heirs me sont teniz par le raison des manoirs de Broghton et de Newinton pres de Banneburi, &c. C' an douziesme le roy Ed. fils au tres noble roy Edward[k]

Robert de Burcester, clerk, granted and confirmed to Christian daughter of Simon Germayne of Bigenhull, and William her son, those two messuages with one cottage, which were new built between his great gate and the messuage of John Ford, in the town of Burcester, to hold during the life of either of them, paying four shillings yearly during the life of the said Robert, and after his decease one pound of cummin to his heirs or assigns at the feast of Michaelmas, for all services and demands; by deed dated at Burcester on Wednesday the feast of St. Peter *ad vincula*, in the beginning of 12. Ed. II.

Noverint universi Christi fideles quod ego Robertus de Burcester clericus dedi concessi et hoc præsenti scripto meo confirmavi Christianæ quondam filiæ Simonis Germayn de Bigenhull et Willielmo filio suo illa duo messuagia cum uno cotagio quæ de novo construuntur inter magnam portam meam et messuagium Johannis Ford in villa de Berencester; habend. et tenend. prædicta messuagia et cotagium cum

An. MCCCXIX. 12, 13. Edw. II.

Tho. de Tynton p'b'r pres. per abb. et conv. de Barlinges ad eccl. de Midlington vac. per resign. Joh. de Tynton nomine permutationis quam idem Joh. de ipsa eccl'ia cum eccl'ia de Gretham quam prefatus Thomas titulo institutionis prius tenuerat fecit auctorizante ep'o rite factam alias minime dimissurus, ad eand. eccl'iam est admissus, 9. kal. Jul. 1319. Reg. Dalderby.

Tho. de Baunburgh p'b'r pres. per abb. et conv. de Elnestow ad eccl. de Godington vac. per mort. mag'ri Ric'i. 3. kal. Dec. 1319.

Pat. 12. Edw. II. Rex.—*T. ep'o Linc. salut. Licet nuper credentes eccl'iam de Acle vestra dioc. nostri patronatus vacasse dilec-*

tum cl'icum n'rum Gilbertum de Ebor. vobis presentaverimus ad eandem rogantes quatenus ipsum Gilbertum ad eccl'iam predictam admitteretis et personam institueretis in eadem; quia tamen nobis constat q'd dilectus nobis in Christo Will'us de Wrotham percelebris memorie d'num E. quondam regem Anglie patrem n'rum ad eccl. de Brehull v're dioc. extunc presentatus et ad ipsam ac predictam eccl'iam de Acle que sub una cadunt presentatione virtute presentationis ad eccl'iam predictam de Brehull de se facta admissus et institutus fuit in eadem et adhuc viget corporea sospitate presentationem de prefato Gilb'to ad eccl'iam predictam de Acle per nos factam ut est dictum duximus revocandam. 31. Jul.

[k] Ashmole, MS.

*curtilagio et pertinentiis de me et hæredibus meis et assignatis præ-
dictis Willielmo et Christianæ quamdiu vixerint vel vixerit alteruter
ipsorum libere quiete bene et in pace reddendo inde annuatim mihi
prædicto Roberto ad totam vitam meam quatuor solidos argenti annuatim et post decessum meum volo quod solvant hæredibus et assignatis
meis unam libram cimini ad festum Sancti Michaelis pro omnibus servitiis sæcularibus et demandis. Et ego prædictus Robertus et hæredes
mei et assignati prædicta duo messuagia et cotagium cum curtilagio
et pertinent. prædictis Christianæ et Willielmo contra omnes gentes
warantizabimus acquietabimus et quamdiu ipsi vixerint vel vixerit
alteruter ipsorum defendemus. Post terminum vero vitæ dictorum
Christianæ et Willielmi supradicta messuagia cotagium cum curtilagio
et pertinentiis ad me vel ad hæredes meos sine contradictione revertantur. In cujus rei testimonium huic præsenti scripto sigillum meum
est appensum. Hiis testibus; Johanne de la Forde de Berencester,
Johanne Philip de eadem, Simone Germayn de Bigenhull, Ricardo de
Blake de eadem, Johanne le Leche de Berencester, et aliis. Datum
apud Berencester die Martis in festo Sancti Petri ad vincula. Anno
regni regis Edwardi filii regis Edwardi duodecimo intrante*[1].

William Burward of Oakle granted to Sir John Handlo, knight,
of Borstall, his part of five swathes in a meadow called Bikmore,
within the said village of Oakle, in consideration of eleven shillings
in silver. *Hiis testibus; Johanne le Brun, Nicholao de Esses, Johanne Ferebraz, Richardo de Luches, Nigello Travers, Johanne Necle
de Arncot, et multis aliis*[m].

Roger uncle to Richard d'Amorie lord of the manor of Bucknell,
having married Elizabeth third sister and one of the coheirs to Gilbert de Clare earl of Glocester, niece to the king, had a grant from
the king to him and his said wife and their heirs in general entail of
the manor of Halghton in com. Oxon, late the possession of Edmund
earl of Cornwall, which grant was confirmed in the parliament held
at York, 13. Ed. II. by which means the said manor of Halghton

[1] Ex Orig. penes hon. D. Guil. Glynne, Bar.   [m] Ex Chartular. de Borstall, MS. f. 11.

passed to their eldest daughter and heir Elizabeth, married 10. Ed. III. to Thomas lord Bardolf; and so in 45. of Ed. III. to their son and heir William lord Bardolf; and in 13. Ric. II. to Thomas lord Bardolf; and 6. Hen. IV. to Ann his daughter and heir, married to Sir William Clifford : as appeared by inquisition made 10. Hen. IV. [n]

Sir Richard d'Amory of Bucknell procured licence from the king for a market every week, upon the Monday at his manor of Ubbele in com. Som. and à fair there yearly on the eve, day, and morrow after the feast of St. Bartholomew the apostle [o].

Queen Eleanor, late wife to king Henry the Third, had formerly out of entire affection to Thomas earl of Lancaster, and Henry his brother, her grandsons, given to them and their heirs a certain part of the earldom of Province, which by right of inheritance descended to her from her father and mother, with jurisdiction of a meer and mixed empire, and all rights and privileges thereto belonging, of which our Thomas earl of Lancaster now obtained a confirmation from the king, bearing date June the fifth [p].

In the same year the said earl attended the king in his expedition against the Scots; where, at the siege of Berwick, the king unadvisedly said, that he would make Hugh le Despenser governor of the castle, and Roger d'Amory of the town, when taken. Which was so much resented by Thomas earl of Lancaster, that with several of his forces he deserted the king; for which the king's army proclaimed him a traitor. His retreat hindered the taking of the town [q].

An. MCCCXX. 13, 14. *Edward II.*

The king by letters dated at York the first of July, required Tho-

An. MCCCXX. 13, 14. Edw. II.
Andreas de Cotesford cap. pres. per priorem et conv. de Kenilworth ad eccl. de Hethe per resign. And. de la Hyde. 16. kal. Jul. 1320.

Joh. de Okle capellan. pres. per d'num Hen. le Tyeys mil. ad eccl. de Oke vac. per mort. Ric'i de Suthampton. 2. non. Mar. 1320.

[n] R. Dods. MS. vol. 40. p. 159.   [o] Dugd. Bar. tom. 2. p. 100. a.   [p] Ib. tom. 1. p. 780. b.   [q] Tho. Walsing. sub an.

mas earl of Lancaster to choose out of his feudatory tenants two
thousand foot-men well armed, and to bring them to the king at
Newcastle-upon-Tyne, and pay attendance for one month, to commence from the feast of the nativity of St. John the Baptist [r]

Walter Burcester, clerk, designing to give unto the priory of Burcester one messuage, ten acres of arable land, four acres of meadow,
and twenty-five shillings yearly rent, with other appertenances in
Grymesbury and Werkworth, petitioned for the king's consent to
dispense with the statute of mortmain. Upon which an inquisition
was ordered, called *ad quod damnum,* &c. and the jury returned, that
it would not be to the damage of the king, if he gave leave to Walter
Burcester, clerk, to make the said grant to the prior and convent of
Burcester, and their successors for ever [s].

The king in this year confirmed a charter of Hen. III. to the abbey of Oseney, which rehearses and ratifies the possession of two hides
of land in Ernicot (now Arncot) in the parish of Ambrosden [t].

Some land in this village of Arncot had been given by king Ethelred, an. 993, to the abbey of Abendon, com. Berks, by express charter, to which these witnesses subscribed. *Ego Dunstan archiepiscopus confirmavi. Ego Oswald archiepiscopus confirmavi. Ego Athel-
wold episcopus impressi. Ego Ælfstan episcopus subscripsi. Ego Athel-
gar episcopus consolidavi. Ego Ælfstan episcopus adquievi. Ego Æl-
fear episcopus non renui. Ego Ælfric episcopus concessi. Ego Athulf
episcopus subscripsi. Ego Æscuin episcopus impressi. Ego Uulfgar
episcopus consignavi* [u].

Richard d'Amory lord of the manor of Bucknell, and Roger d'A-
mory his uncle, were now both in the wars of Scotland [x]. This latter
was one who entered into the association with the earls of Lancaster,
Hereford, &c. against the two Spencers [y].

About this time died Alan de Plugenet, lord of the manors of Pi-

[r] El. Ashmole, MS.   [s] R. Dods. MS. vol. 86. f. 126.   [t] Mon. Ang. tom. 2. p. 110.
[u] B. Twine, MS. C. 2. p. 391. in Bib. C. C. C.   [x] Dugd. Bar. tom. 2. p. 100.   [y] Tho.
de la Moor, ed. 2. sub an.

dington and Hedingdon, leaving Joan de Bohun his sister and heir, who doing her homage in 19. Ed. II. had livery of the lands of her inheritance; and dying without issue in 1. Ed. III. her estate descended to Sir Richard de la Bere, knight, son of Richard de la Bere, brother of the whole blood to Alan Plugenet her father. But the said manor of Pidington now reverted to the crown, and the king bestowed it on his indulged friend Hugh Despenser, sen. who granted it to his kinsman Sir John de Handlo of Borstall, to hold during his life[z]. This manor was by injustice and court interest detained from the prior and canons of St. Frideswide, who had the legal title to it, by the donation of Simon St. Liz the first earl of Huntendon, confirmed by Malcolm king of Scots in possession of the said honor, or rather first given by the said king Malcolm, and ratified by Simon the third earl of Northampton and Huntendon. The confirming charters of Hen. II. of Thomas Becket archbishop of Canterbury, and earl Simon, which should have been recited in their respective place, deserve to be here inserted.

Henricus rex Anglie et dux Normannie et Aquitanie et comes Andigavie archiepiscopis episcopis, &c. salutem. Sciatis me concessisse et presenti carta confirmasse Deo et S. Marie et ecclesie S. Frideswyde, de Oxon. et canonicis ibidem Deo servientibus villam de Pydentona in Oxenfordscira quam Malcolmus rex Scotie eis concessit et dedit in perpetuam elemosinam et carta sua confirmavit, ita ut Johanna soror Thome Bassett eam teneat in vita sua et quamdiu vixerit servicium inde debitum canonicis predictis reddat, et post decessum ejus villa predicta canonicis remaneat cum pertinenciis suis in perpetuam elemosinam et possessionem. Quare volo et firmiter precipio quod predicta ecclesia et canonici ejusdem ecclesie predictam villam cum omnibus pertinenciis habeant et teneant in bosco et plano in pratis et pascuis in aquis et molendinis in viis et semitis et in omnibus aliis locis et aliis rebus ad eam pertinentibus ita bene et in pace libere quiete plenarie et integre et honorifice et rationabiliter cum omnibus libertatibus ac liberis consue-

---

[z] Ex Chartul. S. Frideswydæ, p. 118.

tudinibus suis sicut carta Malcolmi regis Scotie testatur. Hiis testibus, &c.[a]

Thomas Dei gracia Cantuariensis ecclesie minister humilis universis
S. matris ecclesie filiis salutem. Collata sanctis ac venerabilibus locis
beneficia cum graciarum debemus accione quod ad nos pertinet confo-
vere. Ea propter donacionem illam quam dilectus filius noster Malcolmus illustris rex Scotorum fecit ecclesie S. Frideswyde in Oxenford
de villa de Pydentona ratam habentes, et juxta cartam ejusdem regis
Scotie nostri scripti munimine confirmantes, statuimus ne quis ejusdem
ecclesie canonicos in hujus ville sive rerum adjacencium possessione
contra cartam domini nostri regis Anglie Henrici et cartam dicti re
gis Scotie concutere vel aliquibus exaccionibus indebitis vexare pre-
sumat. Valete[b].

Comes Simon omnibus hominibus suis Francis et Anglis tam clericis
quam laicis salutem. Sciatis me dedisse Deo et Sancte Marie et ecclesie
S. Frideswide Oxon. et canonicis ibidem Deo serviencibus in liberam
et perpetuam elemosinam villam Pydintonam in Oxenfordscira pro salute mea et patris et matris mee et omnium antecessorum et successorum
meorum, ita ut Johanna in vita sua teneat et servicium inde debitum
canonicis predictis reddat, post decessum vero prefate Johanne villa
predicta eisdem canonicis remaneat in perpetuam possessionem et elemosinam cum omnibus pertinenciis suis aliis in bosco et plano in pascuis in pasturis et cum omnibus pertinenciis suis aliis que ad eandem
villam pertinent. Hiis subscriptis testibus ; Hereberto filio Athelardi
Waltero de D. &c.[c]

But after this charter made by Simon St. Liz, the third earl of
Huntendon and Northampton, he seized and detained the said village of Pidington ; upon which grievance the canons of St. Frideswide made their complaint to pope Alexander the Third, who sent
letters to the archbishop of Canterbury his legate, and the bishop of
Chichester, commanding them to see restitution made to the said
prior and canons ; and till such restitution should be given, he forbid

---

[a] Ex Chartul. S. Frideswydæ, p. 118.   [b] Ibid. p. 117.   [c] Ibid.

all divine offices to be celebrated within the fee, under which the said village of Pidington was contained.

Alexander episcopus servus servorum Dei venerabilibus fratribus Cantuariensi archiepiscopo apostolice sedis legato et Cicestrensi episcopo salutem et apostolicam benedictionem. Ex parte prioris et fratrum ecclesie S. Frideswyde ad aures nostras noveritis pervenisse, quod cum bone memorie Malcolmus quondam Scotie rex eidem ecclesie villam de Pydintona cum universis pertinenciis suis in perpetuam elemosinam contulisset et scripti sui munimine confirmasset ita quidem quod Johanna nobilis mulier in vita sua eandem villam teneret et servicium quod de predicta villa eidem regi debuerat prefate ecclesie solveret: Willielmus frater ejus qui sibi in regno successit eandem villam prescripte ecclesie abstulit, et postmodum David frater ejus qui honorem de Huntindon tenuit prescriptam villam que ad ipsum honorem spectare dinoscitur injuste detinuit, et nunc comes Simon contra do minum qui prescripte ecclesie pretaxatam villam scripti sui robore confirmaverat in sue salutis periculum detinet occupatam. Quum igitur quod Deo semel offertur non debet ei temeritate qualicunque subtrahi vel auferri, fraternitati vestre per apostolica scripta precipiendo mandamus, quatenus inquisita veritate rei si vobis constiterit eandem villam memorate ecclesie violenter ablatam fuisse eidem ecclesie villam ipsam auctoritate nostra contradiccione et appellacione cessante restitui faciatis, et deinde siquis adversus prefatum priorem et fratres exinde agere voluerit, causam audiatis et fine debito terminetis. Si vero ad mandatum nostrum prelibata villa eidem ecclesie non fuerit restituta, in feodo sub quo eadem continetur donec ipsa villa ecclesiæ appellatione remota restituatur dominica prohibeatis officia celebrari. Dat. Ferentium, &c. [d]

An. MCCCXXI. 14, 15. *Edward II.*

The king now confirmed that charter of king John which re hearsed and ratified the grant of Thomas de S. Walery, lord of the

---

[d] Ex Chartul. S. Frideswydæ, p. 117.

manor of Ambrosden, of the manor of * Mixbury to the abbey of
Oseney : in which parish Wido de Areins, son of Bernard de Areins,
had given six virgates of land, with villanage and appertenances to
the said abbey of Oseney ; who paid to the successive barons of St.
Walery, homage, relief, and scutage for two knight's fees in Mixbury and Newton-Purcel, and half a knight's fee in Hampton-
Gay, with suit at their court of the said barony, till Edmund earl
of Cornwall released some part of their service by indenture in 20.
Ed. I.

*Omnibus Christi fidelibus ad quorum noticiam presentes litere per-
venerint Edmundus comes Cornubie salutem in domino. Noverit universitas vestra quod cum petissemus de abbate de Oseney homagium
relevium et scutagium de duobus feodis militum in Mixeburi et Ni-
weton-Purcel et de dimidio feodo militis in Hampton-Gay unde idem
abbas cognovit quod tenet de nobis terras et tenementa sua in Mixeburi et Niweton-Purcell per servicium dimidii feodi militis, et medietatem manerii de Hampton-Gay per servicium dimidii feodi militis*

An. mcccxxi. 14, 15. Edw. II.
Joh. Sporowe acol. pres. per d'num Joh.
de Insula mil. ad eccl. de Heyford Waryn
vac. per resign. Joh. de Welleton. 3. kal.
Mart. 1321.
* Rectores eccl'iæ de Mixbury com. Oxon.
Wibertus cl'icus ad eccl'iam de Mixebir.
ad pres. nobilis viri R. com. Drocarum.
Rot. Hug. Wells. pont. 13.
26. Octob. 1425. Dominus Cant. admisit
mag'rum Joh'em Norton decretorum doc-
torem ad eccl. de Mixbury, Linc. dioc. ad
pres. D. Joh'is Roffen. ep'i. Reg. Chichele,
261.
1501. 1. Maii. Mag'r Ric'us Carpenter,
LL. pres. per Ric. Roff, ep'um ad eccl. de
Mixbury vac. per mort. mag'ri David Persons. Reg. Smyth, Linc.

1503. 18. Sept. Mag'r Hugo Saunders,
S. T. P. pres. per Ric. Roff. ep'um ad eccl.
de Mixbury per mort. Ric'i Carpenter. ib.
1513. 5. Apr. Mag'r Jacobus Gilbert ad
pres. Joh'is ep'i Roff. admiss. ad eccl. de
Mixbury vac. per resign. mag'ri Hugonis
Saunders. ib.
Permutatio inter dom. Tho. de Branktre
rectorem eccl'iæ de Mixbury et mag. Joh.
de Dalton rectorem eccl'iæ S. Albani in
Wodestrete, London. 12. kal. Maii. 1364.
Reg. Bokingham, ep'i Linc.
Hen. Waryn de Buckyngham presbiter
presentatus per Tho. ep'um Roff. ad eccl.
de Mixeburi per resign. D. Joh. de Dalton
ex causa permutationis de ipsa cum eccl'ia
de Hoghton magna ejusdem dioc. 13. cal.
Aug. 1367. ib.

et faciendo sectam ad curiam nostram de North-Oseneye de tribus
septimanis in tres septimanas. Nos pro salute anime nostre et anima-
rum antecessorum nostrorum remisimus et quietumclamavimus pro no-
bis et heredibus nostris prefato abbati et successoribus suis abbatibus
de Osen. servicia quæ a predicto abbate petebamus et quod de cetero de
eo petere poterimus de uno feodo militis et dimidio in villis predictis
ultra servicium unius feodi militis quod predictus abbas nobis facere
recognovit sicut predictum est . . . . . *Ita tamen quod predictus abbas et*
successores sui abbates de Oseney faciant nobis et heredibus nostris om
nia alia servicia que pertinent ad unum feodum militis videlicet pro
terris et tenementis que idem abbas tenet in Mixeburi et Niweton
Purcell servicia que pertinent ad dimidium feodum militis·et pro me-
dietate manerii de Hampton-Gay servicia que pertinent ad dimidium
feodum militis et sectam ad curiam nostram de North-Oseney de tri-
bus septimanis in tres septimanas exceptis tantummodo homagio et re-
levio de terris et tenementis predictis. Remisimus etiam et quietum
clamavimus pro nobis et heredibus nostris predicto abbati et successo-
ribus suis homagium et scutagium quod aliquo modo ab eis petere po-
tuimus de terris et tenementis quæ tenentur de feodo nostro de Evere.
Ita tamen quod faciant nobis et heredibus nostris omnia alia servicia
que ad predicta terras et tenementa pertinent et nobis inde debentur.
In cujus rei testimonium tam nos quam predicte abbas de Oseney et
ejusdem loci conventus presenti scripto in modum cirographi confecto
sigilla nostra apposuimus alternatim. Dat. primo die Januarii anno
regni regis Edwardi vicesimo ᶜ.

I do not question but this village of Mixbury (anciently called
Meoxberie) took its name from the old word ꟽeox, (*i. e.* in the
middle, or between, or mixture, whence *mixen* or *maxen,* a dunghill,)
and *berie,* an open plain, the place being so situate on a wide spacious plain, through which ran the confines of the Mercian and West-
Saxon kingdoms. It is true, Sir Henry Spelman in the name of

ᶜ Ex Chartul. de Oseney penes decan. et capit. Æd. Christi, Oxon.

places confounds the termination of *berie* with that of *burg* and *bury*, as if the appellative of any ancient town : whereas the true sense of the word *berie* is a wide, open, campaign place, as from sufficient authorities is proved by the learned Du Fresne, both in his Glossary [f], and his Notes on the Life of St. Lewis [g]; where he observes that Beria S. Edmundi, mentioned by Mat. Paris, *sub an.* 1174, is not to be taken for the town, but the campaign, or adjoining plain.   To this and his other remarks on that word might be added, that many flat and wide meadows, and other grounds, are still called by this name of the *berie*, and *berie* field.   So the spacious mead between Oxford and Giftelei, or Ifley, was in the reign of king Athelstan called *beri;* when it was pretended to be recovered by a miracle to the late owners, the abbot and convent of Abingdon [h].

The barons who had entered into an association against the two invidious favourites Despensers, father and son, met at Sherborn, under the command of Thomas earl of Lancaster, and thence marched to St. Alban's, and returned through these parts of the country, as appears from this; that one of the army, who was chiefly concerned in a design of plundering the monastery of St. Alban's, died in his march at Ailsbury, com. Bucks [i].   The barons, when they had stayed at St. Alban's three days, sent the bishops of London, Salisbury, Hereford, Ely, and Chichester, to the king at London, with proposals that he would banish the Despensers, as traitors to the kingdom, and would send letters of indemnity for them and their adherents.   The king not assenting to these terms, the earl of Lancaster with his forces marched to the city, and quartered in the suburbs, till he had leave to enter within the walls: and then, by the mediation of the queen and bishops, the king did agree to the banishment of the Spensers, and letters of pardon were granted, and the barons returned to their allegiance and respective houses [k].   But the lord Badlesmere's servants refusing to admit the queen into the castle of Leeds in Kent, this

[f] Gloss. Lat. in voce *beria*.   [g] Not. ad S. Lud. vitam, p. 89.   [h] B. Twine, MS. C. 2. p. 253.   [i] Tho. Walsing. sub an.   [k] Ibid.

renewed the flame; and at Christmas the king was with one army at
Cirencester, and the earl of Lancaster at the head of another near
Bampton[1]. During these fatal heats, there were solemn justs performed at Whitney, com. Oxon, between Humphrey Bohun earl of
Hereford on the one side, and Aymer Valence earl of Pembroke on
the other; which latter in 8. Ed. II. obtained a licence from the king
to make a castle of his house at Bampton in this county. When
queen Isabel was going to take possession of Leeds castle, the lord
Badlesmere, owner, was then at * Whitney, and sent from thence some

* Rectores eccl'iæ de Witteney com. Oxon.
1219. Dionisius clericus ad eccl. de Wit-
teneia ad pres. d'ni Winton ep'i per resign.
mag'ri Humfredi de Midliers qui habuit
custodiam ejusd. Rot. Hug. Well. pont. 11.

Mag'r Helyas de Glovernia subdiac. ad
eccl. de Witteneya ad pres. mag'ri Barthol.
Winton et Luc. Surrei archid'orum procu-
ratorum ep'i Winton. Rot. Hug. Well.
pont. 19.

Mag'r Will. de S. Mariæ eccl'ia ad eccl.
de Winten ad pres. P. ep'i Winton. Rot.
Rob. Grosthead. anno 2. (1236.)

Rad. Grosset. subdec. prepositus Augustens. ad eccl. de Wytteneia ad pres. regis
ratione ep'atus Winton. vacantis. Rot. Rob.
Grosthead. anno 9. (1243.)

Will'us Wachi de Cambriaco pres. per
dom. regem ratione ep'atus Winton in
manu sua existent. ad eccl. de Witteneya
vac. per resign. mag'ri Petri de Cambriaco.

Will. de Witteneya p'b'r ad vicar. de
Witteneya vac. per mort. Gilb'ti ad pres.
procuratoris Guill'i dicti Vach rectoris
ejusd. 1262. Rot. Ric. Gravesend. anno 4.

Will'us Vacce nepos mag'ri Will'i Vacce
de Chambriaco per provis. papal fit rector

eccl. de Witney per resign. Will'i Vacce de
Cambriaco in curia Romana admissus. Id.
Feb. 1310. Reg. Dalderby.

Mag'r Tho. de Tessunt subd. pres. per
J. ep'um Winton. ad eccl. de Witteney
vac. per resign. Will'i Vacce de Cambriaco
ultimi rectoris ejusd. nomine permutationis
quam idem Will'us cum eccl'ia de Hag-
worthingham quam prefatus mag'r Thomas
prius tenuerat, ad dictam eccl. de Witteney
admissus est. 17. kal. Dec. 1318. ib.

Joh. de Orleton p'b'r pres. per Adam.
Winton. ep'um ad eccl. de Witteney Linc.
dioc. vac. per mort. mag'ri Tho. de Tes-
sunte. 14. kal. Apr. 1336. Reg. Burgwersh.

Permutatio inter Joh. de Orleton rector.
eccl. de Wytteney et mag'rum Joh. de Trillek
rector. eccl'iæ de Brocdon Wigorn. dioc. de
patronatu ep'i Wigorn. 9. kal. Apr. 1339.
ib.

Rogerus Folyot p'b'r pres. per Adam.
ep'um Winton ad eccl. de Wytteney vac.
per dimissionem Joh. Trillek. 7. kal. Octob. 1340. ib.

Mag. Rob. de Wykford cl'icus pres. per
Will. Winton ep'um ad eccl. de Wytte-

[1] Tho. Walsing. sub an.

forces to the said castle, appointing Thomas de Aldine constable, with orders to defend it to the last extremity ; while he himself, with the barons of that party, marched to Kingston upon Thames, with design to proceed and relieve the castle : but before this resolution could be effected, the place was surrendered [m]

Roger d'Amory, the uncle, was of the barons' party ; for which the said Roger was after attainted, and his manor of Kenynton, in com.

neye per mort. d'ni Rog. Foliot. 4. id. Jun. 1359. Reg. Ginewell.

Permutatio inter mag. Rob. de Wycford rector. eccl. de Witteney dioc. Linc. et d'num Joh. de Bleobury rector. eccl. de Felgham Cicestr. dioc. admiss. 4. kal. Aug. 1359. ib.

Joh. de Crekkelade admissus ad eccl. de Wythendon Wigorn. dioc. et Joh. Frenche rectorem eccl'iæ de Witteney ex permutat. 31. Jan. 1369. Reg. Bokingham.

Mag'r Joh. Frenshe rector eccl'iæ de Wytteneye et Joh. de Kelleseye rector eccl'iæ de Uppingham permutant. 5. Mart. 1370. ib.

Nich. de Wykeham licentiatus in legibus presb'r pres. per Will. ep'um Winton. ad eccl. de Witteneye per mort. mag'ri Joh. de Kelseye. admiss. 3. Sept. 1373. ib.

Nich. Wykeham rector eccl'iæ de Wytnay presentat vicarium ad dictam eccl'iam. 13. Aug. 1390.

Joh. Frank capellanus pres. per Henr. ep'um Winton. ad eccl. de Wytteney. 27. Nov. 1414. Reg. Repingdon.

—— Catryk rector eccl'iæ de Wytteney. 1422. Reg. Flemmyng.

Joh. Laceby p'b'r pres. per Rob. Catryk rectorem eccl. de Wytteney ad vicariam ejusdem per mortem Tho. Curson. 22. Oct.

1434. Reg. Gray.

Mag'r Joh. Cokkys p'b'r pres. per Will. Waynflet prepositum coll. regal. B. Mariæ de Etona custodem ep'atus Winton. vacantis ad eccl. de Wytteney per mort. D. mag'ri Will'i Estcour, admiss. ult. Apr. 1447. Reg. Alnewyk.

Mag'r Leonel Wodevile pres. per Will. Winton. ep'um ad eccl. de Wytteney per mortem mag'ri Joh. Cokks. 4. Apr. 1475. Reg. Rotherham.

Mag'r Edw. Cheyny decr. doctor p'b'r pres. per Will. Winton. ep'um ad eccl. de Witteney per resign. mag'ri Leonelli Wodevile. 11. Dec. 1479. Reg. Rotherham.

Mag'r Nich'us West LL.D. p'b'r pres. per Ric. Winton. ep'um ad eccl. de Witney per mortem mag'ri Edw. Cheyney. 4. Aug. 1502. Reg. Smith.

D'n's Georg. Gray cl'icus pres. per ep'um Winton. ad eccl'iam de Wittney per consecr. Nich'i West in ep'um Elien. 12 Nov. 1515. Reg. Alwater.

Mag'r Ric. Sydnor, A. M. pres. per Ric. Winton. ep'um ad eccl. de Wytteney per resign. d'ni Geo. Gray. 6. Jan. 1519. ib.

1536. 15. Mart. Joh. Underhill. S. T. P. ad eccl. de Witney. Reg. Whitgift ar'ep'i Cant.

[m] Jo. Leland, Collectan. tom. 1. p. 328.

Berks, given to Hugh Despenser, sen. earl of Winchester; but Richard d'Amory, his nephew, of Bucknell, adhered to the king; which Richard d'Amory, banneret, had been this summer in the wars of Scotland, and received for the service of himself four shillings a day, for two knights two shillings, and for thirteen other soldiers one shilling *per diem*, for forty days; from the fourth of Aug. to the thirteenth of Sept. forty-two pounds: as also forty-four pounds received for the like military service by his knight Sir Roger de Nonnewike at York, Nov. 7. as appears from the accounts of Roger de Waltham, keeper of the king's wardrobe [n].

Thomas earl of Lancaster, with his associated barons, (of whom many had returned to the king's service,) marched to Gloucester, thence to Burton upon Trent, and so to his castle at Tutbury. The king with his forces in pursuit of them marched to Coventry; thence to Litchfield; to which place the two Spensers with recruits came in to him. The earl of Lancaster placed some foot to maintain the bridge at Burton, which obliged the king to pass the Trent at Walton: when the earl found the king's army had passed the river, he drew out his men from the castle in order to engage; but when he perceived that one of his retinue, Sir Robert Holland, who was bringing in five hundred men to his assistance, had carried them over to the king, he fled northwards; and before the king's forces could overtake him, he got to Boroughbrigge in Yorkshire, where he found the country people in arms under the conduct of William lord Latimer, governor of York, and Sir Andrew de Harcla, governor of Carlisle; where, after a short skirmish, Humphrey de Bohun earl of Hereford was slain, and the earl of Lancaster taken prisoner, and carried to Pontfract, to the king and the two Spensers; and three days after, was in implacable haste condemned to be hanged, drawn, and quartered: but in honour to his great birth the sentence was mitigated into the loss of his head; and on 11. calends of Apr. this noble patriot, being carried to a hill without the town on a lean white jade

[n] R. Dods. MS. vol. 35. p. 125.

without a bridle, was made there to kneel, and when he directed his
face to the east, was compelled to turn toward Scotland, while a villain of London cut off his head °. Of the death of this great peer,
the king himself did soon repent. Many miracles were reported to
be done in the place where he was buried, and a beautiful church
was there erected to the honour of his memory. The common
people had so great a veneration for him, that they worshipped his
picture, drawn on a tablet in St. Paul's cathedral in London, till the
king, by special letter to the bishop of London, dated at York the
28th of June, 16. Ed. II. inhibited that practice. His attainder was
annulled in the first parliament, 1. Ed. III.; and the opinion of his
merits so far prevailed, that in 33. Ed. III. it was generally believed
.that miracles were done at his tomb, and that blood issued out of
it ᵖ. Nay, in 3. Ed. III. Edmund earl of Kent, having some occasions
at the court of Rome, held a discourse with pope John XXII. at
Avignion, and informed his holiness, how Almighty God had done
many notable miracles for the sake of Thomas earl of Lancaster, and
therefore prayed that his body might be translated. But the pope
would not consent, until he should be better certified by the clergy
of England what miracles had been so done, and what credit was
to be given to them ᑫ. In the history of W. de Pakinton, treasurer to
the Black Prince, there is a chapter of the miracles which God
wrought for Thomas earl of Lancaster at the place where he was beheaded.

One of our historians makes it a moot case, whether he deserved
the honour to be reputed a saint. *De Thomæ comitis Lancastriæ
meritis, an inter sanctos sit annumerandus, crebra in vulgo discepta-
tio est : aliis quidem asseverantibus quod sic, eo quod elemosinis in-
dulsit ; quod religiosos honoraverit ; quod pro justa querela, ut videbatur, usque ad mortem certaverit ; quod eciam ejus insectatores parvo*

° Hist. W. de Pakinton apud J. Lel. Collect. tom. 1. p. 669.   ᵖ Tho. Wal. sub an.
1322. et Dugd. Bar. tom. 1. p. 781, 782.   ᑫ Barnes, Hist. Ed. III. p. 39.

*post tempore duraverunt, immo dira morte perierunt. Aliis vero in con-
trarium sentientibus, hominem videlicet conjugatum neglecta uxore sua
generosa innumeras mulierculas polluere; offendentes vel leviter in
eum morti mandare; ordinum fugitivos legisque transgressores ne lege
plecterentur pertinaciter fovere: cuncta denique agenda sua ad nutum
unius secretarii sui passim committere; tempus quoque certandi usque
ad mortem pro justitia defensanda inermiter fugientem non debere
sanctum censeri, præsertim cum invitus comprehensus passus fuerit:
set oblationum donaria et miraculorum simulacra quæ in loco suæ de-
capitationis in præsentiarum celebrantur, qualem in posterum habebunt exitum sæcula videbunt post futura*[r].

The arms of Thomas earl of Lancaster were gules, three lions passant gardant or, a label of five points ermine. The arms of Lacy,
field quartered or, and gules; lion rampant purpure.

In this year, Humphrey de Bohun earl of Hereford, and Roger de
Mortimer, with many other nobles, prosecuting their revenge on
Hugh Despenser the elder, fell upon the lands and estate of his
kinsman John de Handlo lord of Borstall, and committed great
spoil and rapine, because he had been one of the chief counsellors of
the said Hugh Despenser[s].

An. MCCCXXII.   15, 16.   *Edward* II.

Alice daughter and heir of William Longspe earl of Salisbury and
Lincoln, upon her marriage with Thomas earl of Lancaster, had been
endowed at the church door with the castle and borough of New-
castle-under-Line, the towns of Penkhill, Sheprugg, Walstatton, and
Clayton, in com. Staff. and all other hamlets belonging to the said
castle and borough, as also with divers manors and lordships lying in
other counties, of which she had livery soon after her husband's
death, resigning to the king all her right to the lordships of Winterbourn, Ambresbury, and Troubrigge in com. Wilts, Caneford in com.

[r] Hen. de Knyghton inter X. Script. 2540.   [s] Jo. Lel. Collect. MS. vol. 1. p. 328.

Dorset, Henstrigge and Charlton in com. Som. which were of her
inheritance[t]: the manors of Burcester and Midlington continuing
to her, as the hereditary estate from her father, as appears by this
record.

*Universis Christi fidelibus ad quos presens scriptum pervenerit Ale-
sia que fuit uxor Thome quondam com. Lanc. et filia et heres Henrici
de Lacy quondam comitis Linc. salutem. Noveritis me concessisse, &c.
excellentissimo principi et domino meo Edwardo regi Anglie, &c. quod
maneria de Ambresbury, Winterbourn, Troubrigges, cum pertin. in
com. Wilts. et maner. de Caneford in com. Dorset. et maner. de Hen-
gistesrigge et Cherleton in com. Som. cum villis et hamlettis terris tenementis hundredis et wapentagiis, &c. que Johannes de Warrena
comes Surregie tenet ad terminum vite sue de hereditate mea post decessum ejusdem com. domino meo Edwardo regi remaneant[u].* All
which king Edward the Third did after grant to William earl of Salisbury, and his heirs general[x].

At the end of this year, Richard Serich granted and confirmed to
the prior and canons of Burcester and their successors one messuage
and nine acres of arable land, lying in the town and fields of Burcester, with gardens, curtilages, meadows, and other appertenances,
which he held from John Puff, to have and to hold to the said prior
and canons from the capital lord of the fee for the usual service, by
charter dated the 24th of March, 16. Ed. II.

*Sciant præsentes et futuri quod ego Ricardus Serich dedi et hac
præsenti charta mea confirmavi priori et canonicis de Berencester et
successoribus suis unum messuagium et novem acras terræ arabilis jacentes in villa et campis de Berencester cum gardinis curtilagiis pratis
haiis muris fossatis et omnibus aliis ubique pertinentiis, quæ quidem
messuagia et terras habui de dono et feoffamento Johannis Puff habend. et tenend. prædicta messuagium et terram cum omnibus suis pertinentiis supradictis priori et conventui et successoribus suis de capita-*

[t] Dugd. Bar. tom. 1. p. 782. [u] Ex Chartulario abbat. de Barlinges, MS. [x] R. Dods.
MS. vol. 97. f. 149.

libus dominis feodi per servitia inde debita et consueta libere quietè et in pace in perpetuum. Et ego prædictus Ricardus Serich et hære- des mei prædicta messuagium terram et prata cum omnibus pertinen- tiis supradictis prædictis priori et conventui et successoribus suis con- tra omnes gentes warantizabimus acquietabimus et in perpetuum de- fendemus. In cujus rei testimonium huic præsenti chartæ sigillum meum apposui. Hiis testibus; Henrico de Bowcles, Ricardo de Bur- cester, Johanne le Leche de eadem, Thoma Honetoun de Stratton, An- drea de Stamford, Roberto Broun, Johanne Abbod, et aliis. Datum vicesimo quarto die Martii, anno regni regis Edwardi filii regis Ed- wardi sexto decimo [y]

Henry le Teis, lord of the manor of Grendon, having took part with Thomas earl of Lancaster in the northern insurrection, suffered death at London, as others of the confederates did in several places, leaving Alice his sister and heir, then the wife of Warine de l'Isle, of full age [z]. And by inquisition taken 1. Ed. III. it was found that the said Henry le Tyeis held the manor of Alwerton and Tywerwell, in the county of Cornwall, which, together with the manor of Sherborn, in com. Oxon, were held of the manor of S. Walery de North- Oseney; as also the manor of Chilton, in com. Berks, held of the honour of Walingford; and that Alice the wife of Warine de l'Isle was his sister and heir [a]

An. MCCCXXIII. 16, 17. *Edward II.*

By an inquisition now taken in Kent it appeared, that Guy Ferre, lately deceased, held the manor of Godindon, in com. Oxon, to him- self and heirs, by the gift of king Ed. I. [b] Out of the profits of which manor, Edmund le Botiller, who died on the feast of St. Michael this 16th of Ed. II. had six pounds, eighteen shillings, and sixpence; as appears by another inquisition taken in this county of Oxon, wherein the jurors found that Edmund le Botiller, who died on the feast of

[y] Ex Orig. penes D. Guil. Glynne, Bar.   [z] Dugd. Bar. tom. 2. p. 21.   [a] R. Dods. MS. vol. 82. p. 70.   [b] Ib. vol. 51. p. 101.

St. Michael, 16. Ed. *II.* and his heir, then in ward to the king, held the manor of Fretwell, in com. Oxon, and v1ʹ. xviiiˢ. v1ᵈ. of the rents, assize, and other profits arising from the manor of Godindon, in the said county of Oxon, which Guy de Ferre held to himself and to the heirs of his body, by the gift of Edward, father to the present king, in the twenty-sixth year of his reign ᶜ.

In an account of the knight's fees of John de Hastings, it is recited that Roger de Grey at this time held half a knight's fee in Pedington, within the parish of Ambrosden : and that Laurence de Preston held one knight's fee in Preston, Hakelinton, Horton, Pidington, Quenton, and Wotton ᵈ.

The Knights Templars, who had caught up nine thousand manors in this kingdom, being dissolved an. 1312. and all their lands escheated to the king; in this year, by act of parliament, all their late possessions in England were given to the Knights Hospitallers of St. John's of Jerusalem, *Ne in pios usus erogata contra donatorum voluntatem in alios usus distraherentur* ᵉ : by which means the manor of Meriton came to this new order.

Alice widow of Thomas earl of Lancaster quitted her whole right in the castle of Donington to the king, and by the name of Alice countess of Lincoln and Salisbury, gave to the canons of Barlings in com. Lincoln, in her pure widowhood, her manor of Swaton in that county, with the advowson of that church ᶠ. Soon after she married to Eubulo le Strange, (a younger son to John le Strange of Knokyn, the fourth of that name, and of Maud his wife, daughter and heir to Roger d'Eivil ᵍ,) with whom (as was reported) she had been familiar while repudiated from the earl of Lancaster; but taking this second husband without the royal consent, the king seized into his hands whatever she possessed or could claim of the inheritance of her father; nor would the king be satisfied till she had by fine released to him and his heirs all the lands and rights which descended to her

ᶜ R. Dods. MS. Rot. Pip. vol. 17. f. 112.   ᵈ R. Dods. MS. vol. 86. f. 129.   ᵉ Camden, in Trinob.   ᶠ Ex Cartulario Abb. de Barlings. R. Dods. MS. vol. 78. f. 16.   ᵍ Ib. f. 667. b.

from her father in the counties of Lancaster, Chester, and York ;
and to Hugh Despenser the younger, the castle and dominion of
Denbigh in Wales, and the castle of Bolingbrook with its appertenances, and all other lands in that county, and in many other parts
of England. Which Hugh Despenser in 15. Ed. II. had a grant of
the manor of Brustlesham, in com. Berks, late Thomas earl of Lancaster's, attainted. And in 16. Ed. II. had a charter for a fair yearly
at his manor of Boreford in this county, for the space of seven days
preceding the nativity of St. John the Baptist, the day, and eight
days following [h] ; at which time he obtained a grant of twenty pounds
yearly rent issuing out of the said manor of Burford, late John Giffard's, attainted : he had likewise the manors of Finnmere and Shal-
deswell, which had belonged to William Tuchet, hanged at York in
15. Ed. II.   So as by these great alienations, the said Alice had not
above three thousand marks *per an.* of her hereditary estate, which
had been formerly more than ten thousand marks *per an.* [i]

After Christmas, a conspiracy was formed among the followers of
the late earl of Lancaster and the barons, to release all persons in
one night who had been committed to prison upon that occasion. A
party of these conspirators came to the castle of Walingford, where
Maurice de Berkley and Hugh de Audley (lord of the manor of
Stratton-Audley) were in custody, and got into the castle by a
postern gate toward the river of Thames [k].   Upon this alarm, the
king sent orders to Richard d'Amory, lord of the manor of Bucknell
and steward of the king's household, who was then in Lincolnshire,
to come with forces to the said castle, and expel from thence the
king's enemies.   For which service he after received from the master
of the wardrobe for the expences of himself and retinue, from the
24th of Jan. (at which time he received those orders) to the 29th
day of that month, during which time he stayed for the coming of
his men, one hundred and seventeen shillings.   And afterwards for

h Dugd. Bar. tom. 1. p. 392. b.   i MS. in Bib. Bod. James, vol. 27.   k Tho. Wals.
sub an.

nineteen men at arms, of which three were knights, from the thirtieth
day of Jan. to the fifteenth of March, computing thirty-five days,
during which he continued his stay partly in besieging the castle, and
partly in defence of it, after the expulsion of the king's enemies, forty-
five pounds ten shillings, at 4ˢ. *per diem* for himself, 2ˢ. for each
knight, and 12ᵈ. for every common soldier: in all 51ˡ. 7ˢ. as appears
by the accounts of Roger de Waltham, master of the king's wardrobe [l].

The said Hugh de Aldithley, when he made his escape, was received into the king's favour by the interest of his son's wife, who
was the king's niece, *viz.* Margaret, one of the daughters and coheirs
of Gilbert earl of Glocester, and widow of Piers de Gaveston earl of
Cornwall, married to Hugh de Audley le Fitz. Soon after which
time the said Hugh the father died, leaving the said Hugh his eldest
son by Isolda the widow of Walter Balun: he left another son,
James, who succeeded in the manor of Stratton-Audley [m]

John de St. John, lord of the manors of Staunton-St.-John's and
Great Barton, departed this life, leaving John his son and heir fifteen
years of age; and Alice his widow, who after married to Reginald
de Pavely, lord of the manor of Wendlebury, and patron of that
church [n].

An. MCCCXXIV. 17, 18. *Edward II.*

Alice wife of Eubulo le Strange had livery (as daughter and heir
to Henry de Lacy earl of Lincoln) of the court of the fee of de la
Hay, and the gaol standing before the gate of Lincoln castle: as
also an annuity of twenty pounds for the third penny of Lincoln:
all which, by reason of the forfeiture of her late husband, had been
seized into the king's hands [o].

It is a mistake in Mr. Fern to pretend, that when Thomas earl of
Lancaster died without issue, his countess Alice, heir of the Lacies,

[l] R. Dods. MS. vol. 35. p. 126.   [m] El Ashmole, MS.   [n] Dugd. Bar. tom. 2. p. 10.
[o] Ib. tom. 2. p. 782. b.

took to her second husband one Hugh de Fresnes in Arthois, who was called commonly (by what right, says he, I know not, for he was never created) earl of Lincoln [p]. This is misrepresented, her second husband was certainly Eubulo le Strange.

Several of the friends and adherents to Thomas earl of Lancaster were still prosecuted for being concerned in that cause. Among whom there is a remarkable story of Robert de Chliderhou, parson of the church of Wigan in Lanc. who for thirty years had been clerk of the chancery, and afterwards the escheater within Trent; who was now tried at Wigan upon the charge of treason; that at his own proper cost he had sent in to the assistance of Thomas earl of Lancaster two men with arms and horses, viz. his own son Adam de Chliderhou, and John son of John de Knolle, and with them four other men armed with swords, daggers, bows, and arrows. And that the said Robert, in a sermon to his parishioners in the church of Wigan, had publicly told them, that they were the liege men of the said earl, and by their allegiance were bound to assist the said earl in his enterprise, which was just, and the king's cause unjust; and that he would absolve all who went to the aid of that earl. Of which accusation he was found guilty: and, being manuprized, did in the mean time compound for his life by a very large fine [q].

John de Sutton, lord of Dudley castle, was imprisoned by Hugh Despenser, jun. under colour that he had been of that party, till he had compounded by passing away to Hugh, the father, his manor of Eykering, in com. Not. and to Hugh, the son, his castle of Dudley, with other manors. So Oliver de Ingham was glad to compound for the castle of Shokelach, and lordship of Malpass, in com. Cest.

Sir Richard d'Amory, resident at his lordship of Bucknell, nigh Burcester, being a great favourite of his prince, obtained a grant from him, dated March 4, anno regni xi. for the custody of assize of bread and beer within the city and suburbs of Oxford, paying yearly to the

---

p Ferne's Lacies Nobility, p. 129.　　q Ex ipso Autog. in R. Dods. MS. vol. 76. f. 95.
r Dugd. Bar. tom. 1. p. 393.

exchequer one hundred shillings[s]· But on complaint of the university and city, the king, by letters dated March 20, 1324. conveyed the said privilege to the chancellor and mayor. And for compensation of this loss, Sir Richard d'Amory had the custody of the lands of John de Ferrers during the minority of Robert de Ferrers[t], his son and heir by Hawyse, the niece and heir of Cecilie de Muscegros[u].

An. MCCCXXV. 18, 19. *Edward II.*

About this time an account was taken of the tenants, rents, and services within the manor of Berencester, of which the original register, in eight parchment folios, is preserved in the hands of my worthy friend Mr. John Coker, lord of the manor of Bisiter King's-End.

BERENCESTER. *Libere tenentes hæreditarie. Johannes le Veche et Agnes uxor sua tenent unum messuagium et unum curtilagium quod est inter terram quondam Emmæ Bartelett et terram Johannis le Bakere. Tenent etiam unam acram terræ, unde dimidia acra jacet subter Buchamwey inter terram Hugonis Elyot et terram Willielmi Hamond: et alia dimidia acra jacet in terra quæ vocatur Grascroftfurlong et extendit versus Cesterton inter terram Walteri de Langleye et terram Willielmi Hamond et redd. inde per annum ob. ad pascha. Quod quidem messuagium et curtilagium et terram iidem Johannes et Agnes habent ex dimissione Nicholai le Rede et Annoræ uxoris suæ per chartam suam, reddendo inde capitali Domino ob. ut supradictum est: et tenent per formam statuti prout in curia tenta apud Berencester die Martis proxime post festum Sancti Dionysii anno regni regis Edwardi filii regis Ed. IX[mo.] plenius continetur, quo die idem Johannes fecit fidelitatem. Idem Johannes tenet unum messuagium et dimidiam vir-*

An. MCCCXXV. 18, 19. Edw. II.   Hethe vac. per mort. d'ni Andr. de Cote-
Mag'r Will. de Pontesbur pres. per pri-   ford. 4. kal. Mart. 1325.
orem et conv. de Kenilworth ad eccl. de

[s] Wood, Hist. et Antiq. Un. Oxon. sub an. 1321.   [t] Dugd. Bar. tom. 2. p. 100.   [u] Ib. tom. 1. p. 265. b.

gatam terræ per homagium et fidelitatem quod Hugo atte Ford capellanus quondam tenuit, et quod idem Hugo habuit ex dono Margeriæ atte Ford matris suæ, quæ dictam terram de domina tenuit in capite reddendo per annum II^s· VI^d. *ad quatuor anni terminos, videlicet ad festa S. Michaelis, nativitatis Domini, annuntiationis beatæ Mariæ, et nativitatis S. Johannis Baptistæ, per æquales portiones.*

Galfridus de Langleye filius domini Johannis de Langleye domini de Bigenhull tenet unum messuagium et unam virgatam terræ cum prato in Berencester quod vocatur le Palmerslond, videlicet illud messuagium et illam virgatam terræ cum prato quod Thomas William aliquando de ipso tenuit in Berencester, et reddit inde per an. VI^s. *ad terminos prædictos. Quod quidem messuagium et virgata terræ cum prato jacet particulariter in campo ut sequitur, videlicet, una acra jacet juxta murum cänonicorum inter terram Johannis Pistoris et terram Nicholai le Grey, et una acra supra la Hulle inter terram priorissæ et terram Thomæ filii Willielmi. Item duæ acræ super Longelond juxta* le woðe wey *inter terram quondam domini Johannis de Langleye et* le woðe wey. *Item tres acræ et dimidia apud* le fisbponð *juxta terram Nicholai le Grey. Item duæ acræ et dimidia super le Croftland inter terram dicti Nicholai et terram Johannis Pistoris. Item una acra super Cuteschomemor inter terram priorissæ et terram Roberti Elyot. Item una acra apud* le mulnewey *juxta terram prædicti Nicholai et Aliciæ viduæ. Item una acra apud le Wowelond juxta terram Johannis de la Ford et terram Johannis filii Walteri. Item una acra quæ jacet inter terram Aliciæ Heirhiches et terram Thomæ filii Willielmi. Item una acra in Bodemore juxta terram priorissæ. Item tres acræ super Hesneford inter terram Nicholai le Grey et terram Simonis le Frend. Item tres acræ apud Fishthorne inter terram Aliciæ viduæ et terram Walteri Cavel. Item una acra super Crocwellforlonge inter terram Nicholai le Grey et terram Radulphi ad capud villæ. Item duæ acræ super Eldeforde inter terram Nicholai le Grey et terram Nicholai Germayn. Item tres acræ super Hynacre inter terram priorissæ et terram Walteri Cavel. Item tres acræ super Imbelowe inter terram Nicholai le Grey et Kyngesmere. Item una acra super Haggethorn juxta terram Nicholai le Grey. Item una acra super Pudwellforlong inter terram priorissæ et terram prædicti Nicholai.*

Pratum prædictæ virgatæ terræ pertinens jacet particulariter ut sequitur : videlicet, duæ acræ et dimidia super Rowelowe inter terram prioris de Berencester et terram Nicholai le Grey. Item una acra vocata Henedacre jacet in Kynsedeham. Item tres acræ apud le Whitheyes inter Helenesmede et terram dominæ priorissæ. Prior de Berencester tenet duas acras terræ de prædicta virgata acræ quas habuit in escambio de Waltero de Langleye et simul jacent apud Eldeford in campo boreali inter terram Nicholai Germayn et terram Nicholai de Saford.

Johannes filius Thomæ Abbod tenet per quoddam scriptum indentatum factum Thomæ Abbod et hæredibus de corpore suo procreatis sub nomine Agnetis quondam priorissæ et sui conventus unum messuagium cum curtilagio ubi manet, quod situm est inter messuagium quod Robertus le Webbe aliquando tenuit et gablam capitalis messuagii quod H. Faber aliquando tenuit, et reddit per annum xii^d. et sectam curiæ. —Idem Johannes tenet aliud messuagium cum curtilagio ubi manet per quoddam scriptum indentatum factum sub nomine Isabellæ quondam priorissæ et sui conventus Thomæ Abbod et hæredibus de corpore, procreatis quod situm est inter messuagium quod Henricus Faber aliquando tenuit et magnam portam dominæ priorissæ, et reddit inde per annum ad terminum suum iii^s. vi^d. et sectam curiæ. Idem Johannes tenet unam placeam terræ ex transverso curtilagii sui ad capud boveriæ dominæ priorissæ ubi ingressus et egressus ad croftum priorissæ de manerio suo fieri solebat, et reddit inde per annum ad festum S. Michaelis ii^d. et tenet sine charta. Item Johannes et Juliana uxor sua tenent per quoddam scriptum indentatum sub nomine Matildis priorissæ et sui conventus factum eidem Johanni et Julianæ et hæredibus de corpore dicti Johannis legitime procreatis unum messuagium cum curtilagio quod quondam Rogerus le Mayne tenuit juxta messuagium domini de Bigenhull quod tenet de priorissa. Tenent etiam per idem scriptum decem acras terræ de dicta priorissa in campo de Berencester,

quarum duæ acræ jacent apud Eldeford inter terram prioris de Be-
rencester et terram Nicholai de Saford: et una acra et dimidia et una
roda jacent super Morforlong inter terram Gilberti de Stratton et ter-
ram Nicholai le May, et una roda jacet apud Levenchesdich inter
terram domini de Bigenhull et terram Johannis Mich, et duæ acræ et
dimidia jacent super Lyothynacre de quibus dimidia acra jacet inter
terram comit. Lyncoln et terram Hamondi......et una acra jacet
inter terram dicti Hamondi et terram Johannis atte Ford: et una acra
jacet inter terram Johannis Cavel et......et una acra vocata Cut-
tacre jacet super Mangethorn inter terram Johannis Pines et terram
Agnetis le Blake: et dimidia acra jacet juxta Buchamwey inter ter-
ram Johannis atte Ford et terram Johannis Mich: et dimidia acra ja-
cet ibidem inter terram Willielmi Cavel et terram Roberti Michel: et
dimidia acra jacet ibidem inter terram Johannis Knyght et Willielmi
Cavel: et una acra jacet super Goldforlong inter terram domini de
Bigenhull et terram Roberti Michel, et reddit per annum ad quatuor
terminos x^s. vi^d

Robertus filius Johannis le Smith tenet unum messuagium juxta cu-
riam dominæ priorissæ, et reddit inde per annum ad terminos præ-
dictos iii^s. *et sectam curiæ.*

Willielmus filius Johannis Squier tenet unum messuagium cum cur-
tilagio sibi et hæredibus de corpore legitime procreatis per quoddam
scriptum indentatum factum sub nomine Agnetis priorissæ de Mar-
kyate et sui conventus, quod messuagium cum curtilagio quondam fuit
Hugonis Coci de Berencester, et reddit inde per annum ad terminos
prædictos ii^s· *et sectam curiæ.*

Johannes Goldes tenet duo messuagia et quatuor acras terræ qua-
rum una acra jacet super Buchamwey inter terram Nicholai le Saford
et terram Roberti Thames: et una acra jacet atte Melleweysend inter
terram Johannis Gavel et terram Johannis de Aston: et una acra
jacet super Nynacre inter terram dominæ priorissæ quam Petrus
Galewei tenet et terram Andreæ le Rooke: et dimidia acra jacet super
le Melleweysend inter terram Johannis de Aston et terram Nicholai le
Saford: et dimidia acra extendit usque Twyseledwey inter terram

priorissæ et terram Andreæ le Rooke: et reddit inde per annum ad terminos prædictos vi². *et sectam curiæ.*

Summa reddituum liberorum tenentium hæreditarie xxxiv². vii^d. *ob. unde pro termino S. Michaelis* viii². viii^d. *ob. pro termino nativitatis* viii². vii^d. *ob. pro termino annuntiationis* viii². viii^d. *et pro termino nativitatis S. Joh. Bapt.* viii². vii^d. *ob.*

Libere Tenentes ad terminum vitæ Cotag.

Matildis le Taillur tenet per rotulum curiæ unum messuagium cum curtilagio ad terminum vitæ, et reddit inde per annum ad quatuor terminos prædictos iv². *et sectam curiæ.*

Isabella Mandi tenet unum messuagium cum curtilagio per rotulum curiæ ad terminum vitæ suæ, et reddit per annum ad terminos præ dictos ii². *et sectam curiæ.*

Johannes Monekes et Matildis uxor sua tenent per scriptum indentatum ad terminum vitæ eorum unum messuagium cum curtilagio, et reddunt per annum iii². *et sectam curiæ.*

Johannes le Baker et Christiana uxor ejus tenent per scriptum indentatum ad terminum vitæ eorum quatuor domos cum curtilagiis et unum furnum cum secta custumaria ad eundem: et reddunt per annum ad terminos prædictos ix². *et sectam curiæ. Summa* xviii²....

Terræ de dominicis dimissæ ad terminum vitæ.

Johannes Abbot tenet ad terminum vitæ suæ per rotulum curiæ unam acram et unam rodam terræ prout jacent in campo in quinque parcellis unde una roda jacet inter terram Nicholai prepositi de Bigen hull et terram Roberti Michell de Bigenhull, et extendit usque Oldedich: et alia roda jacet inter terram prædicti Nicholai et terram Johannis Rooke super Shottedown, et extendit super Longeland: et alia roda jacet inter terram Roberti Michell de Berencester et extendit usque Longelond: et alia roda jacet juxta terram Nicholai predicti de Bigenhull et extendit super Oldedich: et alia roda jacet ad inferius capud del Oldedich juxta le Gappe *inter terram Nicholai ad* Pontem

*et terram Roberti Elyot : et reddit inde per annum ad terminos præ-
dictos* xviii[d]

Idem Johannes tenet ad terminum vitæ suæ per rotulum curiæ x.
*acras et unam rodam terræ quas quondam Johannes Faber tenuit qua-
rum sex acræ jacent in Rydiforlong in le Reidemor juxta Oxenford-
wey : et dimidia acra jacet super Overdemershelond : et una acra et
dimidia acra et una roda simul jacent juxta Cuttacre inter terram
Walteri Sebern et le Brodewey quæ ducit versus Bikenhull : et dimidia acra jacet super Cuttacre inter terram Willielmi Hamond nativi
dominæ et terram Willielmi le Blake : et dimidia acra jacet super
Magethorn juxta terram Nicholai de Saford nativi dominæ : et quatuor rodæ terræ jacent super le Staneputtes inter terram Rogeri le
Reve et terram Johannis James : et una roda jacet ultra Overlonglond
inter terram Rogeri le Reve et ...... et una acra jacet in the Nether-
brech inter terram Nicholai le Reve et ......*

*Idem Johannes tenet per rotulum curiæ unam acram et dimidiam
terræ unde una acra jacet super Strongforlong inter terram Walteri
Sebern et Orcherdeforlong : et dimidia acra jacet apud Oldemore inter
terram Hamondi atte Nunende et Roberti Germeyn nativorum dominæ,
et reddit inde per annum ad terminos prædictos* vii[s]. vi[d].

*Idem Johannes tenet ad terminum vitæ suæ per rotulum curiæ duas
acras terræ apud Gibelyng juxta terram quondam Johannis de Bigenhull ex parte australi, et reddit per annum ad terminos prædictos* xi[d].

*Johannes le Bakere et uxor sua tenent octo acras terræ arabilis per
rotulum curiæ ad voluntatem dominæ, quarum duæ acræ jacent inter
terram Thomæ Rook et terram Thomæ William et extendit super
Bukamwey : et duæ acræ jacent in le Morforlong inter terram Johannis atte Forde et terram quæ fuit Roberti Elyot : et duæ acræ
jacent apud Mangethorn, quarum una acra jacet inter terram Thomæ
William et terram Willielmi Cavel : et alia acra jacet inter terram
Willielmi Cavel et terram Willielmi Frankleyn : et dimidia acra et una
roda jacent super Cornhull inter terram Agnetis le Blake et terram
Willielmi le Blake : et una roda jacet inter terram Simonis Germeyn*

et terram Nicholai prædicti: et una acra jacet super Cornhull inter terram dominæ priorissæ et terram Johannis Wattes, et reddunt inde per annum ad terminos prædictos iv^s. xi^d

Nicholaus le Blake tenet per scriptum indentatum ad terminum vitæ suæ et Agnetis uxoris ejus duodecem acras et unam rodam terræ, quarum sex acræ jacent super Waterforlong, et duæ rodæ jacent juxta viam scilicet le Gores *super Shorteforlong: et dimidia acra apud Kyngesmere: et una acra apud Longelondes: et una acra apud Hangateshull scilicet Foreshete: et una acra et dimidia super Waterforlong propinquiores Berencester: et duæ rodæ super Waterforlong in Lallesden: et duæ acræ in Lallesden, et una roda* in the broke *ultra Bigenhull: et reddit inde per annum ad terminos prædictos* vii^s. vi^d.

Simon Germeyn et Matildis uxor ejus tenent per scriptum indentatum ad terminum vitæ eorundem xvi. *acras terræ, quarum una acra jacet in Southfeld super Grascroftforlong: et duæ acræ super Lutlemorforlong: et una acra* in le fforlong *versus Bigenhull: et duæ acræ et dimidia super Hodesforlong: et dimidia acra quæ vocatur Brodehalfsacre in Tachemullewey: et una acra super Merforlong propinquior Berencester: et tres acræ in Northfeld super Brokforlong: et duæ acræ super Waterforlong: et una acra in Lallesden: et duæ acræ in le Breche: et reddunt inde per annum ad terminos prædictos* x^s.

Johannes de Lacy et Petronilla uxor ejus tenent per rotulum curiæ duas acras terræ simul jacentes super Overhynacre inter terram dom. com. Lincoln. et terram Johannis Rooke in campo del North, et reddunt per annum xiv^d.

Johannes de Aston tenet quatuor acras terræ et dimidiam quas Johannes de Bigenhull aliquando tenuit, quarum dimidia acra jacet super Overdenyshlond juxta terram Johannis Hargar: et alia dimidia acra jacet ibidem juxta terram Johannis Whyn: et dimidia acra jacet apud Mulleweylonde juxta terram Johannis Goldes: et una acra et dimidia jacent apud Cornhull juxta terram quondam Johannis le Bakere tenentem de domina: et dimidia acra jacet apud Seynt Edburghes-grene-wey *juxta terram Johannis Abbot: et una acra apud*

Netherdenyshelond juxta terram Simonis Warde: et reddit per annum II[s]. x[d]. *ob. q.*

Willielmus le Blake nativus dominæ tenet ad voluntatem illas tres acras quas dominus Willielmus vicarius aliquando tenuit, et post ipsum Johannes Faber et Isabella uxor ejus aliquando tenuerunt : quarum una acra jacet in le Morforlong juxta Sidenhal : et dimidia acra jacet juxta Stanfordewey : et alia dimidia acra jacet . . . . . . et alia dimidia acra apud Eldeford ; et alia dimidia acra super Overdenyshelond : reddit per annum II'. III[d].

Willielmus Cavel et Nicholaus de Saford nativi dominæ tenent quatuor acras terræ quas Rogerus Morain aliquando tenuit, quarum duæ acræ jacent in le Northfeld apud Cotemanleye : et reddunt per annum ad terminos prædictos II[s]. VIII[d]. *et tenetur per rotulum ad voluntatem.*

Willielmus Cavel nativus tenet quatuor acras terræ per rotulum curiæ, quarum una acra jacet super Hangeteshulle juxta terram Nicholai le Blake : et una acra inter terram quandam Simonis Germeyn et Agnetis le Blake, et abuttat super prædictam acram : et dimidia acra in Lallesden : et dimidia acra super Middleforlong inter terram Nicholai atte Brigge et Roberti Germeyn : et una acra super Middleforlong inter terram Nicholai le Blake et Simonis Germeyn : reddit per annum II[s]. VIII[d].

Robertus le Frend nativus dominæ tenet per rotulum curiæ ad voluntatem quinque acras terræ, quarum una acra jacet super Wadforlong inter terram Simonis Germeyn et terram dicti Roberti : et una acra jacet in eadem cultura inter terram Roberti Baudi et terram . . . . . . et dimidia acra jacet super le Croftelond inter terram Johannis atte Forde et terram Johannis Walter, et extendit super le Wodeweye : et dimidia acra jacet super Eldefeld proxime la More inter terram Johannis James et Walteri Sebern : et una acra jacet super Netherdenyshelond inter terram Johannis Knyght et terram . . . . et una acra super Shorteforlong inter terram   reddit per annum II[s]. x[d].

Petrus Galewar nativus dominæ tenet ad terminum vitæ suæ et uxoris ejus sex acras terræ quarum duæ acræ et dimidia simul jacent super le Netherynacre inter terram Roberti Germeyn et terram Johannis Goldes: et duæ acræ jacent in la Morforlong inter dom. Johan. de Langele et Johan. Erbich: *et dimidia acra jacet in le Shorteforlong* aboue the olɒ ɒych *inter Robertum Germeyn et Johannem Stevene: et una acra extendit super Imbelow* grene wey *inter dominum de Bigenhull et Johannem de Saford: reddit per annum ad quatuor terminos* iv'. vi^d *per acram* ix^d.

Summa acrarum ad terminum vitæ dimisarum, octoginta acræ dimidia una roda.

Robertus Elyot capellanus filius Roberti Elyot nuper defuncti nativi dominæ qui tenuit in bondagio duo messuagia et duas dimidias virgatas terræ de domina, tenet unum messuagium et dimidiam virgatam terræ de prædictis duobus messuagiis et duabus dimidiis virgatis terræ, quod quidem messuagium situm est juxta tenementum quondam Johannis Syrich: et dicta dimidia virgata terræ continet xxii. *acras arabiles et unam acram unam rodam unum parcellum apud Shrofdeles, duæ* Swathes *dicti prati jacent ut sequitur . . . . dimidia acra jacet in Southfeld in cultura atte Spore juxta terram domini de Bigenhull: et una roda apud Gadewey juxta terram prædicti domini: et una roda in Oredoune juxta terram Willielmi Cavel ex parte una et terram Nicholai atte Brigge: et una roda super Strongforlong juxta terram Petri Galowar: et apud Wowelond dimidia acra juxta terram priorissæ de Merkyate: et apud Godeforlong dimidia acra inter terram Petri Galewar et Walteri Sebern: et dimidia acra* bi Lesemore side *juxta terram domini de Bigenhull: et apud Funleslo una roda juxta terram Walteri Sebern: et apud le Foxhal dimidia acra juxta terram Roberti Thames: et ibidem dimidia acra juxta terram Simonis Germeyn: et ibidem dimidia acra juxta terram Johannis Eylrich: et una acra ibidem juxta terram P. Galewar: et dimidia acra atte Twiseledewey juxta terram Johannis atte Brigge: et dimidia acra ultra le Twiseledewey juxta terram Johannis le Rooke: et dimidia acra apud Shorteforlong juxta terram Johannis Walter: et dimidia acra apud Brademor juxta terram Roberti le Friend: et dimidia acra ibidem juxta terram Walteri Sebern:*

et dimidia acra ibidem juxta terram Johannis Walter : et dimidia acra ibidem juxta terram dominæ priorissæ : et una acra apud Thoftewellemor juxta terram domini Bigenhull : et in Oldefeld dimidia acra inter terram dominæ et Johannis Walter : item in le Northfeld dimidia acra apud le Wowelond juxta terram Johannis Walter : et una acra super Crocwelleforlong juxta terram Johannis Walter : et dimidia acra super Poukwelleforlong juxta terram Simonis Germeyn : et dimidia acra apud Isenfordhull juxta terram Roberti Wymark : et dimidia acra apud Sidenhal juxta terram Elyæ Coke : et dimidia acra ultra viam Sanctæ Edburgæ juxta terram Roberti le Frend : et dimidia acra apud Stanforde juxta terram Johannis atte Ford : et dimidia acra ibidem juxta terram Roberti Thames : et dimidia acra ibidem juxta viam Sanctæ Edburgæ : et una roda apud Cornhull juxta terram Walteri Sebern : et una roda ibidem juxta terram Andreæ le Rooke : et dimidia acra apud Cotemanlaye juxta terram Johannis atte Forde : et ibidem una roda juxta terram Johannis atte Forde : et apud Gatethorn dimidia acra juxta terram Johannis James : et dimidia acra apud Overbrech juxta terram Simonis Germeyn : et dimidia acra apud Saghesthorn juxta terram Petri Galewar : et dimidia acra ibidem juxta regiam viam : et apud Waltersforlong dimidia acra inter terram Johannis Walter et Walteri Sebern : et dimidia acra in Lallesdon juxta terram Walteri Sebern : et dimidia acra jacet ibidem inter terram Johannis Walter et Walteri Sebern : et dimidia acra apud Kyngesavre juxta terram Roberti Coleyn : et dimidia acra apud Middleforlong juxta terram prioris de Berencester : et dimidia acra ibidem juxta terram Johannis Cavel : et reddit per an. ad terminum ipsius unam marcam et unum adventum curiæ.

A quo quidem prato dimidia roda jacet **atte Witheyes** *juxta pratum prioris : et dimidia acra* **atte Lake** *juxta terram quondam Simonis Germeyn : et una roda* **betwhene Dike** *juxta terram quondam Johannis atte Forde : et una roda atte Rowelowe per sortem ut acciderit inter ipsum Robertum Willielmum fratrem suum, Johannem Walter, et Petrum Galeware : et dimidia roda et dimidia* **Strathe** *apud Shortedolemede : et una parcella apud Shrofdolemed inter ipsum Robertum et*

Willielmum fratrem suum, et continentem ut acciderit per sortem : et duæ swathes apud Mathames cum acciderit per sortem inter communitatem.

Summa reddituum tenentium ad terminum vitæ terras de dominicis LXIV'. VI^d. *ob. q. unde pro termino S. Michaelis,* XVI'. I^d. *ob. q. pro termino natalis domini,* XVI'. I^d. *ob. q. pro termino annunt. &c.*

Redditus et servitia Custumariorum.

Robertus filius Nicholai Germeyn tenet unum messuagium et dimidiam virgatam terræ in bondagio ad voluntatem dominæ, et debet unam aruram in yeme et unam Sarculaturam, et debet unam **Wledbedrip** *pro voluntate dominæ et habebit unum* repastum, *et debet unam falcaturam per dimidiam diem, et virgata terræ integra ejusdem tenuræ habebit* liberam *ad vesperas quæ vocatur* **Evenyngs** *tantam sicut falcator potest per falcem levare et domum portare per ipsam : et dimidia virgata terræ ejusdem tenuræ habebit* liberam *ad vesperas cum quodam socio tantam sicut falcator potest per falcem levare et domum portare, et falcator habebit jentaculum suum de domina priorissa, et ipse Robertus et omnes alii custumarii dominæ liberam falcatam in prato vocato Gilberdesham sine prandio debent tornare et inde fœnum levare et* mulliones *inde facere, et debet quilibet cariare quatuor carucatas fœni ad curiam priorissæ, et habebit unum jentaculum de domina priorissa : et virgata terræ ejusdem conditionis faciet tres* precarias *in autumpno, videlicet precariam sine prandio cum tribus hominibus, et unam precariam sine prandio cum uno homine : et si sit ligator, ad dictas precarias habebit unum garbum seminis de ultimo blado ligato, et debet etiam unam precariam pro voluntate dominæ cum tota familia sua præter uxorem suam ad prandium dominæ, et quotiens ligator habet prandium non habebit garbam : et debet cariare quatuor carucatas bladi in autumpno ad manerium dominæ et habebit unum jentaculum, et debet* talliari *ad festum S. Michaelis pro voluntate dominæ priorissæ, nec debet vendere equum masculum neque bovem de proprio nutrimento suo, neque filium suum ad literaturam ponere, neque filiam*

suam maritare sine licentia et voluntate priorissæ: et si domina pri-
orissa sit præsens, ipse Robertus quæret et cariabit esculenta et potu-
lenta priorissæ pro tempore quo moram fecerit in comitatu pro volun-
tate sua, et reddet etiam per annum ad quatuor terminos consuetos 11ˢ.
v1ᵈ. *et sectam curiæ.*

Willielmus Hamond tenet unum messuagium et dimidiam virga-
tam terræ per idem servitium, et reddit per annum 11ˢ. v1ᵈ.

Willielmus Cavel tenet unum messuagium et dimidiam virgatam
terræ in forma prædicta, et reddit per annum 11ˢ· v1ᵈ

Johannes Cavel tenet unum messuagium et dimidiam virgatam terræ,
et reddit per an. 11ˢ· v1ᵈ

Idem Johannes tenet unum messuagium ad voluntatem dominæ, præ-
ter aliud tenementum prædictum, et reddit per annum 11ˢ.

Robertus Michel tenet unum messuagium et dimid. virgat. terræ ut
supra, et redd. per an. 11ˢ. v1ᵈ.

Robertus le Frend tenet unum messuagium et dimidiam virgatam
terræ per prædictum servitium, et redd. per an. 11ˢ. v1ᵈ.

Roesia quæ fuit uxor Johannis Knyght tenet, &c. ut supra, et red-
dit per an. 11ˢ. v1ᵈ.

Johannes Walter tenet unum messuagium et dimidiam virgatam
terræ, et reddit per an. 11ˢ. v1ᵈ.

Petrus Galeware tenet idem, &c.

Willielmus filius Roberti Elyot tenet idem, &c.

Nicholaus de Saford tenet idem, &c.

Willielmus le Blake tenet idem, &c.

Alicia quæ fuit uxor Ricardi le Grey coterelli et nativi dominæ
tenet unum messuagium duas acras terræ et dimidiam acram prati, et
faciet unam Sarculaturam et unam Wedbedripam et levationem fœni,
et inveniet unum hominem ad mullionem fœni faciendum, sicut supra-
dictus Robertus filius Nicholai, et faciet tres precarias in autumpno
sine cibo, et red. per an. x11ᵈ.

Nicholaus ad Fontem tenet unum messuagium cum crofto et duas
acras terræ et dimidiam acram prati per eadem servitia sicut prædicta
Alicia, et reddit per an. xv111ᵈ. *et sectam.*

Summa reddit. custumariorum et coterellorum XXXIV[s]. VI[d]. *unde pro termino S. Michaelis* VIII[s]. VII[d]. *ob. &c.*

Summa summarum totius redditus prædicti VII[l]. XI[s]. VIII[d]. *q. &c.*

Johannes Abbot tenet unum messuagium et red. inde per annum III[s]. VII[d]. *ad terminos prædictos et sectam curiæ.*

Idem Johannes tenet aliud messuagium quondam Rogeri le Moyne, et reddit inde per an. IV[s]. *ad terminos prædictos.*

Idem Johannes et Juliana uxor sua tenent quatuor acras terræ in feodo per chartam, quarum duæ acræ jacent apud le Cadeford, et una roda apud Liveruchesdich: et duæ acræ et dimidia apud le Morforlong: et reddit inde per an. III[s]. VI[d]. *ad terminos prædictos.*

Idem tenent sex acras terræ arabilis in feodo per chartam, quarum una acra et dimidia jacent juxta Buckinhamewey versus borealem partem: et una acra et dimidia jacent super Overynacre: et una acra quæ vocatur Catacers: et una acra super Goldfurlong: et quatuor butta quæ continent unam acram, &c.

Idem Johannes tenet ad voluntatem dominæ unam acram et unam rodam terræ jacentes in quinque part. quarum una roda jacet inter terram Nicholai præpositi de Bygenhull et terram Roberti Michell de Bygenhull, et extendit usque Olddich: et alia roda inter rodam prædicti Nicholai et terram Johannis Rok super Shortdoun, et extendit usque Longeland: et alia roda juxta terram Nicholai præpositi de Bygenhull, et extendit usque Oldedich: et una roda jacet ad inferius capud del Oldedich juxta le Scappe, inter terram Nicholai ad Pontem et terram Roberti Elyot, reddendo inde annuatim XVIII[d]. *ad terminos consuetos. &c.*

De terris traditis ad firmam.

Johannes Squier tenet duas acras et dimidiam terræ de dominico priorissæ, quarum una acra et dimidia jacent super Overfordeshull: et una acra super Hodesforlong ad terminum vitæ, et reddit inder per an. XXII[d]. *ob.*

Nicholaus le Blake tenet XIII. *acras et unam rodam terræ, quarum*

sex acræ jacent super Waterforlong, et duæ rodæ juxta viam scilicet
les Gores super le Shortforlong, et dimidia acra apud Kyngesmer: et
una acra apud Longelands: et una acra apud Hangateshull scilicet
Foreschetere: et una acra et dimidia super Wateresforlong propin-
quiores Berencestre: et duæ rodæ super Waltersforlong in Lallesdene:
et duæ acræ in Lallesdene, et una roda juxta le Broke *ultra Byken-*
hull: et reddit inde per an. VII^s. VI^d. *ad terminos prædictos, et tene-*
tur ad terminum vitæ suæ et Agnetis uxoris suæ.

Johannes de Astone tenet quatuor acras terræ, quarum una acra
jacet super Overdencheland: et dimidia acra jacet apud Seynt Ed=
burges=grene=wey *juxta terram Johannis Abbot: et dimidia acra apud*
Melestwewende: *et una acra apud Cornhull: et dimidia acra apud*
Stanfords=grenewepe: *et una acra super Netheresdencheland: et*
reddit inde per annum II^s. X^d. &c.

Rogerus Mortimer nativus prioris de Berencester tenet quatuor acras
terræ, quarum duæ acræ jacent in Southfeld apud Oldediches-end:
et duæ acræ jacent in Northfeld apud Colmaneleye: et reddit inde
per an. II^s. VIII^d. *ad terminos prædictos: et tenetur ad terminum vitæ*
suæ.

Henricus Par la custume tenet novem acras et unuam rodam terræ,
quarum quinque acræ jacent super Radyforlong: et dimidia acra
super Overdenchesland: et una acra et dimidia et tres rodæ super
Catacre, &c.

Several donations were now confirmed to the abbey of Egnesham,
com. Oxon, and particularly four hides of land in Chesterton adjoining to Burcester, which had been given by Henry de Oily, son of
Robert, lord of the manor, by this charter.

Notum sit omnibus qui sunt et qui venturi sunt, quod ego Henricus
de Oili concessi et dedi ecclesie Dei et sancte Marie de Egnesham
quatuor hidas terre apud Cestreton villam meam in perpetuam elemo-
sinam pro anima patris mei et Edid sororis mee, duas videlicet in
Brueria et duas in villa Cestreton, liberas et quietas ab omnibus que-
relis excepto murdredo et danegeldo. Testibus Nicholao capellano

meo, Walchelino presbytero de Weston, Nigello de Oili, Widone de Oili, Leonardo de Wittefeld, Willielmo de Cantelu, Petro de Wittefeld, Willielmo filio Ricardi[x].

This church of Chesterton, with those of Weston and Hampton-Gay, &c. had been appropriated to the abbey of Oseney, by Richard bishop of Lincoln, in the year 1263. under this form.

Omnibus Christi fidelibus ad quos presentes litere pervenerint Ricardus miseracione divina Lincolniensis episcopus salutem in Domino sempiternam. Predecessorum nostrorum vestigiis inherentes, qui ad dilectos in Christo filios canonicos S. Marie de Oseneia propter sua devocionis merita et caritatis opera pia affectionis viscera gestabant, ecclesias de Weston, de Cesterton, de Hempton-Gay, de Wallington, et capellas de Burton, et de Forsthull, necnon annuam pensionem decem solidorum ab ecclesia de Ylbestan in quarum antiqua et pacifica possessione existunt in proprios usus perpetuo optinendas concedimus et auctoritate pontificali confirmamus. Salvis in omnibus episcopalibus consuetudinibus et Lincolniensis ecclesie dignitate. In cujus rei testimonium presenti scripto sigillum nostrum duximus apponendum. Datum apud Tynglebrarst—Idibus Junii anno Domini MCCLX. *tercio et pontificatus nostri quinto*[y].

The said church of Hampton-Gay had been appropriated by the patron, Robert Gait, in the time of Hugh the second bishop of Linc. by these letters of request to the said diocesan.

Reverendo patri in Christo et Domino Hugoni Dei gracia Lincolniensi episcopo et officiariis suis Robertus Gayt salutem et debitam cum omni devocione reverenciam. Noverit discrecio vestra quod defuncto G. persona ecclesie de Hempton me eandem ecclesiam vacantem dedisse et concessisse in perpetuam elemosinam abbati et conventui de Oseney, et quoniam in propria persona ad vos non possum, per presentes literas meas dictos canonicos vobis presento, petens et supplicans quatenus ad eandem ecclesiam admittatis[z].

x Ex Chartul. de Egnesham, MS. f. 69.   y Ex Chartul. de Oseney, f. 32.   z Ibid.

An. MCCCXXVI. 19, 20. *Edw. II.* 1. *Edw. III.*

Sir Richard d'Amorie, lord of the manor of Bucknell, who had other large possessions in Godindon, Blechesdon, Weston, and other adjoining parts, for his many faithful services to the king, had the honour to be now first summoned to parliament as a baron. He and his family had the successive prayers and other religious benefits of the abbey of Oseney, by express compact between that convent and Roger d'Amory, when he released to them the manor of Weston; of which conveyance mention is already made *sub an.* MCCLXI. and the fine, which was then passed in the king's court, is fit to be here inserted.

Hec est finalis concordia facta in curia domini regis apud Oxon. a die S. Hilarii in quindecem dies anno regni regis Henrici filii regis Johannis XLV°. *coram Gilberto de Preston, Martino de Littlebyri, et Galfrido de Leunor justiciariis itinerantibus, et aliis domini regis fidelibus tunc ibi presentibus, inter Rogerum de Aumari petentem et Philippum de Wappeleg positum loco suo ad lucrandum vel perdendum, et Ricardum abbatem de Oseneia tenentem, de feodis duorum militum cum pertinenciis exceptis* XXX. *et quinque acris terre et tribus acris prati in Weston unde recogn. magn. ass'c. sum. fuit inter eos in eadem curia, scilicet quod predictus Rogerus recognovit predicta feoda duorum militum scilicet totum manerium de Weston cum pertinenciis ut in dominicis, homagiis, serviciis liberum hominum, wardis, releviis, escaetis, villenagiis cum villanis villenagia illa tenentibus, boscis, planis, pratis, pascuis, pasturis, aquis, stagnis, molendinis, vivariis, piscariis, et omnibus aliis rebus ad predictum manerium pertinentibus, &c. ex ceptis predictis triginta et quinque acris terre et tribus acris prati, esse jus ipsius abbatis et ecclesie sue S. Marie de Oseneya et illud remisit et quietum clamavit de se et heredibus suis predicto abbati et successo ribus suis et ecclesie sue predicte imperpetuum. Et pro hac recogni cione remissione quieta clamacione fine et concordia predictus abbas dedit predicto Rogero trecentum marcas argenti. Et preterea idem*

abbas recepit predictum Rogerum et heredes suos in singulis benefi-
ciis et oracionibus que de cetero fient in ecclesia sua predicta imperpe-
tuum[a].

James de Aldithley, lord of the manor of Stratton-Audley, who
had been in the expedition made into Gascoigne, 18. Ed. II. died
this year without issue, by which the said manor was escheated to the
crown[b]; because his elder brother, Hugh de Aldithley, had his lands
seized, and stood outlawed, for refusing to attend the king: but in
the first of Ed. III. upon his allegation in parliament, that there
were divers errors in his prosecution, all his lands were restored, and
he came then to the enjoyment of the said manor of Stratton[c]. In
which village, the abbey of Egnesham rented their appropriated
tithes to the priory of Burcester at the yearly rent of twelve shillings;
for which sum I have seen this form of receipt.

Noverint universi per presentes nos Jacobum permissione divina ab-
batem monasterii de Egnesham recepisse et habuisse die confectionis
presencium de priore de Burcester duodecim solidos legalis monete pro
decimis in Stratton, videlicet pro crastino S. Michaelis archangeli ul-
timo preterito ante dat. presencium, de quibus quidem duodecim solidis
fatemur nos inde plenarie fore solutos per presentes sigillo nostro con-
signatas[d]

John de St. Amand, lord of the manor of Bloxham, com. Oxon,
and Grendon, in com. Buck. (who in 11. Ed. II. had obtained a licence from the king for a market every week upon the Thursday at
his manor of Wydenay, com. Berks, and a fair there yearly on the
eve, day, and morrow of the purification of the blessed virgin,) had
been summoned to parliament from the sixth to the nineteenth of
Ed. II. inclusive; and died nigh this time, leaving Almaric his son
and heir under age[e]

These parts of the country were much concerned in the approach-
ing revolution, when queen Isabel, with the prince her son, landed at

---

[a] Ex Ghartul. de Oseney, MS. f. 317.   [b] El Ashmole, MS.   [c] Dugd. Bar. tom. 1.
p. 750.   [d] Ex Rental. de Egnesham, MS.   [e] Dugd. Bar. tom. 2. p. 20.

Harwich, and having many of the barons joined to them, came to Oxford, where the bishop of Hereford preached before the Univer_sity on these words, *Caput meum dolet*, with this application, that when the head of a kingdom was sick, there was no cure but divid_ing it from the body[f]. After which the queen (who for some weeks had lódged at Islip[g]) and the prince kept their Christmas at Waling_ford: and after Epiphany held a convention at Westminster, where the young prince, aged fourteen years, was elected king; who, when his father was prevailed with to resign, began his reign on the 20th of January, $132\frac{6}{7}$[h].

That imperious favourite, Hugh Despenser the younger, among other vast possessions lord of the manors of Burcester and Midling_ton, (surrendered to him by Alice countess of Lincoln in her widow_hood,) when his father was beheaded at Bristol on St. Dennis's day in October, fled away with the king, but was taken November 16. at Lantrussen, in Wales, brought to Hereford by Sir Henry Beaumont, and delivered to the queen and her son, where he was executed on a gallows of fifty feet on St. Andrew's eve. And being then quartered, his limbs were sent to four several places, and his head to London bridge. One of our historians does observe, that his execution was done upon a Monday, in revenge of the death of Thomas earl of Lancaster, whose blood had been shed on the same day of the week. By this means the manors of Burcester and Midlington, by consent of the first parliament in the beginning of this reign, fell to the king among other escheats, who kept the said manors, till, in the fifth year of his reign, he restored them to the said Alice and her husband Eubulo le Strange[i].

By the death of Hugh Despenser, sen. and the attainder in this parliament, the manor of Pidington, within the parish of Ambros_den, should by this forfeiture have fallen to the king; but Sir John Handlo, holding the said manor for his life, continued in possession:

---

[f] Tho. de la Moor, Edw. II.   [g] Wood, Antiq. Oxon. l. 1. p. 161.   [h] Tho. Walsing. sub an.   [i] R. Dod. MS. vol. 78. f. 81.

yet when occasion served, in the fourth of Edw. III. he pleaded a lapse to the king to stop the process of the prior and canon of St. Frideswide, who then laid a judicial claim to it [k]

[k] Ex Chartul. S. Frideswidæ, MS. f. 100.

THE END OF THE FIRST VOLUME.

CPSIA information can be obtained
at www.ICGtesting.com
Printed in the USA
LVOW01s1620110116

470118LV00023B/1293/P